YOU'RE NOT OLD ENOUGH SON

An irreverent recollection
of the horror/science fiction/fantasy
scene in the British cinema
1954-1970

YOU'RE NOT OLD ENOUGH SON

An irreverent recollection of the horror/
science fiction/fantasy scene in the British
cinema
1954-1970

by Barry Atkinson

Midnight Marquee Press, Inc.
Baltimore, Maryland

Cover and Interior Design: Susan Svehla

ISBN 1-887664-68-8
Library of Congress Catalog Card Number 2006928700
Manufactured in the United States of America
First Printing by Midnight Marquee Press, Inc., July 2006

Dedication

To my mother for unwittingly developing in me an interest that,
50 years later, bore fruition in the shape of this book.
And to my wife
for her perseverance in checking the countless dates
and facts that constitute the main text.

WHO
WILL
BE
HIS
BRIDE
TONIGHT?
see
DRACULA
ALL NEW
Adults Only X
EASTMAN COLOUR

CONTENTS

8   Introduction

9   That Will Be 1s 6d Please, Sir
        (1954-1958)

19   You're Not Old Enough Son (1958-1960)

28   Sunday, 15 February 1959

31   The Sunday One-Day Program (1961)

37   Trouble at the Embassy (1961)

40   What Shall We See This Sunday? (1962)

54   Sunday, 10 June 1962

59   The Cameo, Cornwall (1963-1965)

67   Nine Days in May (1964)

72   Observations (1965)

77   Foreign Delights (1965-1966)

86   An Evening Out—Greek Style (1965)

90   The Reissues (1966-1967)

94   No Go! (1966)

97   How to Make a Monster Movie (1966)

100 Changes (1967-1968)

103 Highs and Lows (June-July 1968)

108 The Rise and Fall of an Era (1969-1970)

112 Midnight at the Odeon (1969)

114 Reflections—Life After 1970

126 What Shall We See Tonight?
        (24 January 2004)

128 A note on film classification

129 Horror • Science Fiction • Fantasy:
        A personal film checklist

INTRODUCTION

This book is about the cinema but is not a book *on* the cinema. From a very early age and for reasons I have never really fathomed out, I became fascinated by the world of horror, science fiction and fantasy films. Coming from a family of keen cinema-goers, it was probably inevitable that I would end up inheriting their traits, but neither my mother nor my father, or my brothers and sister, were as obsessed by the genre to the extent that I became. Decades before the advent of multimedia entertainment for the younger generation—satellite television, videos, DVDs, computer games, the internet, mobile phones, CDs, a vast array of magazines and other sophisticated equipment for audio and visual purposes—the only form of pleasure available to families was "a trip to the pictures." The cinema reigned supreme—there was nothing else available to amuse us, and television was still in its infancy. The experiences I have written about which took place between 1954 and 1970 no longer exist, yet at the time they formed a major part of my life and many other people's lives as well. Some of the movies described in the following pages have not seen the light of a projection lamp for years. I have brought them out of the attic of my memory and dusted them off, putting them on display as it were, to share a glorious period in the British cinema that has been lost forever.

THAT WILL BE 1s 6d PLEASE, SIR
(1954-1958)

October 1954. The venue—The Crescent cinema in Leatherhead, Surrey, a rather quiet, sedate town with a middle-class population nestling in a fold of the North Downs, surrounded on all sides by miles of beautiful, unspoiled woodlands, wild heathland, the commanding 700-foot-high Box Hill and the scenic River Mole. It was a picturesque future breeding ground for an exceptional kind of fanaticism that would take place among some of the town's younger generation, and one of them in particular; a fanaticism that would, in the course of time, release a darker side of their embryonic personalities. Up on the big screen, Patricia Laffan as Nyah, the PVC-clad alien in *Devil Girl from Mars*, was holding a motley group of character actors and actresses captive with the aid of her tacky-looking robot assistant Chani, in a scene that today would have the more discerning members of the audience rolling about in the aisles with hoots of derisory laughter while the youngsters would be making a bored and hasty retreat to the exits. Way back then in the dark ages, shivers were making their presence felt up and down a very impressionable seven-year-old's spine, even though the film carried a "U" certificate and was thus deemed suitable for people of all ages. This hoary old British low-budget science fiction movie marked my earliest introduction to the world of fantasy cinema. On leaving The Crescent, I grasped my mother's hand and, holding on to her like grim death, walked the mile or so back to the safe comfort of our home, trying to avoid at all costs the churchyard with its gravestones or anybody dressed in black with a passing resemblance to Nyah the alien, as we trooped up the long, tree-lined hill in the

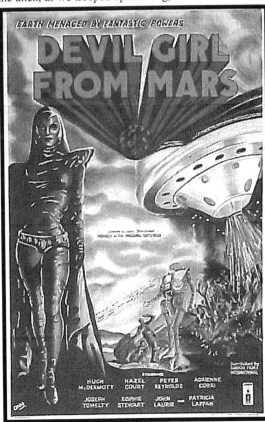

dark to where we lived. I had nightmares for a week. A month later, I sat through Anglo's more superior *Ghost Ship* and was in such a state of high nerves for the following fortnight, spending more time sleeping in my parents' bed than my own, that orders from above were handed out—"You are not seeing any more of *those* type of films until you are a lot older"—a ruling that unfortunately lasted, with one or two exceptions, right up until 1959.

My mother, it has to be said, is the one person above all others whom I hold responsible for my interest in "those type of films" and an early influence on what was to ensue over a period spanning 16 years. A keen cinemagoer who worked as an usherette at the Odeon in Ashford, Kent between 1939 and 1941, she would spend long winter evenings narrating to me, from about the age of five onwards, the complete plots of most of the old *Frankenstein* and *Dracula* movies, which both she and her brother had seen before and after the War. She nourished my inquisitive

FRANKENSTEIN

MIT **BORIS KARLOFF**

nature with fanciful anecdotes of packed houses thrilled at the sight of King Kong loping through the jungle clasping a miniature Fay Wray and recounted the melodramas of the day such as *Murder in the Red Barn* and *Sweeney Todd, the Demon Barber of Fleet Street*. She was the one that stoked the fires of my imagination by acquainting me with these creepy delights, which for kids of my tender years were strictly prohibited—no fairy stories or Rupert the Bear for this young man before bedtime, only tales of Boris Karloff and Bela Lugosi as Frankenstein's monster and Dracula, of Kong battling the planes atop the Empire State Building and of Chaney either lurching around as the Mummy or sprouting hair as the Wolf Man.

And surely there cannot have been another child in the whole of Leatherhead that was privy to the entire scenario of *The Phantom of the Opera*—yet I was! Why she chose to burden me, her first child, with these stories, I never did find out. Perhaps she had a mother's awareness of something out-of-the-ordinary in her offspring's character—certainly, none of her other children were subjected to these narratives and not one of them grew up nursing the sort of fixations or mania that I had to cope with. But for whatever reason (could it be that she simply loved talking about them, and I was a receptive listener?), these extraordinary tales gradually began to work their spells, insidiously worming their way into the nether regions of my mind, cobwebby, half-formed conceptions of a twilight world inhabited by grotesque figures that belonged to a different age than the one I was growing up in. Mum was also an avid reader, devouring mostly crime novels but occasionally science fiction of the H.G. Wells and John Wyndham variety, so I learned all about the Martian invasion of England, not to mention the giant, death-dealing Triffids in Wyndham's book, years before anybody else that I knew had heard of them. It was no small wonder that I developed an extremely vivid perspective of life from very early on, suffering quite frequently from all manner of horrible nightmares. I often woke in the dead of night crying, sweating, or in one case I can recall, vomiting in fear after being pursued down the hallway, in my dreams, by a mass of shapeless forms, shutting myself in the bathroom as these forms clamored outside the door, anxious to lay their hands on a terrified six-year-old. However, the odd uncomfortable night or two never stopped me from pestering my mother to continue with her stories as long as she left a small night-light burning in my bedroom afterward to ward off any more bad visions or nameless phantoms lurking in the dark recesses of my bedroom, waiting just for me! Thus were the seeds being sown for what eventually became for me, up until 1970 anyway, something of an obsession, but in hindsight, I suppose, an innocent enough one—it certainly did me no harm, mentally or otherwise.

Apart from the dubious pleasures to be had from *Devil Girl from Mars* and *Ghost Ship*, my frequent visits to the cinema in the early 1950s were mainly to see the likes of Disney's *Cinderella* and *The Living Desert* or the numerous Westerns and semi-biblical actioners my father was interested in, a custom observed by families all over the United Kingdom who did their utmost to steer their children well clear of anything remotely alarming or disturbing—in their eyes, that is. There was also the weekly trip to the Saturday Morning Picture shows at the Odeon in Epsom that screened, alongside the Popeye and Disney cartoons and the Hopalong Cassidy Westerns, the children's versions of science fiction—*Flash Gordon, Superman, Buck Rogers* and *Rocketman* serials dating from the 1930s and 1940s. These corny old episodes, shown on a "continued next week" format, usually drove the young customers into paroxysms of savage behavior verging on the lawless—sweets hurled at your enemies between balcony and stalls; drinks upset over expensive carpeting; shouting, screaming and fist-fights; and the continual banging of doors as one person after another took full advantage of the toilet facilities. This mass display of boisterousness was only curtailed by threats of "lights up, show's over" by the desperate manager, who was at his wits' end trying to handle such a badly behaved mob in the absence of their parents.

Notwithstanding these relatively exciting forays into a parallel universe on a Saturday morning, where at least you could let off steam for a couple of hours and escape punishment, catching the occasional relatively short trailer to an X-rated horror film was the most I could hope for to liven things up and allow me just a tiny insight into the kind of pictures that my parents were lucky enough to see, and what my mother had been amusing me with since I was five years old. But even these brief snippets began to inflame my interest in the genre. Advertising trailers in the '50s were not the five-minute action-packed "let's give the whole plot away" mini-movies that are screened today. If it was for an adult film being exhibited to a general audience, a few selected scenes lasting about a minute were glimpsed as an appetizer—this was all that was allowed by the censor. As a result of this dictatorial attitude by the censor's office as to what *they* considered suitable for letting loose on the populace in the staid atmosphere of the early 1950s, a single shot of Vincent Price's shadow against a wall as Phyllis Kirk screamed her head off constituted the sole excerpt from Warner Bros.' terrifying *House of Wax*, although this extract alone was enough to raise the hairs on the back of my neck. Likewise, the trailer to the forthcoming attraction at The Crescent of *The Curse of Frankenstein* showing the shadow of Christopher Lee against a wall as Valerie Gaunt screamed *her* head off had a similar effect. Such were the ephemeral but potent images that were to make a lasting impression on a 7- to 10-year-old.

One evening in late 1955, my father returned home from The Crescent after what was for him a rare visit to see something other than his usual beloved Western or war movie. That "something" was *The Quatermass Experiment* and I overheard him telling my mother about a rather unusual incident in the cinema while the film was showing. During the scene where the unfortunate chemist unwraps the raincoat from Richard Wordsworth's alien-infected arm and pays with his life in the most unpleasant way possible, a woman had passed out in the front row and had to be carried from the auditorium by the manager and two assistants, causing a stir among the audience, whose nerves were in a frazzle as it was—Hammer's groundbreaking and phenomenally successful science fiction thriller was considered to be strong viewing at the time, and a faint-hearted customer didn't help matters.

Now *Quatermass* was a name that I was vaguely familiar with. I had called on Tony's house one evening in November, principally to take a nosy look at the television

Carroon's (Richard Wordsworth) ghastly infections caused a bad reaction in some 1950s audience members in *The Quatermass Xperiment*.

BRIAN DONLEVY   JACK WARNER

QUATERMASS XPERIMENT

set that his parents were well off enough to rent, and it so happened that *Quatermass 2* was showing on the BBC (the original TV production). Creeping in through the living room door, the pair of us were honored by the chilling sight of John Robinson as the Professor staring through a porthole at what appeared to be a heaving mass of steamy goo before Tony's parents entered and gently but firmly ushered us out. So curiosity got the better of me and I hot-footed it down to the cinema the next morning to look at the six stills used in those days to publicize and promote the picture that was being shown. These were arranged behind a glass panel in box-like structures, locked at the sides to prevent theft, and usually positioned on the wall outside to give a taste of what could be seen inside—in the case of "X" films, a mouth-watering taste. However, the stills to *The Quatermass Experiment* were a disappointment, showing nothing untoward, and I was left feeling baffled. What was it about this particular film that would cause someone to faint? And why did I feel it was so unfair that *I* wasn't allowed to see it? Anyway, it was no good fretting over the issue—I was eight years old and needed another eight years under my belt before the required age (in the United Kingdom) of 16 to see "X" films. My father also told me later, when I had plucked up sufficient courage to broach the subject of the *Quatermass* disturbance, that *two* women had fainted in the Odeon at Epsom the previous year when *House of Wax* was out on general release. He tantalizingly hinted at the unmasking of a hideously disfigured madman, Vincent Price, near the end as being the reason. More salt rubbed in an ever-festering cinematic wound. Disney films, Westerns and dire British comedies now seemed to pale into insignificance compared to what was on offer to adults and besides, it was almost unheard of for any child under age 10 to go to the cinema in the afternoon or evening unaccompanied—your parents even chaperoned you and picked you up from the popular Saturday morning shows. One was naturally restricted, therefore, to a diet of bland film fodder that parents wanted you to see, or thought you ought to see, rather than the kind of pictures that we schoolboys began to really want to look at—the "monster movies."

1956 came along—my parents saw *Invasion of the Body Snatchers* at The Crescent after I had sat through about a minute of the trailer the week before when Kirk Douglas' *The Indian Fighter* was on. After I drove my mother up the wall, she reluctantly caved in to my incessant demands for a detailed blow-by-blow account of the film, and this was subsequently relayed to my friends at school the next day, as none of their parents had bothered to check it out. Also, the eye-popping poster outside the cinema had us all wondering what this movie, with its over-the-top title, was all about. To hopefully shut me up once and for all, I was given, under protest, a copy of Jack Finney's novelette *The Body Snatchers* on which the picture was based. "Here you are, Barry," said my exasperated mother at the end of her tether, "you'll have some idea now of what kind of film it was." All well and good, but it was the film that I had wanted to see, not the book I was being forced to read, and I felt that Mum was contradicting herself by losing her temper—after all, my "unhealthy" interests were all down to her storytelling in the first place!

In July, my father took me along to *The Ship that Died of Shame* at The Crescent, sincerely believing it to be a war film with a bit more guts to it as the movie was an "A" certificate. Little did he know that there was not a great deal of the Second World War featured in this Ealing production—the story concerned a trio of ex-navy companions who bought their old gunboat from a scrap-yard and used it for various nefarious purposes such as smuggling. The ship, seemingly with a mind of its own, was deteriorating as a result and putting up a resistance to these unlawful activities, self-destructing in the end in protest at its abuse. Dad left the cinema more than a shade disappointed that the picture was not the usual standard war effort, but I was distinctly unsettled by the fact that an inanimate object such as a ship could exert a supernatural influence over human beings, and had difficulty in getting off to sleep for three or four nights—this was one of *those* films which my parents had expressly forbidden me access to two years previously after seeing, ironically enough, another haunted ship saga, *Ghost Ship*. On this occasion I wasn't to blame, as I had had no idea what *The Ship that Died of Shame* was about, and it was Dad who received the sharp edge of my mother's tongue for the next day or so, even though it really wasn't his fault either.

A Sunday in October beheld me gazing open-mouthed at the stills showing the amphibious gill-man overturning a car and menacing a blonde actress in *Revenge of the Creature*, which was the presentation at The Crescent, with people muttering, "Get out of the ruddy way" as they barged past me in their efforts to reach the entrance doors, no doubt wondering what this skinny little kid was doing staring at adult material, particularly as said kid couldn't watch the film anyway. This kid, if the truth be known, was completely dumbfounded by Jack Arnold's creation. What on earth was it? What kind of film was this? Where did it come from? It wasn't from England, that's for sure—it looked nothing like the flicks I was used to seeing. These movies, even if at the moment they only consisted of the occasional film trailer, posters, stills and stories from my parents, were inexorably etching themselves into my brain and would not go away. Fleeting glimpses of forbidden fruit that would one day practically take over the whole, or a large part, of my leisure hours.

In May 1957, *The Curse of Frankenstein* was released to a storm of disgust from the strait-laced English critics ("A charnel-house of a picture" and "Repulsive" were two of the descriptions used), and record-breaking receipts at the box office. The first British horror movie in color was proving to be a sensation in a country where the cinema-going public had become conditioned to sitting through nothing but tame black and white thrillers and Ealing comedies, and more faintings were reported in the press. My parents went to a late-night showing at The Crescent, but when I kept going on at my mother for an account of Hammer's reputedly stomach-churning offering, she would only say, "I can't tell you about it, Barry, and I won't. It was all rather shocking and it made me feel slightly ill. It would give you bad dreams for months, so stop asking me about it." Could this be the same mother who had sat through dozens of old *Frankenstein*, *Dracula* and *Mummy* flicks in the '40s without batting an eyelash? Perhaps, I speculated, the new breed of horror film was a far more terrifying beast.

In the same year, I was passing The Crescent on my way back from the shops when I happened to glance at the stills advertising the new attraction of the week, *20 Million Miles to Earth*. I was immediately transfixed to the spot as though struck by a bolt of lightning. Never in all my

OUT-OF-SPACE CREATURE INVADES THE EARTH!

20 MILLION MILES TO EARTH

WILLIAM HOPPER · JOAN TAYLOR

wildest dreams had I set eyes on anything so excitingly jaw-dropping as the scaly reptilian monster grappling with an elephant in the photograph before me. I was mesmerized by it. Next to the film's title in small lettering was the barrier to me seeing it—"X" certificate. Adults Only. I gazed at the cinema with mixed feelings—so near, yet so far away. Banned, at 10 years of age, from experiencing for myself the wonders unfolding inside (little did I then realize that this one film was to become a personal yardstick for the next 10 years or so). To add insult to injury, my parents paid a visit to see the film two days later and refused point blank to tell me about it afterwards on the grounds that I was still far too young to be bothering with monsters and adult motion pictures. It was very small consolation that I was dragged along to *Three Men in a Boat* soon after, a British comedy outing that made absolutely no impression on me whatsoever as I fell asleep through most of it. And as if that wasn't bad enough, I then had to weather nearly four long hours of *The Ten Commandments* a month later, shaking myself awake during the parting of the Red Sea sequence and then dropping off again. Oh well, I mused—only another six long years to go before I could get around to seeing the likes of *20 Million Miles to Earth* and *The Curse of Frankenstein*.

Back in the school playground, one of our group entertained us by relating how, during the week's run of Ray Harryhausen's space-monster yarn, he had successfully slipped in through the side exit door of The Crescent, which conveniently for him had been left ajar by a careless patron, and had caught a peek of the Venusian creature walking into a barn, before being seized by the manager and forcibly ejected. "At least I've seen part of an 'X' film," he boasted, knowing full well that his one-minute viewing of the picture had made us all as jealous as hell and him into the big hero. He was bombarded for days after with questions about the 60 seconds he had been fortunate enough to catch sight of before leaving the cinema by the short route. (It crossed our minds that maybe we should try The Crescent's side doors to gain entry into a horror film, but the idea was quickly dismissed. If apprehended by the management and our parents were informed, it would have meant detention or the cane, both of which I had endured in the past and had no desire to endure again.) In the meantime, the only gratification to be had along fantasy lines by us non-adults was either reading for the umpteenth time Wells' *The War of the Worlds* and John Wyndham's *The Day of the Triffids* or listening to and being chilled to the bone by *Journey into Space*, broadcast on the Light Program on Monday evenings—we all suffered a few restless nights as a consequence of rocket pilot Jet Morgan's adventures on Mars. Produced by Charles Chilton, this celebrated radio series (at the height of its popularity, it achieved an astonishing audience of nearly six million, dwarfing television viewing figures of that time) charting the exploits of Morgan, Lemmy and Doc in deep space, on the moon and on Mars, was the aural equivalent to *Quatermass*. It had many a lad and lass glued to the wireless set, quaking in terror, their imaginations pushed to the limit as the English space explorers encountered all kinds of obstacles when they voyaged around the solar system, including hostile aliens inhabiting the Red Planet.

There was no getting away from the irrefutable fact that the unattainable "X" film had now taken on the mantle of the Holy Grail among us cinema-going youngsters. Even the titles were intriguing. *House of Wax, Revenge of the Creature, The Curse of Franken-stein, 20 Million Miles to Earth*—how much more provocative they sounded than *Cinderella, Trouble in Store, The Robe* and *The Happiest Days of Your Life*. This was a period in the rather austere, highly self-disciplined '50s when very few of us had television (my family rented their first set in March 1957), pop music for anybody under the age of 30 didn't exist, magazines for the under-30s didn't exist either and therefore the cinema really was the be-all and end-all as far as "what to do to amuse oneself" was concerned. "What's on at the flicks?" became the standard byword for a whole generation in an England utterly devoid of any form of entertainment for overactive children. There was, of course, the radio, or the wireless as it was then known, but this was cluttered up with endless situation comedies and band-type music which most people of my age disliked intensely—it was strictly for the grandparents. The only thing worth tuning in to was *Journey into Space* and, at a stretch, Tony Hancock. The plain truth was that from a "pictures" point of view we had become bored to death with Disney cartoons, Westerns and comedies, the trouble being that if you were heard moaning about your lot, or, heaven forbid, dared to express an opinion, a swift backhander to the ears signified that you were well and truly out of favor. What our mothers and fathers were failing to comprehend was that we urgently needed something a bit more substantial to get our cinematic teeth into, although having said that, the odd surprise did happen now and again.

On a Wednesday in September, I was playing with my model cowboys and Indians on the kitchen table, disregarding everything and everyone around me, when Mum, preparing dinner, spoke out of the blue.

"Barry."

"Yeah?"

"Don't say 'yeah.' Say 'yes.'"

"Sorry. What?"

A deep sigh from my mother who was probably dismayed, as most post-war parents were during those years, by her offspring's declining standards in grasping the basics of the English language.

"I've decided to take you and Roger to the pictures on Saturday for a treat. *Forbidden Planet* is on at The Crescent. I want the pair of you here at 4:00 on the dot. No shenanigans from either of you, especially you." (Staring straight at me.) "The film starts at a quarter to five. So try and make sure you're clean and decent just for once."

The cowboys and Indians were hurriedly forgotten. Did I hear correctly or were my ears deceiving me? *Forbidden Planet*. Not *The Belles of St. Trinian's*, not Norman Wisdom's *Up in the World*, not Disney's *Davy Crockett and the River Pirates*—no, a science fiction film by the sound of it, one that I had never heard of before but a welcome change nonetheless. Needless to say, I somehow managed, with difficulty, to behave myself on the Saturday, keeping well away from my normal pursuits of tree-climbing, building camps in the woods, wading through boggy ponds, soaking my clothes in the river and fighting with our gang's enemies, presenting myself as an unusually spic-and-span 10-year-old at the allotted hour. Mum was suitably impressed, even to the extent of bestowing on me a beaming smile, and we all enjoyed every minute of MGM's fantasy-fest, resulting in me babbling to my schoolfellows ad nauseam with detailed reports on it, as I was the only person in our group who was allowed to see the film.

But this was a solitary affair and only highlighted yet again the fact that all the worthwhile pictures did not carry a "U" certificate—*Forbidden Planet* was an "A." Be that as it may, it was no good trying to sneak into any cinema in our neck of the woods to see an X-rated program. Some of our little clique of fantasy fans had tried to do this and failed miserably. Even the next best thing to an "X," the "A" films, were impossible to see on one's own, although you could get in with an adult. However, it was not much fun being lumbered with a grown-up or even your parents, whether they were considerate to your needs or not. Such was the strict code of conduct practiced in British cinemas during this particular decade. There was absolutely nothing we could do but try to grow older as quickly as possible. But when 1958 arrived, a publication from the United States appeared in the United Kingdom's newsagents that seemed to have a profound effect on myself and many of my friends, firing up our collective imaginations to even greater heights and making us all the more determined to see these prohibited motion pictures, whether we were years under the legal age or not. That publication was Forrest J Ackerman's immortal *Famous Monsters of Filmland*.

As luck would have it, my after-school paper route allowed me access to the most infamous monster magazine of them all, as it was not for sale to persons under 12 years of age, if memory serves me right. Surreptitiously slipping the occasional issue between the papers I was due to deliver on the evening round, and knowing full well that it would be curtains for me if the shopkeeper found out (and even worse if my parents discovered what I had been up to), it was then smuggled into school the following day where, out of sight of any prying teachers who might be afoot, we fledgling film enthusiasts would pore over its hallowed pages with their extraordinary parade of photographs, our eyes on stalks. If ever a publication warranted an "Adults Only" certificate, it was this one. We were left aghast as we turned over page after stunning page of monstrosities from the well-known movies to the obscurities. It captured and enslaved our souls, instilling in us a passion like no other of its kind had done before, or would thereafter. It was, quite simply, *the* catalyst for everything that followed. The marvelous thing about *Famous Monsters* was its knack of providing the same amount of prominent coverage to the grade Z monsters as to the more familiar ones from the classier films. Therefore, the fungus natives from *The Unknown Terror*, the zombie in *The Dead One*, the mutants from *The Unearthly*, *Target Earth!*'s cardboard robots and most of Bert I. Gordon's back-projected, inept-looking creations were right up there with Toho's *Godzilla*, the gill-man from *Creature from the Black Lagoon*, the insect-man in *The Fly*, Ray Harryhausen's Cyclops and Karloff as the Frankenstein monster. All films, good, bad or ugly, were treated as equals—the classics were covered side-by-side with the B's and the Z's. We were also astonished and envious to learn that in the United States, Vampira, a large-breasted female with raven-black hair, arched eyebrows and fingers like talons, hosted a television show devoted entirely to the screening of old '30s and '40s horror films. American youngsters, it seemed, were far more fortunate than their English cousins in having their tastes provided for, as we had absolutely no access to these delights, either on television or the cinema, where we were barred for being too young—the United States did not have the strict censorship laws that we had to suffer. The upside of this, as we discovered later, was that our "X" films were less likely to have been messed around with by the censor, as adults were the only ones who could see them. In America, they played on the whole to a general audience but suffered from severe editing in some cases because of this.

A group decision was arrived at—*these* were the movies that, one way or another, we most definitely *had* to see. Later titles in this field included *Castle of Frankenstein* (1959 onwards and a close runner-up to *Famous Monsters*), *Horror Monsters* (1961-1966), Ackerman's own *Spacemen* (1961-1964), *Monster World* (1964-1966), and *Mad Monsters* (1961-1966), while from the Continent emerged *Cine Fantastique* and *Midi Minuit Fantastique*. But it was Ackerman's groundbreaking and highly influential magazine devoted entirely to the world of fantastic cinema that beyond question turned us on to horror, science fiction and fantasy movies, fascinating us and scaring us in equal measures. For example, Max Schreck as *Nosferatu* put the wind up me for days when I first turned over a page and saw a photo of the stick-like vampire lurking in the shadows, as did Chaney in *The Phantom of the Opera* and Conrad Veidt in *The Cabinet of Dr. Caligari*. Decades old they may well have been, but these ancient classics could still exert a powerful force over innocent young eyes, and any publication that could somehow imbue the rubbery tree-monster in *From Hell It Came* with an air of foreboding surely deserved all the accolades eventually heaped upon it. Until the magazine's arrival in the United Kingdom in 1958, none of us had any prior knowledge of the hundreds of films written about between its lurid covers. We did now! But if these fabulous and unsettling images of aliens, vampires, werewolves, zombies, various Frankenstein monsters, mutants, robots, dinosaurs, assorted creatures and insects the size of office blocks really did exist on celluloid, where were they all and why were they not being shown in England?

As it happens, a few were beginning to emerge from the distributors and being screened—it's just that we had somehow overlooked them until one day in October 1958, John casually mentioned in the school lunch-break to Ian and myself that *The Mole People* was being shown at The Crescent on Sunday, as he had spotted both the stills and poster the previous evening. Our pulses quickened. John suddenly had our undivided attention. "What certificate is it?" we asked eagerly. "An 'A' I think," he replied. Our hearts sank. You had to be 14 and over to see an "A," although an obliging adult could take you in if so inclined. It was all so frustrating, but we nevertheless hatched a plan. I was 11 years old and quite tall for my age. *I* would be the obliging adult taking in two of my friends, both of whom were also 11 but looked it. We would chance it, even though we all knew that The Crescent had garnered a fearsome reputation in our area as far as age and certificates were concerned. Everybody was aware of what could happen once you were inside the foyer—if you bore little or no resemblance to a 14- or 16-year-old and the picture showing was either an "A" or an "X," you were resolutely shown the door. No amount of argument, shouting, stamping of feet or swearing would sway the management. They stood by the letter of the law on this matter and were as immovable as the Rock of Gibraltar, as we were about to discover, on this occasion and many more to follow.

It was with a feeling of severe trepidation, therefore, that we duly arrived outside the cinema at 1:45 p.m. on the Sunday, gathering ourselves together for the baptism of fire. We were three very highly strung boys hoping that this would be the big breakthrough—our very first American fantasy movie. I recalled seeing pictures of the knobby, big-clawed creatures from the film in

Famous Monsters and there was one right in front of me, in the stills behind the glass, straight out of Ackerman's magazine. I turned to stare at the black and white poster that grandly proclaimed: "Deep Inside the Earth! A Lost Civilization! A Million Years Old!" with another of the monsters menacing John Agar. Phew!! Anticipation between us was at fever pitch.

We went in through the swing doors, trying to be as nonchalant as possible, acutely mindful of the reality of the situation—this was uncharted territory! Silence in the foyer as we queued for tickets. The very tall chap in front of me asked for a seat in the back stalls. "That will be 1s 6d please, sir," came an elderly sounding voice from the kiosk. Then, with a lump in my throat and sweaty palms, I realized that it was my turn. Gimlet eyes from a gray-haired lady who appeared to be over 50 bored into me with a searching look as, step by step, I inched forward on trembling legs. Before I had a chance to ask for our tickets, she said, "How old are you, son?" and why was it that I knew exactly she was going to say it? "14," I blurted out. "No, I'm sorry but you're not. I cannot let you in," was her cutting but expected response. I didn't even bother to argue with her. Deflated, we walked out, cursing and resenting the customers who were still lining up to see *The Mole People* and *Curucu, Beast of the Amazon* (also an "A"), almost, ridiculous as it now sounds, on the verge of tears. Again—so near and yet so far. Our first pathetic attempt to sit through a couple of all-American monster movies had ended in complete and utter failure. Would we ever get to see these pictures without waiting a further three to five years before we were legally old enough? What our group eventually termed as the big breakthrough year, after suffering one disappointment after another, was still some way off—for the present, we were just going to have to be patient, although our cunning little minds reasoned that just because we had come up against the proverbial brick wall at The Crescent did not necessarily mean that we would not try to gain entry somewhere else in our quest for cinematic thrills and excitement.

YOU'RE NOT OLD ENOUGH SON
(1958-1960)

December 1958 brought Nigel Kneale's *Quatermass and the Pit* to the nation's television screens, the third in the highly significant series to be broadcast by the BBC and the most ambitious in concept, running for six weeks at 35 minutes per episode. I was the only member of the Atkinson clan allowed to stay up and look at the two fairly innocuous but still creepy opening episodes on the flickering 14-inch black and white monitor in front of me, despite the warning given out at the start of each program by a dour-faced presenter that it was *not* suitable for persons of a nervous disposition. As I huddled up against the fireguard in our living room, the program slowly but ever so surely implanted in my subconscious a growing sense of unease, with goosebumps running up and down my body in spite of the heat from the fire. The name *Quatermass* was synonymous with terror, as everyone knew—I remembered my father's tale of the fainting incident at The Crescent when *The Quatermass Experiment* was showing, and my mother reinforced this by saying that she recollected all the fuss the original serial of the film had made in the country when it was broadcast on the BBC in 1953, although we had no television at the time. By episode 3 of this particular *Quatermass*, entitled "Imps and Demons," I was reduced to a shivering wreck, and after the closing minutes when Andre Morell solemnly intoned, "It's alright. They're dead. They've been dead for a long time," as the camera lingered on the decaying insect-like Martians in the hull of the ancient spaceship, I was informed in no uncertain terms by those on high—"No more!" But I stuck to my guns and insisted that I watch the remaining three episodes because, I argued, *Quatermass and the Pit* was all the rage in England—everyone who was lucky enough to have a television was tuning in to see it and then discussing each episode at great lengths. The police were reporting that crime was down to an all-time low on the nights it was being aired, and several politicians were complaining that parliamentary meetings were making them miss the odd episode, or part of an episode (no video recorders around in those days).

Even the daily newspapers were giving the serial front-page coverage, so great was its impact on the public as a whole. Under no circumstances was I going to be the only person among my circle of friends to miss out on all the action, particularly as it was currently the sole topic of conversation in the school playground. Amazingly, my usually strict parents heard me out and relented. By the end of the series in January 1959, terrified out of my wits and petrified at sleeping all alone (I had my own bedroom in the family home), I was given to sneaking into my brother's bed in the middle of the night after making sure that the rest of the family was asleep, and then creeping back to my room at the crack of dawn, ensuring nothing nasty of an alien nature was concealing itself in the corners or under the bed. This carried on for several nights in a row until the BBC's electrifying serial, with its unnerving and disturbing scenes backed by some hauntingly eerie music, had been purged from my system and life could return to some form of normality. Throughout this time, both my parents and my brother were completely unaware of my nocturnal activities! In fact, so

Andre Morell portrayed Quatermass in the BBC television version of *Quatermass and the Pit*.

shaken was I by *Quatermass and the Pit* that the thought entered my mind that perhaps "X" and "A" certificate movies would have the same effect on me and maybe, just maybe, I ought to pursue less harmful and more conventional interests. One glance at the latest edition of *Famous Monsters of Filmland*, however, dispelled any such thoughts and it was thereafter a return to business as usual as far as our pursuit of the fantasy scene went.

Back in the realms of cinema-land, we became aware that a few of the movies featured in *Famous Monsters* were starting to be shown at The Crescent, but on Sundays only—we didn't latch on to the significance of the Sunday-only programs, which would eventually turn out to play a major role in our lives, until nearly two years later. In February 1959, four of us had another attempt at gaining entry into Leatherhead's one and only cinema when *The Amazing Colossal Man* appeared with an "A" certificate, but again we were turned away as being judged not old enough, which of course we weren't, but that was beside the point! The same thing happened in July—in we trooped to see *The Incredible Shrinking Man*, also rated an "A," and out we trooped a few minutes later, feeling miserable and muttering under our breaths all manner of oaths directed at the female member of the cinema's staff who, after all, was only doing her job, albeit much too successfully for our liking.

The Crescent, we ruefully pondered, was proving to be a very tough nut to crack, and we were becoming fed up with having to be carted along by our respective parents to suffer a succession of "U" features such as *Henry V*, *Above Us the Waves* and yet another Disney movie, *The Shaggy Dog*. "U" films, we said to each other, were just so uninteresting. How could anybody work up any enthusiasm over them? The only purpose they served was to allow us the chance to see, once in a while, the trailer to a forthcoming X-rated picture, which only added to our growing discontentment—a few minutes of *The Fly* and even less of Hammer's latest box office smash, *Dracula*, were tempting morsels that were so far out of reach that they might just as well have been screened on the moon.

As well as the trailers, reviews of movies in the national newspapers sometimes had our fevered imaginations working overtime—but only if it was a write-up to a horror film. These reviews usually came out on a Friday, then repeated on Saturday, and it was on such a day that I was idly flicking through *The Daily Mirror* when the new releases attracted my attention, and one new release in particular—*First Man into Space*. Each film under review was allotted a small photograph, two inches square, and the picture under the description of *First Man into Space* showed what appeared to be a mud-encrusted figure poised menacingly over a terrified woman in the middle of a wood. I stared hard until my eyes began to ache—I couldn't make it out. Was it a man or a monster? Whatever, it was a darned sight more interesting than cartoons, cowboys or soldiers. That night, I cut the page out and took it to school on Monday where, under the lens of a magnifying glass supplied by Billy, the mysterious figure was scrutinized at great length, even if blowing it up by a power of three only made it seem more grainy and obscure. The review told of an astronaut returning to Earth coated with an alien substance that turned him into a blood-drinking killer, so we reasoned that the thing in the wood must be the blood-drinking astronaut—unfortunately, his face was obscured, which was a pity as we really wanted to see what this man, if in fact it was a man, looked like. But the film title alone had us hooked. Blimey, we exclaimed. Fantastic! Is it on around here, and can we see it?

"No good us wanting to see it," I said, dampening everybody's hopes. "It's an 'X'."

"OK, but is it on?" As if being an "X" didn't make a difference!

"I don't bloody know. I'll keep an eye out for it."

But *First Man into Space* never did turn up at our local cinemas, appearing much later on the Sunday circuits, and our group was again left with a deep, resentful feeling of aggravation that out there, splendid movies of a different variety were being screened but at the moment they were out of bounds to 11- and 12-year-olds and would remain so for the foreseeable future.

The three major highlights of a very dispiriting 1959 were the releases of Columbia's surprise hit *The Seventh Voyage of Sinbad* and later on, Hammer's glossy *The Hound of the Baskervilles*, followed by the double feature *The Colossus of New York* with *The Space Children*. Our little collection of fantasy addicts had drooled over the stills to *Sinbad*, which was showing at The Crescent, and I had seen the enticing trailer to the film a week earlier while sitting through Disney's *A Light in the Forest*. Fortunately for me, my mother decided to take both myself and my younger brother to see it as a rare family night out—in 1959, *The Seventh Voyage of Sinbad* carried an "A" certificate. We arrived at the cinema late, in fact 10 minutes into the film. I was so enthralled at the sight of Ray Harryhausen's animated Cyclops roaring away on the big screen that despite the efforts of the usherette vainly trying to shine a dim beam of light with her torch down the packed stalls in the dark, I must have trodden on and tripped over a dozen pair of feet as we blindly made our way to our seats, so riveted was my attention to the action being played out in front of me and not on the audience watching it, much to their annoyance. I was completely bowled over by *Sinbad*—the visuals, the incredible monsters, the music, in

French poster for *7th Voyage of Sinbad*

fact everything—even though we never got around to seeing the first few "missed" minutes, and couldn't stop talking about it to the gang for days afterwards. This was in March. In June, my mother again took me to another "A" movie, *The Hound of the Baskervilles*, my very first Hammer production. For some reason, I remained totally unimpressed. I was too young and not knowledgeable enough to appreciate the lush color, the authentic set design, Cushing and Lee's winning performances and Terence Fisher's expert direction, all of which went straight over my head, so much so that when quizzed at school the next day, the only comment I could make, with a shrug of the shoulders, was, "It was OK, but not very frightening."

A few weeks later, I was taken along to Paramount's *The Colossus of New York*, appearing with *The Space Children*. *Colossus* was rated an "A" and it would have been entirely fruitless to attempt entry at The Crescent on my own, so I dutifully trotted along with my parents, grateful that at least it was something a little bit different from the usual Western or comedy I was used to watching with them, even if both movies failed to leave their mark. Regardless of this, I offered up a silent prayer that perhaps a crossroads had been reached in my cinema-going fortunes and that things might now start looking up.

Despite these initial sorties into the world of fantasy cinema, we still yearned to see the scarier and more "grown-up" movies that appeared between the pages of our ever-increasing collections of *Famous Monsters of Filmland* (most of which had been "borrowed" on a permanent basis from various newsagents and booksellers) but that were proving to be downright elusive. Undoubtedly they were out there somewhere—returning from a trip to the Royal Tournament in London in July, I noticed that *20 Million Miles to Earth* was showing in Cheam, while on a visit to my uncle in Folkestone, we passed a small theater in Hythe that had me craning my

The ABC in Epsom is now an Odeon Twin cinema.

neck in the back seat of the car as the poster outside was advertising *The Return of the Vampire*. Maybe one day...

1960 heralded the start of a new decade and what would eventually turn out to be a key chapter in my life as a committed cinema-goer. First off the starting line, appearing on the major circuits, was 20th Century Fox's highly imaginative, big-budget and very successful *Journey to the Center of the Earth*. A group of us jumped on the bus to Epsom after school, arriving very late at the Odeon and entering the stalls during the scene in the film where James Mason and his fellow explorers are peering down into a glittering crystalline grotto—this evocative sequence, underlined by Bernard Herrmann's magical music, left a lasting impression on me, reinforcing my fascination for all things of a fantastical nature. In those days you could unofficially remain in a cinema until closing time, so we sat through the remainder of the performance together with the whole of the next as well and then left, feeling that we had had our money's worth, particularly as the film was over two hours long. *The Lost World* came around a few weeks later—this was "A" rated but six of us decided to risk it and we all ambled past the ticket kiosk at the ABC in Epsom without being questioned about our ages, rather to our surprise. At last, we thought, a cinema not run on the draconian rules of The Crescent in Leatherhead. Perhaps we should come here more often. We enjoyed this colorful adventure at the time, even though in later years I came to look upon it as a hastily made and rather tedious actioner put together on the back of the commercial success of *Journey to the Center of the Earth*, fatally eschewing the period charm of Sir Arthur Conan Doyle's classic novel. So a couple of highly watchable motion pictures were to be had from what we saw as the usual never-ending sea of mediocrity stretching out before us—but on the 3rd of May 1960, matters abruptly changed for the better and the cinematic breakthrough that I had longed for finally happened.

Hammer's newest nationwide hit, *The Mummy*, was on at The Crescent for three days. Once again, several of us hung around outside the cinema's stately frontage, gawping at the stills and the great poster showing the bandaged menace on the march with a torch beam passing straight through its body. Christopher Lee as Kharis in the swamp was the only still that showed the monster of the title, but it was powerful enough for us to start a little wager in the playground on Tuesday. One Graham Haines placed a bet of five shillings (a vast sum of money for a schoolboy in 1960!) that none of us would have the audacity to sneak in to see the film or, more to the point, persuade old gimlet-eyes behind the kiosk that we were of the proper legal age to be let in, thereby quashing what would be her undoubted protestations to the contrary. A very big challenge indeed, bearing in mind the cinema's repute.

However, unbeknown to the others, I already held a trump card up my sleeve, which I wasn't going to let on about. A few days previously, my father had knocked me for six by actually agreeing, at my request, to take me to see *The Mummy*, even though he would be breaking the law by doing so as I was 13 years and 4 months old—still a very long way off the 16 years you had to be to see an "X" film. What's more, Dad was not only an ex-Royal Marine but a special constable, so for once he would be in breach of his own code of conduct and, quite frankly, not acting as a responsible adult. None of this bothered me, though. For reasons of his own (had he entered into a pact with my mother? "Let him see a horror film. It might stop him going on about them."), he was taking me to see an X-rated picture on Wednesday night and I wasn't going to enter into the whys and wherefores with him. So I craftily took Graham Haines up on his bet, much to the cynical amusement of the rest of the gang who thought that I stood no chance of seeing the film, not at this particular cinema, or any other cinema, come to that.

We arrived at The Crescent just before the 6:00 p.m. showing. "Just walk through the foyer toward the stairs leading to the upstairs circle. I'll get the tickets," said Dad in hushed tones. Feeling extremely agitated and trying to appear as inconspicuous as possible, which wasn't easy under the circumstances, I shuffled toward the stairway on leaden legs, ignoring the ticket kiosk with its grim occupant. As I drew level with the confectionery booth, the woman behind the counter drew me into her gaze and addressed me in a harsh tone.

"Are you 16, son?"

"Yes," I replied, trying to avoid her eyes.

"Are you sure?" she persisted.

"Ask my father. He's getting the tickets."

"Excuse me sir, is your son 16?" she barked across a thankfully more or less empty foyer. This was becoming a bit of an ordeal all round.

"Yes he is," confirmed my father, lying through his back teeth with uncustomary ease.

The hurdle had been overcome—we, or rather I, was in! With the confectionery woman scowling at me, knowing full well that I had "got away with it," we reached the stalls in the circle, settling down in silence in a full house. Nothing happened for a couple of minutes and I began to feel vulnerable, thinking that at any moment a figure would appear from downstairs and throw me out, father or no father. Then, to my relief, the lights dimmed and the certification details appeared behind the slowly parting curtains: *The Mummy*. Certificate X. Adults Only. I shivered in expectation and glanced around, but no one was paying any attention to me, three years underage or not, so I relaxed and sat through nearly 90 minutes of Hammer mayhem, me, at least, feeling exhilarated and stirred by what was happening on the big screen.

As we made our way out, one wag in the queue waiting to get in remarked loudly, "He looks a bit white." The dolt could not have been more wrong. I wasn't in the slightest bit scared, only secretly pleased and smug that I had cracked, with a little help, The Crescent's nut. Dad,

as thoughtful as ever, spared me the embarrassment of watching the second feature, *Bed Without Breakfast*, a long-forgotten sex movie, as he probably thought that it would contain material too risqué for my young eyes. I caught it two years later on a double bill with the ubiquitous *20 Million Miles to Earth* and the only risqué scene in it was the fleeting glimpse of an ample bosom almost hidden from view behind an enormous brassiere. Back at school the next day, I was the hero of the hour. Admitting that yes, it *was* my father who had performed the impossible feat of getting me in at The Crescent, I produced as proof the two ticket stubs to a stunned Graham Haines, who duly coughed up his five shillings while I went on to relate to a disbelieving and admiring crowd a frame-by-frame account of *The Mummy*'s plot.

I had done it once—there was no reason why I could not do it again. *Circus of Horrors* was showing at the ABC in New Malden, a sensationalistic shocker that was playing to packed houses despite adverse comments from the critics concerning its brutal content. Two weeks after successfully negotiating The Crescent's barriers, Chris, his girlfriend and I boarded the bus to New Malden one rain-swept evening to take in the picture. We walked up to the cinema, naively full of self-confidence, noticing the garish, blood-spattered film poster advertising the horrors within—wild-eyed Anton Diffring leering over a half-naked girl with a terrified expression on her face, another girl in a skimpy costume pinioned to a revolving board by several knives, "X certificate—Adults Only" blazoned underneath in big red dripping letters. The light from the foyer flooded into the soaking wet street and over the poster, beckoning us to enter—if we dared. I breathed deeply and gulped back my mounting fear, leading the way up the steps, through the doors, into the warm foyer and heading straight to the booth. This time around, however, there was no Mr. Atkinson senior on hand to come to my aid as the stern-looking man eyed me from behind the glass of the ticket kiosk.

"Three for the back stalls, please," I whispered, my mouth drying up, the self-confidence turning in a split second to self-doubt.

"You're not old enough son," was the quick-fire response.

"Yes I am. I'm 16," I counteracted, trying to sound dismissive but failing miserably.

"You'll have to prove it. Have you got your birth certificate on you?"

"No, of course I haven't." What a stupid question!

"Then I'm sorry but I can't let you and your friends in."

I turned round to Chris and his girlfriend and at the queue forming behind them, who were becoming curious as to what was holding them up. It was no use—this man was not going to budge, not an inch. Perhaps Chris had thought that some of my good fortune in managing to steal in to see *The Mummy* would rub off onto the three of us that particular evening. He was wrong! Feeling thoroughly dejected, we walked back out into the rain and caught the next bus home—the following day at school there was to be, on this occasion, *no* frame-by-frame account of *Circus of Horrors* to relate to my group.

In July, the ever-present *Revenge of the Creature* appeared at the ABC in Fetcham, double-billed with *Man Made Monster*, a really out-of-this-world program to set the blood racing. Would persistence on my part now reap dividends? I was determined to see some of these movies whatever it took, legal or otherwise, so I asked around and decided to swallow my pride by taking some advice from one of our enemies. George was tall and spotty-faced with acne, and could just about pass for a 16-year-old in bad light; furthermore, he had proved it by clocking up several X-rated movies at various local cinemas, mostly of the gangster and sex variety, or what passed for sex in those days—he wasn't interested in horror films. Accordingly, I collared him in the playground one dinner hour.

"How do you manage to get in all the time then? What's the big secret?"

"Well, I'm taller than you for a start," he said, stating the obvious. He then saw how downcast I was looking.

"Right, Barry. Here's how you do it. Lower your voice, try to make it sound deeper and lie about your bloody age. That might do the trick—or it might not."

"Eh? But I've tried doing that. It doesn't work."

"Right. This is what you do. They always ask you when you were born. Lie to them and give them a date. You were born in 1947, weren't you?"

"Yeah." How did he know that?

"Well, if the chap behind the counter says, 'When were you born?' you say…"

I took my cue, performed a quick mental calculation and said, "31st January 1944," even though it didn't sound right.

"Correct. Stick a load of Brylcreem on your hair as well and comb it back like the teddy boys do. It makes you look older."

"OK, if you say so, I'll try it. You've seen a few X films at The Crescent, haven't you?" I asked enviously.

"Yep. I saw *And God Created Woman* there a couple of weeks ago."

"Have you ever tried getting in at the cinema over in Fetcham?"

"No. Never been there. Why, what's on?" he said, frowning.

"Revenge of the Creature."

"Huh," he snorted, showing his contempt for my tastes by slouching off to a group of his friends and leaving me standing on my own.

The big day arrived—Pete and I caught the bus to Fetcham on Sunday, not bothering with the long cycle ride, and arrived five minutes before *Man Made Monster* was about to begin. We took a quick gander at the gill-man and Lon Chaney on the posters outside, with the magic "X"

beside each one, and then crept into the half-empty foyer shaking like leaves, hoping against hope that this cinema, untried and untested, adopted a more benevolent attitude toward its customers, whether they were underage or the correct age. The pair of us approached the ticket kiosk side by side to give each other moral support and, trying to lower my voice to a more manly level, I asked for two tickets for the back stalls. The woman behind the glass stared fixedly at us for what seemed like an age, and then her eyes began darting from me to Pete and back to me again.

"And just how old are you?"

"16."

"And you?" She looked hard at Pete.

"16 as well," he said hoarsely and immediately I thought, "Why couldn't we have said 17 to make it more authentic, or at least different?"

Her eyes stayed on my beleaguered friend.

"When were you born?"

Pete made the mistake of hesitating, although we had rehearsed this scenario the day before so he should have been prepared for the expected grilling. Judging by the look of him, he wasn't! His cheeks had reddened and he was sweating—a sure giveaway that he was trying it on.

"Er, er, the um, 10th of July 1944."

Ignoring him, she turned to me.

"When were you born?"

"The 31st of January 1944," I intoned in my deepest voice, but she wasn't going to be fooled by this hopeless double act that we were putting on for her benefit—and ours!

"I don't believe either of you. Sorry, you'll have to leave."

"Look," I went on, indignantly, "I am 16 years old. We both are!"

"OUT!" she almost screamed, making us flinch. "Stop standing there and wasting my time. I've got other people to serve." As one of those "other people" practically shoved me out of the way to purchase his ticket, no doubt becoming tired at waiting in a queue behind two kids who should have known better and acted their proper ages, Pete and myself hoisted the white flag and left the cinema in defeat, a sense of crushing disappointment weighing heavily on our shoulders with the knowledge that we were being denied the chance to experience one of the legendary *Creature* movies. Perhaps, in hindsight, we had raised our hopes too high with the certainty that we could actually get in to see it.

The Odeon in Cheam was the next unfortunate cinema to receive our unwanted attentions. *Horrors of the Black Museum*, another smash hit that had provoked the stuffy U.K. critics with its lashings of sadistic violence, had been on there for a week and we came up with a pretty foolhardy scheme to obtain our slice of the action. So desperate were we to watch an "X" certificate film that some members of our group were prepared to resort to anything, even bribery and corruption, as long as the end result culminated in us sitting in a darkened auditorium, out of sight and out of mind, being exposed to the thrills and delights of an adult horror movie. George, he with the spotty face who looked 16 and fancied himself as a bit of a hard nut, was cautiously approached in the playground for a second time and offered a substantial sum of money collected from our paper routes and meat routes if he would be so kind as to accompany three of us, including myself, to Cheam on the Saturday, buy *his* ticket and, once inside, let us in through one of the side exit doors. We sincerely believed that this generous offer would appeal to the greedier side of George's nature and that he would play ball with this piece of deception—after all, sticking young defenseless boys' heads down the school toilets to obtain the odd piece of loose change was all part of his deplorable repertoire, so in a way we were stooping to his own low level. In thinking this, though, we were totally wrong. "I've told you lot before. I don't like horror films, so bugger off!" was his acid response and looking directly at me, he said, "No luck with *Revenge of the Creature* then?" With a sneer on his craggy face as he spoke these wounding words, he sloped off to join his own gang, Pete making quite sure he was well out of earshot before telling him to "bugger off" as well.

There was nothing else for it—we would have to go without him. As expected, it was a wasted trip and not, as I had hoped beyond all hope, a case of "third time lucky." Arriving at the cinema just before 7:00 p.m., me, Chris and Pete walked up the imposing steps and pushed open the swing doors to the rather grand foyer, realizing full well that our cards had been marked as soon as we had entered the place because a tall, well-dressed man, obviously the manager judging by his bearing, was looking pointedly in our direction on our wary advance to the ticket counter. I nervously rummaged in my pocket for the correct amount of money, feeling beads of perspiration breaking out on my forehead as he loomed over us, any bravado I may have entertained before we entered the cinema draining away through the soles of my boots now that we were finally inside it.

"Excuse me, lad. Your age, please." This in tones that were uncannily similar to our head teacher at school, especially when he was on the warpath.

"16."

"And yours?"—this to Pete.

"16."

"What about you?"—this to Chris.

"16 years and 3 months."

"Can any of you boys prove that you are 16?"

"No," was our collective response.

"Right. Out you go then. I'm not letting you in."

Off we traipsed into the night, another cinema, another unsuccessful attempt, and no doubt more sarcastic comments from George in the playground on Monday when he would find out that, no, we didn't see *Horrors of the Black Museum* on Saturday and it was all his bloody fault that we had not been able to creep past the kiosk at the Odeon in Cheam—he had been offered a large enough sum to help us but for some strange reason known only to himself had turned it down. An honest hard nut if ever there was one!

But I had the bit between my teeth and wasn't going to be put off so easily in my quest. Remembering that it had been plain sailing getting in to see the A-rated *The Lost World* at the ABC in Epsom, Chris, John, Pete and I decided to try to have a shot at an "X" there—*The Brides of Dracula* was showing in September and John had seen the usual distinctive Hammer poster outside the cinema, a fanged David Peel surrounded by a host of toothsome beauties, all in glorious color with a large X slapped squarely in the middle. Wearing my (at the time) very fashionable

The Cheam Odeon, now a multiplex with three theaters.

three-quarter-length white raincoat, which I personally reckoned added an extra two to three years onto my age, and slicking my hair back with a dollop of grease on the advice of the detestable George, the four of us turned up at 6:30 p.m. and, much to our astonishment, positively breezed through the ABC's barriers without any hassle, even though we were only 13 years and a few months old. Not only were we as pleased as punch, but we had the added bonus of watching what turned out to be one of Hammer's classic vampire thrillers, a full-blooded horror tale that had us clinging to our seats in nervous excitement. As we left the ABC, exiting into the night air in triumphant jubilation, we all voiced the same thought—"Now that was more like it!"

I now had two "X" films under my belt—that was two more than most of my friends at school who had yet to see one (with the exception of George, but he wasn't in our group so he didn't count), although Chris, Pete and John could now boast a solitary success. In John's case, he had tried to sneak in to *The Flesh and the Fiends* at Esher with his girlfriend a couple of weeks previously but had been shown the door (he should have known better—Esher was unknown territory and had not been tested out by the experts), so his much-anticipated second "X" film never materialized. The next day in the playground, I held counsel and my cinema-going public were informed by someone who knew such things that whereas The Crescent in Leatherhead was a "no-go" area as far as "X" and "A" movies were concerned, the ABC in Epsom seemed to welcome you with open arms, as it were. The trouble was that they didn't put on a lot of horror films. Oh well, you couldn't have everything.

As the year drew to a close, my accommodating parents took me along to *The Stranglers of Bombay* at The Crescent, a semi-period horror romp that aroused a certain amount of controversy at the time, as the U.K. censor almost passed it with an "X" certificate but then performed an out-of-character U-turn—there were howls of protests from the rather po'-faced brigade of British film critics when this gruesome catalogue of atrocities eventually went on general release as an "A." This was fine by me, as it gave me the chance to experience all of the ghastly tortures on display that the censor had deemed fit for human consumption, and I found it far livelier than the other Hammer A-rated feature I had seen, *The Hound of the Baskervilles*. Perhaps I preferred my horror films to be in black and white. As it turned out, during the next few years, the vast majority of those that I saw would be.

SUNDAY, 15 FEBRUARY 1959

Saturday, 14 February 1959. Me, Paul, Tony and Dave file slowly up Bridge Street at approximately 5:00 p.m., Nick, my dog, padding forlornly along at our rear, wet and bedraggled. Rain is sheeting down, adding to the already swollen waters of the River Mole which are now steadily rising over the grassy banks, making it a dangerous place for four youngsters and a dog to be. We can only guess that it's 5:00 because none of us have watches—in fact, no one I know owns one. But as it's getting dark, we realize that it must be time to head back home. Besides, after spending the whole day messing about on, and in, the river, we, like the dog, are also wet, muddy and dead beat, and all four of us haven't eaten a scrap of food since leaving our back doors at 8:00 a.m., chewing licorice bubble gum (our favorite) nonstop to stave off the hunger pangs. We haven't had a drink, either, merely a quick sip of water from the Mole—Nick has guzzled his fair share of river water as well, and must be as starving as the rest of us. At the top of Bridge Street, we bear right and march up to the front of The Crescent's dominating frontage that towers loftily above us in the fading light. The current attraction is *Operation Amsterdam*, which doesn't hold any interest—the film that is showing on Sunday, though, does: *The Amazing Colossal Man*. The usual six stills contain two that catch my eye—one shows a man with a pained expression on his face, his clothes in tatters and his skin flayed, the other a bald-headed giant in a loincloth towering over a Las Vegas billboard. The poster, a little way inside the cinema's dimly lit foyer, depicts the same giant causing mayhem, a blonde clutched in one hand, warding off shells from a tank with the other—rather fascinating stuff, we agree. It's an "A" certificate. Neither myself nor the other members of the gang are 14, the age you have to be to see such fodder, but never mind that. I turn to Tony, who is clasping a large glass jam-pot full of greenish river water containing a solitary minnow to his chest, droplets plopping from his saturated hair into the jar.

"Fancy seeing it?"

"I dunno. You can't get in here, can you?"

"Well, we can try it. Paul? Dave? What do you reckon?"

"Yeah, righto. What's on with it?"

I'm not particularly interested in the co-feature, even less so when it turns out to be a war movie, *Tank Commando*, also an "A." After more debate on the subject, I eventually persuade the others that the idea is worth following up, particularly as Sunday can be the most boring day of the week if you are forced to stay in with your parents, so we elect to all meet outside The Crescent at 2:45-ish the next day and attempt the impossible—see a pair of "A" certificates in Surrey's most formidable cinema while being two years under the legal age limit. Even the mere thought of it sends shock waves through my system but I pray, as I trudge up the hill toward home, that luck will be on our side for a change.

Sunday dawns and the rain has stopped. With the morning's routine over with—taking the dog for a run and helping my father in the garden—I make my excuses for missing dinner, something my mother is used to by now, and tramp down the hill to The Crescent dressed in jeans, jumper, an old duffle coat and shoes that have seen better days. Paul, Tony and Dave are lounging around near the majestic building that is our local cinema, looking just as scruffy as I feel. None of us have told our parents that we are spending the afternoon trying to sneak in to see two "A" films—it's best all round if they don't get involved. Perhaps, fingers crossed, our untidy apparel will make us appear older than our 12 years.

However, I'm taking no chances. A man, probably in his twenties, approaches the cinema's steps, eager to view the main feature. So are we—I step directly into his path, addressing him in civil tones.

"Excuse me. Is it alright if we come in with you?" I wave a hand toward my three friends, who put one in mind of the protagonists immortalized within the pages of one of Richmal Crompton's *William* books—ill-groomed, unkempt and shabby. Exactly like myself. He scans us with a hostile expression, taken aback by my apparently bare-faced cheek.

The Amazing Colossal Man and *Cat Girl* ad from *Kinematograph Weekly*

"No, it's not alright. Sorry." Brushing past me, he flounces up the steps, opens the swing doors and disappears into the shadows of the foyer.

"Bloody sod." Tony spits the words out through grimy lips, aimed squarely in the direction of the unhelpful adult's retreating back with venom, voicing our own thoughts, but hold on a minute—another man, older and accompanied by his wife or girlfriend, is walking toward the steps. Let's try again, I mutter to myself.

"Hello. You couldn't take me and my friends in with you, could you?"

"No."

In they go and out we stay. It must be nearly 3:00 now and the film is due to start rolling at any moment. I stare anxiously at the others, sensing deep down that this is a lost cause. Dave breaks the silence in impatient tones:

"Well? This was your idea."

I breathe hard and deep. It's time for battle to commence. "Come on then," I bark, and we walk unsteadily up those daunting steps, throwing wide the cumbersome doors and entering the heavily carpeted foyer, the odor of popcorn, cigarette smoke and cheap perfume making my nostrils twitch. It's deserted—only four slovenly boys finding themselves in a highly vulnerable position, scrutinized by both the lady selling confectionery and the beady-eyed woman behind the glass of the ticket kiosk. In the normal run of events, any persons caught staring at us are regarded with deep suspicion and are told, in so many words, to "Clear off and play marbles." Here though, in these unfamiliar surroundings and not holding home advantage, any such action seems inappropriate, even to us. The paying customers are obviously relaxing in their seats, awaiting the main event. We hesitate—a fatal mistake; it gives us the appearance of a bunch of amateurs at this game of pretense, which of course we are. Tony totters up to the kiosk.

"One ticket please."

"What price ticket do you want?" At the sound of these words, the black clouds begin to disperse. A ray of hope with that question. Have we made it?

"Er...1s 6d please." Then, what we have dreaded happens—the cross-examination!

"You *are* 14?"

"Yeah."

"What is your date of birth?"

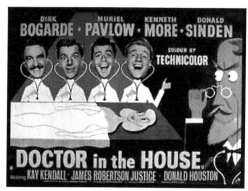

Doctor in the House **was no substitution for** *The Amazing Colossal Man.*

Tony falters. "Er…"

Like a cat that has successfully stalked its prey, she pounces on his hesitation and puts him out of his misery.

"Sorry son. I really don't think you are. And that goes for the rest of you. None of you are old enough. I'm not letting you in."

The black clouds reappear. As we stand there, huddled together like frightened sheep and glaring steadily at gimlet-eyes in the kiosk who glares unflinchingly back, the doors to the auditorium open and the ice-cream lady emerges like a ghost from the gloomy interior—for a brief second, we are honored with a short burst of the thundering soundtrack before the doors swing shut, the soundtrack to a film that on this occasion we are not going to have the pleasure of sitting through. Exiting the warmth of the cinema into the cold winter air, we purposely ignore the stills and poster so as not to lower our spirits any further, Tony swearing loudly at the stone front of The Crescent, using the kind of language that if heard by my father from me would have him reaching for the cane—in this instance, however, it has the effect of restoring our humor a bit.

We can only speculate what a picture with a catchpenny title such as *The Amazing Colossal Man* is about, and how good or bad it is, but surely it has to be far more exciting than *Doctor in the House*, a comedy that I was coerced into going to the previous week with Dave and his parents and which I found markedly unfunny. With hours to spare, we make our way across Bridge Street to the river bemoaning our lot, resolute in our determination to one day see a decent film in that bloody cinema, even if it kills us. (In December 1962, I caught up with Bert I. Gordon's most infamous production at, of all places, The Crescent—after sitting through this pretty average science fiction thriller, with bottom-of-the-barrel special effects, I can quite honestly say that on that Sunday in February 1959, Tony, Paul, Dave and myself had a very lucky escape! The film also gave strength to the old argument among fans that the only thing big about this particular director's works were his initials!)

THE SUNDAY ONE-DAY PROGRAM (1961)

Us hardcore horror, science fiction and fantasy fanatics, which is how we now viewed ourselves (henceforth I shall abbreviate this terminology to HSFF), had accumulated a sizeable collection of magazines devoted to this genre, mostly made up of *Famous Monsters of Filmland* and *Castle of Frankenstein*. We were still mystified as to why the multitude of films written about, categorized, criticized, analyzed and eulogized within these revered pages, not to mention those wonderful photographs that accompanied the text, were not being screened (apart from the odd one or two) in England—well, not where we lived, anyway. The fact was, though, that they were, and had been since the late 1950s. They were right under our very noses and for one reason or another we hadn't really noticed them in the local papers. But one evening in early 1961 I was browsing through the *Leatherhead Advertiser* and observed that The Embassy in Dorking was screening, for one day only on Sunday, *Ghost of Frankenstein* c/w (coupled with) *The Mummy's Curse*. My senses went on high alert. There they were, showing at a cinema only a few miles up the road, two horror movies from the 1940s, typical of the kind that I had read about in the pages of the fanzines we had been immersing ourselves in for months on end. Both were rated "X," but perhaps that was an obstacle that could be surmounted. On the same day, the attraction at the

ABC in Cobham was *The Hypnotic Eye* c/w *The Wasp Woman*. Crikey! Four great films appearing at nearby cinemas on a Sunday, which during that period was supposed to be the quietest day of the week—peace at all times was the unwritten law of the land, to be abided by all, even youngsters bent on the kind of mischief that we used to get up to sometimes. How interesting. Leafing through the paper, it became apparent that quite a few of the other cinemas in the area were open on this day and screening films on a Sunday-only basis—my local The Crescent, the ABC in Fetcham, the ABC in Epsom, and the Odeon in Epsom. Dorking's other cinema, The Pavilion, was closed on the Sabbath. Over the next few weeks, I monitored the situation and there was no doubt about it—some tremendously exciting movies were at long last beginning to materialize in our locality on what became known to our group of fans as the Sunday one-day program circuit.

In the late 1950s and early 1960s, the weekly pattern of film presentations in Britain was vastly different to what the public is used to today. A major release was nearly always shown with a co-feature, the exceptions being the big expensive epics such as *Ben-Hur*, *Spartacus* and *The Ten Commandments*. So, two films plus trailers, a small amount of advertising and occasionally the Pathe News made up a typical afternoon and evening performance. These programs usually ran from Monday to Wednesday, followed by a complete change of films from Thursday to Saturday. Most of the epics ran for a whole week. Sundays, on the other hand, were reserved for the one-day programs and this is where the horror and science fiction film buffs were well catered for, as these Sunday screenings predominately consisted of either two horror/science fiction/fantasy movies or a combination of a horror/science fiction/fantasy feature with a gangster/sex film, most of them X-rated, some "A"s and a smattering of "U"s. The Sunday exhibitions gradually died out in the late '60s and were replaced for a short time by the Saturday late-night shows that put on similar films, but during the years 1961 to 1966, scores of great double bills direct from the pages of *Famous Monsters of Filmland* surfaced to capacity audiences thrilled by these

The Crescent in Leatherhead was a favorite local movie theater.

types of pictures, long before the days when multimillion-dollar computerized digital effects, mass marketing in the media and enough tie-in merchandising on display to sink a ship was sometimes the only way to guarantee a film's commercial success.

A point worth remembering was the number of cinemas that were available to the local community during this period. Our group of cinema-goers had access to The Crescent in Leatherhead, Dorking's Embassy and Pavilion, the Odeon and the ABC in Epsom and the ABCs in Cobham and Fetcham, not forgetting those that were within fairly easy reach on the borders of our home patch, such as in Cheam or New Malden. This proliferation of picture-houses, all within spitting distance of one another, meant that the die-hard HSFF fan very rarely missed out on a double feature as the films circulated like satellites from one cinema to another. For instance, if *The Monster that Challenged the World* c/w *The Vampire* was showing at The Crescent at the same time that *Attack of the 50 Foot Woman* c/w *The Black Scorpion* was playing at The Embassy, Dorking (a favorite watering-hole for this type of fare), you could quite confidently go along to catch The Crescent's program, knowing full well that *Attack of the 50 Foot Woman* would appear at one of the other local cinemas in a few weeks' time, or even sooner. Consequently, very few of these double bills, if any, escaped the net—they always cropped up somewhere within our boundaries.

Many such double bills were stuck together like limpets for years—*Teenage Frankenstein* c/w *Blood Is My Heritage*, *Invasion of the Body Snatchers* c/w *Indestructible Man* and *Frankenstein 1970* c/w *Macabre* were three such samples of the same old pairings repeatedly going the rounds. Others fragmented from one week, or month, to the next. Therefore, *The Deadly Mantis* would appear on a Sunday teamed up with Toho's *Rodan*. Two months later, Universal's popular giant insect thriller could be found sharing the bill with Bert I. Gordon's *The Cyclops*. *Tarantula*, *The Tingler*, *House on Haunted Hill* and *It! The Terror from Beyond Space* were another four examples of movies running over a long period of time with different co-features, although the award for this must surely go to *20 Million Miles to Earth* which, after its initial release in 1957, was continually being shown in cinemas right up until early 1967 with a diverse range of partners, ranging from horror to sex and even adult comedy (Columbia Pictures must have made a small fortune out of this particular production). Over the ensuing years, one could end up by seeing the same film several times over just to catch the different picture it was double billed with at the time!

It is very easy nowadays to dismiss a lot of these films as rubbish, the bottom end, so to speak, of the celluloid market—in fact in some quarters it is fashionable to do so. Although large numbers of them were admittedly produced on fairly low and in many cases minuscule budgets, they displayed in their own individual way a great deal more imagination than their modern-day counterparts, relying to a greater degree on atmosphere and no-nonsense direction rather than a barrage of high-blown special effects. Movies were much briefer, pared to the bone and rarely outstaying their welcome—a running length of approximately 70 to 85 minutes was the norm, with minimal dialogue and characterization before cracking straight on with the storyline, which at least had a beginning, a middle and an end, no matter how routine it might be. A stock of solid and dependable actors—Karloff, Lugosi and Chaney from the '30s and '40s, Marshall Thompson, Richard Denning, John Agar et al. from the '50s, Price, Cushing and Lee—all turned in creditable and believable performances whatever they were starring in, whether it was glossy high-budget or dull low-budget, quite often having to speak dialogue of overwhelming banality while admirably

managing to keep a straight face, and directors including Edward L. Cahn, Nathan Juran, Roger Corman and Jack Arnold turned out some marvelous pieces of work, employing an economy of style with what must have been very restrictive funds.

Above all else, music played a vitally important role—composers such as James Bernard, Hans J. Salter, Bernard Herrmann and a host of others propelled their films along with aggressive, memorable and exciting scores, accentuating the action where necessary to both contribute to the overall mood and compensate for the lack of effects, so unlike the soundtracks of today's pictures, which tend to burble along in the background like meandering streams with nowhere to go. Even the cheaper efforts from the minor studios had half-decent music to listen to. The grade Z bunkum of *Fire Maidens from Outer Space*, *Mesa of Lost Women*, *Robot Monster* and their ilk, which to be quite honest let the side down a bit, did not stand comparison alongside the likes of *Invasion of the Body Snatchers*, *Creature from the Black Lagoon* or *The Incredible Shrinking Man*, just as many of the so-called B movies such as *The Thing that Couldn't Die* deserved some merit in the manner that they were conceived. It didn't matter that many were tatty beyond all description—we had no idea at the time how they were made and had nothing to compare them with anyway; they were simply a form of diversion into a phantasmagoric cosmos that allowed us to indulge our wildest fantasies.

Another fact—these pictures were, on the whole, aimed at an adult audience, hence the abundance of "X" and "A" certificates handed out by the implacable British censor. This also applied to the teenage horror capers churned out in America during the late 1950s—they were also classed as adult material, however juvenile they appeared to the paying customers viewing the silver screen in the United Kingdom. Today the reverse has happened; the younger audience is the one with the spending power at the box office and the newer films reflect this trend in the number of watered-down remakes of X-rated classics such as *The Haunting*, *Godzilla* and *The Mummy* which cannot hold a candle to the original versions—they were far darker and more adult in tone and subject material, and without doubt not suitable for children of that period.

At a time when most modern-day films are transferred straight over to VHS and DVD within a few months of being shown in the cinemas and appear on sale in the shops almost, it seems, with indecent haste, it may come as a surprise to note that a great number of the old horror and science fiction pictures we saw were still being screened commercially on cinema circuits years after release—it was not uncommon to catch a 1930s or 1940s flick at a cinema even in the late 1960s, and nobody at the time thought—"What on earth is *that* movie still showing for?" It was gratefully accepted that one had a golden opportunity to actually see it. Many of the double bills we sat through were composed of films that were often between five and 10 years old, but this wasn't questioned or considered odd—it was a fact of cinema life, plain and simple. People wanted to see them, regardless of age. And see them they did, in very large numbers. During the '60s on a Sunday, cinemas were nearly always packed, with "full house" boards going up outside, queues forming around the block for even the most mundane of double features, patrons standing at the back of the stalls if all the seats had been taken (never mind the fire regulations—if there were any!) and even squatting on the floor between the aisles. As a form of mass entertainment, the cinema reigned supreme—such were the halcyon days of the cinema-going public when standing in the rain outside The Crescent to see *Plan 9 from Outer Space* c/w *The Monster from Green Hell* constituted the high of the week, giving one the same sense of anticipation as filling out a lottery ticket does 40 years later—innocent pleasures indeed!

At last, three long years after purloining my first copy of *Famous Monsters of Filmland* from the newsagents in Leatherhead, one of the pivotal junctures of my teenage existence came to pass—Sunday, 16 July 1961 was the date, a momentous occasion as it marked my first-ever viewing of a pair of bona-fide X-rated all-American horror pictures. On 12 July, in the "what's on at the cinema" section of the local paper, my eyes zeroed in on the following forthcoming attraction:

THE EMBASSY DORKING
Sunday 16th July for one day only
Jeff Morrow   Rex Reason
The Creature Walks Among Us (X)
3.00   6.15   9.10
John Agar   Mara Corday
Tarantula (X)
1.30   4.45   7.45

The news was broadcast to all interested parties at school the next day and the excitement among our group was again intense because three of us had decided that, come hell or high water, we were going to get into this program—it was far too important to miss. We had had enough of mooching about in the playground, bemoaning the fact we were not of an age, in the eyes of the British censor, to watch all of these wonderful movies, and were also becoming increasingly disheartened and embittered at being ejected from one cinema after another in our struggles to see them. Action was urgently needed to restore our sanity, even though The Embassy was an unknown quantity as far as we were concerned—I for one had never actually been there. Would it be as tough to get past the ticket kiosk as The Crescent was still proving to be? Or would it be a walkover like the ABC in Epsom? There was only one way to discover for certain—try the place out.

Although within cycling distance, we decided to take the bus to Dorking on Sunday and joined a very long queue outside the cinema at around 1:25 p.m., John, Chris and I all decked out in our age-enhancing white raincoats, elastic-sided boots and greasy hair, hoping that this particular garb would give us the appearance of 16-year-olds, and not the 14 years and a few months that in reality we were. We hovered around anxiously, looking avidly at the stills outside—the huge spider looming over the desert landscape and the gill-man being studied under a large magnifying glass. The posters to both features looked just as alluring. God, I thought, please let us see these films. I glanced at the crowd. Most of them didn't appear to be that old, although a few grown-ups were included among them. I glanced at my watch. We had been milling around outside doing nothing

MONSTER SPIDER...CRAWLING TERROR 100 FEET HIGH!

TARANTULA!

JOHN AGAR · MARA CORDAY · LEO G. CARROLL

NESTOR PAIVA · ROSS ELLIOTT

for five minutes. This was getting ridiculous. Our nerves were beginning to show. "Right, come on, let's get in there and get it over with," I mumbled to my friends and we finally plucked up the courage to walk through the heavy swing doors. Approaching the kiosk, I steeled myself for the expected rebuff, heart pounding like a steam hammer in my chest. If there had been a term for the word "stress" at that particular moment in time, then I had it in abundance.

"Three 1s 9d tickets please," I croaked through dry lips, handing the woman behind the glass booth the money.

"Thank you. Here are your tickets," she said without even looking at me as she handed over the manna from heaven. Bloody hell—we were in! Without pausing to count our blessings, we entered the pitch-black auditorium 10 minutes into *Tarantula*, just as one of the disfigured victims of Leo G. Carroll's experimental serum staggered into his laboratory—screams of terror from the female members of the audience as we floundered around for three available seats, further screams as the giant spider embarked on its trail of destruction and still more screams (were they genuine? I think they were!) when the gill-man went berserk in Jeff Morrow's house in the climax of *The Creature Walks Among Us*. After the main feature ended, we sat through *Tarantula* again to savor the experience and then caught the bus home on cloud nine. From now on, we said later, The Embassy would be our sole focus of attention—they obviously put profits and the well being of their customers before the authoritarian procedures carried out elsewhere. Good for them—at least there was one cinema close by that would pander to our specific tastes without any fuss and bother. The days of sitting through endless Disney cartoons, dull Westerns, humorless comedies and of falling asleep through *The Ten Commandments* and *Ben-Hur* seemed to be receding fast, thank God.

The word quickly spread around. Forget all about The Crescent—Dorking was the place to be on a Sunday. *The Monolith Monsters* c/w *The Mole People* were the next two A-rated features that five of us saw at The Embassy and then exactly three weeks after that, a tremendous double "X" program—*The Deadly Mantis* c/w *Rodan*, quickly followed by *The Black Sleep* and *Four Boys and a Gun* one week later. This sudden and unexpected run of success went straight to our heads and it was yet another visit to The Crescent, which we had purposely steered clear of for

months, that brought us crashing back down to earth. Foolishly reasoning that the generosity extended to its customers by Dorking's Embassy just might spill over to neighboring Leatherhead, Pete, Robert and I decided to see the X-rated *Monster on the Campus* there on a Sunday in September, playing with the British motor-racing thriller *Checkpoint*. It was no good—gimlet-eyes, in her self-appointed role as guardian of the nation's law-abiding principles (or the youth of that nation) wouldn't allow us in to see the picture at any price, so with our unused ticket money jingling in the pockets of our white raincoats, we left the cinema in disgust, the surrounding streets echoing to an outburst of unmentionable adjectives and expletives at the injustice of it all as we made our way back to our respective homes, with the prospect of the usual Sunday afternoon custom of listening to the radio followed by a late dinner lowering our already battered morales.

Despite this irritating setback, the year ended on a high note with the controversial release of The King Brothers' monster flick, *Gorgo*. The distributors had battled in vain with the unrelenting British censor to reduce the film's rating from an "X" to an "A," but the powers that be dug their collective heels in, pronouncing *Gorgo* to be much too frightening for a younger audience, and it therefore remained out of bounds to all persons under age 16, thousands of whom had been itching to see it, including our gang of enthusiasts. The main reason being the sensational poster that depicted a massive claw towering over the London skyline with the blurbs—"This is the BIG one!" and "Gigantic in Every Way!" I had also shamelessly pinched the paperback novel from a bookshop in Leatherhead (it wasn't on sale to youngsters), which featured on the front and rear covers two very striking photographs of the monster storming through the London streets. The one major difference between the book of the film and the film itself, although we were initially unaware of this, could be summed up in three letters—sex! *Lady Chatterley's Lover* had nothing on *Gorgo* and after reading it, we fervently hoped that the abundant pages of steamy goings-on would be included in the movie—as it turned out, they were unfortunately nowhere to be seen. (The publications in book form of *Konga*, *The Man Who Could Cheat Death*, *The Revenge of Frankenstein* and *Reptilicus* were all written in a similar vein, with photos from the films on the covers and raunchy chapters that would have you sweating under your collars. Again, none of these sex scenes ever finished up in the completed production.)

We made up our minds as a result of this heady mixture of sex, hype and imagery that the King Brothers' much-trumpeted monster-on-the-loose feature was one that would not, under any circumstances, escape our net, the main drawback being that it was showing at the imposing Odeon in Epsom—if it was an Odeon, we speculated, they were probably even stricter than an independent cinema such as The Crescent when it came to kids like us sneaking in to adult movies. It was a daunting prospect, no doubt about it, but me, Chris, Dave and Mark decided to give it a go and much to our surprise had no trouble whatsoever from the management as we sauntered into the large foyer, collecting our tickets with a mixture of relief and self-satisfaction. After suffering the pretty dire co-feature, *Terror in the Haunted House*, we experienced an exhilarating buzz when the main film came on, sitting goggle-eyed through the ear-splitting action on the Odeon's big screen as Gorgo's colossal mother obliterated most of the U.K.'s capital city in an attempt to rescue her imprisoned infant. Lapping up every minute of the commotion unraveling before us, we had to keep reminding ourselves when sitting and hiding in the darkened auditorium surrounded by people a lot older than us that we were still a year or so under the legal age for being in a cinema when pictures like this were showing, and therefore shouldn't really have been there at all.

You're Not Old Enough Son

TROUBLE AT THE EMBASSY (1961)

Now that we have discovered an outlet to satisfy our demands for the type of films we have craved to see for what seems like an eternity, Dorking's Embassy cinema becomes the center of our universe, at least on a Sunday, although visits there during the week will become a regular occurrence over the next 12 months. The local papers reach the shops on a Thursday, or late Wednesday, and in this Thursday's edition, The Embassy is laying on another spiffing double bill on Sunday, *Revenge of the Creature* c/w *The Mad Ghoul*—I'm particularly keen on catching the *Creature* feature, having been turfed out of the ABC in Fetcham over a year ago on an abortive trip to see it. Plans are drawn up as usual during school hours—me, Chris, Pete, Dave, Ian, Tony and Barry F. all decide to catch this momentous presentation, with the rendezvous point being The Crescent at noon on the Sunday in question.

Luckily for a November day, the afternoon is clear of rain as the seven of us, our largest group yet to a horror outing, set off in convoy along the Leatherhead-Dorking highway, dressed up in a motley assortment of garb—white raincoats, jeans, tight gray trousers, corduroy jackets and boots. We reach the town at 1:15 p.m., to be greeted by a substantial crowd swarming around outside the cinema. Big crowds are expected when high-caliber fare such as this is being shown, but this is a larger gathering than normal and we join it after securing our bikes to the railings by the cinema's side wall. There is a buzz in the air—the stills to both films are galvanizing, the posters mouth-watering, and these double "X" programs are so intoxicating that I mentally rub my hands together in expectation of what is in store for me and my pals inside, now that we are able to *get* inside. God, I say to myself, this is so much more satisfying than having to cope with three hours of *Spartacus*, which is the fate that befell me the other week in Epsom on a family trip to the pictures. But little do we realize that this heady atmosphere is about to be shattered. Trouble is on the way and we are on the brink of experiencing the sort of mischief that has been in and out of the news headlines in England for the past couple of years.

At 1:25 p.m., just as the doors start to open, a distant rumble is heard, increasing in crescendo to a roar as coming toward us from the High Street like a black posse from hell appear a horde of rough-looking youths on motorbikes, steering their machines in the direction of The Embassy, much to the consternation of the queues, including myself, who wish to view two Universal horror flicks in relative peace and quiet, or what passes for peace and quiet in these times. The 15 assorted motorbikes grind to a halt on the pavement by the billboards, engines are switched off and the riders with their pillion passengers survey the crowd like a pack of hungry wolves.

"Christ. I hope that lot don't come in."—this from an understandably worried Ian. "Well," I reply, summing up this state of affairs, "there's not a lot we can do about it if they do, is there."

The doors now fully open, we file in, the youths still seated ominously on their machines, not moving. Once inside the comfort zone of the foyer, they are quickly forgotten as we eagerly grab our tickets, smiling as three young lads are ordered to leave at once for being underage (as all seven of us are) and making for the rear stalls. People are still trooping in as the lights dim, the heavy brown curtains draw slowly back and the old '40s Universal logo showing the graphics circling the globe flashes up, signifying the

start to 1943's *The Mad Ghoul*. All goes swimmingly well at first, the audience engrossed as George Zucco sends out wild-eyed zombie David Bruce to indulge in a spot of grave-robbing to obtain fresh hearts for his devious experiments. Then, halfway into the action, shadowy figures can be made out moving silently down the sides of the auditorium toward the left-hand exit doors. The doors are opened with a clunk of the release bar, a chink of gray light filters through into the darkness and more shadowy figures enter illegally, the heavy barred doors slamming shut behind them with a resounding crash that draws everybody's attention away from the horrors on the screen to the very real horrors that might occur at any moment off the screen.

"What are that lot up to now?" whispers Tony nervously.

"I don't bloody know." Impatience is creeping in, but I can't check it. "Hell, I came here to see a film, not a bunch of troublemakers."

The troublemakers embark on their spell of mayhem. About a dozen of them, after wandering around the sides, back and front of the auditorium, home in on a group of lads in a row of seats near the middle that they have obviously been searching for. In they wade, fists flying, abuse hurled, seats springing back into the upright position as startled patrons in the vicinity stand up (and therefore rather inconsiderately obstruct our view) to flee the scene as a pitched battle ensues. Fortunately we are near the back, but it's virtually impossible to focus one's attention on *The Mad Ghoul* or anything else for that matter with this going on. Without warning, the doors to the auditorium swing open, the film suddenly stops and the lights come on as the manager and two assistants stride in, bellowing orders to the gang who, totally against type, stop what they are doing and promptly walk out, barging past the manager and leaving the cinema in an uproar.

"Please calm down ladies and gentlemen. The film will recommence in five minutes."

With these reassuring words, all those present do their best to settle into their seats, including the lads who were assaulted in the first place and, true to the manager's promise, the co-feature restarts, though not at the exact moment it was rudely interrupted, and *The Mad Ghoul* ends with me having lost the main thread of the plot due to the earlier commotion. There is a short break (I make a note that *The War of the Worlds* and *Detective Story* are on in a fortnight) and the better-known '50s Universal logo appears as *Revenge of the Creature* kicks off. However, to our dismay and anger, *this* is also disturbed as the gill-man is escaping from the Miami Seaquarium—somebody has opened the right-hand exit doors and allowed six of the motorcycle gang to enter the theater, where they scamper over to the group who were on the receiving end in the earlier fracas and repeat the exercise all over again. Five minutes of yelling, shouting and general pandemonium is curtailed by the arrival of the police—all six miscreants and the set-upon lads are marched out with a certain degree of force. Thankfully, *Revenge of the Creature* rolls on, yet again I fume because several vital minutes have been missed, the amphibious menace now on the prowl in the Miami streets. As John Agar and a dozen police officers pour a hail of bullets into the gill-man in the finale, Chris leans over Tony in my direction.

"We seeing *The Mad Ghoul* again, Baz?"

"Yeah. As we couldn't bloody well see most of it first time round, why not?"

The decision made, us seven HSFF addicts stay put for not only a second helping of Universal's zombie thriller but, for good measure, second helpings of the main feature as well, more as a caution to avoid any trouble that could be brewing outside the cinema than seeing two horror pictures twice in succession, although both titles are admittedly well worth another look.

7:40 p.m. *Revenge of the Creature* finishes and we exit The Embassy in the dark November evening. Outside, several bobbies are patrolling the road but there is no sign of the motorcycle gang, and seven 14-year-olds breathe a collective sigh of relief—but not for long. Four of our group have no lights fitted on their bikes and to reach the main road, one has to pass right under the noses of the law, who do not take kindly to kids cycling at night without any visible means of illumination to other road users.

"Just walk the bikes past them. Perhaps they won't notice anything," says Chris sensibly, which is what we do, giving us a few anxious minutes. The police that night undoubtedly have bigger fish to fry and despite receiving a searching stare from them, we manage to reach the corner of the High Street and make good our escape, those of us with lights cycling fore-and-aft of those without, reaching Leatherhead with no further mishaps.

An eventful afternoon and evening, then—The Embassy incident is even mentioned in the locals the following week, the phrase "gang reprisal" referred to as a possible cause. I make quite sure that my parents don't set eyes on the offending article by removing the appropriate page from the paper. As with most youths my age, I am given more or less a free rein to do what I like, when I like. But one hint of involvement in gang warfare, unintentional or not, will cut short my cinematic activities for a very long time, free rein or no free rein, and it is better for all concerned that my guardians do not learn of the trouble at The Embassy on that particular day in November. Besides, *The Beast with A Million Eyes* and *The Phantom from 10,000 Leagues* beckon next week and I have no wish to blow my chances of seeing yet another fascinating double bill, however good or bad the films may be (and these two in fact turned out to be pretty awful!

WHAT SHALL WE SEE THIS SUNDAY? (1962)

Was it our imagination, or had most of our local cinemas received a psychic plea over the ether from a group of cinema-mad teenagers in Surrey? Whatever the reason, all of a sudden the floodgates opened as the seemingly entire back catalogue of horror, fantasy and science fiction movies from Universal International, American International, Allied Artists, United Artists, Columbia, Warner Bros., Paramount, RKO-Radio, Anglo Amalgamated, MGM and the minor league studios surfaced in Southern England, apparently overnight! An embarrassment of riches unveiled themselves from January 1962 onwards, so that all of our hard-earned cash from a wide variety of Saturday morning and evening jobs, plus pocket money from our parents if they were in a good enough mood, was spent at the cinema, and mostly on Sundays. Scrutinizing the newspapers each week, our bicycles worked overtime as with a kind of military precision we pedaled from one venue to another in pursuit of our dreams, catching the bus to the destinations that were further afield or if it was raining. It was as if the gods from above had finally taken pity on the nation's entertainment-starved youth and given them an outlet for their pent-up energy.

Mouth-watering delights were to be had, and many of these emanated from The Embassy in Dorking, kicking off in January with *I Was A Teenage Werewolf* c/w *It Conquered the World*. This one cinema, above all others, consistently provided the goods throughout the year and many a Sunday was spent there. *Attack of the 50 Foot Woman* c/w *The Black Scorpion*, *The Tingler* c/w *Attack of the Puppet People*, *Teenage Frankenstein* c/w *Blood Is My Heritage*, *Invasion of the Hell Creatures* c/w *Day the World Ended*, *It! The Terror from Beyond Space* c/w *Curse of the Faceless Man*, *Back from the Dead* c/w *The Disembodied* and, at long last, *20 Million Miles to Earth*—the list was endless. A few oldies from the 1940s also put in an appearance to get the juices flowing, including *House of Dracula*, *Dead Men Walk*, *The Wolf Man* and *The Mummy's Tomb*. It was truly the beginning of a golden age in fantasy cinema-going.

Sundays were now spent cycling frantically to Dorking, Epsom, Fetcham and Cobham, with bus trips to Cheam and New Malden. We snubbed, for obvious reasons, The Crescent. Extensive lists were drawn up of the movies we had seen and even missed on the off chance that we would locate them somewhere in our area, thus ensuring that they did not slip through our fingers (we turned a blind eye to the statement "Persons Under 16 Cannot be Admitted to this Program," which followed practically every double bill mentioned in the papers, as this would have mentally hindered our efforts to see them all). Our respective parents never became involved in any of this frenetic, time-consuming and expensive activity—the fact that we were out from under their feet after what, for them, had been a busy week was all that mattered. Us youngsters had a great deal of freedom at our disposal back then and used every single minute of it—after all, there was nothing to stay indoors for. You never heard the words "What shall we do today?" cross anyone's lips.

In addition to the Sunday one-day circuit, the weekly releases also had to be slotted into our hectic timetables in between schoolwork, household chores and paper routes: *The Pit and the Pendulum*, *The Day the Earth Caught Fire*, *The Hands of Orlac*, *The Time Machine*, *Voyage to the Bottom of the Sea*, *The Premature Burial*, Hammer's disappointing *The Phantom of the Opera*, *Tales of Terror* and others added to our viewing pleasures. The one stumbling block remained, as ever, Leatherhead's Crescent cinema, now christened The Fortress and an impregnable one at that. Apart from sneaking in to see *The Mummy* in 1960 with considerable help from my father, I had still not managed to chalk up another "X" film there—neither had any of my friends, much to our chagrin, because even this cinema was showing some classics on Sundays. *When Worlds Collide*, *It Came from Beneath the Sea*, *Conquest of Space* and a special screening of *The Thief of Bagdad* we caught, but all were rated "U" certificate, which we now felt was beneath us, however good these movies (which admittedly we *did* class as essential viewing) turned out to be. *Creature from the Black Lagoon, The Leech Woman, The Werewolf* and *The Alligator People* we had to miss out on at the time, not only because of the adult ratings awarded to them but also this particular cinema's attitude in not allowing underage clients to enter their domain to see such fare.

It was during the early part of 1962 that an obsessive streak, which in all probability had lain dormant for many years but had now decided to surface due to this unforeseen deluge of goodies, manifested itself in my behavior, giving cause for concern among my friends, thankfully for a short time only on this occasion, although this darker side to my character was to affect my lifestyle, on and off, during the next few years. A large group of us had gone along to The Crescent as the Sunday screening happened to be *This Island Earth*, with an Audie Murphy Western the support feature. Universal's noisy, colorful science fiction actioner was without doubt extremely impressive, "U" certificate notwithstanding, but what really grabbed my attention in the interval was the trailer to *The Alligator People*, the attraction the following Sunday. It was a "U" trailer to an "X" film—however, in 1962, "U" trailers dared to show far more than those one-minute fiascos in the mid-1950s and this one certainly did. "It's the BIG Shocker in Screaming Horrorscope!" the slogans announced, as a man sporting what appeared to be an alligator's head ran through a swamp. *She Devil* was on with it, but that looked far less promising. This brief extract from *The Alligator People* stuck in my mind, staying there throughout the Western and refusing to go away, even intruding upon the scenes where Audie Murphy was blazing away with his six-guns.

We left the cinema after the performance had ended, and I turned to Dave.

"What about that trailer to *The Alligator People*?"

"Well—what about it?"

"We've got to see it."

Ian, Pete, Tony and Chris had joined us and we headed toward the High Street. Ian spoke.

"Got to see what?"

"That film on next Sunday."

"*The Alligator People*? You know you can't."

"Why? What do you mean—can't?"

"'Cause it's The Crescent, you blithering idiot. You've tried. We all have. The only reason you saw *The Mummy* there a couple of years ago was because your old man helped out, if you remember. They just won't let anybody in who's not old enough. They've got principles."

"Sod their principles. I've *got* to see it."

Pete chipped in. "Give it a miss, Baz. The Embassy might have something decent on."

"Not *The Alligator People*."

Ian was becoming rattled with my intransigent mood.

"Look, the bloody *Alligator People* will probably be on there in a couple of weeks."

"And it might not. They don't all go from one cinema to the other. *The Werewolf* hasn't turned up anywhere else yet and we skipped that one not so long ago, if *you* remember."

"Well—I'm not going."—Ian

"I ain't either."—Dave

"Nor me. I'm fed up trying to get in at The Crescent. I'm sick and tired of the bloody place to be honest."—Chris.

"Please your bloody selves. I'll go on my own."

We had now reached the end of the High Street and stood there, ready to disperse in our six different ways—we all resided in various areas of the town. Tony examined me intently—the others were studying me as well.

"You feeling alright Baz?"

"Yeah. Why?"

"You don't look too good. Calm down, mate. You're letting these films get to you. You can't see every one of them, you know."

I made no comment to this remark—a nagging throb was developing at the back of my neck, the beginning of a migraine attack, and all I could think of was that image of the man with the alligator head. It was bugging me—could it merely be that the unconquerable Crescent was showing the film and that the hatred I felt toward the cinema's hard-headed approach over "X" pictures was somehow affecting my mental state? Maybe that was it. I did seem to be running around in circles (or cycling around), chasing one double bill here, and another there, like a man possessed. Perhaps it was time to slow down a bit for the sake of my sanity. Pete gave me a friendly cuff on the shoulders.

"Come on Baz. Cheer up, mate. We'll see something else next week. The Crescent's not worth all the bloody bother."

I managed a weak smile, sighed and we departed, me trudging up through the side roads to home, deep in thought. The lads were right, of course. Bugger The Crescent—let's stick with The Embassy and the great fodder that they were presenting week after week, which one could

Hitchcock's *Psycho* received the dreaded X rating in the U.K., keeping young horror fans out of the theater.

see without any trouble at all. I would pay my respects to them next Sunday. Leatherhead's one and only cinema could go to hell for all I cared.

Which is what I did. *The Alligator People* went by the board—*Attack of the 50 Foot Woman* and *The Black Scorpion* more than made up for its loss at The Embassy, and it was a long time before I caught up with Fox's monster thriller featuring that man with the head of an alligator who had caused just a spot of ill-feeling between myself and my mates.

When Hitchcock's X-rated, much talked-about *Psycho* had a three-day run at The Crescent in March, the temptation was so great that, despite the cinema's now infamous policy of age-discrimination, we made up our minds to take another gamble on the place and slip in to see for ourselves what had shocked the critics and what was continuing to shock the public into paying huge amounts of money to attend this classic thriller. *Psycho* was still raking in a fortune at the box office months after its initial release. Once more, four of us joined a large crowd at around 7:00 p.m. on Saturday, eying up the life-size cardboard cut-out of the portly director informing one and all that "Positively no one is allowed in during the last 15 minutes." Would we be allowed in during the whole 109 minutes? The answer was a resounding "No!" As we filed into the foyer, we spotted old gimlet-eyes in her customary position behind the glass of the ticket kiosk, but we never made it as far as her because the manager, a middle-aged man with a severe-looking demeanor who was probably ex-army, began casting his own beady eyes over the customers as they were queuing for tickets, weeding out the ones that, in his opinion, should not have been there. We didn't stand a chance—marching straight over to our little group, he snarled, baring his teeth.

"Right you four, out you go."

"But we're 16," we retorted, but these words fell on deaf ears—he must have heard that particular phrase a thousand times before.

"Sorry—you are not allowed in."

Then Pete retaliated angrily. "Listen mate. We got in at the bloody Embassy last week and saw two 'X' films." The manager's face almost turned purple at this rebuke.

"I'm not interested in what you were doing last week," he shouted. "You're holding people up. Out you go and don't argue, otherwise I will call the police."

That was the end of our night out—no *Psycho* for us that evening. Shambling off in barely suppressed fury, Chris suddenly turned and yelled at the top of his voice, "Push off, you silly old sod!" and as we bolted through The Crescent's swing doors, all hope of us ever seeing any "X" films at that particular cinema evaporated in the chilly winter air. But our unruly friend wasn't finished yet—in front of several terrified spectators, he lunged out with a booted foot at the Alfred Hitchcock effigy, sending it tumbling to the ground where it hit the paving stones with a loud "Thwack!" Chris had told us that he was sick and tired of The Crescent and he obviously meant it! For a second or two, we stood stock still, frozen in time by this act of vandalism, however much in our view it was warranted. Then we snapped out of the trance and sprinted away like criminals on the run, praying that there were no bobbies on the beat in the vicinity of the place.

However, Chris' feathers had been severely ruffled by this incident. His displeasure at what he saw as The Crescent's high-minded approach as opposed to The Embassy's liberal-minded approach over "X" pictures festered for days like an open wound, and on Wednesday in the playground, he summoned us to a council of war to bounce his latest idea, or more precisely act of vengeance, off us—one night, very late, those of us kicked out of *Psycho* would convene outside the cinema when the street lights were out and the place was closed, break the glass to the panels containing the stills to the current attraction, and relieve the cinema of their promotional photographs, whether the film was a science fiction thriller, Western or comedy—that didn't matter, as long as we had them and The Crescent did not. But we were horrified and demurred, arguing the case against this plot.

OK, petty pilfering was part and parcel of our teenage existence—cigarettes, sweets, toys, paperbacks and monster magazines were occasionally lifted from the shelves of numerous shops in our area and never put back. Stealing items from Leatherhead's major entertainment center was a different kettle of fish. Anyway, we continued, how could we possibly sneak out of our homes at midnight or thereabouts and return undetected? Even my parents would be alerted to the fact that I was up to no good *and* there was also the ever-present patrolling copper to contend with. So the scheme was dropped, although deep down, Chris' plan was secretly admired for its sheer nerve—it certainly would have been one up for our group against a cinema that was the bane of our cinematic life. In hindsight, though, The Crescent's strict stance was understandable. Any cinema found to be letting in underage juveniles to adult movies could have their license revoked and face a stiff fine; besides, young persons of a questionable age were simply not allowed to "get away with it" as discipline was the name of the game in early 1960s England.

Everyone knew the score and it became a kind of contest between cinema management and youth—"Do we let them in or show them the door?"—almost a game of one-upmanship, if you like.

So we settled into a routine of sorts. The phrase "What shall we see this Sunday?" became commonplace in the playground as we perused the local papers to find out what was on and where. The program that got the nod was usually chosen on the Thursday or Friday before we left school by me, now classed as the chief expert in these matters, and then it was a case of meeting up around midday on Sunday, dressed in attire that hopefully made us look older than we really were, and either catching a bus or cycling to the town where the main attraction was appearing. Actually getting out of one's home on this particular day of the week was just as important as seeing two horror flicks—slumped in an armchair waiting for dinner to be dished up at the ungodly hour of 2:30 p.m. while Billy Cotton yelled "Wakey wakey!" from the radio's

Small locals, like the Manchester, New Oxford, cinemas provided teenagers an escape from dull Sunday afternoon family rituals.

tiny cloth-covered speaker, or having to listen to your parents chuckling uncontrollably at *The Glums*, a youngster could quite literally die from terminal boredom if there was nothing on at the pictures. The Sunday cinema circuit was a means of escape from this yawn-inducing post-war ritual carried out in millions of homes throughout England, and even threats of "Well, if you must insist on going out, you can forget all about dinner" made not one iota of difference to my plans for the day—I was off with my chums to participate in another and more fulfilling kind of world, a world that did not involve other members of my family, and that's all there was to it!

It was an altogether completely different experience to pay a visit to the cinema in the early 1960s to what it is like today. One usually queued up in orderly fashion before the dreaded ticket kiosk and was given a small, colored ticket (either mauve or pink, but why I'll never know) similar to those handed out on a bus. A rudimentary program advertising the forthcoming attractions for the next month could be had for a small sum—there were no glossy film magazines on sale, although these began to appear in the mid-1960s. A funereal silence hung over the foyer like a shroud, unlike these days when customers are subjected to a profusion of noise and light, an aural and visual assault on the senses, all part of the hard sell that is the hallmark of the modern-day multicomplex auditoria. The confectionery booth had a minimum of sweets and drinks (usually KiaOra orange and nothing else!) to be proffered to patrons.

The auditorium itself was dark and musty-smelling, only a dim glow permeating from the exit signs, a few scattered lights and the curtain covering the screen—one felt engulfed by the sheer size of it. When the film came on, the lights went off and it was as black as a coal cellar;

no wonder usherettes were on hand to guide you to your seats with their tiny torches, as you would never have found out where you were supposed to be sitting otherwise. Minute circles of red light indicated the furtive smoking of cigarettes, most of which, it has to be admitted, had been nicked from the shelves of Woolworth's in Leatherhead and a few newsagents in the neighboring towns. As a result, the little metal ash-trays between the seats, which dug into your knees if you were slouching and not sitting, rapidly filled up with the evil-smelling butt-ends from countless Woodbines and Senior Service coffin-nails, as they were then called (and with valid reason!). Good behavior had to be observed at all times—any rowdiness and you were out, ejected by a manager who had most probably seen military action in the Second World War and wouldn't stand any nonsense from unruly customers, no matter how little of the picture they had seen. And woe betide anybody foolhardy enough to try to let their friends in through the side exit doors—if you were caught, police action was threatened or, much, much worse, a telephone call to your parents (luckily mine were not yet on the 'phone, but I never attempted this act of subterfuge anyway, although I did contemplate doing it on more than one occasion).

On the Sunday circuit, you sat down after obtaining your ticket, eager for the curtains to roll back to reveal the certification details—"This is to certify that such-and-such a film has been granted the following certificate: X Adults Only." Before that happened, pop records of the day were played over and over again for several minutes—Sandy Nelson's "Let There Be Drums," Cliff Richard's "The Young Ones," Chris Montez's "Let's Dance," Pat Boone's "Speedy Gonzales" and the Shadows' latest hits were a few that spring to mind. Also, rather appropriately, "Monster Mash" by Bobby "Boris" Pickett and the Cryptkickers boomed out with lyrics that made one cringe in embarrassment, even if they were aimed at the people who loved horror movies. Then the records stopped, a stygian darkness descended and the co-feature was screened. A minimum of adverts comprising a few photographs plus "what's on next week/Sunday" were shown after the co-feature had ended, and then it was straight into the main feature. Owing to the relatively short running length of many of the films we saw, these double bills were generally screened three times from 1:30 p.m. onwards, with the program finishing about 10:30 to 11:00 p.m. Ice creams

The spelling *Xperiment* was Hammer's jab at British censorship of horror films.

were served by the usherette during the brief intervals between performances, but even this was carried out in the dark, leading to much swearing and cursing as people blundered into one another trying to locate their seats in the stalls, which wasn't easy as most theaters were built on extremely large and cavernous lines.

In theory, you could stay in the cinema all afternoon and evening, which we quite often did. Lights didn't go up between performances as they do nowadays—you paid your 1s 9d and got more than your money's worth. Full houselights came on when the program had finally ended, resulting in a mad dash for the exits (and fresh air) by youngsters of our age who showed a complete lack of respect for "God Save the Queen"—only one or two older patrons stood stock-still, paying reverence to the Monarchy, when this crackled out through the speakers. The Sunday-only programs nearly always played to a full house—they were the blockbusters of their day, as it were, and this, as I have mentioned before, was the only form of entertainment available to the nation's youth 40 years ago. It is no small wonder that many of the low-budget quickies appearing from America made huge profits for their producers and backers, as there was really nothing else for us to spend our money on.

Both of my brothers were still far too young to see adult films and David, in particular, made a devoted listener as he always insisted that I give him a detailed report on those that I had seen the previous week while walking our dog in the nearby woods on a Sunday morning. I also rubbed his jealous nose in it by telling him with great pleasure about the goodies I was due to be entertained by in the afternoon, usually at the ubiquitous Embassy in Dorking, which was within easy cycling distance of where most of my friends and I lived. The Crescent was the only one that could be reached on foot and was annoyingly screening some excellent movies during this period—annoying because our repeated undertakings to actually get into the place had all fallen on stony ground. One such Sunday double bill had *Night of the Demon* paired with *20 Million Miles to Earth*, heavily advertised outside with posters and billboards, which must have had the desired effect as a vast crowd of people (which was a common-enough phenomenon in the early 1960s) stretched right around the back of the building into the adjoining road, which wasn't surprising—this was a program to excite even the most jaded of horror fans. The Crescent was certainly going to reap a bumper box office return that day! Three of us looked longingly at the posters, knowing that it would be a waste of our collective time to try to get in to see this double feature, shrugged our shoulders and cycled over to The Embassy, where we sat through our own great pair of science fiction thrillers—*The Monster that Challenged the World* c/w *The Vampire*, which, true to form, eventually turned up at The Crescent several weeks later!

Then on Sunday the 8th of April, *Quatermass 2* was the attraction at The Crescent, showing with a brutal Edward G. Robinson gangster flick, *Black Tuesday*. Both were rated "X." As a change in tactics, I made up my mind to go solo on this one and have another stab at breaching, yet again, the cinema's formidable walls. On went the raincoat, the Brylcreem, the fluorescent socks (usually yellow) and the winkle-pickers. Full of self-assurance and with a score of "X" films now under my belt that boosted my confidence, I entered the foyer with a small crowd, walked straight up to the kiosk, fixed old gimlet-eyes with my very own icy scowl and spoke masterfully:

"One ticket for the back stalls, please."

She looked up, squinting, but even she must have realized by now that people do get older over a given period of time if, in fact, she recognized me from my innumerable and ultimately barren attempts at getting past her. After all, it was almost four long weary years ago when she had first refused to let me in to *The Mole People*, and a great deal of cinematic water had gone under the bridge since then. Thankfully, and remembering the invective hurled at him by Chris when we had been thrown out of *Psycho*, the manager was, on this occasion, nowhere to be seen—he was the one person I was dreading to meet rather than the little old dear in front of me. "2s 6d, please," she said in clipped tones. I had cracked it at last! I was probably more over-the-moon at knocking down The Fortress' defenses than actually seeing *Quatermass 2*, and boy did I brag about it at school the next day. From then on, Leatherhead's one and only cinema posed us no problems as far as X-rated movies were concerned—at the end of May, five of our group (all still underage, but that was of no importance!) waltzed in there to see Toho's *Rodan*, showing with the turgid political thriller *The Great Man*, without any difficulty at all. It had been a very long time coming, but it was worth it!

Just to prove to The Crescent that the shoe was now well and truly on the other foot, I took a stroll down there one Sunday to see what turned out to be a pretty run-of-the-mill pair of "A" certificate offerings, *Spacemaster X-7* c/w *The Unknown Terror*. Outside, hovering around by the stills with worried looks on their faces, were five young boys, clearly waiting for some charitable soul to show a little compassion and act as their escort past that intimidating ticket kiosk. Looking at them, I smiled. That was me, I thought to myself, not so long ago. Now *I* was the experienced one and they were the beginners, probably dying to see *their* first pair of American fantasy movies. I walked over to them and they turned around in hopeful expectation.

"How old are you lot?"

"10. 8. 10. 11. 9," came a chorus of replies.

"Fancy seeing these, do you?"

"Yeah!" came the second chorus, in unison this time.

"Come on, then," I said, and they filed in behind me, dutifully handing over their money, which I thrust in the direction of gimlet-eyes with more than a touch of bitterness in my actions, as if to say—"I've had years trying to get into this place so don't mess around any longer because it's me, yes *me*, this time helping these kids in." The five youngsters sat by my side, chatting and whispering excitedly through every lame minute of both films, which they enjoyed at any rate, even if I found them to be distinctly below average. As we left the cinema after the end of the afternoon's performance, I wisely informed them that there were far better pictures on offer than the two they had just seen, but unfortunately for them, they were all "X" certificates, to which they replied, "Thanks for taking us in, we liked them," before disappearing from sight down the High Street. At least on this occasion, I had done my bit and had been, for a change, the obliging adult.

One night, John, Dave and I hopped on the bus and headed out to the ABC in Kingston to catch *Whatever Happened to Baby Jane?*, which quite frankly I had no desire to see but the other two did as they had read the excellent reviews and thought that it might make a welcome break from all the monster fodder we had been subjected to for the past few months. It's just as well that I didn't fancy the movie—a well-built six-foot-plus doorman was having no truck from us and we were turned away before we even had a chance to gain entry into the foyer. Secretly I was glad because, although rated an "X," I had read that it was far too long and talkative for my own preferences and I never did get around to seeing it in a cinema. John and Dave, though, were a touch miffed and sat in a sulky silence on the long journey home while I reflected that the stern measures previously encountered at The Crescent were clearly practiced elsewhere, notably in Kingston!

The final occasion on which I was ever refused entry to an "X" certificate film was an abortive trip in October to see *Doctor Blood's Coffin*, a gory British horror outing that was showing at the ABC in New Malden, the cinema that had turned me away from *Circus of Horrors*. I expostulated with the manager to no avail, exiting through the doors only a couple of minutes after entering them. Leaving the ABC, it seemed both mystifying and extremely infuriating that while I was able to come and go in most of the cinemas throughout our area, the odd one or two were still digging their heels in by continuing to exercise their inflexible attitudes. But in reality I couldn't have cared less because with my 16th birthday not too far away, the constant worry of "can I get in or can't I?" was now a fast-receding problem that belonged in the past—this also applied itself to my friends and fellow fanatics, who were all approximately the same age as myself. The world of the adult cinema was now my oyster!

Did any of these films give me the jitters? No, not really, although after watching *I Bury the Living* at The Crescent one Sunday evening in November, the three of us who had sat through this neat little chiller decided, as a dare or a test of courage, to walk home via Leatherhead church with its yew tree-covered cemetery. As most of the action in *I Bury the Living* took place in the middle of a cemetery, we suffered an unaccustomed attack of nerves and fled through the ghostly gravestones bathed in moonlight, half afraid that Richard Boone would be lurking around a corner, ready to fall upon us. So no, I was never really scared, only thrilled, excited, captivated and charmed. But the same cannot be said for one member of our gang.

Pete, Dave, John and I had cycled over to The Embassy to take in *Invasion of the Hell Creatures* c/w *Day the World Ended*, another popular pairing on the Sunday circuit in those days. Settled comfortably in our seats as *Day the World Ended* got underway, John started having, rather tiresomely, a fit of the creeps, fidgeting in his seat despite the fact that the movie's three-eyed mutant had yet to make an appearance. When the monster's claw suddenly came into view across the big screen, in Superscope to boot, John, apparently, had had enough and turned to speak to me.

"Barry, I'm off. I can't sit here and look at this," he whispered in the darkness.

"Don't be silly. And be quiet—I'm trying to concentrate on the film."

"I'm not being silly. I can't watch it. I'm going home."

"You can't go. Our bikes are all chained up together by the exit door."

"Who's got the key to the lock?"

"Dave."

"Ask him if I can have the key."

"Dave. John's had enough, he's scared (chuckle). He wants to borrow the key to unlock the chain so that he can go home."

"Sssssshhh," from someone behind.

"Well he bloody well can't. If he unlocks the bikes, how will he get the key to us without coming back into the cinema?"

I turned to John. "Sorry mate, no go. You'll just have to sit it out," and to his eternal credit he did, cowering behind the seats when the monster finally ventured onto the set during the last 10 minutes of Roger Corman's post-apocalyptic thriller. Somewhat amusingly, he even closed his eyes at a few of the ridiculous scenes in *Invasion of the Hell Creatures*, a semi-comical piece of science fiction nonsense that hardly merited, in my lofty opinion, an "X" certificate from the British censor. As we expected

Me (right) and a friend in 1963 on the road to the Cameo

after this little drama, John, looking pale and ill on leaving The Embassy, did not make a point of accompanying us on future visits to the kind of pictures that we raved about but which reduced him to a nervous wreck!

And did any of them make us laugh? No—well, not at first they didn't. Only later did I find a lot of them humorous for all the wrong reasons, especially when The Cameo in Cornwall decided to put on a series of grade Z movies which included some really diabolical efforts worthy of amusement. But that was some time off. So no—we didn't laugh when Roger Corman's Venusian monster was wheeled out of its cave during the climax of *It Conquered the World*, looking for all the world like the perambulating model it obviously was; we didn't laugh at the silly little aliens scuttling around and trying unsuccessfully to be scary in *Invasion of the Hell Creatures*; we didn't laugh at the ridiculous camp costumes on display in *The Mole People*; not even Allison Hayes as the unconvincing giant in *Attack of the 50 Foot Woman* made us laugh. Flaws, warts and all were overlooked, not noticed or ignored—these films were treated seriously and with a certain amount of reverence, and when gazing up at the black and white images on the giant screens in the Odeons, ABCs and Dorking's Embassy, I quite often had to mentally pinch myself to ensure that I wasn't dreaming. The pages of *Famous Monsters of Filmland* were coming alive before my very eyes—making a mockery of the worst of them would come later. For now, I was utterly wrapped up in every corny second of their 70-minute running time.

Which is more than can be said of George and his mob. Sniggering behind our backs or, if there were only two or three of us about, in front of our faces, they pointed out scornfully that what we were wasting our time and money on were not proper "X" films at all. No, they said, trying unsuccessfully to give the impression of having far more knowledge on the subject than they actually possessed, proper "X" films contained near-nudity, sex and a few choice swear words, not silly great insects, stupid monsters and mad doctors. Why not try something along the lines of *Saturday Night and Sunday Morning* or *The Loneliness of the Long Distance Runner*, they suggested—*real* adult pictures and British as well, not that American rubbish we kept on rushing off to every Sunday afternoon to see. As George and his acolytes wandered off, profanities were hurled at their backs for the insults and derision aimed at our number one form of entertainment, and I for one had no inclination whatsoever to look at Albert Finney rollicking around in bed with Rachel Roberts, "X" or no "X"—an animated giant scorpion attacking the Mexican military would, for now, give me the bigger thrill!

Once in a while, an almost eccentric pairing of two completely different classes of movie would occur that made little or no sense to the seasoned cinema-goer. On 25 November, The Crescent (now no longer The Fortress) was showing as its Sunday presentation a Rod Steiger Western entitled *Run of the Arrow*, which carried a "U" certificate. Fair enough. But playing second billing to it was Universal's *The Creature Walks Among Us*, rated an "X." So you had the strange situation where on the one hand a person had to be 16 and over to see the co-feature, while the main feature was considered fit for a general audience—an anomaly in cinema terms if ever there was one. Pete and myself, at a loose end that day, decided to watch it, and as we ambled into an unusually quiet foyer, we chanced upon a heated argument taking place between old gimlet-eyes in the ticket kiosk and a lad who must have been all of 12 years old.

"But I only want to see *Run of the Arrow*."

"I'm sorry, but I cannot let you in." Pete and I exchanged grins. How many times had we heard her say that over the past few years?

"Why not?" the youth persisted.

"Because the program has an X film showing with it and you are not old enough to see adult films."

"I'm not interested in the X film. I just want to see the Western."

"I'm sorry, it's not possible."

He wasn't going to give up. "Please let me have a ticket for *Run of the Arrow*. I won't watch the other film, I promise—I'll come out."

"I cannot let you in to see one film. Do you want me to call the manager?"

Perplexed and thwarted by that cold-hearted devil behind the glass booth, the hapless Western fan slunk off with his tail between his legs (although later we had a sneaking suspicion that the supposed Western fan was in fact a horror fan and really wanted to see the *Creature* movie. In other words, he was trying it on). We were a bit puzzled ourselves as to the reasons, if any, behind this lopsided program—not giving a hoot about *Run of the Arrow*, we sat through the gill-man feature and then walked out. For once, The Crescent had had their money's worth out of us.

My parents were, for the most part, oblivious to my Sunday HSFF outings and also to the weekly, or twice-weekly, trips to The Crescent, the Odeon and ABC in Epsom, Dorking's Embassy and the others that I frequented on a regular basis. I was one less pair of feet to get in their way, and if I wished to squander all my money on the pictures and monster magazines, so be it. My fanatical interests were therefore tolerated as long as they didn't interfere with the smooth running of the household. On one occasion, though, a prank born out of sheer stupidity well and truly upset the family applecart and I was severely lambasted over the incident for months after because of it.

Carole, my seven-year-old sister, owned a doll. Nothing unusual in that—but the doll itself was highly unusual, a Spanish model over three feet tall that went under the name of Pandora. Given to her as a Christmas present, this uncannily lifelike figure, propped up against her bedroom wall, had a disturbing aura about it, almost as if it was aware of one's presence—and this was years before I had seen *Dead of Night* and *Devil Doll*! Pandora eerily took on the appearance of a fifth member of the family, hated by my younger brother Dave with a vengeance, who swore blind that the doll's large round blue unblinking eyes followed his every movement when he had to go into Carole's room to retrieve a toy from their shared playbox. "One day," he whispered to me maliciously, "I'm going to drag it into the woods and take it apart piece by piece." I sympathized with Dave—I wasn't too keen on the thing myself. It was like having a dead body in the home and the doll would make you jump out of your skin if Carole moved it out of her room and into another without notifying us. Therefore, it was on a visit to The Embassy in Dorking one Sunday that a plan of my own took shape in my mind; to destroy what was after all an inanimate object, albeit a rather sinister one, so that we, or more precisely Dave and myself, could all sleep easily in our beds.

Invasion of the Body Snatchers c/w *Indestructible Man* was a big favorite on the Sunday circuit and after taking in both films twice over the space of six weeks, evil thoughts entered my head on the cycle home from Dorking regarding Pandora. At the climax to *Indestructible Man*, Lon Chaney is trapped in sewers and fried by police flamethrowers, clambering onto a gantry and exposing his flayed features to the audience. This would be the fate to befall Pandora— when the family was out on one of their jaunts, the deadly doll would receive a roasting just as Chaney had done, and perhaps then it could be disposed of. How all this would be explained to my parents I gave no heed to—I just wanted rid of it once and for all.

Two weeks later, a Sunday presented me with the opportunity to carry out the dirty deed. *Teenage Frankenstein* and *Blood Is My Heritage* was the attraction at The Crescent, but I had caught this double bill twice before and could afford to give it a miss, particularly as the rest of the family were off on a ramble to the River Mole in the afternoon. At 12:30 p.m., I had the place to myself. Pandora was carried from my sister's bedroom, stripped, and hauled across the lawn to the smoldering remains of my father's early morning bonfire. I tossed her onto the glowing embers and stood back. Nothing happened at first. Then, little by little, tiny tongues of flame licked the rigid plastic limbs, which began to bubble up and melt, caving in on themselves and blackening in the heat. The flames took hold and Pandora succumbed in the blaze, or at least her body did—the head remained more or less intact. Grotesquely blistered, scorched and partly melted, but intact all the same. Just like Lon Chaney's face in *Indestructible Man*. Off came the head, the torso and limbs lying amidst the dying flames, resembling something far more flesh-crawling than anything I had seen in a dozen horror movies. Pandora's head, or what was left of it, was then taken back indoors, sluiced clean under the cold water tap, and, in a complete fit of madness on my part, placed neatly under Carole's clean linen bedsheets, near the underside edge of her pillow but not visible. Perhaps I thought that this might be amusing to all parties concerned—I was about to be proved how mistaken I was!

The family arrived back early, around 4:00 p.m., while I was busy poring over homework on the kitchen table, trying my hardest to act normally. When my parents entered the kitchen, I realized in a sudden flash that what I had done was utterly despicable, but it was too late for regrets—a prolonged scream pierced the relative silence. Carole, lying down on her bed for a nap, had pulled back the coverlet, only to find a head from hell staring back at her through empty eye sockets, the "skin" blackened, twisted and misshapen. In all honesty, it would not have looked out of place gracing the front cover of *Famous Monsters of Filmland*. The screams continued, subsiding into heavy sobs. Everybody except myself piled into her room to find out the cause of this distressing uproar—even the dog was affected, crouching on the floor with both ears pinned back. I sat rigidly in my chair, waiting for the inevitable confrontation to begin—I didn't have to wait long. Dad stormed into the kitchen, incandescent rage written all over his face.

"Who the hell was responsible for that?" he roared.

"I'm sorry Dad, it was me."

"For Christ's sake, why? What on earth possessed you to do it?" Dad had blasphemed, his temper getting the better of him.

"I don't know."

"What do you mean—you don't know?"

"I just don't."

"Where's the rest of Carole's doll?"

"On the bonfire."

Suddenly David appeared in the doorway behind Dad's broad back, a smirk on his cherubic features, and I had to quickly suppress a smile. I was in deep trouble and grinning would only make matters worse. Mum was the next person to take over the interrogation as Dad paced backwards and forwards across the room, dreaming up a suitable form of punishment to fit this heinous crime.

"I suppose you got this awful idea from one of those horror films you and your friends are always glued to every wretched Sunday."

"No," I lied.

"Well, no more pocket money for you. Not until this doll has been replaced. For goodness sake, Barry, grow up—I despair of you sometimes. Your sister's almost hysterical with fright in there and you're the one that's to blame. And wipe that smile of your face—this isn't at all funny."

And so the incriminations rumbled on. Carole had to spend the next week or so sleeping in my parents' bed to help her over the ordeal and I escaped retribution, getting off far more lightly than I ever thought possible, perhaps due to the fact that, unbeknown to us children, a major move was in the cards and those in charge had far more important issues to contend with than a malicious jape carried out by their elder son who should have known better, considering his age. However, I had learned my lesson and this would be one episode of life imitating the arts (or, in horror terms, what passed as the arts) that would never be repeated.

The year was drawing to a close and in December I experienced my second bout of 1960s violence in a cinema. A popular double bill comprising *Behemoth the Sea Monster* and *The Cyclops* was on at the ABC in Cobham and as usual was playing to a large, appreciative house. We were enjoying the scenes of the radioactive dinosaur stomping through the London streets when, out of the blue, the back doors leading to the foyer swung open and about 20 teddy boys suddenly announced their presence by marching menacingly down the central aisle, each, for some unearthly reason known only to themselves, holding a lighted candle, as if acting out some ancient ritual to a pagan god. The audience's attention to Willis O'Brien's animated monster movie ceased forthwith. As we sat there in fearful apprehension of what was going to happen next, the manager rushed in with two burly assistants and all hell broke loose, with seats being ripped, dangerous-looking objects hurled from one aisle to the other and general pandemonium ensuing as everybody either ducked back out of sight or made for the exits. I never did find out how this group of "teds" ever managed to make their way past the manager in the first place, or what the ruckus was about, but it was all over in 10 minutes and was, in its own way, a great deal more terrifying than anything Gene Evans and company were combating on the big screen. Incidentally, the film kept rolling throughout all the in-house entertainment, although nobody was actually watching it at the time!

It was in December as well that my parents dropped a bombshell. My father had been offered a job in the West Country and we were going to "up sticks" and move to a small village on the outskirts of Redruth at the end of January in the New Year. From a purely personal point of view, my heart sank and depression set in. The cinemas that had served me well over the past few years were now to become a distant memory. What could I look forward to in Cornwall, a county that I knew absolutely nothing about? "Not a lot," stated one of my friends who had

spent two weeks' holiday with his family in Newquay on the North Coast the previous year. "There's nothing down there."

With his less than reassuring words echoing in my ears, I decided to make the most of what was on offer in my area before the far from anticipated moving date arrived. 1962 ended with two visits to The Crescent, first to catch *The Fall of the House of Usher* c/w *The Amazing Colossal Man* and then, a week later, *Demons of the Swamp* c/w *War of the Colossal Beast*. These were the very last movies I ever saw at The Crescent—the

cinema, originally built in 1939, was demolished in 1967 and with it went all of the dramas and dreams that had been acted out there; of countless kids like myself battling against the odds to see films that they were categorically forbidden, by law, to look at; of repeated arguments with irate managers and certain elderly female ticket staff; of trying desperately to cajole any adult, however unsavory-looking they were, to take us in past the barriers; and of having to endure the organist rising up out of the depths to entertain us in the breaks between performances—all vanished, much as the pictures that they had screened would do by the end of the decade.

In compensation for this loss, The Thorndike Theater was erected in its place. *Monster on the Campus* c/w *Cult of the Cobra* turned out to be my final double bill at the old faithful Embassy in Dorking, during the first week of January 1963 when England found herself covered under a perpetual blanket of snow in the worst winter since 1947. Despite a warning from my parents that, "You shouldn't be going out *anywhere* in this weather," I really wasn't prepared to forgo what I considered to be a final opportunity to sit through two Universal horror films *and* say farewell to my beloved cinema prior to being shunted off to the nether regions of the country where this type of fodder, or even a decent movie-house, might not exist. Therefore, ignoring the sound advice handed out for my own safety more than anything else, Tony and myself manfully managed, by skating, sliding and cycling through intermittent sleet showers, to see the program, taking twice as long as usual to reach Dorking and three times as long to cycle back on roads whose tarmac was hidden under a thick layer of compacted ice and slush, making us feel like a couple of extras from *Scott of the Antarctic*. As with The Crescent, The Embassy fell victim to the property developers and was eventually razed to the ground—a Jehovah's Witness temple now stands on the site where eager crowds once milled and jostled in order to sit through the latest Sunday offerings from Universal International, American International and Allied Artists. During 1962, I had somehow managed to rack up 125 movies, most of which belonged to the fantasy genre. Would 1963, with its impending move to pastures new, prove to be a dead loss as far as this particular HSFF fanatic was concerned? I sincerely hoped against all hope that it wouldn't be.

SUNDAY, 10 JUNE 1962

8:00 a.m. Jump out of bed. Wash, then dress—white T-shirt, old green V-necked pullover and jeans with turn-ups. Breakfast—cornflakes (sometimes two hard-boiled eggs and buttered bread) and a cup of tea. Our dog Nick, sprawled on the kitchen floor, is eyeing me in anticipation of his Sunday walk, if I'm in the mood. I am—both parents are becoming snappy already with four kids milling around under their feet and hindering their progress as they go about their household duties. "Why don't you go out, the sun's shining"—this from my mother, directed at both me and my two brothers. Carole, my sister, stays in—even in these less-violent times, little girls do not wander off on their own. 9:00 a.m. "Come on Dave, hurry up and get ready, will you? I'm taking Nick for a walk up Witch's Wood." At the mention of the word walk, Nick, a Red Setter/Dobermann cross with a temperament to match both breeds goes berserk, scrabbling at the back door and leaping out into the garden when the door is opened to prevent further damage to the woodwork, barking his head off. Scuffed shoes are put on, a combination chain and leather lead is attached to Nick's collar and Dave and I set off, the dog straining on his lead from the start and receiving several wallops to his rump in an effort to calm him down a bit, to no great effect. We walk (in my case, I am pulled) up the unmade road, down a twisting flinty footpath, turn left along a yew tree-lined lane, cross the main road with not a car in sight and enter the extensive woods bordering Givons Grove and Headley Heath. Dave breaks the silence.

"Can you tell me about one of those films you've seen?"

"Which one? I've seen loads."

"That one you saw about the giant flying reptile."

Pause to think. "What? Oh, yeah. *Rodan*."

"Yeah. That one."

As Nick is given the release from his lead that he was waiting for 15 minutes ago, hurtling off down the narrow trail and stopping every few moments to sniff at some unknown scent, I become, not for the first time on these Sunday morning jaunts, storyteller.

You're Not Old Enough Son

"Well, it starts off with an atomic bomb going off in the Pacific Ocean. This causes lots of collapses in a Japanese coal mine. It's really creepy at the beginning of the film 'cause these Japs go wading down some flooded tunnels and get pulled under by something you don't see—actually, *I* thought at first it was one of the flying monsters, although it wasn't. What it turns out to be is a type of gigantic caterpillar."

"Blimey! What do they look like?"

"Er, huge eyes, claws and pincers, twice as large as a man. Anyway, these caterpillars or bugs, whatever they are, attack the miners and the army and are finally destroyed in a battle in the mine tunnels. One of the miners gets lost when the roof of a tunnel caves in and is found later suffering from loss of memory."

"What about Rodan?"

"Hang on a minute. They don't appear yet—there are two of them, by the way. Suddenly, these strange objects are spotted flying around causing destruction, and the army thinks that they're flying saucers. Then the hero gets his memory back and remembers stumbling into a vast cavern and seeing one of the monsters hatching from its egg. There are loads more of the bugs in there as well and this particular Rodan starts eating some of them."

By this time, we are in the aptly named Witch's Wood, a shadowy area of woodland that seems dark even on a sunny day like today—it's the reddish-brown hue of the yew trees with their deep green foliage that lend it such a forbidding aspect. Nick is busy investigating one tree after another, probably, knowing him, on the lookout for rabbits. As we plod along, I continue.

"These flying reptiles emerge from the volcano they are living in and one of the monsters attacks this city, which is a fantastic part of the film. Buildings and bridges collapsing all over the place and cars and tanks being tossed around."

"Huh. How do they get killed?"

"Well, as I said, they hide out in a volcano and the army eventually find them. They wait 'til the pair of them are in their hiding place and then blast it with rockets and bombs. The volcano erupts and the Rodans die in the molten lava."

"Oh. What was on with it?"

"*The Deadly Mantis.*"

"Can you tell me about that one?"

We are now over two miles from home, on the fringes of Mickleham Downs, silent unbroken woodland stretching in all directions, many of

the copses hiding deep craters in the chalk, a legacy of German bombing raids over Southern England during the war. Ruined brick buildings and ancient-looking flint walls of unknown origin stand amidst the trees and it is common knowledge that a young boy was murdered and his body dumped here two years previously. There is a stillness in the atmosphere—a baleful stillness. I stop dead in my tracks and call the dog over for protection. You can never be quite sure—some odd-looking people have been spotted roaming about in these woods recently, and we appear to be the only two human beings for miles around.

"Well?" Dave, a lot younger than me, isn't bothered by acres of woods, bomb craters, collapsed ruins, possible deviants and a murder. All he is interested in is a Universal monster flick made five years ago. Undoubtedly, his imagination is not working overtime unlike mine, which senses an aura of malevolence behind every bush and tree in spite of the sun—a case of too many horror films in a short space of time adding to my feeling of unease. Funny—I've never been spooked out here before. Perhaps these movies *are* affecting me after all.

"Oh, yes. Well, there's a volcanic eruption near the North Pole that causes the ice to melt, and one big block of ice contains this bloody great preying mantis that thaws out and goes on a rampage. It attacks a military base, scares the living daylights out of the Eskimos and flies south toward Washington. Are you listening to this?" Dave is lobbing lumps of flint down a chalky gap in the undergrowth, Nick charging after them and retrieving the sharp stones between fanged jaws.

"Yeah. Go on."

But I'm losing patience now with storytelling, conscious of how far we have rambled from our house, so I hurry things up.

"The monster up-ends a bus and finally gets gassed in New York's Holland Park tunnel—I think it's called the Holland Park tunnel—and that's it."

"That wasn't very long. What was that film you saw last week?" Dave is not giving up, but his persistence is beginning to wear a bit thin.

"*Day the World Ended.*"

"What was that all about?"

"I'll tell you about it when we go out again. I haven't got time now. Where's Nick?" After retrieving our dog who has, as usual, strayed off the chosen route and become disoriented in a dense patch of thickets, I calculate that we have covered a much greater distance than I intended, so decide to head back home, or sanctuary as I now see it. This doesn't please Dave at all.

"Why are we going home now? It's too early."

"Because I'm off this afternoon."

"Where—the pictures?" More questions!

"That's right. The Embassy over in Dorking. *It! The Terror from Beyond Space* is on. Sounds good, doesn't it?"

"Yep. I wish I could go and see it with you."

"Sorry, Dave. I could try and smuggle you in under my coat but I don't think it will work."

We arrive back around 11:30 a.m. The kitchen is beginning to steam up as Mum prepares dinner, aiming for the dreaded 2:30 p.m. time slot, and a male voice is crooning a love song on the wireless. A typical Sunday pall hangs in the air—let's get out of here, I say to myself, before boredom sets in.

"Mum, I'm going out this afternoon."

"Where?"—as if she doesn't already know.

"Dorking, to the pictures. I'm meeting Pete, David and Ian outside The Crescent about 12:00."

"Well, dinner will be ready soon."

"I'll have it when I come back." A resigned look from my mother, as if she's thinking (and she probably is), "What's the use?"

"Fine. I'll keep it warm for you. What time *will* you be back?"

"Late." One plate over the dinner, balanced on a saucepan of warm water, will await me on my return.

No response from Mum, but at least I've had the good manners to inform her of my where-abouts for the rest of the day. I wash and change into my teenage garb—brightly colored socks, tight trousers, shirt, tie, three-quarter-length white raincoat and gusset-sided boots—typical early 1960s pre-Beatles fashion. My bike, a blue Dawes five-speed racer in spotless condition, is hauled out of the garden shed. Time for a quick cup of tea, and then it's a free-wheeling downhill ride to The Crescent, including a diversion to Wiggleys to grab some sweets, where my three friends are waiting. Off we cycle to Dorking on a road virtually devoid of traffic, reaching The Embassy cinema at 1:15 p.m. Our four bikes are chained to the railings by the side of the building and we stroll round to the front of the cinema to mingle with a sizeable crowd. One or two youngsters well under the age of 16 are in among the throng, plainly agitated at the ordeal ahead and trying hard not to be noticed. I ignore these nervous-looking kids—I've been through all of that myself, many times before. Tough luck on them if they don't get in, I think, somewhat uncharitably. We study the poster to *It! The Terror from Beyond Space*, which shows a planet with a rocketship planted on the surface, a weird nonhuman figure poised over it, threatening and alarming. Hmmm. Looks interesting. Unfortunately, there's no poster for *Curse of the Faceless Man*, the support feature, and the stills to both movies don't give too much away either. We enter through the heavy swing doors, approaching the kiosk.

"Four 2s 3d tickets, please."

"Thank you. Here are your tickets." On this particular day, I am 15 years and 5 months old and not 16, the required legal age in the United Kingdom to see an "X" film, and it gives me a rush of adrenalin just to be there, flouting the law.

In we go, opting for four seats in the rear stalls. The gloomy auditorium is filling up quickly now; rather oddly, no music is playing for a change, and it is deathly quiet.

"Want a fag?" asks Ian.

"Yeah," from the three of us.

We all light up. Untipped Senior Service, as strong as they come, pinched last week from Smiths in Leatherhead admits Ian without the slightest hint of remorse. Nearly full now, and as the time approaches 1:30 p.m., the dim lights fade as the certification details of the support feature appear behind the curtains, which now open with a creak of rollers to reveal the United Artists logo on the massive screen. Loud title music blasts out during the credits sequence—not only loud, but harsh, in full-on mono. Sixty-six minutes later, *Curse of the Faceless Man* finishes. Short, sweet and fairly enjoyable—I've certainly seen a lot worse.

"What did you think of it, Baz?" this addressed to myself by Pete as they all look upon me as the specialist in films such as the one we have just seen.

"Not bad. Yeah—pretty good really. You?"

"Yeah. Good."

"What about you, Ian?"

"I thought it was alright."

"Dave?"

"OK. I hope the other one is going to be a bit better."

Ian passes more ciggies around and we drag deeply on them in contentment. Most of the seats are now occupied by customers murmuring to one another as what passes for the adverts come up on the screen, three minutes of stills promoting local businesses which everybody blithely ignores. Then "what's on next Sunday"—the brief, bombastic trailers to *Indestructible Man* and *Invasion of the Body Snatchers*, a double bill I have already seen in Cobham several weeks previously. This is followed by "what's on next week"—the Peter Sellers sex-comedy *The Waltz of the Toreodors* which doesn't appeal one jot. The forthcoming attractions over and done with, the

curtains draw themselves over the screen just as the certification details to the main feature appear, and promptly draw back again. Wham!! The *It!* graphics almost leap out of the picture in imitation 3-D style, backed by a deafening musical soundtrack that thunders over the audience, and we know that we are in for an entertaining 70 minutes or so. Our assumptions are correct—the film makes a big impression on all four of us and we give it the thumbs up when it ends.

At 4:30 p.m., the dimmish lights flicker on for a few minutes and some people begin to file out, although we don't and stay put, having made up our minds to see both movies again and get our money's worth. The darkness descends and the ice-cream lady makes her first appearance of the afternoon just below the right-hand edge of the screen, dwarfed by its dimensions, even more so when *Curse of the Faceless Man* commences its 4:45 p.m. showing, customers still queuing for treats as the credits roll. After buying their ice creams, people are groping their way back to where they think their seats are, annoying those of us who are trying to concentrate on the action up front.

A new customer of considerable height positions himself in front of Pete, who gets the needle as this person's head is blocking off a small part of the picture—small but irritating all the same. Pete leans forward and orders the bloke to sit further down in his seat. The chap turns angrily around, sees four faces glaring at him in the light reflected from the screen, chooses not to argue and obeys, sliding down out of sight. At around 6:00 p.m., following the trailers and adverts, *It!* is shown for the second time and at 7:15, after Marshall Thompson and company have defeated the baggy-suited alien, we rise from our seats and leave, the cool evening breeze acting like a tonic after nearly six hours of sitting in The Embassy's smoke-filled atmosphere. The bikes are unchained and we cycle off home, an easygoing three-mile ride ahead of us. Back in Leatherhead, it's "See you tomorrow" to my mates, and a fast pedal uphill to the family residence.

8:45 p.m. Carole, Dave and Roger have retired to bed, and my parents are watching television. Only Nick is there to welcome me, jumping up and licking my face. Dinner is a congealed mass under a plate placed on top of a saucepan—slices of beef, mashed potato, cabbage, carrots and gravy that cooled off hours ago. No pudding—I obviously miss out on that which, in a way, serves me right. Never mind. I'm famished, so the gas stove is lit, the water in the saucepan boils, the meal warms up and reaches a stage whereby one constituent separates from the other, and the whole lot is then wolfed down in five minutes flat. My parents are probably completely unaware of the fact that I have been in for half an hour, so I make my presence known by bidding them goodnight and turning in at 9:30. Another Sunday, another two "X" films under my belt. As I drift off, my last thoughts are—"Shall I make arrangements with the gang to see *Invasion of the Body Snatchers* next week at Dorking, or *Frankenstein 1970* at Epsom?" Then sleep, at long last, intervenes.

You're Not Old Enough Son

THE CAMEO, CORNWALL (1963-1965)

The Redruth district of West Cornwall did not in fact turn out to be, as I had been led to believe by my mates in Leatherhead, a cinematic backwater, despite its forbidding landscape of lonely, windswept moors, gray-stone hamlets and abandoned mines littering the countryside, totally unlike, in every respect, the leafy, wooded Surrey area I had left behind. Redruth itself had The Regal, a large Odeon-sized theater (its other cinema, The Gem, lay rotting in a backstreet and had been derelict for years). The King's cinema was to be found in Camborne, a couple of miles up the road, and Truro boasted two, The Palace and The Plaza. Helston, on the road to The Lizard, had The Flora. As if that wasn't enough, Falmouth mirrored Epsom in that it had both an Odeon and an ABC; so, far from being an entertainment desert, this part of the country was virtually the equal in cinema terms to the Leatherhead/Dorking/Epsom district where I had so recently lived.

From the Sunday one-day program point of view, however, the outlook was less promising—only the two Falmouth cinemas were open on this particular day of the week; the rest were closed. It wasn't all bad news, though. The Regal, I soon discovered, seemed to specialize in showing at regular intervals not only the major movies that were on general release, but also those that came under the heading of "very rarely seen elsewhere." *Flight of the Lost Balloon* c/w *The Amazing Transparent Man* was the first such double bill I caught there, a duff pair of fantasy efforts that disappeared off the face of the earth soon after their appearance in Redruth. As I sat there mentally tearing both films to shreds, scoring low marks for script, acting, music and direction, the cinema's spacious auditorium was filled with the sounds of The Beatles, Gerry and the Pacemakers and other hits of the period blaring out between performances, replacing the Shadows, Pat Boone and Sandy Nelson that I had been used to hearing at The Embassy not so long ago.

Other appealing and unusual features that appeared at The Regal over the next few months included *First Spaceship on Venus*, *Reptilicus*, *King Kong vs. Godzilla* and *Jason and the Golden Fleece*. They also had a preference for screening the continental horror movies that were beginning to infiltrate themselves onto some cinema circuits in the United Kingdom during this period.

The Plaza in Truro

YOU'LL GASP WITH
HORROR...
A SPINE-TINGLING
MOTION PICTURE
only the
atom age
could
produce!

ATOM AGE
VAMPiRE

...BEFORE
YOUR VERY EYES
THE TERRIFYING TRANSFORMATION
OF MAN INTO MONSTER!

SUSANNE LORET · ALBERT LUPO A TOPAZ FILM CORP. RELEASE

Atom Age Vampire was released as *Seddok—Son of Satan* in Britain.

These films, originating from France, Spain and Italy, were more or less based on Hammer's successful output but with the accent firmly on sadism and sleaze—beautifully photographed in either glorious color or monochrome, they were let down in their presentation by some truly atrocious dubbing inflicted upon them by their British distributors. *Seddok—Son of Satan* was a prime example—a well-directed surgical-cum-horror thriller centered around the theme of Jekyll and Hyde, ruined by some hilariously stilted English that would have had the original scriptwriters blushing in their seats! Nevertheless, at least The Regal was putting on this type of product if no one else was, and *Drops of Blood* appeared soon after *Seddok*, another stylish Italian/French production concerning a mad doctor, blood transfusions and corpses turned into stone statues, a favorite storyline from across the water. In the meantime, both the Odeon and ABC in Falmouth were supplying similar fodder on Sundays to what The Crescent and The Embassy in far-away Surrey had been reliably serving up month after month.

The first double bills I took in there were *The Fiend Who Walked the West* c/w *She Devil* at the Odeon on 5 May, and *Kronos* c/w *The Unknown Terror* at the ABC three weeks later. Not bad for starters, I thought—two entertaining main features coupled with two mediocre co-features, screened in comfortable, roomy cinemas. I fervently hoped that future jollies would present themselves in Falmouth during the weeks to come—this in fact turned out to be the case.

At Cornwall Technical College, a couple of the chaps in my class were interested in the fantasy scene and soon we were comparing notes and buying copies of *Famous Monsters of Filmland* magazine together with others of a similar nature that were flooding the market and adding to our burgeoning collections. Now that I could watch the once inaccessible "X" movie at my leisure, the fun, and even to some extent the challenge, had inevitably diminished compared to the heady old days between 1958 and 1962 when uncertainty was de rigueur as you approached a chosen venue with the one thought uppermost in your mind—"Can I get in to see it?" These films were assessed more critically now and we resorted to compiling our own reviews and comments in any spare time left over between college work. But unbeknown to myself, and even to the Cornish lads who had lived in the Redruth-Camborne area for years, a cinematic jewel in the crown was lurking in the vicinity which over the next two years or so was to prove an absolute gold mine as far as my kind of films were concerned.

The Palace cinema or, as we came to know it, The Cameo (a local name that the cinema became stuck with), was situated down a side road off the main Redruth-Camborne highway near Pool, in a small suburb of Camborne known as South Roskear. Originally built in 1920 under the name of Vincent's Hippodrome, it became a full-fledged cinema in 1924 and was the first in the county to screen a talking motion picture—Al Jolson's *The Jazz Singer*. During the 1960s, it gained quite a cult reputation among aficionados in Cornwall because it dared to incorporate into its busy schedules many categories of film deemed too risqué to be shown anywhere else. More importantly (for me), it also broke the trend of the traditional big-chain cinemas and screened old HSFF movies—*very* old HSFF movies as a matter of fact. Out from the vaults they came, vintage delights and low-grade chillers from the '30s and '40s, obscure B efforts from the '50s and the more extreme examples of the continental horror/sex features that The Regal down the road had on once in a while. I never did find out the name of the proprietor of this remarkable little cinema, but I am eternally grateful to him (or her) for allowing me to see on the big screen many of Universal's classic horror movies from the Karloff/Lugosi/Chaney era before they were consigned to VHS, DVD or, in some cases, a black hole from whence they never reappeared.

I wasn't aware of The Cameo's existence until one Saturday in September. Steve, who like me was a stranger to these parts, told me that he had been cycling back from Camborne, looked to his left for no apparent reason, and seen the cinema's prominent display sign down the road leading to South Roskear village. Out of interest, he had diverted his proposed route home to The Cameo to bring back the news that Columbia's crowd-pleaser, *20 Million Miles to Earth*, was starting on Monday for a couple of days, teamed up with *The Creature with the Atom Brain*. I checked the local paper—yes, there it was, tucked away in small print under the adverts for the larger cinemas in the area. I had already sat through Ray Harryhausen's monster flick a few times but that didn't concern me in the slightest, as it was a great piece of entertainment in my book and the second feature had never crossed my path, which made it the perfect excuse to go. Accordingly, on Tuesday after college, we cycled over to South Roskear to watch both films and, just as importantly, suss out The Cameo, hidden away as it was from the main road.

What struck me immediately was its size—a small, compact theater that included a tiny balcony featuring a row of double seats ideally suited for courting couples. Overall, the complete auditorium probably contained seating space for around 100 customers. Normally there was only one showing per evening of a feature film, be it horror, science fiction, Western, sex or a war movie, commencing around 6:30 p.m. Three to four minutes of adverts and "what's on next week" accompanied the main attraction. No usherettes were on call—confectionery was on sale in the petite foyer. Sometimes the programs ran for a couple of days, or one day, or a whole week. There seemed to be no set order, just a case of—"If it's popular, we'll show it for more than one day." A week after our initial visit to the Columbia double bill, Roger Vadim's rather flimsy excuse

The Palace cinema, fondly known as The Cameo

for a vampire thriller, *Blood and Roses*, was shown with *The Vampire and the Ballerina* and a week later a rare chance to catch up with Hammer's *The Curse of Frankenstein*, which had been given a two-day run. That made three visits to The Cameo in a month.

They appeared to be jumping onto the popular horror bandwagon and I had noticed that on each of my three visits, the cinema had been full to capacity, proving, if proof were needed, that the public at that time really did appreciate this kind of movie fare. It had another full house when Richard Cunha's glorious schlock-horror feature, *Frankenstein's Daughter*, appeared, double billed with *Invaders from Mars*. According to a long-serving patron of The Cameo whom we met one evening, the good news was that the cinema was going to show "some really old movies next year—*Frankenstein* and *Dracula*, so I've been told," the bad news being that most of my pocket money was now being spent over at South Roskear and on the bus fare to get there—one could cycle from St. Day where we lived, but it was a strenuous four miles or so. A Saturday job boosted my income, which was just as well as 1964 came around the corner and with it a veritable treasure trove of goodies being offered to the cinema-goer from probably the smallest movie-house in Cornwall.

At the end of 1963, Independent Television screened in four weekly segments Karel Zeman's highly evocative *Cesta Do Praveku*, or *Journey to a Primeval Age*, a charming fantasy telling of four boys who travel down the "river of time," passing through several geological time zones and encountering many species of prehistoric life. This was extremely unusual—television as a whole did not show any decent films in the early 1960s, only antique British or American thrillers, and certainly nothing of an adult nature. It was also remarkable to have Zeman's classic chopped up into four episodes instead of being broadcast as one complete movie. Moreover, it was screened in the children's slot at 5:00 p.m. rather than the evening. Not that this made any difference—scene for scene, this enchanting piece of work from the noted Czechoslovakian director imbedded itself in my memory for a very long time afterwards, in particular the stop-motion animation, cruder than Harryhausen's creations but just as effective and rewarding.

1964 arrived, but there were no signs yet of the promised feast being served up by The Cameo—perhaps, I wondered, they were having trouble with distribution rights to these undisputed classics, if they were what I imagined them to be. So for now, the old movies remained out of sight. What this cinema did start to put on, though, was just as gratifying, catering to my tastes in more ways than one—rare B efforts and grade Z weirdos from the 1950s, starting in February with *The Beast of Yucca Flats* c/w *Vice Squad*. A succession of these were unleashed on the loyal but bemused patrons over the next 12 months, many of which I am sure would never have seen the light of day anywhere else. *The Astounding She-Monster* was the next presentation after Tor Johnson's lamentable science fiction thriller, followed by *Fire Maidens from Outer Space*, *The Dead One*, *Killers from Space*, *The Gargon Terror, Bride of the Monster* and *Mesa of Lost Women*, all of them woefully inadequate in every department but in a masochistic kind of way quite fun to watch.

In fact, many of these particular types of picture, emanating from the Ed Wood school of filmmaking and knocked out by the small independents, had interesting ideas that were not wholly developed by their backers because of one major problem—a lack of money (and, some might add, a lack of talent!). With their muffled soundtracks, corny dialogue, rudimentary direction, play-it-by-numbers acting, ludicrous storylines and impoverished effects, it was sometimes impossible to believe that the British censor would be so mean as to award them the "X" or "A" certificate but award them he did, and most were indeed considered suitable for an adult audience only. However, despite their multitude of faults, we enjoyed them—at least they were different! (One such program had *Queen of Outer Space* as the main attraction, rated "U." The co-feature was an "X"—*The Disembodied*. Any persons under 16 hoping for a glimpse of Zsa Zsa Gabor in a skimpy space costume were therefore prevented from doing so because the movie on with it was for adults only. In the long run, they didn't miss out on all that much, but this clash of certificates was both baffling and inconsistent and didn't really serve any useful purpose other than to get people's backs up!)

In addition to these bottom-of-the-barrel productions, the ABC in Falmouth began to screen a series of top-notch programs on the Sunday circuit, getting the show on the road in January with *Monster on the Campus* c/w *The Land Unknown*, continuing with *Horrors of the Black Museum* c/w *It! The Terror from Beyond Space* and carrying on throughout the rest of the year with similar treats, ending with a flourish in December with *Blood of the Vampire* c/w *Behemoth the Sea Monster*. The Palace (no relation to The Cameo), a smallish, rather outmoded theater in Truro, joined the general flow with the others—Robert Clarke's classic '50s B movie *The Hideous Sun Demon* popped up there for a three-day showing in May, double billed with *Beyond the Time Barrier*. Hot on its heels came *Back from the Dead*, *Attack of the Puppet People*, *The Quatermass Experiment*, *The Monster of Piedras Blancas* and *House on Haunted Hill*.

This bonanza of delights was similar to 1962's deluge, or indeed a continuation of it, the upshot being that my leisure hours took on all the aspects of a highly complicated juggling act when these programs were appearing, because I *had* to see them. I suppose on looking back that it was comparable to an addiction of sorts, only my particular fix wasn't anything as drastic as drugs or drink, only horror and monster films! Blow homework, revision, dwindling funds and a loss of family life; ever since laying my hands on a copy of *Famous Monsters of Filmland* way back in 1958, I had yearned to see these movies and now that they were out on release at my local cinemas, within sight and sound as it were, I was not, under any circumstances, going to miss out on them. Cycling between St. Day, Redruth, Truro and Camborne and bussing it to Falmouth became the normal way of life for a small group of us, and occasionally our long-suffering girlfriends were dragged along to see for themselves just what all the fuss was about—Cornwall, I surmised, was being just as lucrative, in an offbeat system probably unique to the county, as the Leatherhead area had been in screening this sort of fare. Let's not forget the regular weekly releases either—*Jason and the Argonauts*, *The Day of the Triffids*, *Black Zoo*, *Captain Sinbad* and *Journey to the Seventh Planet* among others; all of these had to be fitted in as well. At this rate, I told myself, 1962's mammoth total of 125 films in a year was going to be well and truly broken, if not shattered.

There were so many grade-A double bills available to the public during 1964 in this relatively remote part of West Cornwall, including Hammer's latest pairing *The Evil of Frankenstein* c/w

Nightmare. Showing at The Regal for five days, this was a steppingstone for my brother Roger as it was his first acquaintance with the world of the X-rated movie, even though he was not quite 15 at the time. Me and a mate, Mike, managed to smuggle him in without any trouble—The Regal was no Crescent, being quite lax in its attitude toward who saw what and when. But Roger did us no favors whatsoever by doing a "John," my friend who had cowered in terror through most of *Day the World Ended* in 1962, actually kneeling in front of his seat with his back to the screen and refusing to look at one second of *Nightmare*, much to the acute embarrassment of Mike and myself. When *The Evil of Frankenstein* eventually came on, he peered through his fingers until Kiwi Kingston appeared as the monster and then promptly ducked behind the seat in front vowing, on leaving the cinema, never to sit through anything like that ever again. It later turned out that Roger, although pretty much a committed cinema-goer, never became smitten with the horror bug—David, on the other hand, who was several years younger than me, inherited my tastes and grew up to develop into an ardent fan, although by the time he had reached the proper age to see "X" movies, most of the older classics had begun to disappear from the cinema circuits.

The big disappointment of the year had to be the re-release of two Ray Harryhausen Columbia movies that potentially had all the makings of a tremendously exciting double program: *The Seventh Voyage of Sinbad* with *The Three Worlds of Gulliver*. I took David along to the Odeon in Falmouth to see them; this was his introduction to both the world of fantasy cinema and stop-motion animation, which *Sinbad* had in abundance—or it *did* have. I never did rate the *Gulliver* feature very much and found it a bit of a bore. There was too much talk going on in the second half, and the film only came to life, in my opinion, when a diminutive Kerwin Mathews fought a baby alligator on a table top in the country of Brobdingnag, proving that a lack of the master's stop-motion creations would sometimes make for dull viewing. But I was horrified at what the distributors had done to *Sinbad*. Being shorn of its more severe "A" rating and reduced to a "U" meant that several key scenes had either been heavily tampered with or were omitted altogether on the assumption that these missing scenes were too frightening for a younger audience. Most of the four-armed snake woman segment had vanished; Sinbad recruiting men in the local gaol yard for his return trip to Colossa was nowhere to be seen; the Cyclops roasting a sailor over a fire was cut from the print; the entire skeleton duel sequence had been edited out of existence; and the death of the dragon at the end had also been sliced up. It was the worst piece of butchery carried out on, let's face it, a major motion picture that I have ever had the misfortune to encounter in a cinema. David, of course, was blissfully unaware of this and reveled in both films, but I was left wondering whether or not the British censor at that time had a screw loose (in 1975, the film was restored to its original full-length, uncut version and given another successful re-release).

Alwyn, a big HSFF fan, and I joined *The Horror Film Club of Great Britain* in November. With its headquarters situated in Bath, members received for a yearly subscription a badge and a very basic but entertaining-enough journal every few months, with quality sketches replacing photographs. Letters were exchanged, lists of films compared, analyzed and debated, and it was nice to know that somewhere out there were other people with similar obsessions who were keen enough to form a club to cater to the fans. I was asked to submit some reviews for the journal a few years later but unfortunately never got around to doing it. But the club journal was no *Famous Monsters of Filmland*, which continued to maintain an incredibly high standard year after year and remained the benchmark to which all others aspired.

In January 1965, the eagerly awaited event finally got underway at The Cameo—*Frankenstein* c/w *Son of Dracula* was screened over two days (the co-feature was wrongly billed as an "X" instead of an "A," a common error made during this period because of the multitude of different films sporting different ratings). Did this herald the beginning of the promised run of "really old movies"? It certainly did! Universal International's back catalogue suddenly shook off two decades of dust and appeared at South Roskear's little gem as Karloff's original 1931 horror flick was quickly followed by *House of Frankenstein, House of Dracula, Frankenstein Meets the Wolf Man, Dracula's Daughter, The Mummy's Ghost, Abbott and Costello Meet Dr. Jekyll and Mr. Hyde, The Invisible Man's Revenge, Abbott and Costello Meet Frankenstein, The Mad Ghoul* and many others. What a treat and also a novelty it was to experience the thrill of seeing these venerable classics up on the big screen (well, big for The Cameo anyway, but who was complaining), in seemingly mint condition as well.

Some were screened as double bills for one night only—others ran for two or three nights. *Werewolf of London* came and went, as did Boris Karloff's wearisome Columbia mad doctor movies and a few antiquated features from Warner Bros., Paramount and MGM. Even several of PRC's moth-eaten old potboilers from the 1940s cropped up, from where heaven alone knows. Could there honestly be another cinema anywhere else in the United Kingdom in 1965 that had as its main presentation on a Saturday night *The Mad Monster* double billed with *Devil Bat's Daughter*? I very much doubted it. On my frequent visits to The Cameo during this particular year, it was akin to stepping back in time as practically their entire output, or a considerable part of it, seemed to date from the '30s and '40s. Occasionally, though, a more modern-day picture was shown, usually of the continental variety (*Castle of Blood* and *The Terror of Dr. Hichcock*), or even a Western or war movie, to remind the audience that the cinema had not, in fact, become trapped in a 1930s/1940s horror time warp and was capable of screening newer material.

Not to be outdone by The Cameo's truly outlandish and mind-boggling policy of being completely at odds with every other cinema in the region, The Regal in Redruth decided to stage a Horror Week in the same month. On the Saturday before this momentous occasion in the annals of local Cornish cinema was to take place, I perused the advertising billboard outside the cinema's facade where the following films were listed as the forthcoming attractions:

Monday: *The Revenge of Frankenstein* c/w *Murder By Contract*
Tuesday: *The H-Man* c/w *The Creature with the Atom Brain*
Wednesday: *The Tingler* c/w *20 Million Miles to Earth*
Thursday: *The Werewolf* c/w *Underworld USA*
Friday: *Night of the Demon* c/w *The Stranglers of Bombay*
Saturday: *The Camp on Blood Island* c/w *The Big Heat*

Hmmm. All Columbia productions with a couple of gangster flicks and a war film (albeit a sadistic one) thrown in to balance the mix—the description Horror Week was therefore a bit of a misnomer, and *The Stranglers of Bombay* had been incorrectly billed as an "X," being a very bloodthirsty "A." Never mind. In its own way it was quite a unique (and brave) piece of programming by the management of The Regal, and it goes without saying that very little college work was performed by myself over those six days—somehow, in between revision for GCE mock O-level exams, I managed to go to five of the six showings, with Mike and Alwyn seeing a couple each. I gave *The Camp on Blood Island* a miss as I had no wish to sit through it again, having caught it with *The Revenge of Frankenstein* at the ABC in Falmouth a few months previously. Including *The Return*

The Haunted and the Hunted **was released in the U.S. as** *Dementia 13*.

of the Vampire c/w *Jack the Ripper* at The Cameo five days later and *The Haunted and the Hunted* c/w *The Crawling Hand* on the Sunday at Falmouth's ABC, I had clocked up an astonishing 14 movies in two weeks, which even for me was an all-time record.

My relentless enthusiasm to see everything on offer eventually brought about a kind of downfall of sorts, health-wise that is. On Sunday, 2 May, I noticed in the local rag that the two Falmouth cinemas were both showing attractive double "X" bills—the Odeon had *It! The Terror from Beyond Space* c/w *Curse of the Faceless Man* while *20 Million Miles to Earth*

(again!) c/w *Boy's Night Out* were the movies being shown across town at the ABC. I checked the times, calculating that if I left the Odeon at 4:30 p.m. after *It!* finished I could catch half of *Boy's Night Out* and the whole of *20 Million Miles to Earth* at the ABC. I decided in the morning, therefore, to see both programs in a single day and also cycle the eight miles to Falmouth, as the bus service could be unreliable at times on a weekend, even though the weather looked unsuitable for a reasonably long bike ride.

Unfortunately, the heavens opened as I set out from home and by the time I reached the town I was soaked to the skin. Chaining my blue Dawes racer to the railings near the Odeon, I more or less dried out through Edward L. Cahn's two mini-classics but was drenched in another downpour on walking over to the ABC. Again, my clothes slowly began to dry in the dark, cozy warmth of the auditorium as I enjoyed watching Harryhausen's Venusian monster making mincemeat out of the Roman ruins for what seemed to be the hundredth time. It was dark when I left the cinema and I now had to face the prospect of a grueling eight-mile-or-so cycle back to St. Day, made worse by the fact that most of it would be uphill—pedaling like a dervish against a fierce headwind with rapidly diminishing stamina due to a complete lack of food since breakfast that morning. It didn't stop raining the whole time I was on the road and I arrived home in the same state I had been in several hours earlier, wet through and thoroughly exhausted, collapsing into bed without eating any dinner. The outcome was a weight loss of several pounds, a week's sick leave from college, and a severe bout of tonsillitis that lasted, on and off, right through to the end of my O-level exams in June. "That will teach you" was the only rebuke that I ever received from my parents for this foolhardy display of cinema-madness, which is how I think they looked upon it at the time. And for once in my life, I had to agree with them!

NINE DAYS IN MAY (1964)

Hallelujah—the weekend has arrived after a hard five-days' slog at 'tech; my deliberations immediately turn to the world of the cinema, having had more than enough of the world of English, Maths and Science over the past week. Let's hope my cinema-going fortunes are going to be a damned sight more productive than last Sunday when, thanks to a puncture in the rear tire of my racer coupled with a torrential band of rain sweeping across the countryside, I was annoyingly prevented from reaching Falmouth where *The Thing that Couldn't Die* was showing at the ABC with *Girls on the Loose*. It isn't often that a movie escapes the net and when it does, it hurts. Forrest J Ackerman's magazine has informed me that Universal's film is about a devilish Elizabethan head dug up on a ranch by a young woman who possesses psychic powers; the head then forces her to search for its body to enable it to resume dabbling in the black arts. It all sounds very tasty and I've bloody well had to pass on it. Therefore, I'm going to make amends, starting today, Saturday. *The Hideous Sun Demon* is completing a three-day run at The Palace in Truro with *Beyond the Time Barrier*. I've rung my cinema-going fraternity and they are all to a man engaged. It's a lovely sunny day and I shouldn't really be burying myself in the darkness of a cinema for three hours; the trouble is, a glimpse of Robert Clarke made up as the mutated lizard-man in *Famous Monsters* (that magazine has got a lot to answer for!) convinces me that I cannot afford to let this relatively little-seen feature slip through my fingers, beautiful weather or not. My bike, freshly cleaned, oiled and repaired, is taken out of the shed and off I go, descending the steep hill leading out of the village, pushing the machine past the gaunt ruins of Killifreth and Wheal Busy mines on my approach to Chacewater, pumping like mad up the gradients to a fairly level stretch of road and finally dropping down into Truro after an hour and a quarter.

The Palace is tucked away in a side road at the rear of a parade of shops, similar to The Cameo near Camborne, and I cycle up to its old-fashioned facade at about 2:00 p.m., chaining my bike to a nearby railing. This is a small, independent theater with a cramped and slightly claustrophobic auditorium smelling disturbingly of mildew and old age. For a change, there's hardly anybody about. In fact, it's positively deserted—merely myself and about 11 other patrons in the place. That's not surprising really on a day like today, when most normal people are making tracks for the beach. But the beach can wait. It will be there tomorrow, and the next day, and the day after that—*The Hideous Sun Demon* won't be. I

pay up, installing myself in the back row as the co-feature, *Beyond the Time Barrier*, comes on, a watered-down version of *World Without End* boasting cardboard sets, mediocre effects and inferior acting. To make matters worse, the print is in an awfully poor state, jumping and scratchy, with an indistinct soundtrack. I am not impressed, although, to be fair, it *is* diverting in a juvenile kind of way. A few adverts, the trailers to future presentations, a brief interval and then the main feature reveals itself as the curtains jangle apart. Yet again, difficulties are experienced in trying to make out the dialogue the actors are mouthing (what is it about these cheapo sci-fi movies and their rough soundtracks?), although Robert Clarke's scaly monster livens up the proceedings and the climax, with Clarke being chased by the police up a large gas tank to his death, reminds me of a sequence I recollect seeing in *Quatermass 2*, lifting this B movie out of the ordinary and into the realms of the acceptable. Pretty good, I reflect on leaving The Palace—it's a pity the rest of the lads were not there to savor it.

Back indoors, the phone rings. It's Mike, telling me that *Gorgo* is on at the ABC in Falmouth tomorrow. Do I fancy going to see it? I mentally berate myself for not noticing this alluring attraction in the local paper; otherwise, it would have been me calling him, and a few others too, so I answer in the affirmative.

"What's on with it?"

"Not a horror film I'm afraid. Something called *Passport To Shame*. It might be OK 'cause it's an' X'. Sure you can make it, or are you off out with your folks? Steve is, 'cause I rang him a few minutes ago."

"No, I am *not* off out with the family."

"Alright then—keep your hair on. I'll be over about half-eleven."

The next morning, with the fine weather continuing, Mike pedals into the village and knocks on our door at 11 a.m. after a four-mile hike from Camborne. Because he's got an additional eight ahead of him, and the route to Falmouth is quite arduous, nothing like the much easier ride into Truro and longer as well, refreshments are ordered—tea and sandwiches, after which we set off and eventually coast into the center of town about 1:00 p.m. We padlock our bikes to the railings in the square and stroll over to the ABC, where a sizeable crowd is waiting for the doors to open, as opposed to the 12 or 13 customers who sat through *The Hideous Sun Demon* yesterday. Settled in our seats, we put up with Diana Dors' sordid tale of vice, *Passport To Shame*, which I admit passes the time adequately, if nothing else. After the ads and the trailers (I note that *Doctor Blood's Coffin* is next Sunday's presentation), *Gorgo* appears, a noisy British monster caper, easily the equal in every department to anything of its ilk that has emerged from Japan or America, however short (79 minutes) it runs. Both of us are keen on a replay by staying seated for the next performance, meaning an extra dose of Diana Dors to wade through, and on account of this we drop the idea, leave the auditorium and wearily cycle back home, wondering why on earth we sometimes punish ourselves in this way just to see a movie I personally have watched twice before. On the other hand, that's what commitment is all about, surely. On reaching the village, Mike is fed and watered to revitalize him in preparation for his return stint to Camborne. Before he departs, he says, "You going to The Cameo next week, Baz?"

That's funny—The Cameo hasn't been mentioned all afternoon in any of our conversations and Mike chooses to bring it up now, prior to setting off. Great!

"I wasn't going to. Why, what's on there?"

"*The Demon Doctor*."

Bugger! I grab the paper and, yes, there it is in the local cinema columns; worryingly, I have once more overlooked another morsel. Perhaps too much college work is addling my brain. Yes—Monday and Tuesday: *The Demon Doctor* and *Varan the Unbelievable*. An on-the-spot decision is required.

"Yep. OK, we'll go Tuesday. See you at college tomorrow," and Mike heaves himself onto his six-speed racer, shooting off in the direction of Redruth and Camborne.

Tuesday arrives. I catch the bus home from college, change, and skip dinner, telling my mother that I'll eat out (which I won't, and never do—horror films have priority over food any day of the week). Jumping on the next bus leaving the village, I alight at Pool and race up the long hill to The Cameo, where I am pleased to observe a large group of people hustling and jostling by the posters. It's always satisfying to experience these movies during a full house; the atmosphere is, to a certain degree, more conducive to one's enjoyment and pleasure of what is actually on display, even when it's as dire a piece of work as *The Astounding She-Monster* or *The Beast of Yucca Flats*. Mike and Steve are waiting there, so in we go, picking three seats at the rear of the cinema's tiny auditorium, as I tend to suffer from headaches and a stiff neck if too near the front. The lights go down and *Varan the Unbelievable* commences. "Unbelievable" is the word for the state of the print—it is in a lamentable condition, severe editing no doubt the cause; either that, or the censor's scissors have been at work. The first few minutes bear little resemblance to what comes after, and the dubbing, as usual with these Japanese monster flicks, leaves a lot

to be desired. Regardless of these shortcomings, the movie records a high rating between us. The special effects, albeit not up to *Godzilla* standards, are heaps better than those in *Gigantis the Fire Monster*, seen a few weeks earlier at The Cameo, and the dark photography gives it a nightmarish air. The monster is a corker as well. We are pleasantly surprised, especially as I've never heard of this one before now.

The lights come up and in the five-minute interval, I partake of an orange drink and a packet of crisps—my meager dinner for the day. Then it's *The Demon Doctor*, a continental horror movie that also receives our seal of approval—inconsistent dubbing, weird musical soundtrack and corny acting it may have, but it's filmed with oodles of style and sadistic glee, and the doctor's pop-eyed assistant Morpho is a real scream, somehow managing to grab all the nubile young women needed for Howard Vernon's experiments even though he's as blind as a bat. At least it's streets apart from most other movies of this breed, with a quirky touch all of its own. After it finishes we go our separate ways, agreeing that this was one hell of a double bill that we have been fortunate enough to attend.

That's a total of six films in four days—hard to contemplate in this day and age, yes, but not in 1964 with so many cinemas about providing an unending supply of horror and monster fodder. West Cornwall, it seems, has latched onto the plain truth, one which we fans could have told the distributors all about—this category of motion picture is big business, however ineptly made the product often turns out to be. They're on everywhere—one glance at the entertainment section of *The West Briton* shows a sea of X-rated pictures spread over the whole of West Cornwall: *Murder Incorporated* c/w *Dead Men Walk*, *The Tomb of Ligeia* c/w *Black Sabbath*, *Peeping Tom* c/w *Girls from the Mambo Bar*, Universal's "big double shock horror bill," *House of Frankenstein* c/w *House of Dracula*, *Lord of the Flies* c/w *Lola*. It's no wonder that some choice tidbits get overlooked in the mad scramble to catch as many as possible. Moreover, The Regal in Redruth is screening *The Castle of Terror* at the end of the week, and I'm debating whether or not to go. Mike says "no." He's stony-broke, and I'm still in funds—just. Therefore, I promise myself to pop along on Friday, as I've spotted photos of the film's hooded madman in *Castle of Frankenstein* and it looks appetizing.

On Friday (happily a college-free day) I walk the hilly two miles into Redruth—the bike is out of action with another puncture, and I could do with the exercise! There's a pitifully small crowd at The Regal—mind you, cinema managers do not expect the afternoon slot to be a big draw anyway, and a few senior citizens are buying their tickets, probably wondering what *The Castle of Terror* and the support feature, *Horror*, are all about. A lot more gory and terrifying than the old *Frankenstein* movies that they saw when they were my age, I think to myself as I buy my

ticket. Let's hope for their sakes that they can stomach them. In a virtually empty cinema, the curtains draw back and *Horror* kicks off, a confusing continental thriller concerning the spooky comings and goings in an old mansion, apparently all to do with a young girl's inheritance. It doesn't make a great deal of sense and I wonder whether the oldies in the audience can fathom out the convoluted plot—the nice black and white photography saves it from becoming just another routine program filler.

The Castle of Terror, on the other hand, is far livelier, and in color—a full-blooded Gothic horror melodrama featuring Christopher Lee in a bit role who really doesn't do a lot, harboring the sinister secret behind a series of horribly gruesome murders carried out by a grotesquely disfigured maniac prowling menacingly around in the castle's dungeons. Atrocious dubbing abounds, the color is bright and flashy and the soundtrack bombastic throughout. Typical French/Italian fare of the period—Hammer Films meet Edgar Allan Poe, with sadism and bloodshed thrown in to titillate the audience. Very fetching, but I wouldn't particularly wish to see it a second time, I guess, as I leave The Regal and hoof it back up Fore Street toward the village and home—the continental horror movies are watchable in their own freakish way, but the continual emphasis on butchery and torture, together with those terrible dubbed soundtracks, does begin to pall after a while.

La Vergine di Norimberga **was retitled** *The Castle of Terror* **for the U.K.**

Sunday dawns, bright and sunny. The family are finalizing their plans for a day out in St. Ives—except for me, that is. I haven't forgotten that *Doctor Blood's Coffin* is being shown at the ABC in Falmouth, a feature that I was refused entry to in October 1962, which means that I've a score to settle and really must make the effort to see the film before it disappears off the circuits. This is one movie that does not count as a "regular" and it is only the third occasion I've spotted it out on release.

"And precisely where are you off to on this lovely day?" This from my mother when it becomes abundantly clear to her from my movements that I have no intention of joining the family trip to St. Ives.

"The pictures in Falmouth."

"What? Again?"

"Yes."

"Blimey, Barry, how many times have you been to the pictures recently?"

"Um. This'll be the fifth." I'm starting to feel anxious now under Mum's barrage of questioning and she hasn't finished yet.

"I take it you can afford all these trips. And don't neglect your college work, will you."

"Don't worry about that. I've finished my revision for the week. And I *have* got the money to go."

"You're not trying to break some kind of record, are you?"

I sigh. "No—it's simply a hobby," and seemingly satisfied at last, Mum gives me a pointed stare (probably thinking, quite rightly, that this cinema-mania is of her own making and realizing that, in hindsight, she was acting unwisely in telling me all those terrible stories years and years ago), before going about her business, ensuring that the wicker hamper that will be hauled to St. Ives beach is bulging with sandwiches, cakes and soft drinks, none of which I will be sharing in. While the family are busy getting ready, I ring a few friends—strangely, everybody seems to be occupied with other things, and as my bike is still laid low with a flat tire, I take the next bus to Falmouth, arriving in the town center at 1:15 p.m.

Despite the glorious sunshine, this double bill has amazingly drawn a large crowd and I head for the rear stalls. The support feature, *Macumba Love*, comes and goes—a colorful but instantly forgettable voodoo potboiler that begins to fade from my memory long before it ends. "What's on next Sunday" looks inviting—*I Married A Monster from Outer Space* c/w *Never Let Go*; nevertheless, these two will have to wait because the credits are rolling for *Doctor Blood's Coffin* and I become drawn not only into Kieron Moore's over-the-top performance in the title role (a young medic with a penchant for illegal heart surgery), but the setting of the film itself, which takes place, rather unusually, in a small Cornish village. In fact, over the next 92 minutes, I play a guessing game while the action lurches from one gory scene to the next, as in "guess which scene is filmed where." Most of it, I determine later, is shot in and around the St. Just and Botallack district, with the abandoned mines scattered over the bleak cliffs providing an unusual backdrop to Moore's ghastly activities. A very energetic horror outing, I conclude when leaving the ABC, and Hazel Court is her usual ravishing self.

Ten films in nine days. Total cost approximately one pound eight shillings—it's me who is now stony-broke. Ten films, and I haven't watched a single minute of television—the cinema is all-persuasive and all-conquering. One day, this never-ending supply of HSFF fodder will cease to exist; even I realize that—it surely cannot go on forever. But while it *does* exist, I will continue to be subservient to its calling, paying reverence wherever I can to the genre that quite often threatens to dominate my existence at the expense of all others.

With this in mind, I make a firm resolution to curtail, for the next seven days if possible, any further trips to the cinema by knuckling down and concentrating on family life and all that it entails. Even as this thought materializes, my subconscious is goading me on, reminding me of next Sunday's attraction at the ABC, let alone the features that may be showing at The Regal, The Cameo, The King's in Camborne…

You're Not Old Enough Son

OBSERVATIONS (1965)

Since 16 July 1961, that decisive day when I successfully negotiated the ticket kiosk at The Embassy in Dorking and saw *The Creature Walks Among Us* with *Tarantula*, I had managed to chalk up a fair number of HSFF movies comprising the classic, the excellent, the ordinary and the awful and had now reached a stage whereby the analytical region of my brain began to intrude into the pleasure zones while watching a particular film. I still gained an enormous amount of satisfaction from them, but along with the enjoyment came the examination of contents—if it was a feature that I took a dislike to, it was more of a dissection of contents. My friends became used to me murmuring, "What's the reasoning behind that shot?" or, "There's too much music going on," and I was ordered on more than one occasion to "shut up" and keep my opinions to myself until at least the program had ended—only then was I allowed to talk about the afternoon's entertainment shortcomings in detail.

Seeing one film after another, sometimes several in the space of a few weeks, patterns started to become apparent in their presentations—the way they were put together, the scripts, how plots were composed, the music, whether or not the actors turned in good performances, and how long it took for the monster to appear. All these various attributes, and the merits or otherwise of numerous horror and fantasy fare, were evaluated and discussed at great length between our group, with as much cogitation and brainwork going on as the time spent in studying for our GCE exams. We were a bunch of lads who deep down probably nursed aspirations of becoming film directors and producers, although some of the stuff we sat through we reckoned, with a certain amount of haughty disdain, that a 12-year-old could have done a better job. The bulk of our input were the movies of the 1950s, the two decades preceding that making up a smaller percentage of what we had seen. Imitation magazines under the preposterous titles of *Monsters of the Night* and *X-Rated Horrors* were cobbled together in the forlorn hope that perhaps one day they might vie for attention with the likes of *Castle of Frankenstein* on the bookshelves, even though these flimsy sheets bashed out on an ancient manual typewriter contained no photographs, only sketches and drawings. Despite this harmless enough debating and differences in our points of view, we did hold firm opinions on the fantasy film as a form of art and had noticed unmistakable traits in the field. The following list that we drew up at the time highlighted both these and one or two of our own beliefs regarding certain movies:

a) Universal International appeared to be the leader in the genre, from their classic '30s and '40s output—*Dracula*, *Frankenstein* and the rest—to their science fiction thrillers of the '50s. Their productions were classier than the rest of the pack, with better directors, producers, actors and music.

b) Allied Artists was the runner-up, with a hefty output during the 1950s, followed by American International, Columbia and United Artists. Behind them came the independents—Howco, Pacific International, Astor, Regal International and Favorite Films among them.

c) The big studios—Paramount, Warner Bros., 20th Century Fox and others—also produced horror and science fiction, but on a lesser scale.

d) Hammer flew the flag for Britain in the field of horror; a few minor studios produced minor films in keeping with their lower profiles.

e) As with the '40s, the '50s had a stock of actors and actresses circulating from one production to another—Richard Denning, John Agar, Richard Carlson, William Hopper, Kenneth Tobey, Marshall Thompson, Allison Hayes, Mara Corday and Lori Nelson, to name but a few.

f) Low-grade efforts from the likes of Ed Wood, Jerry Warren and Robert Clarke all seemed to be burdened with muffled, barely audible soundtracks.

g) Producer/director pairings were quite common in the '50s—Robert E. Kent/Edward L. Cahn and John Croydon/Robert Day being two examples.

h) Ray Harryhausen's animated monsters were streets ahead of anybody else's efforts in this highly specialized area of filmmaking. But when his creations were not onscreen, his films could suffer from bouts of *longueur* in between the action.

i) The old *Frankenstein* and *Dracula* movies, although great fun to watch, were not all that frightening. Throughout these films, there was one actor who always gave a pleasing performance, however good or bad the production was—Boris Karloff. George Zucco was another such actor—solid and dependable.

j) 1960s science fiction films, on the whole, were execrable.

k) Many of Hammer's movies of the '60s were likewise in a sorry state.

l) It usually took about 25 minutes for the monster to appear.

m) The worst-looking fake giant spider appeared in *Mesa of Lost Women*, with the arthropod in *Missile to the Moon* a close runner-up.

n) Why did *Macabre* run for years on the Sunday circuit when it was such a thoroughly boring picture?

o) Bert I. Gordon's special effects were, on the whole, pretty abysmal and never really improved from one film to the next.

p) The music scores to the '40s and '50s movies were tremendously impressive, almost mini-symphonies in themselves. The films relied heavily on them for atmosphere, mood and momentum. The '60s saw the rot set in, probably due to the new "swinging" culture with its mania for pop-art and James Bond-type soundtracks.

q) The vampires in pre-1950s movies had no fangs.

r) The Japanese Toho productions suffered from appalling dubbing.

s) Similarly, the English dubbed onto the soundtracks of the continental horror features was even worse.

t) Whenever a view of Earth was shown in a space movie, it always featured the North and South American continents.

u) The two main causes for monsters to appear were the A bomb and volcanic activity.

v) Despite severe criticism in some quarters, Brian Donlevy *did* make an effective Quatermass.

w) Many films of the '50s had both an American title and an English title, which could sometimes cause confusion in the "what's on next week" columns. For example, *Blood of Dracula* in the United States evolved into *Blood Is My Heritage* in the United Kingdom, *The Hideous Sun Demon* changed to *Blood on His Lips*, *Invasion of the Saucer Men* became *Invasion of the Hell Creatures*, and *Terror in the Midnight Sun* turned up as *Invasion of the Animal People*, although most of the prints we saw were the U.S. versions. Some foreign movies were even lumbered with three separate titles: Riccardo Freda's *I Vampiri* was featured as *The Devil's Commandment* in the United States and *Lust of the Vampire* in the United Kingdom. This disparity in names more or less ceased in the 1960s, with movies being released under a universally recognized title.

x) Allison Hayes, Shawn Smith, Sally Todd, Lori Nelson, Leigh Snowden and Mara Corday were all gorgeous. But what became of them when the 1950s ended?

y) Lon Chaney Jr. was completely miscast as the *Son of Dracula*.

z) Tor Johnson's most wooden of all wooden performances had to be Lobo in *The Unearthly*.

We also came to accept the fact that inflated high-flown trailers did not necessarily mean that the complete article was worth seeing. It was all well and good that the adverts for *The Bride and the Beast* promised "the most exciting safari of modern times" and "one of the great horror stories of our time," when Allied Artists' absurd woman-into-ape picture quite patently failed to deliver any of these superlatives to the audience. And did Bert I. Gordon's *King Dinosaur* really contain "Wondrous sights your eyes have never seen 'til now"? No, it didn't! But this was all part of the fun, and we quickly came to view these excerpts with a jaundiced eye, knowing full well that in many cases, an 80-minute-long feature film would not live up to the expectations exhibited in its promotional trailer.

Without the aid of any sort of literature on the cinema (England's rather high-brow *Films and Filming*, not readily available in our far-west area of Cornwall unless on subscription, was about the only informative piece of reading that actually reviewed films on an adult level), our knowledge of the medium was only really gained by what we had seen the previous week at The Cameo or The Palace. Themes that ran from one decade to the next began to emerge, soaking into our brains like ink on blotting paper, and we started to form our own conclusions, conclusions no doubt already written about in numerous articles elsewhere, but which *we* certainly had not come across in our small circle. The 1930s and 1940s were the periods in which the "Mad Doctor" movies flourished (*The Mad Ghoul*/*The Monster Maker*), along with the man-into-ape or ape-into-man scenario (*The Return of the Ape Man*/*Dr. Renault's Secret*), with Universal's *Frankenstein* and *Dracula* series coursing along from one year to the next. The arrival of the 1950s ushered in cinema's Atomic Age—flying saucers, aliens invading the Earth, robots, monsters on the loose, gigantic insects, mutations, space travel and mad scientists replacing the mad doctors of yesteryear.

Together with this veritable explosion of fantasy came the decade's obsession with hypnotism (*The Search for Bridey Murphy*/*The Hypnotic Eye*), regression (*I Was a Teenage Werewolf*/*Blood Is My Heritage*), disembodied heads (*The Thing that Couldn't Die*/*The Man Without a Body*), man-into-monster (*Monster on the Campus*/*The Vampire*), and rejuvenation (*Lust of the Vampire*/*The Wasp Woman*). Perennial favorites Frankenstein and Dracula were still popular, albeit in far more bloodthirsty formats than the old Universal versions. The 1960s, or what we had experienced of the output of "the swinging decade" up to 1965, was churning out practically everything in color but with no definable ideas of its own—in fact, it was a disorganized mishmash of everything the previous three decades had produced, and made with far less flair. We concluded that the '50s was *our* favored era—it was fortunate that we had a rare opportunity (with a lot of help from The Cameo) to actually see movies made as far back as 1935 and 1942, but for sheer quantity of vicarious thrills of the type thrown at us by *Famous Monsters of Filmland*, the 1950s took some beating—certainly the '60s was proving to be a major let-down in terms of quality product.

Many of the films that we saw seemed to be constructed on very similar lines, and again this was a characteristic of the cycle of '50s monster-on-the-loose movies—it was often a case of "same old story, different monster." We often had a laugh comparing one with another, and if we were to briefly run through the plot developments of two of the '50s' more illustrious efforts, *The Black Scorpion* and *20 Million Miles to Earth*, these similarities stick out like a sore thumb, even though they were produced by different companies, had different directors, different actors and different scriptwriters:

The Black Scorpion

0-2 mins. A somber voice intones opening pre-credit sequence, the scene-setter to what follows. In this picture, it's volcanic activity (an old favorite).

7 mins. Mysterious destruction of houses and automobiles by something unknown.

20 mins. Richard Denning and Mara Corday make eye contact. Possible romance developing.

30 mins. Denning flirts with Corday.

33 mins. The monster (or in this case monsters) makes its first appearance.

40 mins. The film now concentrates on man/military combating the monsters.

82 mins. The final showdown—the army versus giant scorpion in well-known setting. This time it's Mexico City's bullring.

88 mins. Monster is defeated—Denning puts his arm around Corday and they walk off into the distance, with a final close-up of the monster's corpse.

20 Million Miles to Earth

0-1 min. A somber voice intones opening pre-credit sequence, the scene-setter. Here, it's a rocket hurtling toward Earth with an unknown cargo on board.

3-10 mins. Rocketship crashes into the sea—mysterious object washes up.

18 mins. Joan Taylor and William Hopper meet and sparks fly.

22 mins. The baby Ymir makes its appearance.

35 mins. The monster escapes from its cage and goes on a rampage.

42 mins. Hopper and Taylor meet again and the attraction is mutual.

47 mins. The film now concentrates on man/military combating the monster.

75 mins. The final showdown in well-known setting—this time it's the Coliseum in Rome.

82 mins. Monster is defeated—Hopper and Taylor walk off in each other's arms, with a final close-up of the Ymir's corpse.

Them!, *The Deadly Mantis*, *The Beast from 20,000 Fathoms*, *Godzilla*, *Earth vs. the Spider*, *The Monster that Challenged the World*—the same tried and trusted formula was used, with little variation in plot. The budget, in the end, dictated how effective this was all going to be when the finished product appeared on the big screen.

In a way, the romantic side of many of these features could also become slightly irritating, repetitive and far-fetched—John Agar hitting it off immediately with Mara Corday (*Tarantula*), Rex Reason admiring Jeff Morrow's wife Leigh Snowden (*The Creature Walks Among Us*), Shawn Smith fancying would-be murderer Marshall Thompson (*It! The Terror from Beyond Space*), Shawn Smith (again!) avoiding a love-struck Jock Mahoney (*The Land Unknown*), and Touch Connors homing in on Lori Nelson (*Day the World Ended*). Then one had to put up with the incessant verbal sniping going on between Richard Denning and Richard Carlson over the lovely Julie Adams in *Creature from the Black Lagoon*. Still, the films *were* aimed at an adult audience (in the United Kingdom at least), and a few moments of harmless titillation for the grown-ups sandwiched between the action didn't go amiss—most of the female leads in these pictures were attractive anyway.

The other thing that annoyed us, unreasonably perhaps but it still did, was the "let's get the projector out for a brief lesson in animal behavior" syndrome, particularly prevalent in the '50s giant insect thrillers. Once it had been established by the authorities that there was something nasty lurking in the vicinity that was responsible for the usual spate of unexplained deaths, disappearances and trashed vehicles, a projector just had to be produced and the authorities, the army, the hero and the heroine all summoned and instructed to sit or stand in a darkened room while a scientist/doctor decked out in a white coat went to great and sometimes very boring lengths to explain that whatever the giant spider/lizard/locust/mantis/mollusc/ant was up to out there, it was only mirroring the behavior patterns of Earth's more lowly, and certainly much smaller, counterparts as per the film that was rolling before them.

CENTURIES OF PASSION PENT UP IN HIS SAVAGE HEART!

CREATURE FROM THE BLACK LAGOON

RICHARD CARLSON JULIA ADAMS

Therefore, it was solemnly declared, if we knew how to destroy the normal wildlife in their habitats, we could eliminate the gargantuan versions that were creating havoc. All very interesting, no doubt, but these potted natural history episodes rankled—they held up the action, and film excerpts of insects and lizards could be experienced in college during Biology. We didn't need to know about them within the confines of a cinema. Even superior classics such as *Them!* and *Tarantula* were cursed with this affliction. Surely, we reasoned, the film producers at the time must have realized that any audiences watching their product were intelligent enough to work all this out for themselves without the need to have it spelled out for them.

So we argued, expostulated, praised the worthy, panned the lousy—in short, a small group of fantasy fans became unqualified film critics, even taking to task the reviews of the more eminent pundits whose comments regarding HSFF movies both past and present, in newspapers and magazines, we might not necessarily agree with. We had developed our own judgments from countless trips to the cinema and now had an unshakable belief in our ability to determine what we would class as an acceptable and satisfactory piece of celluloid when we saw it without being told otherwise by some so-called expert. Highfaluting standards maybe, but at least we were trying to get the measure of these films as they really were and not how other people saw them.

FOREIGN DELIGHTS (1965-1966)

After finishing my exams, I totally ignored my parents' advice about continuing with further education and the benefits it would bring me in later years and decided to enlist in the merchant navy to broaden my horizons and see a bit of the world, passing the necessary interview and a strict medical and joining the crew of the P & O Orient liner *Chusan* in July 1965 at Tilbury, Essex. No more visits to The Cameo and the Sunday one-day programs in Falmouth were to figure in my life for the next four months, when you were granted a week's shore leave in addition to the odd day or two between cruises.

Returning to Cornwall from Southampton (where we normally berthed after cruising) on my first break, I managed to catch *Attack of the Crab Monsters* c/w *Not of this Earth* at the ABC in Falmouth at the beginning of November, and *Caltiki the Immortal Monster* at The Palace the same week, but that's about as far as it went for the remainder of the year. Steve told me that in my absence, The Cameo had presented a special one-off showing of *The Mask* in 3-D, complete with cardboard glasses containing the notorious red and green lenses. It wasn't so much a case of missing the movie that peeved me slightly when I heard this piece of news (a stinker, according to Steve) but the experience of seeing it in three-dimension, which would have been quite something.

Southampton's abundant collection of cinemas were chock-a-block with only the current releases, most of which I wasn't all that bothered with—there was regrettably no Hampshire equivalent of The Cameo tucked away down a side street showing a few golden oldies, or none that I ever discovered, and the only science fiction film I saw there on the rare occasions that I didn't travel down to the West Country on leave was *Crack in the World*, a dullish sci-fi thriller from Paramount. Once abroad, though, some amusing incidents relating to the fantasy scene occurred that without a shadow of a doubt would not have manifested themselves either in Surrey or Cornwall.

In September, our ship docked at Piraeus in Greece, the main port for Athens, a city I was looking forward to visiting, specifically to explore the ancient ruins at the site of the Acropolis. With a whole day at our disposal, a party of us strolled along the bustling waterfront and passed what appeared to be a newsagent (or a Greek version of one) situated in a parade of shops. We halted in our tracks and wandered in to have a browse and there on the shelves, much to my amazement, were a number of dusty editions of *Famous Monsters of Filmland* and *Mad Monsters*, in English as well. A sudden wave of nostalgia swept over me and I bought five copies, much to the quizzical stares of my fellow cabin-mates, who were at that moment in time completely unaware of my particular bent. Ginger, a cockney hailing from London's East End, broke the awkward silence.

"What do you want those for?"

"I'm interested in them."

"Eh?"

"I like the old horror movies. Always have. I didn't realize you could buy these magazines over here."

He shrugged. "Oh well, it's your money."

Leaving the shop and continuing our walk up the main highway, we chanced upon three cinemas near a left-hand fork that headed toward Athens, two side-by-side and the third situated around the corner in an adjacent road. We sidled up to them in the morning heat. Faded film posters were plastered all over the facade, giving the place the appearance of an advertising hoarding: *The Broken Land, The Quick Gun, No Name on the Bullet, The Secret of Monte Cristo, The 300 Spartans, Goliath and the Barbarians*—the locals evidently liked their Westerns and adventure movies. We peered around the corner at the ramshackle theater in the next street, called The Elysian.

Another surprise, the second of the morning—it was showing a horror film, *The Diabolical Dr. Satan*, which was playing with, of all things, John Wayne's famous Western *Rio Bravo*, surely one the most bizarre double billings in the history of the cinema! We looked at our watches. With still a couple of hours or so left before we were due to go into Athens, we decided more out of sheer curiosity than anything else to see it (although watching a horror flick on foreign soil was a big notch on my belt, as far as I was concerned). In broken English, we determined from the man in the dilapidated foyer that *Dr. Satan* was due to start in two minutes, so we paid up seven drachmas each and entered the dim, claustrophobic auditorium, if one could use the term to describe this hovel. The floor was made up of part earth, part concrete, several children were running around (obviously no "X" ratings out here, then), the seats were in a state of disrepair and, in a scene straight out of an old British comedy caper, several chickens were roaming up and down the aisles looking for food.

When the film began to roll, at least one-third of it was projected onto the ceiling. What a flea-

pit! Fortunately, the movie we saw was in dubbed English with Greek subtitles, so we more or less had some idea of what was going on—at least *I* did, because although the print and viewing conditions were appalling by U.K. standards, it dawned on me after about five minutes that this was in fact *The Demon Doctor* in another guise, which I had seen over a year previously at The Cameo (in very different surroundings, I might add) with *Varan the Unbelievable*. Fancy, I thought, catching up with it in a cinema like this. After the movie ended, we didn't fancy sitting through over two hours, or even two minutes, of *Rio Bravo* in that decrepit place, and as the hot sunshine beckoned, along

Behind this rundown theater in Piraeus, Greece in 1965 was another showing *The Diabolical Dr. Satan*.

You're Not Old Enough Son

with Greece's capital city, we sneaked out through a side exit door so as not to draw attention to ourselves, blinking furiously in the unaccustomed brilliance of light. Still, it was a novel experience to have been there all the same.

On 23 October, our ship paid another call to Piraeus and four of us made our way over to the cinemas that we had unearthed on our previous trip. A large and pretty magnificent poster of *The Evil of Frankenstein* was outside one of the theaters, along with those depicting the Westerns, the biblical dramas and the war films that the Greeks obviously relished. Swiftly coming to the conclusion that this poster would look great on the cabin wall among all the pictures of naked females torn out of dozens of porn magazines, and egged on by my mates, I approached a swarthy-looking man whom I took to be the proprietor of the place, addressing him in civil tones, very much aware that I was the stranger in foreign climes.

"Excuse me. How much can I give you for the poster?"

"Pardon?" He gave me a puzzled look.

Pointing upwards, I repeated the request. "I'd like to buy that poster. How much?"

He grinned, no doubt thinking that I was completely mad.

"OK. It's not a problem. You give me 10 shillings."

"Alright," I agreed, and delving into my wallet, I found the relevant note and gave it to him. He disappeared into the bowels of the cinema and reappeared with a pair of rusty old ladders, unfolded them, propped them up against the wall, took the poster down, rolled it up and handed it over, much to the bewilderment of a crowd of locals who must have been wondering what on earth was going on between the manager of a cinema and four recognizably English lads. After letting me have the poster, he vanished again and emerged with three film stills, one from *Creature from the Black Lagoon*, another from *House of Dracula* and a third from *Unknown Island*. How he had come into possession of these valuables, God alone knows, but if he wanted to pass them on to me, so be it. I thanked him profusely and took my spoils back to the ship. But this unexpected bounty wasn't going to be repeated—when I returned to the same cinema several months later and espied the poster from *The Brides of Dracula* outside, the apparently new owner gave me such a filthy look when I tried to tempt him into parting with it that I beat a hasty retreat and never went back there again.

The Evil of Frankenstein must have been doing the rounds in the Mediterranean during this period. On a visit to the Isle of Capri, a bunch of us took a taxi to the very top of the island and as we were walking down a road in the sweltering heat toward the island's famous Blue Grotto, we passed a small cinema almost hidden from sight behind a bank of exotic-looking shrubs and cacti that was showing *La Rivolta di Frankenstein*—Hammer's colorful and popular productions really got around! In fact, their movies turned up quite frequently all over the place, as our ship cruised from port to port, proving that the revenue they brought in quite rightly earned the company the Queen's Award for Industry. Advertised by flashy and vulgar posters that bore little resemblance to their British counterparts, giving them the aspect of a continental movie, the likes of *The Brides of Dracula*, *The Curse of the Werewolf*, *The Stranglers of Bombay*, *The Plague of the Zombies* and *The Mummy* (more of that one later) were to be discovered being screened in such far-off places as Smyrna in Turkey, Naples in Italy, Barbados in the Caribbean and Sydney in Australia. The venues where these films were showing also ranged from the sublime (Sydney, a very spacious, swank cinema) to the ridiculous (Smyrna, a run-down building on a dusty road opposite a vast open-air bazaar).

The *Chusan*'s four-month world cruise commenced in December and it was on our long voyage out to Australia and the Far East via the Panama Canal and America's West Coast that I was introduced to the pleasures to be had from 8mm film excerpts in running lengths of 200 feet lasting eight minutes, and 50 feet lasting two minutes. Packaged in smart little boxes featuring the original film poster on the cover, these mini-silent extracts consisted of either one complete scene from a particular film, or several very short segments. In a period long before the advent of VHS and DVD, where the taping and buying of movies would be taken for granted by the consumer, the one and only way to watch a picture, however short, in the comfort of one's home was to purchase these little reels of film, unless you were wealthy enough to own a 16mm sound projection system, which was way beyond my financial means.

Variations on the format included two 200-foot reels, one 400-foot reel, and two 400-foot reels. There was also a 160-foot reel, although this was not quite as popular as the other lengths. The real oddity was a 400-foot reel with a flexi-disc synchronized soundtrack, a truly archaic (even for 1965) method of screening a sound film on a silent projector if ever there was one—Heath Robinson himself must have invented it! The main idea was to place a stylus onto the disc, which itself had to be weighted down with a coin to prevent it from slipping off the turntable, at the precise moment that a black marker appeared just before the opening credits on the film. One second out and the ensuing results could be highly amusing to anyone watching it. I was to find out just how mirth inducing this process could be in the coming weeks.

I first came across these mini-movies in Woolworth's, San Francisco, at the end of December when a number of us ventured forth on a shopping expedition, ostensibly to buy some souvenirs for our families back home but also to treat ourselves to anything unusual that happened to catch our eye. These certainly caught mine, to the extent that, briefly at least, *my* family back home was all but forgotten! There were quite a few on display and I quickly purchased half a dozen, even though I had no means of showing them, having to be content with peering at the tiny frames of film containing minute images of Harryhausen's Cyclops, the gill-man, Michael Landon changing into the teenage werewolf and, luxury of luxuries, the Ymir standing atop of Rome's Coliseum as I held the film up to the cabin lights on my return to the ship later in the day, much to the amusement of the lads in our cabin.

Heading back down the main thoroughfare from Woolworth's and feeling dead chuffed by my unanticipated booty of celluloid (a bag full of gold coins would have given me less bliss and satisfaction than those treasured boxes of films did), we passed a cinema, The Regal (a distant relative of The Regal thousands of miles away in Redruth, I wondered?) which was screening four horror movies in one evening—*The Wasp Woman*, *Earth vs. the Spider*, *The Bride and the Beast* and Hitchcock's *The Birds*. Not even The Cameo could manage that! Noticing that none of the films carried any kind of a rating (in England, *The Wasp Woman* and *The Birds* were "X" certificates; the other two were rated "A"), we bundled in to see them, the woman behind the ticket booth quite taken aback by five English lads queuing up with the locals.

Events took an unexpected and quite dramatic turn when halfway through the performance, two police officers burst in through the doors to the auditorium, ran down the main aisle and pounced on a man who was slouching suspiciously in the front row, marching him out in handcuffs after a brief scuffle. What *that* was all about, heaven only knew, but it was a darned sight more stimulating than the awful *The Bride and the Beast*, which we were sitting through at the time. The next day, I threw monetary caution to the wind, buying several more boxed sets of mini-movies and promising myself that a projector would be top of my shopping list when we called in at Hong Kong, as it was rumored that all electrical items there were considerably less expensive than anywhere else on the planet, which turned out to be correct. When the ship docked in Hong Kong's teeming port for three days in February 1966, said projector was duly purchased, together with a heavy, robust screen and several more movies. We were now fully equipped and ready for a film show!

Every person on board had a nickname. It was par for the course—you either went along with it or were ridiculed mercilessly if you objected to the alternative nomenclature that you were eventually saddled with. For example, if you were blessed with ginger hair, you were called Ginger for obvious reasons (and there were a monumental number of Gingers among the crew on our ship). Now that all the lads in the cabin knew of my highly peculiar (to them) pursuits, I had to resign myself to the fact that my new moniker would henceforth be Drac, whether I liked it or not. Around and above my bunk were a few film posters I had sketched direct from those featured in *Famous Monsters of Filmland*; the still from *Creature from the Black Lagoon* was stuck on one of the bulkheads.

It was common knowledge that I alone had the necessary hardware capable of producing a slightly different and more unusual form of entertainment to cheer us all up during the long evenings when we were at sea between ports—crew films were becoming tedious, with dreary offerings such as Morecambe and Wise's *The Intelligence Men*, *The Man from the Diner's Club* and *Bye Bye Birdie* making for an extremely dull viewing program after a hard day's toil serving food to the rather green-looking paying customers while the ship rolled slowly from side to side in a heavy swell—this motion was guaranteed to upset even the hardiest of stomachs and I wasn't alone in not being immune to it. Accordingly, two Horror Nights were arranged in February to spice things up a bit and, dare I say it, bring some much-needed glamour and excitement into our routine existence, particularly as the five-day passage across the Pacific from Yokohama to Hawaii would be, so we were gravely informed by the old lags who knew such things, a very long haul indeed. At my disposal were the following movies that I had purchased in San Francisco, Hong Kong and Tokyo:

200-foot reels
The Deadly Mantis
Battle of the Giants (clips from *One Million B.C.*)
One Million B.C. (more clips from said movie)
Creature from the Black Lagoon
Revenge of the Creature
It Came from Outer Space
The Seventh Voyage of Sinbad
Jason and the Argonauts
First Men in the Moon (in color)
The Revenge of Frankenstein (in color)
This Island Earth
Battle of the Planets (extracts from *This Island Earth*)
20 Million Miles to Earth
The Werewolf
Curse of the Demon
Rodan

160-foot reels
Tarantula
The Creature Walks Among Us
Varan the Unbelievable
The Thing from Another World

50-foot reels
Earth vs. the Spider
The Undead
I Was A Teenage Werewolf
War of the Colossal Beast

400-foot reels with flexi-disc soundtrack
Dracula (the Hammer version)
The Curse of Frankenstein

As if these were not enough to satisfy the prospective audience, I also had two 400-foot reels of the 1925 version of *The Lost World* up my sleeve in the eventuality of everybody being so enraptured with the show that the request for "more!" would echo around the cabin walls. To promote this rather unique event on board ship, a large poster drawn up by me went on display in the crew room:

TONIGHT AND TOMORROW NIGHT
IN CABIN P.52
"HORROR NIGHT"
SEE "CREATURE FROM THE BLACK LAGOON"
"THE REVENGE OF FRANKENSTEIN'"—in Color!
"DRACULA"—in Sound!
AND MANY MORE!
PRICE OF ADMISSION: YOUR SPARE CHANGE (ANY CURRENCY OK)
OR TWO CANS OF BEER
STARTS: 9:30 P.M.
FINISHES: VERY LATE!
NO BAD BEHAVIOR PLEASE!

On the first night's performance, our cabin was crammed full of bodies to the proverbial rafters and bulkheads, probably illegally according to maritime law. In fact, hordes of inquisitive customers had to be turned away on the promise of a repeat showing the following evening as long as they turned up early from their duties. So at 9:45 p.m., the cabin door was securely locked against any late stragglers and the equipment set up. At one end of the cabin we erected the screen. At the opposite end sat the projector, positioned on a sturdy table top (although good fortune smiled on us and the sea was calm that night, so there were no problems with stability), together with the boxes of mini-movies, the order of what was to be screened being dictated by myself as the main organizer of this shindig.

A record turntable stood nearby for what I planned as the highlight of the night's presentation, the inaptly named "sound movies," which were to be shown last. Everyone settled down in readiness with a can in their hand, squatting on the floor, squashing together on the bunkbeds or standing behind me. While the inevitable drinking was tolerated as long as it didn't get out of hand, smoking was strictly forbidden, as the resulting fog in those cramped quarters would have drawn a murky veil over the proceedings as well as acting as an irritant to the viewing audience. As a mental tribute to my first illustration of American sci-fi/horror at The Embassy in 1961, I loaded up the projector with *Tarantula*, threaded the film leader through the numerous little toothed wheels to the take-up spool, and flipped the switch to the "on" position.

The machine burst into life, throwing a powerful shaft of brilliant light across the cabin as the shortened credits to Jack Arnold's masterpiece flickered onto the large white screen before us. A few minor adjustments to the projector's film-gate and the focusing knob and we were off, the onlookers supplying their own interpretations as to what the soundtrack should be like, even if these translations on the moving pictures unfolding in front of them verged on the tasteless most of the time! Halfway through the show the projector bulb blew, but I had foreseen this happening and had two spares on hand to ensure that the night's viewing didn't grind to a halt. Fortunately, none of the reels jammed and although I had to give the machine a 10-minute break after a couple of hours because the heat radiating from it would have warmed several cabins during the night and not just ours, the projector turned in an admirable and impressive performance.

At last, around 12:30 a.m., it was time for *Dracula* and *The Curse of Frankenstein* in "sound." The synchronized flexi-disc to *Dracula* was placed on the turntable and a weighty American half-dollar coin placed near the disc's center to prevent it from sliding off the turntable mat. For what seemed like the umpteenth time, I threaded the film through to the take-up reel and switched the projector on. As the black marker flashed up, Ginger, standing next to me, carefully lowered the stylus down onto the paper-thin record. Peter Cushing appeared on the screen, opened his mouth to speak and was followed by the words about three seconds later. Sniggers from the audience, who by now were all slightly inebriated (the exception being myself—alcohol was definitely off my agenda this evening). Bugger it! Curbing my impatience, I politely asked Ginger to stop the record while I rewound the film. Let's try again, I said to myself. Once more Peter Cushing came on, but this time Ginger wasn't concentrating hard enough and the soundtrack was at least five seconds adrift of the action. Howls of laughter replaced the sniggers—even I couldn't prevent myself from smiling. Eventually, after two further attempts, we more or less managed to match up the soundtrack to what we were watching; I turned up the volume and we sat through about 30 minutes of talkies as Cushing and Lee slugged it out in both extracts to a somewhat slurred and very tinny musical accompaniment that did little justice to James Bernard's legendary scores but nevertheless produced a rousing climax to a memorable evening.

By the time these had finished it was extremely late and I was feeling exhausted, but the fun wasn't over yet—as the expected cries of, "Let's have some more," reverberated through the cabin, on went *The Lost World* until, at something like 1:45 a.m., lights finally went up, the screen was put away, empty beer cans collected and one very red-hot projector given a well-earned rest. The next evening's show was just as successful, with a handsome profit made in foreign currency and beer that was shared among the eight members of our cabin. Talk was bandied about regarding a third show, but a typhoon sprang up the following day, scuppering any immediate thoughts along these lines as all ship's company were confined below decks and it was difficult enough trying to remain on one's feet, let alone attempt to screen a film. So the rough seas put paid to further plans for another Horror Night, and only one more movie presentation was put together by our cabin, but that was many months later.

Returning to San Francisco on our voyage back to England, some of us spent the afternoon traipsing up and down the streets, aimlessly looking for something diverting to amuse ourselves with, even though there was enough cultural heritage in the city, including the vibrant China-town, to satisfy a whole army of tourists—but not an assortment of bored merchant seamen on the loose. There were an awful lot of cinemas and I noticed that the varied ways in which the Americans exhibited their film presentations were poles apart compared to those in the United Kingdom—well, that appeared to be the case in 'Frisco, anyway. In England, you had the usual two-feature program—out here, there were some truly staggering combinations on offer to the local citizens. One theater that we passed was showing four John Wayne actioners, another had five assorted Westerns, and a third was screening two epics with a combined running time of six hours as a double bill. We came upon a small cinema, The Ritz, whose current attraction consisted of *The Bat*, *From Hell It Came* and *Target Earth!*, none of which I had seen in England. At my insistence, we crowded in and sat through all three films, and this time there were no interruptions from San Francisco's law enforcement officers to disturb the proceedings.

The next morning, we discovered another small theater, The Rio, concealed from view down a side street, and again the performance was beyond belief—Columbia's epic, *Lord Jim*, was the main feature, with *three* horror movies as support features: *The Haunted Strangler*, *First Man into Space* and *Fiend Without a Face*—in our native country, this would have equated to three "X" films co-featured with a "U"! We checked the time, estimating that we could watch the horror flicks and miss *Lord Jim*, which really didn't bother us as we had already sat through it, being one of the questionable delights administered to the crew in leisure time, and found it to be interminably monotonous.

What we failed to take into consideration was that the *Chusan* was embarking on the remain-der of her voyage that day, leaving the Port of San Francisco at 2:00 p.m. Consequently, on leaving the cinema, we found that we only had about 20 minutes to hurry back to the liner before she sailed off, which left us with the real possibility of being stranded on the West Coast of America if we didn't make it to the docks on time. Knowing full well the penalties incurred if this ever happened, which didn't bear thinking about, we stood in the busy street wondering what to do next. Jumping on a tram was out of the question—they were far too slow, so we quickly hailed a taxi and arrived at Fisherman's Wharf literally minutes before the gangway went up, much to our sheer relief. The relief rapidly turned to both fear and distress when we were subsequently marched straight along several decks to the purser's office as the ship departed and given a stern warning that if this ever happened again, we were out on our ears. So much for the power of the horror movie that had almost resulted in four of us losing our employment with the world's biggest shipping line.

Before I left the navy in September 1966, one unusual episode took place when our ship dropped anchor off the Greek island of Rhodes in May. Ginger, Brum (from Birmingham, of course!) and myself were mooching around in the noonday heat when we stumbled across a small open-air cinema in Rhodes Town situated down a narrow, unmade road that was showing (surprise, surprise!) Hammer's *The Mummy*. Six stills were arranged behind a glass case, whose lock was broken, on the wall near the entrance. The door was ajar, so we cautiously crept in unheeded. Once inside, the contrast to the glare of the Mediterranean sunshine had us groping around to prevent any accidental damage to the place, but gradually our eyes became accustomed to the gloom.

A big, bulky projection machine stood sentinel over a dozen chairs, some Greek film pamphlets, a few boxes of soft drinks and dozens of old newspapers scattered over the floor. Upon further investigation in an adjoining room, we spotted several large cans of film stacked in a neat pile against a door, no doubt containing the reels to one of my favorite horror movies. This was confirmed by several labels stuck over the cans with the film's title scribbled on them in English. Standing there in the quietness of the building, the thought suddenly entered our minds—could we take one of the canisters out of the cinema undetected and manage to sneak it on board as a souvenir? I realized of course that the reel inside the canister could not possibly fit onto my small projector and gave no regard to the fact that it would be impossible to smuggle such an object past the customs officials when we docked in Southampton. No—I just wanted one of those reels in my collection.

And the idea was there, hovering between us in the warm air. But then it dissipated as fast as it had materialized; we shrugged our shoulders and walked out. I glanced again at the seductive stills on the whitewashed cinema wall, stills that featured a lot more of Christopher Lee as The Mummy itself than the ones I had once viewed outside The Crescent cinema in the far-off year of 1960. What I wouldn't give to have one or more of those prints for myself. They really would look a treat on display in our cabin, and as for showing them to the clan when I returned to England…I squinted around in the dazzling sunlight—a few tourists were intermingling with the locals, and there wasn't a policeman in sight. Nobody, in fact, remotely aware of our presence. However, I dropped the notion and we returned to the *Chusan* after a day's sightseeing, empty-handed. Many years later, on frequent holidays in the Greek Islands, I realized that to attempt to appropriate those stills or that can of film, no matter how much I desired them, would have been an act of absolute madness as Greek police officers, I was informed on good authority by one who had crossed their path, are not of the kind of disposition to be treated lightly.

AN EVENING OUT—GREEK STYLE (1965)

October—the *Chusan* pulls into the Greek island of Kos at noon, midway through its ump-teenth Mediterranean cruise. As it's October, there isn't the blistering heat normally associated with these islands to welcome the ship's crew and her passengers, although the thermometer on the well deck registers a respectable 83°F. After completing our duties in the galley, Terry, Ginger, Dave and myself head ashore, taking in the town, the shops, the tavernas, the bars and exploring a few scattered ruins bordering the town, consisting of one or two columns and the remains of a temple, banks of prickly pear cacti encroaching upon the ancient stones. Dave, the older of our group and who should therefore exhibit some degree of responsibility over the rest of us, shows a complete disregard for Greek culture by relieving himself all over the revered trunk of the vast Hippocrates Plane Tree, reputedly centuries old and partly held up by scaffolding to prevent it toppling over and expiring in the dust.

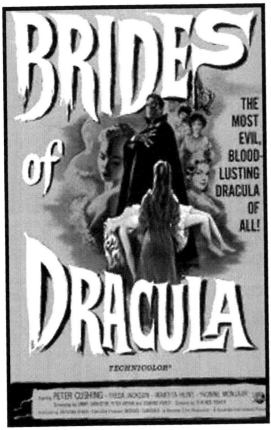

But never mind an oversized tree with a history attached to it—true to form, I'm on the lookout for a cinema, and we eventually root out two. The first is a rickety-looking construc-tion that, in spite of its grim facade, is screening a pretty good double bill—*Twice Told Tales*, which I haven't seen, and *The Castle of Terror*, which I have. Due to the absence of a timetable in the vicinity of this cinema, we can-not fathom out when these films are being presented to the public, or even if the place is open on this particular day of the week—a shame really, as the program most certainly appeals, to me anyway. The second we discover a short distance away, an open-air theater whose main attraction happens to be Hammer's much-vaunted vam-pire chiller, *The Brides of Dracula*. There's a large poster outside together with four stills, the color in the pho-tographs bleached and faded—too much exposure to strong sunlight no doubt the cause of this, and it starts, according to a scrawled note stuck on the door, at 9:00 p.m., twilight in this part of the world at this time of the year, though probably dark enough to view a feature film in these outdoor conditions. I run my eyes over the distinctly non-British poster by the blue-painted door—a Hammer production under the guise of a continental movie; handsome David Peel baring his fangs, surrounded by a bevy of voluptuous, half-naked females, flaunting their ample cleavages. Sex trading places with horror; always a selling point, I suppose.

"Fancy seeing it?" I say idly to the others.

"Christ almighty, Baz, don't you ever bloody give up on these films?"

"Yeah, alright, but I've never been in one of these kind of cinemas. Might be fun."

"If you take my advice, you'll stop banging on about these horror films all the time, otherwise you'll turn into a monster yourself."

"Very funny."

"When is the ship leaving?"

"Midnight, I think."

"I don't know whether it's worth it or not."

"Well, I'm going. I want to see what this" (and I gesture toward the cinema, or what passes for a cinema) "is like. Anyone else coming, or do I go on my own?"

All three grudgingly agree to tag along—at least, I continue, arguing my case, it makes a bloody change to the never-ending succession of bars and girls that normally make up the night's diversions when the ship hits port, and we arrange to meet up after the evening's chores.

The evening shift over and done, we freshen up, change into T-shirts, jeans and plimsolls, and troop down the gangway, dry-witted Brum having joined the entourage of would-be cinema-goers. It's a very pleasant warm, balmy night—however, Kos Town itself isn't exactly buzzing with activity and there's a definite end-of-season feel about the resort, as most of the tavernas are apparently closed for business. Nevertheless, a sizeable crowd of locals greets us upon our arrival at the cinema and as we join them, I take stock of the situation. A whitewashed wall 10 feet high runs the length of the street and, almost as though it were an afterthought, a door-sized hole has been crudely bashed through it, a wooden door fitted in the ragged gap and a ticket booth slapped onto the side, painted in blue, a single overhead light illuminating the proceedings. Basic enough, maybe, but in this climate you can get away with it, whereas in England, you would either be drenched in five minutes from the ever-present rain or freezing to death because of the lack of heat.

After a short while, the door opens and everybody starts to file in. We follow behind them, paying our drachmas to an olive-skinned man who peels off tickets from a big circular roll of the type used on British buses and finding ourselves in a rectangular enclosure filled with dozens of wooden chairs haphazardly arranged more or less in rows, all facing the side wall of an adjacent apartment complex. The wall has a large white square painted on it—this, I correctly assume, is what passes for the screen. Turning round, I spot the projection room, situated in a small block at the rear of the auditorium. Dave cackles loudly.

"Jesus—what a dump!"

"Shut up. You'll get us chucked out."

We grab five chairs near the back and sit down uncomfortably. Kids of about eight or nine, and some even younger by the look of them, are jumping around uncontrollably, their parents or guardians trying to keep them in check. A woman is nursing a baby, and numerous cats are either perched on the wall or dodging in and out of the chair legs, their eyes glowing like miniature lamps. Two scruffily dressed youngsters burst in and scamper down the aisle, laughing and screaming. It's now my turn to chortle.

"What's so amusing?"

"This film was an 'X' in England. I wonder what the certificate is in Greece?"

"I've no idea. Why, it's not important, is it?"

"It is to me."

Immediately upon saying this, a beam of light splitting the gloom signifies that *The Brides of Dracula* is about to begin—only it doesn't. Fifty pairs of eyes are diverted to the wall and a cartoon appears within the white square, a 10-minute Greek version of *Tom and Jerry* spoken in the native tongue as well, lacking the luxury of English subtitles, not that we're the slightest bit interested; all it means is that we sit twiddling our thumbs while the rest of the audience roar their heads off, at what we can only guess. The cartoon finishes and we relax as much as we can in our wooden seats, puffing away on cigarettes and awaiting a good old dose of British Hammer horror, be it in Greek or any other language.

To our dismay, a second cartoon flashes up, this one concerning a little boy creating havoc in his father's garden—in Greek again, no subtitles, and having a similar effect on the locals as the previous one, reducing them to a pack of hysterical nincompoops. We, meanwhile, sit there stony-faced and bored. I glance at my watch—9:30 and still no sign of *The Brides of Dracula*. Is there a problem in showing it, I wonder? I can't take much more of this—I had to endure my fair share of cartoons at The Crescent years ago and have long since outgrown them. All of a sudden, the town's nightlife becomes a very attractive alternative to the ordeal we are being made to suffer, and I'm debating whether or not to walk out and make for the nearest watering hole.

At 9:35 p.m., the intolerable antics of the celluloid urchin thankfully come to an end. Light bulbs strung on overhead cables flicker on, and both adults and children saunter up to an ice-cream stall that has suddenly turned up out of nowhere, buying their treats and plonking themselves down in different seats than the ones they left. Despite the fact that there is now a slight nip in the air, the cicadas are merrily chirruping away, a lament to the summer that has recently departed. A myriad of insect life is circulating round the light bulbs, there is the persistent drone of mosquitoes, and the stars are shining in all their glory. Oh well, I sigh—it *is* different, which is the one thing I was honestly hoping for, the only drawback being that the main feature has yet to get off the ground. My reverie is rudely interrupted by Ginger, complaining, quite understandably, that if the film we actually paid our hard-earned cash to watch doesn't come on soon, he's off to the bars—he hasn't sweated all day in the plate-house just to put up with this claptrap, he adds in no uncertain terms. The way things are going, I might just join him.

Finally, at 9:50, with our patience tested to extreme limits, *The Brides of Dracula* unfolds on the wall before us, the English version, thank goodness, exhibiting Greek subtitles. There it is, one of Hammer's finest offerings, projected against painted stone breeze-blocks in front of five foreign lads, 50 local citizens and a dozen cats, screened in a cinema completely open to the elements. This novel environment does mean that the print lacks depth, contrast and color—as for the soundtrack, four speakers hoisted on poles in the four corners of the building do their utmost to provide an audible backing to what we are gazing at, even if it is light years away from the megawatt sound systems taken for granted in an Odeon or ABC back home. Rather oddly, there is a short intermission some 20 minutes into the movie—fresh supplies of ice-cream are purchased, the locals swap seats once more (is this some form of ritual they re-enact when visiting the cinema, I muse?) and it's then back to David Peel vampirizing his smarmy way through the girls' school while trying to avoid a wily Peter Cushing.

The climax depicting the confrontation between Peel and Cushing brings forth a burst of applause (it seems that the citizens here also take their films seriously), and when the final credits roll, the audience shows its appreciation by handclapping furiously. It's over—altogether, an incomparable (I think) experience, one that I will regale the fraternity with on my return to England and another cinematic notch added to my belt. They may have seen the film in the comfort of a roofed theater—lucky old me has been privileged to see it in a more surreal setting, one not too far removed from the Stone Age.

On leaving the cinema, I decide to investigate the first picture-house that we had come across earlier in the day to satisfy my curiosity as to whether or not it is open, or had been open. Obviously it hasn't been—not a soul in sight, no lights, the whole street in total darkness. It's a pity we're not in Kos tomorrow, otherwise it would be the pictures, Greek style, two nights in a row, if of course the double feature advertised is appearing. But it's no good agonizing over it—besides, I'm forgetting how late it is and the boys are becoming restless, afraid that the ship will leave without us, so we call a halt to the night's adventures.

Strolling back to the dock, I ponder over the machinations involved in the showing of a British horror film over here—the cinema appears to have no name, so who are the distributors? And who is responsible for supervising the shows—only three staff were present during *The Brides of Dracula* as far as I was aware. And why no ratings? Can anyone look at them, no matter how young? Anyhow, my shipmates haven't been all that impressed by the evening's entertainment and voice their opinions—loudly.

"You're not dragging me to any more of these films."—Ginger.

"What a waste of money."—Dave.

"Bloody joke of a cinema. Next time, Baz, you can go on your own."—Terry.

Only Brum, as laconic as ever, shares my aesthetic leanings and thinks that the past few hours have been "reasonably amusing," casually dismissing, with a toss of his head and a withering expression, the snide remarks, jibes and ridicule handed out by our three compatriots as we climb up the steep gangway to our floating home. However, Terry's comments are prophetic in the extreme—there is to be no "next time," and this will count as my one and only foray into the world of the open-air cinema on my travels. As for *The Brides of Dracula*, it will one day in the future cross my path again, turning up in the familiar surroundings of The Cameo in Cornwall many months from now during the great reissue explosion of 1966 and 1967.

THE REISSUES (1966-1967)

I resigned from the navy in September 1966, reacquainting myself with my pals and, from the point of view of the cinema, immersing myself straightaway into the scene that I had left 15 months previously, first of all presenting for a favored few a film show in my living room with a selection of the boxed sets amassed from my time abroad, not perhaps as extravagant as the one held in cabin P.52 a lifetime ago but appreciated by the small audience all the same. Then an invitation was received from *The Horror Film Club of Great Britain* to attend one of their meetings, a three-day convention in Bath, Somerset. A hotel was booked and I caught the train on the last Friday of the month, arriving in the city around midday. At 4:00 p.m., I joined about 20 other devotees at the conference hall booked by the club's leader where, after introducing ourselves, assorted knick-knacks were put up for sale—mainly posters, stills, lobby cards and periodicals.

All persons present were then asked to submit a favorite film or two to a forum for discussion, and this carried on until 11:00 p.m. On Saturday, as well as further exchanges of views and debates taking place concerning everybody's lists of what they had seen (and mine outnumbered most of the others, who were particularly fascinated by my foreign exploits), several antique movies were shown—1925's *The Lost World*, Murnau's silent 1922 classic *Nosferatu*, and Bela Lugosi's creaky old melodrama *Return of the Ape Man* among others. The following day saw more views being aired, an auction of some fairly rare memorabilia and, in the afternoon, further film screenings—*Destination Moon*, *One Million B.C.* and two silent 400-foot reels of *King Kong*, one of the classics that had so far eluded me and had stubbornly refused to surface on any cinema circuit, at least not in the areas that I lived, or had lived, although funnily enough, *The Son of Kong*, the follow-up, *had* appeared.

At the club's suggestion, I also put on five or six of the mini-movies purchased overseas, much to the surprise and amusement of the onlookers, many of whom did not realize that these precious little reels of horror and science fiction film actually existed. The convention wrapped itself up at 11:00 p.m. and I left for Redruth the next day. On reflection, although it was nice to meet fellow aficionados, I felt that we didn't really gel as a group and came away recognizing that I much preferred my own little band of fanatics to being a member of a larger following, who probably had their own codes of conduct which would have clashed with my personal ethics—I was very much a one-man band in those days, too single-minded by half, and tended to go my own way regardless of other people's rules and regulations. This had been my *modus operandi* since the late '50s and I had no intention of changing my habits now.

So it was straight back to both the Sunday circuit and The Cameo, with some first-rate double bills on offer—*Son of Frankenstein* c/w *Tarantula*, Hammer's *Dracula* c/w *The Monolith Monsters*, *Frankenstein 1970* c/w *House on Haunted Hill*, *Gorgo*, paired with Peter Sellers' tough crime thriller *Never Let Go*, *The Four Skulls of Jonathan Drake* c/w *The Black Sleep*, *Frankenstein Meets the Wolf Man* c/w *Cape Fear*, and an eccentric coupling of Karloff's *The Boogie Man Will Get You* with Lugosi's *Lock Up Your Daughters*. The Cameo also presented a rare uncut screening of Franju's *Eyes Without a Face*, and the latest offerings from Hammer, together with Fox's *Fantastic Voyage*, had to be worked into my busy itinerary by some means or another, heedless of cost. This frequently culminated in three trips to the cinema within the space of a week—a season ticket to all theaters concerned would have been a godsend, but in 1966 no such method of payment existed, and a never-ending supply of loose coinage therefore accompanied me on these repeated excursions into the realms of fantasy and horror.

Toward the middle of 1966 and continuing through 1967, some of the major film companies began to reissue, for reasons of their own, a handful of their more celebrated horror and fantasy movies, giving a newer audience what would eventually turn out to be the very last chance to experience the thrill of seeing them in their natural habitat, the cinema, before they eventually found a new lease on life on television (in the United States, that is. In the United Kingdom, they were, and still are, very rarely, if ever, screened). Perhaps they reasoned that there was more

financial mileage to be had from these productions—after all, even in the mid-'60s, a well-made horror film, however far back it was originally released, could still guarantee a big audience and a decent return at the box office.

Probably the first of the reissues to emerge onto the circuits was the pairing of Warner Bros.' brilliant *House of Wax* with the inferior *Phantom of the Rue Morgue*, shown in flat screen and not in their original 3-D format. At long last I could observe for myself the justification behind all those faintings years ago when Phyllis Kirk battered away at Vincent Price's ravaged features—strong stuff for the early 1950s, but not so strong now. Several of the older and more worthy Hammer films reappeared—*The Brides of Dracula* c/w *The Mummy*, *The Curse of Frankenstein* c/w *Dracula*, *The Man Who Could Cheat Death* c/w Paramount's *The Blob* and *The Revenge of Frankenstein* teamed up with, yet again, *The Camp on Blood Island*. *Journey to the Beginning of Time*, the Americanized version of Karel Zeman's classic *Cesta Do Praveku*, also turned up out of the blue in a color-tinted print. The goodies didn't stop there either—*The Day of the Triffids* started doing the rounds with *The Birds*. It was a veritable feast that had me scampering here, there and everywhere on my latest mode of transport, a thoroughly unreliable Lambretta scooter (which had a tendency to break down at night in the middle of nowhere), having become heartily sick and tired of erratic bus services and cycling from one steep hill to the next in the West Country mist and rain.

As another family move loomed on the horizon—a return to the Surrey area from the depths of West Cornwall—I paid what turned out to be my final two visits to The Cameo in November to see, within the space of 10 days, *The Fiend Who Walked the West* c/w *Rodan* and *The Black Scorpion* showing with *Macabre*. These programs summed up perfectly the ethos governing this unique little cinema—marvelous, entertaining double bills playing to a full and appreciative house. It would be sorely missed. (In 1991, The Cameo finally stopped showing films for various reasons and was demolished in August 2003.)

The absolute piece de resistance of all the reissues had to be *King Kong*, rated an "A," double billed with Howard Hawks' highly acclaimed science fiction thriller *The Thing from*

Another World, still carrying the original "X" certificate that it had been awarded in 1951. My family had relocated back to Surrey during the first week of January 1967, and the re-release of the two exalted RKO-Radio classics had featured in the newspapers in December 1966, as this was the first time that *Kong* had been screened in British cinemas, apart from the film festivals, since the very early '50s. It *had* appeared in a solitary edited print on British television while I was overseas, which I had missed out on, so this was a once-in-a-lifetime opportunity to at last pin down one of fantasy's all-time masterpieces, and on the big screen as well.

Having *The Thing* as a co-feature was the icing on the cake, as this was another of those elusive movies that had never been shown, as far as I was aware, on the Sunday one-day circuit or even at The Cameo, a cinema renowned for ferreting out and putting on those hard to find rarities from the '50s. I eagerly scanned the papers for their arrival but didn't have long to wait—they were both on at The Hippodrome in Reigate, commencing on Friday the 20th of January. Proving that my obsessive habits had not changed one iota since the days of 1965 and my five trips in a week to The Regal in Redruth, I went to The Hippodrome on Friday, Monday and Wednesday—dis-

appointingly, all three shows had a below-average audience and I was left wondering whether or not the glamour of these old classics was beginning to wear off, at least for the new breed of mid-'60s paying customers, who seemed unable to relate to, or had little empathy with, movies that were respectively 34 years and 16 years old.

But I couldn't get enough of them—*Kong* made for fantastic viewing in a darkened auditorium and *The Thing* catapulted itself into my personal top 10 list of favorites—and for good measure caught the train to London's Waterloo Station on 30 January, taking in both films for a fourth time at the tiny Classic cinema situated within the confines of the station itself. This last occasion was ruined somewhat by a party of men of questionable sexual gender, unfortunately seated behind me, who shrieked in mock horror every time the "Big Monkey" appeared on the screen, much to the displeasure of the audience and myself in particular. Perhaps they had strayed into the wrong cinema to view the wrong film! Still not satisfied with sitting through four showings of these illustrious and durable features, I paid another visit to Waterloo Station's Classic on Saturday 4 February and watched them all over again with a couple of friends. Finally, for the time being at least, my insatiable thirst for *Kong* had been quenched!

The big mystery (well it was to me, and must have been to other fantasy aficionados) surrounding the undisputed king of all double bills was this—why have an A-rated main feature teamed up with an "X" co-feature? Shades of *Run of the Arrow* c/w *The Creature Walks Among Us* crossed my mind as I reasoned that any *King Kong* fan who was 14 years old and over but not yet 16 was not legally entitled to enter a cinema to see it all the time it was showing with the X-rated Howard Hawks picture. It must have been a source of frustration for the legions of admirers of this fabled movie, who were no doubt dying to see *Kong* in a theater on the silver screen for one last time but were powerless to do so because of the still-strict British censorship laws in force during this period. This struck me as a downright peculiar method of presenting these old classics to a wider audience, and a thoughtless one at that, when it meant that many of the younger members of the general public were denied the chance to experience one of the true greats of the cinema reissued over 30 years after its original release—a very odd practice indeed.

In February, another stupendous double "X" bill materialized to whet the appetite—Paramount's *Psycho* and *The War of the Worlds*, a popular pairing that would be in circulation throughout the United Kingdom for the next two years or so. Several of us traveled up to catch it at the imposing Victoria cinema in London, near the station of the same name. As we entered the rather grandiose foyer, 11 (we counted them) teenagers who were desperate to somehow gain entry and see these two heavyweights of the horror and science fiction genre were in the process of having their dreams destroyed—a very irate manager, with the help of his hefty assistant, was throwing them out into the street for being, in his opinion, underage, despite their vehement arguments to the contrary. Judging by the look of them, he was right! But then I suddenly remembered my own numerous and abortive endeavors at The Crescent many moons ago and couldn't help feeling sorry for their crestfallen state when it eventually dawned on them that on this occasion, it wasn't to be—unfortunately, it was *their* turn to suffer the aggravation caused by the censor's office. Perhaps they should have paid more attention to the advertising outside the cinema, which emphatically stated in big bold letters: "No Persons Under the Age of 16 Permitted to see these Films." Watching these two outstanding pictures in the luxurious surroundings of the Victoria's vast auditorium was not going to be a one-off happening as far as I was concerned—I promptly returned the following evening with my brother Roger and sat there soaking up the atmosphere for a second time.

And still there was no stopping them—Warner Bros.' monster yarn from 1953, *The Beast from 20,000 Fathoms*, resurfaced (literally) with *Rebel Without A Cause* at some cinemas in the South of England, *The Pit and the Pendulum* popped up at a few selected theaters with *The Fall of the House of Usher*, *Journey to the Center of the Earth* appeared, although this fine fantasy had rarely been off the circuits, and *Jason and the Argonauts* commenced another run, qualifying it as one of Ray Harryhausen's most successful features, with a longer shelf life than most of his others, with the special effects wizard's *Mysterious Island* soon following hot on its heels, another popular Columbia fantasy that could still pack them in. Hammer's *The Brides of Dracula* went out on what seemed like its millionth release date since 1960, now teamed up with *Blood of the Vampire*, while *Forbidden Planet* played spasmodically in the provinces. In July, United Artists' *Jack the Giant Killer* was finally given an airing after being shelved for several years because of censorship problems—with a few minor cuts, it was reduced from a possible "X" certificate to an "A" rating and screened in London, where I caught it in a near-empty theater in Oxford Street. *The Horror Club of Great Britain* asked me if I would like to write a review of the movie for the journal, as it only had a limited release outside the London area and never reached Bath where the club was based, but I couldn't muster up much enthusiasm for what I regarded as a watered-down version of *The Seventh Voyage of Sinbad* with inferior special effects to boot, and in the eventuality, I never did put pen to paper.

It was during 1967, however, that despite the plethora of HSFF greats being presented to the newer generation on the circuits, progressive changes in the cinema's climate were becoming noticeable. The storm clouds were gathering, and it was these changes that were to ultimately affect the trends in what audiences now classed as entertainment and bringing to a close the kind of routine I had been used to over the past 13 years.

NO GO! (1966)

"Right. Here we go then. Paper, pens, horror mags, *Horror Film Club of Great Britain* journal. Anything else?"

"Your films."

"Got those. And the projector. They're in my panniers on the jolly old scooter. Now, let's see if we can do a better job this time than those pathetic efforts we turned out last year, which hardly anybody was interested in."

"You sure you want to do this?"

"Yep. I want our thoughts and ideas down on paper. Other people do it—so can we."

"OK. Where do we start?"

"At the beginning."

"Don't act stupid. Where *do* we start?"

"Um. Christ—I don't know. Hang on—let's look at the *Horror Film Club* journal a minute. Right, this is what we'll do. I'll draw the cover when I get home. The Ymir. Or the Cyclops. Maybe a werewolf, or a movie poster. You know, similar to those I did in the navy."

"Yeah, a poster. Great idea. That'll be different. What film though?"

"Perhaps *The Mole People*—no, wait. *The Curse of the Mummy's Tomb*. I've still got that one at home—I'll copy it."

"Good. Now—what can we write about?"

"Er. Well, to start with, we could have a top 10 list of our favorites, both of ours as we're the ones writing the bloody thing, then a couple of film reviews, perhaps a write-up of all these oldies that are appearing at the moment, a sketch or two, some items to sell."

"Sell? Sell what?"

"Well, a few magazines for starters. Mum is moaning about them cluttering the place up and I'm getting bloody cheesed off with it."

"Not *Famous Monsters* though."

"Definitely not—some of the others which are getting a bit dog-eared and torn. Perhaps one or two of my films as well."

"What?"

"Never mind 'what?' Quite a number of them are the worse for wear, and some of them I'm not bothered with anyway."

"For instance?"

"Um. *The Undead. Earth vs. the Spider. War of the Colossal Beast*. There's three."

"You sure you want to get rid of them?"

"Yeah. I don't watch 'em now. The full-length versions weren't much cop either, if you remember."

"Yeah, that's true enough. Right, the typewriter's here. Let's begin."

"OK. Actually, it's probably better if we write it all down first and then type it up afterwards. When it's typed, I'll do the cover and a few drawings inside. Actually, I'm wondering whether we should put photos in to make it more authentic."

"The only way I can think of doing that is to cut some out of our mags, glue them to the pages and that way they'll look alright when we copy the finished article."

"Yeah, and end up with pages full of holes in *Famous Monsters*."

"Sorry—it was only a suggestion."

"There must be another way. Blow it. I'll just have to sketch a few pictures."

"That's alright. You're pretty good at that kind of thing anyway."

"Cheers, mate! Right—10 favorites. I'll make notes as we go along. Fire away."

"Um…*Fantastic Voyage*."

"You only saw that last week."

"So what? Let me bloody finish. Anyway, it was a fab film. *Jason and the Argonauts. Earth vs. the Flying Saucers*."

"All Harryhausen stuff then."

"Yes! *20 Million Miles to Earth*."

"That's definitely one of mine!"

"And don't we all know it! How many is that? Only four. Right, look, this is sodding difficult. I haven't seen the hundreds that you have."

"Didn't you see any when I was in the navy?"

"Actually, I only saw about half a dozen—I don't know why. They didn't seem to be around much."

"It doesn't matter. Carry on."

"Er. Oh, I don't bloody know. *House of Wax*."

"Good film. That'll be in my list. Five."

"*The Land Unknown*—great film. *The Gargon Terror*."

"Eh?"

"Perhaps not. *Gorgo*. Um. *Frankenstein's Daughter*."

"What?"

"Look—I'm struggling. Anyway, it wasn't that bad. I liked it even if you didn't. Alright, I'll change that to *The Evil of Frankenstein*. That's eight. Hang on—*The Brides of Dracula*. Nine. *Godzilla*. 10. Your turn."

"Right—here goes. *20 Million Miles to Earth*, *The Seventh Voyage of Sinbad*, *Tarantula*, *House of Wax*, *House of Frankenstein*, *It! The Terror from Beyond Space*, *Journey to the Center of the Earth*, *The Mummy*, *Rodan*, *Gorgo*—couldn't we make it a top 20? There are loads I've left out."

"Maybe you could but I couldn't. No—we'll stick to a top 10."

"OK. Next—a film review. A new movie—not an old one."

"Right. What about *Chamber of Horrors*?"

"Yeah. Good choice, that. We'll write it up in a minute. Then we'll have a piece on the re-issues. *House of Wax*, *Phantom of the Rue Morgue*, the Hammer films, *The Blob*—any more you can think of?"

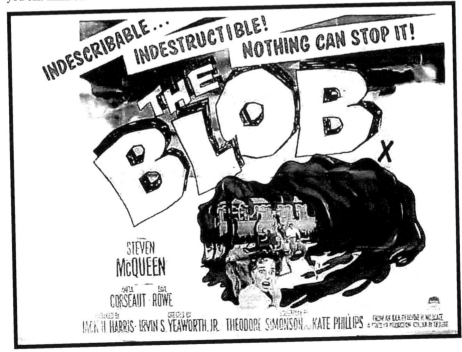

"Not really, although I read some-where that *King Kong* may be out on release at the end of the year."

"Blimey! Where did you read that?"

"Some paper my parents left lying around."

"We can't really review it then—anyway, I haven't seen it."

"I have. It was on television when you were abroad, even though it was cut to ribbons."

"Yes I know! Don't rub it in. Right—is that it?"

"Yep. Don't forget the items for sale."

"I won't. Well" (pause). "Who on earth is going to read this and buy it?"

"Some people might. We could run some copies off at 'tech and flog them—a shilling each. And by the way, we haven't thought of a title yet."

"What about *Double X*? Or—*Creature Features*?"

"Oh I don't know. I'm running out of inspiration, to be quite honest."

"So am I. Let's give up on the idea—it won't come to anything, will it. If you recall, we scrapped all those others that we did before."

"I've still got a couple here, I think."

"Oh, right. Anyway, let's drop it—I can't be bothered. The typewriter's knackered any-way—when you press some of the keys, you get a different letter to the one you want, and they stick. And it needs a new ribbon, which I can't afford, or can you?"

"Nope."

"OK—any decent films around at the moment?"

"Let's have a look in the *West Briton*. Right—here we are. *The Projected Man* is on at The Regal this week. And I think…yes, here it is. *The Cabinet of Caligari* and *Hand of Death*, show-ing at the ABC in Falmouth this Sunday."

"Mmmm. Might see both of them. Come on, let's chuck this lot away and go out." Sound of A4 paper hitting the waste bin as the front door opens…

HOW TO MAKE A MONSTER MOVIE (1966)

Dinosaurus!, *Mighty Joe Young*, *Behemoth the Sea Monster*, *The Beast of Hollow Mountain*, *The Monster from Green Hell* and *Fiend Without a Face*—a selection of movies we had seen that incorporated into their special effects the fascinating realm of stop-motion animation, an area which I had thought about dabbling in from time to time, on a strictly amateur basis, naturally. However, without the knowledge or the expertise needed to bring the monsters in these films to life, and no access to any kind of detailed literature on the subject, we made our own deductions as to what kind of practical process had to be carried out by the effects people to ensure that what the audience eventually saw on the big screen was realistic enough to be regarded as almost lifelike in action and appearance.

For a start, we cinema-goers had noticed that the one common denominator among this menagerie of giant wasps, dinosaurs, crawling brains and a huge ape was that they all moved in a pronounced jerky motion (which wasn't off-putting—it only added to their mystique) as opposed to the smoother action of the obvious men-in-rubber suit monsters that starred in *Godzilla* and *Gorgo*. They also seemed to blend in with the action far more naturally than the men-in-rubber suits movies, however well-executed Toho's brigade of titanic beasts were when stomping around in miniature cities.

As an alternative to stop-motion and rubber suits, titles such as *The Deadly Mantis* and *The Monster that Challenged the World* featured very large models which, we admitted, could pack quite a punch—the popularity of both of these movies on the Sunday circuit proved it. The stop-motion pictures, though, had a more exciting element to them—they stood out from the pack, particularly when compared to the likes of Bert I. Gordon's magnified lizards in *King Dinosaur*, the inferior puppetry of *Reptilicus* or, even worse, the pantomime-looking dummies masquerading as giant spiders in *Missile to the Moon* and *Queen of Outer Space*. Given the choice between *The Black Scorpion* and *The Giant Gila Monster*, Willis O'Brien's animated arachnid flick would win hands down anytime—the effects were that much superior.

One Thursday evening in October, I scootered back from The Cameo after sitting through a thrilling double bill of *20 Million Miles to Earth* and *The Werewolf*. Scanning the credits to

Special effects master Ray Harryhausen with one of his creations

Columbia's space-monster yarn (it was my seventh visit to this movie), I had spotted that the person responsible for the film's special effects, which in this instance were very special indeed, was a certain Ray Harryhausen. The name struck a chord—apart from this movie, where had I seen it mentioned before? Once indoors, I waded through umpteen issues of *Famous Monsters of Filmland* and several editions of F. Maurice Speed's *Film Review* annuals until I came across some of the required information—he was the man associated with *The Seventh Voyage of Sinbad*, *First Men in the Moon, Mysterious Island* and a host of other fantasy box office hits. It transpired that he was without doubt a one-man band and had total control over what his creatures did, which is probably why his visuals were so mesmerizing—they really did turn a lot of people on to this kind of fare.

His method, I discovered after much searching, was to film, using just one single frame at a time, a rubber-coated figure with an internal ball-and-socket skeleton that was painstakingly moved a fraction of an inch between shots. When the completed film was run through a projector, the figure "moved"—jerkily, maybe, but it still gave the illusion of movement. Combined with real actors, front and rear projection, split-screen, scaled-down sets and all manner of optical mattes, this example of cinematic trickery was capable of producing some highly original and memorable images, as I had seen on numerous occasions in a variety of theaters. I then wondered—could this formula be duplicated by anyone as low down on the ladder as myself? I owned a projector and had a few ideas bobbing around in my head—I would give it a go and see what I could conjure up.

First of all, a decent cine-camera was needed. In 1966, these were not cheap, so I ordered one off my mother's catalogue, an easy way of buying expensive items on "tick," making sure that the make of camera I purchased had the facility to shoot not only continuously but at single-frame exposure as well. It arrived a fortnight later, together with a sturdy tripod to ensure a steady image. Several 50-foot rolls of Kodak color film were bought, along with six packs of brown modeling clay. My bedroom was converted into a makeshift studio, as it had a very wide windowsill that captured a great deal of light, even on a dull autumn day. This ledge was to be the playing ground for whatever I chose to perform on it, but my initial stab at coming up with something worthwhile took place on the much larger window sill in the kitchen—a test reel to see what the outcome would look like on a 4-foot-by-4-foot screen.

Not very impressive was the answer. My sister had a bendy Huckleberry Hound—these toys were all the rage in the mid 1960s, a rubber model of a well-known cartoon character about eight inches tall, molded over a wire frame that enabled the owner to bend the figure into any number of poses (not long after, these toys were withdrawn from the shops—the thick wire had a nasty habit of working itself through the soft rubber, thereby presenting a serious hazard to the kiddies playing with them). I picked a reasonably sunny Saturday to take on the role of a film director when the rest of the family were otherwise engaged on an outing to Penzance, and therefore out of my way.

After loading up with film, the camera was screwed onto the tripod and positioned level with the window sill, which was bathed in sunshine—the required amount of brightness, I hoped, that an arc lamp would contribute in a film studio. Huckleberry Hound was sneaked out of my sister's bedroom and placed in an upright posture on the ledge. Click. One frame taken of the blue, rubberized figure standing stationary. I moved both arms upwards a fraction. Click. I moved both arms up a fraction more and bent one leg slightly. Click. I moved the arms and leg again, and turned the head. Click. After several minutes of this, although already it seemed like several years, I lost patience and advanced the film two frames at a time. Then the sun decided to hide behind a cloud. Sod it! More patience lost as I now advanced the film by three frames between shots. Once or twice, Huckleberry toppled over, as if to say, "I've had enough of this nonsense," and because of this, my constant striving to have him in the same place while filming (it's called continuity) went all to pot. In the end I managed, over what felt an inordinately long length of time, to use up the complete reel, all 50 meager feet of it. Huckleberry was hurriedly returned to my sister's playbox before the family came home and discovered what I had been up to, and the precious two minutes of celluloid was removed and packed into its foil wrapping.

On Monday, the film was deposited for processing in Redruth's one and only camera shop and collected the following Saturday afternoon. I couldn't wait to see the results—dinner and television would have to go by the board. I dashed indoors, ignoring my mother's glare as I made for the bedroom. Out came the projector that had served me so well since being bought in Hong Kong many months ago, up went the screen, the little roll of film was taken out of its yellow plastic casing, the white leader was threaded onto the take-up spool, the curtains were drawn to block out the light and the machine was switched on. Oh well—it wasn't *that* bad. Or was it? Huckleberry Hound certainly moved, advancing across the windowsill in a series of erratic, twitchy maneuvers as though heavily under the influence of alcohol, the illumination of the scene constant one second and fluctuating the next, dependent on what the sun was electing to do at the moment of exposure. As a monster, he was about as threatening and plausible as the dinosaurs in *Unknown Island*, and this was definitely one piece of film that would not be shown to my friends—if they were to ever set eyes on it, my credibility would suffer a serious blow.

A greater measure of concentrated effort was required for the next bout of filming. Accordingly, a triceratops was modeled from the clay and some railway track smuggled from my brother's train set, together with two railway carriages and a station waiting room. Over two evenings, I animated, if animation was the right word to use here, the horned dinosaur lumbering past the station building and turning the carriages over with its horns, the whole scene lit by a portable lamp positioned to my right. Using up half of the film on this sequence, I then created a tentacle about six inches long, copied direct from *It Came from Beneath the Sea,* and had this rearing up over the building with one of the carriages in its grip. A few days later, two caterpillars were animated fighting one another and toppling a meccano-built tower in their death throes. This feverish and somewhat furtive activity culminated in two more rolls of film being rushed to Redruth for processing.

A week after picking the films up, I showed them to my pals. They were, I admitted to myself, a vast improvement on Huckleberry Hound. At least they vaguely resembled some of the things we had seen within the confines of a cinema, and we were more than a little bemused at the sight of a clay triceratops waddling over a railway track to attack a toy carriage, the tentacle jerkily folding itself round the same carriage, and two prehistoric caterpillars wrapping themselves around each other—it looked rather captivating, and I received murmurs of approval for my endeavors. However, these primitive attempts at doing a Harryhausen didn't last long—it was all very well moving clay models along a windowsill, but how the hell did you combine this footage with live actors, which in this case would have been us? I gave up—cine film was costly in those days and I didn't have either the time, the inclination or the finances to carry on with a project that some of us had mulled over, which was to somehow produce a little fantasy epic of our own, using the animated models, the natural rugged landscape in which we lived and us as the actors, perhaps even stretching our production, funds permitting, to a 400-foot reel! The idea was shelved. Let's stick to what we are good at, I said, which was to go out and see as many horror and science fiction films as possible.

So there were to be no more animated mini-epics taking place on sunlit window ledges, and the artists responsible for the stop-motion monsters in the movies that we saw could all sleep safely in their beds with the knowledge that a bunch of inexperienced, unprofessional teenagers in West Cornwall would not be queering their pitch and taking up careers in special effects!

CHANGES (1967-1968)

A transitional period appeared to be taking place in Britain's cinemas with regard to the old horror and science fiction films that had been running for what seemed like an eternity, entertaining, on a regular week-in, week-out basis, an entire generation of film buffs such as myself. The Sunday one-day programs were gradually dying out—in the Redhill and Reigate area where I lived, they had ceased to exist, and most of the cinemas in the locality were now closed on a Sunday. In fact, I realized with a growing sense of despondency in early 1967 that the last program I had attended on this once all-important day of the week was *Curse of the Undead* and *The Thing that Couldn't Die* at the ABC in Falmouth in December 1966, prior to my family moving out of Cornwall to Surrey. The familiar classics of the past could still be tracked down but were now being screened as late-night shows instead of on the Sabbath. These shows were usually presented on a Saturday night between 10:30 and 11:00 p.m., about half an hour after the day's main features had ended, and free coffee was occasionally provided to prevent patrons from falling asleep during the performance. Once in a while, one of these late shows would crop up in mid-week. For example, Lugosi's *Dracula*, still commercially going the rounds after a re-

cord-breaking 36 years even if it was showing its age (and unbelievably, in the violent climate of '60s cinema, carrying an "X" certificate), materialized at a midnight showing on a Wednesday in July at The Hippodrome, Reigate with *Creature from the Black Lagoon*. *The Deadly Mantis* c/w *The Land Unknown* was a popular coupling on the late-night circuit, as was *The Quatermass Experiment* c/w *X the Unknown* and *Kiss of the Vampire* c/w *Tarantula*.

Notwithstanding these late shows, which were nowhere near as prolific as the Sunday one-day programs had been in their heyday, there was no doubting the fact that toward the end of 1967 it was becoming increasingly difficult to catch any of the older HSFF features at my local cinemas. Three to four years ago, I had had dozens of splendiferous double bills coming out of my ears with all of my spare time and cash taken up in strategic operations, necessary to ensure that I saw as many of them as humanly possible. Now it was a case of scraping the bottom of the barrel, slogging the whole length of the Old Kent road in London just to be entertained, to use the term loosely, by *The Haunted Strangler* double billed with the crudely made *The Killer Shrews*, hardly a pairing to set the pulses racing, and taking my complaining girlfriend along for the ride. I wound up sitting huddled up in a grubby, freezing theater in Praed Street as *Blood of the Vampire* flickered before me in the less-than-salubrious and half-empty auditorium; discovering a run-down flea-pit in Tooting Bec showing *The Revenge of Frankenstein*, admittedly one of Hammer's finest offerings but a movie I had already seen twice; and taking the train to Streatham to sit through *Invasion of the Body Snatchers*, co-featured with the deplorable *Castle of Evil*.

Slim pickings indeed, and it was plainly clear that most of my cinema-going nowadays was confined to the outskirts of London, the cinemas where I lived having apparently forgotten, or choosing to ignore, any movie produced prior to 1960. In fact, the only bright spot in this tiring and expensive hike around the city's backwaters was tracking down a venue near the West End that was showing for a limited term Wojciech Has' inscrutable three-hour masterpiece *The Saragossa Manuscript*, a truly mind-bending affair that shone like a beacon of light in this never-ending quest to experience once again the pleasure of seeing a decent film presented in equally decent surroundings.

Not only was there a definite change to the kind of cinematic merry-go-round that had played such a paramount role in my life since the mid-'50s, but the overall style of films themselves was undergoing a transformation as well and not, in my opinion, for the better. Prominent among the year's major releases, Warner Bros.' highly influential gangster flick, *Bonnie and Clyde*, had introduced a new and acceptable code of sex and violence to the public, the normally strict British censor bowing to the film producers' wishes that this was realism and should now, in 1967, be allowed to be shown in U.K. cinemas. The overt violence in Arthur Penn's expertly crafted movie then began to filter through to the horror film. No longer was it enough to have a well-told story with a beginning, a middle and an end—a streak of nastiness had to run concurrent alongside the plot, with a few graphically brutal and very gruesome scenes thrown into the mix to titillate the audience.

It sometimes made for unattractive viewing, although even I appreciated the fact that tastes and trends in the cinema did advance over the intervening years. The Hammer films were most affected—gone were the glory days of the 1950s and early 1960s, reflected in classics such as *Dracula* and *The Curse of Frankenstein*. Gore and even rape featured in most of the company's output from the mid-'60s onwards, with an unhealthy predilection for decapitation creeping in as well. The rich, vibrant, inky colors of their original trailblazers had been replaced by an overall blandness in look and design, with repetitive plots and over-familiarization of the same old sets. The freshness had gone—they were beginning to look positively stale.

The current state of the science fiction film fared even worse. All movies seemed to be photographed in garish, pop-art colors, with childish storylines, a fixation for gadgetry, some pretty ghastly James Bond-type musical scores and sets every bit as cardboard-looking as many of their '50s counterparts. They were also far too long. Running lengths had been extended from 70 to 85 minutes, the old norm, to between 95 and 100 minutes and occasionally reaching the two-hour mark, leading to extensive stretches of dull routine sandwiched between the mandatory action—people's attention tended to wander elsewhere during the lulls. At least *World Without End*, *Invisible Invaders* and *The Mole People* were short, sharp and snappy. Even the continental horror productions, after bursting into activity with *The Castle of Terror* and *Black Sabbath* to name but two, had begun to trail off the circuits, and Toho's once mighty series of monster movies were a pale shadow of their former selves, now aimed strictly at the children's market. One began to yearn for the good old black and white days of yore, when *Kronos*, *Revenge of the Creature*, *Giant from the Unknown* and yes, even *Beginning of the End*, were up there on the big screen—they had a kind of crude naiveté that made them appealing but never boring. You could enjoy the fast-paced Universal monster movies and laugh yourself silly at Ed Wood's low-grade attempts at moviemaking, but nobody ever fidgeted in their seats as they did with most of the '60s pictures.

Annoyingly, every film seemed to be jumping onto the James Bond bandwagon and the swinging '60s culture, and when Kubrick's *2001: A Space Odyssey* was released in May 1968, the '50s style of science fiction, already in decline, was sent spinning into oblivion. The majority of sci-fi fans lapped up every single minute of MGM's mammoth space opera, which almost played like a silent movie in parts—quite a few others found it a prodigious exercise in bum-numbing tedium. It was a landmark production in the field, though, paving

the way for the multimillion-dollar spectacles that would become a hallmark for the next decade's output and consigning to the graveyard the likes of *The Terrornauts*, *Duel of the Space Monsters*, *They Came from Beyond Space*, *Captain Nemo and the Underwater City*, *Doctor Who and the Daleks* and other woeful '60s disasters against which the Milner Brothers' *The Phantom from 10,000 Leagues* took on all the characteristics of a masterpiece.

It wasn't all doom and gloom though, and some very respectable pieces of work arose from the ashes amidst the welter of dross—*Robinson Crusoe on Mars* resembled in a lot of ways some of the old 1950s space extravaganzas; *Quatermass and the Pit* was a solidly made and quite scary version of the BBC-TV classic serial; *Planet of the Apes*, a superior old-fashioned slice of hokum, became a deserved box office hit; *Fantastic Voyage* had highly imaginative sets, compensating for an inferior script; and Hammer's *One Million Years B.C.* was at least a bit more challenging than their other lackluster productions put out during this time, benefiting from Ray Harryhausen's splendid special effects. Indicative of a pretty disheartening 12 months, *The Seventh Voyage of Sinbad* was re-released with *The Great St. Trinian's Train Robbery*, and I noted with a feeling of disillusionment that it was the identical butchered print that I had taken my brother to see in 1964. This was one instance where I would have argued that change, in the form of a restored version of this marvelous fantasy, *was* urgently needed.

1968 was an exceedingly thin year indeed for the HSFF film fan, and the outlook was looking decidedly bleak. Apart from Kubrick's space epic and *Planet of the Apes*, there wasn't a great deal to shout about, with the likes of *The Curse of the Crimson Altar*, *The Illustrated Man* and *Son of Godzilla* proving to be depressing fare in the extreme, exhibiting unmistakable signs of a downturn in quality in practically every department—puerile, amateurish, hard-going and unwatchable. The Sunday one-day circuit was now a thing of the past, a rapidly receding memory of past triumphs. I mourned its loss, especially when sitting through such hackneyed potboilers as *The Frozen Dead*, *It!* (*not* the Edward L. Cahn classic but the Roddy McDowell travesty) and a few below-average Hammer movies including *The Devil Rides Out* and *Dracula Has Risen from the Grave*.

In April, a solitary Saturday midnight screening of *The Deadly Mantis* c/w *The Land Unknown* at the Odeon in Redhill appeared to me, at least, like a last-gasp effort to revive the good old times, and *Kiss of the Vampire*, double billed with Universal's ever-popular favorite from 1955, *Tarantula*, popped up in June at the same cinema to revive my flagging spirits. But these turned out to be isolated incidents and rather alarmingly, no other oldies presented themselves again for the remainder of the year in my neck of the woods. Perhaps, I thought to myself, they had literally had their day and it was time to give them a rest. Not surprising really—many had been doing the rounds for years on end and deserved a break. Even my old friend, the perennial *20 Million Miles to Earth* (which I had seen eight times in various cinemas), had vanished off the circuits, surely an omen of sorts that had to be taken seriously. In the meantime, I had to take advantage of what little there was on release, whether it was in Surrey or the back streets of London, and this included a trip to The Times cinema in Baker Street where *King Kong* was being shown with *Peeping Tom*, another curious double billing and again a disparity in certificates—*Kong* was the A-rated picture, while *Peeping Tom* had been awarded an "X."

Reflecting on the years 1967 and 1968, the hard-to-swallow truth hit me that perhaps the horror, science fiction and fantasy area of the cinema was now dead in the water. The current fashion was for "X" certificate detective thrillers (*The Detective*), sub-James Bond adventures (*A Dandy in Aspic*) and soft-porn sex (*The Fox*). *Barbarella* and *Witchfinder General*, although superior to others of their kind, appeared to be throwbacks to another age, and to cap it all I allowed my membership of *The Horror Film Club of Great Britain* to lapse. Although *Famous Monsters of Filmland* and others of its kind could still be bought, the films within their pages were of a type that were fast disappearing from cinema screens all over the country as a new breed of filmmakers and cinema chains took control of what they thought the paying public would prefer to see—certainly, the cycle of '30s, '40s and '50s monster and science fiction movies did not figure on their agendas.

HIGHS AND LOWS (JUNE-JULY 1968)

And so another unsatisfactory month rolls by in what is turning out to be a cheerless year for the HSFF buff. No more Sunday one-day programs and their thrilling double bills to contemplate with relish; the late-night presentations now showing unmistakable signs of drying up; a butchered print of *The Seventh Voyage of Sinbad* going the rounds; awful-beyond-description fare such as *The Terrornauts* being inflicted upon us faithful fans; the current yield of continental horror melodramas exhibiting a steady decline in availability; and not even the combined talents of Lee, Karloff and Barbara Steele were able to prevent *The Curse of the Crimson Altar* from being the farrago that it so obviously is. This isn't what the scene was like between 1962 and 1966, the golden years as I now view them in retrospect—this is cinema purgatory, a worsening in quality all round, and it needs something almighty spectacular to drag it out of the quagmire into which this particular genre is rapidly sinking.

Saturday, 15 June. My partner and I board the train to Victoria Station in London, take the tube to Leicester Square and wend our way through the busy streets to The Casino cinema in Soho's Compton Street where that "something almighty spectacular" is showing in Cinerama—Stanley Kubrick's *2001: A Space Odyssey* (on its initial screening in London, the film was "A" rated and ran for 160 minutes. Once out on general release, it was shorn of 20 minutes, mostly from the Dawn of Man section, and reclassified as a "U"). In the ornate decor of the foyer, we pay for our rather expensive tickets and the glossy brochure that explains in great technical detail how *2001* was conceived, pad up the carpeted stairs to the balcony and sink into our plush seats, gazing in awe at the colossal curtained screen in front of us, which fills both our straight-ahead and peripheral vision.

The classy, well-upholstered theater is surprisingly full for a 1:00 screening and it is so quiet that I reckon that I could probably hear the proverbial pin drop. The patrons, like ourselves, are no doubt wondering what a film looks like in the giant Cinerama format—we are all about to find out. Stygian blackness descends, the curtains swish silently apart almost halfway around the auditorium and "Also Sprach Zarathustra" booms out over the MGM lion and the opening titles in stereophonic sound. I am thunderstruck. As the lengthy Dawn of Man sequence unfolds, one has the illusory sensation of partaking in the action with the apemen, and the space scenes are mind-blowing, each movement of the camera causing you to seemingly move correspondingly with it.

The space station, lending a new meaning to the word realism, appears to

British ad for a re-release of *2001*

revolve right out of the screen into the audience—3-D without the glasses—and during the stargate episode, I can appreciate why London's hippies love this section of the film as it compels me to grip the seat rests as though on a roller-coaster ride—how to get turned on without the aid of drink or drugs. The hotel room climax has me scratching my head in bewilderment and the very final shot of the star child staring at the Earth is both enigmatic and moving. This has been one hell of an experience, I say to myself, as we leave The Casino, widening by miles the gulf between what I have just witnessed and, as an example, Paramount's 1955 *Conquest of Space*, which also features a space station, albeit a pretty amateurish model compared to Kubrick's creation. But this dazzling, awe-inspiring space epic, an incredible achievement in any director's book, has made absolutely no impact on my other half, judging by her caustic comments as we head for the nearest eatery in Leicester Square.

"God, how boring."

"You're joking. Didn't you like it?"

"No I didn't. Actually, I slept through a lot of it, as if *you* didn't notice" (which I hadn't, come to think of it—I was too engrossed in the picture). "No story, no action, nothing. Boring."

I inwardly shrug. Oh well, there's no accounting for taste, even though *I* found it to be wonderfully stimulating and perceived *2001* for what it would become—a milestone in the area of science fiction and special effects wizardry. I wonder what my old cohorts over in Leatherhead would think of it? I suppose it's back to the "X" certificate sex films from now on, but not if I can help it because on the train home, I notice in the *Evening Standard* that *Lady in A Cage* is on at an independent cinema in the New Cross area of London. The certificate intrigues—"X London." This means in essence that England as a whole has banned the movie except the Capital, which has slapped on its own rating, as if to point out to one and all that Londoners are more liberal-minded than anybody else and able to stomach scenes that the rest of the population might shrink from. The following seven days are a holiday, so I broach the subject of a possible trip back on the Tuesday, the carrot dangled before my partner being that the co-feature is *Seventeen*, a controversial sex movie that also has an "X London" certificate. The bait works—Tuesday is penciled in for a visit to New Cross to see a movie that, I find out later that evening, has had its release date postponed for four years because of its disturbing content. I can hardly wait to see it!

Tuesday, 18 June. Up to London we go again, taking the tube from Victoria to New Cross. The cinema, when we eventually locate it, is a run-of-the-mill theater, dirty, shabby and smelly—a real dive. There's virtually nobody about either outside the building or inside the cramped surroundings as *Seventeen* gets underway, although when this risqué, soft-porn feature ends, a few die-hards and shady-looking characters have managed to swell the congregation to a more acceptable level. *Lady in A Cage* is definitely not my cup of tea, ban or no ban, a prolonged exercise in sadistic torment depicting a young James Caan and his gang of thugs terrorizing wheelchair-bound

Olivia De Havilland, closing with the unedifying sight of one of the gang members having his head crushed under the wheels of a car—a crude psycho-shocker with scarcely any merit in its 100-minute running time. William Castle, or even Hitchcock himself, would have made a far better job of that kind of material, I deliberate, as we exit this hovel and make our way across London to Victoria Station and home.

The remainder of the week is cinema-free, giving my finances a well-earned rest, which is just as well because a flurry of activity on the fantasy front in Redhill and Reigate, gleaned from the local papers and a few cinema programs, brings my old obsessions to the surface once again. This is much to the bemusement of my partner who, although enjoying the occasional visit to the cinema, balks at the idea of being towed along to *five* presentations in a little over three weeks (which is what I have planned), not to mention the expense it entails. On the other hand, I never have been one to count the pennies when it comes to the world of fantasy celluloid, and on Saturday 29 June *Witchfinder General* is making an appearance in Reigate at The Majestic with *The Blood Beast Terror* as co-feature.

In addition to this, *Kiss of the Vampire* c/w *Tarantula* is the late-night attraction at Redhill's Odeon, a mile or so separating both cinemas. I rub my hands in glee—these will satisfy me for the time being and fill a void. I decide (after not too much thought on the matter) to grab both

programs by leaving The Majestic at 10:30 p.m. when *Witchfinder General* finishes, sprinting over to the Odeon and catching the double horror bill there which really is too good to miss, particularly as *Tarantula* is a personal favorite. Then, in a flash, I suddenly realize that this "two different film showings in two separate cinemas" scenario has arisen before—in May 1965, flitting between Falmouth's Odeon and ABC in inclement weather and becoming ill with tonsillitis as a result. Needless to say, my partner is taking no part in this ridiculous enterprise verging on lunacy (her words, not mine). It's therefore going to be a solo effort demanding a great deal of stamina, so before I set off, a substantial meal is consumed in the hope that this will enable me to sit through four movies in two cinemas over a seven-hour period—a veritable marathon which even has me, a battle-hardened veteran of countless double-bills finishing at all hours, asking myself whether or not I am up to the task.

Arriving fresh and eager at The Majestic a little before 7:00 p.m., I buy my ticket and put up with the dismal, flat-footed *The Blood Beast Terror* that we customers have to endure in order to make it to the main feature. *Witchfinder General* is screened uncut, Surrey not tampering with the more gratuitous scenes as other areas of the country have done, meaning that every single second of the barbarous violence portrayed in Michael Reeves' period horror-drama remains intact, and exceedingly violent it is, too, especially the gory demise of Vincent Price in the bloody climax, a sequence which, so *The Daily Mirror* informed me recently, has been omitted altogether in some versions.

The film reaches its gruesome conclusion and I quickly head for the exit doors, emerging into the chilly night air and, by a combination of fast walking and running, reaching the Odeon with five minutes to spare, leaping up the steps, snatching a ticket together with a free cup of reviving coffee and collapsing into the rear stalls, breaking out into a cold, dizzy sweat as I try to relax. I haven't the time to figure out if I'm beginning to feel unwell as a consequence of all this racing around—the Universal International logo appears, the credits to *Tarantula* roll, and from the glare thrown out by the screen I can make out that there is a decent crowd in tonight. A surge of pride and nostalgia dispels the oncoming tiredness—Jack Arnold's 13-year-old giant insect thriller can still pack 'em in, even though it seems strange watching it. Strange, because not so long ago this particular film and its kindred were playing everywhere, bedfellows with the main features and up-to-the-minute releases; old companions you could rely on for a good few hours' indulgence. Now they're as rare as hen's teeth, so luxuriate in the picture while you can, I murmur.

Eighty minutes of black and white heaven—it won't be around for much longer. The ending, with the colossal spider ablaze on the edge of town, brings forth a bout of desultory hand-clapping from one joker in the audience (or could it be an appreciative fan?)—a short interval follows before *Kiss of the Vampire* commences, a fine Hammer vampire chiller produced on the cusp of their classic output and their lesser, more mundane mid-'60s efforts. Despite the excellence

of this production, I strain to stay awake during the last 15 minutes, switching to autopilot and viewing the film through drooping eyelids, finally leaving the Odeon at 2:10 a.m., dog-tired and slightly queasy, the exertion expended over the last seven hours having taken its toll—never again, I promise myself, as I force my aching legs to take me in the direction of home, knowing deep down that this promise will be broken once refreshed after a good night's sleep.

Next up on my agenda is a trip the coming Saturday to see *Psycho* and *The War of the Worlds*, a money-spinning double bill that has been in circulation since February of last year and one that has already been graced with my presence three times. My partner raises her eyes skywards, indicating that she will not be joining me—"Surely once is enough"—so on the Saturday, I amble over to Reigate and watch the afternoon performance of two undisputed classics. *The War of the Worlds* in particular shows up the '60s output of science fiction films for what they really are—pretenders to the '50s throne (with the exception of Kubrick's masterpiece). They no longer have the panache that George Pal's brash, comic book spectacle has in spades, and will any of *them* still be around in 15 years' time? I very much doubt it. When viewing Hitchcock's *Psycho* for a fourth stretch, I am always amazed that however many times you see it, you are never quite sure who the murderer is until the final reel, even though Anthony Perkins is the obvious suspect—a master-stroke of deviousness by a director at the peak of his powers.

The next two Saturdays see me traipsing the two miles from our flat into Reigate, once with my partner, and once without. On 13 July, *The Devil Rides Out* is showing with *Slave Girls*, the latest pairing from Hammer, so it must be worthwhile I state unconvincingly, totally aware of what Hammer's present-day fare is like—distinctly under par. She agrees therefore to accompany me to The Majestic. But the Hammer films of 1968 are not up to the standard of the Hammer films of 1958. Ten years have dulled their impact—the same old sets, the same old storylines and the same old cast of stalwarts—the sparkle, the pizzazz, has disappeared. You almost know what's going to happen before it does. *The Devil Rides Out* is admittedly a lot livelier, and in some ways more gripping, than their current crop of *Frankenstein*, *Dracula* and psychodrama offerings, and Christopher Lee as the Duc de Richleau is in commanding form as usual; nevertheless, it still hasn't got "classic" written all over it, and as for *Slave Girls*—a silly Stone Age romp that is destined to remain one of the most forgettable products from the studio ever chosen to be a support feature. I come away feeling decidedly cheated and, not for the first time, calling to mind the days when these films meant something—judging by the half-empty auditorium we have just left, they certainly don't mean a great deal to cinema-goers now.

To appease my partner, I take her to the Odeon in Redhill on Wednesday—Jack Cardiff's much criticized and extremely brutal *The Mercenaries* is the big crowd-puller, containing quite a few graphically sickening scenes that would not look out of place in a Hammer horror movie, fully deserving its "X" rating. And much to my partner's relief, and also to the relief of my bank balance, which has taken a bit of a battering, this frenzied stint of cinema-going terminates, for the present anyway, with yet another outing to Reigate's Majestic to participate in one of Hammer's more unusual features, *The Lost Continent*, teamed up with Warner Bros.' turgid *Peyton Place*-type drama from 1961, *Young and Eager*. *The Lost Continent* receives the thumbs up, the company's second adaptation of a Dennis Wheatley novel in a row. An admirable cast, exotic settings and several out-of-the-ordinary monsters all contribute to what again turns out to be a refreshing change from the *Dracula* and *Frankenstein* series, which is now unfortunately suffering from the "I've seen it all before" syndrome.

This frenetic period has lasted five weeks—an inactive spell now ensues and things settle down a bit. Fourteen films, yes, but not 14 that have been consistent in entertainment value or given me the same amount of pleasure that a similar number would have done five or six years ago. Quite honestly, it has been a chore to sit there and take some of them in, and it is heartbreaking to realize that out of the 14, only two were produced in the 1950s, a decade whose cinematic horror and science fiction output has, at this moment in time, practically ceased to exist as far as the major circuits are concerned. In a little over 12 months' time, they will appear no more.

PRESSBO●K

MAN...WOMAN...AND PREHISTORIC BEAST BATTLE FOR THE SURVIVAL OF THE FITTEST IN THE LIVING HELL THAT IS THE LOST CONTINENT

112 lines x 4 columns (448 lines)
4 columns x 8 inches

MAT—402

THE RISE AND FALL OF AN ERA
(1969-1970)

Perhaps in answer to a telepathic appeal from myself, and maybe from others out there who were worried about the disturbing lack of monster fodder on the cinema circuits, 1969 witnessed a brief but satisfying resurgence of the kind of movies that had received my unrelenting and devoted attention for the past decade and a half—a last throw of the dice, if you like, as if someone from up above was saying, "Let's give them one more airing and then we can shunt them away and concentrate on other more important matters." Before they resurfaced, however, one had to get through the thoroughly distasteful *The Twisted Nerve*, a movie that for once deserved the critical mauling it received, the over-long, talkative but fairly effective *Rosemary's Baby*, Hammer's gruesome and dull outing, *Frankenstein Must Be Destroyed*, and the abysmal *Battle Beneath the Earth*. Then in May, Redhill's Odeon resurrected their Saturday late-night programs after a lengthy fallow spell with *Circus of Horrors*, double billed with *The Pit and the Pendulum*. This was the first time I had seen Anton Diffring's bloodthirsty horror-thriller since being ejected from the ABC New Malden in 1960, but in the end it had been worth the wait, particularly when paired with Roger Corman's splendid slice of Grand Guignol. On a week's holiday in Cornwall in June, *Kiss of the Vampire* c/w *Tarantula*, a very popular latter-day double bill, was on at the ABC in Falmouth and I took my younger brother David to see it—uncannily, *Tarantula* was *his* introduction to the world of the "X" certificate American monster movie, just as it had been mine in 1961, proving that in life, strange coincidences do happen. Dave was still only 15 at the time, but the ABC presented no obstacles as he followed behind me and edged past the ticket kiosk, trying his best to blend in with the rest of the paying customers—could it be, I asked myself, that cinemas were now relaxing the old draconian criteria of years ago in tune with changing times and attitudes? I certainly never used to have as easy a ride in my day!

Back in Surrey, it was now the Odeon in Redhill that was coming up with the goodies, presenting a series of top-notch late-night double features from July onwards—*Theatre of Death* c/w *The Evil Force*, *The Curse of the Werewolf* c/w *Shadow of the Cat*, *Blood of the Vampire* c/w *The Brides of Dracula*, *The Premature Burial* c/w *The Haunted Palace* and once again the last survivors, or so it now seemed, from Universal's golden age of monsterdom, still hanging on in there like grim death, *The Deadly Mantis* c/w *The Land Unknown*. Admittedly, scores of movies I had watched between 1961 and 1966 were no longer being shown, particularly the output of American International, Allied Artists and the small independents, but at least *some* oldies could now be seen, even if it meant staying up at unearthly hours to catch sight of them.

Theatre of Death **was released in the U.S. as** *Blood Fiend.*

The late-night shows usually drew a fair-sized audience (probably all dyed-in-the-wool fanatics like myself) and the knack of trying to stay awake to the bitter end, normally around 2:00 a.m., was to grab a couple of hours' sleep during the afternoon prior to paying the cinema a visit. The free cup of coffee handed out to the customers after they had bought their tickets helped keep the stamina up and ward off the bouts of drowsiness that threatened to cut short the night's viewing pleasures, and there were no adverts or trailers to contend with, which was a blessed relief—one feature finished, there was a five-minute intermission, and then the other feature started. So it was a novel way to experience once again the old classics, but a tiring one also. My own way of coping was to sit bolt upright and concentrate hard—if you just once made the mistake of slumping back into your seat with your knees up in the fetal position and then closing your eyes for a couple of seconds, you were immediately transported to the land of dreams!

In September, Disney's splendid *20,000 Leagues Under the Sea* was given a major re-release in a brand-new, cleaned-up print, and the year ended with two great double bills at the Odeon, *Horrors of the Black Museum* c/w *Konga* and *The Blob* c/w *I Married A Monster from Outer Space*. The chief disappointment amidst the new batch of movies was Harryhausen's *The Val-

On Newquay beach in 1969, prior to a trip to see *Kiss of the Vampire* c/w *Tarantula*.

ley of Gwangi, released in November as a second feature to *The Good Guys and the Bad Guys*, his first film ever to do so. In fact, the special effects maestro was less than happy at having to play second fiddle to a pretty feeble comedy-Western and made his sentiments clear over this in an interview shortly after the film's release. *Gwangi* also received lukewarm reviews from the critics and on viewing it one could understand why—the picture had none of the swagger and spirit of his previous output and, in its own way, seemed to mirror the general lack of interest and enthusiasm being exhibited by the public for this type of feature, which only a few years ago was big box office but was now content to shuffle dejectedly around the circuits playing to half-empty houses, as was the case when I saw it at Reigate's Majestic cinema one wet and windy Saturday afternoon. The whole horror, science fiction and fantasy scene, I sadly contemplated, was steadily but inexorably going downhill—it just wasn't the same anymore.

As I had suspected for some time now, the current spate of oldies being screened principally in Redhill was a short-lived affair—the death-knell had been sounded for the '30s, '40s, '50s and even early '60s HSFF movies. One of the main reasons for their eventual demise, alongside audience antipathy, was television. Up until 1967, only a few films were shown on a weekly basis by the three channels available at the time; BBC, BBC2 and ITV (or ATV as it was then known). Because of moral standards and strict laws governing what was suitable for a television audience as well as in the cinema, these films tended to fall into the mainstream category—Westerns, war movies, musicals, comedies and adventures. During the long British winters, the only reasonably interesting items on offer to film addicts on the "box" were the likes of *Prince of Foxes*, *On the Town*, *She Wore a Yellow Ribbon* and *Twelve O'Clock High*, not to mention repeated showings of England's antique-looking Ealing productions.

Toward the end of 1968, however, and probably in keeping with the more lax code prevailing in the cinema, television finally began to wake up to the fact that there was a more substantial and meatier category of films to be broadcast rather than repeated showings of *The Baby and the Battleship*, and some of the old horror and fantasy features began to show up, usually quite late at night when, it was naively assumed, the younger audience had retired to bed. Hitchcock's *Psycho* had its television premier in October with the kind of warnings given out before the film came on that had preceded *Quatermass and the Pit* in 1958, and *Night of the Demon* soon followed on its heels. In 1969, both BBC and ITV (but ITV in particular) began screening in earnest a whole host of monster fodder, as if to make amends for the years of dross that they had inflicted upon those who could actually afford to rent or even own a television set during this decade.

Several vintage jewels from Universal's tried and trusted back catalogue of golden oldies were put on display. A heavily edited *Behemoth the Sea Monster* stalked across the small screen, as did *The Beast from 20,000 Fathoms*, one or two of the earlier Hammer productions appeared, and my old favorite which had served me well over the years, *20 Million Miles to Earth*, turned up. Nobody that I knew owned a video recorder in 1969, and my lamentable attempts to photograph with a Kodak instamatic camera a few scenes from selected features, particularly Columbia's 1957 monster yarn, produced truly horrendous and very unprofessional results—the high-tech cameras that had the ability to produce the type of photographs that ideally I would have preferred were still some way off.

This influx of goodies on the small screen produced two bizarre coincidences—well, where I lived at any rate. Regardless of whether television was deciding to broadcast one of the old classics or not, some were still in circulation and in April I attended a late-night show at Redhill's Odeon, the fare being *Black Zoo* and the A-rated version of *Behemoth the Sea Monster*, shown under its American title, *The Giant Behemoth*—this contained numerous cuts and edits, meaning that most of the sequences involving the radioactive dinosaur prowling through the London streets were nowhere to be seen, reducing the film's standing, in my opinion. A week later, it cropped up on television, the selfsame shortened print that I had so recently sat through at the Odeon. But for true weirdness, November's late-night showing of *The Curse of the Werewolf* c/w *Shadow of the Cat* took some beating—Hammer's lurid tale of lycanthropy was on at the Odeon at almost exactly the same hour, give or take a few minutes, that it was being broadcast on ITV! I had to pinch myself to see if I wasn't imagining that I saw this in the paper, and whether or not it was a

printing error, but no—the film was on at the pictures *and* television the same evening, and at the same time. Was it worth going, I debated? Yes it certainly was—I had never seen *Shadow of the Cat*, so the Odeon won the day. But as far as I can recall, this strange collision of two different types of media coverage for the identical product did not occur again.

But now that television had latched onto these movies, the cinemas once again began to give them the cold shoulder. In a way, this was understandable. Would any audience in 1969, with a new decade approaching, seriously be expected to, or even want to, fork out hard-earned cash to see either a pair of motion pictures made in 1945 or a cheapskate effort such as *Monster from the Ocean Floor*? I very much doubted it and obviously the cinema chains thought "No, they wouldn't," because 1970 really did bring about the end of an era as far as the old HSFF motion pictures were concerned. Perhaps on realization of this, the final nail in the coffin, I couldn't identify myself with 1970's releases and purposely avoided (at the time) *I, Monster, The Dunwich Horror, Eye of the Cat, Blood on Satan's Claw, The Vampire Lovers* and a few others. I did, though, make a concerted effort to catch what must surely have ranked as Hammer's worst-ever double bill—*The Scars of Dracula* c/w *The Horror of Frankenstein*, two terribly disappointing offerings that seemed, in their own fashion, to sum up the deterioration in the company's current work, although admittedly their output since the mid-'50s had been phenomenal in its consistency.

Not only had the oldies more or less disappeared from the circuits, but the manner in which films were being presented to the public was undergoing a drastic revision as well. The days of the "one major feature" had arrived—these new programs consisted of advertising, now taking on all the aspects of a series of three- to five-minute movies to promote their products, trailers for forthcoming attractions that were also becoming extended in length and content, and the main feature itself. The support picture had been virtually phased out by the big studios, although some double features staggered on for three or four more years, usually composed of a major release coupled with an ex-major release to hopefully pull in the punters. Performances now ran from Monday to Saturday—the Sunday one-day circuit was no more. The Saturday late-night shows started to fizzle out at the end of the year, and cinemas themselves began a series of transmutations to cater to a modern, more discerning class of clientele who wished to associate themselves, to a greater extent, with a cozier, intimate atmosphere in which to experience the wonderful world of celluloid, rather than the cavernous and rather forbidding auditoriums of yesteryear. Smaller, two- or three-in-one theaters began to proliferate with, in many cases, postage stamp-sized screens to match. The massive Odeons and ABCs, most of which were built in the 1930s, were now doomed, being regarded much like the dinosaurs they resembled—old-fashioned and extinct.

On Saturday, 4 July, I went along to the Odeon, Redhill at 10:15 p.m. to catch my very last late-night program there, although I didn't realize it at the time—*The Quatermass Experiment* double billed with *X the Unknown*. The honors for my final midnight performance *anywhere* went to The Regal in Redruth on another holiday in Cornwall in October, a surprising but rewarding pairing of *Psycho* and *Bride of Frankenstein*. *Jason and the Argonauts* was the sole reissue of 1970, although *2001: A Space Odyssey* was still in circulation, and Hammer's juvenile *When Dinosaurs Ruled the Earth* rounded off an extremely dismal year. In compensation, television was showing more and more horror, science fiction and fantasy movies (although this flurry didn't last very long—after a couple of years, they petered out and many were never screened again), but their time at the cinema, apart from film conventions and festivals, was at an end. The curtain had at last come down on them. No longer would packed audiences gasp and even faint at the unmasking of Vincent Price in *House of Wax*; thrill to Ray Harryhausen's Ymir running rampant in Rome; hear the cinema walls reverberate to the deafening sound of Gorgo destroying London; shudder as the grave-robbers disturbed Lon Chaney's tomb and unwittingly revived him in *Frankenstein Meets the Wolf Man*; be enthralled by the original *Godzilla* trampling all over Tokyo; marvel at the pyrotechnics on display in *This Island Earth*; enjoy the shadowy antics of Karloff, Lugosi and Zucco; gape at Kong fighting a Tyrannosaurus in the forest glade; point in derision as the fake spider appeared in *Mesa of Lost Women*; appreciate the expertise of the early Hammer productions; wonder whether Tor Johnson was forever destined to play blank-eyed mutants as in *The Black Sleep*; scream as Richard Wordsworth's infected arm was exposed to view in *The Quatermass Experiment*; become engrossed by the horrors conjured up in Jack Arnold's Universal monster movies; sneer at Bert I. Gordon's effects in *The Amazing Colossal Man*; sit with a wry smile through Richard Cunha's *She Demons*; or laugh their collective heads off at *Teenage Caveman, The Brain from Planet Arous* and *The Flying Serpent*. Flamboyant, colorful, well directed, flatly directed, woodenly acted, well acted, witty, tatty, shoddy, frightening, silly, amazing, noisy, imaginative, dull and absolute rubbish—these are just some of the words to describe the classic period of horror, science fiction and fantasy film which finally ran its course in U.K. cinemas at the very end of 1970.

MIDNIGHT AT THE ODEON (1969)

THE ODEON REDHILL
Monday 10th November for six days
Hywel Bennett: The Virgin Soldiers Cert (X) Adults only
Saturday late-night show commencing 11:00 p.m.
The Deadly Mantis (X) The Land Unknown (X)

The Wednesday edition of *The Surrey Mirror* advertises the latest presentations in Redhill, Reigate, Oxted and Dorking, and this one catches my eye; not the main attraction, *The Virgin Soldiers*, a current box office smash, but the two movies making up the late show. I smile inwardly. *The Deadly Mantis*—I've seen it three times already and the film is 12 years old, still gallantly doing the business on the circuits, raking in a continual supply of cash to fill Universal's bulging coffers. Likewise *The Land Unknown*—this one I've watched twice before and that's 12 years old as well. The staying power of these films is truly incredible—Lugosi's *Dracula*, made 38 years ago, was on at this cinema the other week with *Son of Dracula*, still drawing a fair-sized crowd, who apparently were not bothered by the fact that what they were paying to sit through were two antique products from the '30s and '40s, but it's rare nowadays to catch the old Universal monster and horror flicks. Not so long ago, they filled up the Sunday slots as regular as clockwork. That extremely fertile period seems to have gone forever—a torrent of delights has been reduced to a trickle and it is a case of grabbing everything on offer before the day arrives (and I sense deep down that day is not too far off) when the trickle dries up altogether and becomes a drought. So I make up my mind to take in the late show on Saturday and re-experience the old thrills while I can. My partner, though, doesn't share my passion (or fanaticism) and takes no part in these nocturnal sorties. Any person who goes to the cinema at a time when the rest of the population are tucked up in bed must be in serious need of a psychiatrist, she states quite emphatically. "You can go on your own," she adds, which I normally do anyway.

After getting my head down for a couple of hours in the evening, I wander over to the large Odeon cinema, arriving at roughly 10:30 p.m., just as the customers who have sat through Hywel Bennett's sex-laden army caper spill into the road. Judging by their conversations, several die-hard followers of the monster scene enter the foyer with me for the late performance and hang about aimlessly until the auditorium has emptied. Five more minutes drift past and there are between 30 and 40 people here now, probably dying for a cup of coffee, which is normally given free of charge to the patrons silly enough to want to attend these later-than-late shows. At 10:50 p.m., we are finally allowed to buy our tickets, the coffee lady appears, everyone grabs a polystyrene cup full of the scalding beverage, and we file into the auditorium. Unfortunately, it hasn't been cleared of the evening's accumulation of rubbish—cigarette packets, sweet wrappers and assorted cartons litter the aisles, much to my disgust.

Locating a seat in an area relatively free from this garbage, I settle back, promising myself to stay awake no matter what. It's very quiet—no music is ever played this late at night in the cinema, and only the sound of hushed whisperings disturbs the eerie silence. Darkness descends in a flash and the Universal International logo comes up on the giant Odeon screen in Cinemascope as *The Land Unknown* gets underway, an entertaining, underrated *Lost World*-type adventure frolic boasting decent special effects, an imaginative array of monsters and a very delectable Shawn Smith cavorting around in a skimpy costume, which fairly whizzes along throughout its 78-minute running length. There are no problems with dozing off during this lively offering, although the main ingredient for fighting any bouts of drowsiness, the coffee, has been consumed, and I remind myself that there's another movie to participate in before I can retire to bed.

The Land Unknown finishes and the dim lights flicker on, bathing the surroundings in a warm, cozy glow—very sleep-inducing, and I quickly push *that* thought from my mind. The cinema is three-quarters full—not a bad turnout, really, for a pair of 1950s movies being screened at this ungodly hour. I scan the stalls in the gloom—some of the younger customers are completely

zonked out, slumped in their seats, oblivious to what's going on around them. Just a five-minute pause to boost the stamina levels and then it's 12:30 a.m., the lights fade and *The Deadly Mantis* thunders over the audience, having the same effect as a bucket of cold water. People stir in their seats, shaken from their stupor—stupidly, I do the opposite and make the fatal mistake of letting my eyelids droop for a fraction of a second, feeling, as one does when still awake at midnight, like death warmed up, and for another two or three seconds I am on the point of being sucked into the welcoming vortex of slumber. Pinching myself hard, I snap out of it, sitting up straight and concentrating with every ounce of willpower I can muster as William Hopper and company confront the colossal mantis of the title. It works—somehow, I manage to enjoy for the fourth occasion Universal's entertaining monster insect movie, even if my eyeballs are straining in their sockets for most of the film's 79 minutes, and by the time it ends at 1:50 a.m., I've developed a muzzy, thumping headache. The refrains to The National Anthem strike up, but I'm certainly not interested in listening to it and neither is anybody else as we hobble, stagger and drag our collective way down the Odeon's steep steps, me decidedly groggy, bleary-eyed and nauseous from a pounding head, grateful for the reviving cool draught of the November night air.

I walk the quarter of a mile to our flat very slowly, saying to myself, as I usually do after these late-night excursions, "Is it all worth it?" knowing full well that if an acceptable enough double feature turns up at the Odeon in the future at 11:00 p.m., regardless of whether I've seen both movies before, I will repeat the whole exercise, tiredness or no tiredness. After all, what harm is there in a little sleep deprivation now and again? That's dedication for you, even though this particular night's viewing pleasures result in another migraine laying me low for the whole of Sunday, together with repeated barbed comments from the girlfriend not helping things either. Yes—I admit that the late-night shows *are* killers, a form of masochistic torture in some ways; however, all the time these motion pictures conceived in America's golden age of monsterdom are being screened in my local theaters, I will trot along and pay homage to them because I've developed a sneaking suspicion that they will not be around forevermore. I, and a few fanatics, might enjoy two old black and white monster movies made in 1957 and both coming in at under 80 minutes long, but surely the modern-day audience expects a little bit more for their money. It's called progress—I can't prevent it from happening; on the other hand, I do not feel a part of it.

REFLECTIONS—LIFE AFTER 1970

Everyone has a top 10 list of this or that, depending upon his or her own interests. It's what makes the world go round. Between 1954 and 1970, I saw 450 horror, science fiction and fantasy films at the cinema, so composing a top 10 from such a large variety might be considered rather difficult in the circumstances; I have compromised and come up with a top 20. Any person reading this book will have no difficulties in guessing what that top 20 comprise, but here they are anyway, in alphabetical order—a collection of movies that for no sane or logical reason give me pleasure every time I see them:

The Creature Walks Among Us
The Curse of Frankenstein
Eyes Without a Face
Gorgo
House of Frankenstein
House of Wax
It! The Terror from Beyond Space
Jason and the Argonauts
Journey to the Center of the Earth
Journey to a Primeval Age
King Kong
The Mummy (1959)
The Pit and the Pendulum
Psycho
The Quatermass Experiment
Rodan
The Seventh Voyage of Sinbad
Tarantula
The Thing from Another World
20 Million Miles to Earth

Mexican lobby card for *King Kong*

I was fortunate enough to have sat through some tremendous double bills in my time, so it might be appropriate to run through a top 20 list of favorites, especially as these double features, providing the audience of the day with an abundance of thrills and excitement for the low cost, even then, of a cinema ticket, died out nearly 40 years ago. I therefore pay tribute to the following, in no real order of preference, all of which I not only enjoyed immensely but left me with a feeling that I had received in entertainment value alone more than my money's worth:

King Kong c/w *The Thing from Another World*
The Fiend Who Walked the West c/w *Kronos*
The Creature Walks Among Us c/w *Tarantula*
Horrors of the Black Museum c/w *It! The Terror from Beyond Space*
20 Million Miles to Earth c/w *The Werewolf*
Psycho c/w *Bride of Frankenstein*
The Black Scorpion c/w *Indestructible Man*
House of Frankenstein c/w *House of Dracula*
The Brides of Dracula c/w *The Mummy* (the Hammer version)
The Deadly Mantis c/w *Rodan*
The Demon Doctor c/w *Varan the Unbelievable*
Circus of Horrors c/w *The Pit and the Pendulum*
Blood of the Vampire c/w *Behemoth the Sea Monster*

The Leech Woman c/w *The Incredible Shrinking Man*
The Monolith Monsters c/w *The Mole People*
The Curse of Frankenstein c/w *Dracula* (the Hammer version)
Mighty Joe Young c/w *The Hounds of Zaroff*
Creature from the Black Lagoon c/w *Dracula* (the 1930 version)
Frankenstein Meets the Wolf Man c/w *The Mummy's Curse*
The Birds c/w *The Day of the Triffids*

The prize for the worst double bill that I ever had the misfortune to sit through goes to *Mother Riley Meets the Vampire* c/w *The Devil Bat*, two absolute stinkers that were proudly advertised in the local paper and outside the ABC in Falmouth as "A terrific Bela Lugosi Double!" There *were* others that had me questioning my mental state and wondering what on earth I was playing at shut inside a cinema, putting up with over three hours of drivel when I could have spent the time more constructively with either my mates or my family. On such occasions, when leaving the cinema to the kind of comments directed at the films from my fellow fanatics who had braved them out that wouldn't have been out of place in an army barracks (or on board the *Chusan*!), even my boundless enthusiasm began to ebb. It only needed another visit to a more satisfactory presentation, however, to restore my faith in the subject. Here are 20 patently under-average double bills which had even me fidgeting in my seat.

Curse of the Fly c/w *Duel of the Space Monsters*
Killers from Space c/w *Mesa of Lost Women*
The Horror of Frankenstein c/w *The Scars of Dracula*
The Incredible Petrified World c/w *Man Beast*
Flight of the Lost Balloon c/w *The Amazing Transparent Man*
The Strange World of Planet X c/w *Fire Maidens from Outer Space*
A Bucket of Blood c/w *The Undead*
The Beast with 5 Fingers c/w *The Walking Dead*
The Terrornauts c/w *They Came from Beyond Space*
Corridors of Blood c/w *Nights of Rasputin*

The Giant Claw c/w *Zombies of Mora-Tau*
The Corpse c/w *Psycho Killer*
Mr. Sardonicus c/w *The Hands of Orlac*
Teenage Monster c/w *The Brain from Planet Arous*
The Beast with a Million Eyes c/w *The Phantom from 10,000 Leagues*
Spacemaster X-7 c/w *The Unknown Terror*
The Boogie Man Will Get You c/w *Lock Up Your Daughters*
Earth vs. the Spider c/w *Teenage Caveman*
The Most Dangerous Man Alive c/w *How to Make A Monster*
Frankenstein Created Woman c/w *The Mummy's Shroud*

In spite of this lukewarm fare dished up to the punters, each and every one of the above attractions, however substandard, somehow managed to gather a large crowd, which once again only goes to demonstrate that in the days long before multi-channel television and countless other media diversions, the cinema-going public seemed quite happy to pay for their tickets and sit through a load of old tat such as *Lock Up Your Daughters*, and what's more be entertained by it!

Columbia's *20 Million Miles to Earth* was the one film above all others that featured in an unbroken sequence of double bills spanning nearly 10 years on the circuits, from 1957 right up to 1967—a very popular crowd-puller of its day. What it appeared with in other parts of the country I have no idea, but in the two areas in which I lived, I caught it a total of eight times and spotted it a further four, as follows:

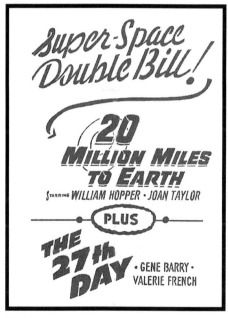

May 1957
20 Million Miles to Earth c/w? The Crescent, Leatherhead (not seen)
July 1959
20 Million Miles to Earth c/w? The Odeon, Cheam (not seen)
May 1961
20 Million Miles to Earth c/w *Underworld USA* The Embassy, Dorking (not seen)
March 1962
20 Million Miles to Earth c/w *Night of the Demon* The Crescent, Leatherhead (not seen)
July 1962
20 Million Miles to Earth c/w *Bed Without Breakfast* The Embassy, Dorking
November 1962
20 Million Miles to Earth c/w *The Big Heat* The ABC, Cobham
April 1963
20 Million Miles to Earth c/w *Live Now, Pay Later* The Odeon, Falmouth
September 1963
20 Million Miles to Earth c/w *The Creature with the Atom Brain* The Cameo, Pool
January 1965
20 Million Miles to Earth c/w *The Tingler* The Regal, Redruth
May 1965
20 Million Miles to Earth c/w *Boy's Night Out* The ABC, Falmouth
October 1966
20 Million Miles to Earth c/w *The Werewolf* The Cameo, Pool

February 1967
20 Million Miles to Earth c/w *House on Haunted Hill* The Odeon, Redhill

This gives some idea of the longevity certain films enjoyed on the circuits before they were retired from duty, given a well-earned rest and then transferred to tape and/or digital disc.

20 Million Miles to Earth wasn't alone in the longevity stakes, and although I cannot claim to have seen any film over 100 times as Ray Harryhausen achieved with *King Kong*, I managed to take in a reasonable number of movies more than once, given the nature of the double bills on offer in those days. Follow-ups to Columbia's sci-fi/monster thriller were *King Kong* (7), *Psycho* (6), *The Brides of Dracula* (6), *Indestructible Man* (6), *The Black Scorpion* (6), *Tarantula* (6), *The War of the Worlds* (5), *The Revenge of Frankenstein* (5), *Invasion of the Body Snatchers* (5), Hammer's *The Mummy* (5), *The Thing from Another World* (5), *It! The Terror from Beyond Space* (4), *The Deadly Mantis* (4), *Journey to the Center of the Earth* (4), *Rodan* (4), *The Werewolf* (4), *Gorgo* (4) and literally dozens of threes, including *The Creature Walks Among Us*, *The Land Unknown*, *Attack of the 50 Foot Woman* and *Behemoth the Sea Monster*. The most popular double bills to hang around on the circuits were *Invasion of the Body Snatchers* c/w *Indestructible Man* (1959-1964), *Teenage Frankenstein* c/w *Blood Is My Heritage* (1958-1963), *Frankenstein 1970* c/w *Macabre* (1958-1964), *The Deadly Mantis* c/w *The Land Unknown* (1965-1969), *Kiss of the Vampire* c/w *Tarantula* (1966-1969) and *The Quatermass Experiment* c/w *X the Unknown* (1964-1970). (In stark contrast to the number of years these films ran, 2004's Kevin Costner Western, *Open Range*—alright, it's not a horror film but serves to illustrate a case in point—was seen by myself on the 21st of March 2004. Two months later, it was on sale in the stores on VHS and DVD!)

Individual scenes within the fantasy film genre *do* stand out—spread over hundreds of movies, these are countless in number. Trawling through my lists, I have come up with a selection of fairly dramatic sequences which have left an impression; inspirational moments adding to the overall excellence of the productions that they featured in:

The Black Scorpion—Richard Denning and Carlos Rivas' descent into the scorpions' nest by way of a rickety cage suspended on the end of a crane, a vast gloomy cavern full of grotesque-looking monsters and eerie sounds. Suspenseful, with some tremendous stop-motion animation work from Willis O'Brien and Peter Peterson.

Bride of Frankenstein—The pastoral interlude whereby Karloff's monster, on the run from the local villagers, is befriended by a blind hermit in the woods. Both touching and amusing.

Dracula—The final confrontation between Peter Cushing (Van Helsing) and Christopher Lee (Dracula) in the vampire's castle. One of horror's, and Hammer's, most famous climaxes.

Gorgo—The 200-foot monster's destruction of London as she searches for her infant. Spectacular, colorful and well staged.

House of Wax—Mad sculptor Vincent Price hobbling after terrified Phyllis Kirk through the deserted fog-shrouded Baltimore streets. Good old-fashioned Gothic thrills and chills.

The Incredible Shrinking Man—Tiny Grant Williams' fight for survival against a (to him) huge spider to gain supremacy over his only means of sustenance, a piece of stale cake—a magical moment in the history of fantasy cinema, brilliantly orchestrated by Jack Arnold.

Jason and the Argonauts—The giant statue Talos creakily turning to stare down at the two Greeks who have dared to enter the treasure chamber that he is guarding. Bernard Herrmann's music and Ray Harryhausen's expertise bring Greek mythology to life in this brooding, atmospheric segment of the film.

Harryhausen's Talos

Journey to the Center of the Earth—Pat Boone discovering the grotto full of giant mushrooms miles beneath the Earth's surface. Imaginative set design underscored once again by Bernard Herrmann's fabulous music.

King Kong—Kong breaking out of the theater, causing pandemonium as he goes on a rampage in New York. Awesome and innovative effects complemented by Max Steiner's rousing music, and hard to believe that this was brought to the screen 70 years ago!

The Monolith Monsters—The skyscraper-sized black crystals toppling and multiplying on the edge of the desert town. For a relatively low-budget film, Clifford Stine's special effects are amazing in their simplicity.

The Mummy—Christopher Lee, dripping with mud, rising unsteadily from the misty swamp as George Pastell reads the Scroll of Life. One of Hammer's most persuasive and unforgettable scenes.

Night of the Demon—The giant fiery demon materializing in the night sky over the treetops during the opening minutes as his next victim looks on in horror. Nerve-tingling supernatural shocks from Jacques Tourneur.

The Quatermass Experiment—Brian Donlevy and colleagues viewing with a growing sense of unease the film of the crew of Q1 on board the rocket and slowly realizing that the astronauts have encountered something sinister in space. Sweaty tension, leaving the audience, and the Professor, to wonder just what that "something" might be.

The Return of the Vampire—Werewolf Matt Willis prowling through a foggy graveyard at the bidding of his master, vampire Bela Lugosi. A typical 1940s spine-tingling sequence.

Rodan—Kenji Sahara stumbling across Rodan's colossal egg in an underground chamber populated by hordes of man-eating insects prior to the giant reptile making its roaring entry. Made during Toho's fertile early years, long before they began to aim their movies at a more juvenile audience.

The Seventh Voyage of Sinbad—The first appearance of the Cyclops on the Isle of Colossa. Harryhausen's Dynamation effects astounded audiences of the day.

Tarantula—The giant spider clambering over a distant hillside as the locals are preparing to dynamite the road to prevent it from reaching the town. Clifford Stine's effects and Henry Mancini's score make for a memorable few minutes of monster mayhem.

The Thing from Another World—The climax in the freezing Quonset hut as a bleeping Geiger counter signals the approach of the alien to beleaguered Kenneth Tobey and his crew.

20 Million Miles to Earth—William Hopper and company's confrontation with the Venusian Ymir in a barn. An expert blend of stop-motion animation and live action in an enclosed setting.

2001: A Space Odyssey—Astronaut Keir Dullea hurtling through the multicolored stargate for what seems like an eternity and ending up in a bizarre, futuristic hotel room. Amidst all the hardware on display, an ambiguous but thought-provoking climax.

I have seen a quite a number of films that I maintain have been unfairly criticized or thought of as too routine. The following is a list of underrated features that I think were rather good, despite, in some instances, their low budgets:

Blood Is My Heritage
Curse of the Faceless Man
The Cyclops
Doctor Blood's Coffin
The Evil of Frankenstein
The Fiend Who Walked the West
The Four Skulls of Jonathan Drake
Frankenstein's Daughter
The Haunted Strangler

The Hideous Sun Demon
I Bury the Living
Indestructible Man
It! The Terror from Beyond Space
The Land Unknown
The Mad Ghoul
The Man Who Could Cheat Death
The Return of the Vampire
The Thing that Couldn't Die
The Vampire
World Without End

Conversely, here are 20 that I felt were distinctly overrated. Certainly, when sitting through them, I went into analytical mode and mentally tore them to pieces!

Barbarella
The Beast with 5 Fingers
The Black Cat
The Curse of the Werewolf
The Damned
Destination Moon
Dr. Terror's House of Horrors
Dracula—Prince of Darkness
Ghost of Frankenstein
The Illustrated Man
Invaders from Mars
It Came from Beneath the Sea
The Magnetic Monster
The Phantom of the Opera (1943)
Rosemary's Baby
Son of Dracula
The Three Worlds of Gulliver
The Tomb of Ligeia
The Walking Dead
When Worlds Collide

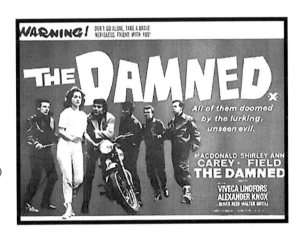

Some memorable fragments of dialogue stick in the memory as well, many, it must be said, quite humorous. Whether or not that was the original intention of the scriptwriters at the time is open to conjecture, but in their own way, they seem to sum up the whole essence of the movies that they were heard in, no matter how short the line was:

Abbott and Costello Meet Frankenstein
Lon Chaney (The Wolf Man): "You don't understand. Every night when the moon is full, I turn into a wolf."
Lou Costello: "Yeah—you and 20 million other guys!"

Bride of Frankenstein
Ernest Thesiger to Karloff's monster in the crypt: "Have a cigar. They're my only weakness."

The Curse of Frankenstein
Peter Cushing to Hazel Court: "Pass the marmalade, would you, Elizabeth?" after his monster has just brutally done away with Valerie Gaunt.

Devil Girl from Mars
Hugh McDermott to landlady of the Scottish inn: "Mrs. Jamieson. May I introduce your latest guest—Miss Nyah. She comes from Mars."
Landlady: "Oh well—that will mean another bed."

House of Frankenstein
Boris Karloff on discovering Frankenstein's monster in a block of ice: "The undying monster! The triumphant climax of Frankenstein's genius!"

House of Wax
Vincent Price to intended victim Phyllis Kirk: "What I need for my Marie Antoinette is you. The real you. Nothing less will satisfy me."

The Incredible Shrinking Man
Grant Williams: "It's easy enough to talk of soul and spirit and essential worth, but not when you're three feet tall."

It! The Terror from Beyond Space
Marshall Thompson: "There's enough voltage in these lines to kill 30 human beings. The only drawback is, the thing isn't human."

Journey to the Center of the Earth
James Mason to an embarrassed Arlene Dahl after bathing in the crystal grotto: "You're wearing 'stays,' are you not?"

King Kong
Robert Armstrong to Frank Reicher: "What's that?" as the Skull Island natives stare at Fay Wray.
Frank Reicher: "He says—look at the golden woman."
Robert Armstrong: "Yeah—blondes are scarce around here."

The Lost World
Claude Rains: "It's a baby Tyrannosaurus!" as a tiny lizard with frills, looking nothing like the offspring of the giant dinosaur, hatches from its egg.

The Mummy
An inebriated Michael Ripper describing something horrible he has just encountered: "I've seen the likes tonight that no mortal eyes shouldn't look at. Ten feet tall he was, swathed in bandages. Came lumbering through that wood like a great bear."

Psycho
Janet Leigh: "Do you go out with friends?"
Anthony Perkins: "Well—a boy's best friend is his mother."

Quatermass and the Pit
Andrew Keir, studying one of the decaying insect-men: "I wonder. A name that's been nearly worn out before anything turned up to claim it. Was this really a Martian?"

Tarantula
Newspaper reporter to John Agar: "I'll have to see that tarantula before I believe it."
John Agar: "You'll see it, Joe. And you'll wish you hadn't!"

Teenage Frankenstein

Whit Bissell to monster, Gary Conway: "Answer me. You have a civil tongue in your head. I know, I sewed it in there!"

The Thing from Another World

Douglas Spencer, on being informed that the hostile alien they have dug out of the ice could be vegetable and not animal: "An intellectual carrot. The mind boggles!"

20 Million Miles to Earth

American Officer: "Colonel Calder here has just returned from an expedition to Venus."
Sicilian Official: "From Venice—perhaps you mean Venezia."
William Hopper: "To Venus. The planet Venus."

The Unearthly

One police officer to another, on surveying the mutants in John Carradine's cellar: "Good Lord. What if they *do* live forever?"

X the Unknown

Dean Jagger to his colleagues: "How do you kill mud?"

And then there were the publicity blurbs on the posters. Even the cheapest slice of old hokum had to be bolstered by outlandish promotional claims on the accompanying poster, stating unequivocally that the movie in question was the greatest piece of entertainment since sliced bread. Of course, many were the opposite—but this didn't prevent the studios from coming up with some pretty outrageous comments in the advertising to lure the public into the cinema to see their product, however awful it might be. Misleading it may have been to describe *Reptilicus* as "Monster from Another Age brings Terror to Mankind!" especially as the monster depicted was a feeble, unconvincing puppet, but the promoters hoped that by describing the film thus, customers would part with their money—if on emerging from the cinema they thought that the poster was criminally deceptive, so be it. So here are just a few overblown blurbs from the hundreds I have come across, all ending with the obligatory exclamation mark, as if to emphasize the importance of the fare on offer:

The Amazing Colossal Man

'Never since King Kong has there been such a Mighty Motion Picture!'

Attack of the Crab Monsters

'Once they were men—now they are land crabs!'

Blood Is My Heritage

'In her eyes—desire! In her veins—the blood of a monster!'

Crack in the World

'Thank God it's only a motion picture!'

The Creature Walks Among Us

'Fury stalks the streets—a city screams in Terror!'

Curse of the Faceless Man

'Entombed for eons—turned to stone...seeking women, women, women!'

The Deadly Mantis
'1,000 tons of insect monster hungering for human prey!'
Fire Maidens from Outer Space
'Science Fiction's Greatest Thrill. Maidens without Men on Mystery Planet!'
Godzilla
'Makes King Kong look like a midget!'
Gorilla at Large
'Get out of his way—before it's too late!'
Half Human
'Half-Man. Half-Beast. All Monster!'
Indestructible Man
'300,000 Volts of Horror!'
It Conquered the World
'Every Man its prisoner—every Woman its slave!'
Macabre
'See it with someone who can carry you home!'
Monster on the Campus
'Every co-ed beauty prey to his fang-slashing passion!'
The Mummy's Shroud
'Beware the beat of the cloth-wrapped feet!'
The Mysterians
'They came from another world—they want 3 kilometers of land—and FIVE of your women!'
Return of the Fly
'Blood curdling giant fly-creature runs amok!'
Terror from the Year 5,000
'From a time unborn—a hideous she-thing!'
War of the Colossal Beast
'The Towering Terror from Hell!'

A good soundtrack to a film has always stirred my imagination. These days, with few exceptions, movie scores have dwindled in importance and the film composer, once a mighty figure in Hollywood, is no longer the all-important person he used to be. In the old days, even a low-budget production required a half-decent soundtrack to both carry it along and paper over the cracks in plot and effects. The more prestigious efforts possessed distinguished scores that lingered in the mind long after one had left the cinema, and here are 20 that still have the power to set the blood coursing through my veins:

Bride of Frankenstein—Franz Waxman
Creature from the Black Lagoon—Hans J. Salter
Dracula (1958)—James Bernard
Eyes Without a Face—Maurice Jarre
Fantastic Voyage—Leonard Rosenman
First Men in the Moon—Laurie Johnson
The Hideous Sun Demon—John Seely
House of Wax—David Buttolph
I Bury the Living—Gerald Fried
Indestructible Man—Albert Glasser
It! The Terror from Beyond Space—Paul Sawtell and Bert Shefter
Jason and the Argonauts—Bernard Herrmann
Journey to the Center of the Earth—Bernard Herrmann
King Kong—Max Steiner

The Mummy (1959)—Frank Reizen-
stein
The Pit and the Pendulum—Les
Baxter
Psycho—Bernard Herrmann
Tarantula—Henry Mancini (credited
to Joseph Gershenson)
The Thing from Another World—
Dimitri Tiomkin
Things to Come—Arthur Bliss

The HSFF genre as such didn't,
of course, grind to a halt after 1970.
It's just that my interest in it did, or at
least it began to wane. As previously
stated, the curtain had come down
on my childhood days of sneaking
into X-rated movies, of cycling
here, there and everywhere to different venues, of actually parting with
my hard-grafted wages and pocket
money to watch and enjoy something as inferior, in cinematic terms, as *Bride of the Monster* or,
on the other hand, experience the initial thrills of Jack Arnold's giant spider trampling over the
desert landscape. This was all now part of my personal history as well as a part of the cinema's
history—the scene from 1970 onwards was a completely different animal as far as my tastes
were concerned. I have therefore ended this book at the dawn of a new decade in which the old
classics ceased to feature in the "what's on next week" columns of the newspapers. In 16 years
of frantic cinema-going, 450 movies belonging to this remarkable and much-maligned category
of the cinema passed before my eyes on the big screen—between 1971 and 2003, a further 32
years of cinema-going, the number totaled a measly 144, only eight of which could be placed in
the category of a golden oldie:

1975—*The Seventh Voyage of Sinbad* is reissued in its original restored length—and not before
time! My six-year-old son is introduced to the world of fantasy cinema, even though he makes a
nuisance of himself by playing around in his seat through most of the film, annoying the people
behind us. In revenge, the Cyclops gives him bad dreams for a week.
1978—*Creature from the Black Lagoon* c/w *It Came from Outer Space* are both given a brief
run, shown in their original 3-D format at selected cinemas. Sitting there wearing the infamous
red and green plastic glasses, the effect, it has to be said, is not all that different to watching
the film in normal flat screen! They are reissued as a double bill in this format again in 1982,
Jack Arnold's gill-man classic reclassified from an "X" to an "A." *House of Wax* also gets a 3-D
screening in the West End and being in color, the effects carry more impact, although no one
passes out during the performances as they did way back in 1954.
1981—*Jason and the Argonauts* is re-released for the umpteenth time with *The 12 Tasks of
Asterix*.
1982—*The War of the Worlds* is double billed with *The Sentinel* for a short airing in London.
1986—A Saturday morning in June at the ABC in Crawley—I dash over there to see a one-off
showing of Fox's splendid fantasy *Journey to the Center of the Earth*. Why a 1959 movie, classic status notwithstanding, should suddenly surface in Crawley, and at this time of the day, is
anybody's guess, but it draws a large audience, mostly people of my age who sit through it and
reminisce about times gone by.

1999—Another Saturday morning in July at Crawley's ABC and, yes, it's *Jason and the Argonauts* again, now 36 years old. Columbia must be raking in the revenue on this one!

2000—Kubrick's masterwork, *2001: A Space Odyssey*, is given a one-day showing in Crawley on a Thursday in July and it's a treat to view the inspiration behind *Star Trek*, *Star Wars* and countless others again on the giant multi-plex screen, in surround-sound as well.

As regards the major year-on-year releases—they have no place within these pages, conceived as they were in an entirely different and more recent period to the one I have written about. Suffice to say that I can literally count on one hand (OK, two hands) the number of films that have made some kind of impact during these later years. I was brought up on a diet of mostly black and white movies that made the most of their minimal budgets and, moreover, still managed to stir the imagination despite their obvious limitations. Fifty million- (and more) dollar productions in widescreen and Dolby wall-to-wall sound, trumpeting the latest computer-generated effects, do not necessarily a good movie make as one critic once remarked, and the majority of the new generation of horror and fantasy features have left me unmoved—verging on the pompous with their "let's have a thrill every five minutes" mentality, they possess no soul, if such a term can be used to describe a piece of celluloid; or, as one reviewer said of *Star Wars* in 1978, "The multitude of modern-day science fiction blockbusters are little more than an empty bag of tricks."

To put it more bluntly, the magic, the fantasy element, whatever one likes to call it, has gone. With every computerized trick-in-the-book explained in great detail in dozens of high-tech magazines, a lot of post-1990 movies resemble gigantic versions of the video games that they are derived from—all flash, bang, wallop and no substance, aimed squarely at the 12-year-old age group. Adults, it appears, have been overlooked, ignored and left behind.

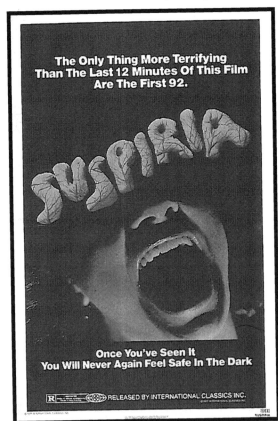

Perhaps the unending succession of '30s, '40s and '50s products had ingrained themselves into my system to such an extent that I had simply lost the appetite for the newer films of the genre. For example, 1979's *Star Trek*, in my estimation as a seasoned fantasy addict, was 132 minutes of stamina-sapping monotony, despite the millions of dollars expended by Paramount in bringing their popular television series to the silver screen—I gained far more satisfaction from Astor's 78-minute *Missile to the Moon*, cooked up in a matter of weeks by Richard Cunha for around 50 thousand bucks, which showed exactly where my allegiances lay. Undoubtedly, though, there were some that I rated highly, even though they were few and far between.

Among them, Dario Argento's gore-fest, *Suspiria* (1976), proved that the continental horror film was very much alive and kicking; Ridley Scott's *Alien* (1979) virtually re-invented the science fiction/horror movie, being a multimillion-dollar throwback to the days of *It! The Terror from Beyond Space*, and H.R. Giger's much-imitated space monster was a humdinger; *The Elephant Man* (1980), an evocative recreation of Victorian London stunningly shot in good old black and white, had a tremendously moving performance by John Hurt in the title role; *The Thing* (1982) and *The Fly* (1986) were decent enough remakes for a change, with innovative and gruesome effects; *Ed Wood* (1994), Tim Burton's bio-pic of the infamous director, perfectly encapsulated the '50s with its cheaper-than-cheap ethics, complemented by Martin Landau's outstanding Bela Lugosi; *Mighty Joe Young* (1999) proved that CGI effects *could* work without being too obvious (and hats off to Disney for allowing the man behind the original, Ray Harryhausen, to feature in a guest appearance); and, more recently, *The Others* (2001), a superbly creepy and extremely atmospheric ghost story that admirably achieved its results with virtually no special effects involved.

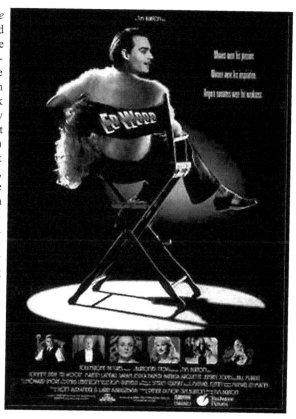

These, together with the occasional new release, keep alive the old spirit of doing things, but as the classics gradually fade into a monochrome twilight, I now have to content myself not with traveling from one cinema to another but with surfing the internet to obtain them on VHS and DVD, mostly from America where they form a considerable part of that country's cultural heritage. Now, on the latest widescreen television equipped with enhanced hi-fi sound and digital technology, I can relive once again in the comfort of my own home the days of *Indestructible Man*, *The Deadly Mantis*, *Rodan*, *The Monster Maker* and their ilk, together with most of the back catalogue of Universal International, Allied Artists, American International and others—a very far cry from The Crescent, The Embassy, The Cameo, the Odeons and the ABCs of yesteryear, maybe, but nevertheless still bringing me as much pleasure and enjoyment as they did when shown on the silver screen 40 years ago.

WHAT SHALL WE SEE TONIGHT?
(24 JANUARY 2004)

"What shall we see tonight?"

"Pardon?"

"Anything on the box?"

"I don't know. Have a look in the paper."

I do. There's nothing on the box—as usual. Time for a film, I reckon. Not a video, though—VHS is on the way out, plummeting in the popularity stakes, and I, along with most of the British public, have been converted to DVD, which I personally rate as more cinema-user friendly than a clumsy reel-to-reel length of magnetic tape housed in a bulky plastic box. Picture quality on a disc is far superior, rendering an overall sheen to even the most obscure piece of old tat from the 1930s, 1940s or 1950s, and what's more doesn't deteriorate with frequent usage. An addition to my collection has recently arrived from the States—Jerry Warren's *The Incredible Petrified World*, originally released in 1959. Apparently knocked out by the director in seven days at a paltry cost, this so-called fantasy relates the tale of four people who discover a labyrinth of tunnels under the bed of the sea when the cable of their diving bell snaps, marooning them on the ocean floor. On our 28-inch-wide flat screen television boasting crystal-clear surround-sound emanating from five speakers, linked up by god-knows how many SCART cables to a slimline top-of-the-range DVD player (cine film and projectors were so much more straightforward, even if the picture on display ranged from the passable to the awful), my wife and I sit through 70 digital minutes of Warren's uncoordinated, undisciplined, woodenly acted, poorly written bunkum, lacking in thrills, drama, decent special effects and exhibiting lousy continuity to boot. While this relic from a bygone age is unfolding before us, we both note the following:

a) John Carradine's experimental diving bell resembles a giant balloon.

b) Carradine is the only person in the film to give some semblance of acting. Robert Clarke and the rest of the outfit simply go through the motions, which isn't really surprising when you consider the state of the script.

c) When the two men and two women emerge from the bell in their diving suits, why doesn't the one chamber flood? There is no other chamber on display—the ladder leads straight from the chamber's floor to the underneath of the bell's escape hatch.

d) One of the men swims back to the diving bell, collects their belongings in a cloth bag, swims out and resurfaces in the caves. However, the clothes are bone dry when the four are next seen wearing them.

e) And if everything is, or should be, soaking wet, how do they manage to light a fire?

f) A clumsily edited insert shot of a monitor lizard doesn't match the tunnels the foursome wander through—it is probably included for shock value. If so, it fails on all counts.

g) And regarding those tunnels—Clarke and company walk up and down the same passage several times with glazed expressions on their faces, almost as if they don't really know what they are supposed to be doing.

h) Warren's camera is, in most of the scenes, stationary. His actors simply move from one side of the set to the other—a very lackadaisical method of directing if ever there was one.

i)   The boat carrying Carradine's diving bell is supposed to be in the middle of the ocean. Yet in one scene, a jetty is clearly seen in the background.

j)   The depth gauge on the boat shows two depths—500 feet and a mysterious 30. The bell separates from the cable at 1,700 feet, although the needle shows the depth to be just over the 500-foot mark.

k)   Maurice Bernard as the hermit sports the worst-looking fake beard in the history of the cinema—and could anybody seriously be expected to survive on a diet of fish for 14 years, in an environment consisting of nothing but water and rock?

l)   The melodramatic poster depicts a giant octopus menacing the divers—the only octopus featured is at the beginning when a scientist is screening footage of a fight between one of the creatures and a shark to a party of colleagues and tediously illustrating to all present the wonders of the deep. (Apparently, a hastily constructed monster octopus was assembled by Warren and his crew, but the end result was so unconvincing that it was never used and scrapped.)

The end credits appear and we exchange glances, grinning from ear to ear. Yes, it *is* undeniably dopey, but in a perverse kind of way we have enjoyed watching it. My wife turns to face me, the grin turning to a look of incredulity.

"Do you honestly mean to tell me that you actually paid to go and see *that* at the pictures?"

"Yes I did," I ruefully admit, and it does indeed seem very hard to believe that on a Sunday in December 1963, a large number of people, including myself, did take the time and the effort to visit the ABC in Falmouth one dull, wet afternoon, hand over good money at the ticket counter, settle themselves in their seats, and relax as Warren's pitiful attempt at entertainment rolled before their eyes.

Over 40 years later, I have experienced it all over again, in the technology of a new era.

A NOTE ON FILM CLASSIFICATION

On 1 January 1937, the British Board of Film Censors introduced the "H" certificate for those films deemed to contain material of a horrific, frightening or adult nature. People under the age of 16 were henceforth prevented from seeing such films, while those awarded the "A" certificate could be seen by 14-year-olds and over—if younger, you had to be accompanied by an adult. "U" films were suitable for all ages. The "H" certificate was replaced by the "X" certificate in January 1951 and all films previously classed as "H" were reclassified as "X." Some films released in the United States during the 1930s and 1940s were banned in Britain for several years or had their release dates delayed because of what the censors viewed as disturbing content. The old horror films of these two decades that surfaced in Southern England during the late 1950s and were screened up to the end of the 1960s were therefore rated as "X" or "A" films, along with their contemporaries from the 1950s onwards. I have given the relevant certification of a film as it was at the time I saw it.

Subsequent changes in times and attitudes have meant that many of these films have had their ratings downgraded—what was considered to be an adult-orientated production decades ago is now, in these more liberal times, PG rated, whereby children can view it with parental guidance. For example, 1961's *Gorgo* carried the "X" certificate and you had to be at least 16 years old to see it. The movie has now been rated as PG on the current video release. However, at the time when *Gorgo* was commercially showing in the cinemas, it was considered to be an "Adults Only" film and subsequently carries the original certificate on my listings.

FILM RATINGS

Countless science fiction, fantasy and horror films of the '30s, '40s and, in particular, the '50s, seem to be dismissed by many critics in numerous movie compendiums as being either the lowest form of entertainment or outright rubbish, the mistake being made of comparing something like *Teenage Frankenstein* to *Twelve Angry Men*, which basically is unfair. The two films belong to completely different genres and are light years apart in ideas and content. My own ratings stay within the HSFF area of the cinema and reflect not only my enjoyment of a particular film but take into consideration the merits or otherwise of direction, acting, special effects, soundtrack and the overall look and impact. Some have made more of an impression on me than others, and it is these that receive a fuller review and comment rather than the mediocre productions that have tended not to stay in the memory. Many cheaply made efforts, including the infamous low-budget B movies, are just as enjoyable in their own right as the more expensively produced ones—just because a film was made in widescreen and color does not make it any better than standard format in black and white. All ratings are obviously drawn from a particular viewer's idea of what constitutes a decent motion picture and as I am no expert in the mechanics of making a film, mine reflect these movies from the fan's or buff's point of view.

*****	Classic Entertainment—has stood the test of time
****	Excellent—very high production values
***	Good—enjoyable without too much class
**	Average—some worthwhile points to recommend it
*	Poor—deficient in practically every department

• HORROR • SCIENCE FICTION •
• FANTASY •
A personal film checklist

Abbott and Costello Meet Dr. Jekyll and Mr. Hyde
Universal 1953; 76 mins; Cert. "X"
CREDITS: Producer: Howard Christie; Director: Charles Lamont
CAST: Bud Abbott; Lou Costello; Boris Karloff; Eddie Parker; Helen Westcott; Craig Stevens
***

Two inexperienced policemen in Victorian London are assigned to catch a killer and meet up with Doctor Jekyll.

The second-best in the series of horror comedies that the silly twosome made in the late 1940s/early 1950s had Karloff playing Doctor Jekyll with relish—he is planning to murder his ward's fiancé, with the duo frantically trying to convince Scotland Yard of Jekyll's intentions. Lou Costello becomes one of the monsters by accidentally sitting on a syringe and at one point a whole load of policemen are transformed into Mister Hydes that end up chasing Abbott and Costello in Keystone Cops style—it's all great fun, and the transformation scenes incorporating Bud Westmore's makeup (the monsters look similar to Westmore's other creations in *Tarantula* and *Monster on the Campus*) were top-notch, forcing the censor at the time to grant the film an "X" certificate in Britain even though in America it played to a juvenile audience.

Abbott and Costello Meet Frankenstein
aka: Abbott and Costello Meet the Ghosts
Universal 1948; 83 mins; Cert. "X"
CREDITS: Producer: Robert Arthur; Director: Charles T. Barton
CAST: Bud Abbott; Lou Costello; Glenn Strange; Bela Lugosi; Lon Chaney Jr.; Lenore Aubert
****

Crates that arrive at a House of Horrors contain Frankenstein's monster, the Wolf Man and Dracula, and Abbott and Costello become pawns in a monstrous game.

This is the all-time great horror comedy and the two pranksters are in what was probably their best form, with Dracula reviving the Frankenstein monster in his castle and planning to control him, with the aid of a mad lady doctor played by Lenore Aubert, by using the brain of Lou Costello. His plan is thwarted by the Wolf Man, Chaney's final appearance in the role. It was also, ironically, the only other occasion that Lugosi ever played Dracula. The film works because the monsters play it straight against the duo's clowning, as though still caught up in an old Universal horror melodrama, a fact that warranted the U.K. censor awarding the film an "X" certificate when it was first released. This was the final appearance of Universal's infamous trio of monsters—they were to be replaced by the much gorier versions that Hammer Films were to produce from 1957 onwards.

"ABBOTT AND COSTELLO MEET THE GHOSTS"
LON CHANEY • BELA LUGOSI • GLENN STRANGE
A UNIVERSAL-INTERNATIONAL PICTURE   G.F.D. RELEASE

The Abominable Snowman
Hammer/20th Century Fox 1957; Regalscope; 91 mins; Cert. "A"
CREDITS: Producer: Aubrey Baring; Director: Val Guest
CAST: Forrest Tucker; Peter Cushing; Robert Brown; Maureen Connell; Richard Wattis; Arnold Marle ***

Against the wishes of his wife, a botanist decides to join forces with a ruthless American and his expedition to locate the Yeti in the Himalayas.

The last of the '50s series of films concerning the Abominable Snowman, this was an intelligent, rather restrained telling of the Yeti fable from Hammer, benefiting from Nigel *Quatermass* Kneale's screenplay and Val Guest's direction. Forrest Tucker was the imported American actor on this occasion, the bombastic leader of an expedition to find the Yetis and clashing with botanist Peter Cushing, as he wants to exploit the creatures for profit after they have been captured. This is at odds with Cushing's own belief that they should be studied in their own environment. The Yetis are depicted as benign, wise beings that can communicate by telepathy, and after one of their number is killed by Robert Brown, the expedition is wiped out and Tucker is buried under an avalanche in reprisal. Cushing is left in peace, the Yetis knowing him to be friendly, and before disappearing into the mountains, all memory of them is erased from Cushing's mind. Thoughtful and talkative, with some compelling black and white photography of the snowbound landscapes, this adaptation of Kneale's 1955 television play *The Creature* was significant in having the horrors toned down, in marked contrast to Hammer's run of X-rated features during this period, and the movie remains one of the company's more laudable efforts from the 1950s.

The Alligator People
20th Century Fox 1959; Cinemascope; 74 mins; Cert. "X"
CREDITS: Producer: Jack Leewood; Director: Roy del Ruth
CAST: Bruce Bennett; Beverly Garland; George Macready; Lon Chaney Jr.; Richard Crane; Frieda Inescort ***

A scientist invents a serum concocted from alligator fluid in the hope that disabled people will grow new limbs, but only succeeds in creating scaly, monstrous humans.

An above average, fast-moving B feature that went the rounds with *Return of the Fly* in the early 1960s on the Sunday circuit. Nurse Beverly Garland, who relates her story under hypnosis to two doctors, plays a bride whose husband, Richard Crane, mysteriously vanishes on their honeymoon. Years later, she traces him to his ancestral home, a remote estate in Louisiana surrounded by swamps, where she discovers that before they married, her husband had survived a terrible accident in a plane crash by acting as a guinea pig for Bruce Bennett's experimental serum, produced from alligator fluid, that replaced damaged and missing limbs. However, the treatment has gruesome side-effects, as Crane begins to turn distinctly reptilian with a liking for human flesh and needs radiation treatment from Bennett's gamma-ray machine to try to prevent him from transforming into one of the creatures that the fluid is derived from. In the film's frenetic climax, demented, alligator-hating Lon Chaney, who lusts after Garland, sabotages the laboratory equipment, causing Crane to mutate into a marauding alligator-man—he eventually sinks to his death in a swamp as his horrified wife looks on. Similar in tone to Fox's *The Fly*, this was a well-made monster movie for its time with some fairly striking makeup and a winning performance from Garland as the distraught wife who uncovers her husband's dreadful secret.

The Amazing Colossal Man
American Intl. 1957; 80 mins; Cert. "A"
CREDITS: Producer/Director: Bert I. Gordon
CAST: Glenn Langan; William Hudson; Cathy Downs; James Seay; Russ Bender; Judd Holdren
***

An army officer who becomes accidentally exposed to a massive dose of radiation following a plutonium bomb explosion grows into a 60-foot giant.

This was without doubt Bert I. Gordon's best-remembered and most successful film and a favorite on the American drive-in circuit, even though, as with all of his other productions, the special effects ranged from the passable to the downright abysmal, with a flamboyant poster promising far more than the movie delivered. After exposure to the radiation, Glenn Langan is taken to a secret military base and kept under guard as he begins to outgrow his surroundings, and even his wife is prevented from seeing him. Once on the loose, the footage of the 60-foot, bad-tempered Langan (who actually turns in a sensitive performance) in a loincloth strolling through Las Vegas, venting his anger by picking up toy cars and wrecking buildings, is not too bad, but the scenes of him pulling out of his foot a giant syringe full of shrinking serum which his friends hope will reduce his size are so ineptly handled that they are laughable. Although at the end the Colossal Man plunges to his supposed death off the Hoover Dam after being blasted by the military, the film was a big hit in the United States and he was back the next year in the follow-up, *War of the Colossal Beast*.

The Amazing Transparent Man
American Intl. 1959; 56 mins; Cert. "U"
CREDITS: Producer: Lester D. Guthrie; Director: Edgar G. Ulmer
CAST: Douglas Kennedy; Marguerite Chapman; James Griffith; Ivan Triesault; Carmel Daniel; Red Morgan **

A criminal and a scientist who have invented a formula to make men invisible use the treatment on a safecracker sprung from jail so that he can steel radium and rob banks undetected to further their experiments.

A very cheap-looking production with one or two flashes of inspiration, especially in the scenes where Douglas Kennedy as the invisible man is on the run from the police and fellow convicts and uses his invisibility to evade capture. James Griffith is the criminal who, in cahoots with scientist Ivan Triesault, plans to create hundreds of invisible people to enable him to take over the world and uses Kennedy as a guinea pig in his experiments, instructing him to break into banks to finance their operations. Using ideas plundered from dozens of other similar movies, and one of the last features to be directed by Ulmer, this quickie was rarely seen in the United

Kingdom and not released until 1963, when it was double billed with another equally long-forgotten film from that period, Nathan Juran's *Flight of the Lost Balloon*.

The Animal World
Warner Bros. 1955; Technicolor; 82 mins; Cert. "U"
CREDITS: Producer/Director: Irwin Allen; Special Effects: Willis O'Brien and Ray Harryhausen; Narrated by Theodore Von Eltz and John Storm **

A semi-documentary charting the evolution of the animal kingdom, including animated dinosaur sequences.

A real oddity this—the only interest really to fantasy fans were the various dinosaurs animated by Harryhausen and O'Brien in the prehistoric section of the film, including an Allosaurus and Brontosaurus, but these were among the poorest of both of their work and shot very quickly because of the film's low budget and time constraints. Large mechanical models were used for close-ups of the monsters fighting, which were even more unrealistic, although some of these scenes were deemed too frightening for a younger audience and suffered at the hands of the censor prior to general release. This was undoubtedly one of Harryhausen's lesser and least-seen efforts, appearing as second feature to *World Without End* in some cinemas during 1965/1966.

Around the World Under the Sea
MGM 1966; Panavision/Metrocolor; 120 mins; Cert. "U"
CREDITS: Producer/Director: Andrew Marton
CAST: Lloyd Bridges; Shirley Eaton; Brian Kelly; Keenan Wynn; David McCallum; Marshall Thompson **

Movements in the Earth's crust produce tidal waves and a super submarine is sent on a mission to plant various sonar devices on the ocean floor to warn of further catastrophes.

This substandard Jules Verne-type fantasy is an earnest but ultimately dull, long-winded production where the script takes over from the action, even though it has a better than average cast and was filmed in attractive locations off the coast of Florida and in the Caribbean. Constant bickering between the male cast over the one female crew member, Shirley Eaton, does not make for good cinema, and the only monster the hydronauts have to battle with is a gigantic moray eel, as well as an active underwater volcano. The submarine itself is well designed though. A big expensive flop when first released.

The Astounding She-Monster
Hollywood Intl. Pictures/American Intl. 1958; 62 mins; Cert. "A"
CREDITS: Producer/Director: Ronnie Ashcroft
CAST: Robert Clarke; Shirley Kilpatrick; Ewing Brown; Kenne Duncan; Marilyn Harvey; Jeanne Tatum **

A female alien arrives on Earth with peaceful intentions but is greeted with hostility.

An infamous low-budget quickie reputedly filmed in less than a week, with Ed Wood Jr. an uncredited consultant, starring Shirley Kilpatrick as the glowing, shimmering but very attractive alien in a skin-tight spacesuit surrounded by a force field, appearing in a forest in the Sierra Madre to preach the word of peace. She encounters wealthy heiress Marilyn Harvey in geologist Robert Clarke's mountain cabin, who has been kidnapped by gangster Kenne Duncan and his cohorts. Killing one of the gang members by her radioactive touch, she is consequently treated as a menace by the other occupants of the lodge. Clarke finally throws an acid bomb at the alien, which melts through her protective metal suit, causing her to disintegrate. After she perishes, her locket is found, validating her mission of goodwill by inviting Earth to join the Council of Planets who have been monitoring our galaxy for decades and wish to eliminate Earth's problems. Kilpatrick's curious way of walking backwards in many of her scenes was apparently the result of her spacesuit being torn and the production team, adhering to a tight shooting schedule, not having the time to repair it! With an over-the-top poster showing the so-called monster to be a cross between Marilyn Monroe and Diana Dors, this camp classic is right up there with 1954's *Devil Girl from Mars* as one of the most unintentionally hilarious female-alien pictures of all time.

Atlantis the Lost Continent
MGM 1961; Metrocolor; 90 mins; Cert. "A"
CREDITS: Producer/Director: George Pal
CAST: Anthony Hall; Joyce Taylor; John Dall; Ed Platt; Frank De Kova; Jay Novello **

A Greek fisherman rescues a young girl who is a princess and travels with her to the lost island of Atlantis.

This ranks as one of George Pal's poorer productions, a hodgepodge of ideas—mad scientists on Atlantis, death rays, moral decadence—and mediocre model work, with footage pinched from *Quo Vadis* to bolster up the action. Anthony Hall is wooden in the role of the young fisherman who rescues Joyce Taylor from a raft and takes her back to an Atlantis ruled by evil John Dall and his minions—he ends up in chains with other slaves, cowed into submission by hypnosis and working in the mines for the minerals needed for Dall's war effort against the rest of the world. The only impressive scenes are at the end, depicting the destruction of Atlantis by a volcanic eruption as Hall escapes to freedom with the princess after leading a rebellion. The film was beset by production problems and not screened in England until the mid-'60s, when it made little impact at the box office.

The Atomic Submarine
Allied Artists 1959; 72 mins; Cert. "A"
CREDITS: Producer: Alex Gordon; Director: Spencer G. Bennet
CAST: Arthur Franz; Brett Halsey; Dick Foran; Tom Conway; Paul Dubov; Bob Steele ***

A submarine sent to investigate the mysterious destruction of shipping in northern waters discovers a flying saucer under the North Pole, piloted by a huge, one-eyed alien intent on taking over the Earth.

Although obviously filmed on a low budget, with much use of newsreel footage (an old stand-by in many of these bargain-basement films), this is a fast-paced little thriller with passable special effects, particularly the scenes of the submarine approaching the flying saucer under the Polar ice cap and the weird, Cyclopean alien with tentacles inside the craft that is intent on invading the Earth and mating, somehow, with Earth women! After lengthy discussions between the crew and the alien, who intones his messages in a very peculiar Shakespearean accent, Commander Brett Halsey blows up the saucer and the alien as it attempts to re-fuel on magnetism from the North Pole, thus saving the world.

Attack of the Crab Monsters

Allied Artists 1957; 70 mins; Cert. "X"

CREDITS: Producer/Director: Roger Corman

CAST: Richard Garland; Pamela Duncan; Russell Johnson; Leslie Bradley; Beech Dickerson; Mel Welles ***

A rescue party sent to a small island to bring back a group of scientists apparently in peril discover that giant mutated crabs have devoured the island's occupants and absorbed their minds.

An early Roger Corman movie that was one of the more successful from this period of his career. The crabs have become mutated by radiation in the seawater and after killing the scientists on the island, consume their heads, luring other victims by using the exact voices of the people that they have devoured. High-voltage electricity fails to kill the monsters and at the end of the film, only one crab, which has become pregnant, is left with three surviving humans on the rapidly sinking island that has been undermined by the crabs. Considering the low budget, the giant crustaceans are quite impressively realized in a fast-moving and inventive monster film that was usually featured with the director's *Not of this Earth* on the Sunday circuit in 1964.

Attack of the 50 Foot Woman

Allied Artists 1958; 66 mins; Cert. "X"

CREDITS: Producer: Bernard Woolner; Director: Nathan Hertz (Nathan Juran)

CAST: Allison Hayes; William Hudson; Yvette Vickers; Roy Gordon; Ken Terrell; George Douglas *

A giant alien lands in the desert, captures a woman and genetically alters her so that she grows to an enormous size.

A cheaply produced turkey, one of the worst films that the normally reliable Nathan Juran ever directed. It concerns Allison Hayes, just released from a mental institution, who tries to convince her philandering husband that she saw an alien spacecraft in the mountains, only for

him to flee when the alien approaches, leaving Hayes to her fate as the alien experiments on her and causes her to start growing at an alarming rate. The production has very little to recommend it—abysmal special effects and poor process work abound, reminding one of a Bert I. Gordon movie, especially the 50-foot woman's ludicrous plastic hand searching for both victims and her adulterous husband and the bald, unrealistic alien in the spacecraft. After killing her husband and wrecking the local town, Hayes eventually perishes on power lines. The film is best remembered now for its memorably tacky title—nothing else. Nevertheless, it was a popular enough addition to the pictures circulating on the Sunday one-day circuit in the early '60s, usually double billed with other Allied Artists productions such as *The Hypnotic Eye* and *House on Haunted Hill.*

Attack of the Puppet People
aka: 6 Inches Tall
American Intl. 1958; 79 mins; Cert. "A"
CREDITS: Producer/Director: Bert I. Gordon
CAST: John Agar; John Hoyt; June Kenny; Michael Mark; Ken Miller; Susan Gordon ***
A mad doll maker shrinks people to a few inches tall as a cure for his loneliness, placing them in marionette shows against their will.

Bert I. Gordon, instead of blowing up his actors to enormous proportions as in most of his other infamous productions, shrunk them in size for a change, but this movie is a bit slow-moving and fails to capitalize on John Hoyt's motives for reducing humans to the size of dolls, although old age and loneliness is hinted at. June Kenny starts work as Hoyt's new secretary and falls for his business associate, John Agar. Agar then mysteriously disappears, and when Kenny finds him, he has been miniaturized to a height of six inches by the doll maker's ray machine. Kenny meets the same fate, the lovers are reunited and form a rebellion with the other shrunken people to overthrow Hoyt and regain their normal height. This was a more cohesive piece of work than some of Gordon's other, shoddier features, although not in the same league as Universal's *The Incredible Shrinking Man,* the benchmark movie on this particular theme.

The Awful Doctor Orloff
aka: The Demon Doctor
Hispamer/Sigma 3 (Spain/France) 1961; 86 mins; Cert. "X"
CREDITS: Producer: Serge Newman; Director: Jesus Franco
CAST: Howard Vernon; Conrado San Martin; Perla Cristal; Maria Silva; Richard Valle; Diana Lorys ****
A deranged doctor captures young women, drains them of blood and skins them in an attempt to restore his daughter's disfigured face.

Jesus Franco's film heralded a new kind of medical science fiction/horror sub-genre—full of sadism, eroticism, torture and sleaze, these movies were a mixture of the more extreme parts of the Hammer horror productions coupled with the sadistic surgery of films such as Franju's *Eyes Without A Face.* Many of these pictures were made on the Continent by Spanish, French and Italian directors, who appreciated the fact that audiences there reveled in these films and they flourished for more than a decade, petering out in the 1970s. In the film, Howard Vernon kidnaps young women with the aid of his blind hunchback assistant Morpho, who then has the task of disposing of the bodies after Vernon has finished with them, a job that he (and the camera) relishes. Morpho kills his master at the end after Vernon has murdered his lover/assistant, whom the hunchback secretly desires—Morpho is then shot dead by the police. All this is played out to the usual weird foreign soundtrack that was a hallmark of this particular type of production. In England, this admittedly stylish film featuring fine black and white photography generally went the rounds as *The Demon Doctor,* atrociously dubbed and with some of the more gratuitously violent scenes missing, appearing at selected cinemas in 1964 on a double bill with *Varan the Unbelievable.*

Back from the Dead
Regal Intl./20th Century Fox 1957; Regalscope; 79 mins; Cert. "X"
CREDITS: Producer: Robert Stabler; Director: Charles Marquis Warren
CAST: Arthur Franz; Peggie Castle; Marsha Hunt; Don Haggerty; Evelyn Scott; Otto Reichow
**

A young woman on her honeymoon is possessed by the spirit of her husband's first wife.

A very dull film about possession, reincarnation and black magic, flatly directed by Warren, who was also responsible for the equally flaccid *The Unknown Terror*. Peggie Castle plays the young wife on her honeymoon taken over by the spirit of Arthur Franz's first wife, who was an evil seducer of men. The person responsible for the possession is Otto Reichow, the head of a satanic cult on the island where they are staying and who is preparing Castle to be a human sacrifice. Marsha Hunt is the wife's sister who eventually brings about the downfall of Reichow and his followers. The combination of ideas in this production was interesting enough, but the handling was let down by the director, who made a real mess out of what could have been an excellent movie.

Barbarella
DeLaurentis/Marianne/Paramount (France/Italy) 1967; Panavision/Technicolor; 98 mins; Cert. "X"
CREDITS: Producer: Dino de Laurentis; Director: Roger Vadim
CAST: Jane Fonda; John Phillip Law; Milo O'Shea; Anita Pallenberg; David Hemmings; Claude Dauphin ***

In the 44th century, space heroine Barbarella is ordered by Earth's president to capture and sabotage the Positronic Ray machine that has fallen into the hands of a lunatic on Planet 16 who could use it to destroy the universe.

A multimillion-dollar *Flash Gordon* is how some critics described this garish, loud, flamboyant, elephantine tribute by Roger Vadim to his (then) wife's sexual attributes. Jane Fonda plays Barbarella, crashing her spaceship onto Planet 16, teaming up with a blind angel (John Phillip Law) and David Hemmings as a resistance leader, and ending up in Milo O'Shea's Orgasmatron, a machine that can kill through too much sexual ecstasy. After many lurid adventures, the climax sees the Positronic Ray machine destroyed and Fonda rescued by Law as Sogo, the city where O'Shea had his empire, is engulfed by a living lake that feeds off evil. Very '60s in its look (the '50s would never have come up with anything like this), the film quickly gained a cult following because of its outlandish sets and design, not to mention the sexual vibes, but the fact remained that the sheer indulgence of it all paled at times and many sci-fi fans were put off by its camp, comic strip leanings. The most effective scene in the whole production is near the beginning when Fonda is attacked by an army of razor-toothed dolls—*Child's Play* was one of a number of later horror movies to capitalize on this creepy sequence. Despite its shortcomings, the film was highly successful when first released.

The Bat
Allied Artists 1959; 80 mins; Cert. "A"
CREDITS: Producer: C.J. Tevlin; Director: Crane Wilbur
CAST: Vincent Price; Agnes Moorehead; John Sutton; Lenita Lane; Elaine Edwards; Gavin Gordon **

A writer of mystery novels rents an old house and finds herself and her guests menaced by a maniac.

One of Vincent Price's weakest films; in fact it resembles for the most part a tired, clapped out Agatha Christie stage play, with all of the guests nervously looking over their shoulders as the killer roams around the house, hoping to scare everybody away so that he/she can search for a hidden fortune, only revealing themselves in the form of a pair of clawed gloves, which go for the jugular vein. Old-fashioned, stagy, lacking in suspense and too talkative, with only

Agnes Moorehead turning in a reasonable performance as the old lady of the house, who unmasks Gavin Gordon as the killer in the final reel.

Battle Beneath the Earth
MGM 1968; Metrocolor; 91 mins; Cert. "U"
CREDITS: Producer: Charles Reynolds; Director: Montgomery Tully
CAST: Kerwin Mathews; Martin Benson; Viviane Ventura; Robert Ayres; Peter Arne; Bessie Love *
The Chinese attempt to invade the United States by tunneling under the continent from a base in the Pacific using laser beams.
A tedious mixture of '60s-style science fiction and sub-James Bond, with a wooden Kerwin Mathews as head of the American forces fighting off the threat of an invasion by the Red Chinese, led by Martin Benson, who are boring tunnels under America from the Pacific seabed. After several noisy battles with laser guns and ray guns taking place in unconvincing underground sets, Mathews detonates a trainload of atom bombs among the invaders and annihilates them. A very unattractive picture indeed from MGM that had a distinctly dated look about it even at the time it was made, with its accent on gadgets and Reds under the bed.

The Beast from 20,000 Fathoms
Warner Bros. 1953; 80 mins; Cert. "X"
CREDITS: Producers: Hal Chester and Jack Dietz; Director: Eugene Lourie; Special Effects: Ray Harryhausen
CAST: Paul Christian; Cecil Kellaway; Paula Raymond; Kenneth Tobey; Lee Van Cleef; King Donovan ****
Awakened from its lair by atomic bomb testing in the Arctic, a prehistoric monster heads south to its ancestral breeding grounds in modern-day New York.
This was Ray Harryhausen's first major feature film in which he took sole charge of the special effects, and also the first of the giant monster-awakes movies that proliferated during the 1950s. After thawing out from the ice, the monster heads south to the Hudson River basin near New York, with Paul Christian, who has caught a glimpse of the beast, having a hard time convincing the authorities of its existence. There are some impressive effects for the time *The Beast* was made—the dinosaur (a Rhedosaurus) rearing up out of the sea and dragging down a cargo boat, the scene where it demolishes a lighthouse, and the climax where the beast rampages through the New York streets, finally meeting a fiery end in a blazing Coney Island amusement park after being shot with a radioactive harpoon. Veteran character actor Cecil Kellaway turns in an engaging performance as an elderly professor who loses his life when the bathysphere he is in gets too close to the monster for comfort. Despite some misgivings at Warner Bros., the film was a huge and unexpected success made on a relatively low budget, with most of the available finances spent on Harryhausen's effects. After disappearing off the cinema circuits for a number of years, the film was re-released in 1967 on a double bill with *Rebel Without A Cause*.

The Beast of Hollow Mountain
Nassour Bros./United Artists (Mexico) 1956;
Regiscope/DeLuxeColor; 80 mins;
Cert. "A"
CREDITS: Producers: Edward and William
Nassour; Directors: Edward Nassour and Ismael
Rodriguez
CAST: Guy Madison; Patricia Medina; Carlos
Rivas; Eduardo Noriega; Julio Villareal; Pascual
Garcia Pena **

In Mexico, an American rancher investigates a series of deaths among cattle and comes across a Tyrannosaurus Rex living in a mountainous area surrounded by swamps.

Guy Madison is the rancher who thinks that his business rival is to blame for his missing cattle, despite the locals believing that something lurking in the nearby mountain is responsible. After a great deal of talking going on, it takes 50 minutes for the monster to make its appearance and when it does it's a major disappointment. The not very large dinosaur is a poorly animated model compared to anything that Ray Harryhausen conjured up, with fuzzy background photography not helping either. After the beast goes on a rampage and attacks the cowboys, Madison eventually lures the monster into the swamp, where it becomes trapped and dies. The film was based on an idea by Willis O'Brien, with cowboys combating a prehistoric monster, and was more or less remade in 1969 by Harryhausen himself as *The Valley of Gwangi*.

The Beast of Yucca Flats
Cardoza/Francis/Crown Intl. 1961; 59 mins; Cert. "X"
CREDITS: Producers: Anthony Cardoza and Coleman Francis; Director: Coleman Francis
CAST: Tor Johnson; Douglas Mellor; Barbara Francis; Bing Stafford; Conrad Brooks; Larry Aten *

A Russian scientist being pursued by agents after defecting to the United States becomes a murderous fiend following exposure to radiation in an A-bomb testing area.

An amateurishly presented, extremely dull-looking thriller, one of a number that ex-Swedish wrestler Tor Johnson made in his short movie career, mostly with the Ed Wood entourage and usually cast as the monster with little or no dialogue—in fact, he doesn't utter a single word in the film, only a series of grunts and snarls. At least he more or less had the main billing in this cheapie, which is itself worthy of a Wood production, boasting wooden acting, appalling continuity and an excruciatingly awful voice-over narration standing in for the script—the jarring soundtrack music is terrible as well. After being exposed to radiation while on the run, Johnson turns into a deranged killer, running around in the desert with a large stick, hiding in a cave and embarking on a killing spree until he is shot dead by the police. There is one scene at the very beginning involving the rape and murder of a girl that bears no relation whatsoever to the remainder of the so-called action—it was that kind of movie, made apparently on the lowest of budgets, completed in a rush by Cardoza and Francis as their funds for the project ran out, and often cited as one of the worst science fiction features ever made.

The Beast with A Million Eyes
ARC/American Intl. 1955; 78 mins; Cert. "A"
CREDITS: Producer: Roger Corman; Director: David Kramarsky
CAST: Paul Birch; Lorna Thayer; Chester Conklin; Donna Cole; Richard Sargeant; Leonard Tarver **

An alien intelligence lands in the desert and takes over the minds of the animals in the area, which then attack humans.

Produced on a paltry budget by Roger Corman, with a lavish poster that promised the audience far more than anything that was actually seen on the big screen, this early effort from American International is probably remembered more for its lurid title than anything else. There are no otherworldly beings or beasts on view as such, although the desert locations exude a certain amount of gloomy atmosphere and menace as various animals that are possessed by the alien and fed on hate attack the main cast. The alien, changed into a rodent at the end of the film, is defeated by thoughts of love as it tries to possess a young courting couple, an emotion that it hates, and it is eventually carried away by an eagle and destroyed.

The Beast with 5 Fingers
Warner Bros. 1946; 90 mins; Cert. "A"
CREDITS: Producer: William Jacobs; Director: Robert Florey
CAST: Peter Lorre; Andrea King; Robert Alda; Victor Francen; J. Carrol Naish; Pedro de Cordoba **
The severed hand of a concert pianist returns from the grave to commit murder.
A big budget, good cast and attractive Italian locations cannot disguise the fact that this is simply not a very creepy or suspenseful film, even though the sight of the hand scuttling around the set is quite telling. A mad master pianist, Victor Francen, tries to strangle his assistant Peter Lorre because of his jealous feelings toward his nurse and later dies in a fall. His severed left hand returns from the grave, killing the contesters of his will, as he has left his estate to his nurse. The ending, when Lorre is revealed as the killer and the hand is a hallucination, is a complete let-down and in fact the actor later criticized Warner Bros. for their handling of this story, stating that it should have been a lot scarier than it turned out to be—it certainly isn't up to the standards set by Universal with their horror fare. The film was being shown at selected cinemas in 1965, double billed with *The Walking Dead.*

Before I Hang
Columbia 1940; 62 mins; Cert. "A"
CREDITS: Producer: Wallace MacDonald; Director: Nick Grinde
CAST: Boris Karloff; Evelyn Keyes; Edward Van Sloan; Bruce Bennett; Don Beddoe; Pedro de Cordoba **
A mad doctor injects himself with an experimental rejuvenation serum to try to find a cure for death and transforms himself into a murderer.
An uninspiring melodrama that was one of a number of fairly predictable "mad doctor" movies that Karloff churned out for Columbia Pictures, all on the familiar theme of restoring one's youth or trying to find a cure for dying. Here he plays Dr. John Garth, sentenced to death for a mercy killing. When he is surprisingly released from prison on the promise that he discontinue his experiments, he administers the serum on himself, becoming youthful once it has taken effect and then changing into a killer, as the serum contained the blood of a convicted murderer. Karloff turns in his customary demented but solid performance, a kind of Jekyll-Hyde character, before being finished off at the end by Bruce Bennett.

Beginning of the End
Republic/AB-PT Productions 1957; Horrorscope; 74 mins; Cert. "A"
CREDITS: Producer/Director: Bert I. Gordon
CAST: Peter Graves; Peggie Castle; James Seay; Thomas B. Henry; Morris Ankrum; Than Wyeen **
Oversized fruit grown in Illinois, modified through radiation treatment by an experimental department of agriculture, cause a pack of locusts that ate the fruit to mutate into giants and attack Chicago.
One of the last of Republic's films, this was a very amateurish-looking Bert I. Gordon picture with low production values featuring back-projected insects fighting the army or swarming over

model buildings, and even photographs of buildings, all to no great effect—in fact, it contains some of the clumsiest trick-work of any of this director's movies. The build-up isn't too bad—trashed vehicles, a town destroyed with no bodies found, a wrecked warehouse that contained food, and snoopy reporter Peggie Castle on the trail of a government cover-up. The opening sequence showing one of the colossal locusts devouring a mute scientist is well staged even by these standards, but from then on the film becomes a risible exercise in low-grade effects and poor process work, with clusters of the bug-eyed menaces scuttling unconvincingly through Chicago's streets. The ending is ridiculous as well, with scientist Peter Graves luring the creatures into Lake Michigan like lemmings, after recording and playing back their mating calls from a boat. This also prevents the military from dropping an atomic bomb on the city to wipe out the monsters, an idea even more preposterous than the hilarious climax.

Behemoth the Sea Monster
aka: The Giant Behemoth
Allied Artists 1958; 80 mins; Cert. "X"
CREDITS: Producer: Ted Lloyd; Directors: Eugene Lourie and Douglas Hickox; Special Effects: Willis O'Brien and Peter Peterson
CAST: Gene Evans; Andre Morell; Henry Vidon; Jack MacGowran; Leigh Madison; John Turner ***

A giant radioactive prehistoric monster, awakened by A-bomb tests, attacks London.

The '50s cycle of "dinosaur on the loose" movies virtually came to an end with this above-average effort directed by Eugene Lourie, who was the man behind the first of such films—*The Beast from 20,000 Fathoms*. Willis O'Brien was brought in to work on the special effects with Peter Peterson and the scenes of the dinosaur (a Palaeosaurus) rearing up out of the Thames, smashing cranes and roaming the city streets, charring humans with its radioactive rays, and the obligatory "monster crashing into electric pylons" shots, are well executed, even though it takes nearly 45 minutes for the beast to fully appear. Less convincing is the phony-looking monster head used when the creature is attacking a ferryboat, which does not resemble the head of the animated monster in the slightest. The dinosaur is killed at the end by a radioactive torpedo fired by Gene Evans in a mini-submarine. Somewhat strangely, the film was severely cut soon after release, with many of O'Brien's sequences of the monster in the London streets missing, together with footage of the victims with radiation burns also omitted, and it was given an "A" certificate, probably because Allied Artists wanted the film to appeal to a wider audience, even in a shortened form. It was possible at one time in the early 1960s to catch both versions at the cinema, the original X-rated movie (which went the rounds with *Blood of the Vampire*), and the "A" version containing the censor's cuts.

Beneath the Planet of the Apes
20th Century Fox 1970; Panavision/DeLuxeColor; 95 mins; Cert. "A"
CREDITS: Producer: Arthur P. Jacobs; Director: Ted Post
CAST: James Franciscus; Linda Harrison; Charlton Heston; Kim Hunter; Victor Buono; Maurice Evans ***

In the far distant future, telepathic mutants ruled by apes live underground and worship a doomsday bomb.

The first of the four sequels to the successful *Planet of the Apes* was the best, even though most of the action was confined to the subterranean remains of New York and the film became a bit claustrophobic as a result. James Franciscus is the lead astronaut on this occasion, appearing in the year 3955 A.D. in search of Charlton Heston and discovering a society of apes in a constant state of argument (as in the first film) while mutated humans capable of telepathy worship the alpha-omega atom bomb. Franciscus meets Heston, who has become unhinged, and after the apes have had a pitched battle with the humans, the astronaut detonates the bomb, annihilating the Earth. The originality of *Planet of the Apes* was missing from this production and there was too much sermonizing from the apes, which dragged the film down slightly, but the underground set designs and color were impressive and the movie was another big hit for Fox, with three more sequels following.

Berserk!
Columbia 1967; Technicolor; 96 mins; Cert. "X"
CREDITS: Producer: Herman Cohen; Director: Jim O'Connolly
CAST: Joan Crawford; Ty Hardin; Michael Gough; Diana Dors; Judy Geeson; Robert Hardy
**

A series of sensational murders at a circus boosts profits, but the owner is the main suspect behind the killings.

An aging Joan Crawford, in a series of unbecoming skimpy costumes that she is obviously too old to wear, plays the owner of a circus where various horrific murders take place. She is the main suspect but not, in the end, the killer, who turns out to be her demented, sexually repressed daughter, Judy Geeson, who was abused as a child by her mother. This was an unattractive, poor man's version of Anglo's *Circus of Horrors*, with a great deal of footage of the real-life Billy Smart's Circus and some horrific killings, such as Diana Dors being sawn in half and Ty Hardin falling onto a bed of spikes. Even Crawford's hammy performance and a solid British support cast could not prevent this from being just another crudely made exploitation movie.

Beyond the Time Barrier
Pacific Intl./American Intl. 1960; 75 mins; Cert. "A"
CREDITS: Producer: Robert Clarke; Director: Edgar G. Ulmer
CAST: Robert Clarke; Darlene Tompkins; Vladimir Sokoloff; John van Dreelan; Arianne Arden; Stephen Bekassy **

A pilot testing an experimental hypersonic aircraft is blasted into the future to the year 2024 and finds himself in a world devastated by a nuclear plague.

A cheaply made but entertaining fantasy that was one of Edgar G. Ulmer's more worthwhile efforts and clearly modeled on Allied Artists' *World Without End*. B movie stalwart Robert Clarke is the pilot breaking through the fifth dimension and arriving on an Earth decimated by a nuclear war in 1971. As in *World Without End*, the peaceful but sterile inhabitants have retreated underground and live in a series of catacombs, while mutants from the war roam the surface. Clarke falls in love with Darlene Tompkins after she rescues him from the mutants' clutches, and eventually helps the Citadel People defeat the mutants. He then returns to his own time by using the "reverse relativity paradox" procedure on his aircraft. Fun to watch in spite of the cardboard sets and wooden acting, the movie turned up on a double bill with *The Hideous Sun Demon* in 1964.

The Birds
Universal 1963; Technicolor; 119 mins; Cert. "X"
CREDITS: Producer/Director: Alfred Hitchcock
CAST: Rod Taylor; Tippi Hedren; Jessica Tandy; Suzanne Pleshette; Charles McGraw; Doodles Weaver ****

On the California coast at Bodega Bay, the inhabitants are suddenly attacked by the local bird population for no apparent reason.

Despite poor color, some distinctly dodgy background process shots, and a drawn out "will they, won't they" love scenario between Rod Taylor and Tippi Hedren, *The Birds* remains one of Hitchcock's key works and also one of his biggest successes. It includes scenes of genuine terror, including the birds' attack on the schoolchildren and the two-minute assault on Hedren in the house, a sequence that took a week to film and had the actress on the brink of a nervous collapse (much, apparently, to Hitchcock's hidden glee). The film does not offer an explanation for the birds' behavior and has no proper ending as such—Taylor and Hedren simply drive away from the house where they have been attacked as the birds cluster in the thousands around the countryside. It is the inherent fear of what would happen if our feathered friends went berserk that Hitchcock cleverly tapped into in this film, rather than a straightforward narrative, and this undoubtedly made it such a hit at the time. It was also the last truly great movie that Hitchcock would make and one of the few suspense films to benefit from having no musical score—only the sound of the birds is heard throughout the picture.

The Black Castle
Universal 1952; 82 mins; Cert. "A"
CREDITS: Producer: William Alland; Director: Nathan Juran
CAST: Boris Karloff; Stephen McNally; Richard Greene; John Hoyt; Lon Chaney Jr.; Paula Corday **

An 18th-century knight avenges the deaths of two of his friends who have died on the whim of a sadistic Viennese Count.

The film is a slow-moving remake of *The Most Dangerous Game* with not enough horror or thrills to sustain much interest, although the sets are lavish enough. A young Richard Greene (in the days before he played Robin Hood on British television) infiltrates the Count's (McNally) castle, complete with torture chambers and a moat full of crocodiles, to avenge the deaths of his comrades, and falls in love with the Count's wife. Karloff is a doctor who helps them escape from McNally's clutches by administering to them a cataleptic drug that gives the appearance of death. Karloff looked completely out of place in this dull, Gothic melodrama that was the first film to be directed by the prolific Nathan Juran.

The Black Cat
aka: House of Doom
Universal 1934; 65 mins; Cert. "X"
CREDITS: Producer: Carl Laemmle Jr.; Director: Edgar G. Ulmer
CAST: Bela Lugosi; Boris Karloff; Jacqueline Wells; David Manners; Herman Bing; Lucille Lund ***

A revengeful doctor with a fear of cats, released from prison after 15 years, hunts down the Satanist who has ruined both his family and his country.

A bizarre exercise in occult terror featuring Universal's two top horror stars in good form, alternating between stylish and stagy, with a convoluted plot that went straight over the heads of much of the audiences of the day and an intrusive semi-classical soundtrack that jars after a while. Karloff is the Satanist and avant-garde architect presiding over a weird, Germanic-looking fortress, practicing Devil worship in his private chapel and hypnotizing David Manners' wife (played by Jacqueline Wells) to be his next ritualistic sacrifice. He also keeps the preserved corpse of the doctor's dead wife in a glass coffin for good measure, and has taken his daughter to be his mistress. Eventually Lugosi, on the side of good for a change, saves Wells from sacrifice and manacles Karloff to a beam, peeling off his skin with a scalpel in revenge. Lugosi is then inadvertently shot by Manners, who flees the place with his wife as the fortress is blown sky-high by the dying doctor. The picture was heavily censored in Britain, with all references to Devil-worshipping cut from the print, and was not a particular success in the United States, as audiences wanted their horror stars to be in more straightforward productions, which after this oddity, they were.

Black Friday
Universal 1940; 70 mins; Cert. "A"
CREDITS: Producer: Burt Kelly; Director: Arthur Lubin
CAST: Boris Karloff; Bela Lugosi; Anne Gwynne; Stanley Ridges; Anne Nagel; Paul Fix **
A surgeon transfers a gangster's brain into a professor injured in a car crash and then persuades him that he is the gangster so that he can locate a cache of hidden money.
Black Friday was an uneasy mix of horror and gangster melodrama that had Stanley Bridges playing the professor who, after Karloff has operated on him, becomes an insane Jekyll-Hyde type schizophrenic. He is then egged on by Karloff, reverting to the gangster's personality and going after the other members of his gang and the cash, which Karloff wants so he can finance a new laboratory. Ridges, who turned in a good performance, replaced Lugosi in the role of the professor, and this was the final double act of the two Kings of Horror for Universal but not one of their more memorable films. Karloff, who narrates the story while awaiting the electric chair, shoots Ridges in the end after the gang members and Lugosi have all been wiped out.

The Black Room
Columbia 1935; 75 mins; Cert. "A"
CREDITS: Producer: Robert North; Director: Roy William Neill
CAST: Boris Karloff; Katherine de Mille; Marian Marsh; Robert Allen; Edward Van Sloan; John Buckler **
An ancient curse prophesizes that the elder son of nobility will be killed by his younger twin.
Karloff starred as the twins in this atmospheric Gothic melodrama that was unfortunately a bit short on excitement and thrills. As Gregor, the younger twin, he returns to his estate where Anton, the older, more despotic, twin resides. Anton has requested his return to the estate to kill him, thus nullifying the curse. Gregor is murdered and thrown into a pit in a remote room of the castle, and the murderous older twin then disguises himself as his dead brother to win the affection of Marian Marsh. However, in the climax, his disguise is discovered, he falls into the pit after being chased by his brother's pet mastiff, and dies on a knife held in his dead twin's hand. Karloff's performance as the twins is one of the most underrated of his Columbia films in this now virtually forgotten thriller.

Black Sabbath
Galatea/Emmepi/American Intl. (Italy/France) 1963; Pathecolor; 99 mins; Cert. "X"
CREDITS: Producer: Salvatore Billitteri; Director Mario Bava
CAST: Boris Karloff; Susy Anderson; Mark Damon; Michele Mercier; Rika Dialina; Jacqueline Pierreux ***
Three horror stories produced in the manner of Corman's *Tales of Terror*, narrated by Boris Karloff.
The first tale, "The Drop of Water," concerns a nurse (Jacqueline Pierreux) who steals a ring from the corpse of a clairvoyant. Back at her home, a dripping tap is heard prior to the dead woman's reactivated corpse appearing, scaring Pierreux to death. The second, "The Telephone,"

tells of a prostitute (Michele Mercier) who is receiving persistant telephone calls from what she thinks is a psychotic client. She asks a girlfriend to stay with her and a man breaks into her apartment, strangling her friend before being killed by Mercier. Then the telephone calls commence again. The third and longest story, "The Wurdalak," stars Karloff as a Russian vampire, coming back from the dead to wipe out his entire family and infecting Mark Damon and his girlfriend with vampirism. For its U.S. release, American International tinkered with all three stories, altering various scenes, dubbing some of the dialogue and even imposing a Les Baxter score over Roberto Nicolosi's original music. It was this tampered version that played at a few selected cinemas in 1964.

The Black Scorpion
Warner Bros. 1957; 88 mins; Cert. "X"
CREDITS: Producers: Frank Melford and Jack Dietz; Director: Edward Ludwig; Special Effects: Willis O'Brien and Peter Peterson
CAST: Richard Denning; Mara Corday; Carlos Rivas; Mario Navarro; Carlos Muzquiz; Pascual Garcia Pena ****

Volcanic activity in Mexico unleashes a horde of giant scorpions onto the local populace; the largest of them heads toward Mexico City in a final confrontation with the army.

Willis O'Brien worked spasmodically on a number of films following 1949's *Mighty Joe Young*, often with other animators, and despite some dim photography, his stop-motion effects highlight a pretty good '50s monster movie concerning a pack of gigantic scorpions released from their underground cave by a volcanic eruption and rampaging through the Mexican countryside. The most memorable part of the film is Richard Denning's nerve-tingling descent into the scorpions' lair inside the volcano—an immense gloomy cavern containing not only the scorpions but a strange caterpillar-type worm with claws and a giant bug-like spider (which resemble ideas left over from previous O'Brien productions). The scorpions' attack and derailment of a train is also well staged, with the largest of the monsters killing the others and heading toward Mexico City for more victims. The explosive climax is a winner as well, with the animated monster attacking the military in Mexico City's bullring before being finished off with a 600-thousand-volt electrified dart fired into its throat by Denning. This was a very popular movie on the Sunday one-day circuit in the early 1960s, often found double billed with either *Attack of the 50 Foot Woman* or *Macabre*.

The Black Sleep
Bel-Air/United Artists 1956; 81 mins; Cert. "X"
CREDITS: Producer: Howard W. Koch; Director: Reginald LeBorg
CAST: Basil Rathbone; Herbert Rudley; Patricia Blake; Bela Lugosi; Akim Tamiroff; Lon Chaney Jr. ***

In 1872, a mad doctor dabbling in unorthodox surgery uses an ancient Eastern cataleptic drug known as "Nind Andhera" to experiment with brain operations, and ends up with a cellar full of deformed freaks.

It's an old-fashioned horror yarn, more '40s than '50s in atmosphere, with Basil Rathbone giving a commanding performance as the unscrupulous Doctor Cadman. He administers the coma-inducing drug to his colleague Herbert Rudley, who is about to be hanged for a murder he didn't commit, reawakening him and forcing him to take part in his experiments on the human brain to find a way to cure his wife, who has a life-threatening brain tumor. Rudley eventually discovers that the subjects of Rathbone's previous botched experiments are either chained up in the cellar of the doctor's house or tend to wander around at will. A semi-galaxy of horror stars were brought in to play the deformed humans—Lon Chaney as a demented strangler, Bela Lugosi (mute throughout, his very last completed film role), Tor Johnson and John Carradine among them. All of the freaks break out

of the dungeon at the end and finish off Rathbone and his comatose wife as the police move in; Rudley is eventually freed as an innocent man.

Black Sunday
aka: Revenge of the Vampire
Galatea/Jolly/American Intl. (Italy) 1960; 83 mins; Cert. "X"
CREDITS: Producer: Massimo De Rita; Director: Mario Bava
CAST: Barbara Steele; Andrea Checchi; Ivo Garrani; Arturo Dominici; John Richardson; Enrico Olivieri ****

A 16th-century witch put to death in an iron maiden mask for committing adultery returns from the dead with her lover to wreak vengeance on the descendants of those who were responsible for her death.

A very stylish Italian horror film that was Bava's debut as a director featuring his favorite actress, the beautiful Barbara Steele, as vampire-witch Princess Asa, who is revived after two centuries when a doctor accidentally drips blood on her remains. Along with her resurrected lover, Arturo Dominici, she goes after Princess Katia, who resembles her, to merge herself with the princess and therefore become one all-powerful being that will exact revenge on her enemies. Steele played both roles. The climax sees the reincarnated witch burned at the stake, putting an end to her reign of terror. The title *Black Sunday* refers to the only day of the year when, according to legend, Satan is allowed to walk the Earth and witches return to persecute their executioners. The film unfolds like a Gothic nightmare, with scenes such as a hearse driving through a misty, phantasmagoric landscape stunningly photographed in black and white. The picture was banned in Britain for several years, as the censor deemed the contents to be too cruel and sexual for public consumption, although on subsequent viewings it is no worse in content than many of the Hammer productions being released around that time.

The Black Torment
Compton Cameo/Tekli 1964; Eastmancolor; 85 mins; Cert. "X"
CREDITS: Producer/Director: Robert Hartford-Davies
CAST: John Turner; Heather Sears; Ann Lynn; Raymond Huntley; Peter Arne; Joseph Tomelty **

A baronet's second wife experiences ghostly happenings that could be attributed to his first wife, who committed suicide.

A period ghost story that has an opulent look about it but is ultimately let down by a logical ending that explains away the hauntings as the act of a madman. John Turner plays an 18th-century nobleman who returns to his castle with his new bride and experiences a series of disturbing events, such as banging on windows, and apparitions of his first wife. It all turns out to be the actions of Turner's mad twin brother who, in collusion with his sister-in-law, is trying to drive the nobleman insane and get him accused of witchcraft so that he can inherit the castle. A good cast was utterly wasted in this unscary, feeble attempt to copy the continental horror movies that were emerging in the United Kingdom during this period.

Black Zoo
Allied Artists 1963; Panavision/Eastmancolor; 88 mins; Cert. "X"
CREDITS: Producer: Herman Cohen; Director: Robert Gordon
CAST: Michael Gough; Rod Lauren; Jeanne Cooper; Elisha Cook Jr.; Edward Platt; Marianna Hill **

The mad owner of a zoo in Los Angeles can communicate with the animals by telepathy and commands them to kill his enemies.

A crudely made shocker with the usual eye-rolling, overacted performance by Michael Gough, who seemed to revel in this type of garish movie during this period. Realizing he can exert his will to train his animals to kill on command, he first dispatches a property developer who wants to take over his site, and then a keeper, Elisha Cook, who has been mistreating the animals in his care. He is finally undone when he attempts to murder his second wife, who wants to leave him but ends up a victim himself when his mute son, Rod Lauren (who witnessed the death of his mother, Gough's first wife, by a lion on his father's orders) sets the animals on him. One hilarious scene has Gough playing a lullaby on his organ to a variety of big cats, completely subservient, sitting on various chairs in his living room, the only bright spot in an otherwise dull, exploitive film.

The Blob
Paramount 1958; DeLuxeColor; 85 mins; Cert. "X"
CREDITS: Producer: Jack H. Harris; Director: Irvin S. Yeaworth Jr.
CAST: Steve McQueen; Aneta Corseaut; Earl Rowe; Olin Howlin; Steven Chase; John Benson ***

A meteor lands on Earth, bringing with it a jelly-like alien life form that absorbs humans and grows to an enormous size.

This juvenile sci-fi outing was notable for introducing a young Steve McQueen to the big screen, and he turned in a personable performance with Aneta Corseaut as a pair of teenage sweethearts who battle the oozing, red gelatinous mass that threatens to wipe out the town's inhabitants after it has landed on the outskirts of a town and devoured a tramp who was foolish enough to prod it with a stick. The best part takes place in the cinema where the teenagers are watching an old Bela Lugosi horror film, unaware that the blob is squeezing itself like red toothpaste through the foyers and holes in the projection walls in search of prey. The monster is frozen at the end by carbon dioxide from extinguishers, and the Air Force transports it to the Arctic to be destroyed. In the early '60s, the film went the rounds in the U.K. with *I Married A Monster from Outer Space*.

Blood and Black Lace
Monarchia/Woolner (Italy/France) 1964; Eastmancolor; 87 mins; Cert. "X"
CREDITS: Producer/Director: Mario Bava
CAST: Eva Bartok; Cameron Mitchell; Thomas Reiner; Giuliana Raffaelli; Claude Danty; Mary Arden ***

A psychotic masked killer murders models working at a fashion salon that is being used as a front for drug peddling.

A sadistic, semi-pornographic continental slasher thriller made 20 years before they became fashionable in the mid-1980s. There is not much of a plot, just a series of very brutal and graphic slayings (a woman having a blade-lined mask placed over her face, another victim having her head pressed against a red-hot stove, and an explicit drowning-in-the-bath sequence) that somehow managed to sneak past the usually strict British censor at the time. The film was eventually released in 1969 with another controversial film of the time, Gala's 1967 sex comedy *Seventeen*. Cameron Mitchell murders the women for the sole reason of satisfying his lust while searching for a diary that details the models' drug intake and sexual preferences. Eventually, Mitchell is killed by the police in this body-strewn and, at the time, quite disturbing picture, one of the more extreme that Bava directed.

Blood and Roses
Documento/Paramount (France/Italy) 1960; Technirama/Technicolor; 87 mins; Cert. "X"
CREDITS: Producer: Raymond Eger; Director: Roger Vadim
CAST: Mel Ferrer; Elsa Martinelli; Anette Vadim; Marc Allegret; Jacques-Rene Chauffard; Alberto Bonucci **

The spirit of a vampire countess possesses a woman who resembles her, and she in turn becomes a vampire.

It may well have been produced in widescreen and color, with a renowned director at the helm, but this version of Sheridan Le Fanu's story *Carmilla* was a tedious bore, only coming alive in the final reel when the modern-day Carmilla, Anette Vadim, perished on a fence post, the screen blooming with her blood. Otherwise, the routine story concerns Vadim as the reincarnated vampire trying to seduce Martinelli and turn her into one of the undead before Mel Ferrer, as her lover, can intervene. In trying to invoke an elegant mood to the vampire legend, the production ends up appearing more as a soft porn movie than a horror flick, totally lacking in thrills and suspense. One was left with the feeling that in another director's hands, this could have been a whole lot better than it eventually turned out.

The Blood Beast Terror
Tigon 1967; Eastmancolor; 88 mins; Cert. "X"
CREDITS: Producer: Arnold L. Miller; Director: Vernon Sewell
CAST: Peter Cushing; Robert Flemyng; Wanda Ventham; David Griffin; Roy Hudd; Vanessa Howard *

A mad entomologist creates a monster death's head moth from experiments with chrysalides.

Robert Flemyng plays a 19th-century professor who is attempting to create a mate for his daughter, Wanda Ventham, as she has the ability to metamorphose into a man-sized moth, capable of killing humans and draining their blood. Peter Cushing is the police inspector on the trail of the killer, who finds a cellar full of bones in Flemyng's house before discovering that the professor has created a mate for his daughter, also with a liking for human blood. The obligatory fire in the house, with the moth-like creatures attracted to the flames, kills off the monsters at the climax. This was a dreary effort all around, with a ropey-looking moth-creature, a weak script and a comic role for Roy Hudd, which seemed out of context to the rest of the picture. Cushing once denounced it as the worst film he had ever appeared in, which says it all. It was originally released with the excellent *Witchfinder General* in the United Kingdom.

Blood Is My Heritage
aka: Blood of Dracula
Anglo Amalgamated/American Intl. 1957; 69 mins; Cert. "X"
CREDITS: Producer: Herman Cohen; Director: Herbert L. Strock
CAST: Sandra Harrison; Louise Lewis; Thomas B. Henry; Heather Ames; Jerry Blaine; Gail Ganley ***

A female student at a high school is hypnotized by her chemistry teacher with an amulet from Carpathia and becomes a vampire.

Sandra Harrison is the student with an explosive temper who falls under the spell of an old amulet used by Louise Lewis to release the beast within her. A briskly made, eerie little horror movie, well directed by Herbert L. Strock, that conjures up some creepy moments (despite the regrettable "Puppy Love" interlude). A young girl in the school basement at night hears footsteps in the shadows behind her before being attacked, and Harrison looks suitably startling as the vampire lurking among the trees and bushes in the school cemetery, waiting to pounce on more victims. The climax sees Harrison in her vampire state strangling Lewis before falling backward onto the broken leg of an upturned table, killing herself and reverting to human form. The film was virtually remade as *I Was A Teenage Werewolf*—the same scriptwriter, the same plot—the difference being that the monster was now a werewolf instead of a vampire. *Blood Is My Heritage* and *Teenage Frankenstein* (also directed by Strock) were a favorite pairing on the Sunday one-day circuit, playing continuously for years in the late 1950s and early 1960s.

Blood of the Vampire
Tempean/Eros/Universal 1958; Eastmancolor; 87 mins; Cert. "X"
CREDITS: Producers: Robert S. Baker and Monty Berman; Director: Henry Cass
CAST: Donald Wolfit; Vincent Ball; Victor Maddern; Barbara Shelley; John Le Mesurier; Andrew Faulds ****

A doctor raised from the dead becomes head of an institution for the insane and carries out experiments on the inmates, who supply him with fresh sources of blood.

Despite the gory opening stake-through-the-heart sequence, there are no vampires as such in this full-blooded horror melodrama, even though Donald Wolfit as the doctor resembles a bulkier Bela Lugosi, with his bushy eyebrows and big hooked nose. He excels in the role of an anemic surgeon who, with the aid of his one-eyed hunchback assistant (memorably played by Victor Maddern), replenishes his supply of blood from the patients in the asylum that he oversees. Vincent Ball is a young doctor unwillingly roped in by Wolfit to assist in his experiments, and the delectable Barbara Shelley is his girlfriend who tries to help him escape from the asylum, only for the pair of them to end up in chains in a dungeon. Wolfit decides to operate on Shelley but Maddern, horrified by his master's actions, frees her and attacks the doctor, who kills him. The lovers flee the asylum with the doctor in pursuit and as they escape, Wolfit, in a bloody climax, is torn to pieces by a pack of ravenous guard dogs. This superior British horror movie was based on the Hammer productions of the day and after its initial release went the rounds for years right up to the end of the 1960s, usually teamed up with *Behemoth the Sea Monster* or, in some instances, Hammer's *The Brides of Dracula*.

The Body Snatcher
RKO-Radio 1945; 78 mins; Cert. "A"
CREDITS: Producer: Val Lewton; Director: Robert Wise
CAST: Boris Karloff; Henry Daniell; Bela Lugosi; Russell Wade; Edith Atwater; Robert Clarke
***

In 19th-century Edinburgh, a coachman supplies a doctor with corpses but has to resort to murder when he cannot lay his hands on more bodies.

A superior Val Lewton production on the well-worn theme of body-snatching, invoking an authentic sense of the murky period in which the film takes place, although a bit short on thrills. Karloff plays the coachman who supplies Henry Daniell with body parts and then attempts to blackmail him with the notion that he (Karloff) would be implicated by the police if the doctor were ever caught. Karloff is murdered, and Daniell places the corpse in the back of the coachman's buggy, driving off to dispose of it. In the ghoulish final moments, the corpse apparently comes to life, scaring Daniell and causing the buggy to topple over a cliff. This final sequence was cut by the British censor but was reinstated in prints that went the rounds in the early 1960s with an "A" rating. *The Body Snatcher* marked the final pairing of Karloff and Lugosi in any film—Lugosi, who only had a minor role in the picture, was now a spent force, suffering from morphine addiction and personal problems, while Karloff's career in the medium carried on more or less successfully for a further 30 years.

The Boogie Man Will Get You
Columbia 1942; 66 mins; Cert. "A"
CREDITS: Producer: Colbert Clarke; Director: Lew Landers
CAST: Boris Karloff; Peter Lorre; Jeff Donnell; Larry Parks; Maxie Rosenbloom; Don Beddoe
**

A mad scientist attempts to create a superbeing from assorted body parts in his basement laboratory.

A semi-spoof, *Arsenic and Old Lace*-type horror-comedy from Karloff, who probably felt that a change was needed and decided not only to send himself up, but Columbia's lame series of mad doctor movies as well. This was a pretty unfunny feature all round, with Karloff and Lorre waylaying traveling salesmen to produce a race of supermen to fight in the war and trying to turn the unfortunate Maxie Rosenbloom into a superman by electricity. The silly climax sees the dead bodies coming alive and putting a stop to the scientist's plans. With a corny script to match the acting, this very dated farce cropped up on the Sunday circuit in the 1960s at a few cinemas with the equally mind-numbing Bela Lugosi effort, *Lock Up Your Daughters*.

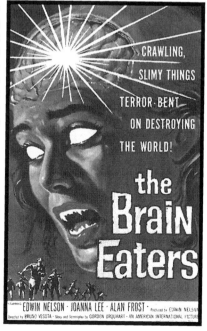

The Brain Eaters
American Intl. 1958; 60 mins; Cert. "A"
CREDITS: Producer: Edwin Nelson; Director: Bruno Vesota
CAST: Edwin Nelson; Alan Frost; Jody Fair; Jack Hill; Leonard Nimoy; Joanna Lee **

Furry parasites from the Earth's center invade a small town and take over the minds of the inhabitants.

A cut-price version of *Invasion of the Body Snatchers* featuring a pack of strange little creatures arriving in a cylinder from the interior of the Earth, boring their way into people's necks and controlling their minds, causing widespread paranoia among the local populace. Ed Nelson finally concludes that electricity can destroy them, even though most of the townsfolk, including his assistant, Joanna Lee, have been taken over by the aliens. Eventually, a falling power cable eliminates the creatures and unfortunately his assistant as well. This was a shoddy adaptation of Robert Heinlein's novel *The Puppet Masters*, which told of an invasion of Earth by creatures from a moon of Saturn and deserved a far better treatment than the film gave. The parasites themselves, resembling furry toys with pipe cleaners as antennae, were among the most pathetic creations seen in any '50s sci-fi movie. Leonard Nimoy of *Star Trek* fame had one of his first roles in this movie—it turned up on the Sunday circuit in 1963 with *The Amazing Colossal Man*.

The Brain from Planet Arous
Howco Intl. 1958; 71 mins; Cert. "A"
CREDITS: Producer: Jacques Marquette; Director: Nathan Hertz (Nathan Juran)
CAST: John Agar; Joyce Meadows; Robert Fuller; Ken Terrell; Thomas B. Henry; Henry Travis
**

A disembodied flying alien brain takes over the body of a scientist to conquer the world.

A juvenile piece of nonsense featuring a strange-looking brain creature with eyes, called Gor, who inhabits John Agar's body after Agar has discovered the thing in a cave. The parasite gives Agar superhuman powers that he demonstrates to the army, such as blasting planes out of the sky with his eyes and blowing up buildings. However, a friendly brain called Vol takes over Agar's dog, who instructs Agar how to get rid of and kill the rogue brain, which has to leave Agar's body every 24 hours to re-form, and Agar, in his normal state, hacks Gor to pieces with an ax. The script is unintentionally amusing and somehow the ubiquitous Agar manages to keep a straight face through the somewhat cheap-looking proceedings.

The Brain that Wouldn't Die
Sterling and Carlton/American Intl. 1959; 81 mins; Cert. "X"
CREDITS: Producer: Rex Carlton; Director: Joseph Green
CAST: Herb Evers; Virginia Leith; Adele Lamont; Bruce Brighton; Doris Brent; Leslie Daniel
**

A scientist keeps the decapitated head of his fiancée alive after an automobile accident and searches for a new body to enable her to live again.

A gorier but sillier version of *Donovan's Brain* with Herb Evers as the mad scientist who keeps a monster in his dungeon, the result of a botched brain transplant, and the head of Virginia Leith in his laboratory, wired up and still capable of speech. With the help of assistant Leslie Daniel, he procures a model, Adele Lamont, to use as his fiancée's new body even though she wants to die in peace. In the end, the creature escapes and sets fire to the laboratory, carrying off the unconscious Lamont, tearing Daniel's arms off and leaving Evers to perish in the blaze. The film went the rounds in 1963 double billed with *Earth vs. the Spider*.

The Bride and the Beast
Allied Artists 1957; 78 mins; Cert. "A"
CREDITS: Producer/Director: Adrian Weiss
CAST: Charlotte Austin; Lance Fuller; Johnny Roth; Jeanne Gerson; Gil Frye; William Justine
**

A big game hunter on honeymoon is unaware that his new wife is the reincarnation of a gorilla.

A preposterous slice of nonsense whose script was provided by Edward D. Wood Jr., the doyen of grade Z horror movies of the '50s—Les Baxter's bombastic score, Weiss' fast-paced direction and Charlotte Austin's above-average performance just about make it watchable. Lance Fuller is puzzled why his wife, Austin, seems able to control his captured ape's wild behavior. The animal is shot when it breaks out of its cage and sneaks into their bedroom with amorous intentions toward her. Worried, Fuller employs a hypnotist to find out the reason behind his wife's dreams of a past existence and, under hypnosis, she reveals that she is the reincarnation of a white gorilla and lived a previous life in the jungle. When the couple embark on an African honeymoon, the movie becomes bogged down in an interminable hunt for two escaped Indian tigers, with extensive stock footage of the natural wildlife. It only picks up again in the climax, when Austin is carried off to a cave inhabited by gorillas, eventually ending up living with them, her bemused husband returning to the States and accepting the fact that he has finally lost her.

Bride of Frankenstein
Universal 1935; 80 mins; Cert. "X"
CREDITS: Producer: Carl Laemmle Jr.; Director: James Whale
CAST: Colin Clive; Boris Karloff; Elsa Lanchester; Ernest Thesiger; Valerie Hobson; Una O'Connor *****

Baron Frankenstein and Dr. Pretorius collaborate in creating a female mate for the Frankenstein monster.

Universal's second Frankenstein outing remains an out-and-out masterpiece of '30s cinema, one of those rare movies where not one second of film is wasted, with all concerned giving wonderful performances in front of and behind the camera. The highlight of this classic has to be the pastoral interlude where Karloff is befriended by a lonely blind hermit living in the woods, who teaches him to appreciate wine, food and music—a superb mixture of pathos and horror, played out to the refrains of "Ave Maria." Elsa Lanchester as the Bride embodies the amazing she-monster in the film's famous climax, a montage of weird camera angles, fast editing and a riotous thunderstorm, all topped off with Franz Waxman's legendary score. Black humor abounds, notably from Ernest Thesiger, who has created miniature human beings that he keeps in bell jars and who eventually assists the Baron in creating a mate for Karloff. In the end, as the Bride rejects her forlorn mate and Karloff mutters the immortal words, "We belong dead," the monster throws a lever and Frankenstein's castle with the laboratory is blown to bits, but you cannot keep a good monster yarn down and a third film, *Son of Frankenstein*, was released four years later. In the United Kingdom, *Bride of Frankenstein* was the least-seen picture from Universal's *Frankenstein* series, only surfacing in 1969/1970 and playing with Hitchcock's *Psycho* at selected theaters.

Bride of the Monster
aka: Bride of the Atom
Banner/DCA 1955; 69 mins; Cert. "X"
CREDITS: Producer/Director: Edward D. Wood Jr.
CAST: Bela Lugosi; Tor Johnson; Tony Mc-Coy; Loretta King; William Benedict; Harvey Dunn *

A scientist invents an atomic ray machine to create superhuman beings, but only succeeds in turning animals and men into monsters.

Another grade Z bottom-of-the-basement production by the King of the Awful, Edward Wood (although producer/director Jerry Warren ran him a close second), apparently filmed in just five days with his "star" Lugosi as the mad scientist who, with Tibetan assistant Tor Johnson, is attempting to create superbeings by harnessing atomic energy to a ray machine. The scene where Lugosi, ill at the time of shooting, wrestles with a giant fake octopus in a swamp is both implausible and comical, while ex-Swedish wrestler Johnson goes through his normal heavyweight monster routine and is killed by Lugosi in the end when he rescues reporter Loretta King from his clutches. Lugosi, after Johnson has turned the ray on him, eventually explodes in an atomic cloud (cue for more poached newsreel footage), and the whole concept, like Wood's other films, resembles for the most part a very amateurish home movie.

The Brides of Dracula
Hammer/Universal 1960; Technicolor; 85 mins; Cert. "X"
CREDITS: Producer: Anthony Hinds; Director: Terence Fisher
CAST: Peter Cushing; David Peel; Yvonne Monlaur; Martita Hunt; Freda Jackson; Andree Melly *****

A disciple of Dracula is inadvertently set free from imprisonment in his castle by a young woman and goes on a rampage at a nearby girls' school.

One of the top-notch Hammer Gothic thrillers of the late 1950s/early 1960s, produced at a time before over-familiarization with their sets and storylines made them all appear a bit jaded. Although Dracula wasn't featured (Christopher Lee allegedly refused to play the Count because of a fear of typecasting), good-looking David Peel made a mesmeric Baron Meinster and his duels with Peter Cushing, who reprised his role as Van Helsing, are every bit as good as those between Cushing and Lee in *Dracula*. This is especially true in the scene in the old mill when Cushing, attacked by Peel, has to burn off the bite marks on his neck with a branding iron to prevent himself from becoming one of the undead. Martita Hunt is also excellent as Peel's mother, who suffers the indignity of being bitten by her own son after he is released and becoming a vampire, pleading with Cushing to free her tortured soul. The climax sees Cushing spraying holy water over the vampire and the horribly scarred Peel perishing under the shadow of the cross cast by the mill's sails. The film was photographed in rich Technicolor and well-mounted, with a commendable sense of the period in which the action took place, and expertly directed by Terence Fisher. It is held in the same high esteem by many fans as 1958's *Dracula*. Strangely, having made his mark in this film, the handsome Peel seemed to vanish without a trace from the British cinema.

A Bucket of Blood
American Intl. 1959; 66 mins; Cert. "A"
CREDITS: Producer/Director: Roger Corman
CAST: Dick Miller; Antony Carbone; Barboura Morris; Julian Burton; John Brinkley; Ed Nelson
**
A dim-witted waiter in a coffee shop frequented by teenagers turns to murder to emulate the whiz kids that he serves, making clay models from his victims.

This is a horror-comedy spoof of *House of Wax*, filmed in five days by Corman and starring Dick Miller (one of the stalwarts of his productions). Miller is a dumb waiter who first kills a cat and covers it in modeling clay and then, through a series of murders that are mostly accidents, ends up covering the bodies with clay, becoming a sort of celebrity as a result. He is finally found out when a fingernail is discovered beneath the clay and the face of one of his murdered models is recognized. In a fit of pique he hangs himself, becoming a clay model to join the others. The beatnik generation depicted in the film now seems terribly dated and the movie resembles at best a low-budget television show that one can find either amusing or irritating by turns.

The Cabinet of Caligari
20th Century Fox 1962; Cinemascope; 105 mins; Cert. "X"
CREDITS: Producer/Director: Roger Kay
CAST: Dan O'Herlihy; Glynis Johns; Dick Davalos; Lawrence Dobkin; Constance Ford; Estelle Winwood **
A young woman breaks down in her car near an old country house and is held prisoner there by a sinister doctor.

This film had virtually nothing to do with the 1919 classic and is really an essay in repressed sexual fantasies. Glynis Johns undergoes a series of nightmarish events when she is put up in an isolated house by Dr. Caligari, played by Dan O'Herlihy. She finds herself drugged and a virtual prisoner in the place and experiences various disturbing happenings all relating to sex and death, with a handsome young man the catalyst for what is going on. In the end, she discovers that she is an old lady, a patient in a mental home suffering from sexual repression, and that O'Herlihy, who is supposedly keeping her prisoner in the house, is in reality the doctor treating her. A few distorted sets gave a nod in the direction of the 1919 *Caligari*, but otherwise this fairly well-made psychological thriller was sometimes too talkative and overwrought to maintain the interest.

Caltiki the Immortal Monster
Galatea/Climax/Allied Artists (Italy) 1959; 76 mins; Cert. "X"
CREDITS: Producer: Samuel Schneider; Directors: Riccardo Freda and Lee Kresel
CAST: John Merivale; Didi Perego; Gerard Herter; Daniela Rocca; Giacomo Rossi-Stuart; Gay Pearl **
Archaeologists discover an amorphous creature in a pool inside an ancient Mayan temple. After a specimen is taken back to the laboratory, it rejuvenates and goes on a rampage.

Director Riccardo Freda's one and only foray into science fiction was loosely based both on *The Quatermass Experiment* and *The Blob* and was one of the first continental horror mov-

ies aimed at the American market. A team of archaeologists led by John Merivale enters the Mayan city of Tikel, abandoned in 607 A.D., and stumbles across a mysterious pool that harbors a flesh-eating monster. After it is destroyed, a piece of the creature is taken back to the laboratory in Mexico City where it comes alive. According to an inscription found near the pool, a radioactive meteorite from a comet that landed on Earth centuries ago caused the blob-type thing to grow to an enormous size. The monster attacks Merivale's wife after crawling through the city, and is finally wiped out by the military, which uses flamethrowers to burn it to death. The picture was shot in Spain by an apparently uninterested Freda and was a flop when first released, turning up in the United Kingdom in 1963 at a few selected cinemas.

Captain Clegg
aka: Night Creatures
Hammer/Universal 1962; Technicolor; 81 mins; Cert. "A"
CREDITS: Producer: John Temple-Smith; Director: Peter Graham Scott
CAST: Peter Cushing; Yvonne Romain; Patrick Allen; Oliver Reed; Michael Ripper; Martin Benson ***

In the 18th century, a vicar presiding over a village on the Romney Marshes is a retired pirate who is involved with the villagers in a smuggling ring.

A lively period romp that was originally released with *The Phantom of the Opera* in the United Kingdom. Oliver Reed and Yvonne Romain are the romantic couple caught up with Peter Cushing as the vicar, who leads the villagers on smuggling raids in the Romney Marshes, dressed up as the luminous, ghostly marsh phantoms on horseback to scare the local population so they can carry on their nefarious activities undisturbed. Patrick Allen plays the army officer who eventually unmasks Cushing as the infamous Clegg, thought to have died many years before, and puts a stop to the smuggling. Atmospheric, stylish, with some fine Olde English sets and eerie scenes on the misty marshes, this was perhaps a better production by Hammer than the main movie it was featured with.

Captain Nemo and the Underwater City
MGM 1969; Panavision/Metrocolor; 106 mins; Cert. "U"
CREDITS: Producer: Bertram Ostrer; Director: James Hill
CAST: Robert Ryan; Nanette Newman; Chuck Connors; Luciana Paluzzi; Kenneth Connor; Bill Fraser **

Survivors from a shipwreck are taken in the Nautilus to an undersea kingdom ruled by Captain Nemo.

Yet another adventure film featuring Captain Nemo from *20,000 Leagues Under the Sea* and typical of many fantasy movies made during this period—tacky color, a wordy script and squarely aimed at a very young audience. The six survivors of the shipwreck are transported in Nemo's submarine to his undersea city. Robert Ryan is unconvincing as Nemo. The dome-like undersea kingdom of Templemer is well conceived, and the main story concerns the survivors' greed as Nemo's oxygen-making plant turns rocks into gold. A rebellion is quelled and the visitors, after evading a giant manta ray, return to the surface, promising never to tell anyone of the whereabouts of Nemo's city.

Captain Sinbad
King Bros./MGM 1963; Wonderscope/Eastmancolor; 85 mins; Cert. "A"
CREDITS: Producers: Frank and Maurice King; Director: Byron Haskin
CAST: Guy Williams; Heidi Bruhl; Pedro Armendariz; John Crawford; Abraham Sofaer; Helmut Schneider ***
Captain Sinbad returns to his kingdom to find that it is being ruled over by an evil sultan.
Although it's nowhere near in the same league as *The Seventh Voyage of Sinbad*, this American–West German co-production is an enjoyable, colorful fantasy that would have benefited greatly from a few Harryhausen-type special effects to boost the visuals. Guy Williams plays an energetic Sinbad, who, with the aid of an aged magician, has to fight invisible monsters, birdmen, a three-headed dragon and, best of all, a giant mailed fist, to reach a tower outside the city of Baristan where the sultan (Pedro Armendariz), owner of a magical ring, has a princess captive and his own evil heart locked in the tower. The magician eventually helps Sinbad usurp the sultan, save the princess and regain his kingdom. The film only had a limited release in England during 1964 and was not too successful at the time.

Castle of Blood
aka: La Danza Macabra
Vulsinia Films/Woolner (France/Italy) 1964; 87 mins; Cert. "X"
CREDITS: Producer: Marco Vicario; Director: Antonio Margheriti
CAST: Barbara Steele; Georges Riviere; Margrete Robsham; Umberto Raho; Sylvia Sorrente; Silvano Tranquili ***
A journalist encounters Edgar Allan Poe in London, who proposes a wager that the young man spend the night in a reputedly haunted castle that nobody has returned from alive.
Margheriti's first horror outing was an atmospheric and erotic thriller starring Georges Riviere as the journalist who decides to take Poe up on his offer. He soon finds to his terror that ghosts *do* inhabit the place—they are the malevolent spirits of people who were involved in sexual intrigues and, as a result, suffered violent deaths. With its scenes of lesbianism between Barbara Steele and Margrete Robsham, and Sylvia Sorrente flaunting her naked body, this was typical continental movie fare of the day, well photographed in black and white with a jarring musical score by Riz Ortolani. Only the usual appalling dubbing spoiled it. In the end, Riviere attempts to escape from the castle as he realizes that the phantoms need human blood to exist, but he impales himself on a gatepost after being chased by a ghoulish Steele; Poe discovers his corpse in the morning. Margheriti, Vicario and Ortolani were reunited during 1964 for *The Castle of Terror*, the director's second and more successful feature—*Castle of Blood* went the rounds at various small cinemas in 1964, double billed with, in some instances, American International's *The Terror*.

Castle of Evil
United Pictures 1966; Eastmancolor; 81 mins; Cert. "X"
CREDITS: Producer: Earle Lyon; Director: Francis D. Lyon
CAST: Scott Brady; Lisa Gaye; Virginia Mayo; David Brian; Hugh Marlowe; William Thourlby
*
A disfigured scientist creates a humanoid robot in his own image before he dies, with which to kill members of his family who are in his will.
A very dreary effort, with no suspense, poor color and flatly directed by Lyon—a kind of cut-price variation on the old *The Cat and the Canary* scenario. Three people on a remote Caribbean island are relatives of mad scientist William Thourlby, who has programmed his robot double to discover which of the three was responsible for his disfigurement and subsequent death. The

tedious action is played out in Agatha Christie style before Scott Brady blasts the robot with a laser gun. The film had a very limited release in England on a double bill with, rather incongruously, Allied Artists' classic *Invasion of the Body Snatchers*.

The Castle of Terror
aka: The Virgin of Nuremberg
Zodiac/Gladiator/Compton Cameo (France/Italy) 1964; Totalscope/Eastmancolor; 83 mins; Cert. "X"
CREDITS: Producer: Marco Vicario; Director: Antonio Margheriti
CAST: Rossana Podesta; Georges Riviere; Christopher Lee; Jim Dolan; Anny Delli Uberti; Mirko Valentin ****

The arrival of the owner of a reputedly haunted castle on the Rhine with his new wife triggers off a series of gruesome murders performed by a crazed victim of Nazi surgical-torture.

The Castle of Terror was one of a number of continental horror movies that appeared spasmodically in the United Kingdom during the early to mid-1960s, and was a typical example of the genre—handsomely photographed, badly dubbed, normally in widescreen and very violent, with the accent firmly on sadism. Mirko Valentin plays the hideously disfigured and insane "The Punisher," who periodically emerges from deep within the castle's vaults to torture women as a result of his surgical treatment at the hands of the Nazis during the war. The film more or less consists of Rossana Podesta running and hiding from the hooded maniac in the depths of the gloomy castle as the grotesque, skull-like Valentin embarks on a reign of terror that includes putting a cage containing a starving rat over a victim's face and placing another woman into an iron maiden. Christopher Lee has a bit part as a benevolent, disfigured servant who finally helps Podesta and Georges Riviere to escape from the clutches of the mad torturer and pays with his own life, as the castle and Valentin go up in flames. The film, directed in rough and ready style by Margheriti and with a score from Riz Ortolani guaranteed to jolt the audience, resembled a typical Hammer production of the day but came across more powerfully—it played with another feature from the Continent during 1964, the aptly titled *Horror*.

Cat Girl
Anglo Amalgamated 1957; 75 mins; Cert. "A"
CREDITS: Producers: Lou Rusoff and Herbert Smith; Director: Alfred Shaughnessy
CAST: Barbara Shelley; Robert Ayres; Kay Callard; Paddy Webster; Jack May; Ernest Milton **

A woman inherits a family curse whereby she can transfer her spirit into a leopard when threatened.

A low-key, virtually forgotten little British version of *The Cat People* featuring Barbara Shelley in her very first horror role before she became the stalwart of many of the Hammer

films of the '60s. Shelley discovers that her husband is having an affair and, full of suppressed emotion, transforms her spirit into a leopard to kill those persons who have crossed her path. There is one startling scene in the picture when Shelley views with pleasure the phantom leopard savaging her husband and his lover, an impressive sequence for a low budget mid-'50s British thriller. She dies in the end when as the leopard, she is run down by her psychiatrist, who gets out of his car to find not a large cat in the road but a dead Shelley.

The Cat People
RKO-Radio 1942; 74 mins; Cert. "A"
CREDITS: Producer: Val Lewton; Director: Jacques Tourneur
CAST: Simone Simon; Tom Conway; Kent Smith; Jack Holt; Alan Napier; Jane Randolph
****

A beautiful young girl from Serbia is convinced that when sexually threatened, she can change into a large predatory cat with the power to kill.

Between 1942 and 1946, Val Lewton produced a series of low-key, psychological horror movies for RKO-Radio, the finest of which was *The Cat People*. Simone Simon played the beautiful heroine, obsessed with the idea that she is descended from a race of Balkan women who can change their form when their passions are aroused. Kent Smith is the unfortunate man who marries her but finds that she is unable to consummate the marriage, forcing him to consult a psychiatrist, Tom Conway, to find out what troubles her. Conway is eventually killed by Simon who, after wounding herself, dies among the big cats in a zoo. There are no transformation scenes in the movie, just loads of suspense and tension by the suggestion of something unseen lurking in the shadows, all directed skillfully by Jacques Tourneur, particularly in the scene where the cat creature stalks Smith's mistress in a basement swimming pool. A mini-masterpiece of '40s horror and suspense.

Chamber of Horrors
Warner Bros. 1966; Warnercolor; 99 mins; Cert. "X"
CREDITS: Producer/Director: Hy Averback
CAST: Patrick O'Neal; Cesare Danova; Laura Devon; Wilfred Hyde-White; Suzy Parker; Patrice Wymore ***

Two amateur criminologists track down The Baltimore Strangler, an insane killer on the loose in the city.

Originally a pilot television production based on *House of Wax* but considered too horrific for a TV broadcast, *Chamber of Horrors* was expanded into a full-length feature film and was quite successful when first released. Patrick O'Neal is a homicidal maniac who is arrested as he is about to marry his girlfriend, who has been strangled. He escapes arrest by cutting off his own hand and attaching to the stump a variety of weapons to murder all those who cross his path. Eventually, he comes to grief impaled on the hook of his own wax image, as he is about to murder Cesare Danova. O'Neal was excellent in the part, although no Vincent Price, but the film was let down by the silly gimmicks of "The Fear Flasher" and "The Horror Horn," warning audiences of the murders to be committed, which were greeted with derisory chuckles when the film first played in British cinemas.

Circus of Fear
aka: Psycho Circus
Henley (Germany) 1967; Eastmancolor; 65 mins; Cert. "A"
CREDITS: Producer: Harry Alan Towers; Director: John Moxey
CAST: Christopher Lee; Leo Genn; Anthony Newlands; Maurice Kaufmann; Heinz Drache; Klaus Kinski **

A series of robberies and murders lead the police to suspect a circus of harboring a killer.

Released with Hammer's *Quatermass and the Pit*, this German co-produced oddity was a mixture of detective story, circus melodrama and a very mild horror thriller. Christopher Lee, in an almost forgotten role and spending most of his short time in the movie wearing a black balaclava, played Gregor, the mutilated hooded lion tamer who was the leader of a gang of thieves (the circus was used as a cover for his activities). There is a *Freaks* type of plot running through the film, the German version of which differs slightly from the U.K. print. This was a fairly humdrum B movie, with a cut-price circus set and a good cast trying its hardest to liven things up, with very little success.

Circus of Horrors
Anglo Amagamated 1960; Eastmancolor; 91 mins; Cert. "X"
CREDITS: Producers: Julian Wintle and Leslie Parkyn; Director: Sidney Hayers
CAST: Anton Diffring; Yvonne Monlaur; Erika Remberg; Donald Pleasance; Collette Wilde; Conrad Phillips ****

A mad plastic surgeon flees to France after a series of botched operations but continues his activities under the cover of a circus.

A big hit in its day, this brash, melodramatic horror movie was carried along by a typical eye-rolling performance by Anton Diffring as the plastic surgeon on the run from the police, who stocks a circus purloined from Donald Pleasance with criminals and collects along the way an assortment of disfigured women he can operate on. If they step out of line, reject his advances, or try to leave the circus, they perish in a series of arranged accidents, such as a trapeze artist falling to her death and another who becomes the victim of a knife-thrower. Even the woman that Diffring falls in love with, Yvonne Romain, whom he operated on as a small girl, ends up being torn to shreds by lions. As a result of these "accidents," the profits of Diffring's circus hit the roof when curious crowds flock to see if any more deaths occur. Eventually, his long-suffering and scarred lover, Wilde, jealous of all the attention that the surgeon is lavishing on various other women and fed up with his broken promises to restore her looks, runs him down outside the Temple of Beauty as he is being pursued by the police after being mauled by a gorilla. Piling on all the nasty goings-on with gusto, this was a sensationalistic and exploitive picture that was very much in the vein of Anglo's *Horrors of the Black Museum*, made a year earlier.

City of the Dead
aka: Horror Hotel
Vulcan/TransLux 1960; 76 mins; Cert. "X"
CREDITS: Producer: Donald Taylor; Director: John Llewellyn Moxey
CAST: Christopher Lee; Betta St. John; Patricia Jessel; Dennis Lotis; Valentine Dyall; Tom Naylor ***

A resurrected witch in Massachusetts runs a coven at a local inn.

Although set in America, the film was shot at the Shepperton studios in the United Kingdom with a vast amount of dry ice to give plenty of atmosphere to the scenes of the witches wandering around the decaying village in their habits. Christopher Lee played a professor and the leader of the coven, luring one of his students to the inn on the pretext that she carries out research into local occult legends, only to have her sacrificed to the returned witch, Patricia Jessel. The student's brother, Tom Naylor, arrives at the village and eventually disposes of the witch and her coven by casting the shadow of the cross on them as he himself dies. The film was not a success at the time of release, probably because although good to look at, it lacked thrills and suspense, and only appeared spasmodically at selected cinemas in 1963, double billed with *The Mobster*.

City Under the Sea
aka: War Gods of the Deep
American Intl. 1965; Colorscope/Eastmancolor; 84 mins; Cert. "U"
CREDITS: Producer: Daniel Haller; Director: Jacques Tourneur
CAST: Vincent Price; Tab Hunter; Susan Hart; David Tomlinson; John Le Mesurier; Henry Oscar **

An American heiress in Cornwall is kidnapped and taken to the lost undersea kingdom of Lyonesse.

An unsuccessful mixture of Jules Verne and Edgar Allan Poe, including comic interludes from David Tomlinson, making for a somewhat childish and corny adventure fantasy, with cardboard-looking sets, poor color photography and a humdrum script. Vincent Price is the Nemo-like ruler of the lost city off the Cornish coast, believing Susan Hart to be the reincarnation of his dead wife who has been taken to his kingdom by gill-men through a secret underground passage.

Hunter and Tomlinson are the men who go after Hart to rescue her. Price is a sea captain from the 17th century who, along with his crew, has been kept alive by the quality of the air in the city. The three captives eventually escape as a volcano threatens to destroy Lyonesse. The film was the last to be directed by Jacques Tourneur, the man behind such classics as *The Cat People* and *Night of the Demon*.

The Colossus of New York
Paramount 1958; 70 mins; Cert. "A"
CREDITS: Producer: William Alland;
Director: Eugene Lourie
CAST: John Baragrey; Mala Powers;
Otto Kruger; Charles Herbert; Ed Wolff;
Ross Martin ***

An eminent scientist who is killed in a car crash has his brain transplanted into a 12-foot-high robot so that he may carry on with his research, but the mechanical man goes berserk and runs amok in New York.

After Ross Martin as the scientist is hit by a car, his father and brother preserve his brain and transplant it into the body of a robot to enable him to continue with his work, but the brain malfunctions through frustration and anger and the mechanical man goes out of control instead. A better than average robot-on-the-loose movie with some effective scenes of the metal giant running rampant in the United Nations buildings, blasting everything in sight with rays from his eyes and causing panic among the crowds. There are also a few moving moments in the picture when Ed Wolff as the robot tries to communicate with his son after the transplant, and in the end, Wolff instructs his own small son to pull a lever that will destroy him. The film was on a double bill with Jack Arnold's *The Space Children* when first released.

The Conquest of Space
Paramount 1955; Technicolor; 80 mins; Cert. "U"
CREDITS: Producer: George Pal; Director: Byron Haskin
CAST: Walter Brooke; William Hopper; Eric Fleming; Mickey Shaughnessy; Phil Foster; Benson Fong **

In 1980, astronauts from a giant space station orbiting the Earth voyage to Mars.

Not all of George Pal's ideas on future space travel were used by Paramount when producing this film because of cost, and the shots of the space station above the planet and the various spacecraft serviced by the station may have looked realistic in 1955 but today appear rather dated and amateurish. The film is bogged down by too much discussion in the first half and only comes alive when the crew journeys to Mars which, along with the Martian landscape, is well depicted. The trip is almost sabotaged by the captain, who believes it blasphemous to journey to another planet, and this contributes to the only bit of suspense in the picture. *The Conquest of*

Space was not a success and severed Pal's connections with Paramount—science fiction movies dealing with space on a realistic level were dropped for the remainder of the decade as being deemed not good box office material.

The Corpse
Abacus/Canon 1969; Technicolor; 90 mins; Cert. "X"
CREDITS: Producer: Gabrielle Beaumont; Director: Viktor Ritelis
CAST: Michael Gough; Yvonne Mitchell: Simon Gough; Sharon Gurney; David Butler; Nicholas Jones **

A bullying father murdered by his wife and daughter returns from the dead to terrorize them all over again.

A bizarre movie that plays more like an "X" certificate 1960s sitcom than a feature film, with virtually no plot and static direction—tyrannical Michael Gough is raised from the dead and makes life hell for his family, and that's about it. The film appears to be just an excuse to show the emotions of fear, nervousness and terror brought on by someone's totally unreasonable behavior, in this case Gough's, who once again gives another over-the-top performance. At the end of a very long 90 minutes, the father resumes his role as the head of the by now shell-shocked family that he has terrorized. A real oddity, and a not very successful one, that was given a limited release in Britain with the unappetizing American murder thriller *Psycho Killer*.

Corridors of Blood
Amalgamated Productions/MGM 1958; 87 mins; Cert. "X"
CREDITS: Producers: John Croydon and Charles F. Vetter Jr.; Director: Robert Day
CAST: Boris Karloff; Francis Mathews; Betta St. John; Francis de Wolff; Christopher Lee; Finlay Currie **

A doctor attempts to find a method to perform painless operations before the advent of anesthetic.

Karloff plays a doctor in Victorian London who is determined to discover a way to operate painlessly on the sick by experimentating with certain opiates. In the process, he becomes a drug addict and is eventually blackmailed by Christopher Lee, a graverobber, into signing false death certificates so that corpses can be sold to hospitals. Despite the authentic period design and good cast, this was a heavy-handed, ponderous medical-horror drama that was nothing more than a catalogue of amputated limbs and mutilations, as an increasingly deranged Karloff hacked away at his agonized patients—even the one-time King of Horror looked uncomfortable in it. Lee stabs Karloff to death in the end during a police raid on the graverobber's premises, and Karloff's son carries on his work to better use than his father. Made back-to-back with the superior *The Haunted Strangler*, the picture ranks as one of Croydon and Day's most unattractive efforts and was not given a release date until 1962.

Corruption
Columbia 1967; Technicolor; 91 mins; Cert. "X"
CREDITS: Producer: Peter Newbrook; Director: Robert Hartford-Davies
CAST: Peter Cushing; Sue Lloyd; Noel Trevarthen; Kate O'Mara; Vanessa Howard; David Lodge **

A mad surgeon murders women to obtain a gland he needs to restore the scarred face of his lover.

A gory British version of the type of continental sadistic surgical movies that were proliferating during this period, such as *The Awful Dr. Orloff* and *Seddok—Son of Satan*, but lacking in flair, with poor color photography. Peter Cushing played a baddie this time, who accidentally scars his fiancée's face at a party and has to resort to murder to obtain the glands he needs to restore her beauty, decapitating prostitutes and keeping their heads in his fridge. There is a vicious murder on a train, and the film seems to wallow in its own excesses. The ridiculous ending has a gang of teenagers breaking into Cushing's house and being wiped out by his laser drill—Cushing then wakes up and takes Sue Lloyd to a party, where the whole scenario commences again, as in *Dead of Night*. A crude exploitation movie, and one of the nastiest that Cushing appeared in during his long career in horror films.

The Cosmic Man
Allied Artists 1958; 72 mins; Cert. "A"
CREDITS: Producer: Robert A. Terry;
Director: Herbert Greene
CAST: John Carradine; Bruce Bennett;
Angela Greene; Paul Langton; Lyn
Osborn; Scotty Morrow **

A friendly alien sent to Earth to spread harmony among humans is greeted with hostility instead.

A low-budget quickie, vaguely reminiscent of *The Day the Earth Stood Still*, which just about works because of Carradine's sepulchral performance as the alien, dressed in a raincoat, hat and dark glasses and who has a negative image, casting a white shadow.
He arrives on Earth to preach the gospel of peace, to no avail. The poor special effects reflect themselves in Carradine's spaceship, which resembles nothing more than a giant ping-pong ball. Even his curing a crippled boy to prove his peaceful intentions does not prevent the military from bombarding the orb with magnetic deflectors, causing Carradine and his vessel to simply vanish at the end of the film, leaving his young friend, the cured little boy, to mourn his going.

Count Yorga, Vampire
Erica/American Intl. 1970; Technicolor; 91 mins; Cert. "X"
CREDITS: Producer: Michael Macready; Director: Bob Kelljan
CAST: Robert Quarry; Roger Perry; Michael Macready; Donna Anders; Michael Murphy; Judith Lang ***

A suave stranger who arrives in Los Angeles is a vampire count.

"America's answer to Count Dracula" is how one critic described this low-key but good-to-look-at vampire chiller, with an excellent performance by Robert Quarry, doing a Christopher Lee as Count Yorga, holding séances in his mansion as a ruse to ensnare more female victims into his sect. The movie is a bit too dark sometimes as most of the action takes place in Quarry's gloomy old mansion at night, with Donna Anders and Judith Lang falling under the bloodsucker's spell and Perry and Macready as the heroes trying to rescue them. Quarry is eventually defeated along with the vampirized Lang, but the film was such an unexpected success that it led to a follow-up in 1971, *The Return of Count Yorga*.

Crack in the World
Paramount 1965; Technicolor; 96 mins; Cert. "U"
CREDITS: Producers: Bernard Glasser and Lester A. Sansom; Director: Andrew Marton
CAST: Dana Andrews; Jeanette Scott; Kieron Moore; Alexander Knox; Peter Damon; Gary Lasdun ***

An attempt to tap the energy at the Earth's core causes a huge crack to appear in the ocean floor, causing widespread destruction around the world.

A 1960s disaster movie made before they began to mushroom in the 1970s. Dana Andrews is the scientist dying of cancer who, as the brains behind Project Inner Space, has caused the calamity, resulting in widespread tidal waves and earthquakes. A nuclear bomb is lowered down a volcano into the path of the crack, but this only succeeds in blowing a huge chunk of the planet into space, forming a new moon, and diverting the split into another direction. A second bomb is lowered into the crack, and eventually the Earth falls into pieces, with only Moore and Scott as the unlikely survivors on the new planet. The special effects are fine in a garish '60s manner, but the film almost grinds to a halt in dealing with the love triangle between the three leads and this spoils an otherwise colorful production.

The Crawling Hand
Hansen Enterprises/Regal Intl. 1963; 89 mins; Cert. "X"
CREDITS: Producer: Joseph F. Robertson; Director: Herbert L. Strock
CAST: Peter Breck; Kent Taylor; Arline Judge; Rod Lauren; Allison Hayes; Alan Hale Jr. ***
    Parts of a rocketship crash-land on a Florida beach and only the astronaut's arm and hand survive intact, infected with an alien force that gives it a life of its own.
    A low-budget but fairly diverting sci-fi movie directed by Strock, the man responsible for *Teenage Frankenstein* and *Blood Is My Heritage*. A space center commander (Peter Breck) is puzzled by his astronauts perishing in deep space when returning from the moon. When the base is forced to destroy an Earth-bound rocket with a deranged astronaut on board, students Rod Lauren and his girlfriend discover the dead astronaut's arm on a beach, which has been infected with an alien force responsible for the deaths in space; the murderous limb now possesses the ability to strangle people. When Lauren takes the limb back to his lodgings, it kills Lauren's landlady, also turning the student into a Jekyll-Hyde type maniac, with dark circles appearing under his eyes to signify that he has changed. Lauren then carries out a series of near-homicidal attacks before taking the limb to a deserted beach where, in front of the police, Beck and Taylor, he has a fit and finds himself cured. The arm, badly chewed by cats, is subsequently shipped off to Washington for analysis. The pace of the film is too slow at times and would have benefited by being at least 10 minutes shorter to make it more watchable. The movie appeared on the Sunday circuit in 1965 double billed with *The Haunted and the Hunted*.

The Creation of the Humanoids
Genie/Emerson 1962: Eastmancolor; 75 mins; Cert. "X"
CREDITS: Producers: Wesley E. Barry and Edward J. Kay; Director: Wesley E. Barry
CAST: Don Megowan; Frances McCann; Erica Elliott; Don Doolittle; Dudley Manlove **
    After World War Three, sophisticated robots that run the world demand equal rights with the humans they outnumber.
    An intriguing, minor sci-fi outing that is unfortunately let down by its stagy production values, with Don Megowan playing a scientist who becomes frustrated by man's over-reliance on the androids (known as Clickers), even though they number far more than the remnants of human society left after the war. When his daughter falls in love with one of them, he discovers that a scientist is infusing them with human blood to make them fertile, and replacing the remainder of the sterile human race with robots. The blue-skinned, hairless robots rebel against the humans and Megowan eventually finds out that he himself is an advanced model of one of the androids, capable of procreation. This had a limited release in the United Kingdom during 1964, double billed with *The Human Duplicators*.

Creature from the Black Lagoon
Universal 1953; Orig. in 3-D; 79 mins; Cert. "X"
CREDITS: Producer: William Alland; Director: Jack Arnold
CAST: Richard Carlson; Richard Denning; Julie Adams; Whit Bissell; Nestor Paiva; Ben Chapman *****
    A team of anthropologists journeys up a remote backwater in the Amazon jungle to capture the legendary gill-man, who has been terrorizing the local populace.

The archetypal 1950s creature-feature, originally shown in 3-D and now proved to be a very influential movie that inspired a host of modern-day directors including Steven Spielberg (who was a big fan of Jack Arnold's moody masterpiece). It became a massive hit for Universal when first released. The amphibious creature, designed by Bud Westmore, was played by Ricou Browning underwater (who could hold his breath for five minutes) and Ben Chapman on land and became one of the decade's most enduring characters, spawning two sequels. James C. Haven's superb underwater photography in the sequences featuring the creature in its watery element transforms the forbidden lagoon into a world of mystery and terror, making the monster appear pale, leprous and menacing. On land, the gill-man material-izes as a dark, avenging devil, terrorizing the small group of scientists marooned on their boat in the lagoon and carrying off Julie Adams to his lair before being shot and sink-ing beneath the waters to a supposed death. The director managed to create a brooding atmosphere out of the claustrophobic jungle settings, assisted by Hans J. Salter's full-blooded and much imitated score. In 1978 and 1982, this seminal horror film was given a limited showing in London in its original 3-D format, double billed with *It Came from Outer Space*.

The Creature Walks Among Us
Universal 1956; 78 mins; Cert. "X"
CREDITS: Producer: William Alland; Di-rector: John Sherwood
CAST: Jeff Morrow; Rex Reason; Leigh Snowden; Gregg Palmer; Don Megowan; Ricou Browning ***

The gill-man is recaptured in the everglades and undergoes a transformation into a more man-like creature.

Jack Arnold, who probably would have done a better job of it, did not direct the last in the *Creature* series of movies. The creature, again played underwater by Ricou Browning, is transformed into a lumbering Frankenstein-type monster by being doused in kerosene when it attacks Jeff Morrow's boat in a remote lagoon, and portrayed on land by Don Megowan. Once metamorphosed, the gill-man is taken to San Francisco and placed in an electrified pen, where Morrow and fellow scientists debate on its future. Unfortunately, the film has to have a love, or lust, interest going on between Morrow, Reason, Palmer and Leigh Snowden, which drags the pace a bit, but in compensation there is an exciting piece of action at the end when the monster escapes from his prison and runs amok in Morrow's house before finally hurling his tormentor from the verandah to his death. The final shot of the bullet-ridden creature gasping and lurching down a sandbank toward the open sea and certain death, as his lungs will not function underwater, is a classic of its type. Ironically, out of the three *Creature* films, this was the most popular on the Sunday one-day circuit in the United Kingdom, appearing frequently between 1960 and 1965 with other Universal favorites such as *Tarantula*, *The Deadly Mantis* and *Monster on the Campus*.

The Creature with the Atom Brain
Clover/Columbia 1955; 69 mins; Cert. "X"
CREDITS: Producer: Sam Katzman; Director: Edward L. Cahn
CAST: Richard Denning; Angela Stevens; Harry Lauter; Michael Granger; Gregory Gay; Karl Davis **

A Nazi scientist creates superbeings powered by atomic energy instead of brains.

A fast-moving but ultimately preposterous and heavy-going movie concerning a mad doctor, Gregory Gay, and a gangster, Michael Granger, attempting to rule the world by replacing dead men's brains with atomic energy, making them seven times stronger than a normal human. Granger also uses the atom-powered zombies to rob banks. Karl Davis is the main giant with the atom brain who goes on a rampage, and when police doctor Richard Denning discovers the man responsible, Gay sends out a whole army of his zombies to wreck the local town before they are all gunned down by the police—an unintentionally hilarious but gruesome climax. The film often went the rounds with *The H-Man*, *20 Million Miles to Earth* and *The Werewolf* in the early '60s.

Crescendo
Hammer/Seven Arts 1969; Technicolor; 95 mins; Cert. "X"
CREDITS: Producer: Michael Carreras; Director: Alan Gibson
CAST: Stephanie Powers; James Olsen; Jane Lapotaire; Joss Ackland; Margaretta Scott; Kirsten Betts *

A music student visits a composer's house in France and triggers a series of strange events.

This was the last of the '60s Hammer psychodramas and by now the formula had become decidedly stale. This time around, Powers was the imported American star, a piano student engaged in writing a thesis on a dead composer's life and becoming entangled with his strange family—his widow, Scott, her drug-addicted, half-paralyzed son, Olsen, and his lunatic brother locked away in the attic. When the maid who administers to the old lady is killed, it soon transpires that Powers has been lured to the house as a mate for the locked-away brother. With liberal doses of sex and violence to boost the weak plot, this was a film-it-by-numbers thriller, dull and tiresome by turns, that went the rounds in 1970 on a double bill with *Taste the Blood of Dracula*.

Cry of the Banshee
American Intl. 1970; Technicolor; 87 mins; Cert. "X"
CREDITS: Producers: James H. Nicholson and Samuel Z. Arkoff; Director: Daniel Haller
CAST: Vincent Price; Essy Persson; Hugh Griffith; Elisabeth Bergner; Patrick Mower; Hilary Dwyer **

In the 16th century, an English magistrate who is attempting to crush the rise of witchcraft in the country finds himself the target of an avenging demon sent by a local coven to destroy him.

Released in England on a double bill with *Count Yorga, Vampire*, this was a somewhat un-imaginative and dreary occult thriller, padded out with plenty of nudity and violence to keep the audiences of the time happy. Price played the magistrate, coming up against a mysterious young man, Patrick Mower, who befriends Hilary Dwyer, Price's sexy young daughter, so that he can worm his way into the magistrate's household. Mower is in fact an avenging devil sent by the coven's high priestess Elisabeth Bergner and can transform himself into a hideous monster at her command. Eventually Price as the witch persecutor is slain along with the rest of his family, Bergner is slaughtered, and Mower as the demon survives the lot of them.

Cult of the Cobra
Universal 1955; 82 mins; Cert. "X"
CREDITS: Producer: Howard Pine; Director: Francis D. Lyon
CAST: Faith Domergue; David Janssen; Marshall Thompson; Jack Kelly; Richard Long; Kathleen Hughes **

Six American GIs are cursed by the high priest of a cobra cult in India, and on their return to America, they begin to die in mysterious circumstances.

Although well made with an excellent cast, the premise of "woman turns into snake" (the main plotline in this film) was just not horrific enough to sustain much interest. When the GIs, who have intruded upon a forbidden Indian temple that is the home of a secret sect of cobra-worshippers, return to the United States, Faith Domergue, a high priestess, follows them to seek retribution. She has the ability to change herself into a deadly King Cobra and dispatches four of the soldiers by snakebite before falling for Marshall Thompson. Richard Long saves Thompson from a certain death by hurling the snake, just as it is about to attack, from a window to its death, only to see it change back into a lifeless Domergue. This was one of the lesser Universal horror movies of the '50s, with little suspense and no proper monster to excite an audience, appearing on the Sunday one-day circuit in the 1960s with other Universal productions such as *Revenge of the Creature* and *Monster on the Campus*.

The Curse of Frankenstein
Hammer/Warner Bros. 1957; Eastmancolor; 83 mins; Cert. "X"
CREDITS: Producer: Anthony Hinds; Director: Terence Fisher
CAST: Peter Cushing; Christopher Lee; Robert Urquhart; Hazel Court; Valerie Gaunt; Melvyn Hayes *****

Baron Frankenstein, with the aid of his unwilling assistant, creates a murderous being from various dead bodies.

Following the commercial and critical success of *The Quatermass Experiment*, Hammer turned their attentions to the old Universal classics and revamped the original *Frankenstein* in garish Eastmancolor, delivering to the British cinema-going public a severe jolt after years of monotonous, black and white post-war thrillers. The film came complete with severed hands, eyeballs and brains in jars and a gruesome-looking creature devoid of all personality, totally unlike the Karloff version. It also boasted a superbly mannered performance by Peter Cushing as the Baron, totally focused on his work at the expense of everyone else, including his long-suffering partner Hazel Court, and Christopher Lee was tremendous as the creature, even though he was plastered under layers of makeup. His appearance was further "improved" midway through the film when he was shot in the face after escaping from the laboratory and found roaming in the woods. Despite (or because of) reports of people fainting or feeling ill when watching the picture, and critics denouncing the film as "'disgusting" and "grotesque," it made an absolute fortune when first released both in Britain and America and carved out careers in horror films for both Cushing and Lee. Adverse comments notwithstanding, there was no denying the fact that it was an extremely stylish production, well directed by Terence Fisher, and it still ranks as one of Hammer's best-ever and most influential pieces of work.

The Curse of the Crimson Altar
aka: The Crimson Cult
Tigon/American Intl. 1968; Eastmancolor; 89 mins; Cert. "X"
CREDITS: Producer: Louis M. Heywood; Director: Vernon Sewell
CAST: Boris Karloff; Barbara Steele; Christopher Lee; Mark Eden; Virginia Wetherell; Rupert Davies *

A man searching for his missing brother encounters a cult of Devil-worshippers in a country house.

It must have seemed a good idea, on paper at least, to have Karloff, Lee and Steele appearing together in one film, but the finished product turned out to be a stinker, a mixture of everything the three stars had made previously, with liberal doses (as the '60s demanded) of whipping, sex and naked women to spice it all up. Mark Eden played the innocent man, Lee was the sinister leader of a gang of Satanists who believed himself to be a warlock, and Karloff was an expert in the occult. As for Steele, she reprised her role from Mario Bava's *Black Sunday*, playing a reincarnated 17th-century witch called Lavinia, her good looks almost unrecognizable under a layer of green face paint and wearing an outlandish golden ram headpiece. Some of the ideas used were also pinched from Bava's classic, implying that Eden's ancestors were the original executors of Lavinia. Lee and Steele plan to sacrifice Eden and his brother for their past misdeeds, but Karloff comes to the rescue and the Satanists perish as the house goes up in flames, with Lee changing into a witch as he expires. A shoddy, messy film that was both dull and derivative in every department and was also a flop at the box office when first released.

Curse of the Faceless Man
United Artists 1958; 66 mins; Cert. "X"
CREDITS: Producer: Robert E. Kent; Director: Edward L. Cahn
CAST: Richard Anderson; Adele Mara; Felix Locher; Elaine Edwards; Gar Moore; Bob Bryant
***

The calcified body of a gladiator buried for 2,000 years under the ashes of Pompeii comes alive and seeks out the reincarnation of his lost love.

An interesting cross between *The Mummy* and *The Golem*, with Bob Bryant as the stone-encased figure lumbering after Elaine Edwards, who just happens to be the image of the senator's daughter whom he loved centuries ago and who has dreams of a past existence relayed to her by a telepathic Bryant. Richard Anderson plays her boyfriend, scientific curator of the museum to which Bryant is taken. A neat little thriller with some eerie moments as the gladiator slowly comes to life, first strangling the truck driver who is transporting it to the museum, then roaming the museum in search of a sacred medallion, and finally carrying off Edwards to the sea in the climax and acting out a 2,000-year-old drama in the belief that he is saving her from an erupting Vesuvius—he dissolves in the water while Edwards escapes. This film was double billed with *It! The Terror from Beyond Space* in the early 1960s and these two movies, both directed by Cahn, were a popular crowd-puller on the Sunday one-day circuit.

Curse of the Fly
Lippert/20th Century Fox 1965; Cinemascope; 86 mins; Cert. "X"
CREDITS: Producers: Robert L. Lippert and Jack Parsons; Director: Don Sharp

CAST: Brian Donlevy; George Baker; Carole Gray; Michael Graham; Rachel Kempson; Jeremy Wilkins **

A scientist experimenting with a matter-transmitting machine physically distorts the people he transmits.

This, the last of the *Fly* movies, was the least believable, released in the United Kingdom with the abysmal *The Duel of the Space Monsters* and bearing little resemblance to the previous two films in the series. Donlevy and Baker are creating all kinds of monstrosities in their transmitting machine, including a man who ages to a skeleton in a few seconds, and two people transmitted who end up as one pulsating mass of flesh. The mutations are kept in a cellar but escape to wreak vengeance, and Donlevy ends up being transmitted to London to discover that his son has destroyed the only booth there; he finds himself lost forever in the fourth dimension. There are no fly-monsters in this film, Robert Lippert having purchased the title from Fox to use in the production, which is workman-like but not as inventive or imaginative as *The Fly* or *Return of the Fly*.

The Curse of the Mummy's Tomb
Hammer/Columbia 1964; Techniscope/Technicolor; 80 mins; Cert. "X"
CREDITS: Producer/Director: Michael Carreras
CAST: Fred Clark; Terence Morgan; Ronald Howard; Jeanne Rowland; George Pastell; Dickie Owen ****

The mummy of Pharaoh Ra-Anteff is taken to London and put on display but comes alive and goes on a rampage.

Hammer's second *Mummy* film was a lavish, big-budget affair, not quite up to the standard of their 1959 classic but still excellent entertainment. American showman Clark brings the mummy to England as a sideshow, despite Egyptian George Pastell, reprising his role from the 1959 movie, giving out the usual warnings that are ignored by the showman. Soon the mummy disappears periodically from where it is housed by Clark, prowling the foggy, dimly lit London streets, killing anyone who gets in its way and hunting down Terence Morgan, who just happens to be the reincarnation of his long-dead brother, responsible for the pharaoh's death 5,000 years ago. The climax sees the mummy fighting to the death with Morgan in the London sewers, with Jeanne Roland a horrified spectator. The film was originally released as second billing to *The Gorgon* in the United Kingdom, making a very good box office return for Hammer.

Curse of the Undead
Universal 1959; 79 mins; Cert. "X"
CREDITS: Producer: Joseph Gershenson; Director: Edward Dein
CAST: Michael Pate; Eric Fleming; Kathleen Crowley; John Hoyt; Bruce Gordon; Edward Binns ***

A strange gunslinger who arrives in a town in the Old West is a Spanish vampire.

An intriguing combination of a Western and horror film, and in its own low-budget way quite unique—it certainly wasn't repeated in any subsequent movies during the '50s and '60s.

Michael Pate plays a mysterious gunman dressed head to toe in black, who is hired by a female rancher being terrorized by a ruthless land baron who has murdered her father and brother. Pate somehow manages to win all of his gunfights even when shot first, and soon after his arrival young women in the town are found dying through a loss of blood. The gunslinger, being a vampire nobleman, is obviously allergic to sunlight although he does walk around when the sun is out. He falls for the rancher Kathleen Crowley, wishing her to become one of the undead and join him in immortality, before priest Eric Fleming (of *Rawhide* fame) shoots him dead with a bullet that contains a piece of the crucifix. There are no fangs or blood on show, but it works and is an underrated film from the Universal back catalogue of horror. In the United Kingdom, it appeared regularly on the Sunday circuit, usually with *The Thing that Couldn't Die.*

The Curse of the Werewolf
Hammer/Universal 1961; Technicolor; 91 mins; Cert. "X"
CREDITS: Producer: Anthony Hinds; Director: Terence Fisher
CAST: Clifford Evans; Oliver Reed; Yvonne Romain; Anthony Dawson; Richard Wordsworth; Michael Ripper ***

While in prison, a peasant girl is raped by a beggar and the resulting baby boy grows up to become a werewolf.

Hammer's first foray into the world of lycanthropy was loosely based on Guy Endore's novel *The Werewolf of Paris*, but unlike the book piled on the gruesome effects and transferred the location to 18th-century Spain. Yvonne Romain, after being assaulted in a filthy dungeon by a very foul Richard Wordsworth, gives birth to a boy who grows up to become Oliver Reed, looked after by a kindly doctor, Clifford Evans. Attractive to most of the girls in the village, Reed's fiery temper always gets the better of him. He eventually ends up in jail toward the end of the film, changing into a ferocious werewolf in the full moon, breaking out of his cell and going on a rampage in the village before Evans kills him in a bell-tower with a silver bullet. Reed conveyed the plight of lycanthropy well, his dark, brooding good looks just right for the part, although in some ways the film was cruder and less distinguished than Hammer's other productions of this period and suffered some minor cuts at the hands of the strict British censor. Nevertheless, it was another big hit for the company and a colorful addition to the Hammer stable.

Curucu, Beast of the Amazon
Jewell Enterprises/Universal 1956; Technicolor; 76 mins; Cert. "A"
CREDITS: Producers: Richard Kay and Harry Rybnick; Director: Curt Siodmak
CAST: John Bromfield; Beverly Garland; Tom Payne; Harvey Chalk; Sergio de Oliviera; Wilson Viana **

Two explorers who journey up the Amazon River in search of a cure for cancer meet a plantation owner deep in the jungle. His workers are deserting him because of a local legend concerning a monster known as Curucu that can kill if disturbed from its territory.

Made in Technicolor on location in Brazil and given a bigger budget than a lot of other Universal productions of the day, *Curucu* patently fails to deliver in the most important department. The so-called monster is tribal chieftain Tom Payne in disguise, scaring off the local native workforce so that his people can still live in a primitive state. Apart from that, there is a boring love interest going on between Bromfield and Garland as the two explorers trying to figure out why the natives are fleeing the plantation in droves from a mythical monster, and the film is not helped by a terribly twee South American tune as the background musical score. This monster-cum-adventure hodgepodge was originally released in America with *The Mole People* and turned up in the United Kingdom the late '50s and early '60s with both *The Monolith Monsters* and *The Mole People*.

The Cyclops
Allied Artists 1957; 75 mins; Cert. "X"
CREDITS: Producer/Director: Bert I. Gordon
CAST: James Craig; Lon Chaney Jr.; Gloria Talbott; Tom Drake; Dean Parkin ***

An expedition to a remote valley in Central America in search of a missing airman discovers that radiation has caused the animals to grow to an enormous size, and the missing man is a disfigured 25-foot giant.

This was one of Bert I. Gordon's more entertaining efforts, even though the one-eyed giant bore a striking resemblance to the monster in Gordon's own *War of the Colossal Beast.* In fact, Dean Parkin played the monster in both films. James Craig mounts an expedition to the Central American jungles in order to locate Gloria Talbott's fiancé, missing when his plane came down in a remote valley. The expedition encounters oversized snakes and rodents, mutations caused by the effects of radiation in the valley. The disfigured giant that terrorizes them is eventually blinded by a torch that Craig thrusts into the giant's eye. The expedition flees the valley and a horrified Talbott finally realizes that the monster is her missing fiancé. Plenty of back-projected and split-screen animals abound, and as usual with all of this particular director's films, these varied from the sublime to the ridiculous. Nevertheless, a better than average monster movie from Gordon for a change.

Daleks—Invasion Earth 2150 A.D.
Aaru/British Lion 1966; Techniscope/Technicolor; 84 mins; Cert. "U"
CREDITS: Producers: Max J. Rosenberg and Milton Subotsky; Director: Gordon Flemyng
CAST: Peter Cushing; Bernard Cribbens; Ray Brooks; Andrew Keir; Jill Curzon; Eddie Powell **

Dr. Who, his two granddaughters and a policeman are transported in the Tardis (his time machine) to a London in the future, where the Daleks plan to detonate a bomb in the Earth's interior and use the planet as a gigantic spaceship.

Although a distinct improvement on the previous Dr. Who film, this picture still suffered from the usual '60s malaise of gaudy color, a swinging James Bond-type score and plastic-looking sets. Policeman Bernard Cribbens, taking over the comedy role from Roy Castle in the first Dr. Who outing, mistakes the Tardis for a real police-box and transports Cushing and his granddaughters to London in the year 2150, where they find the city devastated by an alien disease and the Daleks patrolling the streets. The robotic menaces are planning to use the Earth as a vast spaceship by detonating a bomb in the planet's interior, and are using robo-men slaves as their workforce. Cushing organizes a rebellion to crush the invaders, and in the climax, Ray Brooks manages to deflect the bomb away from the Earth's center, creating a strong magnetic field that destroys the Daleks. The film performed poorly at the box office and the producers abandoned their plans to film a third Dalek movie based on Terry Nation's story *The Chase.*

The Damned
Hammer/Columbia 1963; Hammerscope; 87 mins; Cert. "X"
CREDITS: Producer: Anthony Hinds; Director: Joseph Losey
CAST: Oliver Reed; McDonald Carey; Shirley Ann Field; Viveca Lindfors; Alexander Knox; James Villiers ***

Radioactive children are kept hidden in a remote cave by scientists testing the effects of surviving in a post-nuclear world.

A not too successful mixture of science fiction and 1960s youth rebellion, which features an early performance by Oliver Reed as the leader of a gang of motorcyclists who chase an American couple, Carey and Field, to a cliff edge for kicks. There in a cave, the couple discovers a secret laboratory full of children being tended by scientists in radiation suits to learn what the effects would be on humans after an atomic war. Alexander Knox plays the cold-blooded scientist running the project, and Viveca Lindfors is his equally compassionless girlfriend, who spends her time creating strange, post-apocalypse sculptures. The two Americans attempt to free the imprisoned children at the end, but realize that they themselves have become contaminated with radiation and wander off to their doom, watched by a hovering helicopter. Although intelligently made, with some somber photography of the bleak English seascapes, this was just too depressing a film to make any impact at the box office when it was originally released, although it has grown in status over the years.

Dark Eyes of London
aka: The Human Monster
Pathe/Argyle 1939; 76 mins; Cert. "X"
CREDITS: Producer: John Argyle; Director: Walter Summers
CAST: Hugh Williams; Bela Lugosi; Greta Gynt; Wilfred Walter; Edmond Ryan; Alexander Field ***

A sinister doctor who runs a home for the blind sends out a mute giant to drown victims for their insurance money.

Bela Lugosi traveled to England to play the dual role of the proprietor of the Dearborn Institute for the Blind, removing his whiskery disguise to become Dr. Orloff, an insurance swindler. He sends out his mute, ugly thug (Wilfred Walter) to drown his victims in a tank before dumping their bodies in the Thames. Hugh Williams, as a detective, and Greta Gynt follow the trail of her missing father, who has fallen foul of Lugosi's activities. When Orloff orders the hulking killer to murder the mute's only friend who is aware of the doctor's insurance scam, the hulk kills Lugosi instead. This horrific and occasionally nasty little thriller was the first film to be awarded the "H" certificate in England, but later played in the early '60s as an X-rated movie, usually double billed with Dead Men Walk.

Daughter of Dr. Jekyll
Allied Artists 1957; 74 mins; Cert. "X"
CREDITS: Producer: Jack Pollexfen; Director: Edgar G. Ulmer
CAST: John Agar; Gloria Talbott; Arthur Shields; John Dierkes; Martha Wentworth; Mollie McCart **

A girl who arrives in England to claim her inheritance is informed that her deceased father was the infamous Doctor Jekyll.

Somewhere along the line, the scriptwriters decided to abandon the original Jekyll-Hyde concept and turn this into a werewolf movie instead, and it is a very long way into the film before Talbott is told about her father's experiments in dual personality. She is then suspected as the person responsible for a spate of killings that coincided with her arrival. The real culprit turns out to be Arthur Shields, Talbott's guardian, who changes into a werewolf after taking Jekyll's potion. At the end, he gets a stake through the heart from the villagers, even though in the final shot he appears to have survived. A different treatment of the Robert Louis Stevenson novel, only partly successful and panned by the critics when first released, the picture turned up on the Sunday circuit in 1962 with *The Atomic Submarine*.

The Day Mars Invaded Earth
20th Century Fox 1962; Cinemascope; 70 mins; Cert. "A"
CREDITS: Producer/Director: Maury Dexter
CAST: Kent Taylor; Marie Windsor; William Mims; Betty Beall; Lowell Brown; Greg Shank **

After a communication probe is sent to Mars, the Martians invade the Earth, taking over humans by reducing their bodies to ash and creating replicas.

A third-rate variation on *Invasion of the Body Snatchers* sees Kent Taylor and Marie Windsor as a pair of holidaymakers returning to their town and seeing doubles of their friends and family. The doubles are Martians, intelligent beings of energy traveling by radio beams, who are duplicating and killing off humans to prevent them from exploring and colonizing their planet. Unusually, the film ends with the invaders triumphant and Earth doomed. Cheap and not really inventive, the film was double billed with *Hercules at the Center of the Earth* and had a spasmodic release in the mid-'60s.

The Day of the Triffids
Allied Artists 1963; Cinemascope/Eastmancolor; 94 mins; Cert. "X"
CREDITS: Producer: George Pitcher; Director: Steve Sekely
CAST: Howard Keel; Janette Scott; Kieron Moore; Nicole Maurey; Janina Faye; Mervyn Johns ***

A shower of meteorites renders most of the world blind, and a species of giant man-eating plant turns on a defenseless mankind.

John Wyndham's celebrated early 1950s novel (on which this film was based) was very much in the mold of H.G. Wells' *The War of the Worlds*, an end-of-the-world saga set in the English Home Counties. This somewhat simplistic, rough and ready adaptation (ruined in parts by Ron Goodwin's ear-blasting score) eschewed most of Wyndham's thought-provoking ideas and went all out for monster thrills and mayhem, even including a sequence running side-by-side with the main events concerning a couple marooned at a lighthouse (marine biologist Moore and his wife, Scott) being menaced by the Triffids and defeating them with seawater that was never actually included in Wyndham's novel. Howard Keel was the imported American star this time, recovering from a minor eye operation and waking up in the hospital to a silent London populated by sightless citizens blinded by the meteorite's cosmic rays. Rescuing young Janina Faye from the aftermath of a train crash, he heads off to France and ends up trying to lead a small band of sighted and blind people to safety by avoiding the lurching creatures with their lashing stingers. The climax, which is a bit of a cop-out (in the book, the Triffids survive), has Keel luring hundreds of the plants that have surrounded a house in Spain, where his group have taken refuge, over a cliff to a watery death (they are lured by music from an ice cream van that attracts them). He then rejoins his group in southern Spain. The Triffids themselves, resembling giant seven-foot-high lumbering vegetables with highly colorful heads, were a popular addition to the science fiction/horror catalogue, and the film was a big hit at the U.K. box office when first released with *The Legion's Last Patrol*.

The Day the Earth Caught Fire
British Lion 1961; Dyaliscope; 99 mins; Cert. "X"
CREDITS: Producer/Director: Val Guest
CAST: Edward Judd; Leo McKern; Janet Munro; Michael Goodliffe; Arthur Christiansen; Reginald Beckwith ****

Atomic bomb tests knock the Earth off its axis and it begins to drift toward the sun, threatening all life on the planet.

A superior, intelligent although talkative Britsh science fiction "end of the world" movie directed in semi-documentary fashion by Val Guest that was a big hit when first released. The central part of the film depicting journalists slowly beginning to realize just what is behind the meteoric rise in temperatures and the River Thames drying up is given added realism and drama by the casting of Arthur Christiansen, ex-editor of *The Daily Express*, as boss of the newspaper that breaks the news. Edward Judd as a boozy journalist and Janet Munro supply the love interest, and there is a tense mood of impending catastrophe as, in the end, four bombs are detonated to shift the planet back into the correct orbit. The result of this is never shown—the film pessimistically ends with two newspaper headlines—"World Saved" and "World Doomed."

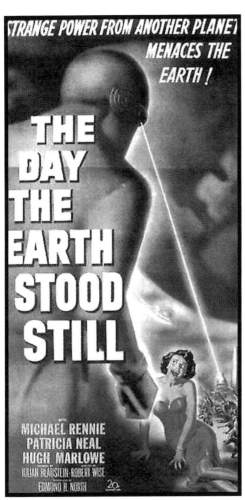

The Day the Earth Stood Still
20th Century Fox 1951; 92 mins; Cert. "U"
CREDITS: Producer: Julian Blaustein; Director: Robert Wise
CAST: Michael Rennie; Patricia Neal; Hugh Marlowe; Sam Jaffe; Billy Gray; James Seay ****

A flying saucer lands in Washington and the world is warned by a friendly alien that atomic wars must cease forthwith; otherwise, extraterrestrial action will follow.

One of the more literate science fiction films of the 1950s, not overly exciting (in fact, it tends to sag in the middle) but expertly put together, with "Klaatu Barada Nikto," the command that Michael Rennie gives to his robot assistant, Gort, becoming a cult phrase among science fiction buffs. The scenes of the saucer landing in front of the massed ranks of military in Washington, of Gort blasting the army with a ray from his helmet, and of the world's power supply "standing still" for 30 minutes as a sign of Rennie's powers, add to the sense of unease that mankind is being manipulated by a superior being. It is only when Rennie befriends widow Patricia Neal and her son that the movie loses momentum. After being shot by the military, Rennie is restored to life by Gort and, with a parting message to Earth again warning of the consequences of any more warlike behavior, flies off into space. Bernard Herrmann contributed to the production one of the earliest of his fantasy scores, and a fine one at that.

Day the World Ended
American Intl. 1956; Superscope; 81 mins; Cert. "X"
CREDITS: Producer/Director: Roger Corman
CAST: Richard Denning; Lori Nelson; Adele Jergens; Touch Connors; Paul Birch; Jonathan
Haze ***

Seven disparate survivors from a nuclear holocaust gather together in a mountain retreat
that is shielded from radioactive fallout and are menaced by telepathic mutants who live in the
surrounding woods.

One of the foremost of the Roger Corman films of the 1950s—a fast-paced post-apocalyptic
thriller with an intelligent script and well acted by the small cast. The oddly assorted group, including a geologist and a gangster who end up fighting over Lori Nelson, squabble among themselves
in their hideout as their food and water is running out, while in the surrounding woods, radiation
is causing everything to mutate. There are some eerie moments as the three-eyed flesh-eating
monster, roaming in the woods surrounding the retreat, tries to lure the survivors out of their cabin
by telepathy, and a good build-up of tension and suspense as one of the bickering survivors begins
to mutate into one of the creatures. The end of the film sees the mutant dissolving in a downpour
of pure, nonradioactive rain after it has abducted the delectable Nelson, who, with Richard Denning, walks away from the cabin to what they hope is a new and better world to live in.

Dead Men Walk
PRC 1943; 64 mins; Cert. "X"
CREDITS: Producer: Sigmund Neufeld; Director: Sam Newfield
CAST: George Zucco; Mary Carlisle; Dwight Frye; Nedrick Young; Robert Strange; Fern Em-
mett ***

The corpse of a man's twin brother who in life dabbled in black magic and sorcery rises
from the dead as a vampire and seeks vengeance.

George Zucco starred as the twins in this fast-moving B feature, produced by the Neufeld/
Newfield partnership and obviously modeled on Universal's output of the time. This was the
only time Zucco ever played a monster—most of his roles were of the mad doctor type. The
vampire twin, assisted by maniacal hunchback Dwight Frye (virtually reprising his character from
Dracula), rises from his coffin, swearing vengeance on his doctor brother, who was responsible
for his death. He attempts to vampirize his niece, Mary Carlisle, but a gold cross she is wearing
thwarts his attempts. Other people in the town fall victim to him before both twins perish in the
evil brother's house, which catches fire at cockcrow. Frye is crushed to death under an altar stone
as the enraged local inhabitants look on in shock. This dimly lit but atmospheric little horror
thriller was one of the better efforts to come out of the PRC studios during the '40s, and Zucco
was once again excellent as both the doctor and the bloodsucking twin.

Dead of Night
Ealing 1945; 120 mins; Cert. "A"
CREDITS: Producer: Michael Balcon; Directors: Alberto Cavalcanti, Basil Deardon, Robert
Hamer and Charles Chrichton
CAST: Mervyn Johns; Michael Redgrave; Googie Withers; Frederick Valk; Sally Ann Howes;
Elizabeth Welch ****

An architect who visits a cottage in the country is told a number of supernatural tales by the
occupants, only to wake up and find that he is reliving the experience all over again.

Many critics claim that this film is overrated, but it still remains a unique British exercise
in terror, with a sterling cast to carry it along, not to mention its four renowned directors. The
tales told to Mervyn Johns range from the comic, concerning two golfers (which, on hindsight,
is out of context with the remainder of the film), to the spine chilling, as in the room with a large,
ornate mirror that reflects a past tragedy. This is perhaps the finest of the stories, although it has

been overshadowed by the final tale, in which his own dummy possesses Michael Redgrave as a ventriloquist. The "circle of terror" motif, which was a mainstay of many a horror film of the 1960s, appears here as Johns, after hearing the stories, tries to strangle one of the guests in the house. He is then woken up by his telephone ringing, with the caller informing him that he has to visit a cottage, which of course is where the film started. The picture was highly successful at the time, probably because the British censor had placed an embargo on horror movies being shown in the United Kingdom during the War, which meant that the cinema-going public had had enough of musicals and routine thrillers by the time the War had ended and needed something more substantial to get their cinematic teeth into, which *Dead of Night* duly provided.

The Dead One
Mardis Gras/Favorite Films 1961; Ultrascope/Eastmancolor; 71 mins; Cert. "X"
CREDITS: Producer/Director: Barry Mahon
CAST: John McKay; Linda Ormond; Monica Davis; Clyde Kelley; Darlene Myrick **
A woman resurrects her dead brother as a zombie to kill her cousin, who plans to inherit her estate.
An uninspiring voodoo thriller commencing with a tour of New Orleans' strip clubs, used solely by Barry Mahon as a means of titillating the audience. Monica Davis is the woman who resuscitates her dead brother, Clyde Kelley, to use him to murder her cousin and his wife, but the zombie only ends up by slaying a bellydancer, whom he mistakes for the cousin's wife, and is shot by the police, disintegrating in the sun as Davis also gets killed. Kelley's zombie makeup and the widescreen color photography are about the only plus factors in this cheap-looking movie that was originally released on a double bill with *The Monster of Piedras Blancas*.

The Deadly Bees
Amicus/Paramount 1966; Technicolor; 83 mins; Cert. "X"
CREDITS: Producers: Max J. Rosenberg and Milton Subotsky; Director: Freddie Francis
CAST: Suzanna Leigh; Frank Finlay; Guy Doleman; Catherine Finn; John Harvey; Katy Wild
*
A female rock singer holidays at a remote farm on a Scottish island where an insane beekeeper has created a strain of killer bees.
One of the worst of the Amicus productions of the '60s, flatly directed by Freddie Francis, who must have had little empathy with this kind of uninspiring material to work on. Suzanna Leigh plays a singer, encountering Frank Finlay as the beekeeper who sets his insects on anyone who tries to escape off the island. After several people have died due to extensive stings to their faces, Leigh herself is attacked in a scene pinched straight out of Hitchcock's *The Birds*, but she and Guy Doleman manage to finally set the bees on their creator, who is stung to death. The film originally ran for over two hours, but was trimmed down for general release and adds weight to the argument that bees are probably the least engrossing of any movie monsters ever to hit the big screen.

The Deadly Mantis
Universal 1957; 79 mins; Cert. "X"
CREDITS: Producer: William Alland; Director: Nathan Juran
CAST: Craig Stevens; Alix Talton; William Hopper; Donald Randolph; Florenz Ames; Pat Conway ****
Following volcanic activity, a gigantic preying mantis thaws from an iceberg in the Arctic and heads south along the Gulf Stream toward the tropics, leaving a trail of devastation in its wake.
The Deadly Mantis is out in the forefront among the 1950s cycle of giant insect films, with splendid special effects by Clifford Stine. It includes scenes of the colossal mantis buzzing over the frozen wastes, causing panic among the Eskimos, attacking aircraft and ships, demolishing an Arctic research station, popping up on radar screens, and landing in a mist-shrouded Washington,

overturning buses and climbing up the Washington Monument. After much deliberation by the experts, palaeontologist William Hopper finally deduces what the creature is from a huge spur that has broken off from one of its legs. The climax sees Hopper, Commander Craig Stevens and the military fighting the monster in Manhattan's Holland Tunnel, destroying it with poison gas, although in the final shot, Alix Talton, taking a flash photograph of the corpse, almost gets crushed by one of the insect's massive feelers as it convulses after expiring. This was a very popular addition to Universal's creature-features of the '50s and a big favorite on both the Sunday one-day circuit and the late-night shows in the early and late 1960s, usually double billed with *The Land Unknown*.

Demons of the Swamp
aka: Attack of the Giant Leeches
Anglo Amalgamated/American
Intl. 1959; 62 mins; Cert. "X"
CREDITS: Producer: Gene Corman; Director: Bernard L. Kowalski
CAST: Ken Clark; Yvette Vickers; Michael Emmet; Bruno Ve Sota; Jan Shepherd; Tyler McVey **
Giant leeches in a remote Florida swamp devour humans.

Most of this picture concerns a triangular love story between Clark, Vickers and Emmet, a barman, resulting in the lovers being forced into a swamp where giant mutated leeches dwell. The leeches are the result of genetic changes due to pollution from Cape Canaveral, and although the swamps give the film some air of authenticity, the monsters themselves are unbelievably fake looking and very hard to see in the murky underwater scenes, where they live in caves. The only gruesome parts of the film are the mutilated bodies covered in sucker marks floating to the surface of the swamp after being sucked dry of blood by the leeches. After numerous arguments between the cast of rednecks as to whether or not it is ecologically correct to destroy the area even though it is populated by man-eating leeches, the swamps are blown up, destroying the monsters. It's a dull, unimaginative horror movie showing a lack of skill in most departments—one or two scary moments just about save it from being a stinker.

Destination Moon
Eagle Lion 1950; Technicolor; 91 mins; Cert. "U"
CREDITS: Producer: George Pal; Director: Irving Pichel
CAST: John Archer; Warner Anderson; Dick Wesson; Tom Powers; Erin O'Brien-Moore; Ted Warde ***
A space crew's first flight to the moon and the hazards they encounter on landing.

A sober, semi-documentary George Pal production that tells of the first manned rocket to the moon, with rather wooden performances by the leads and a stodgy, half-jokey script that grates on the nerves after a while, although the lunar landscape itself looks starkly impressive, based on the paintings of astronomical artist Chesley Bonestell. On landing, the crew has problems with a lack of fuel, thus jeopardizing their eventual take off, but in the end, they find the means to do this without endangering life and the need to jettison all of their supplies. It all looks rather dated now, but the film earned Pal an Oscar for Best Special Effects and was a big success when first released.

The Devil Bat
PRC 1940; 69 mins; Cert. "A"
CREDITS: Producer: Jack Gallagher; Director: Jean Yarbrough
CAST: Bela Lugosi; Suzanne Karen; Dave O'Brien; Hal Price; Donald Kerr; Guy Usher **

A physician creates giant bats from electricity and then trains the creatures to seek out and kill his enemies, who are wearing a particular scent.

A typical B potboiler of its day, with Lugosi going through his usual leering, demented-scientist routine, creating the bats by electrical currents in his laboratory and sending them on their way to attack and kill all those who cross his path. He ends up a victim of his own making as the odor, a special aftershave, gets onto his body by mistake and he is dispatched by one of his own creations. A creaky old horror melodrama, very stagy to look at, and one of many churned out by this small independent film company during the '40s—it was virtually remade by PRC in 1946 as *The Flying Serpent*.

Devil Bat's Daughter
PRC 1946; 67 mins; Cert. "A"
CREDITS: Producer/Director: Frank Wisbar
CAST: Eddie Kane; Rosemary La Planche; John James; Molly Lamont; Michael Hale; Edward Cassidy **

An unscrupulous psychiatrist murders his wife but puts the blame on a young woman in his charge, who imagines herself to be a vampire.

PRC's belated follow-up to *The Devil Bat* was another fairly low-key effort from the studio, made six years after the Lugosi picture. La Planche, Lugosi's daughter, fears that she has inherited not only her father's interest in vampires and bats but also his murderous tendencies, and has nightmares about him. She enlists the help of psychiatrist Eddie Kane, who attempts to drive her mad, as he wants to exploit her fears. Kane murders his wife through jealousy and gets the police to believe that his patient carried out the crime, but is found out in the end. For some strange reason, Lugosi's name from the previous film is also cleared, making him out to be a harmless research scientist, and La Planche, having vindicated her father, becomes a normal young woman. This pedestrian thriller was still being shown as late as 1965 on a double bill with *The Mad Monster* at various small cinemas that specialized in screening these old movies.

Devil Doll
Gala/Anglo Amalgamated 1964; 80 mins; Cert. "X"
CREDITS: Producer/Director: Lindsay Shonteff
CAST: Bryant Halliday; William Sylvester; Sandra Dorne; Yvonne Romain; Frances de Wollf; Karel Stepanek **

A famous ventriloquist murders his partner and transfers his soul to his dummy—he then plans to do the same to a girl he likes.

A low-key variation of the old ventriloquist's dummy motif, always good for the odd shock or two because of the notion of a doll-like figure coming to life. Bryant Halliday has already transferred the soul of his murdered partner into Hugo, the dummy, and has designs on Yvonne Romain, hypnotizing her to like him because he wants her soul transferred as well into a female dummy. Halliday's mistress becomes jealous, so the dummy murders her, and Romain's boyfriend, William Sylvester, smells a rat, starting an investigation into the ventriloquist. Eventually, Hugo the dummy brings about the downfall of his master, who has become mentally and physically weakened by his act, and transfers the soul of the dead partner back into Halliday. As with a lot of minor horror movies made during this period, *Devil Doll* now looks more dated than many 1950s low-budget films, mainly due to its swinging '60s mood that is at odds with the storyline. Nevertheless, it does manage to conjure up some spooky moments, especially in the scenes of the walking and talking dummy, which, unfortunately, vaguely resembles Alfred E. Neuman of *MAD Magazine* fame.

Devil Girl from Mars
Danziger/Spartan 1954; 77 mins; Cert. "U"
CREDITS: Producers: Edward J. Danziger and Harry Lee Danziger; Director: David MacDonald
CAST: Patricia Laffan; Hazel Court; Peter Reynolds; Hugh McDermott; Adrienne Corri; Joseph Tomelty ***

An assorted group of people staying at a remote inn in the Scottish Highlands is menaced by a female Martian and her robot, who have landed on Earth to kidnap men for breeding purposes.

A camp British classic that has Patricia Laffan as the alien Nyah, dressed from head to foot in a black PVC cloak, boots, a very short skirt and tights, landing in Scotland and, aided by her robot assistant Chani, creating a force field around a studio-bound Scottish inn so that she can kidnap the males her race of people need to survive on Mars following an atomic war. The effects are cheap but effective in a Dr. Who-type of way, with a splendid flying saucer and Chani the robot resembling a large refrigerator on legs who has the ability to fire off thunderbolts from his head. After most of the cast have either unsuccessfully attempted to escape or kill the alien, the climax sees Laffan taking one of the characters, a convict, on board the spacecraft and threatening to decimate the inn and its occupants with a death ray as she heads for London and more victims. However, on instructions from a professor among the group, the convict manages to interrupt the ship's power source and it explodes after taking off, wiping out everyone on board. Stagy-looking, featuring some hilariously stilted dialogue spoken by a decent cast, a rambunctious score by Edwin Astley, and an astonishingly wooden but oddly arresting performance from Laffan, spouting streams of scientific jargon with a deadpan delivery, this largely forgotten British science fiction movie really has to be seen to be believed.

The Devil Rides Out
Hammer/Warner Bros. 1968; Technicolor; 95 mins; Cert. "X"
CREDITS: Producer: Anthony Nelson-Keys; Director: Terence Fisher
CAST: Christopher Lee; Charles Gray; Patrick Mower; Leon Greene; Sarah Lawson; Gwen Ffrangcon-Davies ****

The Duc de Richleau goes into battle with a black magician who is trying to initiate his friends into a circle of Satanists.

A superior latter-day Hammer production based on Dennis Wheatley's celebrated black magic novel and one of a series he wrote featuring the character of de Richleau. Christopher Lee is excellent in the role of the Duc, while Charles Gray is splendidly suave and sinister as the Satanist Mocata, playing a game of cat and mouse with Lee with the souls of Patrick Mower and his girlfriend at stake. Lee rescues the pair from a ritual in a house in the suburbs of London that conjures up a deadly apparition, and later breaks up a mass on Salisbury Plain when the Devil himself puts in an appearance. The highlight of the film occurs when Lee and his companions are trapped within the pentagram, a mystic circle, in Gray's house, warding off an onslaught of supernatural apparitions including a giant spider and Death on horseback. The rather confusing climax (it helps

if you have read the book) has Gray becoming a victim of the Angel of Death, who was unable to claim de Richleau as a victim, and time itself being reversed so that the Duc and his friends can lead a normal existence. Despite the meticulous attention to detail in this picture, it failed to set the box office alight and Hammer abandoned their plans to film any more of Wheatley's black magic stories, although they had one more stab at the genre with 1976's *To the Devil A Daughter*.

Devils of Darkness
Planet 1965; Eastmancolor; 90 mins; Cert. "X"
CREDITS: Producer: Tom Blakeley; Director: Lance Comfort
CAST: William Sylvester; Tracy Reed; Hubert Noel; Carole Gray; Diane Decker; Victor Brooks
**

In Brittany, a vampire count and his Gypsy bride prey on holidaymakers.

A minor league vampire movie, taking place, apart from the prologue, in a contemporary setting, produced by independent film company Planet. Hubert Noel is the French bloodsucker Count Sinistre, who is revived on All Souls Eve after being put to death nearly 400 years ago by the local villagers. William Sylvester plays a writer who obtains the medallion that sustains the vampire's existence after a woman he has befriended is abducted by the Count and murdered, with the vampire sect subsequently following him to England, as they want the medallion back to continue their devilish work. In the end, the Devils of Darkness cult is destroyed by lightning in an underground crypt as they are about to sacrifice Tracy Reed, Noel disintegrating into a ravaged corpse when he is caught in the rising sun's rays that throw the shadow of a cross over him. Made on an obvious shoestring budget compared to the Hammer and Amicus productions of the time, which it was clearly modeled on, this thriller tried its hardest to be colorful, exciting and suspenseful but unfortunately fell flat in all departments—and Noel as Count Sinistre ranks as one of the *least* sinister vampires in horror screen history.

The Diabolical Doctor Z
Hesperia/Speva (Spain/France) 1965; 86 mins; Cert. "X"
CREDITS: Producers: Serge Silberman and Michel Safra; Director: Jesus Franco
CAST: Mabel Karr; Fernando Montes; Estella Blain; Antonio J. Escribano; Howard Vernon; Guy Mairesse ***

The daughter of a mad scientist who has died after inventing a mind-control machine takes over her father's work and vows to avenge his death.

Another foreign exercise in sadism by Jesus Franco, with Mabel Karr as the scientist's daughter. She controls a dancer, Estella Blain, with long deadly fingernails, as a revenge tool for her father's death. The mind-control machine sinks needles into people's flesh to change their personalities and nearly finishes off the hero, Fernando Montes, before the police rescue him after exposing Karr as the mad killer. The film is filled with umpteen shots of the gloomy old house where Karr resides with a room full of dolls, and degenerates toward the end into a series of disjointed and chaotic scenes filled with savage imagery (a woman being mutilated by Karr), with the usual weird soundtrack, a hallmark of Franco's movies.

Diary of A Madman
United Artists 1963; Technicolor; 96 mins; Cert. "X"
CREDITS: Producer: Robert E. Kent; Director: Reginald LeBorg
CAST: Vincent Price; Nancy Kovak; Christopher Warfield; Elaine Devry; Lewis Martin; Ian Wolfe **

A French magistrate is possessed by the evil spirit of a criminal that compels him to commit murder.

Vincent Price plays a French judge who accidentally kills a murderer after being attacked in the man's cell, and is taken over by the Horla, an evil spirit that feeds on a person's torments. Price begins to experience ghostly hallucinations and manifestations of his dead wife and ends up decapitating model Nancy Kovak after taking up sculpture as a hobby. All this is told in the form of a diary as the magistrate finally decides to kill himself in a fire to destroy the spirit that is urging him to murder. Despite Price's usual energetic performance, this was a rather unsatisfactory effort all round, carelessly directed by LeBorg, with extremely ineffective color photography, especially in the scenes showing the Horla's victims bathed in a green light. The film, not shown in the United Kingdom until 1965, was not a success at the box office.

Dinosaurus!
Fairview/Universal 1960; Cinemascope/DeLuxeColor; 85 mins; Cert. "A"
CREDITS: Producer: Jack H. Harris; Director: Irvin S. Yeaworth Jr.
CAST: Ward Ramsey; Gregg Martell; Paul Lukather; Kristina Hanson; Alan Roberts; Fred Engleberry **

Workers on an island in the tropics unearth two dinosaurs and an apeman, which are then revived by lightning.

A passable juvenile monster yarn, made on a fairly limited budget judging by the variable special effects. The Neanderthal man takes up the best part of the film, running around and making a nuisance of himself, breaking into houses and trying to come to grips with the modern world while befriending a young boy. The two dinosaurs, a friendly Brontosaurus and an unfriendly Tyrannosaurus, make their appearances toward the end of the film. These were animated by Wah Chang, Tim Barr and Gene Warren, and although quite adequate are not in the Ray Harryhausen league. The apeman falls to his death in a mineshaft, the Brontosaurus sinks in a swamp, and the Tyrannosaurus has a battle with a crane and is forced over the edge of a cliff, where it perishes. Yeaworth, who directed this rather lightweight fantasy, was the man behind the more successful *The Blob* and *The Evil Force*.

The Disembodied
Allied Artists 1957; 66 mins; Cert. "X"
CREDITS: Producer: Ben Schwalb; Director: Walter Grauman
CAST: Allison Hayes; Paul Burke; Eugenia Paul; John Wengraf; Robert Christopher; Joel Marston ***

A scientist working in the tropics is unaware that his wife possesses voodoo powers.

A weird mixture of a jungle and a voodoo picture, with the ubiquitous Allison Hayes holed up in the jungle with her scientist husband, John Wengraf, whom she detests. She discovers that she has the power to work magic spells and, unbeknown to her husband, becomes a native voodoo queen known as Tonda. When a party of visitors arrives at their jungle outpost, Hayes begins to seduce the men, falling for Paul Burke. Showing the others her magic by cutting out the heart of a native and using it to cure one of the visitors who has been mauled by a lion, she then tries to coerce Burke into murdering her husband. When he refuses, she sets him up to be a voodoo sacrifice, but Hayes herself is murdered at the ritual by the dead native's mate, who is bent on revenge. The fake jungle sets, risible dialogue and an over-the-top performance by Hayes put this firmly into the "camp classic" class, and the film was double billed with *The Cyclops* and other Allied Artists movies on the U.K. Sunday circuit between 1962 and 1965.

Doctor Blood's Coffin
United Artists 1960; Eastmancolor; 92 mins; Cert. "X"
CREDITS: Producer: George Fowler; Director: Sidney J. Furie
CAST: Kieron Moore; Hazel Court; Ian Hunter; Fred Johnson; Kenneth J. Warren; Paul Stockman ***

In a small Cornish village, a young doctor practices unorthodox heart surgery on the living by administering to them a cataleptic drug.

A colorful and lurid British horror movie featuring an edgy, overwrought performance by Kieron Moore in the title role of the young doctor. He joins his father's medical practice in a remote Cornish village and then attempts to revive the dead by taking the living hearts from selected local villagers (whom he first puts in a coma by administering a potion originating from the Orinoco in South America), killing anyone who happens to get in his way. The film, a big hit in England when first released, was shot rather unusually around the St. Just area of Cornwall and makes good location use of the old ruined mines on the coast as a backdrop to Moore's nefarious activities, where he has set up a laboratory in an abandoned mine, keeping various bodies in suspended animation to experiment on. As the death toll mounts, his operations culminate in him digging up the body of nurse Hazel Court's dead husband, giving it a new heart, and bringing it back to life in front of her as proof of his work, where upon the reactivated decaying corpse strangles Moore and Court escapes to the beach, where the police are waiting.

Dr. Renault's Secret
20th Century Fox 1942; 58 mins; Cert. "A"
CREDITS: Producer: Sol M. Wurtzel; Director: Harry Lachman
CAST: George Zucco; J. Carol Naish; Lynne Roberts; John Shepherd; Jack Norton; Mike Mazurki ***

A young man visits his fiancée in a remote French village and meets the mysterious assistant of a doctor who has been dabbling in genetic experiments.

20th Century Fox jumped onto the '40s horror bandwagon with this low-key chiller in which George Zucco played a French professor who has conducted experiments on an ape from Java and changed him into apeman J. Carrol Naish, now Zucco's handyman. Naish is attracted in a forlorn sort of way to Zucco's niece, Lynne Roberts. When a local man is murdered who has changed hotel rooms with her boyfriend John Shepherd, Naish becomes the chief suspect. Mike Mazurki turns out to be the villain, eventually trying to abduct Roberts, whom he has designs on, and is foiled by the apeman, who is killed trying to save the girl. Well acted by a good cast, with Naish excellent as the lonely victim of Zucco's experiments, this was a minor effort compared to the full-blooded horror movies being turned out by Universal and the other big studios, but nevertheless an interesting addition to the old ape-into-man scenario.

Dr. Terror's House of Horrors
Amicus 1964; Techniscope/Technicolor; 98 mins; Cert. "X"
CREDITS: Producers: Milton Subotsky and Max J. Rosenberg; Director: Freddie Francis
CAST: Peter Cushing; Christopher Lee; Donald Sutherland; Roy Castle; Neil McCallum; Alan Freeman **

An eccentric old man in a railway carriage tells the fortunes of five fellow passengers and turns out in the end to be Death himself.

This was the first of the Amicus compendium series of horror films and perhaps the weakest, despite the high budget and the obvious care and attention lavished upon it. The most compelling scenes are in the train carriage, with Peter Cushing portraying Death, and at the climax as the passengers realize when alighting onto a deserted platform that they are all dead, with Cushing revealing himself to be the harbinger of doom. The five stories, all variations on the old horror stand-bys, concerning a werewolf, a man-eating vine, voodoo rituals, a dismembered hand, and a vampire, were admittedly well performed by a decent cast, yet none of them were particularly horrific, suspenseful or hair-raising for a film of this type, although the movie was entertaining enough to be a big hit at the box office. Later titles in the series were *Torture Garden*, *Asylum*, *Tales from the Crypt* and *The Vault of Horror*, all of which were a distinct improvement on this picture.

Doctor Who and the Daleks
Aaru/British Lion 1965; Tech-
niscope/Technicolor; 83 mins;
Cert. "U"
CREDITS: Producers: Max J.
Rosenberg and Milton Subotsky;
Director: Gordon Flemyng
CAST: Peter Cushing; Roy
Castle; Jennie Linden; Roberta
Tovey; Barrie Ingham; Geoffrey
Toone **

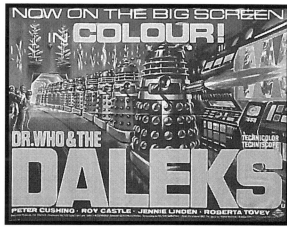

Doctor Who and his com-
panions are transported in the
Tardis to the planet Skaro, where
the robotic Daleks rule over the
Thals.

The big-screen version of the popular BBC television serial turned out to be a brightly colored tacky romp, sporting a ghastly swinging '60s soundtrack, pantomime-looking sets and an awkward, bumbling performance from Peter Cushing as the eccentric Doctor. While at the Doctor's residence in the West Country, Roy Castle accidentally presses the forward lever in Cushing's time machine, the Tardis, and he, Cushing, Jennie Linden and Roberta Tovey are shot forward to Skaro, a planet devastated by a neutron war caused by the Daleks, who are also enslaving the effeminate and ineffectual Thals and preparing to use another bomb to decimate the population. After much frantic running around and escaping from the Daleks and their ray guns in various multicolored sets, the robotic terrors and their bomb are vanquished and the Thals saved from extinction. The picture was moderately successful, being squarely aimed at a children's audience, but was not looked upon favorably by die-hard Dr. Who fans, who found it lacked gravitas and was far too juvenile for their liking.

Doppelganger
aka: Journey to the Far Side of the Sun
Universal 1969; Cinemascope/DeLuxeColor; 101 mins; Cert. "A"
CREDITS: Producers: Gerry and Sylvia Anderson; Director: Robert Parrish
CAST: Ian Hendry; Roy Thinnes; Lynn Loring; Patrick Wymark; Herbert Lom; Ed Bishop **

A planet that is the exact double of Earth is discovered orbiting the far side of the sun, where everything is opposite to our own planet.

The idea of a parallel Earth is an ingenious one, with Ian Hendry and Roy Thinnes as the astronauts traveling to the planet on the other side of the sun only to discover that everything is the same as the Earth but in reverse, such as people driving on the opposite side of the road and writing backwards. Thinnes eventually tries to return to his home planet in a special spacecraft built on the "other" Earth, but the mother ship orbiting the planet rejects the vessel because it has reverse polarity, sending the ship crashing into the space complex from whence Thinnes originally set out, creating an explosive climax as the complex blows up. Despite the exciting ending, the film floundered in the middle through too much philosophical talk concerning the differences between the two worlds and finished up being rather dull. The special effects by the Anderson team who were responsible for *Thunderbirds* were excellent but did nothing to enliven a somewhat stodgy production, and the film had a typically end-of-the-'60s air about it.

Dracula

Universal 1931; 84 mins; Cert. "X"

CREDITS: Producer: Carl Laemmle Jr.; Director: Tod Browning

CAST: Bela Lugosi; Edward Van Sloan; David Manners; Dwight Frye; Helen Chandler; Herbert Bunston ****

A vampire count in Transylvania travels to England in search of new victims.

A legendary motion picture that made an instant star out of Bela Lugosi and set Universal Pictures on the road to horror that was to last throughout the '30s and '40s. The first part of the movie is the most memorable—Dracula's castle is a splendid Gothic creation, with its vast staircase, cobwebs and dark corners, Lugosi gives a wonderfully sinister, leering performance as the Count, speaking such marvelous lines as "I never drink—wine!" Tod Browning's camera roams around this gloomy edifice and its crypt with the three ghostly wives of the vampire drifting about in the darkness. However, when the action moves from the Count's castle to England, the film betrays its stage origins and becomes very pedestrian and, at times, boring, and surely a legendary villain such as Dracula deserves a far better demise than an off-screen groan. Nevertheless, this was a landmark horror production and it is worth noting that it was one of the oldest commercially made films still being shown in cinemas in England during the late 1960s. It appeared on one midnight screening in Surrey in 1967, double billed with *Creature from the Black Lagoon*.

Dracula

aka: Horror of Dracula

Hammer/Universal 1958; Technicolor; 82 mins; Cert. "X"

CREDITS: Producer: Anthony Hinds; Director: Terence Fisher

CAST: Peter Cushing; Christopher Lee; Michael Gough; Melissa Stribling; Valerie Gaunt; John Van Eyssen *****

An estate agent travels to a remote castle in Transylvania, aware that the owner is a vampire count whose reign he must terminate.

After the worldwide success of *The Curse of Frankenstein*, Hammer Films turned their new-found expertise to another classic tale of Gothic horror and produced *Dracula*. From the opening scenes showing blood spattering over Dracula's coffin to the sound of James Bernard's bombastic musical score, audiences of the time were left in no doubt that this was to be an altogether more radical treatment of the Bram Stoker novel from the old horror movies of the previous decade—stakes through the heart and bloody fangs were the order of the day, with numerous reports of faintings in British cinemas when the film was first released, leading to a barrage of criticism from the press and stern rebukes from the censor's office. The action was retained in Transylvania and Christopher Lee made an impressive Count—tall, attractive and well spoken, with Peter Cushing also putting in a classy piece of acting as a rather practical, conceited Van Helsing. Dracula's first appearance as the vampire, with fangs bared and bloodshot eyeballs, looking like a demon from hell, is a classic, as is the final confrontation between Cushing and Lee when Dracula is caught in a shaft of sunlight and disintegrates—a superb climax. There is also a hint of sex as the bloodsucking Lee appears in Lucy's bedroom, evoking the physical attraction between vampire and victim. This handsomely photographed and very stylish version of the old legend became one of Hammer's most highly influential productions (particularly among directors in France, Italy and Spain) and provided them with another massive hit at the box office, both in the United Kingdom and America.

Dracula Has Risen from the Grave
Hammer/Warner Bros. 1968; Technicolor;
92 mins; Cert. "X"
CREDITS: Producer: Aida Young; Director:
Freddie Francis
CAST: Christopher Lee; Veronica Carlson;
Rupert Davies; Barbara Ewing; Barry An-
drews; Ewan Hopper ***

A priest visits Dracula's castle and accidentally revives the vampire, who seeks
out new victims in the nearby town.

Lee's third outing as Dracula is marginally better than *Dracula—Prince of
Darkness* and certainly a lot gorier, but still
lacks the flair of the 1958 classic. Two priests travel to the vampire's castle to attach a cross onto
the wall to ward off evil. One slips and falls onto the frozen moat, and blood from his wounds
revives Dracula, whose body lies under the ice. The vampire then embarks on the usual reign of
terror, lusting after Veronica Carlson, enslaving Barbara Ewing as one of his own, and making
an enemy out of Rupert Davies as a man of the cloth. The film is a bit tedious and heavy-handed
in the middle, relying on the usual '60s predilection for sex and lashings of gore, and is only
redeemed by its gruesome climax whereby after being chased to his castle after he has abducted
Carlson, Lee is pushed off the battlements and impaled on a giant crucifix in the surrounding
abyss, gushing copious quantities of blood in his death throes.

Dracula—Prince of Darkness
Hammer/Warner Bros. 1965; Techniscope/Technicolor; 90 mins; Cert. "X"
CREDITS: Producer: Anthony Nelson-Keys; Director: Terence Fisher
CAST: Christopher Lee; Barbara Shelley: Francis Mathews; Andrew Keir; Suzan Farmer; Charles
Tingwell **

A group of stranded travelers find themselves guests at a castle whose previous owner was
Count Dracula.

A disappointingly lackluster and belated sequel to Hammer's 1958 classic, unwisely filmed in
widescreen, with Christopher Lee strangely silent and anonymous as Dracula and a long opening
40 minutes in which very little happens. Dracula is revived by his sinister servant Phillip Latham,
who cuts Charles Tingwell's throat and uses the blood to mix with the vampire's ashes. He goes
after the other members of the group, vampirizing the luscious Barbara Shelley, who has to be
staked to free her of the vampire's curse. When Dracula's coffin tumbles from a carriage onto
the castle's frozen moat after he has fled from a nearby monastery with Suzan Farmer as his
next intended victim, Andrew Keir, a monk who has entered the castle to help the travelers, fires
a gun at the ice on which Lee is standing; it cracks and the Count disappears under the rushing
water, perishing as a result. The overall dullness of the production was shown up by tagging
on at the beginning of the film the final duel between Peter Cushing and Lee in the far superior
1958 version—this also contrasted the flamboyancy of Hammer's '50s movies as opposed to the
staleness of some of their mid-'60s efforts.

Dracula's Daughter
Universal 1936; 72 mins; Cert. "A"
CREDITS: Producer: E.M. Asher; Director: Lambert Hillyer
CAST: Otto Kruger; Gloria Holden; Marguerite Churchill; Edward Van Sloan; Irving Pichel;
Nan Gray ***

The daughter of Count Dracula arrives in England to reclaim his body.

The first sequel to the 1931 *Dracula* was an atmospheric but slow-moving film, with Gloria Holden starring as the Count's daughter and Edward Van Sloan reprising his role as Van Helsing, imprisoned by the police for the supposed murder of Dracula and his unwilling slave, Renfield. Holden wants to become normal and tries to fall in love with Kruger while kidnapping his fiancée, but her guardian, Pichel, becomes jealous, shoots an arrow at Kruger, and only succeeds in killing Holden. There is a subtle, and for 1936 daring, lesbian scene in the film when Holden instructs a model who resembles her to take her top off for a portrait—unusual for a movie made in this era. But the film on the whole, while good to look at, doesn't really grab the attention and only muddies the waters of the Dracula myth.

Drops of Blood
aka: Mill of the Stone Women
Galatea/Parade (Italy/France) 1960; Techniscope/Technicolor; 94 mins; Cert. "X"
CREDITS: Producer: Gianpaolo Bigazzi; Director: Giorgio Ferroni
CAST: Pierre Brice; Scilla Gabel; Wolfgang Preiss; Dany Carrel; Herbert Boehme; Marco Guglielmi ****
In 1912, a young art student visits a windmill with a carousel of beautiful statues in Holland to research its history, unaware that the figures are in fact the corpses of murdered women, drained of blood by a mad professor in an attempt to cure his daughter of a blood disorder.
A macabre and beautifully photographed continental horror melodrama starring Wolfgang Preiss in Bela Lugosi mode as the doctor who kidnaps young women and drains their blood, which he uses to try to cure his dying daughter, Scilla Gabel, who requires a contant supply of transfusions. As a cover-up for his deeds, he and his criminal assistant have petrified the corpses, exhibiting them as statues of notorious women on the carousel, which has made the mill famous in the area. Pierre Brice is the student who meets and falls in love with Gabel, unaware that she is one of the living dead, kept alive by the blood of the murdered women. A necrophiliac's delight, with several scenes showing Preiss at work in his gloomy old mill, surrounded by various wax-coated body parts and naked corpses—some of these scenes were cut from U.S. and U.K. prints. The fiery climax sees the doctor's final experiment failing to restore his daughter—in a fit of madness, he burns the mill to the ground, the carousel going up in flames with the corpses of the women gruesomely exposed behind the wax (à la *House of Wax*) in the conflagration. This very stylish film, boasting an atmospheric score by Carlo Innocenzi, had a limited release in England in 1963, going the rounds with Compton Cameo's X-rated murder thriller *Confess Dr. Corda*.

Duel of the Space Monsters
aka: Frankenstein Meets the Space Monster
Futurama/Vernon/Seneca 1965; 75 mins; Cert. "X"
CREDITS: Producer: Robert McCarty; Director: Robert Gaffney
CAST: James Karen; Nancy Marshall; Robert Reilly; Marilyn Hanold; Lou Cutell; David Kerman *
An android-astronaut with a damaged brain goes haywire and encounters aliens intent on taking over the Earth.
A ridiculously ragged, disjointed and badly acted movie that has nothing whatsoever to do with *Frankenstein* (its American title) and cannot even be recommended to die-hard fans of the dreadful—it even received an "X" rating in Britain despite the banal content! An alien Princess, Marilyn Hanold, with a bald, dwarf assistant who has pointed ears, has arrived on Earth for the usual old reason—she requires humans, and in particular young women, to replenish a dying world. Their silly-looking pet called Mull terrorizes various people before the rewired astronaut, whose brain was damaged by the aliens when they shot his craft out of the sky, destroys Hanold and her spacecraft after releasing the captured girls. A real farrago of a picture produced in Puerto Rico, with a hilarious opening sequence whereby the android is introduced to the press, only to seize up in mid-sentence. It played second billing to *Curse of the Fly* in 1965/1966.

The Earth Dies Screaming
Lippert/Planet 1964; 62 mins; Cert. "A"
CREDITS: Producers: Robert L. Lippert and Jack Parsons; Director: Terence Fisher
CAST: William Parker; Virginia Field; Dennis Price; Thorley Walters; Vanda Godsell; Anna Palk **

An American pilot lands near an English village to find that most humans have been wiped out and alien robots are walking the streets.

The first in a trio of films that Terence Fisher of Hammer Horror fame made for the small, independent company of Planet. Although produced on a minuscule budget, the movie is quite effective and well acted by a small cast, who give it their all despite the amateurish special effects and cheap-looking sets, which give the movie the appearance of an extended television film. A band of survivors battles both the robots, which resemble the cyber-men from a Dr. Who series and can kill by touch, and the blank-eyed corpses that they reactivate as zombies, led by Dennis Price. Eventually, their main power source, which is controlled from an old army barracks, is destroyed along with the robots, and the surviving humans look forward to civilization being rebuilt.

Earth vs. the Flying Saucers
Columbia 1956; 83 mins; Cert. "A"
CREDITS: Producer: Charles H. Schneer; Director: Fred F. Sears; Special Effects: Ray Harryhausen
CAST: Hugh Marlowe; Joan Taylor; Morris Ankrum; Harry Lauter; Donald Curtis; John Zaremba ***

Aliens from a dying planet arrive at an airbase. When they are fired upon, a fleet of flying saucers attacks Earth.

Years before films such as *Close Encounters of the Third Kind* and *Independence Day* came along, Ray Harryhausen's animated flying saucers were the most realistic seen in the cinema, remarkable when one considers that the film was made in 1956! Robotic-looking aliens arrive at an airbase, which they destroy with ray guns after being met with a hostile reception. The visitors then instruct their fleet to invade Earth, giving humans 56 days to capitulate. The shots of the saucers swooping over the countryside, attacking Washington and destroying several well-known landmarks, are an extraordinary achievement even by today's standards and more than make up for the wooden acting, pedestrian direction and poor musical score. High-frequency sound aimed at the saucers is the weapon that finally destroys the invaders, bringing their spacecraft crashing to the ground in scenes reminiscent of the Martian war machines meeting their end in *The War of the Worlds*.

Earth vs. the Spider
American Intl. 1958; 73 mins; Cert. "A"
CREDITS: Producer/Director: Bert I. Gordon
CAST: Edward Kemmer; June Kenny; Gene Roth; Hal Torey; Sally Fraser; Gene Persson **

A spider that has grown to a huge size by radiation hides in a cave and attacks a small town.

You could say that this was Bert I. Gordon's vastly inferior version of Universal's *Tarantula* aimed at the teenage end of the market, with the special effects the usual haphazard mixture of split-screen techniques, models and miniature sets, all trampled on by a magnified spider. Tracked down to its home in a cave and sedated with DDT by the local sheriff, the monster tarantula is taken to the nearby town and kept in the school gymnasium, but is woken by loud rock 'n' roll music from a teenage dance. Revived, it terrorizes the town and its inhabitants, sucking the fluids from its victims and crawling back to its cave. A group of all-American teenagers enters the spider's lair at the end of the film (note the spider's web made out of strands of rope!) and destroys the creature in the hilarious, badly managed climax.

The Evil Force
aka: 4D Man
Fairview/Universal 1959; DeLuxeColor; 85 mins; Cert. "X"
CREDITS: Producer: Jack H. Harris; Director: Irvin S. Yeaworth Jr.
CAST: Robert Lansing; Lee Meriwether; Robert Strauss; James Congdon; Edgar Stehli; Jasper Deeter ***

A scientist develops a method of transmitting objects through solid matter and when his brother uses the machine, he discovers that he has the ability to penetrate matter using his brain patterns.

An interesting theme which is not fully expanded upon, in this nevertheless lively production starring James Congdon as a scientist who has invented a means of penetrating steel plates with objects such as metal rods and pencils. After his laboratory is accidentally destroyed in a fire, Congdon teams up with his research scientist brother, Robert Lansing (who has just invented a synthetic metal called cargonite) to continue with his experiments. But when attractive Lee Meriwether, Lansing's fiancée, falls for Congdon, Lansing uses his brother's machine for his own purposes out of jealousy, discovering that his hyperactive brainwaves enable him to pass through windows, walls and doors without the aid of a machine. Lansing finds to his cost that this ages him at an alarming rate and has to resort to draining the life force from other people to remain eternally youthful, reducing them to shriveled corpses in the process while also embarking on a string of thefts and slowly turning mad. In the end, after killing several people to regain his looks, he is shot by his fiancée, ages rapidly and disappears into a wall of cargonite, presumably perishing as a result. In a fast-moving picture, with Lansing excellent in the title role, the only thing to spoil matters somewhat is a jazzy '60s-type score that dissipates the overall feeling of mood and tension.

The Evil of Frankenstein
Hammer/Universal 1964; Eastmancolor; 84 mins; Cert. "X"
CREDITS: Producer: Anthony Hinds; Director: Terence Fisher
CAST: Peter Cushing; Peter Woodthorpe; Duncan Lamont; Kiwi Kingston; Sandor Eles; Katy Wild ****

Baron Frankenstein returns to his castle and reactivates the monster that has been preserved in a glacier.

For the first time, Hammer Films was allowed to incorporate some of the Karloff-type features in their monster's makeup through striking a deal with Universal, and Kiwi Kingston does indeed resemble the original Jack Pierce conception, although slightly more ragged around the edges. The plot also used some of the old Universal stand-bys and themes, such as the villagers attacking the castle once the monster is on the loose. Peter Woodthorpe is the hypnotist who is asked by Peter Cushing to try to unlock the creature's mind after it has been brought back to life after being thawed from the ice, but Woodthorpe decides to use the monster for his own nefarious activities and only succeeds in driving it mad, as the monster embarks on a series of thefts and murder. The climax sees the monster destroy the laboratory and engulf himself and his creator in flames. The film is great to look at, with a  marvelous period laboratory harking back to the company's '50s productions, a decent monster for a change, and the usual commanding performance from Peter Cushing as the Baron. This, though, was really the last of the intelligently crafted Hammer Frankenstein productions—it was unfortunately all downhill for the remaining films in this series.

Eyes Without A Face
aka: Les Yeux Sans Visage
Champs Elysees/Lux (France) 1959; 90 mins; Cert. "X"
CREDITS: Producer: Jules Borkon; Director: Georges Franju
CAST: Pierre Brasseur; Edith Scob; Alida Valli; Juliette Mayniel; Beatrice Altariba; Francois Guerin *****
A doctor kidnaps young women to perform skin grafts on his daughter, whose face has become hideously disfigured in a car crash.

Reviled when first shown in the United Kindom by critics who found the film "a nasty and nauseous experience," and severely cut and dubbed for release in America under the title *The Horror Chamber of Dr. Faustus*, Franju's somber foray into the cinematic world of illegal surgery is now rightly viewed as a masterpiece and the forerunner (together with Franco's *The Awful Dr. Orloff*) of a long line of surgical horror films that proliferated in European cinema during the 1960s. The critics' main cause for complaint was a lengthy skin grafting sequence in the middle of the film, shot seemingly in one unflinching take and causing several people to faint when the movie was first screened in Britain. The film's elements of stalking, kidnapping and murder can still have a disturbing effect on an audience today. Combined with this is the haunting performance of Edith Scob as the daughter who, with her doll-like mask hiding her ravaged features, wanders around the house as if in a Gothic fairy tale. Pierre Brasseur plays the doctor, who needs a constant supply of women as the skin grafts on his daughter's face refuse to stay permanent. In a spine-chilling scene, the audience is shown a series of photographs of Scob's face, changing from a beautiful young woman after an operation to a disfigured mess as the grafts deteriorate. The horrific but strangely moving climax sees Scob accepting her fate and wandering out of the house after turning a kennel full of ravenous dogs onto her father, doves wheeling around her wraith-like figure. Filmed in stark black and white by Eugene Shuftan, with a nerve-jangling, insidious score by Maurice Jarre, this is the classic film of its genre to emerge from the Continent—a powerful blend of horror and poetry.

The Fall of the House of Usher
American Intl. 1960; Cinemascope/Eastmancolor; 85 mins; Cert. "X"
CREDITS: Producer/Director: Roger Corman
CAST: Vincent Price; Mark Damon; Myrna Fahey; Harry Ellerbe; Bill Borzage ****

A nobleman buries alive his sister, who suffers from catalepsy, but she returns from the grave to wreak vengeance.

The first of the Roger Corman adaptations of the works of Edgar Allan Poe is also one of his finest. Vincent Price was to be the mainstay of many of Corman's '60s features and here he plays the head of the House of Usher, visited by a friend (Mark Damon) who wishes to see his loved one, Price's sister (Myrna Fahey), just as she is about to be interred by Price, who thinks she is suffering from a family curse of insanity. Fahey later awakes from her tomb in a bloodstained shroud, totally deranged, and kills her brother as the whole mansion crumbles around them and sinks into the mire. This was an exemplary, colorful production all round, conveying slowly and carefully the air of madness and Gothic gloom that symbolized most of Poe's works, although admittedly it was a very long way from the original story. Price gave a noble performance as white-haired Roderick Usher, one that he bettered in Corman's next foray into Poe, the superior *The Pit and the Pendulum*.

Fanatic
aka: Die! Die! My Darling
Hammer/Columbia 1965; Technicolor; 96 mins; Cert. "X"
CREDITS: Producer: Anthony Hinds; Director: Silvio Narizzano
CAST: Tallulah Bankhead; Maurice Kaufman; Stefanie Powers; Peter Vaughn; Yootha Joyce; Donald Sutherland **

A young woman visits the mother of her dead fiancé and finds herself a prisoner of the old lady, who is an insanely religious fanatic.

An over-long and at times tedious psycho-thriller, in which Bankhead appears to be doing an impersonation of Bette Davis in *Whatever Happened to Baby Jane?* Stephanie Powers is taken prisoner and kept in the attic by the madwoman, who attempts to purify her by spouting large chunks of the Bible and forcing her to participate in a mock wedding ceremony so that she can join her fiancé in paradise. Vaughn plays a servant who wants to kill Bankhead, and Sutherland plays an imbecilic gardener. This uninteresting and unattractive mishmash of a drama was one of a series of psychological melodramas that Hammer produced in the wake of *Psycho* and was Bankhead's final film.

The Fantastic Disappearing Man
aka: The Return of Dracula
United Artists 1957; 77 mins; Cert. "X"
CREDITS: Producers: Jules Levy and Arthur Gardner; Director: Paul Landres
CAST: Francis Lederer; Ray Stricklyn; Norma Eberhardt; Jimmie Baird; Greta Granstedt; John Wengraf ***

Dracula leaves Transylvania and takes up residence in a small Californian town to claim more victims.

Paul Landres, who had previously directed *The Vampire*, came up with another variation on the vampire myth in this arresting shocker, with Francis Lederer as Dracula assuming the identity of a painter he has dispatched and going on a rampage in a small town. He wheedles himself into the home of the murdered painter's American cousins. He attempts to convert Norma Eberhardt into one of the undead, killing her cat for starters and rising from his coffin at night, taking on the form of a wolf and a misty vapor. Meanwhile, an investigator from the immigration department is on his trail, as the body of the painter has been dis-

You're Not Old Enough Son

covered. The climax sees Lederer pursued by Eberhardt's boyfriend and falling into a mineshaft, impaling himself on a wooden stake and disintegrating into a skeleton. This was an absorbing take on the old vampire story set in a contemporary setting for a change.

Fantastic Voyage
20th Century Fox 1966; Cinemascope/DeLuxeColor; 100 mins; Cert. "A"
CREDITS: Producer: Saul David; Director: Richard Fleischer
CAST: Stephen Boyd; Raquel Welch; Donald Pleasance; Edmond O'Brien; Arthur O'Connell; Arthur Kennedy *****
A team of scientists is miniaturized and injected into the body of a leading scientist to remove a life-threatening blood clot in his brain.

One of the 1960s' top-ranking fantasy films, with vivid, innovative and meticulously researched sets detailing the interior of the human body, especially in the footage showing the tiny submarine passing through a frozen heart, the journey down the bloodstream with plasma and other organisms pulsating with light, and the views of the lungs, resembling vast gray caverns, as the crew replenish their supply of oxygen. Scenes like these earned the film an Oscar for special effects, even though many of the back-projected process shots were a bit obvious. Having Donald Pleasance as an agent sent to sabotage the mission was a regrettable intrusion, but it fit in with this particular decade's obsession with spying. Pleasance pays with his life, is absorbed by antibodies and the team, after clearing the blood clot from the scientist's brain by a laser beam, escapes through the tear ducts just as they are on the verge of returning to normal size. Leonard Rosenman provided a suitably dreamlike, enchanting musical score to complement the action in a fairly unique picture that was a massive hit at the box office—its only disappointments were a rather weak script and some wooden performances from the leads.

The Fiend Who Walked the West
20th Century Fox 1958; Cinemascope; 101 mins; Cert. "X"
CREDITS: Producer: Herbert B. Swope Jr.; Director: Gordon Douglas
CAST: Robert Evans; Hugh O'Brian; Linda Cristal; Dolores Michaels; Stephen McNally; Edward Andrews ****
On learning of a cache of stolen loot from a fellow cellmate, a psychopathic young cowboy embarks on a trail of murder to locate the money when he is released from prison.

This was a very violent psycho-Western for the time, a kind of unusual remake of *Kiss of Death*, well directed by Gordon Douglas, with Robert Evans playing baby-faced sadistic killer Felix Griffin who, on his release from prison, terrorizes his way across the West to locate the money stolen by Hugh O'Brian and his gang. Once Evans has unearthed the money, he gleefully carries on killing various people connected with the loot, and homes in lustfully on O'Brian's wife. However, he is gunned down in a hail of bullets by O'Brian, who has been released from jail on condition that he goes straight and has to somehow deal with the psychopath before he does any more harm. Evans (who dominates the picture, whether you take to his crazy performance or not) eventually went on to bigger and better things as boss of Paramount Pictures—this film, one of the very first adult-oriented Westerns to receive an "X" certificate in the United Kingdom, was made when he was just another up-and-coming young actor. A very popular addition to the Sunday one-day circuit programs in the early to mid-1960s, the movie benefited from a combined Bernard Herrmann stock score and Leon Klatzkin's stirring theme music that complemented the brutal action.

Fiend Without A Face
British Amalgamated/MGM 1958; 74 mins; Cert. "X"
CREDITS: Producer: John Croydon; Director: Arthur Crabtree
CAST: Marshall Thompson; Terence Kilburn; Kim Parker; Peter Madden; Kynaston Reeves; Michael Balfour ***

At an airbase in Canada, a scientist creates deadly invisible monsters from his thoughts via a machine that uses energy from the base, and they eventually materialize into mobile brains.

The ubiquitous Marshall Thompson stars in this unusual shocker concerning mysterious deaths occurring in the vicinity of a Canadian air force base. Professor Kynaston Reeves has been tapping into the base's power plant to try to preserve his mind after death, but has only succeeded in creating invisible "thought" creatures that suck people's brains from the back of their heads to survive. The picture is notable for the memorable and nightmarish climax, when the animated flying and crawling brains materialize and attack a group of people in a house before Thompson blows up the power station, depriving the brains of energy and causing them to shrivel up and die. The early scenes of people being attacked by the invisible creatures in the woods also pack a punch, and the film had the austere, somber air that symbolized the worthier of the British science fiction films to come out of this period.

Fire Maidens from Outer Space
Criterion/Topaz/Eros 1955; 80 mins; Cert. "U"
CREDITS: Producer: George Fowler; Director: Cy Roth
CAST: Anthony Dexter; Susan Shaw; Paul Carpenter; Harry Fowler; Sydney Tafler; Owen Berry *

Space explorers answering a signal sent to Earth land on the 13th moon of Jupiter and discover the descendants of the lost city of Atlantis, who wish to return to Earth and provide Prossus, their ruler, with a new empire.

An awful film that beggars belief, one of the most inept science fiction films ever made, and certainly one of the worst British ones. The flight deck of the rocketship is reminiscent of the interior of an old aeroplane, and when the astronauts land on the planet, they stroll through what suspiciously looks like an English meadow instead of an alien landscape. The female survivors of Atlantis prance around in diaphanous costumes to the music of Borodin (the Polovtsian dances, or *Stranger in Paradise*), menaced by, without doubt, the unscariest-looking monster of any '50s science fiction production, a man in a one-piece costume with fangs, who eventually dies by falling into a fiery pit. After Prossus is disposed of, one of the girls is finally taken back to Earth with a promise that the rest of them will be collected later. It makes one wonder whether or not the cast had trouble keeping straight faces when they were making this monumental space turkey.

First Man into Space
British Amalgamated/MGM 1959; 77 mins; Cert. "X"
CREDITS: Producers: John Croydon and Charles F. Vetter Jr.; Director: Robert Day
CAST: Marshall Thompson; Marla Landi; Bill Edwards; Robert Ayres; Carl Jaffe; Bill Nagy ***

America's first test pilot into space goes much further in his rocket than expected and returns to Earth a mineral-encrusted fiend, killing and robbing blood banks to survive.

There are shades of *The Quatermass Experiment* in this brisk production, with Bill Edwards as the cocky test pilot who ignores his superiors, taking his rocket deeper into space than allowed and promptly vanishing from the radar screens when the craft passes through a cloud of living space dust. The remains of his rocket, coated with a strange, glistening rock-like substance, are later discovered in a woodland and then a spate of gruesome murders breaks out, with the victims slashed to pieces and drained of blood—even a field of slaughtered cattle is found by the police.

Edwards has, in fact, returned with his rocket, lurching around in his rock-like spacesuit, murdering one person after the other and breaking into blood banks to obtain his supply of plasma to survive in Earth's atmosphere. His brother, Marshall Thompson, eventually lures him into a high altitude chamber at the airbase to try to cure him, but although the organism that coats Edwards' body is destroyed, he is starved of oxygen in the process and expires while apologizing for the murders he has committed. One of a number of films made by Day and producer John Croydon, this remains one of their more superior accomplishments and was quite successful on first release.

First Men in the Moon
Columbia 1964; Panavision/Pathecolor; 107 mins; Cert. "U"
CREDITS: Producer: Charles H. Schneer; Director: Nathan Juran; Special Effects: Ray Harryhausen
CAST: Edward Judd; Lionel Jeffries; Martha Hyer; Betty McDowell; Miles Malleson; Hugh McDermott ****

American and British astronauts carrying out the first landing on the moon find evidence of a previous expedition, and a man in an English nursing home recounts a journey to the moon made with an eccentric scientist in 1899.

Due to apparent problems filming his models in Panavision, Ray Harryhausen kept the stop-motion animation to a minimum in this colorful and enjoyable version of the H.G. Wells classic novel and concentrated instead on creating the Selenites' world within a world, a stunning vista of crystal caverns, hexagonal cities and mysterious shafts filled with sunlight. The film takes quite a long time to get going, but once on the Earth's barren satellite, the pace quickens and the three explorers are left to marvel at the Selenites' underground domain. The only animated creature (apart from the Selenite leaders) is the giant caterpillar-like mooncalf, farmed and slaughtered by the moon people for its flesh. Lionel Jeffries' sphere that transports the trio to the moon is a marvelous Victorian contraption, and the production overall is of a very high standard, particularly when compared to other fare released around this period. The poignant ending has Jeffries remaining on the moon and unwittingly wiping out the Selenites with bacteria from his cold. Musically, Bernard Herrmann wasn't around this time, but Laurie Johnson's score is a delight, especially the main title theme.

First Spaceship on Venus
DEFA/Lluzjon/Crown Intl. (E. Germany/Poland) 1959; Totalscope/Technicolor; 109 mins; Cert. "U"
CREDITS: Producer: Hugo Grimaldi; Director: Kurt Matzig
CAST: Yoko Tani; Oldrich Lukes; Julisu Ongewa; Ignacy Machowski; Kurt Rackleman; Michail Postnikov **

Scientists send a spaceship to Venus to investigate a mysterious magnetic message emanating from the planet.

A film with a somewhat checkered history—although produced in 1959, it was not seen in England until 1963, when it was released at selected cinemas with the comedy *Nurse on Wheels*, and the print shown was considerably shorter than the American version, which ran longer than the original film. The spacecraft itself is a graceful, dart-like vessel. Once on Venus, the crew discovers the remains of an extinct civilization, wiped out by atomic weapons that they were

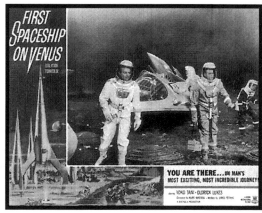

planning to use against Earth. The depiction of Venus, with its strange landscape, volcanos and a ruined city, is excellent, but because of the numerous cuts in the U.K. print, the film appeared muddled and disjointed and this, together with the terrible dubbing, made it difficult to follow what was going on or indeed what the storyline was all about.

The Flesh and the Fiends
aka: Mania
Triad/Pacemaker/Regal Intl. 1960; Dyaliscope; 97 mins; Cert. "X"
CREDITS: Producers: Robert S. Baker and Monty Berman; Director: John Gilling
CAST: Peter Cushing; June Laverick; Donald Pleasance; Dermot Walsh; Billie Whitelaw; George Rose ***
In 19th-century Edinburgh, Dr. Knox purchases corpses from the notorious graverobbers Burke and Hare.
A gorier, more sadistic version of RKO's *The Body Snatcher* with Peter Cushing playing Dr. Knox who, as with his portrayal of Baron Frankenstein, is a coldly determined scientist needing cadavers for his experiments, even turning a blind eye when the graverobbers resort to murder to supply him with more bodies. After prostitute Billie Whitelaw is slaughtered in a particularly disturbing scene that upset the British censor, Hare is caught and gives evidence against Knox who, after defending himself, is let off and becomes an eminent surgeon. Hare is eventually lynched by a mob, while Burke is hanged. The slums of Edinburgh are grimly depicted in stark black and white, and Cushing gives another fine performance as the doctor, although Pleasance and Rose overact like mad as the graverobbers.

Flight of the Lost Balloon
Woolner/Allied Artists 1961; Cinemascope/Eastmancolor; 91 mins; Cert. "U"
CREDITS: Producers: Jacques Marquette and Bernard Woolner; Director: Nathan Juran
CAST: Marshall Thompson; Mala Powers; James Lanphier; Douglas Kennedy; Robert Gillette; Felippe Birriel **
A crew of assorted adventurers journeys by balloon to a remote kingdom in Arabia to rescue a companion who is being kept prisoner by an Arab leader.
A half-baked fantasy adventure film loosely based on Jules Verne's *Five Weeks in A Balloon*. Marshall Thompson and his motley group of friends fly over the African continent and find themselves in a lost kingdom ruled by a mad Arab—after a few adventures, the companion is rescued and flown back to England. Jim Danforth had a hand in some of the special effects, such as the Arab leader clinging onto the balloon as it goes airborne, but the film, although given a bigger budget by Allied Artists than a lot of their other releases, with pleasing color and locations, was not a success and was rarely seen in England. It did the rounds in 1963 teamed with another routine effort, *The Amazing Transparent Man*.

The Fly
20th Century Fox 1958; Cinemascope/Eastmancolor; 94 mins; Cert. "X"
CREDITS: Producer/Director: Kurt Neumann
CAST: David Hedison; Vincent Price; Patricia Owens; Herbert Marshall; Kathleen Freeman; Charles Herbert ****
A scientist invents a matter-transmitting machine, but a fly becomes trapped in one of the pods, and when he transports himself, he emerges part man, part fly.
Fox had one of the biggest and most unexpected hits of the 1950s on their hands when this film was first released, taking the company totally by surprise and compensating for some of their more expensive failures. The story may seem far-fetched and the opening 30 minutes is slow moving, but a good cast and script carry it through because all concerned decided to treat the subject as serious from the outset and not camp it up. David Hedison is the unfortunate scientist experimenting with transmitting objects from one machine to another, emerging from a

transmitter pod with the head and arm of a blowfly and pleading with his wife, played by Patricia Owens, to either catch the fly, which will then enable him to reverse the procedure, or put an end to his misery. He winds up being crushed to death under a hydraulic press, a very stomach-churning scene for 1958, which formed the prologue to the action that was to follow. The climax, which has the mutated fly (sporting Hedison's face) in a web crying, "Help me! Help me!" as he is about to be eaten by a spider before a horrified Herbert Marshall

finally smashes both insects with a rock, is a classic of kitsch but, within the context of the rest of the film, it works. Vincent Price as Hedison's bewildered brother was on the side of good this time, adding a welcome touch of gravitas to the outlandish proceedings.

The Flying Serpent
PRC 1946; 59 mins; Cert. "A"
CREDITS: Producer: Sigmund Neufeld; Director: Sherman Scott (Sam Newfield)
CAST: George Zucco; Hope Kramer; Eddie Acuff; Ralph Lewis; Henry Hall; James Metcalf
**

In Mexico, a crazed archaeologist discovers a winged Aztec serpent guarding the treasure of Montezuma and uses it to kill anyone who attempts to learn of the whereabouts of the fortune in gold and gems.

One of a series of Neufeld-produced horror yarns for PRC, this mind-boggling slice of old hokum has George Zucco, who single-handedly carries the picture with his usual solid performance, capturing the feathered reptile Quetzacoatl in a treasure chamber and training it to kill his colleagues, who are also trying to lay their hands on the treasure by planting one of the creature's feathers on an intended victim. The flying reptile then attacks the person, tears his throat out and drains him of blood before retrieving the feather. The serpent looks ridiculous enough, a ropey creation that in some scenes is clearly being hauled over the set on wires. This was more or less a retread of PRC's *The Devil Bat*, but with a different monster, and had exactly the same ending—Zucco accidentally grabs one of the feathers after trying to murder his stepdaughter and is torn apart by the monster, which is then shot dead.

Forbidden Planet
MGM 1956; Cinemascope/Eastmancolor; 98 mins; Cert. "A"
CREDITS: Producer: Nicholas Nayfack; Director: Fred M. Wilcox
CAST: Leslie Nielsen; Walter Pidgeon; Anne Francis; Warren Stevens; Jack Kelly; Earl Holliman *****

In 2200 A.D., a spaceship lands on the far distant planet of Altair 4 to find that the only inhabitants left from a previous expedition are a scientist, his daughter and a robot, who are carrying out research into the remnants of an ancient civilization known as the Krel that destroyed itself centuries ago.

The acting may be slightly wooden and some of the dialogue stilted, but *Forbidden Planet* still remains one of the '50s' finest science fiction movies and a very influential motion picture. The movie is a feast of beautifully colored visuals and spectacular sets, most of which were created by the Walt Disney studios—the opening shots of the ship approaching the planet in darkness, the strange alien landscape with its green sky and distant cliffs, the underground cities and power plants of the long dead Krel, and the invisible Id monster created from Walter Pidgeon's mind stomping up a canyon before being blasted by ray guns, all backed by a weird electronic soundtrack created by Bebe and Louis Barron. Robby the Robot was probably the most famous robot to feature in any fantasy film, going on to star in *The Invisible Boy* and a host of American television programs—a mechanical celebrity of sorts. The love scenerio between Nielsen and Francis is a bit corny, although typically '50s, but this does nothing to detract from a film that is fantastic to look at and remains the blueprint for many television science fiction serials to emerge in the 1960s, in particular *Star Trek*.

The Four Skulls of Jonathan Drake
United Artists 1959; 70 mins; Cert. "X"
CREDITS: Producer: Robert E. Kent; Director: Edward L. Cahn
CAST: Edward Franz; Valerie French; Henry Daniell; Grant Richards; Paul Cavanagh; Howard Wendell ***

A family lives under a 200-year-old curse whereby the male members are decapitated when they approach their 60th birthday.

And it's all down to the fact that the descendants of the family wiped out a tribe of Ecuadorian headhunters, after which time, the male offspring have had their heads removed after dying. Edward Franz realizes at his brother's funeral that he is next in line to be cursed in this way, as the head of the body is missing. Awakened one night, he is attacked by a native zombie and asks Grant Richards, a police officer, to investigate. He discovers that anthropologist Henry Daniell is really a 180-year-old witch doctor who collects the heads of the family to replace his own and therefore remain eternally alive. Eventually, after the witch doctor has kidnapped Franz's daughter in an attempt to get at him, Franz calls upon the powers of voodoo and decapitates Daniell, who then crumbles to dust. This fast-moving occult thriller from the Kent/Cahn team, well directed with excellent zombie makeup and a literate script, was a popular feature on the Sunday circuit in 1966, often double billed with *The Black Sleep*.

Frankenstein
Universal 1931; 71 mins; Cert. "X"
CREDITS: Producer: Carl Laemmle Jr.; Director: James Whale
CAST: Colin Clive; Boris Karloff; Mae Clark; Edward Van Sloan; Lionel Belmore; Dwight Frye *****

A research scientist creates a living being from corpses and body parts.

The original James Whale production of Mary Shelley's novel is one of the most significant films of the genre ever made, its themes echoing down the years and still being used in movies right up to the present day. Bela Lugosi turned down the role of the monster but Karloff, a two-bit extra at the time spotted by Whale in the studio's canteen, made it his own in legendary makeup by Jack B. Pierce, first seen in a three-shot zoom as the monster walks into the laboratory backwards and turns around to face his creators. Karloff brought pathos to the role, especially in the scene (subsequently cut but restored years later) when he throws the little girl into the lake after he sees her doing the same with flower petals. The monster perishes inside a blazing mill in the fiery climax, but somehow survives, as the massive success of this picture virtually demanded a sequel. *Frankenstein* may seem very primitive by today's standards, and it cries out for some kind of musical score, but it still remains one of the key works of '30s cinema. In England, it was re-released in the early 1960s under the banner "Science's Original Monster Terror!" and was double billed either with *Son of Dracula* or Karloff's *The Mummy*.

Frankenstein Created Woman
Hammer/Warner Bros. 1966; Technicolor; 92 mins; Cert. "X"
CREDITS: Producer: Anthony Nelson-Keys; Director: Terence Fisher
CAST: Peter Cushing; Susan Denberg; Thorley Walters; Robert Morris; Peter Blythe; Barry Warren **

The Baron gives a dead girl the soul of her lover and she sets about exacting vengeance on the youths responsible for both her father's and lover's deaths.

As a film per se, this was reasonable enough—but as a *Frankenstein* film, it was a distinct disappointment. Good-looking and decently photographed it may have been, but by now the formula had become rather derivative and this ranks as probably the least interesting of Hammer's 1960s *Frankenstein* movies, with no monster as such. Peter Cushing attempts to prove that there is life after death by transferring the soul of his decapitated assistant, Robert Morris, into the body of deformed Susan Denberg, who has killed herself in remorse by drowning after Morris has been guillotined for a murder he didn't commit. He succeeds, but the operation turns Denberg, now a blonde beauty thanks to an operation carried out by Cushing and Walters, into a murderer herself. She uses her female wiles to lure the three perpetrators of the crime and her male strength to decapitate and knife them in revenge. The particularly weak ending has Denberg jumping into a fast-flowing river from a cliff, repeating her own original death, while Cushing glances down at the torrent and just walks away, leaving much of the audience at the time to ponder the question—"Is that it?"

Frankenstein Meets the Wolf Man
Universal 1943; 74 mins; Cert. "X"
CREDITS: Producer: George Waggner; Director: Roy William Neill
CAST: Lon Chaney Jr.; Bela Lugosi; Patric Knowles; Ilona Massey; Lionel Atwill; Maria Ouspenskaya ****

The Wolf Man, Lawrence Talbot, travels to Vasaria to seek a cure for lycanthropy and encounters both the Frankenstein monster and the Baron's daughter.

The first of Universal's films featuring more than one monster was a very lively horror romp, inventive and fast-moving with a classic opening scene set in a wind-swept cemetery in which two graverobbers break into the Talbot family crypt, sweeping away the wolfsbane from Lawrence Talbot's coffin and reactivating the Wolf Man. Imaginative set design and laboratory sequences, tremendous transformation shots of Chaney changing into the Wolf Man, and a rousing score by Hans J. Salter make this one of the outstanding productions in Universal's long line of *Frankenstein* movies. Unfortunately, Lugosi, who had originally turned down the role in 1931, was patently miscast as the monster, so much so that a stunt double had to be used in the more strenuous shots of him fighting with the Wolf Man. The frenetic climax has doctor Patric

Knowles reviving the monster to his full power in the Baron's old castle. Chaney, still not cured, turns into the Wolf Man and one of the villagers blows up a dam and floods the laboratory as the two monsters battle to the death. They are swept away on a tidal wave of water and debris, but the film was so successful that they were back a year later in *House of Frankenstein*.

Frankenstein Must Be Destroyed
Hammer/Warner Pathe 1969; Technicolor; 97 mins; Cert. "X"
CREDITS: Producer: Anthony Nelson-Keys; Director: Terence Fisher
CAST: Peter Cushing; Veronica Carlson; Freddie Jones; Thorley Walters; Maxine Audley; Simon Ward ***
     Baron Frankenstein, with the assistance of a young doctor, experiments in brain transplants with disastrous results.
     A lively and macabre addition to Hammer's *Frankenstein* series, a definite improvement on *Frankenstein Created Woman* but not all that much better, although Freddie Jones turns in a sympathetic performance as the doctor who has the brain of an insane professor transplanted into his body and goes mad as a result, destroying Peter Cushing in a fiery blaze at the end. By now, Cushing's character had become an embittered, hard-boiled scientist, and he was to play the role only one more time, in 1973's *Frankenstein and the Monster from Hell*. The transplant scenes were considered quite graphic at the time, as was a nasty decapitation sequence, but the fantasy elements of the previous films were missing, with gore and even rape taking over to coincide with the new trend of violence prevalent in late-1960s cinema. Hammer joined in with this trend, but their films gradually suffered in quality as the decade wore on.

Frankenstein 1970
Allied Artists 1958; Cinemascope; 83 mins; Cert. "X"
CREDITS: Producer: Aubrey Schenck; Director: Howard W. Koch
CAST: Boris Karloff; Tom Duggan; Charlotte Austin; Jana Lund; Don Barry; Irwin Berke **
     A film crew stays in a castle owned by a descendent of Frankenstein who, unaware by them, is creating another monster.
     Frankenstein 1970 is notable for its brilliant opening sequence, in which a terrified girl is pursued through woods by the Frankenstein monster. It turns out to be a television crew making a movie about the *Frankenstein* legend; they wish to use Karloff's castle as a film set. Karloff plays the Baron, renting out his castle to finance his experiments in reactivating his original creature. For most of the film, the monster lumbers about swathed in bandages, totally blind. Karloff, in a subplot, has also been left scarred by Nazi torturers who have unhinged his mind, and he proceeds to murder members of the crew to obtain body parts for his creation. After his manservant, two members of the crew and then his confidante have been dispatched, the police storm the castle. The climax sees Frankenstein and the monster perishing in a cloud of radioactive steam from his atomic reactor. When the bandages are peeled back from the dead monster's face, the creature resembles Karloff, who was trying to create his own image. After the splendid opening five minutes, this ended up as a rather plodding updating of the well-worn story, woodenly acted by the cast except for Karloff, who very rarely gave a bad performance in any film. It was, however, one of Allied Artists' more successful horror productions, going the rounds for years in the early '60s, usually with *Macabre*.

Frankenstein's Daughter
Layton/Astor 1958; 85 mins; Cert. "X"
CREDITS: Producer: Marc Frederic; Director: Richard E. Cunha
CAST: Sandra Knight; John Ashley; Donald Murphy; Sally Todd; Harold Lloyd Jr.; Felix Locher ***
     An old doctor's mad assistant creates both a drug that turns people into monsters and a creature out of body parts.

Not really related to any other *Frankenstein* film, *Frankenstein's Daughter* is an insane mix of Jekyll-Hyde and teenage schlock-horror movie all rolled into one, and in its own crazy way is quite engaging. Felix Locher is the doctor experimenting with a formula to cure the aging process. Unbeknown to him, his assistant Donald Murphy, a descendant of the Frankenstein family, is creating his own drug, spiking Sandra Knight's drink and turning her into a wild-haired, wild-eyed maniac with very bad teeth and bushy eyebrows. He also murders Sally Todd after she turns down his advances, stitching her head onto a body he has created to produce one of the ugliest-looking monsters of the '50s. Framing the old doctor for theft to get him out of the way, Murphy then has to coax his creation back into the laboratory after it escapes and lumbers about, killing people. At the end, Knight almost becomes one of the monster's victims, but boyfriend John Ashley comes to the rescue, throwing a vial full of acid into Murphy's face while the monster goes up in flames. A genuinely underrated camp classic knocked out in 10 days by Richard Cunha, it had a limited release in England; it appeared in 1963 on an odd double bill with *Invaders from Mars*.

From Hell It Came
Allied Artists 1957; 71 mins; Cert. "X"
CREDITS: Producer: Jack Milner; Director: Dan Milner
CAST: Todd Andrews; Tina Carver; John McNamara; Linda Watkins; Gregg Palmer; Suzanne Ridgway **

A man condemned to death by a witch doctor on a Pacific Island is brought back to life by radiation as a perambulating tree stump.

The infamous walking tree movie of the '50s. Believe it or not, the first half is quite promising as scientists dig up and view the weird-looking scowling stump growing out of the ground, wondering what it could be. It used to be Gregg Palmer, killed by a tribal chief after being caught dallying with the local women, the native sticking a knife in Palmer's heart and burying him upright in a coffin. Radiation fallout from nuclear tests has drifted onto the island, causing his body to fuse with the wood and mutate into a living tree. The stump is taken back to Todd Andrews' laboratory and given a blood transfusion, which reactivates it, but when the thing eventually breaks loose and starts prowling the island looking for victims and slaughtering the local natives, the film becomes comical for all the wrong reasons. Paul Blaisdell designed the tree-monster—he was the man responsible for many of the creatures in the early Roger Corman movies such as the mutants in *Day the World Ended*. At the end, Andrews fires a bullet at the sacred dagger wedged in the tree-monster's "heart"—the monster topples backwards into a swamp and is destroyed. Absurd it may have been, but it fared slightly better than the Milner Brothers' earlier effort, the abysmal *The Phantom from 10,000 Leagues*.

The Frozen Dead
Goldstar/Seven Arts/Warner Bros. 1966; Eastmancolor; 95 mins; Cert. "X"
CREDITS: Producer/Director: Herbert J. Leder
CAST: Dana Andrews; Kathleen Breck; Anna Palk; Philip Gilbert; Alan Tilvern; Karel Stepanek **

A scientist attempts to revive the frozen bodies of Nazi soldiers so he can rule the world.

A flatly directed and tiresome horror movie, typical of many a mid-1960s production whereby gruesome effects replaced plotlines and imaginative flair. It concerns a scientist, Dana Andrews, who has preserved hundreds of German corpses in suspended animation since the end of the Second World War (and in their uniforms!), hoping to restore them to life and revive the Third Reich. All of the action takes place in and around a country mansion, with dismembered limbs kept alive and even the functioning decapitated head of a young girl thrown in for good measure. Andrews communicates with it by telepathy to refine his animation techniques and carry out research on the human brain, as most of the frozen corpses are brain-damaged. The preposterous climax sees the head telepathically controlling the assorted limbs, which strangle Andrews and his assistant before they can revive the German corpses.

The Gamma People
Columbia 1955; 79 mins; Cert. "A"
CREDITS: Producer: John Gossage; Director: John Gilling
CAST: Paul Douglas; Eva Bartok; Leslie Phillips; Walter Rilla; Martin Miller; Phillip Leaver
**

A newspaper reporter and a photographer uncover a plot in Eastern Europe to turn children into geniuses with gamma rays for the benefit of the state.

This was a lackluster, Cold War-type thriller that focused on Paul Douglas' and Leslie Phillips' attempts to free the small Balkan state of Gudavia from Walter Rilla's dictatorship, whereby the rays he is using on children are producing not only a few geniuses (which he wants to use to run the state), but a whole lot of mindless zombies running riot. Needless to say, this insane plot is foiled in the closing reels. The film was briskly directed by Gilling but lacked suspense, was too long-winded, and lapsed into comedy in some sequences, which ruined the overall mood. It also failed to capitalize on its obvious anti-Communist message.

The Gargon Terror
aka: Teenagers from Outer Space
Topor Corporation/Warner Bros. 1958; 87 mins; Cert. "X"
CREDITS: Producer/Director: Tom Graeff
CAST: David Love; Dawn Anderson; Bryant Grant; Harvey B. Dunn; Tom Lockyear; Helen Sage **

Teenage aliens land on Earth and unleash Gargons on the countryside to graze on humans, hoping that the creatures will then increase in size, breed, and become the aliens' source of food supply.

An alien clambering out of a tinny flying saucer wearing what suspiciously looks like a motorcycle crash helmet; ray guns that reduce humans to skeletons; monster lobsters that are only seen as shadows; and an incredibly stilted script—Tom Graeff's inept sci-fi production was so bad it was enjoyable. The Gargon of the title is a species of lobster that grows into a giant and attacks the local inhabitants of a small town after being unleashed from a flying saucer. One of the human-looking aliens, amusingly called Derek and played by David Love in a cheapskate space uniform, decides in a fit of alien conscience that what his race are doing is morally wrong and escapes from the others, falls in love with local girl Dawn Anderson, betrays his comrades and their intentions and, full of guilt about the devastation the monster is causing, destroys the Gargon with a disintegrating ray. He then sacrifices himself by guiding the alien's fleet of flying saucers with their cargo of Gargons on a tractor beam into the side of a mountain, where they are annihilated in an explosion. This tacky B movie with abysmal effects (and none of the aliens resembled teenagers!) appeared at selected cinemas in 1964, usually double billed with *Gigantis the Fire Monster*.

Ghost of Frankenstein
Universal 1942; 68 mins; Cert. "X"
CREDITS: Producer: George Waggner; Director: Earle C. Kenton
CAST: Lon Chaney Jr.; Cedric Hardwicke; Ralph Bellamy; Lionel Atwill; Evelyn Ankers; Bela Lugosi **
Frankenstein's monster is discovered in a sulfur pit by Ygor the shepherd and revived by lightning, and when Ygor's brain is transplanted by mistake into his body, he is driven mad.
Lon Chaney Jr. took over the role of the monster in the fourth Universal *Frankenstein* film, and some say the worst. The film is directed by Kenton with little imagination or verve, and Chaney's monster, dug out of the sulfur pit by Ygor and revived when lightning strikes the electrodes in his neck, is a rather glum, soulless robot compared to Karloff's previous, more sensitive, performances. Lugosi reprised his role as Ygor, Cedric Hardwicke was yet another offspring of the Baron, and Lionell Atwill played the doctor's evil assistant, substituting a donar's brain with the shepherd's which, when placed unwittingly in Chaney's head by Hardwicke, causes the monster to go blind and mad. At the end, the laboratory catches fire after Chaney runs riot and a falling beam crushes him to death. After this somewhat drab entry into the *Frankenstein* series, Universal decided to spice up the action in the next movie with the addition of another monster, the far livelier *Frankenstein Meets the Wolf Man*.

Ghost Ship
Abtcon/Anglo Amalgamated 1952; 69 mins; Cert. "A"
CREDITS: Producer/Director: Vernon Sewell
CAST: Dermot Walsh; Hazel Court; Hugh Burden; John Robinson; Hugh Latimer; Joss Ackland ***
A young couple purchases a yacht that has the reputation of being haunted.
Actually filmed on Vernon Sewell's own yacht, this low-key but quite goose-pimply British thriller has Dermot Walsh and Hazel Court as the young couple buying a boat, only to have most of the crew resigning from their positions as the ship is reputed to be haunted—it was previously found at sea with no one on board. A medium, Hugh Burden, is brought in to investigate, and he reveals that the previous owner murdered his wife and her lover as he overheard them plotting to kill him. The bodies were then hidden on the vessel in a water tank. Eventually, Walsh and the crew find the bodies and then one of the crewmembers confesses to being the real murderer and kills himself. Flashbacks were used to tell the story of the previous occupants of the yacht, and this was one of Sewell's earlier and more atmospheric pictures—he virtually remade it in 1961's *House of Mystery*.

The Giant Claw
Clover/Columbia 1957; 76 mins; Cert. "A"
CREDITS: Producer: Sam Katzman; Director: Fred F. Sears
CAST: Jeff Morrow; Mara Corday; Louis D. Merrill; Morris Ankrum; Edgar Barrier; Robert Shayne *
A huge buzzard-like bird flies to Earth from outer space and attacks New York.

The Giant Claw represents the bottom end of the fantasy-horror market, a truly ludicrous movie surprisingly made by a major film company with terrible special effects and poor production values, knocked out in just two weeks. The bird itself is mostly seen as only one claw or a flurry of feathers—when it is visible, it resembles a giant stuffed turkey, a good description of this picture. The monster has a force field that renders it impervious to radar, lands in New York and lays an egg, which scientists destroy. The bird then goes on a rampage until Jeff Morrow invents a special device that can project a beam into the monster's force field, and when the scientist pierces this, the creature crashes into the sea and lifts one claw into the air as it sinks, a befitting end to an abysmal creature-feature.

Giant from the Unknown
Screencraft/Astor 1958; 77 mins; Cert. "X"
CREDITS: Producer: Arthur A. Jacobs; Director: Richard E. Cunha
CAST: Edward Kemmer; Sally Fraser; Buddy Baer; Morris Ankrum; Bob Steele; Joline Brand
***

A giant 500-century-old Spanish conquistador is revived from the dead by lightning and goes on a rampage.

A geologist and archaeologist arrive in a small town in the California hills to investigate the rumors of a spirit that is causing the inhabitants to become fearful and superstitious of something in the woods near the Devil's Gap area. The local sheriff, meanwhile, is also trying to find out what is causing the animals in the area to be slaughtered horribly—one of the villagers has also been found hacked to pieces. The spirit turns out to be a giant Spaniard called Vargas, played by six-foot-plus Buddy Baer. He is discovered in his grave by Edward Kemmer, but when lightning strikes his body during a storm, the bearded giant is reactivated and goes on a killing spree with his ax through the local town, causing mayhem until finally Kemmer confronts the giant on a narrow bridge, pushing him to his death in the torrent below. Richard Cunha's first feature film was a rough and ready affair, although entertaining enough, benefiting greatly from Albert Glasser's thunderous soundtrack, and went the rounds in 1964 with Toho's *Half Human*.

The Giant Gila Monster
HPC 1959; 74 mins; Cert. "A"
CREDITS: Producer: Ken Curtis; Director: Ray Kellogg
CAST: Dan Sullivan; Lisa Simone; Jerry Cortwright; Shug Fisher; Beverly Thurman; Fred Graham **

A gigantic lizard that has lived in the New Mexican desert for years emerges and runs amok.

A bottom-of-the-basement monster movie made by the same team that was behind the equally inept *The Killer Shrews*. The film seems to be just an excuse for an obnoxious bunch of hotrodders and assorted characters to race around and mouth stupid lines while a live, magnified lizard appears out of the desert and wanders over models of railways and buildings, stomping through a teenage dance hall until Dan Sullivan fills his hotrod full of nitroglycerine, points it in

You're Not Old Enough Son

the direction of the monster and sends it flying, ramming the lizard and blowing it to smithereens. Some half-decent black and white photography makes it marginally more watchable than *The Killer Shrews*, with which it appeared on a double bill when first released.

Godzilla
Toho/Eros (Japan) 1954; 81 mins; Cert. "X"
CREDITS: Producer: Tomoyuki Tanaka; Director: Inoshiro Honda
CAST: Akira Takarada; Akihiko Hirata; Takashi Shimura; Momoko Kochi; Fuyuki Murakami; Sachio Sakai ****

A 400-foot radioactive prehistoric monster, awakened in the Pacific by atomic bomb tests, leaves his island home and heads for the Japanese mainland to attack Tokyo.

The first of Toho's monster films gave birth to a creation that became almost as famous a name in the world of fantasy cinema as *King Kong*. Unlike the tepid, juvenile remake of 1998, the original *Godzilla* was much more serious and darker in tone and mood, with award-winning special effects as the gigantic fire-breathing monster, first seen causing panic on the island of Odo, proceeds to trample Tokyo underfoot, smashing power lines, upending trains, fighting off jet planes and razing buildings to the ground in an orgy of mayhem and destruction, all at the expense of the plot, which is virtually nonexistent. In the end, Godzilla is reduced to bones by a device created by a scientist that removes oxygen from seawater, although he somehow miraculously survived to feature in another dozen or so other movies. For the American release, additional footage was added featuring Raymond Burr as a reporter, and the film was 17 minutes longer that the original Japanese version, which became a record-breaking hit for Toho.

Godzilla Raids Again
aka: Gigantis the Fire Monster
Toho/Warner Bros. (Japan) 1955; 82 mins; Cert. "X"

CREDITS: Producer: Tomoyuki Tanaka; Director: Motoyoshi Odo
CAST: Hiroshi Koizumi; Yukio Kasama; Setsuko Wakayama; Takashi Shimura; Minuro Chiaki; Mayuri Mokusho **

On an island, Godzilla (or Gigantis) is discovered in battle with another monster, Angurus, as radiation has caused them to reawaken. Both monsters head toward Tokyo and Godzilla, after destroying Angurus, is killed by an avalanche of ice on another snow-covered island.

Toho rush-released this effort to cash in on the phenomenal success of *Godzilla*, but the picture lacks cohesion and the scenes of the two monsters trashing Osaka are poorly lit and murkily photographed. The ending is pretty weak as well, with Godzilla (renamed Gigantis on British and American releases) perishing under a mound of ice on another island when aircraft blast the volcano with rockets, causing an avalanche. The film was not the success the company hoped for, and this persuaded Toho to reunite with director Inoshiro Honda to create their first film in color, the vastly superior *Rodan*, the following year.

Godzilla vs. Mothra
aka: Godzilla vs. the Thing
Toho/American Intl. (Japan) 1964; Techniscope/Technicolor; 94 mins; Cert. "A"
CREDITS: Producer: Tomoyuki Tanaka; Director: Inoshiro Honda
CAST: Akira Takarada; Yuriko Hoshi; Hiroshi Koisumi; Yumi Ito; Emi Ito; Yu Fujiki ***

Mothra's giant egg is washed onto a beach by a hurricane at the same time that Godzilla attacks Japan.

The fourth Godzilla film started the trend in friendly monster movies aimed at a younger audience and is a colorful, noisy enough romp with some excellent special effects but a very long way from the darker, more adult original of 1954—this was reflected in the "A" rating given it. Tiny twins known as the Peanut Sisters, who are the guardians of Mothra, try to enlist the help of the giant moth when Godzilla goes on a rampage, but the aging Mothra is defeated by the monster. It is left to Mothra's two huge larva that hatch from the egg to attack Godzilla, spraying him with sticky threads and sending him crashing to his supposed death over a cliff in the unintentionally hilarious climax.

Gorgo
King Bros./British Lion/MGM 1961; Technicolor; 79 mins; Cert. "X"
CREDITS: Producer: Wilfred Eades; Director: Eugene Lourie
CAST: Bill Travers; William Sylvester; Vincent Winter; Bruce Seton; Martin Benson; Joseph O'Connor ****

Salvage workers capture a 65-foot prehistoric monster off the coast of Ireland and transport

it to London, where it goes on display in Battersea Park. The creature's 200-foot mother follows the trail and proceeds to demolish half of the Capital to retrieve her offspring.

The best British monster movie of its type ever made ("England's answer to *Godzilla*" announced one critic), it is commendably brief compared to other such films so that it gets straight to the action, which is pretty impressive, particularly Gorgo's spectacular destruction of Tower Bridge and Big Ben when rampaging through London. The simplistic story has Travers and Sylvester capturing baby Gorgo and transporting the infant to London where, much against the wishes of scientists who want to study the monster, they are paid a fortune by an entrepreneur to exhibit the beast to the public. The infant's huge mother follows the phosphorescence trail in the sea to the city, causing widespread destruction before rescuing her baby. The end has both mother and infant wading down the Thames toward the open sea and freedom, leaving behind them a London in ruins. Before the film's original release, it was reported in the press that MGM and The King Brothers had argued with the British censor against the film receiving an "X" certificate, possibly on a financial basis—it would have reached a larger audience if it had been an "A" film. However, the censor considered the film to be of sufficient adult content to be certified "X," which it duly was, even though all of the steamy sex included in the book that accompanied the film's first outing on the circuits was omitted from the final production. Admittedly the scenes of Gorgo ploughing through whole blocks of houses with people leaping out of their windows to their deaths do have a nightmarish quality about them and were fairly alarming for the time, but on current video release, the film has been downgraded to a PG rating. The publicity blurbs for 1960 announced the film as "Gigantic in Every Way!" and "This is the Big One!" and it really was the last of the big monster movies ever made in the late '50s/early '60s.

The Gorgon
Hammer/Columbia 1964; Technicolor; 83 mins; Cert. "X"
CREDITS: Producer: Anthony Nelson-Keys; Director: Terence Fisher
CAST: Peter Cushing; Barbara Shelley; Christopher Lee; Richard Pasco; Patrick Troughton; Michael Goodcliffe ****
    Members of a small community in Transylvania live in fear as a number of them have been turned to stone by a mysterious creature.
    One of Hammer's classier and more out of the ordinary productions of the 1960s, with Michael Goodliffe as a professor investigating a series of strange deaths in the village. His son, Richard Pascoe, falls in love with the mysterious Barbara Shelley, who inhabits the gloomy, empty old castle where most of the action takes place with sinister Peter Cushing, the owner who is aware of her dreadful secret. Christopher Lee pops up in a cameo role as the son of one of the victims, who comes to suspect that Shelley is not all that she appears to be. The film has a haunting, dreamlike atmosphere about it and is beautifully shot in Technicolor. The only jarring note: the false-looking snakes in Shelley's hair as she transforms herself into the Gorgon at the climax, turning Cushing to stone before Lee decapitates her, thus destroying the creature.

Gorilla at Large
20th Century Fox 1954; Technicolor; Orig. in 3-D; 93 mins; Cert. "A"
CREDITS: Producer: Robert L. Jacks Director: Harmon Jones
CAST: Cameron Mitchell; Ann Bancroft; Raymond Burr; Lee J. Cobb; Charlotte Austin; Lee Marvin **
    A murderer at loose in a carnival uses an escaped gorilla to cover up his deeds.
    Possibly one of the worst of the '50s 3-D productions, a glossy but overblown amalgamation of a circus, detective and horror movie set in an amusement park, with a good cast all at sea. Lee J. Cobb is a detective investigating two murders at a circus, Burr is the carnival owner, and Lee Marvin appears in an early role as a talkative police officer. Trapeze artist Anne Bancroft is finally revealed as the killer, disguising herself in a gorilla costume. The film's real gorilla is also an actor in costume, and Cameron Mitchell even gets to wear one as well, although he saves Bancroft at the end after she is carried to the top of a roller coaster by the ape and then has to face the law. A tedious and unscary thriller reflected in the "A" rating that it was given in the United Kingdom.

The H-Man
Toho/Columbia (Japan) 1958; Tohoscope/Technicolor; 97 mins; Cert. "X"

CREDITS: Producer: Tomoyuki Tanaka; Director: Inoshiro Honda
CAST: Yumi Shirakawa; Kenji Sahara; Eitaro Hirata; Koreya Senda; Mitsuru Sato; Akihiko Ozawa ***

Radiation from H-bomb tests in the Pacific turns men into liquid blobs that can absorb human flesh.

Temporarily abandoning their giant monster movies, Toho and director Honda ventured into the realm of science fiction with this grisly and garish tale of liquified beings that multiply in the sewers of Tokyo after a ship that has passed through a nuclear testing area has leaked radioactive waste into the city's water system. The gelatinous blobs can dissolve humans for food, and begin to feed on gangsters, who are using the sewer system as a hideout. The oozing monsters are eventually destroyed when police storm the sewers with flamethrowers and set the entire Tokyo sewer system ablaze, killing them in the inferno. In 1964/1965, this flashy and somewhat over-the-top picture was doing the rounds at selected cinemas with *The Creature with the Atom Brain*.

Half Human
Toho/DCA (U.S./Japan) 1955; 72 mins; Cert. "A"
CREDITS: Producer: Tomoyuki Tanaka; Director: Inoshiro Honda (U.S. footage: Kenneth G. Crane)
CAST: Kenji Kasahara; Akira Takarada; Momoko Kochi; Akemi Negishi; John Carradine; Morris Ankrum ***

In Northern Japan, scientists discover that a Yeti-like apeman and his infant inhabit a cave and are shielded from the outside world by a native tribe.

Half Human was probably the best of the '50s Abominable Snowman films, with a well-designed, sympathetic creature featured for a change. A party of skiers discovers the relatively shy Yeti and its infant in the mountains, worshipped by natives. When the infant is captured and shot dead by members of another expedition who visit the spot, the creature runs amok, wiping out most of the party in revenge. Unfortunately, the American version included extra footage featuring the ubiquitous John Carradine and three colleagues who, having purloined the body of the infant, discuss among themselves the events unfolding in the film. As a result, most of the original Japanese dialogue is missing and some scenes bear little resemblence to what Carradine is talking about, thus confusing the issue. The climax has the surviving scientists and tribe members cornering the Yeti in its cave; the monster kills one of the villagers before falling to its death into a volcanic pit.

Hand of Death
20th Century Fox 1962; Cinemascope; 59 mins; Cert. "X"
CREDITS: Producer: Eugene Ling; Director: Gene Nelson
CAST: John Agar; Paula Raymond; Steve Dunne; Roy Gordon; John Alonzo; Butch Patrick ***

A research scientist comes into contact with an experimental nerve gas and turns into a deformed, insane monster whose touch can kill.

One of the last horror/science fiction films that fantasy stalwart John Agar starred in. This little-known effort had him working as a researcher in a laboratory with a chemical gas agent that eventually causes him to kill anything he touches and deforms his features into something resembling a grotesque, bloated pumpkin. Disguising himself in a trenchcoat and fedora, he goes after the people he thinks are responsible for his condition, dispatching them one by one with his puffed-up fingers until he is cornered by the police and shot. A rarely seen film in the

United Kingdom, *Hand of Death* had a limited release in 1966 with *The Cabinet of Caligari* on the Sunday circuit. The film then never saw the light of day and, due to various legalities, was thought to be lost, but it has recently been unearthed and is hopefully being transferred to VHS and DVD for release.

The Hands of Orlac
Riviera/British Lion (U.K./France) 1960; 105 mins; Cert. "A"
CREDITS: Producer: Steven Pallos; Director: Edmond T. Greville
CAST: Mel Ferrer; Lucille Saint-Simon; Dany Carrel; Christopher Lee; Felix Aylmer; Basil Sydney **

A concert pianist is driven to madness because he believes that a murderer's hands have replaced his own, which were badly damaged in a plane crash.

The third version of Maurice Renard's novel is undoubtedly the weakest, with Mel Ferrer playing the crazed pianist who thinks he may have inherited the hands of a strangler. Ferrer flees his house after the operation and becomes involved with Christopher Lee as a magician who blackmails him as a murderer for his own gains. Dany Carrel as Lee's assistant betrays Lee to the police and pays with her life, knifed to death in a cabinet during a stage performance. Eventually, Ferrer is informed that the previous owner of the hands was acquitted of his crimes after he was executed, and he is reunited with his girlfriend. Ferrer turned in a below-par performance in a role that would have suited Lee far better; the film, which is far too long, thus fails to convince.

The Haunted and the Hunted
aka: Dementia 13
American Intl. 1963; 81 mins; Cert. "X"
CREDITS: Producer: Roger Corman; Director: Francis Ford Coppola
CAST: William Campbell; Luana Anders; Mary Mitchell; Bart Patton; Patrick Magee; Barbara Dowling ***

Following an argument about money, a scheming woman causes her husband to suffer a heart attack and dumps his body in a lake. She then pretends to communicate with a dead child in an old Irish castle, to acquire his family's inheritance.

Francis Ford Coppola's first feature film turned out to be a grim little drama set in and around a bleak Irish castle, with Luana Anders professing to be in psychic communication with her late husband's niece, who also died from drowning, in an attempt to drive her mother-in-law mad and get her hands on the estate for her own gains. In carrying out this charade, she triggers an old family secret and is butchered to death in a particularly harrowing scene. Bart Patton turns out to be the ax murderer who had been responsible for his little sister's death, locked away in the castle because of his insanity. Coppola conjures up an air of Gothic madness over the whole proceedings, probably using the production as a framework for his own directorial ambitions, as the picture was cobbled together at the last minute by Corman as a favor to Coppola.

The Haunted Palace
American Intl. 1963; Panavision/Pathecolor; 85 mins; Cert. "X"
CREDITS: Producer/Director: Roger Corman
CAST: Vincent Price; Debra Paget; Lon Chaney Jr.; Leo Gordon; John Dierkes; Elisha Cook Jr. ***

A man arrives at a small New England village as heir to the palatial mansion without realizing that his ancestor was a notorious black magician who was burned alive over 100 years ago.

Corman, after dabbling with five Edgar Allan Poe productions, felt he needed a change of direction and turned his attentions to H.P. Lovecraft. The movie was based very loosely on *The Case of Charles Dexter Ward*. The director's favorite actor, Vincent Price, played Ward, encountering a great deal of hostility from the local villagers and noting various hideously deformed people wandering the streets. Price then falls under the baleful influence of his ancester's portrait, which begins to exert a powerful influence over him. Slowly, Price becomes possessed by his dead ancestor's evil spirit, which seeks revenge through him on the villagers who buried him alive, creating more mutations to rule the Earth as slaves of the Dark Powers. The spirit also revives his dead wife and then orders Price to sacrifice Debra Paget to a monstrous four-armed creature lurking deep within the mansion vaults. Although a little too ambitious and not a great success at the box office, the film is full of striking imagery, with foggy exterior shots of the mutants roaming the streets contrasting with the cobwebby, shadowy interiors of the old mansion. Price also turned in his usual excellent performance as the tormented Dexter Ward.

The Haunted Strangler
aka: Grip of the Strangler
British Amalgamated/MGM 1958; 81 mins; Cert. "X"
CREDITS: Producer: John Croydon; Director: Robert Day
CAST: Boris Karloff; Jean Kent; Elizabeth Allen; Anthony Dawson; Dorothy Gordon; Derek Birch ****

A criminologist/novelist investigating the case of the Haymarket Strangler slowly realizes that he himself is the deranged killer.

The team of John Croydon and Robert Day came up with an absorbing variation on both the Jekyll-Hyde and Jack the Ripper themes in this stylish shocker featuring one of Karloff's most telling performances from this later period of his career. He plays a researcher in old crime cases who believes that the real Haymarket Strangler was never caught, and when a new series of stranglings in the area break out, he begins to suspect that he may be guilty of the murders. Karloff's portrayal of the insane killer is striking because of the lack of makeup—as he becomes

possessed and turns into the strangler, his face becomes twisted down one side, and his body hunched, before he claims more victims. In the end, Karloff realizes that in fact he is the infamous strangler responsible for the fresh killings, and is shot after being chased by the police, falling onto the grave of the man wrongly hanged for his crimes. The film was made back to back with the inferior *Corridors of Blood* and went the rounds in the early '60s, usually double billed with *Fiend Without A Face*.

The Haunting
MGM 1963; Panavision; 112 mins; Cert. "X"
CREDITS: Producer/Director: Robert Wise
CAST: Richard Johnson; Claire Bloom; Julie Harris; Russ Tamblyn; Lois Maxwell; Valentine Dyall *****

A team of assorted psychic investigators assembles in an old New England mansion that has a history of deaths and suicides, and soon team members find themselves under threat from the malevolent influences contained within the house.

Forget the awful 12-rated [akin to the U.S. PG-13) and distinctly unscary 1999 remake, which proved to discerning horror buffs the old adage that multimillion-dollar special effects do not a good movie make. With stark black and white photography and expert direction by Robert Wise, this is one of the screen's greatest-ever supernatural shockers that still retains the power to cause a shudder after repeated viewings. The four investigators who gather in the mansion comprise an anthropologist, Johnson; a skeptic, Tamblyn; and two women susceptible to ESP, Bloom (a repressed lesbian) and Harris. It is the nervous Harris who triggers off a series of frightening phenomena, culminating in her death as the house forces her car to crash when she tries to escape, her spirit undoubtedly destined to be imprisoned with the other ghostly occupants in the mansion. It's not a case of what you see that scares the audience, but what you don't see—no ghosts on display here, just weirdly distorted camera angles, poundings on the doors, pulsating walls and far-off whispering, sobbing voices. The infrared photography of the old mansion in some of the exterior shots also gives the whole place a nightmarish appearance. A superior, well-acted spine-chiller that has rarely been equaled in terms of cinematic terror.

Hercules at the Centre of the Earth
Aka: Hercules in the Haunted World
SPA/Cinemat/Woolner (Italy) 1961; Totalscope/Technicolor; 91 mins; Cert. "A"
CREDITS: Producer: Achille Piazzi; Director: Mario Bava
CAST: Reg Park; Christopher Lee; Giorgio Ardisson; Eleonara Ruffo; Franco Giacobini; Marisa Belli ****

Hercules descends into a mythical world at the Earth's center to obtain a rare stone to cure an insane princess, held under the evil influence of an agent from Hades.

Mario Bava took time off from directing and producing horror films to make this imaginative and vivid fantasy, probably the finest in a series of Hercules movies that proliferated on the Continent during the late '50s and early '60s. Reg Park played Hercules, descending into an underground hell to retrieve the magic stone and a golden apple to prevent the demonic Christopher Lee from draining the girl's blood, which would give him eternal life. Park and Giorgio Ardisson, who plays Theseus, have to battle a rock-man and vampires who inhabit tombs in dark caves on the ghostly island of Hesperides before defeating Lee and the powers of darkness. Despite the poor dubbing that afflicted many of these continental films, this was a beautiful picture to look at, very atmospheric and well directed by Bava.

The Hideous Sun Demon
aka: Blood on His Lips
Clarke King Enterprises/Pacific Intl. 1959; 74 mins; Cert. "X"
CREDITS: Producer: Robert Clarke; Directors: Robert Clarke and Thomas Boutross
CAST: Robert Clarke; Patricia Manning; Nan Peterson; Patrick Whyte; Fred La Porta; Peter Similuk ***

A physicist contaminated by radiation from an experimental isotope turns into a scaly, lizard-like monster when exposed to sunlight.

Robert Clarke, doyen of plenty of '50s B movies, turned producer/director and came up with his most infamous effort from this decade, and the one he is most remembered for. Clarke is the physicist who survives a radiation leak at a research center and afterwards reacts to sunlight by changing into the monster of the title. He spends a great deal of time bemoaning his plight, having to avoid the sun by either retreating to the shadows or inside his house, and meeting a girl singer in a bar while forgetting he has a girlfriend at his laboratory, driving backwards and forwards between the two women and occasionally changing into the creature en route when he is trapped in the sun's rays. Although poorly scripted and produced on a low budget, the picture is redeemed by Clarke's striking makeup as the scaly lizard-man, which was quite an original creation for a picture of this type. In the end, Clarke is pursued by the police after befriending a young girl, who tells her mother where he is hiding, changing into the monster as he emerges from his hideout into the sun and eventually falling to his death from the top of a huge gas tank after being shot. Another plus point is John Seely's rambunctious musical score, which carries the film along nicely.

Homicidal
Columbia 1961; 87 mins; Cert. "X"
CREDITS: Producer/Director: William Castle
CAST: Glenn Corbett; Patricia Breslin; Jean Arless; Eugenie Leontovich; Richard Rust; Alan Bunce ***
A young nurse presides over a household consisting of a paralyzed old lady and a strange young man who harbors psychotic secrets.
William Castle's answer to *Psycho*, this crude but convincing shocker stars Jean Arless as a transvestite killer who, in the opening scenes, murders the Justice of the Peace after he has married her/him to a bellboy for one day only, and then heads for a mansion inhabited by an old lady (Leontovich), a reclusive young man who was tyrannized by his father as a youth, and his half-sister, Patricia Breslin. Arless announces to the family that she and the young man are married, but Breslin and her lover, Glenn Corbett, suspect that Arless is somehow linked to the recent murder of the JP, and are puzzled by the old lady being terrified of Arless. After the demented Arless decapitates the old lady, "she" reveals herself to be the mysterious young man, brought up as a girl to safeguard her inheritance, and to murder anyone who stands in his/her way. The film had a "fright break" two minutes before the end, should anyone want to leave the cinema before the truth about Arless was revealed. This was a typical Castle gimmick introduced in most of his productions to boost profits. In hindsight though, Castle's movie predated the genre of the slasher movies of the 1980s and in this respect can be seen as a minor landmark in this particular field of the horror cinema.

Horror
aka: The Blanchville Monster
Llama/Columbus/Compton Cameo (Spain/Italy) 1963; 88 mins; Cert. "X"
CREDITS: Producer: Alberto Aguilera; Director: Alberto de Martino
CAST: Gerard Tichy; Joan Hills; Leon Anchoriz; Richard Davis; Helga Line; Frank Moran ***
The daughter of a horribly disfigured owner of a castle is afraid her father may fulfill an ancient family curse and kill her before she reaches the age of 21.
A little-seen Spanish horror movie concerning a young college girl, Joan Hills, who travels to see her father in his gloomy old castle, only to be informed that he died in a fire. Various strange people occupy the castle, including her sinister brother, an even odder housekeeper, and a weird doctor. It transpires that the girl's father did not die in the fire—he was horribly scarred and turned insane, believing that his daughter must die before she is 21. The man flees the house and his daughter wakes up, buried alive—it's the old "let's kill the daughter to gain her inheritance" routine again. This was a surprisingly decent Gothic melodrama, released in the United Kingdom in 1964 on a double bill with *The Castle of Terror*.

The Horror of Frankenstein
Hammer/EMI 1970; Technicolor; 95 mins; Cert. "X"
CREDITS: Producer/Director: Jimmy Sangster
CAST: Ralph Bates; Graham James; Dave Prowse; Kate O'Mara; Veronica Carlson; Bernard Archard *
A young Victor Frankenstein creates a murderous being from body parts.
When watching this latter-day Hammer *Frankenstein* film for the first time, a sense of sadness enveloped many viewers, who thought to themselves how far this once-worthy series from the company had gone downhill since the heady days of *The Curse of Frankenstein*. *The Horror*

of Frankenstein fails in every department—a cocky and unlikeable performance from Ralph Bates as the Baron, a weak and ineffective piece of acting from Graham James as his unwilling assistant, an over-the-top Kate O'Mara as Bates' busty, oversexed housemaid, and a daft, unimaginative monster played awkwardly by Dave "Darth Vader" Prowse. There is a complete lack of Gothic atmosphere, the color photography is murky, and a half-jokey script doesn't help matters. The climax sums up the whole dismal affair—while Bates is being questioned by the police over a series of deaths, a little girl accidentally pulls a lever in his laboratory, destroying the monster in a shower of acid. Perhaps Terence Fisher could have made a better job of it. As it is, this undoubtedly ranks as one of Hammer's worst-ever productions and well and truly marked, for them, the end of a golden era of fantasy/horror filmmaking.

Horrors of the Black Museum
Anglo Amalgamated/American Intl. 1959; Cinemascope/Eastmancolor; 95 mins; Cert. "X"
CREDITS: Producers: Herman Cohen and Jack Greenwood; Director: Arthur Crabtree
CAST: Michael Gough; June Cunningham; Graham Curnow; Shirley Ann Field; Geoffrey Keen; Gerald Andersen ****

A writer obsessed with crime drugs his assistant and instructs him by hypnotism to commit various horrific murders so that he can report them to his newspaper and boost sales.

A series of bloody scenes highlight this flamboyant though melodramatic horror thriller, including a pair of binoculars spiking a woman through the eyes, another woman guillotined in her bed, and a man dumped in a bath of acid. All are staged by Graham Curnow as Michael Gough's unwitting assistant, turned into a Jekyll-Hyde monster by Gough, who then writes lurid accounts of them for his newspaper. The mad writer also has a museum in the basement of his house devoted entirely to Scotland Yard's notorious "Black Museum," and even resorts to murder himself, using a pair of ice tongs to slaughter a woman who is blackmailing him. After the police have spent much time scratching their heads wondering who the killer is, Curnow, in his altered state, stabs his girlfriend to death in a fairground, is cornered on girders, and leaps to his own death, plunging a knife into Gough's heart. The film was criticized for being too violent when first released, but this only added to its success at the box office; it was one of a number of movies made around this time where sensational murder acts were the order of the day (Anglo's *Circus of Horrors* was another example). Lacking the imagination and subtle overtones that turned many of the Hammer films of this period into durable classics, *Horrors of the Black Museum* was nonetheless a handsomely mounted if disturbingly brutal addition to the British horror genre.

The Hound of the Baskervilles
Hammer/United Artists 1959; Technicolor; 84 mins; Cert. "A"
CREDITS: Producer: Anthony Hinds; Director: Terence Fisher
CAST: Peter Cushing; Andre Morell; Christopher Lee; Marla Landi; Miles Malleson; David Oxley ****

Sherlock Holmes is asked to solve the mystery of a curse hanging over the Baskerville family on Dartmoor.

This is a sumptuous version of Arthur Conan Doyle's classic yarn that was a big success in its day, with Peter Cushing an authoritative Holmes and Andre Morell as his dependable companion Watson. The pair travels to Dartmoor to investigate the brutal murder of Sir Charles Baskerville,

apparently committed by a legendary giant hound, after being called upon by Christopher Lee, playing Sir Henry Baskerville, who fears he may be the next victim under a family curse. Marla Landi (Lee's lover) and her father turn out to be the culprits—they hate the Baskervilles because of their history of cruelty to the local inhabitants, and use the monstrous hound as a revenge weapon to kill off members of the family. Landi perishes in a swamp at the end after the detective has unraveled the mystery and shot the hound, and Lee is left alone in his house to contemplate a lonely future. Hammer toned down the horrors in this production and instead came up with a lavish, beautifully photographed film that ranks as probably the finest-ever screen treatment of this particular novel.

The Hounds of Zaroff
aka: The Most Dangerous Game
RKO-Radio 1932; 78 mins; Cert. "A"
CREDITS: Producers: Ernest B. Schoedsack and Merian C. Cooper; Directors: Ernest B. Schoedsack and Irving Pichel
CAST: Joel McCrea; Leslie Banks; Fay Wray; Robert Armstrong; Noble Johnson; Hale Hamilton
****
A group of people shipwrecked on a remote island off the Malay Peninsula finds themselves the victims of an insane big game hunter.

A very early chase melodrama, much imitated over the ensuing decades but rarely equaled. Joel McCrea, Fay Wray, Robert Armstrong and the crew of a shipwrecked yacht are lured by a system of fake beacons to the castle of mad Count Zaroff, played by Leslie Banks, who enjoys nothing better than to hunt down his shipwrecked survivors as sport, keeping their mummified heads in his trophy room. Armstrong and the crew are slaughtered, leaving McCrea and Wray to be let loose in the jungle with Banks, after giving them a day's grace, pursuing them with his bow and arrows, a pack of hungry hounds, and a giant mute servant, Noble Johnson. After several narrow escapes, McCrea is presumed killed but returns to Zaroff's castle, wounding the Count by plunging an arrow into his back. He and Fay Wray escape from the island in a motor launch as Banks, dying from his wound, falls from the castle into the pack of ravenous dogs. Made in tandem with early production work on *King Kong*, the movie displayed the same dense, atmospheric jungle settings (painted on glass by Mario Larrinaga and Byron L. Crabbe) that were to appear in Willis O'Brien's masterpiece, as well as an early score by Max Steiner. The British censor for U.K. release cut the trophy-room sequence showing the decapitated heads, and the picture turned up for a solitary screening in 1965 with RKO's *Mighty Joe Young*.

House of Dracula
Universal 1945; 67 mins; Cert. "X"
CREDITS: Producer: Paul Malvern; Director: Erle C. Kenton
CAST: Onslow Stevens; Lon Chaney Jr.; John Carradine; Lionel Atwill; Jane Adams; Glenn Strange ****
A doctor specializing in curing abnormalities receives a visit from Dracula and as a result transforms himself into a nocturnal killer.

Universal's '40s monster cycle virtually came to an end with this truly mind-blowing and inventive follow-up to *House of Frankenstein*, which threw everything into the pot. It includes Dracula (who has come to visit Onslow Stevens in the hope that he can be cured of vampirism); the Wolf Man (whom the doctor cures of lycanthropy); a hunchback nurse; Frankenstein's monster (found in a cave and revived briefly by Stevens); and Stevens himself. Stevens turns into a demented Jekyll and Hyde-type character after carrying out blood transfusions between himself and Dracula, played with far more conviction by Carradine than in *House of Frankenstein*. Dracula's evil control is eventually terminated when the doctor hauls his coffin into the sunlight, the vampire disintegrating into a skeleton, and Stevens is finally shot by a cured Chaney as the Frankenstein monster gets crushed under a beam in the obligatory inferno at the end. The hallucinatory scenes involving Stevens as he turns into a rabid fiend after the blood transfusions and embarks on a reign of terror caused censorship problems in Britain at the time, and the film was banned for several years—it then went the rounds in the 1960s double billed with either *House of Frankenstein* or *The Wolf Man*.

House of Frankenstein
Universal 1944; 71 mins; Cert. "X"
CREDITS: Producer: Paul Malvern; Director: Erle C. Kenton
CAST: Boris Karloff; John Carradine; Lon Chaney Jr.; J. Carrol Naish; George Zucco; Anne Gwynne ****

A mad scientist, Dr. Neimann, escapes from prison, revives Count Dracula and discovers Frankenstein's monster in a cave, which he reactivates in his laboratory. The Wolf Man puts in an appearance as well.

Universal's first compendium of monsters suffers by having a slow-moving first 20 minutes or so, which concentrates mostly on Carradine's portrayal of Dracula, and not a particularly believable one at that—top hat and tails do not make for a scary vampire Count. He goes on a rampage against Karloff's enemies when the doctor, who has murdered George Zucco and taken over the running of his "House of Horrors," removes the stake from his heart on condition that the vampire obey his commands. Once Carradine disintegrates in the sunlight, the film's pace quickens, with Karloff discovering the Wolf Man and the Frankenstein monster (played by Glenn Strange) frozen in a cave beneath the ruins of Frankenstein's castle. After being thawed out, Lon Chaney as the Wolf Man falls in love with a Gypsy girl, much to the chagrin of hunchback J. Carrol Naish, who also loves her but is killed by her with a silver bullet. The Frankenstein monster is brought back to life in the climax, but both he and Karloff perish in a bog after being routed by the local villagers. This rousing horror yarn was so popular that all of the monsters were back the following year in *House of Dracula*. The film also contained another early but memorable score by Hans J. Salter.

House of Horrors
aka: Joan Medford is Missing
Universal 1946; 66 mins; Cert. "X"
CREDITS: Producer: Ben Pivar; Director: Jean Yarbrough
CAST: Martin Koslek; Rondo Hatton; Kent Taylor; Virginia Grey; Alan Napier; Bill Goodwin **

A mad sculptor rescues a deformed killer from a river and uses him to murder those who criticize his work.

This was Rondo Hatton's second appearance as The Creeper. He was a natural for the part, as he suffered from the disfiguring disease of acromegaly (enlargement of the bones of the extremities, face and jaw, caused by overactivity of the pituitary gland) in real life. Rescued from a river by suicidal Martin Koslek, he is first used as a model by the sculptor, who then orders the simple-minded brute to dispose of anyone who dares to express their dislike for his work. When leading art critic Alan Napier is found with his spine snapped, suspicion falls on Koslek, who then has the idea of shopping Hatton to the law. Needless to say, Hatton kills the sculptor and is gunned down by the police as he attempts to abduct Virginia Grey, although he was unaccountably back in 1946's *The Brute Man*. Hatton died the same year that this corny old potboiler was released, and the British censor changed the title to *Joan Medford Is Missing* for its U.K. screening, the movie reverting back to its original title when shown on the Sunday circuit in 1962 with *The Mummy's Hand*.

House of Mystery
Independent Artists/Anglo Amalgamated 1961; 56 mins; Cert. "A"
CREDITS: Producers: Julian Wintle and Leslie Parkyn; Director: Vernon Sewell
CAST: Peter Dyneley; Jane Hylton; Nanette Newman; Maurice Kaufmann; Ronald Hines; Colette Wilde ***

A young couple, about to buy a house at an unusually low price, is informed by an old woman that the place has been the subject of various unexplained occurances.

A low-budget British ghost picture made by Sewell, who also directed the abysmal *The Blood Beast Terror* and the even worse *The Curse of the Crimson Altar*. He did a lot better with this minor effort, which was a virtual remake of the director's own *Ghost Ship*, released in 1952. Ronald Hines and Colette Wilde are the prospective buyers, who are told by the old lady in flashback that ghostly happenings had plagued the previous couple who had owned the house, including lights being switched on and off and the image of a man on their television set. A medium and psychic investigator had been summoned and they discovered that another owner, Peter Dyneley, who was an electrician, had electrocuted his wife and her lover by tampering with the wiring system of the house. As the old woman finishes her story, she promptly disappears in front of the couple, leaving them alone in the booby-trapped house, an unnerving ending to a satisfactory little thriller.

House of the Damned
20th Century Fox 1963; Cinemascope; 63 mins; Cert. "X"
CREDITS: Producer/Director: Maury Dexter
CAST: Ronald Foster; Merry Anders; Richard Crane; Erika Peters; Georgia Schmidt; Richard Kiel **

An architect sent to view an old castle on behalf of a deceased circus showman encounters strange happenings when viewing the property.

The strange happenings are caused by a family of freaks, who have lived in the castle's dungeons for years and are afraid of being thrown out of their abode, wanting to be left alone. Resorting to the tricks of the trade learned in the circus, they are hoping that prospective buyers of the property will think it haunted and go away. Ronald Foster plays the architect who is subjected to a series of disturbing events in the castle, together with his wife and their friends. The end has the freaks (some of whom were genuine), led by Richard Kiel, unveiling themselves and finally admitting that they will have to confront the outside world if they want to survive. A low-budget quickie from Maury Dexter, not all that enterprising, with, for a change, a happy ending.

House of Wax
Warner Bros. 1953; Warnercolor; Orig. in 3-D; 88 mins; Cert. "X"
CREDITS: Producer: Bryan Foy; Director: Andre de Toth
CAST: Vincent Price; Phyllis Kirk; Frank Lovejoy; Carolyn Jones; Roy Roberts; Paul Picerni *****

A sculptor in wax who is hideously disfigured in a fire resorts to stealing corpses from the morgue to exhibit in his new wax museum.

Warner Bros.' superior remake of *Mystery of the Wax Museum* was a huge hit when first released, and the most successful 3-D film ever made. Vincent Price played a gifted sculptor whose partner sets fire to his wax museum as an insurance scam, leaving him to die in the inferno. He survives, mad and horribly disfigured, committing murder, stealing the corpses, and exhibiting them in wax at his new museum, which he aims to shock the public with. Price also becomes fixated with Phyllis Kirk, whom he plans to kill and exhibit as his model of Marie Antoinette. Classic scenes include Price pursuing Kirk through the misty Baltimore streets, his grotesque features only half visible in the shadows; Price in the morgue searching for Carolyn Jones' body; and the unmasking at the climax when Kirk batters away the sculptor's mask, revealing his ravaged face beneath, all filmed in garish Warnercolor. In England, this final scene had quite a few people screaming and passing out in their cinema seats in 1953/1954. The film launched Price on the path of horror for which he became famous, and this is perhaps one of his best-remembered roles. In 1966, the film was re-released for a short period in normal flat screen, going the rounds with *Phantom of the Rue Morgue*.

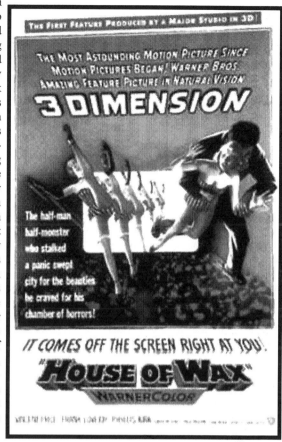

House on Haunted Hill
Allied Artists 1958; 75 mins; Cert. "X"
CREDITS: Producer/Director: William Castle
CAST: Vincent Price; Carol Ohmart; Elisha Cook Jr.; Richard Long; Alan Marshall; Carolyn Craig ****

An eccentric millionaire offers $10,000 to anyone who can survive the entire night at his reputedly haunted mansion.

This is probably William Castle's most infamous production, and certainly his most successful; it was still doing the rounds years after release, often double billed with other Allied Artists features such as *Frankenstein 1970*, *Stakeout on Dope Street* and *Riot in Cell Block Eleven*. Five guests turn up at Price's mansion and are menaced by skeletons, a severed hand, a witch, blood dripping from the ceiling, and other horrors created by Price to scare his guests into submission. Devious Carole Ohmart wants her husband (Price) killed and has plotted with lover Alan Marshall that during all of the ghostly events taking place, he will be shot by a pistol he has supplied guests with in miniature wooden coffins. Price, however, discovers their plan and up-ends the pair into a bath of acid. Castle's gimmick this time around was to have a skeleton trundled out over the heads of the audience when Price turns the tables on his wife and her lover. Great fun, with a wicked sense of black humor running through the picture, and a whole lot more credible in every department than the blood-soaked but unappealing 1999 remake.

How to Make A Monster
American Intl. 1958; Technicolor sequences; 73 mins; Cert. "A"
CREDITS: Producer: Herman Cohen; Director: Herbert L. Strock
CAST: Robert H. Harris; Paul Brinegar; Gary Conway; Walter Reed; Gary Clarke; Morris Ankrum **

After being sacked by his studio, a film makeup artist drugs actors playing the Teenage Werewolf and Teenage Frankenstein and uses them to commit murder.

The same team that produced both *I Was A Teenage Werewolf* and *Teenage Frankenstein* must have put their collective heads together and thought—"Let's have the two monsters in one film." The result is a cobbled-together, nonscary parody of several American International productions of the day, hence the "A" certificate, and the monsters are only weaker versions of those in the original films. They are sent out to murder the men responsible for Robert H. Harris being dismissed from his job. Harris also has a chamber of horrors, disguises himself as an apeman, and even the monster from *The She-Creature* puts in an appearance. In the end, he is killed by his own creations because he threatens to have them stuffed and mounted as exhibits. A lackluster effort with comic overtones that fails to chill or build up any suspense.

The Human Duplicators
Crest/Woolner 1962; Eastmancolor; 81 mins; Cert. "X"
CREDITS: Producers: Hugo Grimaldi and Arthur C. Pierce; Director: Hugo Grimaldi
CAST: George Nadar; Barbara Nicholls; Dolores Faith; George Macready; Richard Kiel; Hugh Beaumont **

A giant alien humanoid is sent to Earth to duplicate humans as androids so that his race can conquer the planet.

Richard Kiel, who was later to find fame as Jaws in two James Bond movies, played the alien Kolos, who takes over George Macready's laboratory so that he can create replicas of human leaders in government and science that will obey his command. The duplicates shatter like pottery when hit violently and are created in special coffins in the laboratory. Kiel eventually decides not to carry out his plans, as he falls in love with a beautiful blind woman whose sight he restores, and the climax sees the duplicates wiped out with a laser beam by George Nadar. A mundane, not very inventive production that had a limited release in the United Kingdom in 1964, going the rounds with *The Creation of the Humanoids*.

The Hunchback of Notre Dame
RKO-Radio 1939; 117 mins; Cert. "A"
CREDITS: Producer: Pandro S. Berman; Director: William Dieterle
CAST: Charles Laughton; Maureen O'Hara; Edmond O'Brien; Cedric Hardwicke; Thomas Mitchell; Alan Marshall *****

A lonely hunchback, the bell-ringer of Notre Dame Cathedral in Paris during the revolution, falls in love with a Gypsy girl.

A superb, evocative production of Victor Hugo's novel, with Laughton unforgettable as Quasimodo, a tremendously moving portrayal that, in the scenes with Maureen O'Hara as Esmeralda in the cathedral, can still bring a tear to the eye, especially when he realizes that no one could possibly be friends with someone as ugly as himself. The film plays like a historical pageant on one hand, featuring its mixture of beggars, thieves, clerics, the King and courtiers, and a horror film on the other. It features a tormented Quasimodo lashed by the whip on instructions from his master (a chilling Cedric Hardwicke), who scuttles around the darkened alleyways like a bloated frog until he rescues Esmeralda from the hangman's noose so that she can have sanctuary within the cathedral's walls. The riotous climax sees O'Hara reunited with O'Brien after two hours of revolt and upheaval, and has Laughton kill the hated Hardwicke. The movie's famous final shot shows Quasimodo mourning his loss from among the cathedral's gargoyles as O'Hara goes off with the crowd. One of the true classics of the 1930s, and superior to the 1923 Lon Chaney version, which in itself was a celebrated film.

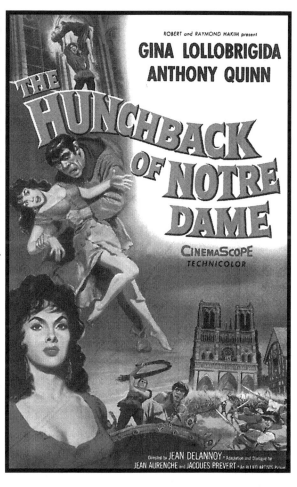

The Hunchback of Notre Dame
aka: Notre Dame de Paris
Paris Films/Allied Artists (France/Italy) 1956; Cinemascope/Eastmancolor; 103 mins; Cert. "A"
CREDITS: Producers: Robert and Raymond Hakim; Director: Jean Delannoy
CAST: Anthony Quinn; Gina Lollobrigida; Jean Danet; Alain Cuny; Jean Tissier; Robert Hirsch **

An international version of the Victor Hugo novel.

And a thoroughly inept one. Gina Lollobrigida played a glamorous if unlikely Esmeralda, the color and widescreen worked well enough, and the picture was beautifully photographed, but Anthony Quinn was hopelessly miscast as Quasimodo, making him appear more like a half-mongol idiot rather than a figure of compassion, as in the 1939 picture. In this movie, which more or less followed the same storyline as the others, Esmeralda passes away and Quinn, discovering her body, cuddles up beside her so that he can die with her. The film opens with the discovery of their remains in a cell. A crude effort that was not a success at the box office and wasn't helped by being badly dubbed when released in the United Kingdom.

The Hypnotic Eye
Allied Artists 1959; 77 mins; Cert. "X"
CREDITS: Producer: Charles B. Bloch; Director: George Blair
CAST: Allison Hayes; Jacques Bergerac; Merry Anders; Marcia Henderson; Joe Partridge; Guy Prescott **

A deranged hypnotist mesmerizes beautiful women and then wills them to mutilate themselves.

A somewhat nasty little picture appealing to misogynists only. The Great Desmond, played by Jacques Bergerac, is coerced by his disfigured girlfried, Allison Hayes, herself a former beauty, to hypnotize young women whom she is jealous of, then take them out on the town after appearing in his stage act. When they return to their homes, Hayes instructs the women to perform a normal act such as taking a shower when the water is scalding, washing their hair in caustic shampoo, or drying their hair over a lighted gas oven, causing them to mutilate themselves. After they come out of their trances, the women have no memory or idea as to why they disfigured themselves in this fashion. "Hypnomagic" was the gimmick used in the film, with numerous close-ups of Bergerac's staring eyes attempting to hypnotize the audience watching it, and although the makeup of the mutilated women was hideously effective, this ended up by being a rather tasteless piece of filmmaking.

Hysteria
Hammer/MGM 1965; 85 mins; Cert. "X"
CREDITS: Producer: Jimmy Sangster; Director: Freddie Francis
CAST: Robert Webber; Anthony Newlands; Jennifer Jayne; Lelia Goldoni; Maurice Denham; Peter Woodthorpe **

A man treated for amnesia after he survives a car crash experiences hallucinations relating to the driver killed in the accident.

Hysteria ranks as one of the poorest in the Hammer series of psychodramas, with a definite "it's all been done before—and better" air about it. American Robert Webber, after suffering from loss of memory in a car accident, becomes involved in a convoluted plot concerning Lelia Goldoni (as the crash victim's widow) and Anthony Newlands (his psychiatrist). Both are trying to frame him, because of his amnesia, for the murder of Newlands' wife. As Webber regains his memory with the help of investigator Maurice Denham, he tricks the pair of them into revealing their nefarious plans at the end of the film. Slow-moving and bland, this jaded effort was one of Sangster and Francis' poorest collaborations and one of the least-remembered Hammer productions of the 1960s.

I Bury the Living
United Artists 1958; 76 mins; Cert. "X"
CREDITS: Producers: Albert Band and Louis Garfinkle; Director: Albert Band
CAST: Richard Boone; Theodore Bikel; Peggy Maurer; Herbert Anderson; Howard Smith; Russ Bender ***
The newly appointed caretaker of a cemetery discovers to his alarm that by sticking black pins into the cemetery map, he possesses the power to cause the death of that particular plot's owner.

Richard Boone plays the chairman of the Immortal Hills cemetery, who takes over the part-time job of caretaker from Theodore Bikel, released after 40 years of loyal service. Boone, to his consternation, realizes that he may be responsible for the deaths of the committee members. The members begin to die like flies when a black pin is inserted into their reserved plots on a wall-sized map of the cemetery, which occasionally pulsates with a weird glow, giving Boone hallucinations. After frantically sticking white pins into the map to try to reactivate the seven dead members, it transpires in the end that Bikel is the man behind the murders, as he was enraged at losing his job after such a long time, taking out his vengeance by dispatching the committee members and shifting the blame onto Boone. Although the trick ending (Bikel imagines the corpses have come alive to seek revenge, only for the police to turn up and confront him) lets the film down slightly, this was a very capable horror-murder-mystery thriller from Albert Band, helped along by an unusually creepy and very noisy musical score from Gerald Fried.

I Married A Monster from Outer Space
Paramount 1958; 78 mins; Cert. "X"
CREDITS: Producer/Director: Gene Fowler Jr.
CAST: Tom Tryon; Gloria Talbott; Ken Lynch; John Eldredge; Valerie Allen; Maxie Rosen-
bloom ***

On the eve of his wedding, a man is kidnapped
by aliens and replaced by a replica, which marries the
woman to try to comprehend human emotion before
taking her and more females from the town to their
home planet for breeding purposes.

Despite the penny dreadful title, this was a dark
and brooding piece of science fiction, well directed
by *I Was A Teenage Werewolf* Gene Fowler Jr. The
plot involves aliens who have come to Earth to kidnap females to repopulate their dying planet and are
able to take on human form. On his way back from
his stag night, Tom Tryon is waylaid by an alien and "taken over." Following his return home,
Gloria Talbott realizes that her fiancé is acting strangely but goes ahead with the wedding anyway. There is a chilling scene in the movie as Tryon, standing on a balcony in a thunderstorm,
reveals his grotesque alien features in a flash of lightning, his unsuspecting wife behind him.
The climax has the townspeople attacking the aliens, some of whom dissolve into messy pools
and evaporate when bitten by dogs, and releasing the humans that have been replicated from the
alien's spaceship. The spacecraft eventually departs the Earth as the invaders realize that they
cannot live on our planet. The film was re-released in 1964 and went the rounds on the Sunday
circuit with *The Blob*.

I Married A Werewolf
aka: Werewolf in A Girl's Dormitory
Royal Films/Compton Cameo/MGM (Italy/Austria) 1961; 83 mins; Cert. "X"
CREDITS: Producer: Guido Giambartolomei; Director: Paolo Heusch
CAST: Carl Schell; Barbara Lass; Maurice Marsac; Curt Lowens; Maureen O'Connor; Mary
McNeeran **

The director of a girls' boarding school is, unbeknown to his friends and colleagues, a
werewolf.

An international collaboration that turned up in the United Kindom in 1965 on a double
bill with the equally obscure *Where Has Poor Mickey Gone?* Curt Lowens plays the werewolf
protected by his mistress Maureen O'Connor, who has to resort to blackmail and murder to cover
up his terrible affliction, as he has a habit of preying on the sexy young students in his care. A
newly arrived teacher, Carl Schell, happens to be an expert in lycanthropy and eventually uncovers Lowen's secret, noting among other things that dogs are scared of him. In the end, after a
number of students have been slaughtered, Schell finishes the werewolf off with a silver bullet.
A darkly photographed, somewhat muddled affair cursed with poor dubbing that had additional
footage added for American release, although the werewolf itself was a pretty ferocious-looking
creation. On the Continent, the movie played under the title of *Lycanthropus*.

I Saw What You Did
Universal 1965; 82 mins; Cert. "X"
CREDITS: Producer/Director: William Castle
CAST: Joan Crawford; Leif Erickson; John Ireland; Patricia Breslin; Andi Garrett; Sharyl Locke
***

Two teenage girls playing pranks on the telephone ring a man on a random call who has
murdered his wife, stating, as a joke, that they both witnessed the killing.

William Castle was in much better form with this straightforward, no-frills picture, the precursor to many of the teenage slasher movies of the 1990s that ran on a similar theme. John Ireland played the murderer who, after disposing of his wife in the shower, believes the two girls have actually witnessed his deed by saying "I saw what you did" on the telephone. With Joan Crawford making a play for him, Ireland then proceeds to track the girls down so he can silence them. There were no gimmicks on display from the director on this occasion, just a plain old adult thriller that was double billed on first release with the sex comedy *A Very Special Favour*.

I Was A Teenage Werewolf
Anglo Amalgamated/American Intl. 1957; 76 mins; Cert. "X"
CREDITS: Producer: Herman Cohen; Director: Gene Fowler Jr.
CAST: Michael Landon; Whit Bissell; Yvonne Lime; Guy Williams; Robert Griffin; Vladimir Sokoloff ***

Under hypnosis, a scientist retrogresses a troubled, rebellious college student who as a result changes into a werewolf and goes on a rampage around the campus.

The title says it all—produced on a paltry budget, this numb-brained classic made an unexpected fortune at the box office when it was first released, raking in more money than many big-budget films of the day. It was also responsible for the trend in so-called teenage horror movies that ran throughout the remainder of the '50s. Whit Bissell plays the doctor experimenting with hypnosis and a secret serum who causes hotheaded student Michael Landon to revert to a primitive state and become a murderous werewolf when alarmed or attracted to females. The movie was briskly directed by Fowler, with moody photography and some effective transformation scenes of Landon metamorphosing from youth to werewolf, dripping saliva from his fangs as he approaches his coed victims. The climax has Landon changing into the monster and killing both Bissell, his creator, and Bissell's assistant just as the police arrive on the scene—he is shot dead and reverts to his normal self.

The Illustrated Man
Warner Bros. 1968; Panavision/Technicolor; 103 mins; Cert. "X"
CREDITS: Producers: Howard B. Kreitsek and Ted Mann; Director: Jack Smight
CAST: Rod Steiger; Claire Bloom; Don Dubbins; Robert Drivas; Jason Evers; Tim Weldon **

A young man encounters a hobo covered in tattoos who is trying to track down the woman who put them there so that he can kill her.

Rod Steiger plays the tattooed tramp, who meets wandering Robert Drivas on the road. When Drivas stares at the tattoos, they appear to come alive and three stories unfold. The first concerns a holographic projection room of the future where wild animals conjured up by children end up eating their parents; the second relates a tale of astronauts trying to survive on a rain-swept Venus; and the third tells of a couple who give their child a suicide pill, as they have been informed that the world is due to end, only to be told after supplying the pill that the world will survive. All three stories deal with death and betrayal, and after viewing them, Drivas attempts to kill Steiger. A supposed morality play, the movie slows up between the stories with too much philosophical talk, and only the segment concerning the astronauts trying to come to grips with the relentless rain on Venus carries any impact. Steiger gives his usual over-mannered performance, but this confusing film was not a success, as its messages seemed to go right over the heads of the audiences watching it.

The Incredible Petrified World
GBM/Governor 1959; 70 mins; Cert. "X"
CREDITS: Producer/Director: Jerry Warren
CAST: John Carradine; Robert Clarke; Allen Windsor; Phyllis Coates; George Skaff; Maurice Bernard **
The crew of a diving bell that accidentally sinks to the ocean floor discovers a strange laby-rinth of underwater caverns and a hermit-like survivor.
A lame fantasy adventure from cheapo producer/director Jerry Warren, filmed largely in Arizona's Colossal Cave over seven days, with a good cast of B movie stalwarts more or less going through the motions. When the cable of John Carradine's experimental diving bell snaps, two men and two women find themselves marooned in a vast system of caves fed by oxygen from volcanic vents. They encounter the bearded, Robinson Crusoe-type survivor of a shipwreck (Maurice Bernard), who has been roaming the caves for 14 years and come across a not too realistic back-projected monitor lizard. Slow-paced with very little action, this would have been a far more promising enterprise if made on a bigger budget—as it is, tedium sets in before the crew are rescued in the end by another diving bell after the hermit is buried under an avalanche of rocks following a volcanic eruption. The movie was shot side by side with *Teenage Zombies*, and the pair of them were originally released together as a double bill in the United States.

The Incredible Shrinking Man
Universal 1957; 81 mins; Cert. "A"
CREDITS: Producer: Albert Zugsmith; Director: Jack Arnold
CAST: Grant Williams; April Kent; Randy Stuart; Paul Langton; Raymond Bailey; William Schallert *****
A man on a boat trip with his wife is accidentally exposed to a strange, radioactive mist and as a result shrinks to a minute size, battling for survival in the cellar of the house he once owned.
Many critics and fans rate this as the pinnacle of Jack Arnold's film career, a thought-provoking fantasy with outstanding effects by Clifford Stine and a philosophical ending that has very few equals. From the opening scene, when  Grant Williams, who gives an engaging performance, is exposed to a silvery mist that envelops his boat, the audience watches in horror as, day by day, he inexora-bly loses height and weight to the consternation of his wife, eventually having to live in a doll's house and be menaced by the household cat. Shrinking to just a few inches tall, he finally becomes trapped in the cellar, where he has to survive against all odds for the rest of his days, his wife and friends believing him to have been killed by the cat. Arnold places Williams in

oversized and utterly convincing sets created by art director Robert Clatworthy, so that the cellar becomes a hostile environment full of obstacles to overcome by the miniature human. Williams has to live in a matchbox, sustaining himself with huge droplets of water from a leaking boiler and hiding there when a spider goes on the prowl. The highlight is his prolonged battle with the spider over the only source of nourishment, a piece of stale cake, his dispatch of the creature on a bench-top counting as one of fantasy cinema's greatest-ever scenes. In the final moving moments, the audience is left to sympathize with Williams as he gazes up at the heavens through a ventilation grill, wondering whether or not there is a place in the universe for him, however small he becomes. A minor classic of '50s fantasy/science fiction, imitated in countless other films but never bettered.

Indestructible Man
Allied Artists 1956; 70 mins; Cert. "X"

CREDITS: Producer/Director: Jack Pollexfen
CAST: Lon Chaney Jr.; Robert Shayne; Marian Carr; Ross Elliott; Casey Adams; Marvin Ellis ***

A scientist experimenting on a cure for cancer reactivates the body of a murderer with a massive dose of electricity and he goes on a rampage, hunting down and killing the associates who sent him to the gas chamber.

A fast-moving horror thriller, a cross between *The Walking Dead* and Chaney's own *Man Made Monster*, filmed in a rough and ready semi-documentary style by Jack Pollexfen and featuring a particularly bombastic soundtrack by Albert Glasser. Chaney is "Butcher" Benton, the convict who goes berserk after being revived by scientists after his execution, mute and impervious to bullets. After tracking down and killing several of his associates and policemen, he gets horribly scarred by flamethrowers in the Los Angeles sewers after locating a cache of stolen loot, and perishes on power cables, trying to give himself more strength. The only dumb point about the movie is the inordinate number of times a close-up of Chaney's squinting eyes is inserted into the action to no great effect. The film was a particular favorite on the Sunday one-day circuit in the early 1960s, usually double billed with *Invasion of the Body Snatchers*.

The Innocents
20th Century Fox 1961; Cinemascope; 99 mins; Cert. "X"
CREDITS: Producer/Director: Jack Clayton
CAST: Deborah Kerr; Martin Stephens; Pamela Franklin; Michael Redgrave; Megs Jenkins; Peter Wyngarde ****

A governess in a lonely house comes to realize that the spirits of two dead servants who were lovers possess the children in her charge.

A literate and somber adaptation of the Henry James novel *The Turn of the Screw*, with some flesh-creeping moments and stark black and white photography, much in the same mold as MGM's *The Haunting*, where suggestive camera-work built up the unease and tension rather than a barrage of special effects. Deborah Kerr is the sexually repressed governess who, when she realizes that the children are possessed, tries to liberate them of their demons, more by terrorizing them than by reason. Eventually, Mark Stephens (of *Village of the Damned* fame) dies, and Pamela Franklin goes mad. Peter Wyngarde is seen briefly as one of the dead lovers, but the film relies more on atmosphere to carry it through, although at times it develops into a shouting match between Kerr and the children, which does have a tendency to destroy the mood. Nevertheless, a sensitive, well-made ghost thriller.

Invaders from Mars
National Pictures Corp./20th Century Fox 1953; Cinecolor; 82 mins; Cert. "A"
CREDITS: Producer: Edward L. Alperson; Director: William Cameron Menzies
CAST: Arthur Franz; Helena Carter; Jimmy Hunt; Leif Erickson; Hilary Brooke; Morris Ankrum
***

A young boy discovers a spaceship in a pit at the bottom of his garden but fails to convince his parents that this is a prelude to an invasion of Earth by Martians.

Science fiction for the younger generation—the Martians are bug-eyed slaves in greenish costumes ruled over by the Supreme Leader, a tentacled head in a glass dome. They have arrived on Earth, as is usual in these films, to replenish their dying planet and control humans by placing a strange crystal device in the back of their necks. After Jimmy Hunt's parents have been taken over by the Martians, he finally convinces a friendly psychologist and the military of the possibilities of an alien invasion. The army eventually enters the spacecraft and, after a battle with the slaves, plants explosives and blows up the ship. The original ending, which had Jimmy Hunt waking up in bed and realizing that he had dreamed the whole thing, then falling asleep only for the story to start all over again, was omitted for the British release, which kept the story intact with no dream ending. The color photography is superb, even though the film overall is a bit juvenile in its concept.

Invasion
Merton Park/American Intl. 1966; 82 mins; Cert. "A"
CREDITS: Producer: Jack Greenwood; Director: Alan Bridges
CAST: Edward Judd; Yoko Tani; Tsai Chin; Valerie Gearon; Lyndon Brook; Eric Young **

Aliens transporting prisoners from one planet to another crash-land on Earth near an English hospital, and when one of the alien prisoners is taken to the hospital, others follow to take him back.

A very minor British offering made on a minuscule budget that nevertheless manages, in its own economical way, to build up an atmosphere of tension. The aliens have crash-landed on Earth while transporting a cargo of prisoners, and when the other aliens demand that the prisoner be handed over to them but are refused, the hospital is surrounded by a force field, which raises the air temperature. More aliens arrive, but Edward Judd escapes from the hospital through the sewers and alerts the army, which destroys the spacecraft and its crew with a missile. Most of the action takes place within the confines of the hospital, and the film is more of an exercise in psychological terror than standard sci-fi fare, resembling at best a British television drama.

Invasion of the Body Snatchers
Allied Artists 1956; Superscope; 80 mins; Cert. "X"
CREDITS: Producer: Walter Wanger; Director: Don Siegel
CAST: Kevin McCarthy; Dana Wynter; King Donovan; Carolyn Jones; Larry Gates; Pat O'Malley
*****

A doctor returns to his hometown and gradually starts to notice that the local inhabitants are behaving abnormally, leading him to discover that alien seed pods have taken over the humans with replicas that lack all emotion.

An enthralling, influential, much-imitated film, brilliantly directed by a young Don Siegel, with telling performances all round and a tremendous score by Carmen Dragon. The build-up of tension and unease is superbly handled by the director as doctor Kevin McCarthy, puzzled by a number of disquieting incidents among the residents, tries to convince his friends that people are somehow acting differently in the town, leading to the chilling sequence when King Donovan uncovers his "new" body on a table in the dining room, ready to possess him when he falls asleep. Doubts about McCarthy's sanity are dispelled during the famous scene in the greenhouse, when the doctor discovers the pods spewing out blank, human bodies ready for possession, which he destroys with a pitchfork. McCarthy and Wynter's flight from the town, now completely taken over by the aliens who display no emotions, is heart-stopping, as is the unhappy moment where McCarthy leaves Wynter in a mine for a short time, only to return and realize in horror that she has been possessed, having fallen asleep in his absence. Against Siegel's wishes, an ending with hospital staff realizing that a terrified McCarthy is telling the truth was tagged on, as Allied Artists thought that the original climax, with McCarthy stumbling across a truckload of pods on the freeway and screaming "You're next!" at the audience, was too downbeat. The film ran for years after release, mainly teamed with Allied Artists' *Indestructible Man*, a popular double bill on the Sunday circuit.

Invasion of the Hell Creatures
aka: Invasion of the Saucer Men
American Intl. 1957; 69 mins; Cert. "X"
CREDITS: Producers: James H. Nicholson and Robert Gurney Jr.; Director: Edward L. Cahn
CAST: Steve Terrell; Frank Gorshin; Gloria Castillo; Raymond Hutton; Russ Bender; Lyn Osborn **

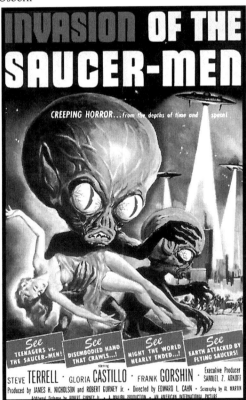

Little green aliens land in a flying saucer near a small American town and menace the local teenagers.

Probably the first semi-comedy science fiction thriller, hence the inclusion of comic Frank Gorshin in the cast, with the strange-looking dwarf aliens with enlarged brain cases and huge eyes scuttling around in the bushes, injecting the teenagers with alcohol from their nails. Despite the light-hearted nature of the movie, the U.K. censor still slapped an "X" rating on it! The film was aimed at the teenage market but is neither funny nor scary—the usual arguments abound between parents and offspring, a sign of '50s teenage rebellion and angst, so that nobody believes the youngsters when they report the aliens in the vicinity, putting it down to drunken behavior (which of course is what the aliens intended). Eventually, the little monsters are defeated by the youths turning their car headlights on them, whereupon they evaporate in the blinding glare—a welcome relief, as most of the movie is shot in darkness. The film was a popular feature of the Sunday one-day programs in 1962, usually double billed with *Day the World Ended*.

Invisible Invaders
United Artists 1959; 67 mins; Cert. "A"
CREDITS: Producer: Robert E. Kent; Director: Edward L. Cahn
CAST: John Agar; Jean Byron; John Carradine; Robert Hutton; Hal Torey; Paul Langton **
Invisible alien invaders from the moon arrive on Earth, taking over the bodies of dead people, who then attack the living.

A fast-paced minor thriller from the prolific team of producer Kent and director Cahn, a forerunner of films such as *Night of the Living Dead*, with Carradine his normal solid self as the leader of the zombies. The invaders have arrived on Earth, as they believe our technology will one day pose a threat to their existence. They proceed to possess the bodies of the dead, causing earthquakes and destruction (an excuse here to insert a lot of stock footage) to try to wipe out the human race. The living dead also go on a rampage until John Agar, holed up in a cave with a group of scientists, discovers that high-frequency sound drives the aliens out of the corpses, destroying them in the process. The aliens are briefly seen as misty clouds as they leave the bodies and perish.

The Invisible Man
Universal 1933; 71 mins; Cert. "A"
CREDITS: Producer: Carl Laemmle Jr.; Director: James Whale
CAST: Claude Rains; Gloria Stuart; Henry Travers; William Harrigan; Una O'Connor; Holmes Herbert ****
A scientist who has found a method to make him invisible turns into a megalomaniac as a result.

A famous version of the H.G. Wells novel, which made a star out of Claude Rains, even though his face wasn't seen until the very end of the film. Arriving at a small English inn, Rains, his face bandaged to disguise the secret of his invisibility, quickly ensconces himself in his room, showing signs of increasingly erratic behavior toward his landlady, Una O'Connor, and her guests. Growing ever more insane, he reveals his invisible state to the startled lodgers and goes on a rampage of mayhem, robbery and murder until shot dead by the police, his body slowly materializing in the snow. The special effects showing Rains' invisibility, achieved by John Fulton, were revolutionary for the time, and the film was such a success that it revived the flagging fortunes of Universal Pictures. Admittedly the first half is a bit creaky, the Invisible Man's continual rants against society tending to become tiresome after a while, and the production is looking its age, but this is still a primitive landmark in screen fantasy.

The Invisible Man Returns
Universal 1940; 81 mins; Cert. "A"
CREDITS: Producer: Kenneth Goldsmith; Director: Joe May
CAST: Cedric Hardwicke; Vincent Price; Nan Grey; John Sutton; Cecil Kellaway; Alan Napier **
The brother of the invisible man, framed for the murder of his brother, uses the invisible serum on himself to find the person responsible for the crime.

Vincent Price stepped into Claude Rains' shoes in this belated and unsatisfactory sequel to the 1933 classic—the film is played out more along the lines of a murder mystery, using John Fulton's much-improved special effects. Price injects himself with Duocaine and escapes from prison after being framed for his brother's death, but suffers from the same maddening side effects as Rains did in the first film. The police shoot him just as the real killer, Cedric Hardwicke, confesses to the crime and falls to his death from a mining truck. This turned out to be a routine production that had little in common with the original film, although it did mark the first appearance of Vincent Price as the lead role in a horror movie.

The Invisible Man's Revenge
Universal 1944; 78 mins; Cert. "X"
CREDITS: Producer/Director: Ford Beebe
CAST: Jon Hall; Lester Mathews; John Carradine; Gale Sondergaard; Evelyn Ankers; Alan Curtis ***

A criminal on the run uses invisibility to exact vengeance on the men who framed him for a crime so that he would lose out on his inheritance.

John Fulton's effects again enlivened the fourth entry in the Invisible Man series and John Hall, who had taken over the part from Vincent Price in 1942's *The Invisible Agent*, carried on in the role. (Price had refused, even at this early stage in his career, to be typecast in horror movies.) Hall, after escaping from an asylum, enlists the aid of a doctor, Carradine, to make him invisible so that he can murder not only those who tried to cheat him out of his inheritance, but also a group of former business partners who attempted to kill him while searching for diamonds in Africa. Hall goes insane from the serum, using fresh supplies of blood to make himself visible, including Carradine's, and is eventually killed by the doctor's Great Dane dog as he attempts a transfusion from another victim. This was the more lurid and full-blooded of the four films but the least successful, forcing Universal to drop any plans for a fifth picture along the same lines.

Island of Terror
Planet/Universal 1966; Eastmancolor; 89 mins; Cert. "X"
CREDITS: Producer: Tom Blakely; Director: Terence Fisher
CAST: Peter Cushing; Edward Judd; Carole Gray; Eddie Byrne; Sam Kydd; Niall MacGinnis ***

A scientist working on a cure for cancer accidentally creates giant mutated viruses that can suck the bones from humans.

This was the second and more cohesive of the three films that Terence Fisher directed for the Planet studios and the most successful at the box office. A corpse without any bones is discovered on a remote Irish island. Peter Cushing (a professor) and Eddie Byrne (a doctor) travel to the island to discover that calcium-feeding monsters are accidentally on the loose from a laboratory, multiplying and threatening to take over the island. The movie mainly consists of Cushing and the rest of the cast attempting to avoid the bone-eating silicates, which resemble the monsters in *Night of the Big Heat* made a year later, although these monsters have tentacles and can crawl. They are eventually destroyed by injecting cattle with a radioactive isotope—the creatures feed on the cattle and die, dissolving into gooey blobs.

Isle of the Dead
RKO-Radio 1945; 72 mins; Cert. "X"
CREDITS: Producer: Val Lewton; Director: Mark Robson
CAST: Boris Karloff; Ellen Drew; Katherine Emery; Marc Cramer; Helene Thimig; Alan Napier ***

In Greece during the war, a general travels to an island where the inhabitants are falling victims to a mysterious plague.

A strange, dark, brooding production from the Val Lewton–Mark Robson team, with Karloff as a Greek general, weakened by the windborne plague while trying to combat the local "vrykolakas" or vampires, on a strange little island inhabited by a disparate group of characters who spend much time wondering who the next victim of the plague will be. The film is very slowly paced and much too talkative, but it does have a certain morbid dreamlike quality about it. There's one nightmarish scene in which one of the plague victims, who is subject to cataleptic fits, is buried alive and screams in her tomb to be freed; it was undoubtedly this harrowing sequence that caused the movie to be banned in Britain for about 10 years until being screened in the early 1960s with RKO's *The Cat People*.

It!
Goldstar/Seven Arts 1966; Eastmancolor; 97 mins; Cert. "X"
CREDITS: Producer/Director: Herbert J. Leder
CAST: Roddy McDowell; Jill Haworth; Paul Maxwell; Aubrey Richards; Ernest Clark; Oliver Johnston **

An insane museum curator discovers that a statue in his care is the legendary Golem, and he reactivates it to wreak havoc in London.

In this inept reworking of the Golem legend, Roddy McDowell seemed totally miscast as the mad curator who realizes that he can control a giant statue in his museum and order it to do his bidding—for reasons of his own, he also keeps the mummified body of his mother in his house, a nod in the direction of *Psycho*. The one decent scene in this drawn-out effort is of the statue toppling Hammersmith Bridge on the telepathic command of McDowell, who also orders the creature to kidnap Jill Haworth, as he is jealous of her interest in Paul Maxwell, who plays an American medieval expert. The production overall is lackluster, with the tree-like Golem (less effective in many ways than the walking stump in *From Hell It Came*!) waddling into the sea at the end and dissolving after McDowell has been destroyed by an atomic bomb dropped on his house. The movie was originally released as second billing to Hammer's *Dracula Has Risen from the Grave*.

It Came from Beneath the Sea
Columbia 1955; 78 mins; Cert. "U"
CREDITS: Producer: Charles H. Schneer; Director: Robert Gordon; Special Effects: Ray Harryhausen
CAST: Kenneth Tobey; Faith Domergue; Ian Keith; Donald Curtis; Harry Lauter; Del Courtney ***

Disturbed by underwater atomic tests, a gigantic octopus emerges from the Mindanao Trench in the Pacific Ocean and attacks San Francisco.

This standard monster-on-the-loose movie is enlivened by Ray Harryhausen's excellent special effects, boosting an otherwise routine production. Harryhausen expertly staged the scenes of the giant octopus (which has only six tentacles) dragging a cargo boat into the depths of the sea and of the monster crawling all over the Golden Gate Bridge before attacking San Francisco, and finally being destroyed by an explosive dart fired by Kenneth Tobey from a submarine. However, the film is let down by the obligatory love interest between Tobey and Faith Domergue, which slows the pace in the mid-picture before the monster appears; by Robert Gordon's flat direction; and by an unimaginative musical score. Despite these shortcomings, this was a big hit for Columbia when first released.

It Came from Outer Space
Universal 1953; Orig. in 3-D; 80 mins; Cert. "A"
CREDITS: Producer: William Alland; Director: Jack Arnold
CAST: Richard Carlson; Barbara Rush; Charles Drake; Kathleen Hughes; Russell Johnson; Joe Sawyer ****

A spaceship crash-lands in the Arizona Desert and aliens replicate the bodies of the local town's inhabitants to use as labor to repair their craft.

Jack Arnold's first science fiction outing for Universal turned out to be a minor classic, using one of his favorite locations for filming, the desert. Richard Carlson plays the scientist and astronomer who ventures out into the desert after seeing what he thinks is a falling meteorite and discovers a massive, globe-like spacecraft in a crater, which is subsequently buried by a rockfall. He is also the first to see the floating, one-eyed amorphous aliens, who are able to take on human form as they wish to employ the local inhabitants as a workforce. The 3-D effect of the aliens enveloping humans as they are replicated is very persuasive, especially as the audience is allowed to "see" from the aliens' perspective. The climax has the townspeople storming the crater to destroy the ship and the aliens, only to be prevented from doing so by Carlson, who has realized that the visitors' intentions are not hostile but indeed peaceful. After the crowd has listened to Carlson, the repaired ship suddenly takes off. The movie was far less violent than Arnold's subsequent films for Universal and because of this, perhaps not as memorable or hard-edged. It was given a brief run in London as late as 1982 in its original 3-D format, double billed with *Creature from the Black Lagoon*.

It Conquered the World
Anglo Amalgamated/American Intl. 1956; 71 mins; Cert. "X"
CREDITS: Producer/Director: Roger Corman
CAST: Peter Graves; Beverly Garland; Lee Van Cleef; Sally Fraser; Charles B. Griffith; Russ Bender ***

A being from Venus hides in a cave and sends out bat-like emissaries that take over people's minds.

An early Roger Corman production that is now famous for the cucumber-like Venusian monster with the big claws, lurking in a cave and being wheeled out at the climax to kill Lee Van Cleef before being blasted by the army and having its eyes burnt out by a blowtorch. Van Cleef, in an early role, is a scientist who guides the Venusian to Earth hoping that it will rule the planet more constructively than Man, but the alien has other ideas and only wants to control the Earth on its own terms, sending out bat creatures that sting people in the back of their necks, turning them into zombies. Despite the corny-looking monster, the film is efficiently directed by Corman, surprisingly well acted by a decent cast, and is quite suspenseful as the bat-mites zoom around looking for their victims to transform mankind into zombie slaves. It was also successful in portraying small-town paranoia à la *Invasion of the Body Snatchers*. In the early 1960s, the picture was double billed with *I Was A Teenage Werewolf* on the Sunday circuit.

It! The Terror from Beyond Space
United Artists 1958; 69 mins; Cert. "X"
CREDITS: Producer: Robert E. Kent; Director: Edward L. Cahn
CAST: Marshall Thompson; Shawn Smith; Kim Spalding; Ann Doran; Dabs Greer; Ray Corrigan ****
A spaceship Earth-bound from Mars with the sole survivor of a previous expedition on board is menaced by a creature from the planet, which proceeds to wipe out the crew one by one.

The plotline that formed the basis to Ridley Scott's *Alien* was reputably taken from this superior sci-fi thriller, perhaps the best-ever effort from producer Robert E. Kent and director Edward L. Cahn, who cooperated on a fair number of films in the 1950s. Marshall Thompson is the only survivor from a previous Mars expedition, being escorted back to Earth for court martial, as the authorities believe that he murdered the members of his crew for food and water. The real culprit, however, gains entry into the ship just before it blasts off. The monster is played by Ray Corrigan, a fearsome-looking *Creature from the Black Lagoon*-type being with large claws. The film is imaginatively photographed by Kenneth Peach, making good use of the ship's cramped interiors and of the intruder prowling around in the shadows looking for victims to drain of marrow and blood while using up the vessel's oxygen supply because of its huge lung capacity. The alien, impervious to grenades, bullets, electric shocks and even a blast from the ship's nuclear reactor, batters its way up through the hatches, forcing the surviving crewmembers to take refuge in the ship's control room. The climax sees Thompson and company trapping the monster in a hatch door and letting the air out of the ship, suffocating the creature to death. Paul Sawtell and Bert Shefter provided one of science fiction's most memorable title scores as well as a full-blooded soundtrack and the film, expertly put together by director Cahn, was often double billed with *Curse of the Faceless Man* on the Sunday one-day programs of the early 1960s.

Jack the Giant Killer
United Artists 1962; Technicolor; 94 mins; Cert. "A"
CREDITS: Producer: Edward Small; Director: Nathan Juran; Special Effects: Jim Danforth
CAST: Kerwin Mathews; Torin Thatcher; Judi Meredith; Walter Burke; Don Beddoe; Roger Mobley ***
An evil magician kidnaps the princess of the King of Old Cornwall, and a farmer's son is given the task of rescuing her from the magician's remote island retreat.

Kerwin Mathews and Torin Thatcher virtually reprised their roles from *The Seventh Voyage of Sinbad* in this colorful but somewhat violent fairy tale, whose release date was delayed in the United Kingdom because of censorship problems. The film was originally to have been awarded an "X" certificate, but United Artists argued that the movie was aimed at a younger audience, so with the censor making a few minor cuts it was eventually passed with an "A" rating in 1967. Nathan Juran, also of *Sinbad* fame, directed and Jim Danforth replaced Ray Harryhausen on the stop-motion special effects. Danforth's animated models were variable—the horned, cloven-hoofed giant that storms the castle in the opening sequence before being slayed by Mathews is excellent, even though it resembles a poorer version of Harryhausen's Cyclops from *Sinbad*, but the fighting sea-serpents at the end look very rubbery and amateurish. The ghostly visitations, demons and ghouls in Thatcher's castle were probably deemed too frightening for younger children and the film is several minutes too long, dragging slightly in the middle. Despite spirited performances all round, the film was not a success and still appears today to be a cut-price version of Harryhausen's Columbia classic of 1958.

Jack the Ripper
Mid Century/Paramount 1959; 88 mins; Cert. "X"
CREDITS: Producers/Directors: Robert S. Baker and Monty Berman
CAST: Lee Patterson; Eddie Byrne; Betty McDowell; Ewen Solon; John Le Mesurier; George Rose **

An American detective assists Scotland Yard in hunting down Whitechapel's notorious killer.

A grim, murky retelling of the Ripper saga, with Lee Patterson as the American trying to help the British police track down the murderer of prostitutes. The culprit in this version of the story is crazed surgeon John Le Mesurier, who has caught venereal disease from one of the women and is carrying out his crimes to rid the London streets of the cause of his ailment. Le Mesurier finally gets crushed to death under an elevator, a scene originally shown in color in some U.K. prints. The film was too downbeat to be much of a success, and turned up occasionally in the mid-'60s on a double bill with *The Return of the Vampire*.

Jason and the Argonauts
Columbia 1963; Technicolor; 104 mins; Cert. "U"
CREDITS: Producer: Charles H. Schneer; Director: Don Chaffey; Special Effects: Ray Harryhausen
CAST: Todd Armstrong; Nancy Kovak; Gary Raymond; Laurence Naismith; Niall MacGinnis; Honor Blackman *****

To regain his right to the throne, Jason assembles a crew of athletes and sets sail in search of the fabled golden fleece in the land of Colchis.

Together with *The Seventh Voyage of Sinbad*, this fabulous piece of Greek mythology marks the peak of Ray Harryhausen's career, a marvelous blend of spectacular special effects, picture-postcard locations (filmed in Italy), and stirring music, held together by a great cast. Many aficionados would say that the finest part of the picture is a third of the way in, when the giant bronze statue of Talos menaces Jason and his crew on the Isle of Bronze. This is also one of Harryhausen's most lengthy animation sequences and the scene where Talos, on his pedestal, turns to stare down at the two Greeks who have dared to disturb his treasure chamber is a classic piece of cinema in anyone's book. The much talked about finale, with Jason and his men battling an army of seven skeletons, took Harryhausen a painstaking four months to film, but again ranks as one of his most famous stop-motion sequences. Todd Armstrong is admittedly a bit wooden in the title role, and the color is muddy at times, but this doesn't detract from the eye-popping visuals, all underlined once again by a rousing Bernard Herrmann score. The film was one of the biggest box office hits of 1963 in the United Kindom and also one of the most financially successful that Schneer and Harryhausen ever produced as a team.

Jason and the Golden Fleece
aka: The Giants of Thessaly
Medallion/Compton Cameo (Italy/France) 1960; Totalscope/Eastmancolor; 97 mins; Cert. "U"
CREDITS: Producer: Virgilio De Blasi; Director: Riccardo Freda
CAST: Roland Carey; Ziva Rodann; Maria Teresa Vianello; Alberto Farnese; Luciano Marin; Cathio Caro ***
Jason and his crew set sail on the Argo to discover the whereabouts of the Golden Fleece.
A typical continental production of the time—bad dubbing, disjointed scenes due to editing, and the usual weird soundtrack music, all filmed in garish color by Riccardo Freda, who took time off from his sadistic horror tales to come up with a reasonably entertaining adventure romp. While not up to the standards of Columbia's *Jason and the Argonauts*, this was still a fair stab at the Greek legend. Setting out to find the Golden Fleece, Jason and his men have to first battle their way through a ferocious storm before encountering an island of seductive witches who can turn men into sheep. There is a not-very-realistic Cyclops that they thwart, and a final uprising against an evil king when the fleece is returned to their homeland. The most exciting sequence in the picture is when Jason has to scale up a gigantic statue to retrieve the fleece; this is worthy of inclusion in the Columbia 1963 classic. A muddled but enjoyable romp, going the rounds in the early '60s with *Samson and the 7 Miracles*.

Journey to A Primeval Age
aka: Cesta Do Praveku
Studio Gottwaldow/New Trends (Czech) 1954; 87 mins; Cert. "U"
CREDITS: Producer/Director: Karel Zeman
CAST: Josef Lukas; Vladimir Bejval; Petr Herrmann; Zdenek Hustak *****
Four boys discover a cave and travel down the "river of time," passing through the various geological ages, encountering much prehistoric life and ending their journey at the dawn of creation.
Karel Zeman's marvelous use of stunning prehistoric dioramas (inspired by the paintings of Czechoslovakian artist Zdenek Burian), stop-motion animation, live action and animatronics to create a bygone world predated the later works of special effects artists such as Ray Harryhausen and films like *Jurassic Park*, but have rarely been equaled in terms of sheer beauty, accuracy and wonder. In fact, it remains one of the very few films of its type to convey to an audience precisely what the primeval world would have looked like—vast silent empty vistas populated by strange-looking beasts, with Man nowhere to be seen. There is no real story as such—the boys act as though they are on an extended adventure, and parts of the film almost resemble a lesson in prehistory as various ancient animals are encountered on their journey down the river that takes them through the ages. Memorable scenes include the four adventurers being attacked by the giant flightless bird Phororhacos, the depiction of the Tertiary period with its parade of prehistoric mammals, the battle between the Ceratosaurus and the Stegosaurus, and the boys wading through the Carboniferous swamps and forests encountering giant amphibians as they search for their missing journal. In 1966, an American producer, William Cayton, picked up the rights to this enchanting classic, added a few scenes of four American boys discovering the cave in Central Park, dubbed it and released the film under the title *Journey to the Beginning of Time* to cash in on the success of Hammer's *One Million Years B.C.* It is generally this version that can be found on various European video releases, and not the original Czech movie.

Journey to the Center of the Earth
20th Century Fox 1959; Cinemascope/DeLuxeColor; 132 mins; Cert. "U"
CREDITS: Producer: Charles Brackett; Director: Henry Levin
CAST: James Mason; Pat Boone; Arlene Dahl; Peter Ronson; Thayer David; Diane Baker
*****

An Edinburgh professor and assorted colleagues follow a 16th-century explorer's trail down an extinct volcano in Iceland to the Earth's center, encountering many wonders on their travels, including dinosaurs, an underground sea, and the lost city of Atlantis.

This expensive, handsomely mounted and very entertaining version of the Jules Verne novel was a big box office winner in 1960, with fine subterranean sets and backdrops, excellent special effects, an unusually witty and lucid script for this type of picture, and a nice sense of the Victorian period in which the story takes place. The film was also notable for its successful use of live lizards as dinosaurs. Not to be overlooked was James Mason's performance as the irascible Professor Lindenbrock, one of the finest and most underrated of his career. Even pop star of the time Pat Boone shone in his role as the professor's nephew, Alex. Mason is the Scottish professor (in the novel, he is German) who discovers a cryptic message scrawled on a plumb bob in a block of lava, which gives clues to a route to the Earth's interior. Despite protests from his academic colleagues, he decides to follow up the message and carry out his own exploration. The movie does take a fair bit of time to get going before the party, together with an evil descendant of Arne Saknussemm, the original explorer, reach the crater and journey into the depths of the volcano, but from then on it is tremendous fun. Particularly impressive is the cavern full of giant mushrooms that Pat Boone discovers, the ruins of Atlantis, and the climax whereby the team are shot out of an active volcano on an altar stone. A great-looking fantasy that also contained a moody, atmospheric score by Bernard Herrmann, which many fans rate as one of his best.

Journey to the Seventh Planet
Cinemagic/American Intl. (Denmark) 1961; Pathecolor; 83 mins; Cert. "A"
CREDITS: Producer/Director: Sidney Pink
CAST: John Agar; Greta Thyssen; Ann Smyrner; Carl Ottosen; Ove Sprogoe; Mimi Heinrich
***

The first manned space voyage to Uranus encounters a giant alien brain capable of creating matter from the astronaut's deep-rooted fears, which it uses to try to force them to leave the planet.

The expedition that lands on Uranus is a multinational team lead by John Agar, and the brain they encounter taps into their subconscious thoughts, sending out images to scare them off—giant fanged rats, a huge spider, and quicksand. All of the crew's girlfriends materialize as well, a mixture of horror and comforting illusions to throw them off guard and to make them consider leaving the planet. In the end, the barrier surrounding the alien is pierced by Agar and his crew, and after freezing the brain with liquid oxygen, it is smashed and destroyed, releasing the crew from their phobias. Produced by the same team that was responsible for the dire *Reptilicus*, this juvenile forerunner of 1972's *Solaris* (and its remake in 2002) admittedly had colorful special effects, even though the acting and script left a lot to be desired, and went the rounds in 1963 with *Marco Polo*.

The Killer Shrews
HPC 1959; 70 mins; Cert. "X"
CREDITS: Producer: Ken Curtis;
Director: Ray Kellogg
CAST: James Best; Ingrid Goude;
Ken Curtis; Baruch Lumet; Gordon McLendon; Henry Dupree *

A scientist on a remote island develops a serum that turns shrews into ferocious dog-sized flesh-eaters.

Bottom-of-the-barrel rubbish featuring several badly executed scenes of the cast trying to escape from the unscary, inept-looking shrews (large dogs in shaggy coats with fangs). Scientist Ken Curtis is trying to reduce the size of humans to solve the world's overpopulation problem, and when seven people are washed up on his island during a hurricane, the giant shrews he has inadvertently created hunt them down, killing most of the cast before the survivors escape the island in a make-shift boat. This tawdry movie was originally released with the equally inept *The Giant Gila Monster* and went the rounds in the late 1960s with *The Haunted Strangler*.

Killers from Space
Planet Filmways/RKO-Radio 1954;
71 mins; Cert. "A"
CREDITS: Producer/Director: W.
Lee Wilder
CAST: Peter Graves; James Seay;
Barbara Bestar; Frank Gerstle; John
Merrick; Shep Manken *

The sole survivor of a plane crash is captured by aliens living in a cave in the Nevada Desert and brainwashed into becoming their emissary on Earth prior to an invasion.

A low-budget sci-fi thriller from Wilder that ranks among the silliest of the decade's output and features probably the '50s' dumbest-looking visitors from outer space. Scientist Peter Graves encounters the bug-eyed aliens from the planet Astron Delta, who are trying to put together a device that will create giant insects and reptiles, which they will then use to conquer the Earth. This will enable them to migrate from their own planet and repopulate ours. Graves is brainwashed by the aliens into committing sabotage at a nearby nuclear testing site, but when the brainwashing technique wears off, he regains his senses and blows up the cave where the aliens are hiding by tampering with a dynamo that supplies them with power. The film was so dreadful that it was not even unintentionally funny. Wilder did slightly better with his other effort, *The Snow Creature*, released in the same year.

King Dinosaur
Zimgor/Lippert 1955; 63 mins; Cert. "A"
CREDITS: Producers: Al Zimbalist and Bert I. Gordon; Director: Bert I. Gordon
CAST: Bill Bryant; Wanda Curtis; Douglas Henderson; Patricia Gallagher **

An expedition manning an experimental rocket is sent to a new planet called Nova, which has entered our solar system; there they encounter dinosaurs and other primitive life forms.

A cut-price Bert I. Gordon production that was apparently knocked out over a weekend at a paltry cost. The first 10 minutes contain at least nine minutes of stock footage showing rockets, military bases and scientists—the crew, two men and two women then take off for the new planet and land in the middle of a pine forest. After much trekking about (cue for more newsreel footage of various forms of wildlife) and encountering both a giant armadillo and a huge back-projected cricket, they eventually discover a subtropical island in the middle of a lake that supports prehistoric life. Bryant and Curtis row over to the island (Henderson is laid low after fighting an alligator) and are menaced by a bevy of magnified lizards until rescued by the other two crew members, a mastodon purloined straight from 1940's *One Million B.C.* also putting in an appearance. Finally, the island and its monsters are wiped out by an atomic bomb planted there by the astronauts. Gordon's first feature as a director was also his cheapest—in a 63-minute movie, the unconvincing dinosaurs didn't get a look in until the final 10 minutes! It must be admitted that the film is fun to see for all the wrong reasons, even though it still ranks as one of the shoddiest monster pictures ever cobbled together in the 1950s.

King Kong
RKO-Radio 1933; 100 mins; Cert. "A"
CREDITS: Producers/Directors: Merian C. Cooper and Ernest B. Schoedsack; Special Effects: Willis O'Brien
CAST: Robert Armstrong; Fay Wray; Bruce Cabot; Frank Reicher; Sam Hardy; Noble Johnson
*****

A crew of adventurers journeys to a remote island in the Indian Ocean populated by prehistoric life and captures a giant ape. They bring the monster back to New York, where it breaks loose and terrorizes the city before being shot off the top of the Empire State building.

The all-time classic monster movie and the pioneering blueprint for everything else that followed of the same genre. Willis O'Brien's groundbreaking special effects, incorporating stop-motion animation, matte paintings, miniature rear and front projection and multiple exposures, paved the way for future artists in this field such as Ray Harryhausen and Jim Danforth. However, the great thing about *Kong* is that the multitude of effects on display do not swamp the story but become an integral part of it. Many of the scenes in *King Kong* have passed into movie folklore—the first appearance of the giant ape on Skull Island as Fay Wray screams her head off; the fight between Kong and the Tyrannosaurus Rex in the forest glade; the break-out from the theater; and of course the climactic battle atop the Empire State building, which can still bring a tear to the most hardened eye as Kong meets his end. Never to be forgotten is Max Steiner's magnificent score, probably a career best and all the more amazing when one considers that the film was made only a few years after the advent of the talkies. The incredible success of this film saved RKO-Radio from bankruptcy and became an enduring legend in cinema history. In 1967, it was re-released for a limited period with *The Thing From Another World* and in 1993 a special edition was released on video containing previously edited footage believed to be too violent for 1930s audiences.

King Kong vs. Godzilla
Toho/Universal (Japan) 1962; Tohoscope/Technicolor; 96 mins; Cert. "X"
CREDITS: Producers: Tomoyuki Tanaka and John Beck; Directors: Inoshiro Honda and Thomas Montgomery
CAST: Michael Keith; James Yagi; Mie Hama; Kenji Sahara; Akihiko Hirata; Ichiro Arishima
***

An atomic bomb frees Godzilla from an iceberg; King Kong is worshipped as a deity on a remote island in the Solomons. The two monsters head toward Tokyo and fight to the death.

This was to be the last of Toho's adult-oriented X-rated monster movies before they turned their attentions to the more juvenile end of the market. A rather tatty-looking Kong is first seen wrestling a giant octopus to defend a group of Japanese fishermen while members of a pharmaceutical company debate whether or not to capture him. Godzilla is the bad guy who invades Tokyo, with Kong escaping from a raft, taking him to captivity, and heading for the city to do battle with him. The scenes of the two monsters trashing Tokyo and fighting on Mount Fuji are very well staged in the usual Toho manner, although the comic antics of the cast let the proceedings down a bit. The film ends with the two heavyweights hurling boulders at each other before an earthquake ejects both monsters into the sea—Godzilla disappears but Kong wades back to the shore. As usual with their major releases, extra footage featuring Michael Keith was added to the American version, and this ranked as one of the best of the dozen or so *Godzilla* movies since the monster's inception in 1954.

Kiss of the Vampire
aka: Kiss of Evil
Hammer/Universal 1963; Eastmancolor; 87 mins; Cert. "X"
CREDITS: Producer: Anthony Hinds; Director: Don Sharp
CAST: Noel Willman; Clifford Evans; Edward de Souza; Jennifer Daniel; Barry Warren; Isobel Black ****

In Bavaria at the turn of the 1900s, a young couple on honeymoon is invited to a party at a sinister castle and become unwittingly trapped by a sect of vampires.

A well-plotted and inventive Hammer vampire film with a spine-chilling and gory climax; the vampire sect and their leader are wiped out by a plague of bats as they gather, white-robed, for a sacrificial ceremony. Once again, Christopher Lee was apparently still refusing vampire roles for fear of typecasting, leaving Noel Willman to give a suave but sinister performance as a disciple of Dracula and leader of the cult of the undead, holding vampiric orgies in his castle. Director Don Sharp cranked up the tension to sweaty levels during the central scene in which Edward de Souza and Jennifer Daniel are lured into the vampire's lair at a party where everyone has donned bird masks, completely unaware that the bloodsuckers are after the wife, whom they plan to use as a sacrifice to the Devil. Clifford Evans was also excellent as the vampire killer Professor Zimmer, taking over the Van Helsing role from Peter Cushing in one of Hammer's more illustrious '60s offerings, reissued in 1969 with Universal's *Tarantula*.

Konga
Anglo Amalgamated/American Intl. 1960; Eastmancolor; 90 mins; Cert. "A"
CREDITS: Producer: Herman Cohen; Director: John Lemont
CAST: Michael Gough; Jess Conrad; Margo Johns; Claire Gordon; Austin Trevor; Jack Watson
***

A demented biologist creates a growth serum that he uses on carnivorous plants and also his pet chimpanzee, which grows to an enormous size and attacks London.

Released in the United Kingom in 1961 to cash in on the success of *Gorgo*, with a lurid novel full of sex scenes (not included in the film) to accompany it. This was a vulgar, childish mad scientist movie with a way-over-the-top performance by Michael Gough as the creator of the serum, embarrassingly lusting after one of his students, and an equally dumb performance by Jess Conrad, although the giant carnivorous plants looked gaudy and fairly nasty. Gough administers serum to his pet chimpanzee, Konga, and lets the animal loose on his enemies, but when the biologist's wife discovers his affair, she gives the chimp a massive dose of the serum to try to control the creature herself. The climax, with the chimp growing to gigantic proportions, crashing through the roof of the house, and stomping off toward Big Ben with Gough in its grip, is the most enjoyable part of the film. The air force puts paid to Konga, and after being destroyed, he shrinks back to normal size, killing Gough in the process.

Kronos
Regal Intl./20th Century Fox 1957; Regalscope; 78 mins; Cert. "A"
CREDITS: Producer/Director: Kurt Neumann
CAST: Jeff Morrow; Barbara Lawrence; George O'Hanlon; John Emery; Morris Ankrum; Kenneth Alton ****

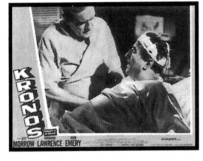

Deposited on a beach in Mexico by a flying saucer, a 100-foot, cube-shaped robot goes on the march, sucking up energy from power stations as a source of food for another planet.

A one-off film this—rarely seen, but one of the real curiosities of '50s sci-fi cinema. A flying saucer takes over the mind of a scientist at a research station, who then transmits details of power plants in the area by thought control to the giant robot left by the saucer on a beach, which has the capacity to feed on and store energy. The sight of the enormous chunk of metal, resembling a giant hydraulic press with a dome-like head and pistons for legs, stomping across the landscape, destroying power stations, blasting planes out of the sky, and even absorbing the energy from an atomic bomb (which the military uses against it), is unique. The sequences showing the rampaging Kronos emitting blasts of electrical charge and causing panic among the local population are impressive. At the end, Jeff Morrow short-circuits the machine by dropping a negative bolt between the robot's two antennae; Kronos absorbs its own energy, implodes, and becomes a mass of twisted metal. It does take almost 30 minutes for the robot to appear, but from then on the action and effects never let up and are helped along by a thundering Paul Sawtell/Bert Shefter soundtrack.

Lady in a Cage
American Entertainments Corp./Paramount 1964; 100 mins; Cert. "X London"
CREDITS: Producer: Luther Davis; Director: Walter Grauman
CAST: Olivia De Havilland; James Caan; Ann Sothern; Jeff Corey; Rafael Campos; Jennifer Billingsley **

A rich and disabled widow becomes trapped in her elevator and is terrorized by a gang of thugs who break into her home.

This thoroughly unpleasant exercise in sadism, which had virtually no plot other than James Caan and his gang breaking into Olivia De Havilland's house and being extremely nasty and brutish to her, failed to gain a general release in the United Kingdom because of its disturbing nature. It only went the rounds at selected cinemas in London in 1968, teamed up with Gala's equally controversial sex-comedy *Seventeen*. De Havilland spends most of the picture crying and screaming her head off, crippled and trapped in her private elevator, while Caan gives a horribly leering performance as the chief thug. In the end, the audience is treated to the nauseating sight of one of the gang members having a car run over his head in graphic detail and another being stabbed in the eyes before the tormented widow is rescued. Although the film played along psycho-thriller lines, the subject matter had very little artistic merit and it failed miserably at the box office because of its prohibitive rating.

The Land Unknown
Universal 1957; Cinemascope; 78 mins; Cert. "X"
CREDITS: Producer: William Alland; Director: Virgil Vogel
CAST: Jock Mahoney; Shawn Smith; William Reynolds; Douglas Kennedy; Phil Harvey; Harry Brandon ****

An expedition sent to Antarctica to investigate a mysterious warm water region crash their helicopter into a Pterodactyl and are forced to land in a hidden tropical valley that has remained unchanged since the Mesozoic period.

Universal's expensive combination of *The Lost World* and *One Million B.C.* was a very lively affair, with square-jawed hero Jock Mahoney and the delightful Shawn Smith being menaced by dinosaurs, man-eating plants and the crazed, lone survivor of a previous expedition in a strange, prehistoric landscape. The film runs the gamut of special effects—a man in a dinosaur suit is the Tyrannosaurus Rex, enlarged back-projected lizards fight to the death, and the man-eating plant is a life-sized model, as is the impressive Elasmosaurus in the lake. Even a Pterodactyl puts in an appearance. The primeval backdrops and dioramas are also imaginatively achieved, with their towering mist-shrouded cliffs, giant trees, waterfalls and jungle vegetation. After landing in the valley, the cast spends a great deal of time fighting and trying to get away from the various monsters and the half-mad survivor who wants Shawn Smith all to himself. Eventually, the team plus the sole survivor repair their helicopter with parts salvaged from the 1945 expedition and escape their primordial prison after a final battle with the Elasmosaurus. This was an inventive "X" certificate variation on the old *Lost World* theme, put together with vigor and style—it played continuously throughout the 1960s in England with either *The Deadly Mantis* or *Monster on the Campus*.

The Last Man on Earth
Alta Vista/American Intl. (Italy) 1963: 86 mins; Cert. "X"
CREDITS: Producer: Robert L. Lippert; Directors: Sydney Salkow and Ubaldo Ragona
CAST: Vincent Price; Franca Bettoia; Emma Danieli; Giacomo Rossi-Stuart; Umberto Rau; Tony Cerevi **

The only survivor of a plague that has wiped out most of mankind has to battle for his existence against hordes of vampire-like zombies.

The first adaptation of Richard Matheson's celebrated novel *I Am Legend* was given an unimaginative and heavy-handed treatment in this dull movie, with Vincent Price delivering, for him, a very restrained performance as the lone survivor who has to locate and destroy the zombie-like humans living in deserted buildings all around him. He finds a girl who has possibly developed an antidote for the plague, but when he accidentally wipes out her group of friends, he is defeated in the end by the mutants who, being so numerous, have formed their own society. The film had various production problems and was not released in England until 1967.

The Leech Woman
Universal 1960; 77 mins; Cert. "X"
CREDITS: Producer: Joseph Gershenson; Director: Edward Dein
CAST: Coleen Gray; Grant Williams; Gloria Talbott; Phillip Terry; John Van Dreelen; Estelle Hemsley ***
A scientist who develops a youth serum from an African plant plans to use his wife as a guinea pig in his experiments, but she has him killed and after taking the serum has to resort to murder to maintain her looks.

One of the best of the latter-day Universal horror movies, with Coleen Gray giving a forceful

performance as the deranged woman who despises her husband, Phillip Terry, so much that she has him sacrificed by an African tribe and then takes the youth serum that he has developed herself. What she doesn't realize is that a new male pineal gland has to be found for the serum to take effect. As the glands only work for a short time, Gray, on returning to America, embarks on a series of murders to obtain her supply of the glands so that she can remain forever beautiful. Grant Williams, Gray's lawyer whom she fancies and wants to prise away from his fiancée, Gloria Talbott, finally discovers her secret and withholds the serum, and at the end she crumbles to dust. This was one of a series of rejuvenation pictures produced in the very early '60s, with some startling makeup showing Gray aging before taking the serum. In 1962, it was going the rounds on the Sunday one-day circuit with *The Incredible Shrinking Man*.

Lock Up Your Daughters
New Realm 1956; 51 mins; Cert. "A"
CREDITS: Producer: Sam Katzman **
This bizarrely produced tribute to Bela Lugosi was made up of footage from six of the films he starred in for Monogram, including *The Ape Man*, *Voodoo Man* and *Return of the Ape Man*, together with fresh scenes of Lugosi never seen before. The whole mediocre exercise, narrated by the man himself shortly before he died, was a very old-fashioned idea of what passed for entertainment, even when it was made, and appeared occasionally on the Sunday one-day circuit in the mid 1960s.

The Lost Continent
Hammer/Seven Arts 1968; Technicolor; 98 mins; Cert. "X"
CREDITS: Producer/Director: Michael Carreras
CAST: Eric Porter; Suzanna Leigh; Hildegard Kneff; Tony Beckley; Nigel Stock; Neil McCallum ****
A tramp steamer with assorted crew and passengers wanders off course and becomes marooned in the Sargasso Sea, encountering monsters and a strange colony remaining from the Spanish Inquisition.

Based on Dennis Wheatley's novel *Unchartered Seas* (although the Spanish Inquisition side of the story did not figure in the book), this was one of Hammer's real oddities of the late '60s, a wonderfully flamboyant movie featuring a strong British cast and some truly outlandish monsters. The Sargasso Sea, a vast area of seaweed in which the occupants of the ship become trapped, harbors carnivorous vines, a giant jellyfish-type creature that crawls all over the ship, and monstrous hermit crabs that inhabit small islands in the sea and attack the passengers when they begin to explore. The squabbling cast are captured by a group of conquistadors who travel over the deadly weed supported by gas-filled balloons strapped to their backs, and are taken to an old galleon on an island where a young, evil descendant of the Spanish throne rules over a lost kingdom, hurling his enemies into the maw of a monster hidden under the weed. The crew and passengers eventually escape his clutches by setting fire to the ship and the vines, freeing the islanders from his tyrannical rule. An unconventional production from Hammer that was a lot more original than some of the usual horror fare they were churning out during this period.

The Lost World
First National/Warner Bros. 1925; 62 mins; No Certificate
CREDITS: Producers: Earl Hudson and Watterson R. Rothacker; Director: Harry O. Hoyt; Special Effects: Willis O'Brien
CAST: Wallace Beery; Lewis Stone; Bessie Love; Lloyd Hughes; Arthur Hoyt; Bull Montana
****

Professor Challenger and assorted colleagues journey to a plateau in the jungles of South America and discover both dinosaurs and the missing link.

This celebrated early silent version of Sir Arthur Conan Doyle's famous novel is rightly renowned for its special effects, conceived and created by Willis O'Brien, who was to work on the classic *King Kong* a few years later. Audiences of the time were astonished to see dinosaurs moving on the screen, all brought to life by stop-motion animation wizardry, although this technique was not fully understood when the film was first released. Some of the remarkable sequences concocted by O'Brien include the sight of dozens of dinosaurs fleeing from an erupting volcano, and the climax that has a Brontosaurus (in the book, it's a Pterodactyl) roaming the London streets and walking onto London Bridge, which collapses under the monster's weight, sending it plummeting into the Thames, scenes that caused a sensation in 1925. A landmark motion picture that was to inspire a host of imitators for the next 50 years until computers replaced the animators and everything became "realistic."

The Lost World
20th Century Fox 1960; Cinemascope/DeLuxeColor; 98 mins; Cert. "A"
CREDITS: Producer/Director: Irwin Allen
CAST: Claude Rains; Michael Rennie; Jill St. John; David Hedison; Fernando Lamas; Ray Stricklyn **

A party of explorers led by Professor Challenger journey to a remote plateau in the Amazon jungle and encounter dinosaurs.

After the critical and commercial success of *Journey to the Center of the Earth*, Fox turned their attentions to Conan Doyle's adventure novel and decided on a remake of the 1925 classic, but made the fatal mistake of updating the action from the early 1900s to modern times and having the explorers flown to the plateau by helicopter. The sight of Jill St. John cavorting about in pink boots and screaming at top volume when she steps into a carnivorous plant seemed to destroy any credibility about this version, and although Claude Rains made a passable Professor Challenger, his character seemed to peter out midway through the film, which then concentrated on the "lost diamonds" story and became downright tedious. Real lizards were used for dinosaurs and these were only partly convincing. At the end, the plateau blows up through volcanic activity and Rains shows the survivors an egg, from which hatches a baby monitor lizard with frills—this, he blithely announces to one and all, is "a baby Tyrannosaurus!" There was some pre-production talk of having Willis O'Brien, the genius behind *King Kong*, supervise the special effects and at one point he was consulted over this, but eventually the idea was vetoed because of the cost and time involved in stop-motion animation. A pity—he could have saved the film from becoming the farrago that it turned out to be, although it was quite successful when first released and Paul Sawtell and Bert Shefter's music was, as usual with these composers, suitably stirring in places.

Lust of the Vampire
aka: I Vampiri
Athena/Titanus/Herts Lion (Italy) 1956; Cinemascope; 78 mins; Cert. "X"
CREDITS: Producers: Ermanno Donati and Luigi Carpentieri; Directors: Riccardo Freda and Mario Bava
CAST: Gianna Maria Canale; Antoine Balpetre; Dario Michaelis; Paul Muller; Carlo D'Angelo; Wandisa Guida ****

A mad doctor murders young women and uses their blood to restore youth to his cousin, a beautiful but aging Countess whom he loves.

The familiar story of retaining one's youth by regular exterior and interior transfusions of blood was given a scientific explanation by Riccardo Freda (in his directorial debut), who argued with the film's producers during filming; Mario Bava actually completed the picture in the final few days of production. This film was the precursor of the French/Italian/Spanish horror genre that flourished in the 1960s and as such was a landmark continental production. Stunning actress Gianna Maria Canale plays the Countess, needing a regular supply of blood to keep her forever young. This is obtained by Antoine Balpetre, who sends out his drug-addicted assistant to kidnap young women, treating their blood with radiation before administering it to Canale. After several women's corpses have been found drained of blood, the police eventually track the pair down in Canale's splendid Gothic castle. The doctor is shot and, deprived of her life-preserving fluid, the Countess ages rapidly into a haggard old crone and dies. This very stylish and, at the time, underrated Italian film, beautifully photographed in stark black and white, was severely cut, atrociously dubbed and released with additional scenes in the United States under the title *The Devil's Commandment*, where it flopped at the box office, while in the United Kingdom it surfaced on the Sunday one-day circuit in 1964 (also with added sequences) as *Lust of the Vampire*, double billed with *Terror in the Midnight Sun*. Hammer's *Countess Dracula* was a virtual remake of *I Vampiri*, although the action in their version took place in a different century.

Macabre
Allied Artists 1958; 73 mins; Cert. "X"
CREDITS: Producer/Director: William Castle
CAST: William Prince; Jim Backus; Jacqueline Scott; Christine White; Phillip Tonge; Susan Morrow **

When a small-town doctor is suspected of the death of his wife and sister, a plan is hatched to scare him to death by convincing him that his daughter has been buried alive.

William Castle's first feature film and also the first to promote one of his infamous gimmicks—this time, it was free life insurance from Lloyds of London if the film fatally scared anybody watching it. Lloyds would never have had to pay out, because this dull thriller is similar in many ways to a padded-out television detective feature, with doctor William Prince finding his patients deserting him in droves because of their suspicions over his wife's and sister's deaths, and then frantically searching a graveyard to see if his daughter has been buried alive. Most of the non-existant action takes place either in an undertaker's office or the cemetery, and numerous flashbacks explaining the reasons his patients have for hating him almost grind the film to a halt. Even the trick ending, with the revelation that the doctor is responsible for the whole charade and that he has been trying to scare his wealthy father-in-law to death to get his hands on his money, is a letdown. Although laborious and too talkative for most of its running time, this was an inexplicably popular choice on the Sunday one-day circuit in the 1960s, usually playing second feature to *Frankenstein 1970*.

Macumba Love
United Artists 1960; Eastmancolor; 86 mins; Cert. "X"
CREDITS: Producer/Director: Douglas Fowley
CAST: Walter Reed; Ziva Rodann; June Wilkinson; Ruth de Souza; Douglas Fowley; William Wellman Jr. **

A writer who travels to Brazil to investigate a series of suspicious deaths becomes a marked man by a sect of voodoo-worshippers.

A tatty piece of melodrama from producer/director Fowley that turned up with *Doctor Blood's Coffin* in 1964 on the Sunday circuit. A writer, Walter Reed, goes to Brazil and accuses the local voodoo practitioners of not only fakery but of being responsible for a gruesome series of murders. By doing so, he becomes their next target. Most of the film consisted of numerous scenes showing hordes of brightly decked-out native women prancing about in a frenzy of singing and chanting, including June Wilkinson and her 44-inch bust, and very little else, although the vivid color photography was quite fetching.

The Mad Ghoul
Universal 1943; 64 mins; Cert. "X"
CREDITS: Producer: Ben Pivar; Director: James P. Hogan
CAST: George Zucco; David Bruce; Evelyn Ankers; Robert Armstrong; Turhan Bey; Milburn Stone ****

A mad scientist dabbling with the effects of an ancient poisonous gas sends out his zombie assistant to rob graves for fresh hearts as an antidote for the victims of his experiments.

An outlandish, fast-paced B movie that managed somehow to throw everything into its relatively short running time—a mad doctor, graverobbing, zombies and even a love triangle. George Zucco plays the doctor who is experimenting with an ancient gas that the Egyptians used for life-preserving purposes, but which turns animals and humans into the living dead. He administers the gas to his young assistant, David Bruce, as Zucco is envious of his relationship with singer Evelyn Ankers and wants her all to himself. Bruce changes periodically into a wild-eyed, parchment-skinned zombie who has to retrieve hearts from freshly buried corpses to enable Zucco to produce a serum that will restore him to his normal self. As the effect is only temporary, more hearts are required and soon the newspapers are screaming "Ghoul!" as several graves are defiled. Zucco also continues to lust after Ankers, who in turn is now going out with Turhan Bey, so the doctor orders Bruce to kill his love rival. Bruce refuses, as he once loved Ankers himself when he was "normal," gives Zucco a whiff of the gas and then, back in his zombie state, attempts to kill Bey onstage during a concert but is shot dead by the police. Zucco, also now changed into one of the living dead, perishes in the end as he tries unsuccessfully to secure a heart from a fresh corpse to use on himself. This was great horror entertainment for the time, with Bruce turning in an uncanny performance as the unfortunate zombie, even though the script was slightly corny. The other plus point was a fine score by Hans J. Salter in a picture that turned out to be the only zombie film produced by Universal in the 1940s.

The Mad Magician
Columbia 1954; Technicolor sequences; Orig. in 3-D; 73 mins; Cert. "X"
CREDITS: Producer: Bryan Foy; Director: John Brahm
CAST: Vincent Price; Mary Murphy; Patrick O'Neal; Eva Gabor; Jay Novello; John Emery
***
An inventor of illusions takes revenge when his employer prevents him from using his own tricks onstage, and another magician seduces his wife.

Vincent Price's second 3-D outing in a year was one of the least remembered of his '50s films and an obvious attempt by Columbia to jump onto the *House of Wax* bandwagon. He plays The Great Gallico, who becomes frustrated when his boss continually prevents him from using his tricks onstage, and then seduces his wife behind his back. To add insult to injury, a rival magician, The Great Rinaldi, steals his ideas and uses them in his stage act. Mad with rage, Price embarks on a killing spree against those responsible for his grievances. Various horrific slayings in 3-D include slicing up his employer with a buzz saw until Price himself is accidentally cremated in a trick coffin put through an incinerator. Price wears a variety of masks to disguise his features, another nod in the direction of *House of Wax*, and some of the scenes were shot in color to heighten the gruesome effect of his vengeful killings.

The Mad Monster
PRC 1942; 77 mins; Cert. "X"
CREDITS: Producer: Sigmund Neufeld; Director: Sam Newfield
CAST: George Zucco; Johnny Downs; Glenn Strange; Anne Nagel; Gordon Demain; Sarah Padden ***
A mad doctor is convinced that injecting humans with wolf's blood will create an invincible army, but he only succeeds in turning a man into a werewolf-type monster.

After Universal's *The Wolf Man* became a big box office hit, PRC knocked out this above-average potboiler in five days to cash in on the success of the Chaney picture. Horror stalwart George Zucco expounds his theories on the benefits of wolf's blood in the human body to an imaginary array of scientists conjured up in his mind. To test his hypothesis, he injects the experimental serum into his dim-witted handyman Pedro, played by lanky Glenn Strange (making his horror debut), who promptly grows fangs and sprouts hair—a sort of cut-price wolf man in dungarees. Zucco has to subdue the monster with a whip and administers to him an antidote at given times, using Strange to kill those who scoff at his ideas. The monster then goes on a rampage, abducting and murdering a small girl until, in the closing scenes, a bolt of lightning causes Zucco's house to go up in flames, and both doctor and the wolf man perish in the conflagration. *The Mad Monster* was not released in the United Kingdom until 1952, as the British censor feared that the public would resist having blood transfusions after seeing the picture, and a statement was released stating that animal blood was never used in transfusions as depicted in the film. On the plus side, it only takes about five minutes for Strange to undergo the transformation from man into monster—not the usual 20 minutes or so as in most other movies of this type.

The Magnetic Monster
United Artists 1953; 76 mins; Cert. "A"
CREDITS: Producer: Ivan Tors; Director: Curt Siodmak
CAST: Richard Carlson; King Donovan; Jean Bryon; Harry Ellerbe; Kathleen Freeman; Leonard Mudie **

An experimental radioactive isotope sucks in energy from its surroundings and increases in size, threatening a nearby town.

An intelligent, low-budget but ultimately rather humdrum thriller using extensive stock footage from 1934's *Gold* in the noisy, frenetic climax, which is the best part of the picture. The isotope created by Leonard Mudie grows in size, magnetizes metal and gives off radiation, killing people in the process. Scientists find that they have to feed the isotope energy to prevent it from destroying the Earth. Eventually, the isotope is taken to an undersea generator and Richard Carlson pumps 900 million volts into the element, rendering it harmless. The film was double billed with *Invisible Invaders* in the early 1960s on the Sunday one-day circuit.

Man Beast
Favorite Films 1955; 67 mins; Cert. "A"
CREDITS: Producer/Director: Jerry Warren
CAST: Rock Madison; George Skaff; Virginia Maynor; Tom Maruzzi; Wong Sim; Lloyd Nelson **

An expedition to the Himalayas to search for a missing climber encounters the Abominable Snowman.

A bargain-basement quickie concocted by Jerry Warren, who joined the Abominable Snowman craze of the mid-'50s and came up with a creature resembling a man in a white gorilla costume. A local guide takes Rock Madison's party to where the Yetis are hiding but, unbeknown to the rest of the group, one of the guides is a half Yeti, the result of a union between a human woman and a Yeti who wants women to procreate with the snowmen to create a super-race. The guide tries to kidnap Virginia Maynor and take her to the Yetis so that she can breed with them to produce a more intelligent species, but unfortunately his plans go wrong as the entire expedition except for Lloyd Nelson and Maynor are wiped out at the end of the film when the creatures attack the expedition. In 1963, the movie appeared with another cheap Warren effort, *The Incredible Petrified World*, on the Sunday circuit.

Man Made Monster
aka: The Electric Man
Universal 1941; 68 mins; Cert. "X"
CREDITS: Producer: Jack Bernhard; Director: George Waggner
CAST: Lon Chaney Jr.; Lionel Atwill; Anne Nagel; Frank Albertson; Samuel S. Hinds; William Davidson ****

A mad scientist gives carnival sideshow performer Chaney—The Electrical Man—a massive dose of electricity and turns him into a human dynamo whose touch can kill.

A fast-paced horror movie, with Lon Chaney solid in the role of the carnival performer, surviving an accident in which a bus crashes into an electricity pylon at the film's beginning and feeding off electric currents in mad electrobiologist Lionel Atwill's laboratory, as the scientist wishes to take advantage of Chaney's high tolerance level to try to create a race of super zombies. Subjected to ever-increasing doses, Chaney becomes deranged and lethal to the touch, requiring repeated charges to survive and stomping around in an insulated rubber suit. Atwill uses his influence over Chaney to force him to murder his unwilling assistant. Chaney then goes to the electric chair but survives, escaping from prison with a glowing head and arms and hunting down Atwill, who perishes from shock on a metal door handle being held by the electric man. After being chased by the police, he finally comes to grief when his rubber suit catches on barbed wire, reducing him to a withered corpse as the current drains out of his body onto the wire. In the 1940s, the British censor's office objected to *any* film having the word "monster" in the title, and it was released as *The Electric Man*, reverting to its original title in the late '50s and early '60s when it was usually screened with *The Wolf Man*, *Revenge of the Creature* or *The Mummy's Curse* on the Sunday circuit.

The Man Who Could Cheat Death
Hammer/Paramount 1959; Technicolor; 83 mins; Cert. "X"
CREDITS: Producer: Anthony Nelson-Keys; Director: Terence Fisher
CAST: Anton Diffring; Hazel Court; Arnold Marle; Christopher Lee; Frances de Wolff; Delphi Lawrence ****

In Paris in 1890, a mad surgeon who is also a sculptor remains youthful by killing people to obtain certain glands that he replaces in his own body every 10 years.

A lurid, underrated Hammer production with a typical eye-rolling performance by Anton Diffring who, when the time approaches to replenish the glands in his body that prevent him from aging, takes a greenish potion that keeps him going and glows with a hellish light, burning people with his touch. The story takes place at the time of Diffring's next transplant. Killing one of his young models and procuring the glands from her body, as the set he had prepared previously had spoiled because the operation had been delayed, he then murders his assistant and confidante Arnold Marle who, appalled at Diffring's unethical and murderous methods, refuses to help him and destroys the life-preserving potion. The surgeon, in desperation, then attempts to persuade his friend Christopher Lee to perform the operation. But Lee is on the side of good this time, suspecting that Diffring has committed murder for his own ends, and pretends that he has transplanted the glands when, in fact, he hasn't. The grisly climax sees the doctor realizing that the glands have not been replaced and decaying rapidly to 104 years old in front of a terrified Hazel Court before going up in flames in an inferno started by one of his victims, a scarred, deranged model. This was a gorier take on *The Picture of Dorian Gray* and one of director Fisher's "forgotten" works from the late 1950s, which seems strange—colorful and well-presented, this horror offering was a lot more competent than many of the Hammer movies that were to appear in the following decade.

The Man Who Turned to Stone
Clover/Columbia 1956; 80 mins; Cert. "X"
CREDITS: Producer: Sam Katzman; Director: Leslie Kardos

CAST: Victor Jory; Charlotte Austin; Frederick Ledebur; Ann Doran; Barbara Wilson; William Hudson **

A group of 18th-century scientists have to take energy from young women to prevent themselves from turning to stone.

A routine outing from quickie stalwart Sam Katzman that has scientist Victor Jory and his colleagues, who have discovered the secret of eternal youth, setting up a reformatory for young women to enable them to steal their life-force via a particularly antiquated-looking electrical device. Jory and Frederick Ledebur proceed with their plan, and soon a number of females are dying from heart attacks as a result of their activities. Eventually, psychiatrist William Hudson uncovers the secret behind the deaths, the reformatory is burned to the ground, and the scientists turn to stone as Charlotte Austin escapes her fate in the nick of time. Flatly directed by Kardos, this run-of-the-mill production cropped up on the Sunday circuit in 1964, double billed with *The Creature with the Atom Brain*.

The Man with X-Ray Eyes
American Intl. 1963; Pathecolor/Spectarama; 88 mins; Cert. "X"
CREDITS: Producer/Director: Roger Corman
CAST: Ray Milland; Harold J. Stone; John Hoyt; Diana Van Der Vlis; Don Rickles; John Dierkes ****

A scientist invents experimental eye drops that give him x-ray vision but which eventually drive him mad.

An excellent performance by Ray Milland lifts this garishly colored film out of the rut and transforms it into a mini-classic. At first, Milland is bemused by the clichéd benefits of x-ray vision—seeing through women's clothing at a party as an example. Then, as he increases the strength of the drops, he begins to view a multi-faceted world (in lurid Spectarama) and goes on the run after killing his boss, who intends to stop Milland in his research by withdrawing funds. Milland eventually hides out in a carnival and poses as a mind reader to escape the law. Driven insane by the almost parallel world of dazzling lights and colors that only he can see, he ends up in a church and eventually tears his eyeballs from his head in biblical fashion, a terrifying end to an unconventional Roger Corman film.

The Man Without A Body
British Filmplays/Eros 1957; 80 mins; Cert. "X"
CREDITS: Producer: Guido Coen; Directors: W. Lee Wilder and Charles Saunders
CAST: Robert Hutton; George Coulouris; Julia Arnell; Nadja Regin; Kim Parker; Sheldon Lawrence **

A scientist restores life to the disembodied head of the prophet Nostradamus to enable him to profit from the head's powers of prediction.

The series of "disembodied head" films of the '50s came up with some real clunkers.

This pretty dull and uninmaginative effort starred George Coulouris as a financier suffering from a brain tumor, who has the bright idea to use the head's powers to predict how his business will fare and then transplant the head onto his own body to enable him to keep living and rule his business empire. One of the more ridulous scenes shows Coulouris arguing with Nostradamus on the ethics of what he has done, with Nostradamus arguing back that his reanimation has been a waste of time. In the end, the head is grafted onto another body and both Coulouris and the resulting monster destroy each other.

Maniac
Hammer/Columbia 1962; Hammerscope; 86 mins; Cert. "X"
CREDITS: Producer: Jimmy Sangster; Director: Michael Carreras
CAST: Kerwin Mathews; Donald Houston; Nadia Gray; Justine Lord; Liliane Brousse; Norman Bird
***

An artist on holiday in the French Carmargue falls in love with a devious woman and agrees to her plan to help a killer, her husband, escape from an asylum.

The second entry in the series of psychological thrillers that Hammer produced following the massive success of *Psycho* at the box office. The somewhat tortuous plot has Kerwin Mathews (of *Sinbad* fame) assisting Nadia Gray in getting her husband out of jail as he was accused of murdering, with an oxyacetylene torch, the man who raped their daughter. After a number of strange events, including another murder with a blowtorch, the culprit turns out to be Donald Houston, Gray's lover, who is trying to start a new life for them; Mathews has been duped into helping them out. Originally released with *The Damned*, this did not rank as one of Hammer's more successful enterprises, although the black and white photography of the Carmargue was strikingly realized and Carreras built up some moments of menace and suspense along the way.

Mark of the Vampire
MGM 1935; 60 mins; Cert. "A"
CREDITS: Producer: E.J. Mannix; Director: Tod Browning
CAST: Bela Lugosi; Lionel Barrymore; Elizabeth Allen; Carol Borland; Lionel Atwill; Jean Hersholt ***

In an attempt to solve a murder in an old house, a police inspector hires actors to portray vampires in order to scare the culprit into confession.

A hauntingly beautiful film to look at, with stunning photography by James Wong Howe and a genuinely startling scene in which Carol Borland drifts across a cobwebby room on giant batwings. In fact, Borland is the best thing in the movie and far more compelling than Lugosi, her blank white features motionless as she glides through the silent night accompanied by a bat, or staring through the windows of the house at her intended victims. The mundane detective story, concerning Lionel Barrymore's efforts to expose the killer of a rich man who, at the end after the charade has been played out, turns out to be Hersholt, seems secondary to the ghostly comings and goings of the vampires. A very atmospheric picture, despite the spoof ending that lessens the film's impact, whereby Lugosi and Borland take off their vampire disguises to reveal themselves as vaudeville performers. It still leaves a lingering sense of the supernatural that stays in the mind long after the movie finishes.

Marooned
Columbia 1970; Panavision/Technicolor; 134 mins; Cert. "A"
CREDITS: Producer: M.J. Frankovich; Director: John Sturges
CAST: Gregory Peck; Richard Crenna; David Janssen; Gene Hackman; James Franciscus; Nancy Kovak **

Three U.S. astronauts become trapped in their spacecraft while returning from a space station orbiting the Earth and an expedition is launched to rescue them.

Trumpeted at the time for its realistic special effects, which earned Columbia an Oscar, this big-budget space opera had all the makings of a great film—a strong cast, a bona-fide director and millions spent on making it. Unfortunately, the end result was a bit of a bore, suffering from the usual '60s affliction of too much gadgetry and talk at the expense of thrills and suspense. Like the spacecraft depicted in the movie, it drifted on for far too long. Gregory Peck and Gene Hackman turned in the best performances, while a wooden David Janssen played the hero, who launches his rescue rocket through the eye of a hurricane, coming to the aid of two of the astronauts (the third, Richard Crenna, took his own life to save his companions). Sturges, well known for his rugged Westerns and exciting war movies, appeared to be all at sea in space and the film, despite the apparent care and attention lavished on it, languished through repeated bouts of tedium, flopping at the box office.

The Masque of the Red Death
American Intl. 1964; Cinemascope/Pathecolor; 89 mins; Cert. "X"
CREDITS: Producer: George Willoughby; Director: Roger Corman
CAST: Vincent Price; Jane Asher; Hazel Court; David Weston; Patrick Magee; Skip Martin ***

In 12th-century Italy, a Prince who is also a Satanist revels in parties and orgies in his castle while outside a plague rages.

This was probably the most expensive and sumptuous of the Corman/Poe productions, although not quite up to the standard of *The Pit and the Pendulum*. Price plays Prince Prospero, a Devil-worshipping sadist, blithely ignoring the pestilence that is sweeping the countryside by holding huge banquets within his castle walls, until Death pays him a visit and the guests start dying like flies as a result. Jane Asher is an innocent young virgin whom Price wishes to initiate into the black arts, and she turns out to be the only survivor as Death decimates the castle and Price himself. Based on the Poe short story of the same name, together with the author's *Hop Frog*, this opulent and highly colorful-looking picture had several minutes of Devil-worshipping sequences involving Hazel Court cut by the British censor when it was first released, although these scenes were restored years later. Originally double billed with *The Man with X-Ray Eyes*, this was a big success at the time.

Master of the World
American Intl. 1961; Magnacolor; 104 mins; Cert. "U"
CREDITS: Producer: James H. Nicholson; Director: William Witney
CAST: Vincent Price; Henry Hull; Charles Bronson; Mary Webster; David Frankham; Vito Scotti **

In 1848, a mad scientist tells the world that if all wars do not cease, he will destroy the planet in his flying machine.

An unsuccessful adaptation of two Jules Verne novels, *Master of the World* and *The Clipper of the Clouds*. The flying machine that Vincent Price uses to convey his anti-war messages, named The Albatross, is a well-conceived creation, and there is a fine cast of eccentrics, including Charles Bronson as a government agent and Henry Hull as a munitions dealer. Price wipes out the Austrian and Egyptian armies as proof of his power, but in the end, Bronson destroys the flying machine and frees the captives. The film, which comes across like an aerial version of *20,000 Leagues Under the Sea*, is spoiled by showing too much stock footage of battles plundered from other movies, tinted to no great effect. It also features extremely poor process work, making the production appear curiously old-fashioned compared to other pictures made during this period. Although this was one of American International's more expensive efforts, it failed to make an impact at the box office, despite another good performance by Price.

The Maze
Allied Artists 1953; Orig. in 3-D; 80 mins; Cert. "X"
CREDITS: Producer: Richard Heermance; Director: William Cameron Menzies
CAST: Richard Carlson; Veronica Hurst; Michael Pate; Hilary Brooke; Lillian Bond; Robin Hughes ***
A man who is the heir to a Scottish ancestral home inherits a family curse whereby the former baronet is a 200-year-old frog.

It sounds like an absurd story, but a good cast and an imaginative director prevent it from becoming a laughing matter. Richard Carlson plays the heir, who realizes on a visit to his Scottish castle that something sinister lurks in a vast maze near the castle. In the center of the maze is a pond to which the baronet, a man-sized frog who has lived for 200 years, has to be taken and bathed regularly by his servants, and eventually by Carlson himself. Carlson finds himself immured in the castle's keep, protected by butler Michael Pate, as the curse that blighted his ancestor, who was born a freak of nature, will be passed on to him. At the end, the grotesque man-frog falls to its death from the top of the castle and Carlson is freed from the curse.

Mesa of Lost Women
Howco Intl. 1953; 69 mins; Cert. "A"
CREDITS: Producers: G. William Perkins and Melvin Gordon; Directors: Herbert Tevos and Ron Ormond
CAST: Jackie Coogan; Allan Nixon; Richard Travis; Mary Hill; Tandra Quinn; Harmon Stevens **
A mad scientist working in an isolated area of Mexico's Meurto desert creates dwarfs, giant spiders and "tarantula" super-women who possess deadly sexual powers.

A bottom-of-the-basement production that boasts one of the worst fake-looking giant spiders in '50s movies—it hides in Jackie Coogan's laboratory behind a screen and you can almost see the strings. Doctor Harmon Stevens escapes from a mental institution after encountering Coogan in his laboratory on the remote Zarpa Mesa and having a breakdown. The scientist is pumping tarantula serum into humans' pituitary glands, transforming women into super-women and men into dwarfs. Twenty-odd minutes into the film, the plot oddly changes tack with scenes of Tandra Quinn, obviously one of Coogan's creations, dancing like mad in a cantina, all dark hair, flashing eyes and deadly fingernails, looking for victims. The demented Harmon then coerces a group of people at gunpoint, including Richard Travis and Mary Hill, to fly to the mesa to enable him to exact revenge on Coogan, but when the plane crashes, they are left stranded and are picked off one by one, falling victims to the tarantula women, a tribe of midgets, and the giant spider. The climax sees Coogan's laboratory being blown sky-high by Harmon and Travis and Hill escaping, leaving one super-female survivor—but this odd, disjointed movie was never going to have a sequel made. The other minus points are Hoyt Curtin's irritating guitar/piano score, which jangles discordantly almost nonstop throughout the entire 69-minute running time, and a corny commentary by Lyle Talbot who, at regular intervals, describes either what the actors are up to or what the story is all about.

Mighty Joe Young
RKO-Radio 1949; 94 mins; Cert. "A"
CREDITS: Producer: Merian C. Cooper; Director: Ernest B. Schoedsack; Special Effects: Willis
O'Brien, Ray Harryhausen and Peter Peterson
CAST: Robert Armstrong; Terry Moore; Ben Johnson; Frank McHugh; Douglas Fowle; Dennis
Green ****

A nightclub owner specializing in sensational acts travels to Africa to bring back to the
United States a giant ape as his new showpiece.

The movie that kick-started the career of stop-motion maestro Ray Harryhausen, who col-
laborated on it with his mentor, Willis *King Kong* O'Brien. Terry Moore is the young girl living
in Africa whose pet is a 15-foot gorilla, brought up by her from a baby. Taken to the States by
unscrupulous showman Robert Armstrong (virtually reprising his role from *Kong*) who wants to
exhibit the gorilla as a new attraction, he becomes the record-breaking star turn in Armstrong's
show. One night, however, he gets miffed with a drunken audience who bombard him with coins
to the tune of "Beautiful Dreamer," breaking out of Armstrong's nightclub in an orgy of violent
destruction. The ape is then hunted by the police, who think he is dangerous and should be ex-
terminated. Joe Young becomes a hero in the end, rescuing children from a burning orphanage,
and returns to a normal life in Africa with Moore and Ben Johnson. The animation of the ape is
both superb and somewhat variable—in the African scenes where the cowboys try to rope him
he appears in some instances slightly smaller than in the nightclub sequences, the outstanding
part of the film. Nevertheless, the picture was awarded an Oscar for best special effects. Harryhausen went on to produce a string of renowned monster and fantasy features, but O'Brien's
career faltered—he always had grandiose ideas that never materialized on the big screen and
only worked spasmodically for the next few years in tandem with other animators on features
such as *The Black Scorpion* and *Behemoth the Sea Monster*.

Missile to the Moon
Layton/Astor 1958; 78 mins; Cert. "A"
CREDITS: Producers: Marc Frederic and George Foley; Director: Richard E. Cunha
CAST: Richard Travis; Cathy Downs; Tommy Cook; K.T. Stevens; Michael Whalen; Gary
Clarke ***

A space rocket with assorted characters on board blasts off to the moon without government
permission and on landing, the crew are captured by a race of Moon Maidens.

Produced by the same team that was responsible for the cult classic *Frankenstein's Daughter*,
this hilarious cheapskate fantasy features Michael Whalen piloting a rocket to the moon against
the U.S. government's wishes, taking with him his assistant, Richard Travis, two convicts hastily
trained to be astronauts, and Cathy Downs as Travis's fiancée. Whalen is killed by a loose piece
of equipment during a meteor storm
and when the ship lands, the remainder
of the crew hides out in a network of
caves to escape the sun's rays. They are
menaced not only by the obligatory giant spider, but a race of rock-creatures
that chase them into the arms of the
moon women. It also transpires that
Whalen was, in fact, an alien who
was planning an invasion of Earth to
replenish the moon's dwindling natural
resources. At first, the women want
the Earth people killed, but romance
rears its head, and some of them assist

in helping the crew escape to Earth. Fleeing from the rock-creatures, they manage to reach the ship and blast off, but not before one of the convicts is caught in the sun's rays, frying him to a crisp. Filmed in California's Red Rock Canyon, featuring fake-looking painted sets that would not have looked out of place in a pantomime, a bevy of ex-beauty queens wearing ridiculous costumes and a truly abysmal giant spider, this was a slice of highly outlandish nonsense from Astor, a hybrid cross between *Fire Maidens from Outer Space* and *Queen of Outer Space* (and more entertaining than both of them) that was screened at selected cinemas in 1964, playing second feature to *The Trollenberg Terror*.

Mr. Sardonicus
Columbia 1961; 89 mins; Cert. "A"
CREDITS: Producer/Director: William Castle
CAST: Guy Rolfe; Ronald Lewis; Audrey Dalton; Oscar Homolka; Erika Peters; Vladimir Sokoloff
**

An aristocrat whose face is fixed in a hideous grimace relates his story to a surgeon in the hope of a cure for his condition.

Castle's film is based on 1928's *The Man Who Laughs* and is one of the director's more restrained and little-seen efforts. Guy Rolfe apparently goes into deep shock after seeing the skeleton of his father move while he is digging up his grave searching for a missing lottery ticket. Rolfe blackmails a surgeon, Ronald Lewis, into trying to find a cure for his fixed grimace, threatening to mutilate Audrey Dalton, who was once Lewis' mistress but is now in his clutches, if he doesn't comply with his demands. Lewis succeeds in restoring Rolfe's face to normality by shock, but Rolfe's mouth is now permanently closed and he foresees himself starving to death. Castle's rather pointless gimmick in this unsuccessful picture was to ask the audience near the end what form of punishment should be given out to Rolfe, even though only one climax had been filmed.

The Mole People
Universal 1956; 78 mins; Cert. "A"
CREDITS: Producer: William Alland; Director: Virgil Vogel
CAST: John Agar; Hugh Beaumont; Cynthia Patrick; Nestor Paiva; Alan Napier; Eddie Parker
***

In Asia, a group of anthropologists discover a ruined city on the summit of a mountain. On descending a deep, narrow shaft, they come upon the subterranean civilization of Sumerians, albinos who rule over a race of quasi-human beasts—the Mole People.

More of a fantasy adventure than a horror movie, the Mole People of the title, with their knobbly skin, bulbous eyes and large claws, were a lesser but nonetheless appealing entrant into Universal's catalogue of 1950s creature-features. Following a prologue featuring Dr. Frank C. Baxter speaking on the wonders believed to exist in the interior of the Earth, John Agar, Hugh Beaumont and Nestor Paiva discover the remnants of the Sumerian civilization inside an Asian mountain, who rule the creatures of the title, making regular sacrifices among their own people to the sun to keep the population down. The scenes of the Sumerians' underground cities are quite impressively realized for a fairly low-budget film of this type, as are the slave fields where the albinos whip the Mole creatures into servitude. The acting and script, though, is rather corny, with the Sumerians in their strange costumes looking like extras from a Cecil B. De Mille biblical production, and it has been quoted that John Agar said to Cynthia Patrick one day on set, "What kind of rubbish are we making here?" only to be "pleasantly surprised" at the finished results. Paiva gets killed by one of the beasts, the other two are captured by the high priests who look upon them as intruders, and Agar falls in love with local blonde Patrick. The Mole beasts revolt against their tormentors in the end, scrambling out of the earth and going on a rampage, while Agar, Beaumont and Patrick escape to the surface, only for the girl to be crushed to death under a falling pillar during an earth tremor. Hans J. Salter supplied an imaginative soundtrack, one of many he contributed to Universal during his long and distinguished career with them.

The Monolith Monsters
Universal 1957; 77 mins; Cert. "A"
CREDITS: Producer: Howard Christie; Director: John Sherwood
CAST: Grant Williams; Lola Albright; Les Tremayne; Trevor Bardette; William Flaherty; Harry Jackson ****

Rock fragments from a meteor that crashes in the desert grow to an enormous size when exposed to water and give off a vapor that turns people to stone.

A suspenseful, underrated classic from Universal suggested from a story by Jack Arnold. Grant Williams discovers crystal fragments from a meteor scattered over the desert floor that absorb silicon and turn people to stone. There are some chilling moments, such as Williams finding his office wrecked and covered with glistening black rock and his partner, on being touched, crashing to the floor like a stone statue, and a small girl who exposes herself to the gas after cleaning a piece of meteor in a rain bucket having her forelimb crystalizing into rock while her parents are found dead among the shattered re-

mains of their farmhouse. Likewise the shots of the alien rock seething in a crater as water floods in and of the fragments growing into gigantic crystals, looming over the desert landscape, build up an atmosphere of impending doom, helped by Clifford Stine's extraordinary special effects and a thunderous Joseph Gershenson soundtrack. There is a thrilling and remarkable climax as the black crystals, grown to a colossal size, topple and multiply themselves on the edge of a small desert town, only to be halted in their tracks by Williams, who blows up a dam, releasing a tidal wave of water that mixes with salt from a nearby mine, thus destroying the monoliths. This was a very popular picture on the U.K Sunday circuit, double billed with a variety of other Universal productions, including *The Mole People* and even Hammer's *Dracula*.

The Monster from Green Hell
Grosse/Krasne/DCA 1957; 71 mins; Cert. "X"
CREDITS: Producer: Al Zimbalist; Director: Kenneth G. Crane
CAST: Jim Davis; Robert E. Griffith; Barbara Turner; Eduardo Ciannelli; Vladimir Sokoloff; Joe Fluellen **

A rocketship containing laboratory insects is exposed to radiation and crashes in Africa, unleashing giant mutated wasps on the local populace.

A low-budget monster movie that tells of an expedition trekking to the African jungle to discover the whereabouts of the missing rocket and encountering huge flightless wasps that menace the party and the local natives before being destroyed in a volcanic eruption. Stop-motion animation of a very rudimentary kind was used to animate the giant insects, but they move very slowly and for most of the scenes, only their enlarged heads are seen. At times, they appear grotesquely out of proportion to the humans they are chasing. The only realistic moment is where one of the giant wasps battles a huge snake and, for some strange reason known only to the film's producers, the final few minutes showing an erupting volcano are in color. The movie turned up occasionally in the early 1960s, usually double billed with Ed Wood's *Plan 9 from Outer Space*.

Monster from the Ocean Floor
Palo Alto/Lippert 1954; 64 mins; Cert. "A"
CREDITS: Producer: Roger Corman; Director: Wyott Ordung
CAST: Stuart Wade; Anne Kimbell; Dick Pinner; Jack Hayes; Wyott Ordung; Inez Palange **
    On an island in the Gulf of Mexico, people disappear during the night of the full moon and local superstition points to an ancient god living beneath the waves.
    This cheapo was Roger Corman's first-ever production, made in six days at a cost of $12,000. Anne Kimbell, an artist who saw the creature while on holiday, and Stuart Wade, a marine biologist, investigate a strange series of deaths and discover that atomic bomb tests have created a giant jellyfish-type sea beast that surfaces when the moon is full and attacks the local populace. The natives believe it to be an ancient Aztec sea-god. Wade eventually destroys the monster by ramming it with a mini-sub, just as it is about to devour Kimbell. An uninspiring little effort, but at least it was aware of its shortcomings and made no pretensions to be otherwise.

The Monster Maker
PRC 1944; 64 mins; Cert. "X"
CREDITS: Producer: Sigmund Neufeld; Director: Sam Newfield
CAST: J. Carrol Naish; Ralph Morgan; Wanda McKay; Tola Birell; Glenn Strange; Sam Flint ***
    A mad doctor injects his enemies with acromegaly germs, causing their features to become grotesquely distorted.
    A somewhat distasteful horror film from the Neufeld/Newfield team, especially as acromegaly is a registered and distressing disease. Naish plays the demented scientist, on the run from Europe after he has killed his wife and her doctor lover and assuming the doctor's identity to protect himself. Ralph Morgan, a concert pianist whose daughter, Wanda McKay, is spurning Naish's advances when he becomes obsessed with her, is the doctor's next unfortunate victim; Naish injects him with the lethal bacteria in revenge and causes Morgan's features and limbs to become horribly distorted as a result. The doctor then informs the pianist that he will administer the necessary antidote to cure him if his daughter will accept his hand in marriage, but McKay refuses to cooperate. Eventually, Morgan is manacled to a bed by Glenn Strange, the doctor's lumbering henchman, and given more threats, but he breaks free, kills Naish and is then given the antidote to his disease by Naish's aide, who sympathizes with his plight. This was one of the better and grimmer of the PRC movies the company produced in the '40s, with a first-rate makeup job on Ralph Morgan as the pianist with the swollen, misshapen features.

The Monster of Piedras Blancas
Vanwick 1958; 71 mins; Cert. "X"
CREDITS: Producer: Jack Kevan; Director: Irvin Berwick
CAST: Les Tremayne; Forrest Lewis; John Harmon; Jeanne Carmen; Don Sullivan; Frank Arvidson ***
    A lighthouse keeper lives with the knowledge that a legendary marine creature inhabiting the caves below the lighthouse could go on a rampage if not fed at regular intervals.
    A nicely done, minor-league B creature-feature with a ferocious monster that bears a passing resemblance to both the *Creature from the Black Lagoon* and *It! The Terror from Beyond Space*.

Nobody believes keeper John Harmon's stories of a seven-foot-tall monster lurking in the caves beneath his lighthouse until it emerges and goes on a killing spree in the local town, gruesomely ripping its victims' heads off and drinking their blood. After several decapitated bodies have been found, causing panic among the small coastal community, the creature abducts Jeanne Carmen, the keeper's daughter, and then enters the lighthouse to exact vengeance on its would-be benefactor. Throwing Harmon to his death from the top of the building, the monster then corners Don Sullivan, Carmen's boyfriend, until she arrives on the scene and blinds it with light from the beacon. Sullivan clubs it on the head with a rifle and the thing plummets into the sea. The movie rambles on a bit in the first half but picks up in the final 15 minutes, when the monster makes its appearance. Jack Kevan, who produced the film and also played the monster, was responsible for not

only this creation, but had a hand in the design of the monsters in the Universal productions of *The Mole People*, *This Island Earth* and *Monster on the Campus*.

Monster of Terror
aka: Die Monster Die!
American Intl. 1965; Panavision/Pathecolor; 89 mins; Cert. "X"
CREDITS: Producers: James H. Nicholson and Samuel Z. Arkoff; Director: Daniel Haller
CAST: Boris Karloff; Nick Adams; Freda Jackson; Suzan Farmer; Terence de Marney; Patrick Magee **

A radioactive meteorite causes plants to grow huge and humans to mutate.

A big-budget but oddly unsatisfactory production loosely based on H.P. Lovecraft's story *The Color Out of Space*. Nick Adams visits fiancée Suzan Farmer at Karloff's house and discovers the reason for his hostile behavior—he has become infected with radiation from the meteor, has a cellar with a mysterious green light emanating from it and a greenhouse full of mutated, carnivorous plants, as well as a disfigured housekeeper. At the end, Karloff goes mad and ends up as a mutation with a glowing green head as Adams and Farmer flee the house. A curious hybrid of science fiction and horror, which doesn't quite come off, it was originally released with Roger Corman's *The Haunted Palace*.

Monster on the Campus
Universal 1958; 77 mins; Cert. "X"
CREDITS: Producer: Joseph Gershenson; Director: Jack Arnold
CAST: Arthur Franz; Joanna Moore; Judson Pratt; Troy Donahue; Nancy Walters; Phil Harvey ***

A professor who injures himself on a prehistoric fish, the coelacanth, turns into a murderous ape-like monster.

Although probably the most lackluster and flatly directed of Jack Arnold's films for Universal, *Monster on the Campus* still had its fair share of unsettling moments and, like most of the other horror efforts produced by the company, ran continuously until the late 1960s on both the Sunday and late-night circuits in the United Kingdom. Arthur Franz imports a radioactive prehistoric fish whose juices can accidentally regress animals into a primeval state. Parts of the movie, such as a dragonfly drinking the fish juice and growing to enormous proportions, and a dog turning into a wolf after lapping up the same substance, are a bit silly, but the man-into-monster scenes are grimly horrific. Franz leaves a trail of corpses in his wake after changing into the monster, first when cutting his hand on the coelacanth's teeth and then later when juice from the fish drips into his pipe and he smokes it! Eventually, to prove that he is responsible for the series of slayings, Franz first photographs himself as the apeman and then transforms himself into the monster before the startled police who shoot him dead, whereupon he changes back from monster to man. A curious fact with this production is the way Universal took various musical tracks from their other films to form a kind of composite music score—parts of the scores of *Tarantula*, *The Incredible Shrinking Man* and *House of Dracula* are featured, a money-saving idea from the company if ever there was one.

The Monster that Challenged the World
United Artists 1957; 85 mins; Cert. "X"
CREDITS: Producers: Arthur Gardner and Jules V. Levy; Director: Arnold Laven
CAST: Tim Holt; Audrey Dalton; Hans Conreid; Barbara Darrow; Casey Adams; Harlan Warde
****
Earthquakes in the Salton Sea area unleash giant caterpillar-like molluscs onto a nearby naval base.

One of the more intelligently made creature-features of the 1950s, efficiently directed in semi-documentary style and boasting a better than average script for a change. The creatures, disturbed from their watery lairs by earthquakes, use the local network of canals and old Indian wells to move around and hunt for human prey. These ingenious mechanically operated monsters, created by Augie Lohman, are very arresting, either when rearing up by the side of a boat to be fended off by a boat hook, creeping into view from under their huge shells, or leaping out of the shadows off-screen to claim more victims, whom they suck dry of all liquids, leaving grotesque dry carcasses everywhere. The monsters are eventually blown to bits when naval divers plant depth charges near their underwater hideouts. The movie has a prolonged and exciting climax, with one of the creatures hatching out of an egg-sack and menacing Audrey Dalton and her daughter in a laboratory before chubby naval commander Tim Holt dispatches it with a blast of steam, plus a little help from a volley of police bullets. *The Monster that Challenged the World* was a popular addition to the Sunday circuit in the early to mid-'60s, often double billed with *The Vampire*.

The Most Dangerous Man Alive
Trans Global/Columbia 1958; 82 mins; Cert. "A"
CREDITS: Producer: Benedict Bogeaus; Director: Allan Dwan
CAST: Ron Randall; Debra Paget; Elaine Stewart; Anthony Caruso; Morris Ankrum; Gregg Palmer **

On escaping from prison, a convict becomes exposed to a cobalt bomb explosion and changes into a man of steel.

One of the lesser of the "mutated gangster" revenge films of the '50s, which was shelved before being released in England in 1963. Ron Randall plays the convict who, suddenly possessed with steel in his veins after being exposed to intense radiation in a bunker, hunts down the men who framed him for his crime and sent him to prison. Impervious to bullets and injury, he finishes them off one by one, but eventually realizes that he has become impotent, much to the distress of his wife, Debra Paget. At the end, realizing that his only emotion is hate, he meets his demise when police flamethrowers reduce him to dust. This turned out to be a poorer version of Allied Artists' *Indestructible Man* and the last film to be directed by Dwan.

Mother Riley Meets the Vampire
aka: My Son the Vampire
Fernwood and Renown 1952; 74 mins; Cert. "A"
CREDITS: Producer/Director: John Gilling
CAST: Arthur Lucan; Bela Lugosi; Dora Bryan; Richard Wattis; Philip Leaver; Ian Wilson **

An insane doctor disguises himself as a vampire and abducts Old Mother Riley in his attempts to take over the world.

The last of the Mother Riley movies starring Arthur Lucan in drag as the Irish washerwoman was an antique-looking comedy-thriller even when first released, although a big hit in the U.K. cinemas at the time. Bela Lugosi sent himself up as a doctor impersonating a vampire, controlling a completely unimaginative robot and inventing a machine that could destroy whole armies. Most of the action took place in Lugosi's gloomy old house, with Lucan eventually foiling the doctor's plans for world domination. Resembling an ancient British farce, this early effort by John Gilling turned up at a few selected cinemas in 1963, giving bemused audiences an opportunity to see two worn-out old screen veterans who were way past their prime slugging it out in a pretty dire picture—the equally inept *The Devil Bat* was the second feature!

The Mummy
Universal 1932; 78 mins; Cert. "X"
CREDITS: Producer: Stanley Bergerman; Director: Karl Freund
CAST: Boris Karloff; David Manners; Zita Johann; Edward Van Sloan; Bramwell Fletcher; Henry Victor ****

Archaeologists accidentally revive the mummy, Im-Ho-Tep, who seeks out the reincarnation of his long-dead princess.

One of the few early '30s true classics of horror that has not dated as much as other films of the same genre made during this period, possessing a strange, dreamlike quality that lifts it above the average fare. Karloff gives a mesmerizing performance both as the bandaged mummy, which is only glimpsed at the beginning of the film, and the stick-like, wizened Ardath Bey, who is seeking a woman to take the place of his love, the Princess Anck-es-en-Amon, in modern-day Egypt. Zita Johann is the object of Karloff's desires, and he plans to kill her to achieve eternal reunion between the two of them, as he believes her to be the reincarnation of his princess, showing her their past lives in a magic pool. In the end, rejecting Ardath Bey's advances, she calls upon Isis for help, and the statue of the goddess reduces the ancient Egyptian to dust and bones in the final few seconds of the picture. A film that enhanced Karloff's reputation as the new King of Horror and, although slow-paced at times, a fascinating period piece.

The Mummy
Hammer/Universal 1959; Technicolor; 88 mins; Cert. "X"
CREDITS: Producer: Michael Carreras; Director: Terence Fisher
CAST: Peter Cushing; Christopher Lee; Yvonne Furneaux; Felix Aylmer; George Pastell; Raymond Huntley *****

Archaeologists break into a forbidden Egyptian tomb and unleash an ancient curse. The 4,000-year-old mummy of Kharis is brought to England and revived, where it proceeds to kill the desecrators of its tomb one by one.

Hammer's flamboyant, updated version of the old Boris Karloff classic was another box office winner for the company and ranks among their all-time top productions. Christopher Lee is superb in the title role of the avenging Kharis, all mud-caked bandages and glaring eyes. That's especially true in the scene where George Pastell reactivates the mummy by reading the scroll of life, and he emerges from the swamp to murder Felix Aylmer in a nursing home before embarking on a series of attacks on Peter Cushing, one of the desecrators of his princess' tomb. A lengthy flashback narrated by Cushing tells how Kharis was buried alive for trying to bring back to life the dead princess. There is also a hint of pathos in the scene where Lee gazes upon Yvonne Furneaux, who resembles the Egyptian princess that he once loved; his six-foot-plus height was never put to better use than in this film. After killing Pastell (who tries to knife Furneaux, realizing that she is preventing the mummy from carrying out his wishes), Lee carries the unconscious girl off to the swamp where she persuades him to release her, just as the local villagers open up on the mummy with their guns. Clasping the scroll of life, Lee sinks to his death beneath the waters. Frank Reizenstein's music was also a major plus point—in fact many fans rate this score as one of the best of any Hammer film, on a par with James Bernard's music for *Dracula*. As usual with the company's other productions from this period, the splendid color photography was another bonus.

The Mummy's Curse
Universal 1944; 62 mins; Cert. "X"
CREDITS: Producer: Ben Pivar; Director: Leslie Goodwins
CAST: Lon Chaney Jr.; Peter Coe; Virginia Christine; Kay Harding; Martin Kosleck; Kurt Katch
****

The mummy of the Princess Ananka emerges from a Louisiana swamp and Kharis the mummy, revived by tana leaves, goes on a rampage.

The last in Universal's series of *Mummy* films that starred Lon Chaney remains the best and the most straightforward of the lot, with less mumbo-jumbo and flashbacks than the previous films and containing a lot more inventive action. Twenty-five years on from the events in *The Mummy's Ghost*, the superstitious local workforce refuse to clear the nearby swamp because they claim it is cursed by the mummy. Meanwhile, Peter Coe reactivates Kharis with a brew made from tana leaves, while, in a remarkably spine-tingling scene, a mud-encrusted Ananka, played this time by Virginia Christine, pulls herself out of the swamp and is restored to her former beauty by the power of sunlight. Kharis goes on the usual rampage in his hunt for the princess, killing anyone who crosses his path, before the bandaged menace, in a showdown in an old monastery, literally brings part of the building crashing down on him. Ananka then reverts to her mummified state and is left alone in her coffin to presumably rest in peace.

The Mummy's Ghost
Universal 1943; 61 mins; Cert. "X"
CREDITS: Producer: Ben Pivar; Director: Reginald LeBorg
CAST: Lon Chaney Jr.; John Carradine; Ramsay Ames; Robert Lowery; Barton McLane; Claire Whitney **

Kharis the mummy is taken to a museum in New England, where he goes in search of the reincarnation of Princess Ananka.

Lon Chaney's second outing as Kharis has him seeking out a local girl, Ramsay Ames, to replace the shriveled-up Princess Ananka housed in the Mapleton Museum in Massachusetts. Kharis abducts the girl for embalming, but John Carradine as the high priest wants the pair of them to live forever by giving them a brew of tana leaves. The usual mayhem follows, with Chaney killing Carradine and marching off to the swamp with the reincarnated princess, who ages rapidly when they both sink beneath the surface. This turned out to be perhaps the weakest and least creative entry in Universal's *Mummy* series.

The Mummy's Hand
Universal 1940; 67 mins; Cert. "X"
CREDITS: Producer: Ben Pivar; Director: Christy Cabanne
CAST: Tom Tyler; Dick Foran; Peggy Moran; Wallace Ford; George Zucco; Eduardo Ciannelli ***

Egyptian archaeologists discover the mummy of Kharis, kept alive for 3,000 years by tana leaves.

The belated sequel to Karloff's *The Mummy* featured Tom Tyler as the bandaged menace Kharis, with Dick Foran and Wallace Ford as the explorers who break into Princess Ananka's burial chamber, unaware that it is cursed. George Zucco is the high priest lusting after Peggy Moran as the reincarnated princess, and he feeds Kharis a brew of tana leaves to revive him so that Kharis can wipe out the desecrators of the princess' tomb. The mummy meets his end by having a brazier full of tana juice tipped over him, setting him ablaze. All of the action took place on the old jungle set of *Green Hell*, and the movie is fast-paced and quite resourceful apart from Tyler's shambling performance as Kharis, which is not all that convincing—the ex-cowboy star was suffering from severe arthritis at the time of filming, and it showed.

The Mummy's Shroud
Hammer/20th Century Fox 1966; DeLuxeColor; 84 mins; Cert. "X"
CREDITS: Producer: Anthony Nelson-Keys; Director: John Gilling
CAST: Andre Morell; David Buck; John Phillips; Elizabeth Sellars; Maggie Kimberly; Roger Delgado **

In 1920, the guardian mummy of a young pharaoh comes alive and proceeds to wipe out the desecrators of its master's tomb.

High production values, nice color, and a good cast vainly attempt to liven up the old legend in this latter-day *Mummy* outing with Andre Morell, financed by egomaniac John Phillips, leading an archaeological expedition to take Kah-To-Bey's mummy back to Cairo, only to be hunted down by Eddie Powell, the pharaoh's tutor Prem, who is revived by Roger Delgado. After the usual catalogue of murders, Maggie Kimberley utters a few magic words from an ancient incantation as the mummy confronts David Buck (learned after a meeting with soothsayer Catherine Lacey), and the thing crumbles into bones and dust. There is a lengthy prologue, similar to that featured in Terence Fisher's *The Mummy*, which tells of the events 4,000 years ago that led to the pharaoh's burial, but on the whole this was a flat-footed, uninspiring entry in the series, low on thrills and featuring a particularly unscary, threadbare-looking mummy. The one plus factor was an outlandish performance by Hammer stalwart Michael Ripper as Phillips' much put-upon agent. The film was originally released as second billing to another of Hammer's weaker efforts, *Frankenstein Created Woman*.

The Mummy's Tomb
Universal 1942; 61 mins; Cert. "X"
CREDITS: Producer: Ben Pivar; Director: Harold Young
CAST: Lon Chaney Jr.; Turhan Bey; Wallace Ford; Dick Foran; John Hubbard; Elyse Knox
***

The mummy of Kharis is brought to America to exact revenge on the desecrators of his tomb.

The bigger and bulkier Lon Chaney took over the role of Kharis from Tom Tyler in this movie, which uses a lot of flashbacks from the previous two *Mummy* films, and even a crowd scene from *Frankenstein*, the action taking place 30 years later as Kharis, brought to Mapleton in Massachusetts, goes after a by now elderly Foran and Ford, the pair of archaeologists who originally broke into his tomb. Turhan Bey as the priest wants to enrol Elyse Knox as a priestess and orders Chaney to hunt her down, but the villagers arrive in a mob and Kharis perishes in a burning mansion. Although Chaney went on to play the role another two times, he was never all that happy in the part, complaining that being buried under a layer of bandages was far too restrictive to bring out any nuances to the character of Kharis.

The Mysterians
Toho/RKO-Radio/MGM (Japan) 1957; Tohoscope/Eastmancolor; 89 mins; Cert. "A"
CREDITS: Producer: Tomoyuki Tanaka; Director: Inoshiro Honda
CAST: Kenji Sahara; Yumi Shirakawa; Akihiko Hirata; Momoko Kochi; Hisayo Ito; Takashi Shimura ****

Aliens arrive on Earth from Mars with a giant robot, intent on abducting Earth women to replenish their dying world, which has been destroyed in a nuclear war.

After the success of *Godzilla* and *Rodan*, Toho turned their attentions to the science fiction genre for their next production and came up with a lively romp based on ideas plundered from a host of American movies. Inhabiting Mars for thousands of years since their home planet, Mysteroid, was destroyed in a nuclear war, the cloaked, masked aliens land on Earth in a flying saucer, unleashing onto the local populace a giant robotic bird (named Mogella in publicity handouts, but not mentioned in the film). The robot goes on a rampage, destroying villages and mountains and having several battles with the military until it trundles across a booby-trapped bridge that blows up, sending the mechanical menace crashing into a ravine. The Mysterians are then wiped out by the army and scientists who use ray guns on them. Superb special effects put this rarely seen feature into Toho's top league of movies, although, as usual, the poor dubbing let it down slightly. It went the rounds at selected cinemas in 1964 double billed with *Captain Sinbad*.

Mysterious Island
Columbia 1961; Technicolor; 100 mins; Cert. "U"
CREDITS: Producer: Charles H. Schneer; Director: Cy Endfield; Special Effects: Ray Harryhausen
CAST: Michael Craig; Michael Callan; Gary Merrill; Percy Herbert; Joan Greenwood; Beth Rogan ****

During the American Civil War, a group of soldiers escape from a Confederate prison in a balloon and after braving a fierce storm land on a remote volcanic island populated by giant animals and Captain Nemo.

Based on the Jules Verne novel that was the author's sequel to *20,000 Leagues Under the Sea*, this was another big success from the team of Schneer and Harryhausen, a noisy, vigorous "Boy's Own" caper with splendid special effects, imaginative locations and a strong cast combating a giant crab, a huge bird and man-sized bees that have been mutated to enormous proportions by Herbert Lom's Captain Nemo to solve the world's need for food. After many adventures, including an attack by pirates on their cliff-top hideout, the island, its monsters and Nemo, who becomes trapped in the Nautilus by falling rocks, are all destroyed in the explosive climax as the volcano erupts, with the soldiers and their women escaping on the pirate ship that Nemo had sunk earlier in the film but then brought to the surface. All the nonstop action is played out to a very deafening Bernard Herrmann nautical-based musical score.

The Nanny
Hammer/Seven Arts 1965; 93 mins; Cert. "X"
CREDITS: Producer: Jimmy Sangster; Director: Seth Holt
CAST: Bette Davis; Jill Bennett; James Villiers; William Dix; Wendy Craig; Pamela Franklin ***

A mad nanny is suspected of murdering a child in her charge.

Hammer's diluted but still effective version of *Whatever Happened to Baby Jane?* features William Dix as a precocious, disturbed boy who supposedly drowned his sister in the bath and who, on his return from a special school, hates his new nanny, Bette Davis, with a vengeance, as she was in fact responsible for his sister's death. The boy's ineffectual mother, Wendy Craig, cannot understand her son's hostility toward Davis. However, when the nanny realizes that the boy is on to her, she grows ever more irrational and puts the whole family in danger, even bumping off Jill Bennett as Craig's sister, who suffers a heart attack when Davis withholds her medication. Davis is superb in the lead role, cutting down on the histrionics for a change and giving a subtle performance in pure evil. Rather ironically, Craig as the weak wife went on to play a nanny herself in a television sitcom during the late 1970s.

The Neanderthal Man
United Artists 1952; 77 mins; Cert. "X"
CREDITS: Producers: Aubrey Wisberry and Jack Pollexfen; Director: E.A. Dupont
CAST: Robert Shayne; Richard Crane; Doris Merric; Joyce Terry; Robert Long; Dick Rich **

A scientist invents a serum that regresses people and animals back to a primeval state, and changes himself into an apeman.

A shoddy-looking effort whose man-into-apeman theme was put to far better use in Universal's *Monster on the Campus*. Scientist Robert Shayne, angry at his ideas on regression being ridiculed by the local scientific society, first changes his housekeeper into a primitive ape-woman and then himself into the monster of the title by taking an experimental serum. There are no transformation sequences on offer here—Shayne simply wears an inflexible mask, and not a very good one either. After going on a murderous rampage, he is killed in the end by another of his creations, a saber-tooth tiger that was once the family cat. In 1964, this uninspiring man-into-monster movie was double billed somewhat oddly at some cinemas with Corman's *The Pit and the Pendulum* and went the rounds for a few months.

The Night Caller
aka: Blood Beast from Outer Space
Armitage Films 1965; 84 mins; Cert. "X"

CREDITS: Producer: Ronald Liles; Director: John Gilling
CAST: John Saxon; Maurice Denham; Alfred Burke; Patricia Haines; John Carson; Jack Watson ***

An alien is sent to Earth from Ganymede, a moon of Jupiter, to kidnap women for genetic experiments.

A commendable '60s British science fiction thriller for a change that manages to be both eerie and persuasive. The film begins with the discovery of an orb-like meteorite in a field, which is then taken to a laboratory where it sprouts weird growths, acting as a teleportation device from which an alien escapes. The humanoid creature sets up an office under the guise of a modeling agency and begins kidnapping women and transporting them to his own world, which has been ravaged by nuclear war and needs a fresh supply of new blood to regenerate the planet. After numerous young women have either vanished or been murdered, the police finally catch up with the alien, called Medra, who is deformed down one side of his face and sports an artificial-looking clawed hand. Unfortunately, the ending peters out, with Medra simply vanishing into thin air, but overall this is a dark little movie made on a low budget by a minor film studio.

Nightmare
Hammer/Universal 1964; Hammerscope; 83 mins; Cert. "X"
CREDITS: Producer: Jimmy Sangster; Director: Freddie Francis
CAST: David Knight; Moira Richmond; Brenda Bruce; Jennie Linden; George A. Cooper; Clytie Jessop ***

A young girl suffers recurring nightmares after witnessing her mad mother killing her father several years previously.

The fourth of Hammer's psycho-thrillers of the '60s with the customary bewildering plot, but well photographed and directed by Freddie Francis. Once more, it was the old "let's scare the girl to death to gain her inheritance" scenario. This time around, the girl's guardian, David Knight, and his mistress, Moira Redmond, are the couple staging a number of disturbing and gruesome events to frighten Jennie Linden to the brink of insanity. The scheme succeeds, and Linden is carted off to an asylum, but then Redmond begins to experience the same happenings, she and her lover fall out, and in the end, Brenda Bruce and the family's chauffeur expose the lovers as criminals. The film played second billing to *The Evil of Frankenstein* when first released.

Night Monster
aka: House of Mystery
Universal 1942; 73 mins; Cert. "A"
CREDITS: Producer/Director: Ford Beebe
CAST: Ralph Morgan; Bela Lugosi; Lionel Atwill; Fay Helm; Irene Hervey; Nils Asther **
A man whose legs were amputated in an operation swears vengeance on the three doctors he holds responsible, rising from his wheelchair on synthetic limbs so that he can murder them.
One of Universal's lesser offerings from the 1940s, a wordy and mildly effective murder mystery with horror overtones boasting a fine cast, with Ralph Morgan playing the crippled head of Ingston Towers growing new but temporary legs by willpower after being in cahoots with mysterious Eastern mystic Nils Asther, who can create new tissue from his thought processes. One of his party tricks is to materialize a skeleton from his mind. Rising from his wheelchair at night, Morgan prowls the misty marshes near the estate, taking out his vengeance on the doctors, whom he blames for his missing limbs, strangling them one by one with prosthetic hands, and anyone else who crosses his path. After a string of murders, his embittered daughter, Fay Helm, riddled with guilt over her father's deadly secret, burns the family mansion to the ground and Morgan is shot dead by Asther as he attempts to strangle Irene Hervey and her boyfriend. Lugosi, although given star billing, was utterly wasted as a butler, wandering around strangely in the background without saying very much. Slow-moving but creepily atmospheric in parts, the film was originally released with The Mummy's Tomb and the title was changed to *House of Mystery* in the United Kingdom, but it then surfaced in the late '50s and early '60s under its original title, double billed with either *The Mummy's Ghost* or *Black Friday*.

Night of the Big Heat
aka: Island of the Burning Damned
Planet 1967; Eastmancolor; 94 mins; Cert. "X"
CREDITS: Producer: Tom Blakeley; Director: Terence Fisher
CAST: Christopher Lee; Patrick Allen; Peter Cushing; Sarah Lawson; Jane Merrow; William Lucas *
Aliens that land on a Scottish island emit intense heat and menace a group of disparate characters in a public house on the island.
The third of Terence Fisher's films for Planet and the worst of the three—a decent cast squabble among themselves with banal dialogue, particularly the trio of Patrick Allen, Sarah Lawson and Jane Merrow, all caught up in a tedious love situation, and Peter Cushing is completely wasted as a doctor who doesn't do a lot. Christopher Lee plays a UFO spotter convinced that the rising temperature on the island is the result of alien activity, and as the death toll mounts among the local populace, with telephone lines and television sets being affected, the audience is left waiting on tenterhooks until the closing minutes to see just what these mysterious aliens look like. They turn out to be large glowing globular blobs moving very slowly over the heather and gorse. A thunderstorm dissolves the creatures in the rain after Lee dies and that's it. A very poorly conceived version of John Lymington's quite successful novel of the time, hindered by some pretty garish color photography.

Night of the Demon
aka: Curse of the Demon
Columbia 1957; 95 mins; Cert. "X"
CREDITS: Producers: Frank Bevis and Hal E. Chester; Director: Jacques Tourneur
CAST: Dana Andrews; Niall MacGinnis; Peggy Cummins; Maurice Denham; Athene Seyler;
Liam Redmond *****

A cynical American psychologist sent to England to investigate a series of mysterious deaths gradually comes to realize that he may be the next victim of a demon from hell after trying to expose an occultist.

This classic movie grips from the onset when a disbeliever who has unwisely crossed Niall MacGinnis is pursued and slain by the giant medieval devil of the title that materializes out of the night sky, cleverly convincing the audience that such things do exist even if Dana Andrews chooses to scoff at the supernatural. Although director Jacques Tourneur objected to the inclusion of the demon at the beginning and end of the film, within the context of the rest of the movie the scenes work and are very well executed. MacGinnis is in superb form as the devious Devil-worshipper, unsuspectingly passing on a parchment of runic symbols to his intended victims, who die at a given time. There are several Alfred Hitchcock-type scenes of pure terror, such as Andrews' flight through darkened woods chased by the invisible demon, the creature, again invisible, stomping along the hallway of Andrews' hotel, and the climax on the railway train as MacGinnis realizes that by unknowingly being handed the parchment, he has become the monster's next victim. He is then pursued down the railway tracks by the fiery demon, which tears him to shreds. An intelligent, expertly crafted thriller that is probably the finest film on demonology ever made—it was a firm favorite on the U.K. horror circuit throughout the 1960s.

Night of the Eagle
aka: Burn, Witch, Burn!
Independent Artists/American Intl. 1961; 86 mins; Cert. "X"

CREDITS: Producer: Albert Fennell; Director: Sidney Hayers
CAST: Peter Wyngarde; Janet Blair; Margaret Johnston; Anthony Nicholls; Colin Gordon; Reginald Beckwith ****

A professor at a college who is skeptical about the occult realizes that his wife is a practicing witch who has been furthering his career by using the black arts.

Peter Wyngarde stars as the professor in this underrated British occult thriller, probably overshadowed by the superior *Night of the Demon* but worthwhile all the same. When he discovers that his wife, Janet Blair, is using magical charms to boost his career prospects, he orders her to destroy them but in doing so invokes the wrath of the head witch of a coven, Margaret Johnston, who also lusts after him. This triggers a series of disturbing events, such as a witch-doll strapped to his chair and his possessed wife attacking him. In the film's memorable climax, a giant stone eagle comes to life and pursues and attacks Wyngarde and his wife in the corridors of the college. The happy ending sees the giant eagle changing back to stone and crashing down onto the head witch, thus breaking the curse. A genuinely chilling little picture, one of the more compelling to come out of the smaller British studios of the early 1960s.

The Night Walker
Universal 1964; 86 mins; Cert. "X"
CREDITS: Producer/Director: William Castle
CAST: Barbara Stanwyck; Hayden Rorke; Robert Taylor; Lloyd Bochner; Judith Meredith; Rochelle Hudson **

An adulterous wife has recurring nightmares concerning her husband, who was killed in an explosion while she was having an affair.

A contrived and artless William Castle psycho-thriller that has Stanwyck tormented not only by visions of her blind, dead husband but an imaginary lover who appears in the shape of Lloyd Bochner. He turns out to be a private eye, hired by her husband before he died. Meanwhile, the real lover, Robert Taylor, is posing as her dead husband to try to lay his hands on her money, and kills the private eye before falling to his own death at the end of the film, leaving Stanwyck alone with her inheritance. A mediocre and not very likeable outing from the director, showing the gradual deterioration in a lot of his films as the '60s wore on.

Nights of Rasputin
Rialto/Faro/Explorer/MGM (Italy/France) 1960; Eastmancolor; 95 mins; Cert. "X"
CREDITS: Producer: Giampaolo Bigazzi; Director: Pierre Chenal
CAST: Edmond Purdom; Gianna Maria Canale; John Drew Barrymore; Jany Clair; Ugo Sasso; Giulia Rubini **

A vagrant monk in Old Russia cures the Tsar's son and inveigles himself into the court for his own power and sexual needs.

This continental version of the Rasputin legend was admittedly a colorful, glossy production, with suave, handsome British actor Edmond Purdom playing the evil monk who wheedles himself into the Russian court and hypnotizes the Tsarina into being his sex slave. However, the familiar inaccuracies riddled the story, and the film concentrated on Rasputin's sexual adventures rather than historical fact. The ending, with the mad monk being stabbed, shot and thrown into a river, was less gruesome than the Hammer 1966 version and Purdom, although turning in a good performance as Rasputin, was no Christopher Lee. After being shelved for a couple of years, the film went the rounds in 1962, playing second feature to *Corridors of Blood*.

Nosferatu
Prana Films (Germany) 1922; 93 mins; No Certificate
CREDITS: Director: F.W. Murnau
CAST: Max Schreck; Alexander Granach; Gustav von Wangenheim; Grete Schroder; G.H. Schnell; Ruth Landshoff *****

A vampire count travels to Bremen and unleashes a plague on the local population.

An unofficial reworking of the Bram Stoker novel featuring one of the most loathsome-looking vampires in screen history, Max Schreck as Count Orlok, with his gaunt features, pointed ears, stick-like body and long clawed talons—a far more powerful figure, it has to be said, than Bela Lugosi in Universal's 1931 adaptation. Stoker's estate and family objected to the making of this film, so by necessity Murnau shifted the action, once out of Transylvania, from London to Bremen. Dracula became Orlok, Renfield took on the guise of Knock, the estate agent, but some parts of the book were retained by the director in his version: the young estate agent, Hutter, traveling to Orlok's castle in the Carpathian Mountains to arrange the sale of property, and the sea voyage on the ship, with the Count rising like a ghostly specter from his coffin and wiping out the crew. The remainder of the picture then moves to Bremen, where the vampire compels an army of rats to spread the plague while he searches for the estate agent's wife to join him as one of the undead. The climax sees Orlok dissolving into a misty vapor in the rays of the rising sun as he is lured by lust into the heroine's bedroom, and the final view is of the ruined battlements of his remote castle. A very early and influential film indeed, whose startling imagery carried on through the next five decades of filmmaking—it was one of the first exponents of the enduring "shadow on the wall" motif, and its air of death and decay has rarely been equaled. The movie was remade in 1979 to far less effect with Klaus Kinski in the title role and was given another release in 1995 in a color-tinted version, sporting a special musical score by James Bernard of Hammer Films fame.

Not of this Earth
Allied Artists 1956; 67 mins; Cert. "X"
CREDITS: Producer/Director: Roger Corman
CAST: Paul Birch; Beverly Garland; Morgan Jones; Jonathan Haze; Ann Carroll; Dick Miller
***

An alien is sent to Earth through a transporter machine to gather human blood for use on a dying planet.

A minor Roger Corman classic, with bulky Paul Birch as the blank-eyed alien wearing sunglasses and looking more like a businessman than a malevolent visitor from another planet. When Birch's blood begins deteriorating, he seeks out victims to replenish his own, leaving drained corpses in his wake and using a bat-like creature as his emissary to claim more victims. The scenes with the transporter machine whereby crates of blood are transported to Birch's dying planet, and also of Birch's superiors on the Planet Davana communicating with him via the machine, resemble episodes of *Star Trek* that were made years later. However, the film, swiftly directed by Corman, has a dark, sinister air to it and at the end Birch, who is attempting to transport a human through the transmitter, dies in a car crash because he experiences pain from the high pitched whine of a following police motorcycle.

The Oblong Box
American Intl. 1969; Eastmancolor; 91 mins; Cert. "X"
CREDITS: Producer/Director: Gordon Hessler
CAST: Vincent Price; Christopher Lee; Hilary Dwyer; Alastair Williamson; Peter Arne; Harry Baird ***

You're Not Old Enough Son

An insane, disfigured man is imprisoned by his brother in the family mansion, but escapes and seeks his revenge.

A grisly revenge tale, started by Michael *Witchfinder General* Reeves (who died during filming) and completed by Gordon Hessler. Alastair Williamson is disfigured by a witch doctor in Africa as retribution for a botched operation that his brother, Vincent Price, performed on a native child. Back in England and imprisoned in the family mansion, he escapes by feigning his own death, having a funeral and bribing a doctor, Christopher Lee, to shelter him while he embarks on a series of brutal slayings. Price is his intended final victim, and gets bitten by the maniac before the killer is shot dead. Price is then horrified to learn that the disfigurement carried by his brother through witchcraft has been passed on to him. This was the first time that Price and Lee had appeared together in a horror film, which was graphically violent for its time, in particular Williamson's savage murder of a prostitute who dares to look at his features under the hood that he wears.

On the Beach
United Artists 1959; 134 mins; Cert. "A"
CREDITS: Producer/Director: Stanley Kramer
CAST: Gregory Peck; Ava Gardner; Fred Astaire; Anthony Perkins; Donna Anderson; Guy Doleman *****

An atomic war has devastated the world and the only survivors left await their fate in Australia as a vast radioactive cloud inexorably drifts toward the continent.

Neville Shute's post-holocaust novel received the big-budget screen treatment—a formidable cast and a director with clout. Gregory Peck played the U.S. naval commander of a submarine, docking in Melbourne and falling for socialite Ava Gardner. Anthony Perkins was a young officer who had trouble coping with his wife's fragile state of mind as radioactive death approached, and even veteran actor Fred Astaire turned in an engaging performance as the playboy who prefers to gas himself seated at the wheel of his favorite racing car rather than take a suicide pill. The real highlight of the whole production is Peck's lengthy mission to California in his submarine to investigate a mysterious radio signal emanating from the city, only to eventually discover that it is nothing more than a window blind's pull-cord blowing in the wind above a transmitter—a crushing and chilling denouement. The scenes of a deserted San Francisco bathed in an eerie grayish monochrome are also disturbingly realistic, and the movie ends on a distinctly downbeat note, with shots of the empty, rubbish-strewn streets of Melbourne, until recently populated by thousands of people who have now all perished in the fallout. A stark end-of-the-world message in a memorable film.

One Million B.C.
aka: Man and his Mate
United Artists 1940; 80 mins; Cert. "A"
CREDITS: Producer: Hal Roach; Directors: Hal Roach and Hal Roach Jr.
CAST: Victor Mature; Carole Landis; Lon Chaney Jr.; John Hubbard; Robert Kent; Nigel de Brulier ***

Two tribes of cave dwellers fight with each other in a world populated with dinosaurs.

Although enlarged, back-projected lizards and even a man in a rubber suit were used as dinosaurs, this was an impressive and highly unusual film for its time, even allowing for the fact that man did not exist at the same period as the prehistoric animals depicted in the movie. The scenes involving the dinosaurs fighting were so popular that they were plagiarized by a score of later fantasy efforts, including *Two Lost Worlds* (1950), *Robot Monster* (1953) and *King Dinosaur* (1955). They even turned up in *Tarzan's Desert Mystery* (1943). After the film's release, there was a complete ban on the use of live lizards, or any other animals, in films such as this one, brought on by the American Society for the Prevention of Cruelty to Animals. The trio of Carole Landis, Victor Mature and a scarred Lon Chaney give their all, battling various monsters and volcanic upheavals and having virtually no dialogue to speak, a theme carried over in the 1966 Hammer remake.

One Million Years B.C.

Hammer/Seven Arts 1966; Technicolor; 100 mins; Cert. "A"

CREDITS: Producer: Michael Carreras; Director: Don Chaffey; Special Effects: Ray Harryhausen

CAST: John Richardson; Raquel Welch; Robert Brown; Percy Herbert; Martine Beswick; Yvonne Horner ****

A remake of the 1940 film with superior special effects.

Hammer employed the services of ace special effects man Ray Harryhausen on their revamp of the old 1940 *One Million B.C.* and his animation and model work, including a giant turtle, a superb baby Allosaurus and a briefly seen Brontosaurus (additional footage of this was omitted at the last moment) was of his usual high standard. Despite Harryhausen's stunning effects, the film was not particularly well received at the time—critics had little regard for the fact that there was no real dialogue—but it seems to have grown in stature over the years and is thought of more highly now than it was in 1966, when the sight of Raquel Welch in a Stone Age bikini caused more than a few laughs. The breathtaking Canary Islands locations dramatically stand in for the prehistoric landscape, and the earthquake at the film's climax is well staged, with Mario Nascimbene providing a stirring score. There is also one eerily chilling scene in the film, when John Richardson and Welch find themselves almost trapped in a gloomy cavern populated by primitive cannibals—a slight touch of the Hammer Horrors here, as opposed to all the bright sunshine in the exterior shots and Harryhausen's glossy dinosaurs. This eventually turned out to be one of Hammer's most successful films of the 1960s.

Panic in Year Zero

American Intl. 1962; 92 mins; Cert. "X"

CREDITS: Producers: Arnold Houghland and Lou Rusoff; Director: Ray Milland

CAST: Ray Milland; Jean Hagen; Frankie Avalon; Mary Mitchell; Joan Freeman; Richard Garland ***

A family on a fishing trip is left marooned when Los Angeles is destroyed by an atomic bomb.

Ray Milland directed himself in this bleak but fairly engrossing post-nuclear holocaust movie. Milland, his wife, son and daughter take up residence in a cave in the hills above Los Angeles and are menaced by survivors of the blast, leading to Frankie Avalon killing some of them after Mary Mitchell has been raped. Milland's family at first cannot understand his hardening attitude toward the survivors—he refuses them food and shelter and reads from a book describing what to do if an atomic bomb goes off. But they eventually come to realize that they are part of a brand new world and the film ends with the usual proclamation—"There Must Be No End—Only a New Beginning."

Paranoiac
Hammer/Universal 1962; Hammerscope; 80 mins; Cert. "X"
CREDITS: Producer: Anthony Hinds; Director: Freddie Francis
CAST: Oliver Reed; Janette Scott; Alexander Devion; Sheila Burrell; Liliane Brousse; Maurice Denham **

A man turns up at a family mansion claiming to be the owner's long lost son who was presumed dead.

A very contrived thriller, borrowing its plot from a number of similar films, including, of course, *Psycho*. Alexander Devion arrives at a mansion claiming to be Janette Scott's brother, which drives her mad as he realizes that she is falling in love with him, even though she believed him to be dead. He then admits that he is an imposter, trying to uncover an insane killer, played by a glowering Oliver Reed, who just happens to be Scott's real brother. A series of mistaken identities ensues, with Reed playing the organ to the walled-up corpse of his brother whom he murdered. Reed is finally exposed in the climax as the killer who was after the family riches after several red herrings and shocks. Although well directed by Freddie Francis, the film was just too confusing to make much sense and despite Reed's heavyweight presence failed to make an impact—it was not released until 1963, when it went the rounds with *Kiss of the Vampire*, and then given a brief run in 1967 with the spy thriller *Deadlier than the Male*.

Peeping Tom
Astor/Anglo Amalgamated 1960; Eastmancolor; 109 mins; Cert. "X"
CREDITS: Producers: Michael Powell and Albert Fennell; Director: Michael Powell
CAST: Carl Boehm; Moira Shearer; Anna Massey; Maxine Audley; Martin Miller; Brenda Bruce ****
A shy young man sadistically treated by his father when he was a boy commits murder and films his victims as they are being killed.
A disturbing movie for the time it was made, heavily criticized for its explicit content. The industry ostracized director Michael Powell as a result, and 20 minutes were cut from the initial release, although these scenes were restored in later prints. Carl Boehm played the mild-mannered photographer, working as a studio focus-puller during the day and by night killing women he has befriended, by using a spike concealed in his 16mm camera, and then viewing the results at home. He takes up with Anna Massey, who unfortunately has the dubious honor of seeing the home footage that his father took of his experiments in sadism, and when the police discover the killer's identity, Boehm spares Massey and films his own suicide. The film obviously seems mild by today's standards, but its voyeuristic nature placed it in the soft porn category and it was not a success when first released, only showing at selected cinemas in the '60s and given a brief re-release in London in 1968, double billed somewhat bizarrely with RKO's *King Kong*.

The Phantom from 10,000 Leagues
Milner/ARC 1955; 81 mins; Cert. "A"
CREDITS: Producers: Jack and Dan Milner;
Director: Dan Milner
CAST: Kent Taylor; Cathy Downs; Rodney
Bell; Michael Whalen; Helene Stanton;
Philip Pine **

A mutated sea-monster guards an under-water deposit of uranium.

A cheapskate production from the Milner brothers starring Kent Taylor as an oceanographer investigating a series of mysterious deaths at a beach resort. Michael Whalen has created the monster responsible for the deaths to protect the precious ore deposit on the seabed for himself so that he can use it in his atomic research, but in the end, dynamite puts paid to him and his creation, although in a nearby laboratory, scientists are creating a similar creature. Too much talk and muddled under-water photography in which the monster, looking like a scaly alligator, is hardly glimpsed made this a very shoddy piece of juvenile hokum that was double billed with *The Beast with A Million Eyes* on the Sunday circuit in the early 1960s.

The Phantom of the Opera
Universal 1925; Color sequences; 79 mins; Cert. "A"
CREDITS: Producer: Carl Laemmle; Director: Rupert Julian
CAST: Lon Chaney; Mary Philbin; Norman Kerry; Snitz Edwards; Gibson Gowland; John Sainpolis *****

A hideously disfigured man lurking beneath the Paris Opera House abducts a singing pro-tégée from the chorus line so that he can become her tutor, but the madman is also insanely in love with the girl.

One of the '20s most celebrated of all horror movies, with Lon Chaney reveling in his most famous role of the masked Phantom, Erik, who terrorizes the opera house and kidnaps Christine, played by Mary Philbin, taking her to his underground lair, a splendid Gothic creation of waterways and arches dominated by the organ that the Phantom plays. The unmasking of Chaney by Philbin, revealing his skull-like features (the reason for his disfigurement was omitted by Universal) is one of horror's greatest moments, causing widespread faintings when the film was originally released. From then on, the movie becomes a might disjointed and melodramatic, although the flamboyant sequence depicting the masked ball, which Chaney attends disguised as The Red Death in an attempt to recapture the love of his life, whom he has set free if she promises never to see her lover again, is almost as good as the unmasking scene. The final moments showing the Phantom being chased through the Paris catacombs and streets, although shot in the vein of a '20s-type serial, are a classic piece of Grand Guignol cinema. He is eventually captured by the mob, beaten to death and thrown into the river. The film was given a short run at selected cinemas in the early 1960s with most of the scenes tinted in two-tone Technicolor, together with an added musical score. Despite a few lulls, it still remains, decades after release, the best-ever version of Gaston Leroux's famous novel.

The Phantom of the Opera
Universal 1943; Technicolor; 92 mins; Cert. "A"
CREDITS: Producer: George Waggner; Director: Arthur Lubin
CAST: Claude Rains; Nelson Eddy; Susanna Foster; Edgar Barrier; Leo Carillo; Fritz Leiber ***

A remake of the 1925 classic.

This time around, Claude Rains took over the Chaney role as Erik the Phantom, the disfigured composer, sporting a rather fetching mask and cape and setting his sights on soprano Susanna Foster. Despite Universal spending a fortune on lavish sets, costume design and color, for which the film won an Oscar, this was a distinctly unscary and not very thrilling film that concentrated far too much on Nelson Eddy's singing and the opera side of things and not enough on the hidden terrors lurking beneath the opera house. Even the unmasking scene revealing the Phantom's acid-scarred features was a disappointment and Rains, although competent in the part, was no Lon Chaney. But at least it fared better than Hammer's limp 1962 version.

The Phantom of the Opera
Hammer/Universal 1962; Technicolor; 84 mins; Cert. "A"
CREDITS: Producer: Anthony Hinds; Director: Terence Fisher
CAST: Herbert Lom; Heather Sears; Edward de Souza; Thorley Walters; Michael Gough; Miles Malleson **

A third film rendition of Gaston Leroux's novel.

It was really only a matter of time before Hammer decided to film their version of the famous tale, but what they came up with was, rather surprisingly for them, a curiously muted, pedestrian and none too creepy adaptation, despite the money spent on making it. It was one of their few films from this period not granted an "X" certificate by the censor, given instead an "A" rating, and perhaps by dampening down the horrors they were hoping to reach a wider audience. If so, they failed, as this was a rare flop for the company. Herbert Lom turned in a reasonable performance as the Phantom who falls for Heather Sears, but Michael Gough looked out of place as the malicious impresario responsible for Lom's hideously burned face, and the unmasking scene was poorly executed by the normally reliable Terence Fisher. The sets were picturesque in the usual Hammer style, although lacking in Gothic splendor, but U.K. audiences preferred their Hammer films with more blood and guts and preferably rated an "X," which is possibly one of the reasons why it ended up a commercial failure.

Phantom of the Rue Morgue
Warner Bros. 1953; Warnercolor; Orig. in 3-D; 84 mins; Cert. "X"
CREDITS: Producer: Henry Blanke; Director: Roy del Ruth
CAST: Karl Malden; Claude Dauphin; Patricia Medina; Steve Forrest; Anthony Caruso; Dolores Dorn **

In 19th-century Paris, a number of brutal murders among young women baffle the police and the culprit turns out to be a mad gorilla controlled by a professor.

The bodies of several murdered girls are discovered by the Paris police in gruesome poses—one is found stuffed up a chimney and another is ripped to pieces in a room full of smashed-up furniture, and all of the corpses have small bells attached to their wrists. The person behind the slayings is a Professor (Karl Malden), who meets the girls, gives them trinkets to win their affections and sends out his trained gorilla to slaughter them if they reject his advances. Psychologist Steve Forrest and fiancée Patricia Medina uncover Malden as the man responsible and when Medina ignores Malden's lustful overtures, he orders the ape to murder her. The creature carries her to the top of a tree after being chased by the police, and leaps off the branches onto Malden, who has the trinkets on him, killing the Professor before being shot dead. This was a gaudy, tasteless and oddly unattractive film with an unappealing, over-the-top performance by Malden, although the period setting was authentic-looking and the murders horribly graphic by early '50s standards. In 1966, the picture was re-released as a double bill with *House of Wax* and was quite successful on its latter-day run.

Pharaoh's Curse
Bel-Air/United Artists 1956; 66 mins; Cert. "X"
CREDITS: Producer: Howard W. Koch; Director: Lee Sholem
CAST: Mark Dane; Ziva Rodann; Terence de Marney; Diane Brewster; George Neise; Ralph Clanton ***

In 1903, an archaeological expedition to the Valley of the Kings in Egypt desecrates the tomb of a royal priest, whose spirit then possesses the body of a native.

A fast-moving combination of *The Mummy* and a supernatural thriller, unusual in not following the conventional route of most of the old *Mummy* films. Despite warnings of dire consequences from Arab girl Ziva Rodann, headstrong George Neise, the expedition's leader, breaks into the tomb of a pharaoh's priest, but when an incision is made in the mummy's bandages, Rodann's brother's spirit enters the body and the murderous priest comes alive, bumping off the members of the expedition while aging rapidly. It is eventually sealed in its tomb with Neise by a fall of rock over the entrance. The mummy itself resembled a withered old man for most of the picture, but this was still an entertaining variation on a familiar theme. It appeared on the Sunday circuit in 1962, double billed with *I Bury the Living*.

The Picture of Dorian Gray
MGM 1945; Technicolor sequences; 111 mins; Cert. "A"
CREDITS: Producer: Pandro S. Berman; Director: Albert Lewin
CAST: Hurd Hatfield; George Sanders; Donna Reed; Angela Lansbury; Peter Lawford; Richard Fraser ****

In Victorian England, a handsome young socialite leads a life of decadence and debauchery and stays forever youthful while in the attic of his house, his portrait shows the ravages of his sinful existence.

A slow-moving but literate adaptation of Oscar Wilde's infamous novel that shocked Victorian society. Hurd Hatfield plays the impossibly handsome Dorian Gray, who coldly drifts through London's social world, discarding with arrogance all those who come into contact with him and causing Angela Lansbury as an infatuated showgirl to kill herself because of his treatment of her. He also murders those who cross him, while all the time, his portrait portrays the real, inner Gray, a creature of lust and sin. The movie also features an excellent performance by George Sanders as his confidante, who continually questions Gray's hedonistic way of life. The famous ending had Gray, realizing at last that he is cursed, stabbing his portrait (a marvelous creation painted by the Albright Brothers) and decaying into a shriveled corpse, filmed in Technicolor for the final sequence. In 1963, the film popped up for a solitary one-day showing with *The World, the Flesh and the Devil*.

The Pit and the Pendulum
American Intl. 1961; Panavision/Pathecolor; 85 mins; Cert. "X"

CREDITS: Producer/Director: Roger Corman

CAST: Vincent Price; Barbara Steele; John Kerr; Luana Anders; Anthony Carbone; Patrick Westwood *****

The son of a Spanish nobleman is convinced that he is slowly going mad by inheriting the traits of his father, who was a notorious torturer during the Inquisition.

Roger Corman's second Poe production ranks as possibly his finest, a highly atmospheric piece of Grand Guignol with Vincent Price hamming it up wonderfully. He is a nobleman who has, unbeknown to his guests, a dungeon full of torture apparatus in his creepy old mansion, with one exceptionally nasty device in the lowest part of the house. Barbara Steele, playing Price's wife, and Anthony Carbone are the pair of lovers trying to drive the nobleman mad to enable them to acquire his fortune and eventually they succeed, although at the cost of their own lives. Carbone falls to his death into the pit after being chased by Price, who now believes himself to be his father, and Steele ends up in an iron maiden. John Kerr plays the innocent victim who finally suffers the horror of the razor-sharp pendulum in the film's harrowing, and now quite infamous, climax. Full of dank, cobwebby corridors, old crypts and people being buried alive, the picture also features one of Price's best-ever roles as the tortured Spanish nobleman. Les Baxter's weird, miasmic clanking soundtrack, particularly when heard over the opening shot of the mansion perched on a mist-shrouded cliff overlooking the ocean, also contributes to the film's aura of doom and decay. In the United Kingdom, when it was first released, patrons were insured for £10,000 if they died of fright while seeing the movie.

The Plague of the Zombies

Hammer/Seven Arts 1965; Technicolor; 91 mins; Cert. "X"

CREDITS: Producer: Anthony Nelson-Keys; Director: John Gilling

CAST: Andre Morell; Diane Clare; Brook Williams; Michael Ripper; Jacqueline Pearce; John Carson ***

The squire of a small Cornish village reduces the inhabitants to zombies so that he can use them as a workforce in his tin mine.

A thrilling slice of Hammer hokum that was a lot more enjoyable than *Dracula—Prince of Darkness*, the film that it was second feature to when first released in 1966. Andre Morell plays a professor called upon by Brook Williams to investigate a strange epidemic in a Cornish village, whereby corpses are apparently coming alive. It turns out that

John Carson is practicing voodoo so that he can use the reanimated corpses as labor in his mine. There are some compelling scenes of the rotting zombies crawling out of their graves and of Diane Clare seeing her dead friend come alive as one of the living dead. There is also the gruesome moment when Jacqueline Pearce is decapitated to save her from becoming a zombie. Eventually, the mine is infiltrated by Morell and set ablaze, causing the zombie workforce to perish in the flames. Made back-to-back with *The Reptile*, the two films were originally intended to be released as a double bill, but this never materialized on the circuits in England.

Plan 9 from Outer Space
Reynolds/DCA 1956; 79 mins; Cert. "X"
CREDITS: Producer/Director: Edward D. Wood Jr.
CAST: Bela Lugosi; Tor Johnson; Vampira; Gregory Walcott; Lyle Talbot; Mona McKinnon
**

Aliens attack the Earth for the ninth attempt, reactivating the dead to use as slaves to attack the living.

Ed Wood's most notorious production, a farrago of bad acting, wooden sets, uneven continuity and lousy special effects. Lugosi, the so-called star of the picture, wasn't even in the film per se—two minutes of footage of him that Wood had shot before he died were included in the finished production and a stand-in took his place, masking his face with a cloak to hide the obvious fact that he was not Lugosi! The aliens looked like rejects from an old Buck Rogers film, the flight deck of their spacecraft resembled the inside of a bus with curtains, and Vampira and Tor Johnson were roped in to play the undead. The flying saucers were rumored to be silver-painted hubcaps and in several scenes, day suddenly changed into night for no apparent reason other than the director thought it artistic to do so. The one almost decent-looking scene is of a blank-eyed Johnson rising from the dead in a cardboard-created cemetery. Despite or because of all of this, the movie isn't quite as atrocious as its reputation warrants and can be enjoyed on a certain masochistic level by fans of the truly dreadful. It is amazing to think, though, that at the time of release, the British censor awarded the film an "X" certificate. In the early 1960s, it did the rounds with another awful Wood effort, *Bride of the Monster*, and also *The Monster from Green Hell*, cropping up again in 1963 with Toho's *Rodan*. In 1994, Tim Burton's homage to the eccentric director, *Ed Wood*, lovingly recreated the making of this camp classic and also featured as a bonus an outstanding Oscar-winning performance by Martin Landau as washed-up horror legend Bela Lugosi in the final days of his career.

Planet of the Apes
20th Century Fox 1968; Panavision/DeLuxeColor; 112 mins; Cert. "A"
CREDITS: Producer: Arthur P. Jacobs; Director: Franklin J. Schaffner
CAST: Charlton Heston; Kim Hunter; Roddy McDowell; Maurice Evans; James Whitmore; James Daly *****

A U.S. spaceship hurtles forward thousands of years and crash-lands on a planet where apes are the masters and humans the slaves.

A big-budget, creditable adaptation of, and in many ways an improvement on, Pierre Boule's pulp novel *Monkey Planet*. After escaping from their wrecked spaceship that crashed on an uncharted planet, Charlton Heston and fellow astronauts find themselves from the onset battling with the warlike apes, finally captured along with other humans and being the subject of curiosity, close scrutiny and, when Heston speaks, hostility. With a team of friendly ape scientists, he is eventually led toward an excavation in the cliffs where strange but familiar artifacts from a seemingly long-dead civilization are being unearthed, and it is only in the final, now memorable scene, when Heston and his female companion are set free and stumble across the half-buried remains of the Statue of Liberty on the shoreline, that he realizes with horror that he is back on Earth in a distant future. The movie was impressively photographed around the national parks of Arizona and Utah and the arresting ape makeup earned the film an Oscar. Despite losing pace slightly in the central part of the film, with too many discussions going on between the apes as to what to do with the astronauts, *Planet of the Apes* was a huge success on first release and spawned four inferior sequels.

The Premature Burial
American Intl. 1961; Panavision/East-mancolor; 81 mins; Cert. "X"
CREDITS: Producer/Director: Roger Corman
CAST: Ray Milland; Hazel Court; Richard Ney; Heather Angel; Alan Napier; John Dierkes **

A man with an inherent fear of being buried alive goes into a cataleptic coma, is thought dead and then buried. Dug up, he exacts revenge on those who interred him alive.

A typically lavish treatment of the Poe story, but in many respects a strangely unsatisfactory film and one of Roger Corman's least effective pieces of work. Ray Milland is the man obsessed with being buried alive, as he believes his father met with a similar fate while in a cataleptic trance. His house is installed with all manner of devices to prevent it from happening to him. His devious wife shocks him into a cataleptic coma, but when he is exhumed, he comes out of the trance, goes insane and takes out his revenge on those who plotted against him. Milland overacts like mad for most of the time and the picture's sole theme of premature interment does not seem strong enough to sustain any suspense—it lacks the Gothic splendor of other Poe adaptations and simply becomes tiresome long before the ending.

The Projected Man
Protelco/Universal 1966; Techniscope/Technicolor; 90 mins; Cert. "X"
CREDITS: Producers: Maurice Foster and John Croydon; Director: Ian Curteis
CAST: Bryant Halliday; Mary Peach; Ronald Allen; Norman Wooland; Derrick De Marney; Sam Kydd ***

A scientist invents a matter-transmitter machine, but when it is sabotaged he emerges from it totally deranged, with one half of his body reversed and a touch that can kill.

A British cut-price version of Fox's *The Fly* that sees Bryant Halliday as the guinea pig looking pretty grotesque when he steps out of the transmitter, as one side of his body has been turned inside out. He can kill with electric force from his touch and plans to exact revenge on those who made his life a misery by previously sabotaging his equipment in front of a committee of scientists, electrocuting them to death. Halliday finally realizes what he has become and destroys himself and his equipment after the police have caught up with him and helped him to his laboratory. The film starts off well enough but goes downhill in the second half, with little suspense to maintain the interest, only numerous shots of Halliday on a rampage, emerging from the shadows with his disfigured features, electrocuting his victims and threatening the lovely Mary Peach.

Psycho
Paramount 1960; 109 mins; Cert. "X"
CREDITS: Producer/Director: Alfred Hitchcock
CAST: Anthony Perkins; Janet Leigh; John Gavin; Vera Miles; Martin Balsam; John McIntire *****

A young woman steels $40,000 from her office and goes on the run, ending up in a lonely run-down motel owned by a young man and his mysterious mother.

Hitchcock, impressed and intrigued by the low-budget black and white horror movies that proliferated during the '50s, decided to bring his own expertise to the genre, although initially against Paramount's wishes, and came up with his most notorious and discussed shocker, endlessly imitated but never bettered and one that can still manage to jangle the nerves after repeated viewings. *Psycho*, the key example of a rather mundane novel being transformed into a brilliant piece of celluloid, was not particularly well received by the critics when first released, probably because it was in stark contrast to the director's highly expensive productions of that time and had no big-name stars in it, though the film made a fortune at the box office in a very short period ("Positively no one allowed in during the last 15 minutes" ran the advertisements as one queued up to see it). Suffice to say that Anthony Perkins' performance as the mother-fixated Norman Bates, Hitchcock's playing with the emotions of the audience, the shower scene, the shocking murders, and the final shot of the mummified corpse of Bates' mother—all have gone down in cinema history to make this the classic horror thriller, and the highest-grossing black and white film ever made. Bernard Herrmann's legendary music is one of the most instantly recognizable of any movie score and forms an integral part of the production, a fact that Hitchcock himself always acknowledged in interviews. Ironically, Perkins became so famous in his portrayal of Bates that it killed stone-dead his up-and-coming career as a romantic lead—audiences just could not accept him in any role other than as a weirdo. The film was given a successful re-release in 1967, double billed with *The War of the Worlds*, and went the rounds in 1968 at selected cinemas as a late-night show, teamed up with, unusually, Universal's *Bride of Frankenstein*. In 1998, Gus Van Sant directed a new version of Hitchcock's masterpiece, scene-for-scene in color, more as an experiment than an homage, using the original Herrmann soundtrack. It was a complete failure, a pointless exercise and above all else proved that *Psycho* was made for the black and white medium, not color.

Psycho Killer
aka: The Psycho Lover
Medford Films 1969; Eastmancolor; 80 mins; Cert. "X"
CREDITS: Producer/Director: Robert Vincent O'Neill
CAST: Lawrence Montaigne; Joanne Meredith; Elizabeth Plumb; Rod Cameron; Neville Brand; Aldo Ray **

A psychiatrist who has grown tired of his wife programs a murdering rapist to kill her.

An extremely distasteful psycho-thriller featuring a surprisingly good cast in which a psychiatrist, Montaigne, takes under his supervision a patient who has committed a number of rape-murders, only for the man to somehow be released from custody on each occasion through apparent lack of evidence. After watching the film *The Manchurian Candidate*, which presents him with ideas, he programs the killer to murder his wife, but when she learns of the plot, she invites the psychiatrist's mistress to the house on the same day that the psychopath is due there, so that she will be murdered in her place. The British censor cut several rather brutal and disturbing scenes from this production and it was eventually given a short, unsuccessful run with *The Corpse*.

The Psychopath
Amicus/Paramount 1965; Techniscope/Technicolor; 83 mins; Cert. "X"

CREDITS: Producers: Max J. Rosenberg and Milton Subotsky; Director: Freddie Francis
CAST: Patrick Wymark; Margaret Johnston; John Standing; Alexander Knox; Judy Huxtable; Don Borisenko ***

A police inspector investigates a series of deaths whereby a small doll is placed by the side of the victim's bodies.

A stylish shocker from Amicus, albeit with a rather far-fetched story concerning a wheel-chair-bound widow, Margaret Johnston, who sends out her demented son, John Standing, to assist her in the murder of the ex-members of an Allied War Commission that tried and executed her husband, who was a German industrialist. Johnston herself is also a knife-wielding killer, able to rise from her wheelchair to commit murder. The dolls, which bear an uncanny resemblance to the victims, are placed next to the bodies and are from Johnston's own vast collection. She finally makes up her son as one of the dolls and places him among the others in her room, where, now totally insane, he murmers the word "mama" in a grotesque finale after he has spared Judy Huxtable, playing a daughter of one of the victims.

Quatermass and the Pit
aka: 5 Million Years to Earth
Hammer/Seven Arts 1967; Technicolor; 97 mins; Cert. "X"
CREDITS: Producer: Anthony Nelson-Keys; Director: Roy Ward Baker
CAST: Andrew Keir; James Donald; Barbara Shelley; Julian Glover; Duncan Lamont; Edwin Richfield *****

Workmen engaged on a London tube extension unearth fossil apemen from the clay and a mysterious object resembling a spacecraft that begins to exert an ancient and powerful force.

First televised on BBC-TV as six 35-minute episodes in December 1958 and January 1959 with Andre Morell in the title role, the third of Nigel Kneale's *Quatermass* serials concerning a mysterious cylinder unearthed during an archaeological dig in London held the entire British nation in its grip, long before the days of multi-channel television, VHS and DVD. Schools complained that schoolchildren were staying up late to watch it (despite warnings given out at the start of each episode that it was unsuitable for people of a nervous disposition), suffering from nightmares as a result and therefore not concentrating on their homework, Parliament was adjourned so that its Ministers of Parliament would not miss an episode, and the police reported empty streets and little crime on the nights it was broadcast. It even made the front-page headlines in some of the daily newspapers. There was to be no black and white cinema version starring Brian Donlevy this time (the general consensus is that Andre Morell's portrayal of the Professor is the definitive one), and although the BBC

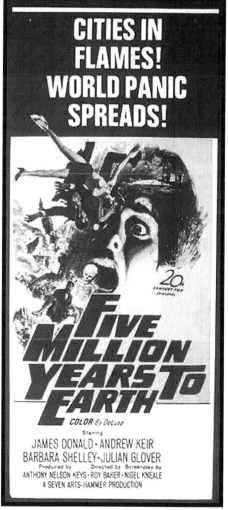

CITIES IN FLAMES! WORLD PANIC SPREADS!

20th CENTURY FOX presents

FIVE MILLION YEARS TO EARTH

COLOR By DeLuxe

Starring
JAMES DONALD · ANDREW KEIR
BARBARA SHELLEY · JULIAN GLOVER
Produced by   Directed by   Screenplay by
ANTHONY NELSON KEYS · ROY BAKER · NIGEL KNEALE
A SEVEN ARTS-HAMMER PRODUCTION

gave Hammer the option to film it in 1961, it took the company several years to bring the serial to the screen; they probably reasoned that Kneale's multitude of ideas involving alien invasion, race-memory, hauntings and telekinetic energy was much too fanciful for a late '50s or early '60s audience. The change of location from the Roman excavations to the extension of Hob's Lane tube station was a stroke of genius, and there are some truly hair-raising moments in the film—the driller, Sladden, fleeing from the Martian spaceship, the whole set erupting around him in poltergeist activity, and the final scenes of a huge Martian figure hovering over London in a miasma of energy while the population, under its control, goes berserk. In other ways, though, the movie is not an improvement on the teleserial—the insect-like Martians are nowhere near as menacing as the originals which, when first seen, really did raise the hackles, and the purging of the Martian hives sequence is a let-down compared to the 1959 version. Although technically the film is well made, with Andrew Keir turning in a solid performance as the Professor, the BBC television adaptation still remains a spine-chilling classic.

The Quatermass Experiment
aka: The Creeping Unknown
Hammer/Exclusive 1955; 82 mins; Cert. "X"
CREDITS: Producer: Anthony Hinds; Director: Val Guest
CAST: Brian Donlevy; Richard Wordsworth; Jack Warner; Margia Dean; David King-Wood; Gordon Jackson *****

The first three-manned British space rocket crash-lands in England with two of its crew missing; the surviving astronaut has been infected by an alien organism that slowly mutates him into something less than human.

The Quatermass Experiment was initially Nigel Kneale's groundbreaking six-part serial on BBC-TV, televised in 1953 and giving the vast majority of the British public that tuned in to see it a severe shock, leading to empty streets and pubs on the nights it was being screened. Hammer's film version was shot in semi-documentary style by Val Guest and was a phenomenal success in both Britain and the United States—it put Hammer on the map and forced the company to concentrate their efforts on horror and science fiction films, and not costume dramas or thrillers as was intended. One of the major talking points that critics argue about is the casting (or mis-

casting, depending on your point of view—it was certainly the opinion of Nigel Kneale) of American actor Brian Donlevy in the title role. Some find his bullying, arrogant performance at odds with the essentially English setting of the film—others insist that Donlevy's hard-nosed man of science is the force that such a story commands. Many science fiction fans are inclined to go with the latter view, believing that Donlevy was right for the role (he was obviously chosen with one eye on the American market despite the rumor that he was continu-ally drunk during filming). On another point, though, the critics were completely unanimous in their praise—gaunt-looking Richard Wordsworth as the infected astronaut changing before our eyes turned in one of the greatest performances of its kind in any 1950s science fiction movie, British or American; he looked weird, even without makeup. The scene where the unsuspecting chemist unwraps the astronaut's coat to reveal a fungoid stump instead of an arm caused faintings in cinemas when the film first came out, and the climax had Wordsworth, now completely mutated into a tentacled monster, being electrocuted on scaffolding in Westminster Abbey. The film was originally released as *The Quatermass Xperiment* to cash in on the relatively new British "X" certificate (a rating that Hammer became obsessed with during this period) and was shown with the French thriller *Rififi*, but in the 1960s it did the rounds teamed with the same company's *X the Unknown*. The movie was such a box office smash that *Quatermass 2* soon went into production and Hammer began to cast their eyes over the old Universal classics with a view to revamping them for a new generation of cinema-goers.

Quatermass 2
aka: Enemy from Space
Hammer/United Artists 1957; 85 mins; Cert. "X"
CREDITS: Producer: Anthony Hinds; Director: Val Guest
CAST: Brian Donlevy; Bryan Forbes; Vera Day; John Longden; Sidney James; William Franklyn
*****

While investigating showers of meteorites that are landing over England, Professor Quatermass discovers that his moonbase project has been replicated at a site near Winnerden Flats and is being used as an acclimatization center for an alien invasion.

The second of the *Quatermass* films (originally broadcast on BBC television in late 1955), with Brian Donlevy reprising the title role, was the bleakest—in fact, with its theme of aliens taking over and controlling the minds of humans, it was nearer in tone to *Invasion of the Body Snatchers* or even *1984*. The Shell Haven Refinery in Essex, with its windswept, gray landscape, was convincingly used as the center of alien operations and there is a growing feeling of sinister alarm about the whole film, with the blustering Professor suspecting that even members of the government have been taken over and are acting in the aliens' interests. The horrifying sight of an MP covered in black poisonous slime, the alien's "food," sliding and staggering to his death among the glittering pipes and machinery at the plant, still packs a punch, as do the scenes of the villagers rioting against the zombie-like guards at the refinery before realizing that one of their number has been turned to pulp in the pipes feeding the aliens in the domes. Sidney James, proving that he could act in serious roles, turned in a winning performance as a boozy but likeable newspaper reporter who pays with his life while trying to expose the refinery for what it is. The ending resorts to standard monster fare, with the giant blob-like aliens escaping from the domes and self-destructing as their asteroid is destroyed by Quatermass' rocket. Overall, *Quatermass 2* is an intelligently made minor classic with some great black and white photography (a hallmark of the Hammer science fiction films from this decade), much underrated in its time and probably overshadowed by the success of *The Curse of Frankenstein* released the same year.

Queen of Outer Space
Allied Artists 1958; Cinemascope/DeLuxeColor; 80 mins; Cert. "U"
CREDITS: Producer: Ben Schwalb; Director: Edward Bernds
CAST: Eric Fleming; Zsa Zsa Gabor; Laurie Mitchell; Paul Birch; Barbara Darrow; Dave Willcock **

An expedition from Earth crash-lands on Venus to find an all-female dominated planet bent on destroying Earth.

It isn't quite as awful as *Fire Maidens from Outer Space*—only the fact that it is in widescreen and color saves it from being so. The film is a ridiculous piece of late '50s camp whimsy that has three astronauts and a scientist landing on Venus and being sentenced to death as spies by Laurie Mitchell as the masked queen of the planet.

Eric Fleming starts an affair with Zsa Zsa Gabor, one of the Venusian women who eventually leads a revolt against Mitchell as she plans to decimate Earth with a ray gun. In the end, the sabotaged ray gun blows up, killing the evil ruler. The garish studio set resembles a tacky tropical jungle, there is plenty of stock footage from *World Without End* (also directed by Bernds but a lot worthier than this!), and the obligatory giant spider makes an appearance. Even the look of the astronauts has been lifted from another film, *Forbidden Planet*. A comic book failure all round.

Rasputin the Mad Monk
Hammer/Seven Arts 1966; Cinemascope/DeLuxeColor; 92 mins; Cert. "X"
CREDITS: Producer: Anthony Nelson-Keys; Director: Don Sharp
CAST: Christopher Lee; Barbara Shelley; Richard Pascoe; Francis Mathews; Derek Francis; Suzan Farmer ***
    A peasant monk with hypnotic powers infiltrates the Court of Tsar Nicholas the Second and uses his influence to manipulate the royal family for his own greed and lust.
    A highly melodramatic and not altogether accurate account of the charlatan monk with a huge sexual appetite, played with evil relish by a heavily bearded Christopher Lee, who wormed his way into the higher echelons of Russian society, only to become a dangerous menace that eventually had to be got rid of. Lee gives a mesmerizing performance in a production that is little more than a catalogue of the atrocities that Rasputin carried out, rather than an exercise in historical authenticity. These include chopping off a man's hand, throwing acid in the face of another, and seducing the Tsarina's lady-in-waiting, Barbara Shelley, who then commits suicide. The ending is suitably over-the-top as befits a Hammer production, with the mad monk being poisoned, stabbed, shot and thrown into a river before finally expiring. Double billed with *The Reptile*, this was only partly successful at the box office—perhaps the subject matter did not really appeal to a wider audience.

The Raven
Universal 1935; 62 mins; Cert. "X"
CREDITS: Producer: David Diamond; Director: Louis Friedlander
CAST: Bela Lugosi; Boris Karloff; Irene Ware; Samuel Hinds; Ian Wolfe; Lester Matthews ***
    A gangster on the run demands a new face from an eminent but insane surgeon and ends up mad and disfigured.
    An enjoyable mixture of horror and Edgar Allan Poe, with Lugosi hamming it up deliciously, playing a mad surgeon obsessed by Poe who keeps a torture chamber in his house as a shrine to the novelist and poet. He also lusts after Irene Ware, whom he operated on after she was disfigured in a car crash. Karloff is the bearded killer, a fugitive from San Quentin, calling on Lugosi and demanding a new face. He ends up terribly scarred after the surgeon tampers with his nerve endings, his features twisted down one side as a result. After becoming the surgeon's unwilling assistant on the promise of a new face, Karloff is eventually shot after saving Ware from Lugosi's clutches, and the surgeon is crushed to death between moving walls. This was a stylish little shocker featuring Universal's two major horror stars—it even threw in a *Pit and the Pendulum*-type sequence toward the end. In 1964, it was screened at selected small cinemas in the United Kingdom with 1934's *The Black Cat*.

The Reptile
Hammer/Seven Arts 1966; Technicolor; 91 mins; Cert. "X"
CREDITS: Producer: Anthony Nelson-Keys; Director: John Gilling
CAST: Noel Willman; Ray Barrett; Jacqueline Pearce; Jennifer Daniel; Michael Ripper; Marne Maitland ***
    A young woman brought back to England from Malaya changes periodically into a hideous snake-creature.

Made back-to-back with *The Plague of the Zombies*, this unusual Hammer movie has a nice atmosphere of unease about it and is slightly different from their normal fare, although it does take time to get going. Noel Willman plays a doctor living in a Cornish village with his mysterious daughter, Jacqueline Pearce, who has the ability to transform herself into a snake-like creature as punishment for her father's lustful desires and after he has gained forbidden knowledge of the black arts in Malaya. Barrett and Daniel are the young couple

who arrive at the village to find out the reason why Barrett's brother has died from a strange bite, which is also claiming other lives. The monster, aroused by heat and sensual emotion, awakens every so often to claim more victims, and then retires to sleep near a sulfur pit in the cellar of the house. Pearce's snake makeup is a bit obvious, but scenes of her writhing in lust on her bed as her servant chants to her are both creepy and loathsome. The obligatory inferno at the climax finishes off Pearce after she has bitten her father to death. A persuasive little chiller, well directed by John Gilling, and originally released with *Rasputin the Mad Monk*.

Reptilicus
Cinemagic/American Intl. (Denmark) 1962; Pathecolor; 90 mins; Cert. "A"
CREDITS: Producer/Director: Sidney Pink
CAST: Carl Ottosen; Ann Smyrner; Mimi Heinrich; Asbjorn Anderson; Marla Behrens; Bent Mejding *

The tail of a prehistoric reptile is discovered in a bog in Lapland and transported to a laboratory where it regenerates itself into the original monster and goes on a rampage in Denmark.

This uninspiring film, ranking among the worst monster-on-the-loose pictures ever produced, has one half-decent scene—that of the oil exploration team digging up the bloody remains of the monster's tail in the wilds of Lapland. After that, the proverbial rot sets in. The remains are taken to Copenhagen and, after being given nutrients, regenerate into the monster during an electrical storm. The creature itself is almost as unconvincing in its appearance as the bird in *The Giant Claw*, resembling a poorly constructed puppet moving and flying around model buildings that supposedly depict Copenhagen. Reptilicus is finally destroyed by having its scales removed after being rendered unconscious and blown up with a poisoned rocket, but pieces of the creature threaten to regenerate all over again into a new monster, paving the way for a sequel that thankfully never materialized. The American version omitted the scenes of Reptilicus flying, as they were so badly conceived, and substituted these with shots of the monster spewing forth green slime over people which were just as fake-looking—the Danish print was also 10 minutes longer.

Return of the Ape Man
Monogram/Favorite Films 1944; 60 mins; Cert. "A"
CREDITS: Producers: Sam Katzman and Jack Dietz; Director: Philip Rosen
CAST: Bela Lugosi; John Carradine; George Zucco; Frank Moran; Michael Ames; Judith Gibson
**

A scientist revives an apeman discovered in the Arctic in a block of ice and gives it another scientist's brain to make it more human.

A typical low-budget potboiler of the 1940s with Lugosi and Carradine going through the motions as a pair of scientists who thaw one of the screen's ropiest-looking apemen, Frank Moran, from the ice and bring him back to life. When Carradine objects to Lugosi inserting a portion of a human brain inside the head of the Neanderthal to advance his mind and cure his antisocial behavior, Lugosi murders him and transplants his brain into the primitive creature, which turns it into a killer, although as a sign of the human traits he has inherited, he gets to play the piano and utter a few words. The apeman goes on a rampage, bumping off Carradine's wife, while Lugosi attempts to control it with the aid of a blowtorch, but eventually the scientist is killed by his creation and they both go up in flames.

Return of the Fly
20th Century Fox 1959; Cinemascope; 78 mins; Cert. "X"
CREDITS: Producer: Bernard Glasser; Director: Edward L. Bernds
CAST: Vincent Price; Brett Halsey; David Frankham; John Sutton; Danielle DeMezt; Pat O'Hara
****

Years after the death of the inventor of the matter-transference machine, his son takes up the experiments and he too becomes part man, part fly.

A fast-paced follow-up to *The Fly* with Vincent Price reprising his role as the brother of the inventor who, to no avail, warns Brett Halsey about the dire consequences of continuing in his father's footsteps. Halsey, however, becomes obsessed with his father's apparatus and soon has the transmitters working with financial help from Price, but following a fight with his criminal assistant, David Frankham, who wants to sell the plans of the experiments to the highest bidder, he and a fly are placed in one of the pods. When Price unknowingly activates the disintegrater/integrater, Halsey emerges as the fly-monster. A snooping police inspector is also dumped into one of the transmitters with a rat, and Frankham destroys the resulting monstrosity. The scenes of Halsey as the fly-creature (he has a much larger head than the monster in the first film) stumbling about in the bushes and creeping around the house are quite eerie. This is one horror movie with a happy ending—Halsey is changed back into a man again and reunited with his girlfriend. The success of *Return of the Fly* called for a third outing, but this wasn't made until 1965—the inferior *Curse of the Fly*.

The Return of the Vampire
Columbia 1943; 69 mins; Cert. "X"
CREDITS: Producer: Sam White; Director: Lew Landers
CAST: Bela Lugosi; Matt Willis; Nina Foch; Frieda Inescort; Gilbert Emery; Miles Mander
****

During the London blitz, workmen accidentally revive a vampire count who, with the aid of his werewolf assistant, befriends a family for more victims.

Dracula aside, the role of the 200-year-old Count Armand Tesla was without doubt Lugosi's finest performance as one of the undead in a densely plotted thriller, with the added bonus of an unwilling werewolf played by Matt Willis. In 1918, a professor researching vampirism and having access to the records relating to Tesla's activities tracks down Lugosi, who has been terrorizing his family, to a cemetery and drives a stake through his heart. The family, who feel sorry for him, befriends Willis, the vampire's werewolf assistant. Over 20 years later during a bombing raid, the stake is removed from Lugosi's corpse and the revived vampire takes out his vengeance on the same family, desiring to enlist Nina Foch as his bride and forcing Willis back into his werewolf state to carry out his wishes. The unfortunate Willis eventually brings about the vampire's demise by dragging him into the sun from his resting place where he promptly disintegrates, a scene cut by the British censor on initial release but restored in later prints. With a cracking opening sequence set in a misty graveyard, this was one of the '40s most outstanding vampire movies and was still being screened theatrically as late as 1966, when it went the rounds in England with *Jack the Ripper*.

The Revenge of Frankenstein
Hammer/Columbia 1958; Technicolor; 91 mins; Cert. "X"
CREDITS: Producer: Anthony Hinds; Director: Terence Fisher
CAST: Peter Cushing; Michael Gwynn; Francis Mathews; Eunice Gayson; Lionel Jeffries; John Welsh *****

Having escaped death by the guillotine, Baron Frankenstein, under the auspices of a medical practice, creates another creature from body parts.

Hammer's follow-up to *The Curse of Frankenstein* was an expensive, well-mounted and highly successful production photographed in rich Technicolor, with Peter Cushing once again excelling himself in the role of the doctor, rescued from the gallows by Karl, his crippled, hunchbacked assistant. As a reward for saving his life, Cushing, with the help of a young doctor played by Francis Mathews, puts the brain of Karl into the "normal" body that he has created, but with disastrous results. When Michael Gwynn as the rather well-mannered creation returns to the laboratory to dispose of his old body, he disturbs the janitor, who beats him so badly that his brain becomes damaged and he slowly begins to degenerate into his previous crippled form, escaping from Cushing's laboratory and committing murder. The climax has Gwynn, now twisted, deformed and crazed, literally gatecrashing a soiree and exposing Frankenstein to the horrified guests. Although the Baron is battered to near death at the end of the movie by his outraged patients, who realize that they have been used by him for spare body parts in his experiments, Mathews performs a transplant operation on his broken body and he emerges in one piece in London as Doctor Franck, meaning that Cushing was back for a third time in 1964's *The Evil of Frankenstein*.

Revenge of the Creature
Universal 1954; Orig. in 3-D; 82 mins; Cert. "X"
CREDITS: Producer: William Alland; Director: Jack Arnold
CAST: John Agar; Lori Nelson; Nestor Paiva; John Bromfield; Robert B. Williams; Dave Willock ****

The creature is captured in a backwater of the Amazon and put on display at a sea-life center in Miami, but it breaks loose and terrorizes the town.

The incredible success of *Creature from the Black Lagoon* produced two sequels, this one being the first that was almost as good as the original and certainly a lot more violent in tone

TERROR IS LOOSE IN THE CITY!

REVENGE OF THE CREATURE

ALL NEW THRILLS! SHOCK! SUSPENSE!

JOHN AGAR · LORI NELSON · JOHN BROMFIELD

NESTOR PAIVA

than its predecessor. Captured and brought back from the Amazon in a coma, the gill-man is revived and kept in a tank in the Ocean Harbor Seaquarium in Miami as the main attraction. Once there, the obligatory love interest between John Agar and Lori Nelson goes on a bit in the middle of the film, with too many shots of visitors staring at the gill-man in his tank chained to the floor, and protracted scenes of Agar and Nelson carrying out experiments in an attempt to humanize the monster. But when the creature escapes from his man-made prison into the dazzling Miami sunlight, causing panic among the crowds, the action quickens up and Jack Arnold expertly manipulates his creation against an urban background instead of the jungles of the previous film. Favorite scene—the creature lurching in on a party where a jazz band is playing, much to the consternation of the customers, and carrying off Lori Nelson. The climax sees the creature again endeavoring to drag Nelson back into the sea, only for it to be gunned down by the police as it frantically tries to swim to safety. Clint Eastwood, in his screen debut, appears for all of two minutes as a laboratory technician with a rat problem!

Robinson Crusoe on Mars
Paramount 1964; Techniscope/Technicolor; 109 mins; Cert. "U"
CREDITS: Producer: Aubrey Schenck; Director: Byron Haskin
CAST: Paul Mantee; Vic Lundin; Adam West ****
    A lone U.S. astronaut becomes marooned on Mars and befriends a native who is on the run from deadly alien spacecraft.
    A surprisingly inventive and quite vivid '60s fantasy, filmed in America's Death Valley to simulate the Martian landscape. Paul Mantee is the sole survivor of an expedition to Mars when his spaceship crashes on the planet. To escape the fierce temperatures of the Martian terrain, he finds a cave to inhabit with his pet monkey and discovers that heating various rocks supplies him with life-preserving oxygen. Vic Lundin plays a slave who escapes the alien ships that visit Mars to exploit the minerals there (the spacecraft resemble the fighting machines in *The War of the Worlds*) and he becomes Mantee's Man Friday. There are some imaginative views of the Martian canals and of the alien spacecraft blasting the pair with rays, forcing them to head north on a long trek toward the Martian pole to locate water and find a way to escape from the planet. When a meteor crashes into the polar cap, it causes the ice to melt, which nearly finishes them off. In the end, they manage to contact another Earth rocket and are presumably rescued.

Robot Monster
Astor 1953; Orig. in 3-D; 63 mins; Cert. "A"
CREDITS: Producer/Director: Phil Tucker
CAST: George Nadar; Claudia Barrett; Gregory Moffett; Selena Royle; John Mylong; Pamela Paulson *
    "Ro-men" have decimated the Earth with ray guns, leaving only six survivors in a battle for survival.
    Tiresome, cheap and virtually unwatchable, *Robot Monster* is in the same league as *Bride of the Monster* and other inferior productions of the 1950s, with the well-publicized monster

turning out to be a man in a gorilla suit wearing a diving helmet with antennae on top of it. The human survivors of the Ro-Men's invasion have invented a serum that makes them immune to the Ro-Man's ray gun and spend most of the film trying to dodge the monster, which forms an unrealistic attachment to Claudia Barrett. Footage from the 1940 *One Million B.C.* is thrown in for good measure as rays used against Earth have reactivated various dinosaurs, and in the end the whole scenario turns out to be a dream—Gregory Moffett wakes up and the nightmare is over. Made at a paltry cost of $20,000 in four days, the film's one saving grace was its mercifully short running time, although it has achieved a cult status among fans of the truly awful over the years.

Rodan
Toho/King Bros./DCA (Japan) 1956; Technicolor; 79 mins; Cert. "X" CREDITS: Producer: Tomoyuki Tanaka; Director: Inoshiro Honda CAST: Kenji Sahara; Yumi Shirakawa; Yasuko Nakata; Akio Kobori; Akihiko Hirata; Minosuki Yamada
*****

Atomic bomb tests in the Pacific cause collapses in a coal mine, unleashing huge caterpillar-type bugs called Meganuron onto the local populace. Also disturbed after centuries of being entombed are two giant flying reptiles that escape from the mine, causing widespread destruction in Japan.

Before Toho began aiming their pictures at a more juvenile audience in the 1960s, making their monsters more friendly, their earlier films such as the original *Godzilla* had a harder edge and a more adult approach; hence *Rodan*'s "X" rating. This was the first Toho production in color, probably ranking as their best and most successful—fast-paced, imaginative, noisy and great fun. It ran for years after release, often billed with a diverse mix of films such as *The Deadly Mantis*, *Plan 9 from Outer Space* or even *The Fiend Who Walked the West*. Following atomic bomb tests in the Pacific, a coal mine in Japan experiences extensive cave-ins, with several miners mysteriously disappearing, their mangled bodies recovered in the flooded passages. The local village is then attacked by a huge species of carnivorous insect that appears to have emerged from the depths of the mine. The early scenes inside the gloomy mine tunnels, before the Meganurons attack the miners and the military, produce a chilling sense of unease. When the bugs are wiped out, Kenji Sahara as Shigeru becomes trapped and lost in another cave-in. Reports then come in of a strange flying object that has caused planes to crash and left two lovers dead on the edge of a volcano. Shigeru is found in a confused state and has lost his memory. He regains it by seeing a bird's egg hatching in a cage and then remembers discovering one of the monster's colossal eggs in a vast chamber, with the giant reptile hatching in a series of roars and pecking at the Meganuron bugs for food. The special effects depicting Rodan's attack on the city of Sasebo are first-class and far less derivative than in later Toho features, and the movie ends in a fiery, explosive climax as the army blasts the volcano where the monsters are hiding, causing an eruption that finally destroys them in the resulting lava flow. The Japanese print was several minutes longer than the U.S. and U.K. versions. Although the Americans added extra footage at the beginning showing A-bomb tests, several edits were made to quicken up the pace of the film that worked, even though the dubbing, as usual, left a lot to be desired.

Rosemary's Baby
Paramount 1968; Technicolor; 137 mins; Cert. "X"
CREDITS: Producer: William Castle; Director: Roman Polanski
CAST: Mia Farrow; John Cassavetes; Ruth Gordon; Ralph Bellamy; Patsy Kelly; Sydney Blackmer ***
A young couple who decide to rent rooms in a block of Manhattan apartments are unwittingly drawn into a coven of Satanists.

John Cassavetes and Mia Farrow move into an apartment in Manhattan that has a sinister reputation. Almost immediately, Cassavetes becomes involved with a circle of Devil-worshippers, who promise him success as an actor on condition that his unsuspecting wife is offered to the Devil for impregnation. One night, she is raped by a demon. When she becomes pregnant, the neighbors embrace Farrow as one of their own, fussing over her and treating her like their daughter. When the baby is born, Rosemary is quickly ushered from the room, but later goes back to an upstairs apartment filled with strangers, hovering over a cot that contains her satanic infant. Farrow finally accepts her fate and cradles the baby in her arms. *Rosemary's Baby* kick-started the cinema's morbid fascination with the Devil, culminating in *The Exorcist*, and has a disturbingly claustrophobic atmosphere about it, although at over two hours long there are moments when the film lapses into tedium and becomes heavy-handed. The rape scene was cut by the British censor but restored to prints a few years later, and Ruth Gordon as the kindly but evil old neighbor won an Oscar for best supporting actress. Veteran director/producer William Castle did a "Hitchcock" and featured himself very briefly outside of the apartment block, standing by a phone booth.

The Saragossa Manuscript
Kamera/Contemporary (Poland) 1964; Dyaliscope; 182 mins; Cert. "X"
CREDITS: Producer: Riszard Straszeuski; Director: Wojciech Jerzy Has
CAST: Zbigniew Cybulski; Kazimierz Opalinski; Iga Cembrzynska; Joanna Jedryka; Slawomir Linder; Miroslawa Lombardo *****
During the Napoleonic Wars, two soldiers on opposing sides in a battle discover a large ornate book in a house that has the ability to tell a multitude of stories woven around the supernatural.

The main character in this intricately plotted masterpiece is Count Alphonse van Worden, played by noted Polish actor Zbigniew Cybulski, embarking on a journey across the arid Spanish mountains to Madrid. He spends the night in a deserted inn and encounters two princesses who may or may not be phantoms. From then on, the film develops into a number of riddles, conundrums and fanciful stories within stories, particularly during the final 90 minutes, whereby at least four tales are unfolding simultaneously, all relating to debauched royalty, bewitching women, ghosts, mystical priests, demons and various intrigues. The ambiguous ending has Cybulski being informed that he has undergone a series of challenges to prove the worth of his soul—he is last seen galloping off into the wilderness in pursuit of the two princesses. Given a limited showing at a few art-house cinemas in the United Kingdom and shorn by 30 minutes (in the United States, the version was almost an hour shorter), Has' surreal epic, superbly photographed in glacial black and white and based on the old campfire storytelling days of years gone by, demanded 100% concentration from the audiences watching it and took no prisoners—one either loved it or loathed it. One thing is certain—its like was never repeated. The full-length director's cut lasting three hours has recently been issued on DVD.

The Scars of Dracula
Hammer/EMI 1970; Technicolor; 96 mins; Cert. "X"
CREDITS: Producer: Aida Young; Director: Roy Ward Baker
CAST: Christopher Lee; Dennis Waterman; Jenny Hanley; Patrick Troughton; Christopher Matthews; Michael Gwynn **
    Revived by a bat vomiting blood over his ashes, Count Dracula proceeds to terrorize the local villagers and a trio of youngsters who have unwittingly strayed into his castle.
    Relocating the action back to a European setting for fresh impetus, Lee's fifth outing as Dracula was another big disappointment. Sadism and brutality had crept into the plot, showing scenes of Lee stabbing his mistress to death, whipping his crippled manservant Patrick Troughton into submission, and a priest being slaughtered by man-eating bats. One or two sequences in the castle were moderately spooky, such as the vampire crawling down the castle walls like a grotesque caped lizard, but the film was woodenly directed by Baker, with unsympathetic performances from the cast except for Lee, who was as solid as ever, even in these trying circumstances. In the climax, Lee is impaled (yet again!) on a lightning rod and topples from the battlements in flames. Despite the movie's shortcomings, it fared slightly better than the abysmal *The Horror of Frankenstein*, with which it originally appeared on a double bill.

Scream and Scream Again
Amicus/American Intl. 1969; Eastmancolor; 94 mins; Cert. "X"
CREDITS: Producers: Max J. Rosenberg and Milton Subotsky; Director: Gordon Hessler
CAST: Vincent Price; Christopher Lee; Alfred Marks; Peter Cushing; Anthony Newlands; Peter Sallis **
    A mad scientist creates superhuman beings out of various synthetic body parts to enable him to control the government with humanoids.
    This was a real ragbag of a film combining surgical horror, repulsive murders and a detective story, none of which really gelled as a whole, the result being a bit of a disjointed mess. Price played a doctor creating humanoids from synthetic body parts composed of real amputated limbs and artificial ones, using a convenient vat of acid to dispose of any unwanted tissue. In probably the most effective sequence, one of his creations, having gone berserk and committed murders in the style of a vampire, is chased by the police, tearing off his own hand from handcuffs to escape the law and eventually disposing of himself in the vat of acid in Price's laboratory. Price himself turns out to be a synthetic humanoid, as does Christopher Lee as a police inspector who, after Price is killed, calls a halt to the investigation, knowing that as one of the humanoids, he can carry on with Price's work. Peter Cushing made an appearance as well. This was the only picture that united the three latter-day stalwarts of horror. The movie appeared to be a patchwork of ideas from several other productions, dressed up in the kind of frantic violence that was a hallmark of late 1960s cinema, and was not a great success when first released; the clumsy title didn't help either.

The Screaming Skull
American Intl. 1958; 68 mins; Cert. "X"
CREDITS: Producer: John Kneubuhl; Director: Alex Nicol
CAST: Alex Nicol; John Hudson; Peggy Webber; Russ Conway; Tony Johnson ***

A man attempts to drive his wife insane when they spend the night in a reputedly haunted house.

Peggy Webber, recently released from a mental institution, is taken to Alex Nicol's creepy old mansion left to him by his first wife, who was killed in mysterious circumstances and who littered the house with dozens of human skulls. Nicol is after Webber's money, and by manipulating the skulls to his own advantage, he hopes to drive her mad and get his hands on her inheritance. She almost teeters on the edge of madness as the skulls start popping up all over the place, but supernatural events intervene and Nicol is himself killed at the end by a horde of phantom skulls that pursue him, one of which bites him to death. Produced on a low budget, the movie went all out for cheap visual effects such as the skulls floating through the air, distorted camera angles and a weird soundtrack, and ended up as a grade B Gothic melodrama, quite atmospheric in its own unassuming way. In the early 1960s, it went the rounds double billed with either *Teenage Caveman* or *Earth vs. the Spider*.

The Search for Bridey Murphy
Paramount 1956; VistaVision; 84 mins; Cert. "X"
CREDITS: Producer: Pat Duggan; Director: Noel Langley
CAST: Louis Hayward; Teresa Wright; Kenneth Tobey; Nancy Gates; Richard Anderson; Tom McKee ****

A doctor, after undertaking an intensive course in the techniques of hypnosis, experiments on a friend's wife, who regresses back to a previous existence as a housemaid in 19th-century Ireland.

This film version of Morey Bernstein's bestseller of the early 1950s, which itself was based on a true story of an American housewife undergoing hypnosis and recounting her past life, is a somewhat wordy affair for the first 20 minutes. Things improve when Louis Hayward hypnotizes Kenneth Tobey's wife, Teresa Wright, who then, over several sessions, relates to Hayward and his astonished friends details of her previous life as an Irish girl called Bridey Murphy, from her birth in 1798 to her death in 1864, and also her existence beyond the grave. Wright gives a nerve-tingling performance in an otherwise pedestrian, workmanlike production as Hayward, ignoring warnings from other doctors, presses her for more information on her previous existence, even regressing her further back to when she was a young child dying from an incurable disease in America. The climax, when Hayward is unable to bring Wright out of her trance and she is caught in her Bridey Murphy persona, is a genuinely disturbing moment, although she becomes her normal self in the end. This was one of a number of "regression through hypnosis" pictures made around the time, and is probably the most rewarding, as it was given the more adult treatment.

Seddok—Son of Satan
aka: Atom Age Vampire
Lyons Film/Topaz (Italy) 1960; 105 mins; Cert. "X"
CREDITS: Producer: Mario Bava; Director: Anton Giulio Majano
CAST: Alberto Lupo; Susanne Loret; Roberto Berta; Sergio Fantoni; Franca Parisi; Andrea Scotti ****

A scientist transforms himself into a hideous, vampire-type monster and murders women, taking from their bodies a certain gland that will enable him to produce a serum to restore a nightclub stripper's face, horribly scarred in a car crash.

A lurid, melodramatic horror movie that effectively played on the Jekyll and Hyde theme and was one of a number of productions to emerge from the Continent which were similar in vein to Franju's *Eyes Without A Face*. Alberto Lupo, who gives a dominating performance, is the scientist experimenting in cures for cancerous deformities caused by radiation, falling in love and becoming totally obsessed with blonde Susanne Loret, a patient admitted to his clinic following a car crash that has left her badly disfigured. When his serum, called Derma 28, fails to restore her ravishing looks permanently, he turns himself into a sadistic monster to cover his tracks, taking glands from the women he kills and producing fresh quantities of the serum in an attempt to prevent Loret's scar tissue from returning. At the end, after several killings and with the singer's looks finally restored, the monster is cornered in a greenhouse after confessing to Loret that he only resorted to murder because he loved her; he is then stabbed to death by his mute assistant, changing back into human form in front of the police. The only horror film that Mario Bava produced rather than directed, *Seddok* was in England in 1963 it ran 18 minutes shorter than the original version and was very badly dubbed in stilted English.

The Seventh Voyage of Sinbad
Columbia 1958; Technicolor; 89 mins; Cert. "A"
CREDITS: Producer: Charles H. Schneer; Director: Nathan Juran; Special Effects: Ray Harryhausen
CAST: Kerwin Mathews; Kathryn Grant; Torin Thatcher; Richard Eyer; Alec Mango; Danny Green *****

Sinbad sets sail and returns to the Isle of Colossa to obtain a fragment of the eggshell from the giant roc which will restore his princess to normal size, and has to battle many monsters in his quest as well as the evil magician Sokurah.

Many critics rate *The Thief of Bagdad* as the ultimate Arabian nights fantasy, but over the years the reputation of *The Seventh Voyage of Sinbad* has put it on equal terms with its illustrious predecessor. A terrific mixture of innovative special effects (in the new process Harryhausen and Schneer termed Dynamation), colorful locations, winning performances from Kerwin Mathews and Torin Thatcher as hero and villain, and a tremendous score by Bernard Herrmann have now made this a perennial classic. The film features one of Harryhausen's favorite creations, the Cyclops, but his rather frightening appearance, together with the famous skeleton sword fight toward the end in the forbidding setting of the magician's castle, warranted the movie being given an "A" certificate from the British censor when first released, although this didn't stop it being a smash hit at the box office. In 1964, the film was severely cut (the complete skeleton duel was missing, as were several scenes involving the Cyclops, the snake-woman and even the dragon's death at the end of the film), reduced to a "U" rating and released on a double bill with *The Three Worlds of Gulliver*. In 1975, however, it was restored to its full length and included all of the scenes in the original 1958 film that were deleted from the 1964 version, even though the "U" certificate was retained, and this fantastic fairy tale relating Sinbad's adventures on the Isle of Colossa with its array of monsters became a hit all over again with a new generation of movie-goers.

Shadow of the Cat
BHP/Hammer/Universal 1961; 79 mins; Cert. "X"
CREDITS: Producer: John Pennington; Director: John Gilling
CAST: Andre Morell; Barbara Shelley; William Lucas; Freda Jackson; Andrew Crawford; Conrad Phillips ***

A husband murders his wife for her money and her pet cat appears to be responsible for a series of killings of the dead wife's enemies.

An unusual, low-budget but competent thriller, parts of which are seen through the feline's point of view, and where the cat is presented as an unstoppable force bent on revenge for the death of its mistress. By cunning stealth, it provokes Morell, Jackson and Crawford, who are behind the murder, into being killed, along with the three corrupt relatives who are brought into the house to dispose of the animal. Barbara Shelley as the victim's niece inherits the family fortune in the end, along with boyfriend Conrad Phillips. A predictable enough story is lifted out of the ordinary by the continual views of the house and its protagonists through the cat's slant-eyed distorted vision, which makes the movie just that little bit different from the usual old murder mystery.

She
Hammer/MGM 1965; Hammerscope/Technicolor; 106 mins; Cert. "A"
CREDITS: Producer: Michael Carreras; Director: Robert Day
CAST: Peter Cushing; John Richardson; Ursula Andress; Bernard Cribbins; Christopher Lee; Rosenda Monteros ***

Two former soldiers and their companion journey to a lost city hidden in a range of African mountains and encounter the immortal Ayeshea—"She who must be obeyed."

A lush, expensively produced version of H. Rider Haggard's classic tale of adventure that was not well received by the critics who probably compared it, somewhat unfairly, to the original RKO 1935 version. Cushing, Richardson and Cribbins play the three adventurers who discover the lost city of Kuma in a remote mountain range in Africa, its race of people ruled by Ursula Andress, with a glowering Christopher Lee as her high priest. Richardson is informed that he is the reincarnation of Ayeshea's long-dead lover and must enter the sacred flame with her that grants immortality every 2,000 years. In the movie's best scene, Ayeshea steps into the blue fires but her immortality is taken from her as she enters the flames twice to coerce Richardson into joining her; as a result, she decays into a haggard old woman, crumbling into dust before the horrified traveler's eyes. Richardson, however, is cursed with immortality and realizes that he has to remain in the city for another 2,000 years before he can die. Although it takes time to get moving, the film looks great, with authentic desert locations and plush sets. However, it does become slightly too wordy in the middle and the overall lack of action no doubt accounted for its less than impressive showing in British cinemas when first released.

The She-Creature
Golden State/American Intl. 1956; 77 mins; Cert. "A"
CREDITS: Producer: Alex Gordon; Director: Edward L. Cahn
CAST: Chester Morris; Tom Conway; Marla English; Cathy Downs; Lance Fuller; Ron Randall ***

A prehistoric female beast that rises from the sea is controlled by a hypnotist and kills at his bidding.

When hypnotist Chester Morris uses his powers to control his assistant Marla English, her previous self in the form of

You're Not Old Enough Son

a female sea-creature emerges from the ocean. Morris manipulates the beast through English and sends it out to commit murder, gaining fame and profit through a promoter by foretelling the crimes before they happen. English, however, falls for Lance Fuller, a young professor who is skeptical about hypnotism and past regression. In the end, jealousy causes the hypnotist to order the monster to do away with his love rival, but it disobeys, killing him instead and disappearing into the sea, leaving English in the arms of Fuller. Obviously filmed on a low budget, this was nevertheless an enjoyable if talkative little B movie, another of the '50s features dealing with hypnotism and regression, well directed by the prolific Edward L. Cahn. The original-looking monster appeared again in a slightly altered form in the 1956 *Voodoo Woman*, also directed by Cahn.

She Demons
Screencraft/Astor 1958; 77 mins; Cert. "X"
CREDITS: Producer: Arthur A. Jacobs; Director: Richard E. Cunha
CAST: Tod Griffin; Irish McCalla; Victor Sen Young; Rudolph Anders; Charlie Opuni; Gene Roth **

A mad Nazi war criminal on a remote island kidnaps young girls from another island to use them in experiments to try to cure his wife's disfigured features.

Frankenstein's Daughter was a cult, camp classic; *Missile to the Moon* an enjoyable, mind-boggling, corny romp; and *Giant from the Unknown* an unusual slice of horror hokum. *She Demons*, on the other hand, was the weakest of director Richard E. Cunha's quartet of movies released in 1958 by Astor, flatly directed with cheaply produced cardboard sets and full of ideas borrowed from a lot of other releases of this period. Four adventurers are shipwrecked on a remote volcanic island and after one of them is killed, the other three encounter mad doctor Rudolph Anders, a Nazi who is transferring the genes of kidnapped beauties to his disfigured wife, hoping to restore her looks. He only succeeds in creating a race of native women with perfect bathing beauty bodies but sporting hideous faces who all act like a pack of wild animals. Anders abducts feisty Irish McCalla to operate on, hoping that her blonde good looks will do the trick, but in the end he is interrupted by a fleet of American bombers that uses the island as target practice—the volcano erupts, Anders, his wife, the Nazis and the disfigured girls are all destroyed and Griffin, McCalla and Victor Sen Young make their escape in the nick of time.

She Devil
Regal Intl./20th Century Fox 1956; Regalscope; 77 mins; Cert. "A"
CREDITS: Producer/Director: Kurt Neumann
CAST: Jack Kelly; Mari Blanchard; Albert Dekker; John Archer; Blossom Rock; Paul Cavanagh **

A woman is cured of tuberculosis with a fruit fly serum, but the side effects cause her to transform herself into a schizophrenic killer.

This was undoubtedly Kurt Neumann's poorest effort, particularly when compared to his other works, *The Fly* and *Kronos*. Mari Blanchard, after taking the serum to cure her of TB, undergoes a personality change, her hair goes from blonde to brunette, and she acquires superhuman strength. She murders the wife of a wealthy businessman, John Archer, whom she then marries, eventually disposing of him in a car crash to benefit from his will. Kelly and Dekker finally stop Blanchard in her tracks, as the two doctors invented the serum, and she is given an antidote that drives out the demons caused by the serum but allows the tuberculosis to return, causing her to die. This was a dreary and not very original version of the Jekyll and Hyde story, turning up occasionally on the Sunday circuit in the 1960s with either *The Unknown Terror* or *The Fiend Who Walked the West*.

The Ship that Died of Shame
Ealing 1955; 91 mins; Cert. "A"
CREDITS: Producers/Directors: Michael Relph and Basil Deardon
CAST: Richard Attenborough; George Baker; Virginia McKenna; Bill Owen; Bernard Lee; Roland Culver ****
A trio of ex-navy companions buys their old wartime gunboat and uses it for smuggling purposes, but the ship itself begins to rebel against their criminal activities.
During the War, Richard Attenborough and his pals are saved on many occasions by the faultless running of their ship, which has an uncanny knack of rescuing them from all kinds of hazards. In peacetime, Attenborough and two of his compatriots rescue the vessel from a scrapyard and resort to a bit of illegal smuggling to help with their finances. Very soon, Attenborough teams up with a ruthless ex-Major and smuggling gives way to both gun-running and aiding murderers to escape the police. As a result of these murky enterprises, the ship begins to deteriorate in looks and performance, as if somehow sensing the unlawful schemes it is being used for, and creates obstacles for the crew to hinder them in their exploits. Finally, after a member of the Coast Guard is killed, the Major is shot by one of Attenborough's buddies and after a fight on deck, Attenborough himself is knocked overboard. As he clings on for safety, the ship lurches in the water and sucks him under the waves to his death. In humiliation, the vessel then destroys itself in the docks. A standard post-war thriller was given the fantasy treatment by Ealing, making the ship mirror the moral decline in its crew—a nautical Dorian Gray as it were—and a fine cast made it all appear so believable, with several eerie moments contributing to one of the more unusual of this company's '50s output, and also one of the least seen.

The Shuttered Room
Warner Bros. 1966; Technicolor; 99 mins; Cert. "X"
CREDITS: Producer: Phillip Hazelton; Director: David Greene
CAST: Carol Lynley; Gig Young; Oliver Reed; Flora Robson; William Devlin; Bernard Kay **

Returning to her New England home with her new husband, a young woman experiences traumatic events connected with her childhood spent in the house.
An unattractive mixture of a "spooky old house" thriller and typical '60s gang violence. Carole Lynley is the woman subjected to taunts from the leader of a group of thugs (an over-the-top Oliver Reed, reprising his role from *The Damned*) and realizing that something nasty lurks in the old mill-house family home in New England. It eventually turns out

to be her sister, insane and disfigured, who has been locked up in chains in a room guarded by an aging aunt, played by Flora Robson, who lets her out on occasion. Although there are some disturbing moments when the audience sees the terrified victims backing away from the sobbing, demented girl's viewpoint in the attic, the constant scenes outside in the glaring sunshine lessen any impact the film may have had and dissipate the air of menace inside the house. Reed is finally responsible for the fire that burns the house down, taking its mad occupant and the aunt with it, although Lynley and Gig Young manage to escape.

The Skull
Amicus/Paramount 1965; Techniscope/Technicolor; 90 mins; Cert. "X"
CREDITS: Producers: Max J. Rosenberg and Milton Subotsky; Director: Freddie Francis
CAST: Patrick Wymark; Peter Cushing; Jill Bennett; Christopher Lee; Michael Gough; Nigel Green ***
    A collector of occult artifacts acquires the skull of the Marquis de Sade from a dealer despite warnings that it has a demonic history.
    A colorful, lurid horror offering from Amicus, the company that gave Hammer a run for their money during the 1960s, concerning the trouble that Peter Cushing brings upon himself when he purchases the skull of the notorious sadist from Patrick Wymark, a dodgy dealer. Fellow collector Christopher Lee warns his friend that the skull casts a deadly spell over anyone who owns it, but Cushing chooses to ignore the advice and soon falls under the object's spell, hallucinating, committing murder and finally having his throat torn out. There are just a shade too many point-of-view shots from the skull's eye-sockets that detract from the main action, although scenes of the menacing skull floating about are eerily unsettling. This was one of the company's more successful pictures made during this period.

Slave Girls
aka: Prehistoric Women
Hammer/Seven Arts 1966; Cinemascope/Technicolor; 74 mins; Cert. "A"
CREDITS: Producer/Director: Michael Carreras
CAST: Martine Beswick; Edina Ronay; Michael Latimer; Carol White; Stephanie Randall; Yvonne Horner *
    A bolt of lightning transports a big game hunter in Africa back to a prehistoric tribe.
    A ridiculous slice of camp hokum, similar to *One Million Years B.C.* without the dinosaurs or *Creatures the World Forgot* without the violence. Michael Latimer is the big-game hunter trying to track down the elusive white rhinoceros and suddenly finding himself among a tribe of prehistoric Amazonian brunettes inhabiting a lost valley with blonde-haired slaves. One of the slaves, Carol White, helps him escape from Beswick's clutches, and another flash of lightning sends him back to the modern world, where he meets a young woman who is the exact double of the slave who rescued him. Twenty-one minutes were cut from the print for the U.K. release of this piece of whimsy that went the rounds as second billing to *The Devil Rides Out*. It remains one of the most bizarre productions from any of Hammer '60s output, almost as if it were put together as an afterthought after the success of *One Million Years B.C.*

The Snake Woman
United Artists 1960; 68 mins; Cert. "A"
CREDITS: Producer: George Fowler; Director: Sidney J. Furie
CAST: John McCarthy; Susan Travers; Geoffrey Danton; Arnold Marle; John Cazabon; Elsie Wagstaff **
    In the 1890s, a woman gives birth to a daughter who, because her mother has been injected with snake venom, can periodically transform herself into a cobra and kill people when threatened.

An uninventive minor thriller from the same team that created all the lurid histrionics in *Doctor Blood's Coffin*. Susan Travers grows up alone after her mother dies in childbirth and her doctor father is killed. A detective, John McCarthy, is sent to a remote village on the moors in the West of England to investigate a series of mysterious killings related to the doctor's death, and hears rumors from the local villagers of a strange snake woman in the area who may be responsible. McCarthy notices that Travers, whom he becomes friendly with, responds in an odd way to the sound of a flute, and he eventually uncovers her as the culprit by charming the killer snake with the same musical instrument, killing it, only for it to change back to the young girl in human form. In 1963, the film, a watered-down forerunner of Hammer's *The Reptile*, briefly went the rounds on a double bill with *The Split*.

The Snow Creature
Planet Filmways/United Artists 1954; 69 mins; Cert. "A"
CREDITS: Producer/Director: W. Lee Wilder
CAST: Paul Langton; Leslie Denison; Teru Shimada; Robert Kino; Robert Hinton; Rollin Moriyama **

In the Himalayas, the wife of a Sherpa is abducted by an Abominable Snowman and on pursuing the creature, the expedition discovers another Yeti, which they capture and take back to Los Angeles.

This, the first of the Abominable Snowman films of the 1950s, was a fast-moving B feature made on a shoestring budget, although still fun to watch, with surprisingly realistic Himalayan settings in the first half to complement the action. After avoiding the traps set by the Yetis in the mountains, one of the beasts is eventually captured in a cave by botanist Paul Langton and his team. It is then transported to Los Angeles, where it breaks loose from its cage and goes on a rampage, hiding out in the city's sewers until it is finally caught in a net and shot by the police. Disappointingly, the movie's main failing is the Yeti itself, which is a bit shabby to say the least, seen mostly in shadow; however, this was still an enjoyable little picture that appeared on a double billing with *The Fantastic Disappearing Man* in 1963 on the Sunday circuit.

Son of Dracula
Universal 1943; 79 mins; Cert. "A"
CREDITS: Producer: Ford Beebe; Director: Robert Siodmak
CAST: Lon Chaney Jr.; Robert Paige; Evelyn Ankers; Frank Craven; J. Edward Bromberg; Louis Allbritten **

Count Dracula's son arrives in America and goes in search of new victims.

A well-mounted, atmospheric movie from the Universal '40s horror stable but, rather unusually for this company, not all that sinister in either mood or tone and Lon Chaney, sporting a moustache, looked far too well-built for the part of a vampire. Calling himself Anthony Alucard (spell it backwards!), he arrives from Budapest as a guest of Louise Allbritten, who soon finds herself under his spell, yearning for immortality with him. This was the first film to feature the vampire changing into a bat, achieved by special effects ace John Fulton, and the scene of Chaney materializing from smoke in his coffin, which glides across the misty water like a ghostly punt, was also nicely done. Robert Paige burns the vampire's coffin at the end and Chaney dies in the rising sun. Scriptwriter Curt Siodmak came up with an admittedly stylish production that had too much talk and very little in the way of thrills, even though the excellent cast gave it their all.

Son of Frankenstein
Universal 1939; 95 mins; Cert. "X"
CREDITS: Producer/Director: Rowland V. Lee
CAST: Basil Rathbone; Boris Karloff: Bela Lugosi; Lionel Atwill; Josephine Hutchinson; Lionel Belmore ****

Frankenstein's son returns to his father's castle and with the aid of Ygor, a broken-necked shepherd, reactivates his father's monster.

One of Universal's most lavishly produced horror films of the 1930s and also, at 95 minutes, one of the longest. Basil Rathbone plays the son, restoring his father's derelict castle and laboratory with the aid of Lugosi as Ygor, who locates the monster in a pit of sulfur. Rathbone, unbeknown to his wife, then periodically sneaks off to the laboratory and sets about reactivating the monster, with Ygor acting as Karloff's nurse. The bizarre angled sets gave the film a distinctly Germanic look and the only minus point about the whole production was Karloff as the monster, mute and slightly nondescript in the role compared to his previous two films in the series, and looking very bulky in a sheepskin jacket. Lionel Atwill is the police inspector who, along with Rathbone in the film's climax, dispatches the monster back into the sulfur pit from whence he came before he can harm Rathbone's little son. Atwill promptly loses his false arm in the process. The film marked the end of Universal's trio of classic *Frankenstein* films—the series continued into the '40s, with new monsters and characters added to boost the appeal at the box office.

Son of Godzilla
Toho/American Intl. (Japan) 1968; Tohoscope/Technicolor; 86 mins; Cert. "A"
CREDITS: Producer: Tomoyuki Tanaka; Director: Jun Fukuda
CAST: Tadao Takashima; Akira Kubo; Bibari Maeda; Akihiko Mirata; Yoshio Tsuchiya; Kenji Sahara **

Godzilla's son is born on an island and is threatened by several monsters.

The Godzilla films produced by Toho had now reached a stage in the late 1960s whereby only a very young audience could appreciate the antics of these rubber-suited monsters on the big screen, the older audience having given up on them many moons ago. This one featured a baby Godzilla, born on an island where weather experiments have caused all of the plants and animals to grow to an enormous size because of the rising temperatures. Godzilla comes to the rescue when the infant is attacked both by a giant spider called Spigon and a huge preying mantis, and the pair are eventually forced to go into hibernation when the scientists freeze the island, which has become too dangerous a place for humans to live. This was a fairly childish addition to the series, with silly comic overtones and a very long way indeed from the 1954 original, having a spasmodic and unsuccessful run in England throughout 1969.

The Son of Kong
RKO-Radio 1933; 70 mins; Cert. "A"
CREDITS: Producer: Merian C. Cooper; Director: Ernest B. Schoedsack; Special Effects: Willis O'Brien
CAST: Robert Armstrong; Helen Mack; Frank Reicher; Noble Johnson; Victor Wong; John Marston ***

Escaping from his creditors, film producer Carl Denham and an assorted crew of adventurers return to Skull Island in search of a rumored horde of treasure and meet up with King Kong's son.

Rush-released to cash in on the enormous success of *King Kong*, the follow-up has its moments but it seems to take an age for Robert Armstrong, Helen Mack and Frank Reicher to reach Skull Island, even though the film is only 70 minutes long. Baby Kong is white-haired, 12 feet high, and friendly toward man, warding off a Styracosaurus and a huge bear after Armstrong rescues him from a swamp. Kong, following Armstrong and company around like a big amiable puppy dog, shows the travelers a vast cave in an old temple containing precious jewels before they are attacked again, this time by a dragon-like dinosaur that Kong defeats. At the picture's climax, an earthquake causes a tidal wave to sweep the island, drowning the ape as Armstrong and company make their escape, with Skull Island finally sinking into the storm-tossed sea. Even though some of the animation in this production was an improvement on *King Kong* and the movie had the same lovingly produced glass backdrops, Willis O'Brien was less than happy with the semi-comic results (it was never, in a million years, going to live up to the reputation of its illustrious predecessor), and despite tinkering with several projects that never saw the light of day did not really work on any other major film until *Mighty Joe Young* in 1949.

The Sorcerors
Tigon 1967; Eastmancolor; 87 mins; Cert. "X"
CREDITS: Producers: Patrick Curtis and Tony Tenser; Director: Michael Reeves
CAST: Boris Karloff; Catherine Lacey; Ian Ogilvy; Elizabeth Ercy; Victor Henry; Susan George
**

An elderly couple possesses a device that enables them to experience various thrills through the taking over of a young man's body.

Karloff and Lacey play the old, staid couple who, through a device coupled with telepathy, live out the experiences of teenager Ian Ogilvy—they can also influence him to carry out further actions according to their whims. The experiment goes horribly wrong when Lacey forces the youth to rob and commit murder to heighten her thrill level. Eventually Karloff, realizing that what they are doing is morally wrong, forces Ogilvy to crash his car and die while on the run from the police for murder, and the resulting explosion burns the old couple to death. Similar to many films of the late '60s, the emphasis here was on sex and violence as opposed to straight storytelling, and the movie featured a particularly vicious and quite graphic moment when Ogilvy stabs Susan George to death with a pair of scissors. The film therefore became just another standard '60s shocker with little to recommend it, and director Reeves' next project was the even more violent, but far superior, *Witchfinder General*.

The Space Children
Paramount 1958; VistaVision; 71 mins; Cert. "U"
CREDITS: Producer: William Alland; Director: Jack Arnold
CAST: Adam Williams; Peggy Webber; Michael Ray; Johnny Crawford; Jackie Coogan; Sandy Descher ***

The children of personnel at a U.S. rocket base dealing with H-bombs that they plan to launch into space are compelled by a telepathic peaceful alien to sabotage the base.

This marked the final science fiction film that Jack Arnold made in the 1950s and the only one given a "U" certificate—a far cry from the "X" certificate horrors of *Creature from the Black Lagoon* and *Tarantula*. The desert landscapes of Arnold's previous movies are here replaced by the windswept California cliffs and restless sea, as the children wander along the shoreline and discover the alien in a cave. It resembles a large glowing brain. Arnold cleverly allows the audience to enter the children's world with their mistrust of adults and their gang mentality, and the alien brain becomes their friend and ally as it employs them to sabotage the launch of an atomic missile. The military eventually confronts the alien and children in the cave, and are told that similar creatures have landed on Earth and immobilized all nuclear weapons. The film was not one of Arnold's more successful features and was released at the time with *The Colossus of New York*.

Spacemaster X-7
Regal Intl./20th Century Fox 1958; Regalscope; 71 mins; Cert. "A"
CREDITS: Producer: Bernard Glasser; Director: Edward Bernds
CAST: Bill Williams; Robert Ellis; Lyn Thomas; Paul Frees; Joan Berry; Thomas B. Henry **

A space satellite returns to Earth from Mars with a strange alien fungus on board that multiplies and consumes everything when mixed with blood.

A *Quatermass*-type story that starts off well enough, with the plastic-looking fungus drooping all over the walls of the space probe and devouring a doctor, Paul Frees, when it mixes with his blood. After Lyn Thomas, the doctor's lover, has unknowingly come into contact with the fungus and tries to flee to Hawaii, the film becomes interminably bogged down in a semi-documentary plot concerned solely with investigating agents trying to track Thomas down before she can spread the fungus spores, which feed on human blood, and destroy the world. She is eventually captured and decontaminated, returning to normal and destroying the alien infestation at the same time. This was a typical cheapish effort from Regal, similar to their other works during the mid to late '50s—once again, the widescreen photography made it watchable.

The Split
aka: The Manster
Breakston/Lopert/United Artists (U.S./Japan) 1959; 72 mins; Cert. "X"
CREDITS: Producer: George P. Breakston; Directors: George P. Breakston and Kenneth G. Crane
CAST: Peter Dyneley; Jane Hylton; Satoshi Nakamura; Terry Zimmern; Jerry Ito; Toyoko Takeichi **

A doctor experimenting with an enzyme causes a man to grow another head, which then becomes a separate creature.

A bizarre American/Japanese co-production that had a limited release in the United Kingdom in 1963 with *The Snake Woman*. Professor Nakamura has already changed his wife into a dwarf and his brother into an albino-type ape by using an experimental enzyme. Peter Dyneley as a newspaper reporter tests some of the enzyme potion on himself that Nakamura has been experimenting with, then begins to sprout hair, fangs, and a weird-looking eye on his shoulder, personifying his evil other-self. The eye then gradually develops into another monstrous head. Now a rampaging monster, he kills the doctor and captures his female assistant, Terry Zimmern, dragging her off to an active volcano, where the gases cause him to split into two separate beings. The hairy monster that emerges pushes the girl into the volcano and Dyneley, restored to normal, hurls the creature to its death into the depths of the volcano.

The Strange Door
Universal 1951; 80 mins; Cert. "A"
CREDITS: Producer: Ted Richmond; Director: Joseph Pevney

CAST: Boris Karloff; Charles Laughton; Sally Forest; Michael Pate; Alan Napier; Paul Cavanagh ***

A 17th-century insane nobleman resides over a castle full of torture instruments, which he uses against his enemies.

A melodramatic slice of hokum that has the feel of an Edgar Allan Poe movie about it, years before Roger Corman entered the scene and directed *The Fall of the House of Usher* and *The Pit and the Pendulum*, both of which in some ways it resembles. Charles Laughton is the nobleman who has his brother, Paul Cavanagh, incarcerated in his dungeon as he dared to marry Laughton's childhood sweetheart, who subsequently died in childbirth. Laughton brings their daughter up as his own and tries to marry her off to a local villain as his long-term plan of revenge. When the villain changes his ways, Laughton goes madder still and throws the pair into his dungeons as well. Karloff has a guest role as a sympathetic butler, somehow managing to avoid being killed by the nobleman and saving the three prisoners as his master sets a series of crushing movable walls in motion to dispose of them—Laughton finally falls to his death in the huge wheel that drives the mechanism. A good cast saves the film from being just another period-cum-horror thriller and Laughton is suitably over-the-top and hammy in the main role.

The Strange World of Planet X
aka: The Cosmic Monster
Artists Alliance/Eros/DCA 1958; 78 mins; Cert. "A"
CREDITS: Producer: George Maynard; Director: Gilbert Gunn
CAST: Forrest Tucker; Gaby Andre; Martin Benson; Alec Mango; Wyndham Goldie; Hugh Latimer *

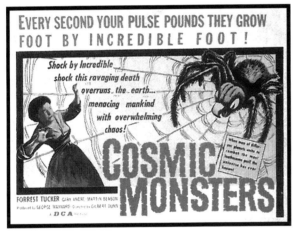

A scientist experimenting with magnetism allows cosmic rays to penetrate Earth's ionosphere, causing the insect life to grow to huge proportions.

An incompetent British effort with abysmal special effects, especially in the unrealistic scenes showing the enlarged insects in the woods, attacking humans. Martin Benson plays a friendly alien who, worried about the effect that the cosmic rays are having on Earth, appears amidst Forrest Tucker and assorted colleagues and eventually seals the hole in the ionosphere, eliminating Alec Mango, the scientist responsible, and causing the giant insects to die. He then loftily declares that the human race is unfit to join the Federation of Planets and takes off in his flying saucer. Based on a BBC television play, this ranks as one of the most dismal, flat-footed British science fiction films released in the late 1950s.

The Stranglers of Bombay
Hammer/Columbia 1960; Megascope; 80 mins; Cert. "A"
CREDITS: Producer: Anthony Nelson-Keys; Director: Terence Fisher
CAST: Guy Rolfe; Andrew Cruickshank; Allan Cuthbertson; Jan Holden; George Pastel; Marne Maitland ****

In 1826, English caravans crossing India are menaced by a sadistic religious cult who rob and strangle their victims.

Guy Rolfe plays a police officer going it alone against the Thuggee Cult, a group of brutal religious fanatics led by George Pastell, who are carrying out raids with alarming ease on caravans traveling into India. As his fellow officers, through fear, bribery and snobbery, do not want to involve themselves in getting rid of the cult and its followers, Rolfe infiltrates the gang on his own, nearly getting himself executed in the process. A tribe hostile to their cause eventually eliminates the cult after yet another caravan and its soldiers have been wiped out in gruesome fashion. Hammer must have been as surprised as the British public was when this film somehow escaped with an "A" certificate from the censor's office after a few minor cuts, as there was talk at the time of the movie being given an "X" rating and no wonder—there was a veritable catalogue of atrocities on display, including a tongue being cut out, eyes being gouged, and scenes of mutilations, stranglings and amputations. Even the scene where Rolfe was spread-eagled in the sand awaiting torture, watched over by a lustful Indian girl, raised a few eyebrows. Whatever merits the film had, and it was undeniably well presented, boasting a rousing score by James Bernard, this still remains one of director Terence Fisher's nastiest and most tasteless pieces of work.

A Study in Terror
Compton Cameo/Tekli/Sir Nigel Productions 1965; Eastmancolor; 95 mins; Cert. "X"
CREDITS: Producer: Herman Cohen; Director: James Hill
CAST: John Neville; Donald Houston; Anthony Quayle; John Fraser; Robert Morley; Frank Finlay **
     Sherlock Holmes and his companion, Doctor Watson, are called upon by the authorities to discover the identity of Jack the Ripper.
     A modernistic Holmes (John Neville, mouthing every Conan Doyle cliché in the book) and a bumbling, hesitant Watson (Donald Houston), after receiving a box of surgical instruments with the scalpel mysteriously missing, race around the foggy London streets as one prostitute after another is butchered to death. This mishmash of several differing styles pitting Conan Doyle's famous detective against England's first serial killer was an interesting premise that refused to gel, even with a stellar cast involved, and ended up coming across as just one more mid-'60s slasher movie. Gruesome shock-horror murders, over-the-top performances and an anachronistic soundtrack (parts of which sounded suspiciously like a jazz score) all contributed to a crude exploitation effort that had little respect for the genre it was aping—the continental horror film. Despite a Hammer-type ending, with scarred prostitute Adrienne Corri and John Fraser as Lord Carfax (finally unmasked as the Ripper) perishing in a burning inn, A Study in Terror lacked atmosphere and a sense of period, and was a fairly unattractive picture to experience—Peter Cushing and Andre Morell did it so much better in 1959.

Tales of Terror
American Intl. 1962; Panavision/Pathecolor; 90 mins; Cert. "X"
CREDITS: Producer/Director: Roger Corman
CAST: Vincent Price; Peter Lorre; Basil Rathbone; Joyce Jameson; Leona Gage; Debra Paget ****
     A trio of Edgar Allan Poe horror stories.
     Three stories unfold in this movie, with no connecting plot to link them. In the first, "Morella," Price plays a man who has mummified his wife, who died in childbirth, and has taken to drinking heavily. Her malevolent spirit enters the body of their daughter, whom Price blames for her death, and she fights with her father, who drops a candle; they both perish in a fire. The second story, "The Black Cat," stars Lorre as a wine taster, walling up Price and Jameson, who have been having an affair behind his back, until the noise of a cat from behind the wall alerts the police and Lorre is found out. The final tale, "The Facts in the Case of Monsieur Valdemar," which is the most enjoyable of the three, is of a sinister hypnotist played by Rathbone who holds Price in a cataleptic trance on his deathbed, as he wants to marry his wife. Price comes out of the trance, dissolving into a putrid, gooey mess over Rathbone, who drops dead from fright. This

was a highly enjoyable compendium of Poe adaptations by Corman, released at the time with *Panic in Year Zero*.

Tarantula
Universal 1955; 80 mins; Cert. "X"
CREDITS: Producer: William Alland; Director: Jack Arnold
CAST: John Agar; Mara Corday; Leo G. Carroll; Nestor Paiva; Ross Elliott; Edward Rand
*****

A spider that has been treated with an experimental growth nutrient escapes from a scientist's laboratory, swiftly grows to an enormous size and terrorizes the countryside before being bombed to death on the outskirts of a desert town.

From the opening shot of a hideously deformed man lurching across the screen to the final scene of the colossal spider blazing in the desert, *Tarantula*, without a shadow of a doubt, is the Number One of the 1950s cycle of giant insect films, tightly plotted with a snappy script and the inventive action boosted by Clifford Stine's tremendous special effects. The movie could just as easily have concentrated on the storyline concerning the effect of the nutrient on humans leading to a grotesque swelling of the features known as acromegaly, but following a fight in the scientist's laboratory that results in the tarantula's case getting smashed, Jack Arnold then has his rapidly growing spider crawling all over the desert landscapes, eating horses, cattle and humans, bringing down power lines and, in an ironic twist, demolishing the house and laboratory from which it escaped. The most impressive scene is near the end when the town's citizens, intent on mining the road to town to stop the monster in its tracks, spot the huge spider crawling over the distant hillside and heading toward them. Lending an air of gravitas to the proceedings, Leo G. Carroll gives his customary excellent low-key performance as the biochemist who, having disposed of two of his colleagues who have become deformed from acromegaly, becomes a victim of his own growth nutrient, his face distorting horribly as a result. There is also a certain amount of sexual chemistry between John Agar and Mara Corday, pneumatically dressed in white throughout the film. Henry Mancini's score, under the supervision of Joseph Gershenson, is in the Hans J. Salter mold—powerful, strident and memorable. A very popular movie on the Sunday circuit, *Tarantula* was still being screened in British cinemas as late as 1969, more often than not with Hammer's *Kiss of the Vampire*.

Target Earth!
Allied Artists 1954; 75 mins; Cert. "A"
CREDITS: Producer: Herman Cohen; Director: Sherman A. Rose
CAST: Richard Denning; Virginia Grey; Richard Reeves; Kathleen Crowley; Whit Bissell; Arthur Space **
A girl awakes to find that the city she lives in is deserted and lethal robots from Venus patrol the streets.
A low-budget science fiction drama that, despite the cardboard-looking robots, which vie with Chani in *Devil Girl from Mars* as the tackiest-looking mechanical villains of the '50s, moves along

briskly enough. Kathleen Crowley stars as the girl who wakes up to find herself in a deserted Chicago with only a few survivors from an alien invasion, among them hero Richard Denning. This disparate group spends a great deal of time arguing among themselves, as they often do in post-apocalyptic thrillers. The lumbering robots can kill humans with a death ray from their helmets—a direct steal from Gort in *The Day the Earth Stood Still*. They are eventually destroyed when scientist Whit Bissell invents an ultrasonic beam that shatters their face-plates, and the military bombard the city with sound waves, rendering them harmless.

Taste of Fear
Hammer/Columbia 1961; 82 mins; Cert. "X"
CREDITS: Producer: Jimmy Sangster; Director: Seth Holt
CAST: Susan Strasberg; Ronald Lewis; Ann Todd; Christopher Lee; Leonard Sachs; Anne Blake ****

A crippled young woman visits her father's villa in the South of France to find that he has mysteriously disappeared.

Taste of Fear marked Hammer's first foray into the world of psychodrama following the worldwide success of *Psycho*. In such movies, confusing plotlines centered on mistaken identities and family secrets, which were used as an excuse for a quota of shocks, jolts, murders and the obligatory trick ending. This one, which was probably the better structured of the lot, had Strasberg in a wheelchair visiting her father and stepmother in his villa. Ann Todd, as the stepmother, informs the girl that her father has gone away, but she then thinks she sees his body in the summerhouse and in the swimming pool. The supposed body then disappears. Christopher Lee is a doctor who informs members of the family that Strasberg's mind is wandering, but she suspects that Ronald Lewis, playing the chauffeur, and her stepmother are trying to kill her for her inheritance. Her assumptions prove to be correct, as they arrange for her car to crash over a cliff, only to be met the next day by Strasberg's look-alike friend who, in collusion with Lee, has returned to the villa to find out why her friend's father had disappeared. An excellent adult thriller that made the most of its French Riviera locations and was well photographed in black and white.

Taste the Blood of Dracula
Hammer/Warner Bros. 1970; Technicolor; 95 mins; Cert. "X"
CREDITS: Producer: Aida Young; Director: Peter Sasdy
CAST: Christopher Lee; Ralph Bates; Geoffrey Keen; Linda Hayden; Martin Jarvis; John Carson ***

In Victorian London, a depraved young lord comes into possession of the ring, cape and dried blood of Dracula and, with the aid of three of his friends, decides to revive the vampire for the sheer excitement such an act will bring to them.

Director Peter Sasdy was one of Hammer's latter-day choices to continue the *Dracula* franchise and, to his credit, came up with a definite improvement on both *Dracula—Prince of Darkness* and *Dracula Has Risen from the Grave*. Ralph Bates, soon to become one of Hammer's leading men, played the arrogant young lord who, after trying to force his companions to drink the vampire's blood, is murdered by them, as they are full of revulsion at what they have done. Lee materializes as Dracula and, to avenge the death of his disciple, seduces the three children of Bates' friends, compelling each to murder their own fathers. Lee perishes in the end when he cuts himself on broken glass and falls into the path of a cross contained within the stained-glass window of the derelict church he is hiding in. Within the context of a turn-of-the-decade Hammer vampire picture, this was a pretty lively production all round with vivid color photography to match the action, but unfortunately after Sasdy's effort, the remaining films in the series were pale imitations of their former selves.

Teenage Caveman
American Intl. 1958; Superama; 65 mins; Cert. "A"
CREDITS: Producer/Director: Roger Corman
CAST: Robert Vaughn; Darrah Marshall; Leslie Bradley; Jonathan Haze; Frank de Kova; Robert Shayne **

A caveman rebels against his tribe and sets out on a journey to discover what lies beyond the forbidden river.

Probably the one film that Robert Vaughn would prefer not to be associated with and also one of Corman's less memorable pictures. Dressed in a rather fetching one-piece costume with a bow and arrow, Vaughn as the young caveman encounters on his travels back-projected lizards from 1940's *One Million B.C.* before chancing upon the fearsome creature from across the river that his tribe was afraid of. This turns out to be a survivor from a nuclear war dressed in an old radiation suit who is still contaminated and whose touch can cause death. In fact, Vaughn and his tribe are the products of a post-nuclear future, the sole survivors of a new mankind. The film ends on an optimistic note, that perhaps mankind can construct a better world than the one they blew up.

Teenage Frankenstein
aka: I Was A Teenage Frankenstein
Anglo Amalgamated/American Intl. 1957; 74 mins; Cert. "X"
CREDITS: Producer: Herman Cohen; Director: Herbert L. Strock
CAST: Whit Bissell; Gary Conway; Phyllis Coates; Robert Burton; George Lynn; John Cliff **

A modern-day descendant of Frankenstein creates a monster from the corpses of teenagers.

Following the unexpected success of *I Was A Teenage Werewolf*, American International rush-released this updated variation of the *Frankenstein* legend, starring young Gary Conway as the monster who has the body of an Adonis and the face of a Halloween mask. Unfortunately, Strock's pedestrian direction lacked the necessary flair and imagination to lift the movie out of a rut, although Whit Bissell turned in an energetic performance as the mad doctor who creates Conway from teenagers involved in car crashes, sending the monster out to obtain a decent-looking head and ordering him to murder his (Bissell's) girlfriend, who has become too inquisitive over his activities. She ends up being disposed of in a cellar full of alligators. There are also quite a few graphically gruesome (for the time) laboratory scenes showing Bissell at work on his creation, not to mention some unforgettable lines of extremely risible dialogue. The climax bursts into Technicolor for all of 10 seconds as Conway, with a brand-new handsome head, backs into a bank of electrodes after killing Bissell, who wants to ship him to England for further experimentation. This fairly drab horror outing ran for years after release in England, a popular feature on the Sunday one-day circuit, more or less permanently double

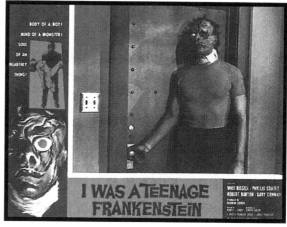

billed with *Blood Is My Heritage*, also directed by Strock but with slightly more vigor.

Teenage Monster
aka: The Meteor Monster
Howco Intl. 1957; 65 mins; Cert. "A"
CREDITS: Producer/Director: Jacques Marquette
CAST: Anne Gwynne; Stuart Wade; Gloria Castillo; Gilbert Perkins; Steven Parker; Charles Courtney *

In a small, midwestern town, rays from a meteorite turn a teenager into a werewolf-like psychopathic killer.

A tatty-looking grade Z travesty, resembling at times nothing more than an amateur home movie, with Gilbert Perkins as the unfortunate hairy monster hiding in his mother's cellar when not leaping about killing people. He is befriended by a waitress who uses him to kill her enemies, as she wants to acquire his mother's gold mine. When she discovers the plot to oust her from her fortune, the boy's mother instructs the monster to kill the waitress, which he does, and is then shot by the police, falling over a cliff to his death. This was one of the cheapest and most mind-numbingly boring productions to emerge from the '50s teenage horror series, originally released with *The Brain from Planet Arous*.

The Terror
American Intl. 1963; Pathecolor; 81 mins; Cert. "X"
CREDITS: Producer/Director: Roger Corman
CAST: Boris Karloff; Jack Nicholson; Sandra Knight; Dick Miller; Jonathan Haze; Dorothy Neuman **

A young officer separated from his regiment during the Napoleonic Wars meets a mysterious girl on a seashore and follows her to a castle, which harbors a terrible secret.

Jack Nicholson, in one of his earliest film roles, is the officer who meets up with the baron of the castle, Karloff, and learns that the girl he has been seeing is the ghost of the baron's young wife, whom he murdered 20 years previously when he caught her with a young man. In a storyline guaranteed to baffle even the most keyed-up of audiences, Karloff turns out to be impersonating the real baron, whom he also murdered years ago for having an affair with his wife. The girl, controlled by a witch, has returned from the grave for revenge. In the end, the crypt becomes flooded, Karloff dies and the girl disintegrates in Nicholson's arms. Corman rattled off this hodgepodge of Poe ideas in just three days on the set of *The Raven*, as he still had the services of Karloff for two days, and it is to his credit that the film is just about watchable, even though it doesn't make a great deal of sense.

Terror from the Year 5,000
aka: Cage of Doom
American Intl. 1958; 74 mins; Cert. "A"
CREDITS: Producer/Director: Robert Gurney Jr.
CAST: Ward Costello; Joyce Holden; John Stratton; Frederic Downs; Fred Herrick; Salome Jens **

Scientists invent a machine that can retrieve objects from the future, and a horribly disfigured woman appears, seeking new men to replenish a dying human race.

An intriguing little film in which Salome Jens as the mutated female skulks around for most of the time disguised as a nurse and hiding her grotesque features, which are only really seen at the end of the movie. She has appeared from the future, seeking new mates to revive a world destroyed by radiation in an atomic war. Escaping from the laboratory and killing both a servant and a nurse with radiation burns, she hypnotizes John Stratton to return with her to the distant future. Her plans are thwarted by Ward Costello who, realizing that she is giving off radiation and contaminating the present surroundings, destroys Jens, Stratton and the transmitter machine. The film is slow-moving and much too talkative but, if made on a bigger budget, could have been a whole lot more exciting than it turned out.

Terror in the Haunted House
Howco Intl./British Lion 1958; 84 mins; Cert. "X"
CREDITS: Producer: William S. Edwards; Director: Harold Daniels
CAST: Gerald Mohr; Cathy O'Donnell; Barry Bernard; William Ching; Johnny Qualen **

A newlywed woman realizes that the mansion she is going to live in is the same building that she has had recurring nightmares about.

A clumsy attempt at psychodrama, this lackluster thriller has Cathy O'Donnell suspecting her husband of foul deeds in his mansion and thinking that for some reason he wishes her dead. It transpires that he is trying to shock her out of a childhood memory block that saw her witnessing the ax-murders of her entire family in the attic, causing her to be traumatized about the event ever since. Her memory returns as she is forced into the attic, remembering at last who the real murderer was—it was William Ching, who then attempts to murder her to keep her quiet. This was a mediocre production, despite a nasty slaying near the end, and was originally released in the United Kingdom in late 1961 as second billing to the King Brothers' monster movie *Gorgo*.

Terror in the Midnight Sun
aka: Invasion of the Animal People
A.B. FortunaFilm/Unger Productions (Sweden) 1960; 73 mins; Cert. "X"
CREDITS: Producer: Bertil Jernberg; Director: Virgil Vogel
CAST: Barbara Wilson; Stan Gester; Robert Burton; Bengt Blomgren; Ake Gonberg; Gosta Pruzelius ***

An alien spacecraft lands in Lapland and a giant, Yeti-like monster is released and goes on a rampage.

In Lapland, a glowing spacecraft crashes into the side of a mountain in a scene shamelessly copied direct from Universal's *It Came from Outer Space*. A team of scientists from Zurich is sent to investigate what the authorities believe to be a meteor, meeting up with snow-troopers, who have discovered giant footprints and wrecked buildings in the area of the landing. Flying out to the meteor's crater, the team realizes that the object is a globular spaceship, the crew of which unleashes a large, hairy beast on the local population. The lumbering giant captures Barbara Wilson, daughter of the team's leader, and takes her to its masters. It then proceeds to smash up a village before eventually being pursued by the locals on skis, who burn it to death. After the creature's demise, the spaceship with its cloaked, bald aliens suddenly flies off without any explanation as to why it landed in the first place. Briskly directed by Virgil Vogel and making excellent use of the snow-covered locations, with eerie sound effects adding to the overall atmosphere, this compelling little movie, Sweden's one and only sci-fi monster flick, went the rounds on the Sunday circuit in 1964 with *Lust of the Vampire*. Unfortunately, in 1962, cheapo producer/director Jerry Warren obtained the rights to *Terror in the Midnight*

Sun and proceeded to chop it up, deleting various scenes, adding new ones and introducing a running commentary by John Carradine, who pontificated on all things scientific which had nothing whatsoever to do with the main plot. Retitled *Invasion of the Animal People* and running 18 minutes shorter than the Swedish picture, this was a classic example of a pretty good monster movie being completely ruined by interfering hands—in this case, Warren's. An additional 25 confusing minutes were later included for television release, but the truncated 55-minute version, a travesty of the original, turned up in 1965 on a double bill with *Indestructible Man*.

Terror Is A Man
Valiant 1959; 89 mins; Cert. "X"
CREDITS: Producers: Kane Lyn and Eddie Romero; Director: Gerry De Leon
CAST: Francis Lederer; Greta Thyssen; Richard Derr; Oscar Keesee; Lilia Duran; Flory Carlos
***

A man shipwrecked on a remote island is menaced by a scientist who conducts experiments in turning animals into half-human creatures.

Richard Derr plays the man washed ashore on the aptly named Blood Island, where Lederer has performed over 200 operations on a tiger to change him into a grotesque man-beast. Derr falls for the scientist's wife, Thyssen. The monster that Lederer created escapes from the laboratory, throwing the scientist over a cliff before being shot, leaving the lovers alone on the island. At the end, the wounded monster is placed in a boat by a sympathetic native and pushed out to sea. A gruesomely efficient American/Philippine co-production that was loosely based on H.G. Wells' *The Island of Dr. Moreau*, this was the first in a series of *Blood Island* movies, which included *The Blood Devils*, *The Bride of Blood* and *The Mad Doctor of Blood Island*, many of which never saw the light of day in Britain.

The Terror of Dr. Hichcock
aka: The Horrible Dr. Hichcock
Panda/Sigma 3/Warner Bros. (Italy) 1962; Totalscope/Technicolor; 88 mins; Cert. "X"
CREDITS: Producers: Luigi Carpentieri and Ermanno Donati; Director: Riccardo Freda
CAST: Robert Flemyng; Barbara Steele; Maria Teresa Vianello; Harriet White; Silvano Tranquili; Spencer Williams ****

A respected but demented doctor administers a drug to his wife so that he can make love to her in a near-death state.

Produced by the same team who were responsible for *Lust of the Vampire*, the erotic-horror overtones of continental cinema probably reached a peak with the release of Riccardo Freda's necrophilia masterpiece. Robert Flemyng is the English doctor of the title, playing weird funeral games with his wife, Maria Teresa Vianello, drugging her with an anesthetic so that she remains comatose while he performs macabre sexual acts. Unfortunately, one night, she apparently expires during the fun and games. Years later, Flemyng returns to his London mansion with his second wife, Barbara Steele (who is unaware of her husband's perverted tastes), only for Vianello to return from the grave, mad and withered-looking. The doctor then attempts to drain the blood from Steele to try to use it to rejuvenate his first wife, whom he still lusts after. The insane pair finally dies in the end as the mansion goes up in flames. Filmed in rich dark colors with lingering camera shots of Steele's tortured face and of Flemyng caressing the corpses of various women in the opening sequences, this disturbing picture (shorn of 12 minutes for U.K. and U.S. release, including the notorious footage of Flemyng raping a dead body) only appeared in a few selected art-house cinemas in 1965, double billed with the equally controversial Yugoslavian film *The Switchboard Operator*.

The Terror of the Tongs
Hammer/Merlin 1961; Technicolor; 79 mins; Cert. "X"
CREDITS: Producer: Kenneth Hyman; Director: Anthony Bushell
CAST: Christopher Lee; Geoffrey Toone; Yvonne Monlaur; Brian Worth; Richard Leech; Milton Reid **

In 1910 Hong Kong, a British merchant sets out to avenge the death of his daughter, who was murdered by a secret Chinese sect.

After the success of *The Stranglers of Bombay*, Hammer quickly followed it up with another dose of Far-Eastern mayhem, featuring Christopher Lee as the evil leader of the Red Dragon Tong, a subversive criminal society in Hong Kong where torture was the name of the game. Geoffrey Toone is the sea captain attempting to infiltrate unnoticed into the Tong stronghold, gaining the affection of Yvonne Monlaur as a Tong slave in the hope that she will lead him to Lee's headquarters, where he can bring the murderers of his daughter to justice. Toone is found out, captured by the Tongs and tortured, but escapes only to discover that the society's influences extend to the East India Company and his superiors, and that he himself has been targeted for execution. Monlaur, at the cost of her own life, eventually helps the captain bring about the downfall of Lee and his group, as the anti-Tong police destroy Lee's headquarters and Lee is dispatched by his own executioner.

Although granted an "X" certificate in Britain, this was a far less satisfactory film than the A-rated *The Stranglers of Bombay*, which Terence Fisher had directed. Bushell's direction verged on the pedestrian, and the picture would have benefited from Fisher's surer touch. Even the atrocities, handled mostly by hulking henchman Milton Reid, were nowhere near as gruesome as in Fisher's film. Lee's performance, though, was first-rate, and secured him the lead role in the series of *Fu Manchu* pictures produced in the mid to late '60s.

The Terrornauts
Embassy/Amicus 1966; Eastmancolor; 75 mins; Cert. "A"
CREDITS: Producers: Max J. Rosenberg and Milton Subotsky; Director: Montgomery Tully
CAST: Simon Oates; Zena Marshall; Charles Hawtrey; Stanley Meadows; Patricia Hayes; Max Adrian **

An office building is transported through space with an assorted group of people and lands in a strange fortress on a man-made asteroid inhabited by the remnants of an alien race.

Amicus produced a series of tacky science fiction movies throughout the '60s that appeared to be aimed at the Dr. Who-type of audience, and this ranked as one of their cheapest efforts.

Simon Oates plays the astronomer trying to contact other life forms, who is informed by tapes in the fortress that if man leaves his planet for exploration, ancient hostilities will commence again, as the fortress is the only artifact remaining from an ancient civilization that was wiped out by another race of aliens that are now en route to Earth. A robot appears and gives the humans various tests; the one alien on show resembles a man in a lobster suit. The fortress eventually instructs the humans to stop the invading force by using the weapons left on the artifact. The set design is unimaginative and the whole film has an amateurish, tired look about it.

Theatre of Death
aka: Blood Fiend
Pennea/Hemisphere 1966; Techniscope/Technicolor; 91 mins; Cert. "X"
CREDITS: Producer: Michael Smedley-Aston; Director: Samuel Gallu
CAST: Christopher Lee; Lelia Goldoni; Jenny Till; Julian Glover; Ivor Dean; Evelyn Laye **

In Paris, a series of murders where all the victims have been stabbed in the neck seem to be connected to a Grand Guignol theater that specializes in sensational acts.

Christopher Lee's performance as Darvas, the head of the theater, is about the only worthwhile point of interest in this erratically directed thriller which has Lee's ward, Jenny Till, committing a series of vampire-type murders because she was force-fed blood as a child to keep her alive when she was trapped in an avalanche. She is also under the hypnotic influence of Lee, who is using her for his own ends in his act. Darvas is the man the police suspect, but when he is murdered by his ward (who realizes that he knows she is the killer), they lose the scent and the murders continue. Till's girlfriend, Lelia Goldoni, finally discovers the truth about her and when the two women confront each other, Till runs off, hiding herself in the theater but under the stage to evade the police. She is then accidentally killed by a voodoo dancer, who inadvertently thrusts a spear into her from above the stage floor during an act. This laborious production, photographed in hideous, flashy color, was not given a wide release in the United Kingdom, only showing at a few cinemas with *The Evil Force*, and it remains one of Lee's most forgettable movies.

Them!
Warner Bros. 1954; 93 mins; Cert. "X"
CREDITS: Producer: David Weisbart; Director: Gordon Douglas
CAST: Edmund Gwenn; James Whitmore; James Arness; Joan Weldon; Onslow Stevens; Chris Drake ****

In the New Mexican desert, mysterious disappearances among the populace are caused by hordes of giant, radiation-mutated ants.

Running a close second to Universal's *Tarantula* but perhaps overshadowed in the eyes of many fans by Jack Arnold's more intricately plotted masterpiece, *Them!* remains one of the finest of the '50s giant insect films. The opening scenes create a chilling mood of suspense, depicting a young girl with a blank expression on her face found wandering alone in the desert by policeman James Whitmore and FBI agent James Arness, who can only mutter "them," wind whistling through an empty, shattered building, and strange twittering noises in the surrounding area. A legion of gigantic ants are discovered to

be the cause, mutated to giant proportions as a result of atom bomb tests in the Nevada desert, and after a skirmish with the army, when the experts think they and their nest have been destroyed, the queen ant turns up in the Los Angeles sewer drains with more eggs that hatch. A terrific final battle then takes place and the monsters are eventually poisoned by gas and burned alive by flamethrowers. The ants, huge life-sized models, were extremely realistic for a film of this type, and Gordon Douglas directed a good cast in a hard-nosed, semi-documentary style reminiscent in many ways of a 1950s detective thriller.

They Came from Beyond Space
Embassy/Amicus 1967; Eastmancolor; 85 mins; Cert. "A"
CREDITS: Producers: Max J. Rosenberg and Milton Subotsky; Director: Freddie Francis
CAST: Michael Gough; Robert Hutton; Jennifer Jayne; Bernard Kay; Geoffrey Wallace; Zia Mohyeddin *

Under cover of a meteor shower in Cornwall, aliens introduce a plague and abduct humans, transporting them to the moon as a workforce for their damaged fleet of spacecraft.

Amicus knocked out this limp effort in tandem with *The Terrornauts* and it shows. The film has unbelievable, shoddy-looking sets (the Master of the Moon's laboratory looks like a bare living room) and an implausible plot, whereby second-rate American actor Robert Hutton, with a metal plate in his skull that is immune to the alien's mind control, is transported to the moon with various scientists and held captive by an embarrassed-looking Michael Gough. Gough plays the Master of the Moon in a becoming robe, who informs them that his race has landed on Earth's satellite and needs humans to repair their crippled fleet. The movie ends with a pact being made between the aliens and Earthlings, who will repair the ships without the need for force. A very worn-out affair that surely had all the members of the cast wondering what on earth they were doing starring in such unimaginative nonsense.

The Thief of Bagdad
London Films 1940; Technicolor; 106 mins; Cert. "U"
CREDITS: Producer: Alexander Korda; Directors: Ludwig Berger, Michael Powell and Tim Whelan
CAST: Sabu; Conrad Veidt; John Justin; June Duprez; Rex Ingram; Allan F. Jeayes *****

In Old Bagdad, a boy thief helps a usurped prince regain the throne to his kingdom from an evil sorceror.

A magnificent, highly colorful spectacle of a type that is rarely, if ever, seen today and certainly retaining its reputation as one of the key British productions of the 1940s. An exuberant Sabu played the young thief of the title, who befriends blind John Justin and embarks on a quest to help him become the rightful ruler of Bagdad. His many adventures include meeting up with Rex Ingram as the cunning genie and battling a huge spider inside a mountain temple to capture a jewel embedded in an idol that can grant the owner a number of wishes. Conrad Veidt, dressed from head to toe in black, made a first-class villain, finally getting his just deserts when Sabu and Justin enter the city on a flying carpet. As he makes his escape on a flying mechanical horse, Sabu fires an arrow and Veidt falls to his death. The whole exotic romp was underlined by Miklos Rozsa's fantastic score. The film runs neck and neck with Columbia's *The Seventh Voyage of Sinbad* as the greatest Arabian Nights adventure ever committed to celluloid.

The Thing from Another World
Winchester Pictures/RKO-Radio 1951; 86 mins; Cert. "X"
CREDITS: Producer: Howard Hawks; Director: Christian Nyby
CAST: Kenneth Tobey; Margaret Sheridan; Dewey Martin; Douglas Spencer; Robert Cornthwaite; James Arness *****

An American scientific research team in the Arctic discovers a flying saucer buried in the polar ice. They accidentally destroy the ship, but the alien pilot is taken back to the camp in a block of ice, where it inadvertently thaws out and terrorizes the base in its search for human blood to survive and procreate.

One of *the* undoubted classics of 1950s science fiction—fast-paced, classy acting and an intelligent if wordy script—*The Thing from Another World* was also one of the first American films to receive the new "X" certificate when it was released in England at the end of 1951. Although Nyby is credited with being the director, the film has the hallmark of Howard Hawks stamped all over the production and has a distinctly Germanic look about it—dark corridors, gloomy interiors and dim lighting. The ferocious being depicted in the film (the shape-changing alien in John W. Campbell's story *Who Goes There?* was transformed in the film to a more conventional space monster) heralded the beginning of a new wave of movies concerned with the so-called "menace from the skies" that ran right through to the end of the decade. Standout scenes include the research team trooping down snow-covered slopes to the buried

saucer in a howling gale, the first sighting of the alien outlined against the door as it roars into the hut and is doused in kerosene, and the chilling climax whereby a rapidly clicking Geiger counter heralds the approach of the monster, which is finally trapped between electrodes and incinerated to a pile of ashes. Not normally associated with this type of film, famed Hollywood composer Dimitri Tiomkin produced one of science fiction's most momentous soundtracks. John Carpenter also used the fiery title lettering in his gory but less memorable 1982 remake. In 1967, the film was re-released on a double bill with RKO's *King Kong*, allowing fantasy fans the opportunity to revel in two of the screen's all-time great movies.

The Thing that Couldn't Die
Universal 1958; 69 mins; Cert. "X"
CREDITS: Producer/Director: Will Cowan
CAST: William Reynolds; Andra Martin; Jeffrey Stone; Robin Hughes; Carolyn Kearney; Forrest Lewis ***

A water-diviner gifted with ESP unearths an old chest containing the severed head of 16th-century Devil-worshipping sailor Gideon Drew.

The Elizabethan chest dug up by Andra Martin on a remote California ranch after being located with a divining rod contains not treasure, as she had hoped, but a sailor's head. Portraying the head is Robin Hughes; the man himself was executed on the orders of Sir Francis Drake in

1579 for dabbling in the occult and witchcraft. The evil-looking head exerts a powerful hypnotic influence, forcing Martin and the ranch dwellers to search for the rest of its body so it can come alive and resume practicing the black arts. When the body is finally located in a coffin and dug up, it is joined to the head, but before it can wreak havoc, the resulting creature is destroyed by an ancient amulet that Martin wears to protect her from evil, and it crumbles into a skeleton. This enjoyable horror-cum-supernatural B thriller was a lot more compelling than many of the other "disembodied head" films churned out in the '50s and appeared regularly in the 1960s on the Sunday one-day circuit, often double billed with other Universal efforts such as *Curse of the Undead* and *Monster on the Campus*.

Things to Come
London Films/United Artists 1936; 130 mins; Cert. "A"
CREDITS: Producer: Alexander Korda; Director: William Cameron Menzies
CAST: Raymond Massey; Cedric Hardwicke; Ralph Richardson; Edward Chapman; Margaretta Scott; Maurice Braddell
*****

A war in 1940 all but decimates mankind, and a new, technological society rises from the ashes with the aim of sending a rocket into space.

Based on the famous H.G. Wells novel, *Things to Come* was a landmark film of the fantasy genre and certainly of British cinema, a one-off, never to be repeated. The film played in three sections, commencing with the outbreak of war in Everytown, Christmas 1940, shot in a semi-documentary style by Menzies and eerily forecasting the real war only three years away from the time the film was made. The town is eventually reduced to rubble and 30 years later, when the war has ended, is visited by Raymond Massey in his futuristic flying machine. His fleet of planes quells a rebellion led by the Boss, Ralph Richardson, subjecting the citizens to the Gas of Peace and making them friendly and more willing to accept the ideas of a new world. Forward to the year 2036, when the movie's visuals kick in, a lengthy and stunning montage of views depicting the construction of a technological Everytown with huge machines at work in a sterile society. Massey again plays Everytown's ruler, worried that this futuristic Utopia has robbed men of their free will, and in the stirring climax, his daughter and Cedric Hardwicke's son are blasted into space from a gigantic cannon to discover whether a more compassionate, caring existence can be formed elsewhere. The film originally ran for over two hours and was not a success at the time, Wells' messages going right over the heads of the audiences of the day, and the version screened at selected cinemas in the early 1960s was edited down to 113 minutes. Mention must also be made of Arthur Bliss' impassioned "Pomp and Circumstance"–type music for this mammoth enterprise, a magnificent score that was a virtual symphony in its own right.

This Island Earth
Universal 1954; Technicolor; 86 mins; Cert. "U"
CREDITS: Producer: William Alland; Director: Joseph Newman
CAST: Jeff Morrow; Faith Domergue; Rex Reason; Lance Fuller; Russell Johnson; Robert Nichols *****
A scientist recruited by mysterious methods to work at a research institution gradually comes to realize that it is being run by aliens who are kidnapping Earth's scientists to restore their war-torn planet of Metaluna.

A full-blooded, expensively produced comic book space opera that boasts colorful visuals and highly imaginative special effects. The film commences in a mystery fashion at first. Rex Reason travels in a pilotless plane to the institute after creating a machine called an interositer as an alien means test. He begins to realize that the strange-looking boffins with the high foreheads, with whom he has to work, are not quite human. When he attempts to escape in a plane, he and Faith Domergue are kidnapped by a flying saucer and transported by Jeff Morrow to Metaluna, where the aliens want to enlist the humans' help in repairing the planet's damaged ionosphere layer, the subject of continuous bombardment by their enemies, the Zahgons. However, Metaluna is a doomed planet, so Morrow, Reason and Domergue, after being menaced by an insectoid mutant slave worker, return to Earth, escaping in their plane as the saucer with Morrow on board crashes into the sea. This was a highly successful Universal production, with vivid scenes depicting the battle-scarred landscape of Metaluna and the saucer's flight through space, although the mutant, a garish cre-

ation with claws and an exposed brain, did look somewhat out of place, as though it had wandered on set from one of Universal's other monster productions. In many ways, this was a significant fantasy film of the '50s, despite being hampered by wooden performances from the leads.

The Three Worlds of Gulliver
Columbia 1959; Technicolor; 99 mins; Cert. "U"
CREDITS: Producer: Charles H. Schneer; Director: Jack Sher; Special Effects: Ray Harryhausen
CAST: Kerwin Mathews; June Thorburn; Jo Morrow; Lee Patterson; Basil Sydney; Gregoire Aslan **

The adventures of Gulliver in the lands of Lilliput and Brobdingnag.

Columbia's follow-up to *The Seventh Voyage of Sinbad* did not turn out to be one of Harryhausen's more memorable features. Kerwin Mathews was a personable enough Gulliver, but the film only concentrated on two of the lands that he visited, emphasizing the contrast by showing him first as a giant in Lilliput, the land of the little people, and then as a tiny human in Brobdingnag, the land of the giants. It seemed to be aimed at a much younger audience than *Sinbad*. The animation was kept to a minimum as most of Harryhausen's effects, and the film's budget, involved placing Mathews in either miniature or oversized sets. Admittedly there is a fine sequence where a diminutive Gulliver fights an alligator-type lizard on a table top, and a huge squirrel is briefly seen near the end before he finally escapes from Brobdingnag, but these scenes aside, the film tended to sag in the middle through too many discussions about what to do with Gulliver, with nowhere near enough action to keep the kids happy. On the plus side was yet another fine score by Bernard Herrmann.

The Time Machine
MGM 1960; Metrocolor; 103 mins; Cert. "A"
CREDITS: Producer/Director: George Pal
CAST: Rod Taylor; Yvette Mimieux; Alan Young; Whit Bissell; Sebastion Cabot; Doris Lloyd
*****

A Victorian scientist invents a machine that can travel backward and forward in time, and has various adventures in the future.

The Time Machine became George Pal's biggest success for MGM and looks fantastic. There is quite an array of Victoriana on display in the opening setting in Rod Taylor's house, and the machine itself is all gleaming brass knobs and dials. Then there is the transformation in the landscapes as Taylor, first stopping in 1917 when a war is being fought and then nearly

falling foul of a nuclear blast in the same war still being waged in 1966, advances to the year 802,701. There he encounters the Eloi, a peaceful but ineffectual race ruled over by the nocturnal Morlocks, who use the humans for both slave labor and food. Many critics say the film goes off the boil once Taylor teams up with the Eloi to battle the Morlocks and rescue the delightful Yvette Mimieux from their clutches, but this was standard fantasy fare at the time, when some form of monster had to be defeated by the hero, and the ensuing years have added to the overall charm of the movie. It does eschew most of the social messages contained in the H.G. Wells novel and alter the original closing chapter, whereby the traveler arrives at the very end of the Earth's existence—Taylor simply returns to his own time, narrates his story to his disbelieving friends, and then heads back to the Eloi and Mimieux. A few minor quibbles notwithstanding, this was a colorful and endearing fantasy that won an Oscar for the effects showing the changing vistas as the machine hurtled through time to a distant future.

The Tingler
Columbia 1959; 82 mins; Cert. "X"
CREDITS: Producer/Director: William Castle
CAST: Vincent Price; Judith Evelyn; Darryl Hickman; Patricia Cutts; Philip Coolidge; Pamela Lincoln ****

A doctor realizes that fear and shock can cause a parasitic crustacean to appear on people's spinal columns, which can only be released by a sudden scream.

Together with *The House on Haunted Hill*, this is probably William Castle's most renowned film, again featuring his favorite actor Vincent Price as the doctor who is convinced that a strange organism appears on the spine during periods of stress and fear, which can ultimately cause death. When he is summoned by a man to treat his sick wife, Judith Evelyn, Price begins to test his theories, as the woman is a deaf mute unable to scream. The couple owns their own cinema specializing in silent films and, by a series of shocks, such as blood running from taps and a disembodied arm rising out of a bath full of blood, Price succeeds in scaring Evelyn to death, separating the scaly creature from her spinal cord and keeping it in a box. It then transpires that in fact the dead woman's husband, Philip Coolidge, was responsible for her death, while Price's wife, in a turnabout to the plot, tries to induce the creature to kill her husband. Eventually the organism escapes and causes panic in the old cinema, killing the projectionist before Price recaptures it and restores it to Evelyn's body, where it dies. Castle's gimmick for this movie was to wire up some seats in various cinemas in America that would then transmit a mild electric shock each time the creature appeared. *The Tingler* was a perennial favorite on the Sunday circuit in the 1960s, often teamed up with other Columbia movies such as *The Werewolf* and *20 Million Miles to Earth*.

The Tomb of Ligeia
American Intl. 1964; Cinemascope/Eastmancolor; 81 mins; Cert. "X"
CREDITS: Producers: Roger Corman and Pat Green; Director: Roger Corman
CAST: Vincent Price; Elizabeth Shepherd; John Westbrook; Derek Francis; Oliver Johnston; Richard Vernon ***

A squire who lives alone in a vast Gothic house is convinced that the spirit of his evil dead wife resides in a cat.

This was to be the last of Corman's Poe films and perhaps the least successful, as by now the formula had become a shade repetitious. Nevertheless, it was handsomely mounted, with a commendable low-key performance from Price. Sporting dark glasses, he mourns the loss of his first wife, Ligeia, and begins to imagine that the family cat is possessed by her spirit, which could also be taking over the identity of his second wife (both played by Elizabeth Shepherd) as a form of vengeance from beyond the grave. Ligeia in fact hypnotized her husband before she died, leaving him in a trance-like state so that he would remain in love with her. The climax has the usual conflagration as the old abbey goes up in flames and Price, now blinded, dies in the arms of his dead wife. This was a more literate study of Poe along the lines of *Jane Eyre*, concentrating on obsession and possession, filmed on location rather than in the studio but, to die-hard horror fans, the movie was too slow-moving, too earnest and lacking in the thrills that hallmarked the other features in the Poe series.

Torture Garden
Amicus/Columbia 1967; Technicolor; 93 mins; Cert. "X"
CREDITS: Producers: Max J. Rosenberg and Milton Subotsky; Director: Freddie Francis
CAST: Burgess Meredith; Jack Palance; Beverly Adams; Peter Cushing; Barbara Ewing; Michael Bryant ***

A group of five visitors to a fairground have their fortunes told by the mysterious Dr. Diablo.

The second Amicus omnibus of horror stories was a slightly superior effort to the disappointing *Dr. Terror's House of Horrors*. Burgess Meredith invites some strangers into his sideshow and relates their fortunes to them in the form of a tale, all of which end in death. The first concerns Michael Bryant, who murders a rich uncle and then falls foul of his uncle's cat, which consumes human heads. The second has Beverly Adams sleeping her way to the top in Hollywood, only to find that her bed partners are automatons with brains, a fate which also befalls her. The third tells of a woman, Barbara Ewing, who falls for a concert pianist, but the piano becomes jealous and crushes her to death. The final fortune, and the best, stars Jack Palance as an obsessive Edgar Allan Poe collector who murders Peter Cushing to obtain his collection, which includes the resuscitated body of Poe himself, preserved in a cobwebby crypt and writing manuscripts. Palance in his glee sets fire to the place, killing himself and the author. The fifth visitor turns mad and kills Diablo, and the visitors run out of the sideshow, but when Palance returns, it transpires that Meredith has staged his own murder and in the end he is revealed as the Devil, and the five visitors are all dead.

Tower of London
Tigon/United Artists 1962; 79 mins; Cert. "X"
CREDITS: Producer: Gene Corman; Director: Roger Corman
CAST: Vincent Price; Joan Freeman; Richard McCauly; Michael Pate; Sandra Knight; Justice Watson **

Richard Duke of Gloucester murders his way through King Edward IV's court.

Roger Corman's rather bland, stagy remake of the Karloff 1939 vehicle came across as more of an adaptation of an Edgar Allan Poe novel than a stab at English history, and for historical accuracy was to some extent suspect. Price plays Richard, the deformed Crookback, slowly going mad and drowning the Duke of Clarence in a vat of wine, torturing a girl for supposed treason and incarcerating the young princes in the Tower of London. He is then haunted by the ghosts of his victims and goes insane, his death being foretold at the Battle of Bosworth. Although the castle in which most of the action takes place is suitably Gothic, and Price overacts like mad as the evil Richard, the film was flatly directed by a seemingly uninterested Corman and shelved until 1967 when it was eventually released on a double bill with *The Sorcerors*.

The Trollenberg Terror
aka: The Crawling Eye
Tempean/Eros 1958; 85 mins; Cert. "X"
CREDITS: Producers: Robert S. Baker and Monty Berman; Director: Quentin Lawrence
CAST: Forrest Tucker; Laurence Payne; Janet Munro; Jennifer Jayne; Warren Mitchell; Andrew
Faulds ***

A strange, radioactive cloud that descends on a Swiss mountain hides tentacled aliens that can communicate by telepathy and threaten to invade the local town.

Based on a '50s BBC-TV serial, this is a pretty good sci-fi thriller, similar in vein to Hammer's *Quatermass* movies. It again features a fading American actor, Forrest Tucker, who, as a United Nations investigator, tries to convince the inhabitants of Trollenberg that deadly creatures from space are lurking up in the mountains following a spate of mysterious deaths among climbers. Janet Munro, a psychic, can also feel a strange telepathic presence in the area. Tucker, Payne and Mitchell, upon investigating the peculiar events, realize that the aliens need a thin atmosphere to survive, and they also learn that a similar cloud that caused identical weird happenings had previously been observed in the Andes. In some of the film's gorier moments, the creatures decapitate anyone venturing too near the cloud. As the town's mountain observatory is attacked by the huge, tentacled jellyfish-type aliens in an exciting climax, Tucker calls up the air force and the cloud is bombed, wiping out the monsters in the process.

20 Million Miles to Earth
Columbia 1957; 82 mins; Cert. "X"
CREDITS: Producer: Charles H. Schneer; Director: Nathan Juran; Special Effects: Ray Harryhausen
CAST: William Hopper; Joan Taylor; Frank Puglia; John Zaremba; Thomas B. Henry; Tito Vuolo *****

The first U.S. spaceship to Venus crash-lands off the coast of Sicily with one human survivor and a specimen of animal life from the planet in the form of an egg. From the egg hatches a hostile, reptile-like creature that rapidly grows in Earth's atmosphere and goes on a rampage in Rome.

Before Charles H. Schneer and Ray Harryhausen turned their attention to the Arabian Nights, Jules Verne and Greek mythology for their ideas, they made adult monster movies and *20 Million Miles to Earth* was the finest of the lot, and the most successful at the box office. The Venusian Ymir (never mentioned by name in the film) was one of Harryhausen's personal favorites, and his animation of this eye-grabbing, savage creature is absolutely superb. A young fisher-boy finds a canister from the crashed rocket washed up in a sea-cave and takes it to a local professor who lives in a caravan with his granddaughter, Joan Taylor. Inside the canister is a gelatinous egg from which a tiny, scaly animal hatches, growing to an enormous size and subsequently being pursued by William Hopper and a posse of police and soldiers, until trapped by a helicopter dropping an electrified net over it. Sedated and taken to Rome, the creature revives when a tray of instruments crashes against the electrical current that is keeping it comatose, and it runs riot through the city, fighting with an elephant, demolishing bridges and making (further) ruins of the Roman ruins, before being shot at the top of the Coliseum. This very popular monster-on-the-loose yarn ran for a decade in the United Kingdom after its initial release, often double billed with other Columbia favorites such as *Night of the Demon* and *The Werewolf*, and even adult movies such as *Boy's Night Out*, and is regarded by many fans as one of the peaks of Harryhausen's illustrious career.

20,000 Leagues Under the Sea
Disney 1954; Cinemascope/Technicolor; 127 mins; Cert. "U"
CREDITS: Producer: Walt Disney; Director: Richard Fleischer
CAST: Kirk Douglas; James Mason; Peter Lorre; Paul Lukas; Robert J. Wilke; Carleton Young
*****

A mysterious sea monster that is destroying ships turns out to be Captain Nemo's futuristic submarine Nautilus, and several men captured and imprisoned on board experience a series of adventures.

This ranks as one of Walt Disney's biggest-ever box office hits, a stirring and spectacular version of the famous Jules Verne novel with an unforgettable cast, including James Mason as the cultured, brooding Nemo and Kirk Douglas as the exuberant harpoonist Ned. The highlight of the film is, of course, the battle with the giant squid, an excitingly choreographed action sequence that stands head and shoulders with the best that the '50s had to offer, which in that decade was an awful lot. The underwater photography is superb, as is the overall design of the film, in particular the Nautilus. The picture mainly deals with Douglas, Lukas and Lorre carrying out various foiled bids to escape from what they see as their prison, leading to another memorable scene where they are chased off a remote Pacific island by an army of cannibals who storm the submarine. The rousing climax sees Nemo's secret island base destroyed by attacking forces and Nemo dying as his beloved craft sinks beneath the waves. The film won two Oscars for special effects and art direction and remains one of the greatest fantasy adventure movies ever made, with a tremendous score by Paul Smith. Running continuously in the cinema from the first date of release, a brand new cleaned-up print was successfully released in the United Kingdom as late as 1969.

Twisted Nerve
Charter/British Lion 1968; Eastmancolor; 118 mins; Cert. "X"
CREDITS: Producers: George W. George and Frank Granat; Director: Roy Boulting
CAST: Hywel Bennett; Hayley Mills; Frank Finlay; Billie Whitelaw; Phyllis Calvert; Barry Foster *

A demented psychopath disguises himself as his retarded brother to murder his stepfather and remain undetected.

The same team that produced the hit 1966 sex-comedy *The Family Way* ended up an extremely unpopular "cropper" with this brutal, distasteful psychodrama that seemed to imply that mongolism could be a root cause of a homicidal nature. A huge barrage of criticism at the time forced the makers to deny any such link at the beginning of the film. Phyllis Calvert has one mongoloid son and has passed on one of the damaged chromosomes to her second son, Hywel Bennett. Bennet, who occasionally lapses into six-year-old mode, murders his stepfather with scissors, axes Billie Whitelaw to death after she makes advances toward him, and then attempts to rape Hayley Mills until the police stop him in time. The late '60s trend in sex, nudity and violence was all here in this thoroughly unpleasant movie, which didn't contain a single redeeming feature, and it is surprising to note that the soundtrack was scored by none other than Bernard Herrmann who, on hindsight, must have balked at lending his name to a production such as this.

The Two Faces of Dr. Jekyll
aka: House of Fright
Hammer/American Intl. 1960;
Megascope/Technicolor; 89 mins;
Cert. "X"
CREDITS: Producer: Michael Carreras; Director: Terence Fisher
CAST: Paul Massie; Dawn Adams; Christopher Lee; David Kossoff; Francis De Wolff; Norma Marla ***

In 1874, an unattractive doctor changes himself into a handsome but evil philanderer.

An interesting version of the Jekyll-Hyde story that has a morose Paul Massie playing a bearded Jekyll turning himself into a handsome, clean-shaven Mr. Hyde, first raping his wife as punishment for having an affair with his best friend (played by Christopher Lee), and eventually killing Lee with a snake that crushes him to death. After his wife commits suicide, he embarks on an affair with Norma Marla, who also dies because of his behavior. The end result is an aging Jekyll, drained of all emotions and a physical wreck, quite alone because of his hedonistic lifestyle as Hyde. Because of the lack of any conventional monster, the film flopped at the box office, even though Fisher concentrated somewhat voyeuristically on the adult themes of Hyde lusting after female flesh. Some of these scenes were cut when the picture was released in America. Lee probably would have done a better job with the lead role, as Massie's performance was rather understated. Nevertheless, an intelligent reworking of the old theme of dual personality, if not a wholly successful one.

Two Lost Worlds
Sterling/Eagle Lion/United Artists 1950; 61 mins; Cert. "U"
CREDITS: Producer: Boris Petroff; Director: Norman Dawn
CAST: James Arness; Laura Elliott; William Kennedy; Gloria Petroff; Thomas Hubbard; Jane Harlan **

In the 1830s, a woman is kidnapped by marauding pirates from a colony in Queensland, Australia, and she and her rescuers become stranded on an island inhabited by dinosaurs.

A long-forgotten fantasy adventure film that was allegedly cobbled together from a pair of pilot shows for a television serial that never saw the light of day. It's an engaging but cheap combination of a pirate movie with a *Lost World* ending. Pirates attack an American clipper and the mate, James (*The Thing*) Arness, who is injured in a battle, is put ashore at a colony in Queensland to convalesce. There he meets Laura Elliott and falls for her, arousing jealous feelings in her fiancé, William Kennedy. The pirates raid the colony, kidnapping Elliott and her friend, and the two love rivals set off in pursuit, snatching the girls back and making off in a small boat, but ending up on a barren volcanic island populated by prehistoric animals. The women and their men do not actually set foot on the island until the final 20 minutes of the film. Once there, they encounter plenty of dinosaurs purloined straight from *One Million B.C.* stock footage. The volcano erupts in the climax, and Arness, Elliott and her sister are rescued by a passing vessel.

2001: A Space Odyssey
MGM 1968; Super Panavision (Orig. in Cinerama)/Metrocolor; 160 mins; Cert. "A"
CREDITS: Producer/Director: Stanley Kubrick
CAST: Keir Dullea; Gary Lockwood; William Sylvester; Leonard Rossiter; Robert Beatty; Daniel Richter *****

An alien artifact in the form of a monolithic slab gives early apemen the impetus to use tools. In the year 2001, another slab discovered on the moon sends out signals in the direction of Jupiter, and a manned spacecraft is sent to investigate the origin of the signals and whether extraterrestrial life exists there.

2001 was without doubt the most momentous and talked about science fiction production of the 1960s, revered by many, thought to be a colossal bore by others. The film was a stunning (for the time) montage of model shots and groundbreaking special effects. Kubrick's use of classical music to evoke the right mood behind the various segments of his visionary space epic was also revolutionary in its concept. The acting was slightly wooden at times, but really played second fiddle to the hardware and the visuals, highlights of which included the breathtaking shot of an ape's bone transforming itself into a sleek rocket falling through space, and the end sequence, which had Keir Dullea's astronaut hurtling through the multicolored stargate (a favorite scene with spaced-out hippies) to find himself in a futuristic hotel room, a unique puzzle in itself. The film was originally shown on the giant Cinerama screen in London and was 160 minutes long with an "A" certificate. On general release, 20 minutes were cut from the print, mostly in the Dawn of Man sequence, and the movie was granted a "U" rating. The '50s and early '60s cycle of cheapo science fiction had already waned by now, but the days of cut-price special effects, of cardboard spacecraft and of rubbery-looking aliens literally ended with the release of Kubrick's masterpiece, which raised the genre to a much higher level. Thereafter, no self-respecting company would dare release a science fiction or fantasy picture with inferior effects and production values; this was reflected in the likes of *Star Wars*, *Star Trek* and their ilk, which emerged in the '70s, big expensive blockbusters with eye-popping visuals (but, some might argue, no better than their '50s predecessors).

The Undead
American Intl. 1956; 71 mins; Cert. "A"
CREDITS: Producer/Director: Roger Corman
CAST: Pamela Duncan; Richard Garland; Allison Hayes; Val Dufour; Dorothy Neumann; Richard Devon **

A psychotherapist regresses a prostitute back to her previous existence as a witch.

Corman's first horror picture was an odd little affair starring Pamela Duncan as the reincarnation of a witch burned at the stake. When she is hypnotized, her voice travels backward through the ages, enabling her ancestor to escape. Duncan and the psychotherapist, Richard Garland, travel back to the Dark Ages to ensure that the witch is burned as planned, to carry on the same threads in Duncan's future, although Duncan wants to save her former self from death even if it means changing the future. Unfortunately for them, the Devil appears after being summoned by another witch and, after Duncan as her former self is executed, he forbids Garland to return to his own time. Full of witches, knights, black cats and people dressed in outlandish costumes, the movie is a mishmash of various ideas, imaginative on a cheap-looking level. It appeared on a double bill with *A Bucket of Blood* in the early 1960s.

The Undying Monster
aka: The Hammond Mystery
20th Century Fox 1942; 63 mins; Cert. "A"
CREDITS: Producer: Bryan Foy; Director: John Brahm
CAST: James Ellison; John Howard; Heather Angel; Holmes Herbert; Bramwell Fletcher; Heather Thatcher ***

The Hammond family lives under the curse of lycanthropy.

Produced to cash in on the success of Universal's *The Wolf Man*, John Brahm's low-key werewolf movie took place in Cornwall. The monster is only really seen at the end of the film, hauling itself up over a cliff-edge in full view of the camera. John Howard plays the heir to the Hammond family, which lives under a curse dating back to the Crusades. One of his ancestors sold his soul to the Devil and had to claim a human life to sustain his own. A local girl is murdered in unusual circumstances and after Scotland Yard is brought in to investigate, Howard finally abducts his sister, who is aware of his terrible secret, before being shot to death by the police when revealing himself to be the wolf man. This studio-bound film was similar in vein to a quaint old British murder mystery of the '40s, well directed by Brahm with the accent on atmosphere and not horror, the set design of the misty cliffs, twisted trees and gloomy old mansion compensating for the lack of action. It's a pity the British censor removed the metamorphosis scene of Howard changing from werewolf to man and also insisted on a change of title, as no film distributor could use the word "monster" in the United Kingdom during the 1940s, although this sequence was restored in later prints, and it was the uncut version that played in a few cinemas during the early '60s.

The Unearthly
Republic/AB-PT Productions 1957; 73 mins; Cert. "X"
CREDITS: Producer/Director: Brooke L. Peters (Boris Petroff)
CAST: John Carradine; Marilyn Buferd; Allison Hayes; Myron Healy; Tor Johnson; Sally Todd
***

A mad doctor experiments on his patients, who think they are being treated for depression, with a series of glandular operations to prolong human life, but only succeeds in creating mutants that he keeps in his cellar.

Very much in the fashion of a '40s-style horror movie, The Unearthly featured John Carradine in one of his more telling roles, compensating for the fact that the film was obviously made on a meager budget, as most of the action took place within the confines of his gloomy old mansion. He plays a doctor trying to discover the secret of eternal life by inserting a new tissue—Gland 27—into his patients, who have been lured to his house by promises of a cure for their depressive illnesses, unaware that he plans to use them as guinea pigs in his experiments instead. Tor Johnson, in a remarkable display of wooden acting even by his standards, plays the doctor's hulking, dim-witted henchman Lobo, a role that he perfected in numerous low-grade efforts during this period. The delectable Allison Hayes is the heroine saved from Carradine's clutches by undercover cop Myron Healy, who falls for her. Sally Todd crops up as the only person seen operated on in the film, transformed into a disfigured mutant after Carradine has finished with her. Carradine is polished off in the end by one of his messed-up patients and the police, in the closing scenes, discover the subjects of Carradine's botched experiments in the cellar, who resemble the animal people in The Island of Lost Souls. Similar in content to The Black Sleep but cheaper looking, with corny dialogue and mediocre acting, the picture is still enjoyable thanks to Carradine's over-the-top performance, which carries the day.

Unearthly Stranger
Independent Artists 1963; 74 mins; Cert. "A"
CREDITS: Producer: Albert Fennell; Director: John Krish
CAST: John Neville; Gabriella Lucidi; Phillip Stone; Patrick Newell; Jean Marsh; Warren Mitchell **

A scientist comes to realize that his new wife is an alien who has been sent to Earth to spearhead an invasion.

Another minor British '60s thriller with virtually no special effects—it plays more like a television serial along the lines of a cut-price version of Invasion of the Body Snatchers. John

Neville plays the newlywed who realizes that there is something odd about his wife, Gabriella Lucidi. She sleeps with her eyes open, never blinks and can handle hot objects without any pain. When she cries, the tears scald her cheeks like acid. She and others like her have been sent to Earth to prevent our scientists from learning a new process of space travel, the knowledge of which they already possess, but she falls in love with her new husband and cannot bring herself to kill him. In the end, the aliens simply vanish into thin air, leaving their clothes behind.

Unknown Island
Cohen Productions/Film Classics 1948; Cinecolor; 76 mins; Cert. "A"
CREDITS: Producer: Albert Jay Cohen; Director: Jack Bernhard
CAST: Barton MacLane; Virginia Grey; Richard Denning; Philip Reed; Richard Wessel; Daniel White **

An assorted crew of adventurers set sail from Singapore for an island that one of their number says is populated by prehistoric animals.

The companions travel to a strange island led by photographer Philip Reed who has flown over it, nervous ex-marine Richard Denning who was shipwrecked there, and Reed's fiancée, Virginia Grey. Once on the island, they encounter various dinosaurs and a giant sloth. This was a corny but enjoyable cross between one of the '40s ever-popular jungle films and *The Lost World*, with echoes of *King Kong* thrown in for good measure, featuring some of the ropiest-looking monsters in screen fantasy history. The ape-like giant sloth and the Tyrannosauri are men in suits, plastic models that hardly move stand in for the other dinosaurs, and some of these are curiously man-sized. What saves the movie from becoming a complete dud is its good use of vibrant color and some decent acting between Denning and Grey as the would-be lovers. The film is more suited to a children's audience than for adults and, in its own amateurish way, is quite fun to watch. After a climactic battle between the sloth and a Tyrannosaurus, which is certainly *not* in the *King Kong* class, the four survivors escape the island and Denning and Grey fall into each other's arms in true '40s romantic fashion.

The Unknown Terror
Regal Intl./20th Century Fox 1957; Regalscope; 77 mins; Cert. "A"
CREDITS: Producer: Robert Stabler; Director: Charles Marquis Warren
CAST: John Howard; Mala Powers; Paul Richards; Gerald Milton; Duane Gray; May Wynn **

In the Caribbean jungle, the legendary Cave of Death is being used by a scientist to nurture a strange fungus with deadly properties.

A run-of-the-mill production starring Gerald Milton as a crazed scientist carrying out experiments with the hallucinogenic fungus discovered in the remote Cave of Death on a jungle island in the Caribbean. Both he and his native wife, May Wynn, study the effects of the fungus on humans, turning the local natives who are due to be sacrificed in tribal rituals into mutant monsters that resemble nothing more than men with foamy soapsuds all over their faces.

Mala Powers is the woman landing on the island with husband John Howard to investigate her brother's mysterious disappearance at the hands of Milton. The climax has Howard and Powers blowing up the cave to prevent the fungus from multiplying, spreading to the other islands and taking over the world, as it has become immune to the effects of fresh air. Although ploddingly directed by Warren, the movie was a popular enough choice on the Sunday circuit in the 1960s, often going the rounds with *Kronos* or *Spacemaster X-7*—the passable widescreen photography saved it from being just another program filler.

Unknown World
Yordan Enterprises/Lippert 1950; 74 mins; Cert. "U"
CREDITS: Producers: J.R. Rabin and I.A. Block; Director: Terrell O. Morse
CAST: Bruce Kellogg; Marilyn Nash; Victor Kilian; Jim Bannon; Otto Waldis; George Baxter
**

A scientist invents a giant boring machine to escape into the Earth's center should there be fallout from a nuclear war.

After a talky first half, with Victor Kilian going on at great lengths as he explains his ideas to a team of scientists on the means whereby the human race could escape to a refuge in the Earth's central crust from a possible atomic war, this rather mundane and poorly directed picture gathers pace once the crew are in the Cyclotram boring machine heading for the interior of the Earth to seek out such a refuge. A gigantic cavern is eventually found 1,640 miles into the Earth's center, but the atmosphere there renders human reproduction sterile, and a volcanic eruption forces the expedition back to the surface. The sequences inside the cavern were filmed in the famous Carlsbad Caverns in New Mexico and are the only imaginative moments in an otherwise routine and fairly uninteresting production, which, on a larger budget, would have turned out to be a far more enterprising picture.

The Valley of Gwangi
Warner Bros. 1968; Technicolor; 95 mins; Cert. "A"
CREDITS: Producer: Charles H. Schneer; Director: James O'Connolly; Special Effects: Ray Harryhausen
CAST: James Franciscus; Gila Nolan; Laurence Naismith; Richard Carlson; Freda Jackson; Gustavo Rojo ***

In the early 1900s, a traveling circus troupe in Mexico discovers a hidden valley populated by prehistoric animals.

Harryhausen's main ideas for *Gwangi* originated from an aborted Willis O'Brien project of the 1940s and although the film has a strong cast, and the special effects are up to the maestro's usual high standards, not to mention a rousing Elmer Bernstein–type score by Jerome Moross, it has a distinct "I've seen it all before" air about it. The constant bickering between lovebirds James Franciscus and Gila Nolan palls in the first part of the movie, which only picks up once the tiny prehistoric horse Eohippus leads the party into the scenically splendid Forbidden Valley. The scenes of Gwangi doing battle with a Styracosaurus, escaping from the circus and fighting an elephant, and the climax where the dinosaur is burned to death in a cathedral, are first-rate, but Harryhausen was less than pleased when the film was released as second billing to a comedy Western *The Good Guys and the Bad Guys*, his first feature to do so. It didn't perform well at the box office either—if made 10 years earlier, it would have been a smash hit. *The Valley of Gwangi* really marked the end of the golden age of the Schneer/Harryhausen team and although their films carried on into the 1970s, they would never again recapture the critical and commercial success of their previous productions made at a time when computer-enhanced digital effects did not exist. Harryhausen was a one-man band as far as special effects were concerned.

The Vampire
aka: Mark of the Vampire
United Artists 1957; 76 mins; Cert. "X"
CREDITS: Producers: Arthur Gardner and Jules Levy; Director: Paul Landres
CAST: John Beal; Coleen Gray; Kenneth Tobey; Dabbs Greer; Lydia Reed; Paul Brinegar
****

A doctor accidentally takes pills given to him by an elderly, dying scientist that have been distilled from the blood of vampire bats, and turns into a modern-day vampire.

Although standard horror fare—man takes an untested substance and then changes into a monster—this was a well-made chiller, updating the vampire legend to a contemporary setting to fit in with the new wave of science fiction movies that marked this decade, similar to what Columbia did with *The Werewolf* (1956). John Beal, excellent in the title role, is the unfortunate doctor who slowly realizes that he may be the person behind a spate of mysterious deaths whereby all of the victims have died from heart attacks and a rare blood disease. He becomes addicted to the pills left by an old scientist, transforming himself into a crazed killer and prowling the shadowy streets looking for human prey, resembling more of a grotesque Jekyll-Hyde figure than a vampire with his twisted, distorted, wrinkled features and shaggy hair. At one point he feeds one of his victims into a furnace to remove evidence that he is the murderer that the police are hunting. The obligatory shooting at the end by the police finishes Beal off. Rarely seen in the United Kingdom, the film went the rounds on the Sunday one-day circuit in 1962 with *The Monster that Challenged the World*. Gerald Fried's thunderous score underlined the proceedings nicely.

The Vampire and the Ballerina
C.E.F. Consorzio/United Artists (Italy) 1960; 86 mins; Cert. "X"
CREDITS: Producer: Bruna Bolognesi; Director: Renato Polselli
CAST: Helene Remy; Maria Luisa Rolando; Walter Brandi; Tina Gloriana; Iscaro Revaiol; John Turner ***

A troupe of ballet dancers takes refuge in a castle during a storm and falls prey to a vampire countess and her vampire servant.

An erotic vampire tale from Italy that not only had a beautiful vampiress, Maria Luisa Rolando, but an ugly vampire in Walter Brandi, who played her domineering servant. The two of them carry out a love-hate relationship while preying sexually on two of the ballerinas in particular, Helene Remy and Tina Gloriana. Most of the film is taken up with the duel of wits between Rolando and Brandi, and the dancers themselves comically resemble a group of strippers, but Brandi's vampire makeup is sufficiently monstrous to make him one of the screen's more grotesque bloodsuckers. After most of the troupe has been attacked by the lecherous vampires, the countess and her servant perish in the sun at the end of the picture. This was a sexploitive variation on Riccardo Freda's *Lust of the Vampire* that appeared at cinemas specializing in the continental sex and horror-type of movie in the early to mid-1960s—it turned up on one occasion double billed with *Blood and Roses*.

Varan the Unbelievable
Toho/Cory and Dallas/Crown Intl. (Japan) 1958; Tohoscope; 70 mins; Cert. "X"
CREDITS: Producers: Tomoyuki Tanaka and Jerry A. Baerwitz; Director: Inoshiro Honda
CAST: Kozo Nomura; Myron Healy; Tsuruko Kobayashi; Ayumi Sonoda; Koreya Senda; Akihiko Hirata ***

Experiments on an island to remove salt water from a lake cause a giant prehistoric, spiky reptile to emerge and head toward mainland Japan, leaving a trail of devastation in its wake.

One of the rarest of Toho's X-rated '50s monster movies, produced very much in the nightmarish darker tone that made *Godzilla* such a classic. This particular beast first emerges from a lake and destroys the island where Myron Healy and his Japanese wife are experimenting with chemicals to produce fresh water from saltwater, much against the wishes of the local populace, who believe that his experiments will disturb the monster from its lair. The creature then has several battles with the military in Oneida City on the mainland before swallowing a large quantity of balloons filled with explosives and falling onto a truckload of bombs which are detonated, causing it to plunge back into the sea, presumably dying as a result of its injuries. The film, which had some impressive special effects for the day, ran in several differing lengths and even various versions, depending on which country it was shown in, and was not released in Britain until the early 1960s in a murkily photographed, almost incoherent, badly edited version, double billed with *The Awful Dr. Orloff* (*The Demon Doctor*). The original Japanese feature did not contain many of the scenes included in the American print and was almost a different film altogether, running 17 minutes longer than the U.K. release.

Village of the Damned
MGM 1960; 78 mins; Cert. "A"
CREDITS: Producer: Ronald Kinnoch; Director: Wolf Rilla
CAST: George Sanders; Barbara Shelley; Martin Stephens; Michael Gwynn; John Phillips; Laurence Naismith ***

The entire population of a small English village falls into a coma for 24 hours after a force field has surrounded the local countryside—when they awake, every woman in the village has been made pregnant by an alien force.

Based on John Wyndham's popular novel *The Midwich Cuckoos*, this is a relatively short version of the book and has a typically understated British look to it, but what saves it from becoming just a routine thriller is a decent cast, good photography and brisk direction by Wolf Rilla—the film certainly doesn't hang about. The women give birth to children, all who possess extrasensory powers, can communicate with each other by telepathy, are highly intelligent from a very early age, and have blond hair. They also display a group mentality when threatened, killing anyone by thought control who crosses their path. After several unnerving incidents when the children demonstrate their powers to the adults, schoolteacher George Sanders and his wife, Barbara Shelley, come to realize that they are malevolent aliens who could pose a threat to Earth. Sanders eventually lures them all into the local school where he has planted a bomb, and they are blown up and destroyed along with him. The film was a box office hit and a sequel, *Children of the Damned*, was made three years later.

Voodoo Woman
Carmel/American Intl. 1956; 77 mins; Cert. "A"
CREDITS: Producer: Alex Gordon; Director: Edward L. Cahn
CAST: Tom Conway; Marla English; Touch Connors; Lance Fuller; Mary Ellen Kaye; Paul Dubov *

A mad scientist in the jungle experiments with the local women to turn them into slaves, but creates monsters instead.

A dull-looking feature mostly shot at night, with Marla English as the monster, resembling the being in *The She-Creature* with shaggy hair, staring eyes and a body like a gorilla. Tom Conway plays the scientist who turns English, the leader of an expedition looking for gold in the jungle, into the monster of the title, after unsuccessfully trying the same experiment on his wife. It is never made apparent quite why Conway is trying to create a female super-race by a mixture of voodoo and science to be controlled by telepathy, and he is finally killed by English after she learns that there is no gold in the area, who then falls into a blazing pit in the climax to a pretty feeble B movie, one of the worst to be directed by the normally reliable Edward L. Cahn. It appeared on the Sunday one-day circuit in 1963 with *Terror from the Year 5,000*.

Voyage to the Bottom of the Sea
20th Century Fox 1961; Cinemascope/DeLuxeColor; 105 mins; Cert. "U"
CREDITS: Producer/Director: Irwin Allen
CAST: Walter Pidgeon; Joan Fontaine; Peter Lorre; Michael Ansara; Barbara Eden; Robert Sterling ****

An experimental atomic submarine surfaces on a trial run to discover that the Earth is in imminent danger of perishing under a blazing belt of radiation caused by meteoric bombardment of the Van Allen Belt.

A glossy, big-budget action movie that spawned a television series in the United States, with Richard Basehart replacing Walter Pidgeon as Commander Nelson of the nuclear submarine Seaview. The submarine (which cost Fox $40,000 to make and was also used in the TV series that followed), with its assorted crew and passengers that spend a great deal of time squabbling, sets sail for the Pacific (against government orders) with the aim of firing a missile into the Van Allen Belt to quell the inferno before the ice-caps melt and destroy the planet. The special effects and underwater photography are top-notch, with the Seaview negotiating dozens of submerged mines in one sequence and fighting off a huge octopus that attaches itself to the hull. A giant squid they encounter, though, is poorly conceived. Eventually, Pidgeon, who turns in a solid performance as the grumpy commander, fires the rocket, extinguishing the flames and saving the world from disaster despite saboteur Joan Fontaine's attempts to stop him. It's just a pity that Frankie Avalon had to sing over the title credits (Paul Sawtell and Bert Shefter provided an otherwise excellent score), the only blight in an otherwise lengthy, fun-packed undersea romp that was a massive hit at the U.K. box office when first released.

The Vulture
Homeric/Iliad/Paramount 1966; 91 mins; Cert. "A"
CREDITS: Producer/Director: Lawrence Huntington
CAST: Akim Tamiroff; Robert Hutton; Broderick Crawford; Diane Clare; Philip Friend; Annette Carrell **

A scientist changes himself into a murderous vulture-man to kill the people responsible for burying his ancestor alive.

A very odd British/American/Canadian collaboration that had a limited release in the United Kingdom in 1967. In Cornwall, Akim Tamiroff plays a scientist who trains a matter-transmitter machine onto the place where his ancestor was buried alive with his familiar (a vulture), 200 years previously, for practicing witchcraft. The spot is also rumored to contain a horde of Spanish treasure. The result is that the scientist becomes the half-vulture, half-man monster of the title, setting out to destroy the descendants of those responsible for interring his ancestor alive. Soon mutilated sheep are found with black feathers near their corpses, and gold coins are scattered over the countryside. Diane Clare is the last surviving descendant, who is saved from Tamiroff's clutches by Robert Hutton before the monster is finally shot. Poorly scripted and woodenly acted by a surprisingly good cast who are completely ill at ease, this plays along similar lines to the equally inept *The Blood Beast Terror* by having one of the most unconvincing and unscary-looking monsters of any '60s horror movie. Tamiroff wears a large black cloak for most of the film's running time to cover his feathers, although somehow he has managed to retain his human features, and a pair of giant rubber claws is used when the vulture swoops on a victim. The picture was originally filmed in color for television release, but was screened theatrically in black and white at selected cinemas.

The Walking Dead
Warner Bros. 1936; 66 mins; Cert. "A"
CREDITS: Producer: Lou Edelman; Director: Michael Curtiz
CAST: Boris Karloff; Edmund Gwenn; Barton McLane; Margurite Churchill; Ricardo Cortez; Warren Hull **

A convict executed for a murder he did not commit is reactivated by a scientist and sets out to take revenge on those who framed him.

Another in the long line of horror-gangster melodramas churned out by the major studios during the '30s and '40s, many of them starring Karloff, who could always be called upon to turn in a convincing performance, however derivative the plots and material were. After Karloff has been executed in the electric chair, scientist Edmund Gwenn gives Karloff a mechanical heart and the reactivated convict, turned insane by revenge, seeks out those who framed him for murder, scaring them to death one by one until he expires, taking his secret with him. A very predictable outing is bolstered as usual by Karloff's customary solid presence and some atmospheric photography, but although there are a few suspenseful scenes, the movie overall is fairly lame and lacks impact. It was virtually remade by Columbia in 1939 as *The Man They Could Not Hang*.

War of the Colossal Beast
aka: The Terror Strikes
Carmel/American Intl. 1958; 68 mins; Cert. "A"
CREDITS: Producer/Director: Bert I. Gordon
CAST: Roger Pace; Sally Fraser; Russ Bender; Dean Parkin; Charles Stewart; George Becwar **

Thought to have died by falling off the Hoover Dam, the Colossal Man turns up in New Mexico, horribly disfigured and mad.

Bert I. Gordon's sequel to *The Amazing Colossal Man* is an uninspiring, flatly directed effort, even with the added attraction of having the 60-foot giant's face half caved in, and a damaged brain to boot. Dean Parkin, who was also the disfigured monster in Gordon's *The Cyclops*, plays the Colossal Man this time. As usual, the production is full of the token use of model cars and trucks together with phony back-projected shots and liberal employment of the split-screen technique, a trademark of Gordon's pictures. The giant, discovered in the mountains of New Mexico by his sister, is captured by eating a truckload of drugged bread and transported to Los Angeles, where he breaks out of an aircraft hangar and goes on a rampage—cue the extensive footage from *The Amazing Colossal Man* as the giant slowly remembers who he is. The end sees the Colossal Man, full of remorse for the destruction he has caused, killing himself on high tension wires, a scene that in the original release burst into Technicolor for about 20 seconds.

The War of the Worlds
Paramount 1953; Technicolor; 85 mins; Cert. "X"
CREDITS: Producer: George Pal; Director: Byron Haskin
CAST: Gene Barry; Ann Robinson; Les Tremayne; Paul Frees; Carolyn Jones; Jack Kruschen
*****

Mysterious cylinders land in the California desert, paving the way for an invasion of Earth by Martians.

H.G. Wells' quintessentially English novel had the Martians striding across the Home Counties on tripod machines and reducing London to ruins in the late 1800s. George Pal transferred the story to America and the year 1953, placing the Martians in aerodynamic war machines that hovered on anti-matter beams, emitting death rays and forming around themselves an invincible force field. This was slam-bang comic book science fiction, noisy, colorful and full of battles as Earth tries to fight the Martians off, even using the atom bomb to no effect, only to find that in the end, the humble microorganisms in the atmosphere bring about their eventual demise. Highlights are the first confrontation between the army and the invaders, a spectacular shoot-out that still puts many modern-day fantasy movies to shame (including the tepid *Independence Day*), and the sequences featuring Gene Barry and Ann Robinson trapped in a deserted house, surrounded by cylinders and Martian war machines, not to mention the first glimpse of a one-eyed Martian itself—the moment when Robinson is touched on the shoulder by the inquisitive alien is one of science fiction's most memorable scenes. The climax sees the war machines crashing into the streets of Los Angeles as the Martians succumb to the planet's natural bacteria. Pal received an Academy Award for best special effects, even though these may look a bit on the dated side today, and the film remains one of the key sci-fi productions of the 1950s, the only downside being the religious motif running side by side with all the ear-splitting action, which grates after a while. In 1967, it was given a successful release with Hitchcock's *Psycho*, a truly stupendous double bill that ran in the United Kingdom for well over a year.

The Wasp Woman
Filmgroup/Allied Artists 1959; 73 mins; Cert. "X"
CREDITS: Producer/Director: Roger Corman
CAST: Susan Cabot; Barboura Morris; Fred Eisley; Michael Mark; Frank Wolff; William Roerick ***

A scientist invents a cosmetic cream from Royal Jelly enzymes that transforms a woman into a giant killer wasp.

Susan Cabot plays the dowdy head of an ailing cosmetics company who uses the experimental rejuvenating cream invented by Michael Mark on her face, as she believes that she is not growing old gracefully and that the product will boost the company's profits. It works at first, restoring her beauty, but then she changes into a wasp-like monster with a desire to vampirize those she kills, bumping off one member of the staff after another. When she finally corners one of her employees, Barboura Morris, to claim her as a victim, the scientist arrives on the scene and throws carbolic acid in the creature's face, pushing it out of an office window where, unable to fly, Cabot as the monster falls to her death. This was an excellent, fast-moving Corman quickie, another variation on the rejuvenation theme that was popular in cinemas at the time, made just before he decided to concentrate his efforts on the works of Edgar Allan Poe. Cabot was also surprisingly good in the title role.

The Werewolf
Clover/Columbia 1956; 83 mins; Cert. "X"
CREDITS: Producer: Sam Katzman; Director: Fred F. Sears
CAST: Steven Ritch; Joyce Holden; Don Megowan; Kim Charney; Eleonore Tanin; Harry Lauter ****

Scientists inject an experimental serum into a man saved from a car crash to test a cure for radiation sickness, but only succeed in turning him into a werewolf.

Columbia updated the werewolf legend in this production to fit in with the new atomic age theme in the cinema, combining it with contemporary science to explain Steven Ritch's transformation into a werewolf rather than the supernatural folklore of the old 1940s horror movies. The result was a superior sci-fi/horror outing filmed at a crackling pace, with the wolf man prowling the darkened streets and terrorizing the Big Bear Lake region of California in search of food and help and being treated as an outcast by the scientists who have created him. There is one tremendous scene when the tortured Ritch changes from man into werewolf in a prison cell and slays the two scientists responsible for his plight. After breaking out of jail and escaping into the snow-laden woods, he is eventually cornered on a dam and shot by the police. Making good use of the stark, wooded Big Bear Lake locations, this modernization of the old fable was also used as a motif by United Artists to some degree of success in 1957's The Vampire.

Werewolf of London
Universal 1935; 75 mins; Cert. "X"
CREDITS: Producer: Stanley Bergerman; Director: Stuart Walker
CAST: Henry Hull; Warner Oland; Valerie Hobson; Lester Matthews; Spring Byington; J.M. Kerrigan ***

In Tibet, a young botanist is bitten by a werewolf and on his return to London finds himself cursed with lycanthropy.

The first major film version of the werewolf legend featured Henry Hull as a young botanist searching for a rare bloom in Tibet, the Mariphasa lupino lumino, unaware that it is an antidote for lycanthropy. The werewolf that attacks him, Warner Oland, follows him to London to retrieve the plant and by now Hull, himself cursed by being infected by Oland, is prowling the streets, howling in his room and looking for victims. He eventually kills Oland but is shot by the police and changes from wolf to man before their eyes. It may seem very slow-moving and primitive by today's standards, but the picture was remarkable for Jack Pierce's painstaking six-hour makeup job on Hull as the werewolf, and John Fulton's transformation scenes were also revolutionary for the day, although overshadowed six years later by the superior effects in The Wolf Man.

Wheel of Fire

aka: Pyro

SWP/Esamer/Paramount (U.S./Spain) 1963; Pathecolor; 91 mins; Cert. "X"

CREDITS: Producers: Sidney J. Pink and Richard C. Meyer; Director: Julio Coll

CAST: Barry Sullivan; Martha Hyer; Soledad Miranda; Sherry Moreland; Luis Prendes; Fernando Hilbeck **

The wife and daughter of an American engineer in Spain are burned to death in a fire started by his jealous ex-mistress—the husband, horribly disfigured, dons a mask and seeks revenge.

Released in the United States under the title *Pyro*, the wheel in the U.K. version of the picture refers to the generator that Barry Sullivan is constructing in Spain. While out looking for a property to house his family, he prevents a young woman from burning her house down, as she needs the insurance money to survive. He falls in love with her and then rejects her when the passion gets too hot for comfort. Feeling spurned, she then takes revenge by setting fire to his house, resulting in the death of his wife and child and his disfigurement. Donning a mask that makes him appear normal, Sullivan, now deranged, stalks her and her child to carry out his revenge. This was an uninspiring Spanish-American co-production that was originally released in 1965 with *Love with the Proper Stranger.*

When Dinosaurs Ruled the Earth

Hammer/Seven Arts 1969; Technicolor; 100 mins; Cert. "A"

CREDITS: Producer: Aida Young; Director: Val Guest; Special Effects: Jim Danforth

CAST: Victoria Vetri; Robin Hawden; Patrick Allen; Sean Caffrey; Drewe Henley; Magda Konopka **

In prehistoric times, a young cave girl is swept out to sea by a tidal wave and, when washed ashore, is adopted by a baby dinosaur.

This flaccid monster-romp was just another rehash of *One Million Years B.C.* with hardly any narrative save that of Victoria Vetri and Robin Hawden from warring tribes falling in love and being menaced by Patrick Allen and his tribe, who want Vetri back with them. Jim Danforth's stop-motion animation is excellent—giant crabs, a Triceratops, a Plesiosaurus that attacks a fishing village and the dinosaur family that befriend Vetri are almost up to Ray Harryhausen standards and these, together with some colorful scenery and locations, are really the only reasons to watch this piece of Stone Age nonsense.

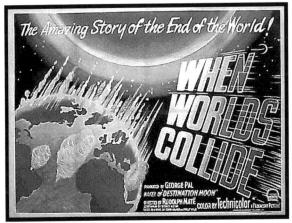

When Worlds Collide
Paramount 1951; Technicolor; 82 mins; Cert. "U"
CREDITS: Producer: George Pal; Director: Rudolph Mate
CAST: Richard Derr; Barbara Rush; John Hoyt; Mary Murphy; Laura Elliott; Larry Keating ***

A planetary system consisting of a new star and planetoid enters the solar system, causing widespread chaos on Earth, and a small group of survivors launch a rocket to populate the new planet.

A fairly impressive George Pal fantasy. A star, Bellus, collides with the Earth, causing tidal waves in New York and volcanic eruptions, just as heroic Richard Derr and an assorted group of scientists take off in their rocket and land on the new planet, Zyra, which turns out to be another paradise in which man can plan a future. The film does take a while to get up steam and is too talkative at times, with the love interest between Derr and Barbara Rush slowing things up, but the remarkable (for their day) special effects, showing a tidal wave devastating Times Square in New York and other scenes of destruction, earned Pal another Oscar, although the picture was not quite the spectacular that Paramount had hoped for. In retrospect, the film was a direct ancestor of disaster films such as Paramount's *Deep Impact* and Buena Vista's *Armageddon*, made over 40 years later but still incorporating the same themes of mass destruction on Earth.

Where Has Poor Mickey Gone?
Ledeck and Indigo/Compton Cameo 1964; 59 mins; Cert. "X"
CREDITS: Producer/Director: Gerry Levy
CAST: Warren Mitchell; John Malcolm; Raymond Armstrong; John Challis; Christopher Robbie; Karol Hagar **

An eccentric magician causes the members of a teenage gang who are making his life hell by their antagonistic behavior disappear into a magic cabinet.

A long-forgotten but interesting oddity from Gerry Levy starring Warren Mitchell in the days before he became famous as Alf Garnett on British television. Mitchell is a stage magician tormented in his basement workshop by a gang of teenage hoodlums and, by magic, he causes them to disappear one by one into one of his stage props, a large mysterious cabinet. Virtually filmed in one room, this was apparently shot in a week on a shoestring budget and appeared in the mid-'60s with *I Married A Werewolf* at selected cinemas.

Witchcraft
Lippert/20th Century Fox 1964; 79 mins; Cert. "X"
CREDITS: Producers: Robert Lippert and Jack Parsons; Director: Don Sharp
CAST: Jack Hedley; Lon Chaney Jr.; Jill Dixon; David Weston; Marie Ney; Yvette Rees ***

A company plans to remove a cemetery for development purposes, but the local witches come alive to stop the scheme from taking place.

The film tells the tale of two families of witches—the Laniers, whose company are bulldozing the old graveyard, and the Whitlocks, who own it. Old rivalries that date back to the 17th century rise to the surface as Lon Chaney, head of the Whitlocks, plans to take revenge on Jack Hedley as head of the other family. He calls upon the witches to rise up and revolt against the desecration of their ground. Yvette Rees plays a malevolent, reincarnated witch turning up in the rear seats of people's cars, causing them to fatally crash. The climax sees the Whitlocks perishing under boiling oil as Hedley's wife is rescued from their clutches during a black mass ceremony. This atmospheric, underrated film by Don Sharp, with moody black and white photography, was not a particular success and only had a limited release in the United Kingdom, double billed with *House of the Damned*.

The Witches
aka: The Devil's Own
Hammer/Seven Arts 1966; Technicolor; 91 mins; Cert. "X"
CREDITS: Producer: Anthony Nelson-Keys; Director: Cyril Frankel
CAST: Joan Fontaine; Alec McCowen; Kay Walsh; Ann Bell; Ingrid Brett; John Collin **

A woman traumatized by a voodoo priest in Africa returns to England to take up a teaching post, but discovers a coven of witches at the school.

A lackluster Hammer tale of the occult that is neither chilling nor particularly thrilling as Joan Fontaine discovers that Kay Walsh and Alec McCowen, who run the school where she has just started work as a teacher, are witches who have planned to have her initiated as one of their own. Walsh also wants to sacrifice one of the pupils, a virgin, to grant her immortality. After a great deal of melodramatic running around, Fontaine eventually kills Walsh and the coven disbands. Fontaine, with a perpetual frown on her face, seems miscast in the role, and the whole production comes across as an adult-oriented St. Trinians film without the laughter, almost totally lacking in excitement, suspense and entertainment.

Witchfinder General
aka: The Conqueror Worm
Tigon/American Intl. 1968; Eastmancolor; 87 mins; Cert. "X"
CREDITS: Producers: Arnold L. Miller and Louis M. Heyward; Director: Michael Reeves
CAST: Vincent Price; Ian Ogilvy; Hilary Dwyer; Rupert Davies; Patrick Wymark; Wilfred Brambell ****

A lawyer in 1645 travels the countryside falsely persecuting women as witches to profit from the number he burns at the stake.

A stylish period shocker featuring Vincent Price in one of his most notorious roles—a violent, bloody film that was savagely edited soon after release, although the uncut version played in London for a time. Price is the self-proclaimed Witchfinder General, causing panic in rural England because of his propensity for accusing any young woman of witchcraft to mainly satisfy his sadistic traits, and also for the money he makes from doing it. All of this culminates in graphic scenes of hangings, torture and burnings at the stake, which are not for the faint-hearted. Ian Ogilvy, a young Cromwellian soldier, and his girlfriend Hilary Dwyer portray the couple who fall foul of Price's pathological urges. Ogilvy ends up in a dungeon while Dwyer is tortured. Young up-and-coming director Michael Reeves piled on the gore, probably taking full advantage of the new code of violence in late 1960s cinema, especially in the climax when Price meets his just deserts at the hands of Ogilvy, who hacks him to pieces with an ax and stamps out his eyes with his boots before another inmate of the prison shoots the bloodied tormentor to put him out of his agony. This harrowing scene was almost completely missing from the heavily cut version. Despite the gruesomeness of it all, it remains an authentic-looking and well-photographed recreation of a particularly troubled period in British history.

The Wolf Man
Universal 1941; 71 mins; Cert. "X"
CREDITS: Producer/Director: George Waggner
CAST: Claude Rains; Lon Chaney Jr.; Evelyn Ankers; Ralph Bellamy; Maria Ouspenskaya; Bela Lugosi ****

In Wales, the heir to an ancestral home is attacked by a Gypsy werewolf and changes into one himself when there is a full moon.

Six years after the release of *Werewolf of London*, Universal kick-started the whole werewolf legend all over again in this opulent horror film and Lon Chaney, playing the cursed Lawrence Talbot, made the "hairy one" his own (often referring to the Wolf Man as his baby), starring in the role five times. A sterling cast of stalwarts included Claude Rains as Chaney's father, Lugosi as the Gypsy werewolf that Chaney kills with a silver-topped cane, and Russian character actress

Maria Ouspenskaya as the old Gypsy soothsayer. It is she who warns Chaney what may happen to him when the moon is full. His transformation scenes took six hours to film, although the full change is only really seen once toward the end, and the fact that Chaney has previously been glimpsed as the Wolf Man prowling around a misty, not very authentic-looking Welsh landscape does lessen the impact. Claude Rains eventually clubs Chaney to death with the same cane used on Lugosi, but the film was so popular that Chaney was back playing the role two years later in *Frankenstein Meets the Wolf Man*.

The World, the Flesh and the Devil
MGM 1958; Cinemascope; 95 mins; Cert. "A"
CREDITS: Producer: George Englund; Director: Ranald MacDougall
CAST: Harry Belafonte; Inger Stevens; Mel Ferrer **

A man trapped underground for days in a mining accident reaches the surface to discover that the world's population has been wiped out by atomic war.

It has been suggested that this post-Holocaust film was inspired by M.P. Shiel's classic 1901 end-of-the-world novel *The Purple Cloud*, but in fact it bears little resemblance. Shiel's almost impenetrable saga is one of the great unfilmed works of fantasy fiction—a young doctor on an expedition to the Arctic returns south from the North Pole to find that the world has been decimated by a vast cloud of cyanide gas. Utterly alone, he roams the continents, torching cities and slowly going mad until he comes across a sole female survivor whom he cannot at first relate to. This movie had Belafonte meeting up with Mel Ferrer and Inger Stevens in a deserted New York, sparking off racial tensions among the trio until they all walked off in harmony at the end. The empty New York streets are dramatically realized, but the film is much too talkative, with endless shots of racist Ferrer trying to hunt down Belafonte, and the sudden ending is disappointingly weak. The extraordinary images conjured up in Shiel's long-forgotten novel are still waiting to be put onto the big screen.

World Without End
Allied Artists 1956; Cinemascope/Technicolor; 81 mins; Cert. "A"
CREDITS: Producer: Richard Heermance; Director: Edward Bernds
CAST: Hugh Marlowe; Nancy Gates; Rod Taylor; Lisa Montell; Christopher Dark; Nelson Leigh ****

After orbiting Mars, a spaceship accidentally accelerates and breaks through a time warp, landing on Earth in the year 2508 to find that an atomic war has driven mankind underground, with hostile mutants roaming the surface.

Allied Artists pulled out all the stops and came up with a colorful and expensive (for them) fantasy, a kind of variation on *The Time Machine* and a lively, underrated movie. Hugh Marlowe is the captain of the spaceship jettisoned through a time warp and crashing onto what appears to be a deserted planet with his three fellow astronauts. After encountering a huge species of spider in a cave and fighting off hordes of one-eyed, caveman-type mutants, they chance upon a cemetery and deduce from the dates on the gravestones that they are back on Earth in a far distant future. The astronauts then discover that the peaceful remnants of human civilization have moved underground into a series of interconnecting caves, impotent because of radiation fallout from the war in 2188 and living in fear from the constant threat of the mutants prowling the surface. Marlowe, after falling in love with Nancy Gates, which causes jealousy to rear its ugly head among the ineffectual humans, eventually persuades the Underground People to take up arms and fight, and they destroy the mutants in a battle with homemade bazookas after Marlowe has defeated the mutant leader in an arm-to-arm contest. The final scenes show the humans trying to rebuild their life on the surface of the Earth. Although the script left a lot to be desired, this was solid, entertaining hokum and was one of a number of fantasy films produced in the '50s whose overall designs were much plagiarized by television serials such as *Star Trek* and *Lost in Space* during the 1960s.

X the Unknown
Hammer/Exclusive/RKO-Radio 1956; 80 mins; Cert. "X"
CREDITS: Producer: Anthony Hinds; Director: Leslie Norman
CAST: Dean Jagger; Edward Chapman; Leo McKern; William Lucas; Anthony Newley; Jameson Clark ***

In the Scottish Highlands, a living primeval mud creature periodically surfaces from deep within the Earth to seek out radioactive material to feed on.

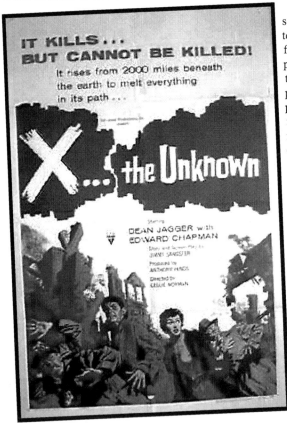

An austere piece of British science fiction, very similar in style to Hammer's first two *Quatermass* films (the company, in fact, approached Nigel Kneale to use the Quatermass character in this production but he refused them permission). Dean Jagger was the imported American actor playing a research scientist, failing to convince the locals that something sinister is causing people to melt and the local landscape to cave in after a boy sees his friend burned to death by the radioactive creature and reports it to the scientist. When Jagger's assistant descends into a deep fissure to find out precisely what is down there, the dormant monster emerges from its lair to cause havoc on the surrounding countryside, breaking through a concrete barrier constructed by the army to seal the fissure. *X* itself is a slimy, glowing blob, quite impressively shot considering the restrictive special effects budget, oozing over walls and down country lanes, moving toward the local power station to gain energy and stripping the flesh off anybody foolhardy enough to approach it. The climax sees Jagger luring the thing out of the abyss with a cobalt isotope and bombarding the blob with electric rays, blowing it to bits and rendering the radioactivity in the area harmless. Originally released in the United Kingdom with the French thriller *Les Diaboliques*, this sober documentary-type Hammer outing boasting fine black and white photography was more or less permanently double billed with *The Quatermass Experiment* from the middle of the 1960s and was a favorite midnight screening as late as 1969 in some cinemas.

Zombies of Mora-Tau
aka: The Dead that Walk
Clover/Columbia 1957; 71 mins; Cert. "A"
CREDITS: Producer: Sam Katzman; Director: Edward L. Cahn
CAST: Gregg Palmer; Allison Hayes; Joel Ashley; Autumn Russell; Morris Ankrum; Ray Corrigan **

A team of adventurers searching for diamonds on the ocean floor finds its way barred by underwater zombies in coffins who are guarding the treasure.

A low-budget zombie-adventure picture that ranked as one of director Edward L. Cahn's lesser efforts during his considerable output throughout the 1950s. Ashley, Hayes, Ankrum and Palmer are the four treasure hunters searching for a deposit of diamonds on the seabed off the coast of an African island. They discover that 10 members of a previous expedition have, under a native curse, been turned into zombies and are warding off anyone foolish enough to try to lay their hands on the stones. Despite warnings from Autumn Russell's grandmother, who lives on the island, that they could be the next to be cursed, the team attempts to retrieve the treasure and the voodoo rituals start again, with Hayes earmarked as the next zombie victim. The zombies are eventually made to vanish when the sunken ship they are guarding is destroyed. Amateurish underwater photography (filmed apparently through an aquarium fish tank) and wooden acting contribute to a very average thriller that turned up on the Sunday circuit in 1964 with the terrible *The Giant Claw*.

**If you enjoyed this book,
call or write for a free catalog
Midnight
Marquee Press
9721 Britinay Lane
Baltimore, MD 21234**

**410-665-1198
www.midmar.com**

Made in the USA
Charleston, SC
18 October 2011